UNCOVERING EUROPEAN PRIVATE LAW

Uncovering European Private Law

A Student Handbook

Edited by Marija Bartl, Laura Burgers,
and Chantal Mak

OpenBook Publishers

https://www.openbookpublishers.com

All external links were active at the time of publication unless otherwise stated and have been archived via the Internet Archive Wayback Machine at https://archive.org/web

Digital material and resources associated with this volume are available at https://doi.org/10.11647/OBP.0448#resources

Information about any revised edition of this work will be provided at https://doi.org/10.11647/OBP.0448

ISBN Paperback: 978-1-80511-505-2
ISBN Hardback: 978-1-80511-506-9
ISBN PDF: 978-1-80511-507-6
ISBN HTML: 978-1-80511-509-0
ISBN EPUB: 978-1-80511-508-3

DOI: 10.11647/OBP.0448

Cover image: Black redstart with a bright red tail (2023), https://unsplash.com/illustrations/black-redstart-with-a-bright-red-tail-drinks-water-from-the-lake-reflected-in-the-mirror-water-stylization-TxrxnAAfRdc, licensed under the Unsplash+ License

Cover design: Jeevanjot Kaur Nagpal

Contents

V. METHODS

Contributor Biographies

Editors

Prof. Dr. Marija Bartl is Professor of Transnational Private Law at the Amsterdam Law School and the Director of the Amsterdam Centre for Transformative Private Law (ACT). She is a (co)president of European Law Unbound-Society and the editor of *European Law Open*. She has taught several courses, including 'European Contract Law', 'Private Law in European and International Perspective', 'Law as a Change-Maker', and 'Making Markets Beyond the State'. Bartl has held appointments as a Fernand Braudel Fellow at the European University Institute, a Fellow at the Institute of Advanced Studies in Nantes, Visiting Fellow at the Harvard Law School, Boston University and the Max Planck Institute for Comparative Law in Hamburg. She has recently published an open access monograph *Reimagining prosperity: Toward a New Imaginary of Law and Political Economy in the EU* (CUP, 2024). Currently, Bartl is working on her ERC-funded project 'Law as a Vehicle for Social Change: Mainstreaming Non-Extractive Economic Practices (N-EXTLAW)', exploring how private law may help mainstream 'non-extractive economic practices'. See https://www.uva.nl/profiel/b/a/m.bartl/m.bartl.html

Dr. Laura Burgers works as an Assistant Professor at the Amsterdam Law School and ACT. Her research is situated at the intersection of sustainability issues, private law, fundamental rights, and legal theory. Her interests include climate litigation, rights of future generations and rights of nature. She teaches in the University of Amsterdam's (UvA) private law programmes, supervises an Environmental Justice Clinic and coordinates a five-hundred-student bachelor course on law and sustainability. She works often with societal partners including the artistic-philosophical collective Embassy of the North Sea. She is one of the national experts in the United Nations (UN) program Harmony with Nature. See https://www.uva.nl/en/profile/b/u/l.e.burgers/l.e.burgers.html

Prof. Dr. Chantal Mak is Professor of Private Law, specialising in fundamental rights and private law, at the Amsterdam Law School and ACT. She is a teacher and former programme director of the LL.M. in transnational and European Private Law at the Amsterdam Law School. Her research focuses on the legal-theoretical and constitutional legal framework for private law in Europe, with a special interest for the role of the judiciary in European Private Law. See https://www.uva.nl/profiel/m/a/c.mak/c.mak.html

Authors

Dr. Jaap Baaij is an Associate Professor at the Montaigne Centre for Rule of Law and Administration of Justice and the Molengraaff Institute for Private Law of the University of Utrecht. His interdisciplinary research concentrates on the state's utilisation of contract law and civil procedural law to advance—or curb—private-market lawmaking through alternative dispute resolution. At this interface of public and private governance, he combines doctrinal analyses with empirical research, political theory, language philosophy, and comparative law to take on themes related to contract interpretation, cross-border commercial transactions and arbitration, corporate social responsibility, and transnational legal theory. He obtained his Ph.D. cum laude at the University of Amsterdam, at the Centre for the Study of European Contract Law (CSECL), the predecessor of ACT. He also obtained a J.D. from Yale Law School. See https://www.uu.nl/staff/CJWBaaij

Michael Bakker, LL.M. is PhD Fellow at the Amsterdam Law School and ACT. In his research, he focuses on the role of shareholders and the general meeting with respect to the sustainability/ESG strategy and policy of publicly listed companies. He is a lecturer in corporate and commercial law. He holds master's degrees in law (LL.M.) and finance (M.Sc.) from the University of Amsterdam and he was a visiting student at Columbia Law School. See https://www.uva.nl/profiel/b/a/m.h.c.bakker/m.h.c.bakker.html#Profiel

Dr. Guido Comparato is a Reader in Private Law at Birkbeck College, University of London. He was previously a Lecturer in Commercial Law at Brunel University London and a Postdoctoral Research Associate at the European University Institute. He holds a PhD in law from the University of Amsterdam. See https://www.bbk.ac.uk/our-staff/profile/9148851/guido-comparato

Dr. Antonio Davola is Assistant Professor in Economic Law at the University 'Aldo Moro' of Bari and Adjunct Professor at LUISS Guido Carli University in Rome. He holds a Ph.D. in Law and Technology from Sant'Anna School of Advanced Studies in Pisa, an LL.M. from Yale Law School, and in 2020 he was Marie Sklodowska Curie Individual Fellow at the University of Amsterdam with his project 'FairPersonalization'. His main areas of interest involve financial markets regulation, competition law, consumer protection, and the governance of new technologies. He devotes significant attention to the application of experimental and empirical analysis to consumer protection, consistently with a research approach strongly focused on Law and Economics.

Dr. Talya Deibel is Senior Postdoctoral Researcher at University College Cork (UCC). She received her LL.M. degree in law and economics (2012) and her Ph.D. in private law (2012) from Bilkent University. After completing her Ph.D., she held various postdoctoral positions across Europe, including at the Oxford Institute of European and Comparative Law, the Unidroit Institute, and the Amsterdam Centre for Transformative Private Law. Before joining UCC, she taught Roman law, foundations of private law, and comparative law at Bilkent University, where she also served as the

Chair of Legal History. Talya's interdisciplinary research revitalizes the fundamentals of European private law and legal philosophy, particularly in the context of emerging technologies such as artificial intelligence (AI) and neurotechnology. See https://research.ucc.ie/profiles/tdeibel@ucc.ie

Dr. Irina Domurath is is Assistant Professor at the Department of Political Science, Law and International Studies of the University of Padova. Previously, she held positions at the Central University of Chile, the University of Amsterdam, and the University of Copenhagen. She works on the political economy of European Private Law, with a focus on consumer and data protection, consumer finance, and access to housing. She is currently executing a project on 'Radical Privacy in European Private Law', financed by the Ministry of Higher Education and Research of Italy, under the 'Rita Levi Montalcini' Program. See https://www.ucentral.cl/facultades-y-carreras/facdeh/santiago/investigadora-irina-domurath

Prof. Dr. Martijn Hesselink has been Professor of Transnational Law and Theory at the European University Institute as of September 2019. Prior to joining the EUI, he was Professor of European Private Law at the University of Amsterdam, where he was also the founding Director of the Centre for the Study of European Contract Law (CSECL, predecessor of ACT). Professor Hesselink in an Editor of *European Law Open*. He served as a member of the European Commission's expert group on European contract law and wrote numerous studies, reports, and briefing notes on matters of contract law and consumer law for the Legal Affairs Committee of the European Parliament. Professor Hesselink has been a Visiting Professor or Fellow at several universities, including René Descartes (Paris V), Roma Tre, Católica Global School of Law (Lisbon), Panthéon-Sorbonne (Paris I), Sciences Po (Paris), Columbia Law School (New York), and the Institute for European and Comparative Law (Oxford). See https://www.eui.eu/people?id=martijn-hesselink

Nena van der Horst, LL.M., works as a PhD Candidate at the Amsterdam Law School and ACT, on Prof. Marija Bartl's ERC-funded project 'Law as a Vehicle for Social Change: Mainstreaming Non-Extractive Economic Practices'. In this project she is writing a PhD thesis on the relation between profit distributions to shareholders and corporate purpose. Nena has a background in private law and economics. She obtained both her master's degree in Dutch law (cum laude) and her master's degree in economics at the Radboud University in Nijmegen (The Netherlands). She also teaches various company law courses. See https://www.uva.nl/en/profile/h/o/n.vanderhorst/n.van-der-horst.html

Dr. Jennifer de Lange-Collins has practiced as a lawyer for more than twenty years. In 2015, she joined the Amsterdam Law School, where she now teaches on Dutch and English masters courses including Financial Law and Finance, Security and Insolvency. In 2024, she defended her PhD dissertation, completed at ACT, in which she explored the intersection between sustainability and financial law, with a particular focus on the role of EU financial regulation.

Prof. Dr. Marco B. M. Loos is Professor of Private Law, in particular of European consumer law, at the Amsterdam Law School and ACT. He studied Law at the University of Amsterdam (1987–1993) and subsequently wrote his Ph.D. thesis at Utrecht University (1993–1998). From 1997 to 2001 he worked as a lecturer at Tilburg University. He has worked at the University of Amsterdam since 2002, and since 2005 as a Full Professor. In addition, he currently is a member of the Board of Governors of the Consumentenbond (since 2015) and of the Stichting Voortgezet Onderwijs Amsterdam-Zuid (a combination of three schools of secondary education in Amsterdam, since 2021), and of the Stichting toetsing verzekeraars (since 2022; from 2018–2022 he was a member of the Stichting's Board). Furthermore, he is a member of the Dutch Social-Economic Council's Commission on Consumer Affairs (Commissie voor Consumenten-aangelegenheden, Sociaal-Economische Raad, since 2022) and of the Board of the Ius Commune Research School (since 2023, third term). He is also a Deputy Judge at the Court of Appeal of 's Hertogenbosch (since 2015). Previously, he has been a member of several bodies for alternative dispute resolution. Loos specialises in European and Dutch contract law and European and Dutch consumer law. He publishes regularly on subjects of European consumer law, including standard contract terms, digital content, consumer sales, and enforcement of consumer law. See https://www.uva.nl/profiel/l/o/m.b.m.loos/m.b.m.loos.html

Prof. Dr. Joasia Luzak is Professor of Private Law, the Director of the Centre for European Legal Studies (CELS), and Director of Global Engagement for the Law School of the University of Exeter. She is also a Guest Associate Professor at the Amsterdam Centre for Transformative Private Law (ACT) at the University of Amsterdam. At this university, as of 2015, she was a Deputy Director of the Centre for the Study of European Contract Law (predecessor of ACT), as well as the Director of the European Private Law LL.M. program. Her research interests include European consumer law, contract law, and law on internet and digital markets. See https://experts.exeter.ac.uk/25252-joasia-luzak

Prof. Dr. Marieke Oderkerk is Professor of Private International Law and Comparative Law at Vrije Universiteit Amsterdam. Her research covers a wide range of topics including doctrinal notions of private international law (PIL) and international family law. In 1999, she obtained a Ph.D. on a topic related to comparative legal research methodology at the University of Amsterdam. From 1998 until the end of 2000, she was a University Lecturer at the Molengraaff Institute for Private Law of Utrecht University. She then joined the University of Amsterdam as Assistant Professor from October 2000 and as Associate Professor from April 2010 onwards. She was Research Coordinator of the Amsterdam Institute of Private Law between 2005–2008. In January 2009, she joined the Centre for the Study of European Contract Law (now ACT). From July 2019 to 2022, she was program director of the Master Privaatrecht (UvA). On 1 August 2022, she was appointed Full Professor of Private International Law and Comparative

Law at the Vrije Universiteit Amsterdam and is part-time Associate Professor at the University of Amsterdam. Furthermore, in 2013 she was installed as Deputy Judge at the Amsterdam Court of Appeal. See https://research.vu.nl/en/persons/marieke-oderkerk

Dr. Marleen van Uchelen is Associate Professor at the Amsterdam Law School and ACT. She specialises in company law and the laws on various legal entities, including social enterprises, foundations, and associations. Marleen obtained her doctorate in 2018; her doctoral thesis is called 'The Role and Position of the Supervisory Board of the Dutch Foundation'. Besides teaching, she works in the notarial practice and advises on governance and governance structures, especially in the semi-public sector (amongst others health care institutions) and the non-profit sector (amongst others cultural institutions). Marleen regularly publishes in various academic journals and contributes to book publications. See https://www.uva.nl/profiel/s/c/m.j.schipper/m.j.van-uchelen.html

Eva Vermeulen is a Ph.D. researcher in property law with an interest in policy and political philosophy at the Amsterdam Law School and ACT. In her thesis, she studies if and how theories of distributive justice should be considered in the legal institution of property, using distributive injustices in Dutch housing as a case study. Her other research interests include the role of private law in addressing sustainability challenges, such as corporate accountability, green finance, and climate action, as well as the interaction between public policy and private law. She now works as a policy strategy advisor at De Nederlandsche Bank, the supervisory institution of the Netherlands, where she focuses on the climate transition strategy and sustainability-related financial risks. See https://nl.linkedin.com/in/evaelizavermeulen

Prof. Dr. Rolef de Weijs is Professor in Insolvency Law at the Amsterdam Law School and ACT. He holds a master's in law and philosophy from Groningen University and an LL.M. degree from Harvard Law School. He also participated in the Japan Prize Winners' Programme. He did his Ph.D. research at the Amsterdam Institute for Private law. In 2010, he defended his Ph.D. thesis 'Faillissementspauliana, Insolvenzanfechtung & Transaction Avoidance in Insolvencies'. De Weijs specialises in insolvency law, corporate law, and corporate finance. De Weijs practices law as an attorney and a court appointed trustee in bankruptcy at Houthoff, a law firm in Amsterdam. See https://www.uva.nl/profiel/w/e/r.j.deweijs/r.j.deweijs.html

I. INTRODUCTION

1. The Evolving Concept of Private Law in Europe

Laura Burgers, Marija Bartl, and Chantal Mak

Abstract

This introduction aims to set out some of the basic concepts of European private law, while providing a common ground for the rest of the handbook *Uncovering European Private Law.* The introduction starts by defining some key terms, such as private law, private autonomy, or freedom of contract, and then proceeds to unpack important processes and developments that have marked the constitution of private law in Europe, including materialisation and constitutionalisation of private law, as well as the Europeanisation and instrumentalisation of private law through positive and negative integration. Building on the reading of these terms and processes, we propose to understand European private law not only as a multi-level legal field but also a way of looking at private law that is necessarily transdisciplinary, comparative and contextual.

The handbook *Uncovering European Private Law* will allow you to do one of the very essential things in life, namely, to explain to others why your (future) area of expertise—European private law—is absolutely fascinating. Parties and family gatherings will never be boring again. The book's objective is to introduce you to important and topical debates in European private law, ranging from anti-discrimination, digital justice, sustainability to financial crises, data protection, and global supply chains. But before we delve into those, this introduction aims to refresh your memory on some key concepts in the area of private law in Europe. The aim is, firstly, to set common ground for the rest of the book. Secondly, we explain our specific understanding of the concept of European private law, which combines its study as a legal field with a necessarily transdisciplinary, comparative, and contextual approach.

Thus, the central question of this chapter is: what do we mean by European private law? We break up this question into smaller aspects. In Section 1, we discuss what the *private* in private law stands for. In Section 2, we introduce (and immediately relativise) the private legal principle of private autonomy to get a

 https://doi.org/10.11647/OBP.0448.01

better idea of the implications of calling something private *law*. In Section 3, we discuss the lawmaker in private law not only being national but also *European*. In Section 4, we integrate these reflections into a formulation of the meaning of European private law for the purposes of this handbook.

1. The 'Private' in Private Law

'Everyone has three lives: a public life, a private life and a secret life', according to Gabriel García Márquez (1927–2014), a Colombian writer and winner of the Nobel prize in literature.[1] Though Márquez most likely did not think of it this way, we find the distinction between these three can serve as a metaphor to reflect on the concept of private law.

Public life is regulated by public law. Public law is typically understood as the law that regulates relationships between citizens, on the one hand, and public authorities handling in their public capacity on the other. Examples include constitutional law, setting out the main institutions of the State; administrative law, regulating how administrations take decisions and how citizens can object to these; and criminal law, stipulating which crimes are punishable by law. The legal relationship between a citizen, on the one hand, and public authorities on the other is frequently described as a 'vertical' relationship.

People's *private* lives are regulated by private law. Private law is typically understood as the law that regulates relationships between two or more private parties (i.e. individual humans, companies, associations, foundations etc.) or a public actor acting in a private capacity.[2] Examples include contract law, regulating the legal enforceability of agreements between parties acting in their private capacity; tort law, setting out conditions under which wrongdoing by one party to another should be compensated; company law, unfolding the conditions under which a legal person can legally function; property law, containing rules on, inter alia, transfer of ownership; and family law, regulating affairs like marriage, divorce, and guardianship over minors. The legal relationship between two or more parties acting in their private capacity is frequently described as a 'horizontal' relationship.

---

1 He reportedly told this to his biographer who inquired after a Parisian lover of Márquez. Cf. J. Wilson, 'Gabriel Garcia Marquez—A Life, by Gerald Martin', *The Independent* (24 October 2008), https://www.independent.co.uk/arts-entertainment/books/reviews/gabriel-garc-237-a-m-225-rquez-a-life-by-gerald-martin-5358667.html

2 This definition is common in civil law systems (see also below). In a similar fashion, Jan Smit defines private law as 'a unified whole of which the main branches—on contract, tort, property, family, and inheritance—are governed by conflicts between individual autonomy and countervailing principles. J. M. Smits, *Advanced Introduction to Private Law* (Cheltenham: Edward Elgar Publishing, 2017). The Harvard Law School's *Project on the Foundations of Private Law*'s definition comes rather close to ours too but refers to the common law (see below): '"Private law" embraces the traditionally common law subjects (property, contracts, and torts), as well as related subjects that are more heavily statutory, such as intellectual property and commercial law. It also includes areas of study that are today less familiar to students and scholars, including unjust enrichment, restitution, equity, and remedies.'. Cf. Harvard Law School, 'Project on the Foundations of Private Law', *Harvard University*, https://blogs.harvard.edu/privatelaw/

Note that private law also applies to public parties when they act in their private capacity. When you buy a chair, you handle it in your capacity as a private party, for example as a consumer or on behalf of a company. Likewise, a state agency may act in a private capacity when entering into a contract ordering chairs for its employees.

It is likely that people do not want anyone to interfere in their personal or secret lives, implying that interference through the means of law is unwanted as well. This observation helps us to reflect on the meaning of the 'private' in private law: private does not necessarily mean secret in this context. Marriage is usually not secret, nor is it to start a company or a foundation, or even to enter into a contract. The 'private' in private law rather refers to the capacity of actors entering into legal relationships not being public.

Privatisation—the process of handing over state activities to private parties—can make it difficult to determine whether a certain actor is handling in its private capacity. For example, the management of public transport and prisons, and the provision of energy and water, used to be in the hands of the public authorities in most states, but many such activities have been privatised.[3] Private companies thus often exercise a public function.

We will see time and again in this book how the so-called 'public/private divide' (i.e. the doctrinal distinction between public and private law) is constantly challenged by various 'struggles for recognition' by different subordinated groups,[4] as well as broader societal developments such as globalisation, privatisation, financialisation, digitalisation, and more. (See, for example, Chapter 7 on a new, social concept of ownership by Eva Vermeulen; Chapter 10 on social enterprises by Nena van der Horst and Marleen van Uchelen; Chapter 11 on financial crises by Guido Comparato and Chapter 13 by Antonio Davola on data subjects). Moreover, areas like economic law, including competition law, do not always fall clearly within either the category public or private as defined above.

At the same time, we may reflect on the concept and reach of 'law'. Insofar as people's personal or secret lives should be free from interventions, they remain outside of the scope of the law. Both public and private law, thus, have limits.

Think of the social sphere: The law does not, for example, attach consequences to your friend missing a lunch appointment.

Furthermore, consider the hiring of a painter for your house, a gardener for the backyard, or a babysitter for one's children. Public law establishes certain rules for such services, for instance regarding working hours and safety. Private law governs the contractual relationship, which, inter alia, concerns payment and working conditions. Since the hiring of services for one's home and family are of a personal nature, one may to some extent distinguish among applicants on the basis of personal preferences—including those that in the context of employment by a public authority or private company would not be allowed under non-discrimination law. As we shall see, however, it is a subject of debate where to draw the boundaries of law in such cases.[5]

---

3 See also D. Parker, *The Official History of Privatisation Vol. I: The Formative Years 1970–1987* (London: Routledge, 2009).

4 A. Honneth, *The Struggle for Recognition: The Moral Grammar of Social Conflicts* (Cambridge: John Wiley and Sons, 2018). In this seminal work, Honneth argues that the recognition of certain groups as rights holders is important for questions of distributive justice.

5 H. Collins, 'The Vanishing Freedom to Choose a Contractual Partner', *Law and Contemporary Problems*

2. Private Autonomy as a General Principle of Private Law

Every jurisdiction has its own particularities, but it is possible to enumerate some general principles of private law. Whole bodies of literature exist on this topic; we only present it briefly, focusing on one overarching principle with influence on both substantive and procedural private law, namely that of private autonomy.

Another important private law principle, especially dominant in continental Europe, is that of good faith. (See Chapter 6 on *bona fides* by Talya Deibel.) Other private law principles include *pacta sunt servanda* (agreements must be kept), private property, equality of the parties, and freedom of contract. Many of these principles are interrelated.

a. Substantive Side of Private Autonomy

Substantively speaking, the principle of private autonomy finds expression in inter alia, the contract law principle of freedom of contract, according to which parties are free to decide (1) whether they want to enter into a contract; (2) with whom they want to enter into a contract; and (3) what the substance of that contract may be.

This principle assumes a certain equality between the parties. We call this *formal equality*, i.e. equality before the law.

In the 19th century, the sociologist Max Weber asserted that *formality* offers legitimacy to the law.[6] He understood legitimacy as legality: according to Weber, the law is legitimate (i.e. people accept its authority and are willing to obey) when it is 1) systematic; 2) general; and 3) complete. That is, the law should offer an all-encompassing system that is formulated so as to apply generally without being tailored to specific situations, and yet be so complete that judges do not need to resort to personal convictions to be able to apply the rules.[7] Many private legal rules meet these requirements, for instance, the rule that property can be transferred from one legal subject to another.

In reality, power imbalances may exist between parties. At the end of the 19th century and over the course of the 20th, specific fields of private law emerged that aim to repair such power imbalances and thus to realise (some) *substantive* or *material equality* as well. Prominent examples include labour law, consumer law, and tenancy law.

Have you ever entered into a negotiation with Amazon, Facebook, WhatsApp, or other large companies on the general terms and conditions of your usage of their products and services? Very likely, the answer is no. Such products and services are often offered on a 'take it or leave it' basis. Consumer law has the aim to recover some of the power imbalance between you—the consumer—and business entities.

Other power imbalances exist in labour relations, especially where an individual worker performs a task that can be easily performed by others as well. Labour law

---

76.2 (2013), 71–88 (p. 71).

6 On Weber, cf. S. H. Kim, 'Max Weber', in E. N. Zalta (ed.), *The Stanford Encyclopedia of Philosophy (Summer 2021 Edition)*, https://plato.stanford.edu/archives/sum2021/entries/weber/

7 See e.g., A. J. Hoekema, *Legitimiteit door legaliteit, over het recht van de overheid* (Nijmegen: Ars Aequi Libri, 1991), p. 15.

therefore protects workers. Likewise, tenancy law protects tenants against the power of homeowners to, for instance, arbitrarily evict them from rented homes.

Thus, whilst contract law, traditionally speaking, was there to facilitate the legal enforcement of commitments between private parties deemed equal, with the introduction of fields like labour law, tenancy law and consumer law, private law took on another goal, namely the promotion of material or substantive equality. This can be called the 'social' or 'societal' dimension of private law. To the extent that the promotion is taken up by the judiciary, this is often called the 'materialisation' of private law (*Materialisierung* in German): private law application does not happen purely formally but involves the realisation of material goals.

This social dimension is not unique to contract law but occurred in other fields of private law as well. Take tort law. From the end of the 19th century and in the course of the 20th century, most tort law systems adopted variants of strict liability next to fault liability.[8] Thus, in some situations, they let go of the requirement of fault: a tort law obligation to pay damages can also arise out of a certain responsibility. For example, in principle, employers are liable for damage caused by faults of their employees, even if the employers themselves made no mistakes—one reason for this being that employers are more likely to be able to afford the damages than an individual employee. Car owners are at least partially liable when they end up in an accident, even if the accident was not their fault, because of the risk they took on by driving. Also, in principle, producers are made liable for products that turn out to be deficient within a certain period of time after the purchase, even if it is unclear whether there is actually a fault made in the production process. Hence, formal equality is let go to promote material equality as the end result.

Various authors are critical of the materialisation of private law. They feel that private law should merely be used to achieve *corrective justice*, i.e. to restore a just situation between two parties acting in their private capacity. They oppose the usage of private law to achieve *distributive justice*, i.e. to distribute (financial) means between different parties in society.[9] (See also Chapter 2 on justice in European private law by Martijn Hesselink).

Throughout the second half of the 20th century, another development gained traction, namely the constitutionalisation of private law. This concept refers to the horizontal application of fundamental, constitutional or human rights. These rights primarily pertain to the public law domain and are meant to protect citizens against state power. The goal of constitutionalisation is to ensure that material imbalances between private parties do not impede the enjoyment of fundamental rights. Private actors, thus, to some extent have to heed the public interest. (See also Chapter 5 on human rights in private law by Chantal Mak).

---

8 The distinction between fault and strict liability is however not that sharp in practice, see C. Van Dam, 'Strict Liability', in *European Tort Law*, 2nd edn (Oxford: Oxford University Press, 2013), pp. 297–306.

9 Cf. Notably E. Weinbrib, *The Idea of Private Law* (Oxford: Oxford University Press, 1995).

The application of human rights in private law often requires courts to conduct a balancing of rights and interests.[10] For example, the question has arisen whether the right not to be discriminated against based on sexual preference might be invoked against a Catholic bakery refusing to bake a cake celebrating gay marriage.[11] It is not difficult to see that such an application of the fundamental right not to be discriminated against would clash with the Catholic baker's private autonomy or freedom of contract. Thus, a case like this challenges a principle originally thought of as essential for contract law specifically and private law generally. It is also interesting to reflect on the question of whether this balancing of interests is different depending on whether the bakery is a small, family-owned business or a large chain.

b. Procedural Side of Private Autonomy

The procedural side of the principle of private autonomy has implications for civil procedure. It is for the parties to delimit the boundaries of the legal dispute. This is different from public law proceedings, in, say criminal law, where judges typically may research and inquire further about the facts of their own motion, and where the public prosecutor can choose to take a private party (i.e. an alleged criminal) to court. In private law, one of the parties decides what part of their conflict they want to take to court, and whether they want to do that at all.

In private law proceedings, judges usually rely on the facts put forward by the parties; they deem true those facts presented to them that were not (convincingly) disputed. This is true for civil procedure throughout Europe. Although there is no specific term for this in English, other languages designate it as a concept: *lijdelijkheid* in Dutch, for example, or the *principe dispositif* in French, the *Dispositionsmaxime* in German, *disposisjonsprinsippet* in Norwegian.

Materialisation can also impact this procedural side of private autonomy. For instance, in consumer law, in certain circumstances judges are required to *ex officio*—of their own motion, not because one of the parties asked to do so—check whether the general terms and conditions of a company are unfair under European Union (EU) law. It is thought that this is necessary, inter alia, because the length and technicality of general terms and conditions make them often incomprehensible for consumers. That is, if judges do not assess the fairness of such terms *ex officio*, it is likely that this will not happen at all, as consumers will not challenge terms that they have not read or understood.[12] (See Chapter 9 on consumers in European private law by Joasia Luzak.)

In private international law—the legal field regulating the applicable law, competent court and enforcement in cross-border private legal conflicts—the principle of party

10 H. Collins, 'On the (In)compatibility of Human Rights Discourse and Private Law', in H.-W. Micklitz (ed.), *Constitutionalization of European Private Law* (Oxford: Oxford University Press, 2014), pp. 49–51.

11 European Court of Human Rights, fourth section decision, Application no. 18860/19, *Gareth LEE against the United Kingdom*, 7 December 2021.

12 This duty for judges to check compliance with the law *ex officio* applies to the bulk of European consumer law, with the limitations that the problem with consumer law must be material to the dispute at stake (i.e. no general court check); and that the intensity of the duty is connected to how much difference it can make: for example, if there is no remedy for the violation to be ascertained, then there is also little reason to act *ex officio*.

autonomy exists for the domain of contracts. This means that parties who enter into a contract, are free to negotiate what law applies to their contract and to which court or arbiter they will resort in case of conflict. Note that this principle is not applicable in, for instance, tort law. There it is usually the place where the tort took place, or where the damage occurs, that determines the applicable law and the competent court.

The rules of private international law can thus render several courts, at the time, competent. So-called 'forum shopping' refers to the practice of certain parties to select the court that is most likely to rule in their favour. Sometimes, when a party is sued before one court, it starts proceedings in another court to block the first case. Parties with enough financial resources and/or legal knowledge and capacity can thus set the odds in their own favour. Hence, one could consider forum shopping as (mis)use of this procedural side of private autonomy.

3. The Maker of Private Law in Europe

a. Public and Private Lawmakers

In case you buy something, and the other party does not deliver, it is contract law that allows you to enforce your contract. The conditions under which one can enforce contracts are laid down in contract law, which is made by the public authorities. Contract law can be either codified in legislation or developed by the judiciary in case-law; the same holds true for other fields of private law, such as tort law, property law, company law, and family law.

Thus, in this book, we understand private law as law made by public authorities, i.e. legislatures and judiciaries.[13] Sometimes, people refer to private law when they speak of rules made by private parties. We understand these kinds of rules to fall within the sphere of freedom of contract or self-regulation (e.g. codes of conduct drafted by companies in a certain sector) that is shaped by publicly enacted rules of public and private law.

Rules made by private parties can be laid down in a contract. For example, when a group of neighbours enters into an enforceable agreement not to vacuum clean on Sundays, they create a 'private law' amongst themselves to behave accordingly. Thus, the *substance of contracts* is sometimes referred to as 'private law' (though not in this book).

Private law understood this way can also take other shapes. For example, many large multinationals subscribe to the OECD guidelines, pledging that they will respect human rights and environmental law. This type of *self-regulation* is quite common. It is not meant to be legally enforceable and can therefore not be considered a contract.

Private standard-setting happens in all kinds of areas: for example, food producers develop their own logos for 'healthy' foods and electricity providers adopt common standards for the connectivity of charging stations for electronic vehicles. By some authors, such *standardisation by the private sector* is also called private law.

13 So, in addition to what we have been noting above in Section 1 on the difficulty of drawing a sharp line between private and public law, the *secret life of private law* may be that it is in fact public law.

In continental Europe, private law is often codified in national civil codes. 'Civil law' is frequently used as a synonym for 'private law'. Civil procedural law is typically laid down in codes of civil procedure. It refers to procedural rules in private legal disputes and contains rules on, for example: evidence, possibilities for appeals, and enforcement of judgments.

Note that 'civil law' is a term that is also used more generally to depict the legal systems of those states that have adopted a civil code (i.e. one comprehensive legal text containing private law provisions). In Europe, these are mostly the continental states. Civil law can refer to the legal system of those states as a whole—including private *and* public law. Using the term like this, civil law systems are contrasted to (mostly Anglo-American) common law systems, which do not have civil codes. Civil law systems are characterised by an emphasis of general rules laid down in legislation, and by *deductive* legal reasoning, applying a general rule to a specific case. Common law systems are characterised by an emphasis on judge-made law and by *inductive* legal reasoning, distilling general rules from specific cases. There are also other 'legal families'. Often, for instance, the Nordic countries are described as a separate category. (See also Chapter 16 on comparative law by Marieke Oderkerk.)

b. Europeanisation of Private Law

Within EU Member States, the public authorities who make laws that impact private legal relationships are not only national authorities, but also the EU and its institutions. The increasing influence exercised by the EU on national private laws is a process called 'Europeanisation' of private law.

EU law consists of:

- the constitutive treaties, i.e. the international agreements between the 27 Member States that constitute the EU as such, also known as primary EU law:
    - the Treaty on the European Union (TEU);
    - the Treaty on the Functioning of the European Union (TFEU);
    - the Charter of Fundamental Rights of the European Union (CFREU);
- secondary EU law, i.e. law enacted by the EU institutions that were created by the constitutive treaties. Such laws can take the shape of:
    - Regulations;
    - Directives;
    - Decisions;
- the interpretations of primary as well as secondary EU law by the Court of Justice of the European Union (CJEU) in its case-law.

The most usual way of intervention of the CJEU in private law is through the so-called 'preliminary reference procedure'. This procedure denotes a possibility, and at times an obligation, for national courts to refer questions of interpretation of EU law to the CJEU.

> The CJEU has the final interpretative authority in the matters of EU law. Furthermore, in principle, EU law (and its interpretations), take precedence over national law, including constitutional law ('primacy of EU law').[14]

EU law does *not* as such distinguish between private law and public law.[15] All EU legal sources can however influence private legal relationships. After all, the EU goal of establishing the internal market is dependent on private law facilitating market transactions—without, for instance, financial law, contract law, company law, and property law it would be difficult to sustain this market.[16]

> The goal to establish this EU-wide market might seem politically neutral at first sight because it merely aims at economic cooperation. Likewise, the ostensibly technical rules of private law may look politically neutral. Yet, as argued convincingly by Katharina Pistor, private law *enables* the market to exist, and therefore, private law is anything but neutral: it has been used to create capital by the *haves* and they have thus contributed to the growing material, social and political inequality. In turn, changes in private law can also effectively change the distribution of wealth, power, and environmental harms.[17] (See also Chapter 15 on private law and the political economy by Marija Bartl.)
>
> Indeed, to put central the goal of establishing an internal market, might marginalise other goals that one could deem essential for European societies. Social justice is one of them (see further below), but one could equally think of environmental sustainability. Whilst a high level of consumer protection might be effective for the promotion of the internal market, it is not precisely environmentally sustainable to ship goods around over large distances, nor to replace rather than repair broken consumer goods. The European Commission is aware of this and issued a 'Green New Deal' in December 2019, a series of policy proposals which should address inter alia these questions. (See also Chapter 14 on EU sustainable finance regulation by Jennifer de Lange-Collins.)

The constitutive treaties of the EU can exercise influence on private legal relationships through, firstly, so-called negative integration of the internal market. That is, they forbid cartels and national regulation that pose barriers to the four 'fundamental freedoms' of the EU, which should facilitate the goal of the EU to create an internal market:

1. the free movement of persons;
2. the free movement of goods;
3. the free movement of capital; and
4. the free movement of services.

---

14 The CJEU also has the competence to, inter alia, rule in cases instigated by the European Commission against EU Member States, or in cases against the EU institutions. See Articles 251–281 TFEU.

15 Even in national legal systems this distinction is mostly made by scholars. In EU law, there is no separate codification of rules of private law, but nor is there in many common law systems.

16 C. U. Schmid, 'The Instrumentalization Thesis in a Nutshell', in C. Joerges and T. Ralli (eds), *European Constitutionalism without Private Law; Private Law without Democracy* (Oslo: ARENA, 2011), pp. 17–27.

17 See K. Pistor, *The Code of Capital; How the Law Creates Wealth and Inequality* (Princeton, NJ: Princeton University Press, 2019).

Negative integration is aimed at national deregulation, that is, at removing barriers to the cross-border movement of persons, goods, services, and capital. These barriers, which EU law thus requires be removed, can have their origin in what is seen as private law at a national level, or they have their origin in rules that influence private legal relationships (see Chapter 3 on negative integration by Jaap Baaij).

The *Bosman* ruling may serve as an example. Jean-Marc Bosman was a professional football player. The rules of the UEFA, the FIFA, and the Belgian football association allowed his club to ask for a very high transfer sum to be paid, even though his contract had already expired. Bosman argued this prevented his free establishment as a worker, because the sum was so high that it effectively prevented him from working for another football club. The CJEU agreed, and thus the free movement of workers applied horizontally in the conflict between Bosman and the football associations.[18]

Secondly, *general principles of EU law* that, according to the CJEU, flow from these fundamental freedoms may apply directly between private parties, notably the prohibition of discrimination.

The *Mangold* case, on age discrimination, can serve as an example. Mangold argued that he was discriminated against on the basis of age since, unlike younger employees, he could not get a permanent position. The employer invoked German labour legislation stipulating that no objective reason was needed to refuse permanent positions to people above fifty-two. This piece of legislation aimed to improve the flexibility of the labour market for older employees. Yet according to Mangold, the relevant provision was discriminatory. The CJEU agreed, saying that non-discrimination is a general principle of EU law. Mangold could thus invoke this general principle of EU law in the legal proceedings against his employer, requiring the national law to be set aside.[19]

Thirdly, horizontal application of certain provisions of the CFREU can impact private legal relationships. Such horizontal application of the CFREU constitutes a form of the aforementioned constitutionalisation (see Chapter 5 on human rights in private law by Chantal Mak).

Note the difference and overlap between the fundamental freedoms, general principles of EU law like non-discrimination, and fundamental rights. *Fundamental freedoms* are foundational for the internal market. *Fundamental rights* are foundational for the democratic rule of law and human dignity. *The general principle of non-discrimination* might be foundational for both—non-discrimination is not only a general principle of EU law, but also a human right recognised in, for instance, the United Nations International Covenant on Civil and Political Rights.

In the past decades, many authors and organisations have expressed criticism

18 Case C-415/93 *Union royale belge des sociétés de football association ASBL v Jean-Marc Bosman, Royal club liégeois SA v Jean-Marc Bosman and others and Union des associations européennes de football (UEFA) v Jean-Marc Bosman* [1995] ECLI:EU:C:1995:463.

19 Case C-144/04 *Werner Mangold v Rüdiger Helm* [2005] ECLI:EU:C:2005:709. An interesting aspect of this case is that it was actually constructed. Mangold's employer, who was a lawyer, had earlier challenged the German labour legislation, claiming it violated EU law. He and Mangold created this case and it triggered the prejudicial question by the German Court to the CJEU. So, in fact, they were both proved right.

towards the EU for merely focusing on the economic aim of establishing the internal market.[20] This critique is often labelled as the 'social deficit' of the EU. Partly in response hereto, the EU had the CFREU enter into force in 2009. Yet the problem of the social deficit seems not fully solved, as will be discussed in a number of chapters in this book (see, for example, Chapter 12 on housing by Irina Dorumath).

Secondary EU law can exercise influence on private legal relationships through so-called positive integration, i.e. by creating new EU-wide rules—these rules may fall within areas that affect the private laws of the Member States. For example, the EU adopted the Consumer Rights Directive, which influences the national contract laws of the Member States, as well as the Commercial Agency Directive, which influences national company law (see Chapter 4 on positive integration by Marco Loos).

EU law can have 'direct vertical effect', 'direct horizontal effect', or 'indirect horizontal effect', depending on the circumstances.

Decisions and regulations are pieces of EU law that do not need implementation to have direct effect in the Member States in vertical as well as horizontal relationships. In other words, the parties to a dispute can invoke these pieces of legislation as soon as they are enacted by the EU and have entered into force.

Directives are dependent upon implementation by the State and do not, in principle, have a direct effect in horizontal nor vertical relationships. Thus, parties can only invoke them in a legal dispute once these directives are transplanted in the national law. In case Member States implement directives too late, however, private parties may invoke them against public authorities under certain conditions (vertical direct effect). Moreover, the CJEU interpreted a number of *treaty provisions* to apply directly, some in only vertical relationships, some in horizontal relationships as well.

Subject to certain conditions, *treaty provisions and directives* can also have an indirect effect on private legal relationships. The notion 'indirect horizontal effect' is used to refer to various phenomena.[21] These include: 1) there is an obligation on part of the State to prevent impediments to fundamental rights and freedoms in private legal relationships; 2) the national judiciary interprets open norms that do apply between private parties in line with the relevant EU provisions, a practice known as 'harmonious' or 'consistent interpretation'.[22]

Implementation of EU law can differ between Member States. State liability, for instance, is usually a matter of administrative (i.e. public) law in Italy, whereas in the Netherlands, the default is to sue the State in tort (i.e. private) proceedings. This is related to the EU law principle of procedural autonomy, which does not refer to the autonomy of parties to a conflict, but rather to the autonomy of EU Member States to implement and enforce EU law in a way they deem fit.[23]

---

20 See, for instance, the contributions to D. Kochenov, G. de Búrca and A. Williams (eds), *Europe's Justice Deficit?* (Oxford: Hart Publishing, 2015).

21 Cf. A. Hartkamp, 'The Effect of the EC Treaty in Private Law: On Direct and Indirect Horizontal Effects of Primary Community Law', *European Review of Private Law* 18.2 (2010), 527–548.

22 If it is not possible to interpret national law in conformity with EU law, courts may, in certain circumstances, be required to set aside national law. In that case, the effect of EU law may be considered to be direct rather than indirect.

23 See also B. Krans and A. Nylund (eds), *Procedural Autonomy across Europe*, 1st edn (Antwerp: Intersentia, 2021).

4. The Meaning of 'European Private Law'

The term 'European private law' can be understood in several ways. Firstly, in a narrow sense, it may refer to *EU law* impacting private legal relations, i.e. law emanating from the EU level, or 'EU private law'. This comprises treaty provisions, secondary law (most importantly directives) and CJEU case law on matters that, according to the national laws of Member States, fall within the scope of private law.[24]

For a long time, it was thought that to promote the EU's goal of the single market, it would be convenient to have one set of rules that would govern all private law transactions within the EU. For over two decades, from 1989 onwards, attempts were made to draft a civil code for the European Union. However, no consensus could be reached, which in turn exposed how legally and politically salient issues of private law are, and what importance civil codes have for national identities.[25] It also raised the question of the competence of the EU, as it was debated whether the treaties offered a legal basis for the EU to enact such comprehensive legislation in the field of private law.[26] Nonetheless, the harmonisation of law continued in specific areas of private law. This resulted in numerous EU legal instruments, mostly directives.

> In other words, the integration of the internal market by means of harmonising the private laws of the EU Member States is nowadays rather fragmented. Instruments include the Product Liability Directive, the Doorstep Selling Directive, the Package Travel Directive, the Unfair Terms Directive, the Regulation on the law applicable to contractual obligations (Rome I), the Consumer Rights Directive, the Digital Content and Distance Sales Directives, and many more.

Although a European civil code was never realised, the process towards it has underlined the importance of research on European private law in a second sense, namely on what constitutes the 'common core' of the private law systems in the EU Member States.[27] National systems of private law in Europe display overlap, as they are all to varying degrees influenced by Roman law and medieval canon law. This overlap is furthered, of course, by the fact that EU law is applicable in all Member States, with the CJEU issuing common interpretation.

> Within the inter-European research project, *The Common Core of European Private Law*, numerous books have been published that search for similarities and differences in the national systems of private law in Europe.[28]

In a third, wider sense, European private law is understood as the field of law

---

24 Recall that EU law itself does not make a distinction between public and private law.

25 Cf. also M. Hesselink, 'The Politics of a European Civil Code', *European Law Journal* 10.6 (2004), 675–697 (p. 675).

26 In case you are interested in the debate, see also P. Legrand, 'Against a European Civil Code', *Modern Law Review* 66.1 (1997), 44–63; H. Collins, *The European Civil Code: The Way Forward* (Cambridge: Cambridge University Press, 2014).

27 For more information on the project, cf. Common-core, 'Welcome to The Common Core of European Private Law', *Common-core* (2020), https://common-core.org/.

28 Ibid.

comprising the rules governing private legal disputes within the multi-level legal order of both EU law and national private laws.[29] In other words, European private law includes national private laws, EU (private) law, and the interplay between the two. This wider sense comes closest to how we perceive European private law for the purposes of this book.

In our view, the latter is the most appealing approach for it allows us to understand better the positive law, as well as many scholarly critiques to European private law. It allows for a thorough understanding of the positive law because EU law and national law are co-dependent: national private law cannot be interpreted without the understanding of the transformations brought about by EU law, including the role of the CJEU, while EU private law depends for both its full meaning and enforcement on national private laws.

At the same time, the broader definition also helps us understand scholarly critiques, which express a fear that EU law threatens the coherence, essence or autonomy of national private laws.

> A number of authors, including notably Christoph Ulrich Schmid, are very critical of private law being used as an instrument by EU law to achieve the goal of the internal market, a process called instrumentalisation of private law.[30] According to Schmid, national private law leans on a specific type of justice, namely commutative justice, i.e. justice *between the parties*, free from external considerations. 'The party relationship must not be instrumentalised by external collective goals', he writes.[31] Yet that is precisely what happens when national private law is used as an instrument to give effect to EU law aiming to establish the internal market. With the Europeanisation of private law, Schmid posits, private law is instrumentalised 'excessively'.

At this point, it is good to note that our approach to European private law in this handbook goes beyond understanding European private law only as a substantive field of law, such as 'German company law' or 'French tort law' once might have been. Importantly, we see European private law also as a certain way of *looking at* private law, as an approach to study questions of private law in Europe, which requires a method that can be transdisciplinary, comparative, and contextual.

The method can be *transdisciplinary,* because it is not confined to one legal discipline: international law, EU law, as well as national law, is of relevance for the study of private law in Europe. As private law is delineated differently in the Member States, scholars of European private law cannot remain in the private law silo. The method can be *comparative,* because European private law might work out differently in various Member States—an awareness of similarities and differences is therefore vital to understand European private law's operation and impact. Lastly, the method can be *contextual,* because studying European private law requires an awareness of

29 Cf. C. Mak, 'Rights and Remedies—Article 47 EUCFR and Effective Judicial Protection in European Private Law Matters', *Amsterdam Law School Legal Studies Research Paper* 2012.88 (2012), https://papers.ssrn.com/abstract=2126551

30 Schmid, 'The Instrumentalization Thesis in a Nutshell'.

31 Ibid., p. 22.

at least the political, historical, sociological, and economic context in which it comes about.

European private law is fundamentally interested in the boundary struggles between what is public and what is private, what is individual and what is collective, across boundaries of various political communities. It is a field where different conceptions of justice clash, not only between the EU and the Member States, but also amongst and within the Member States, and (as everywhere) between scholars. Such clashing conceptions of justice do often lead to high controversies, concerning the interpretation of the law by the CJEU and national courts, which can reveal (or obscure) the political and economic stakes behind the law.

For example, our approach allows us to qualify the so-called *People's Climate Case* against the EU as a case relevant for the study of European private law. In this case, a number of families from all over Europe brought a case against the European Commission and the European Parliament, before the CJEU, for failing to formulate effective climate policy. The claim was based on Article 340 TFEU—which lends its inspiration from national tort law systems. The case brings together elements of national tort law, European secondary legislation, provisions from the CFREU, international climate change law as well as climate science. Thus, a transdisciplinary (and even interdisciplinary) approach is necessary to comprehend this case.[32] Moreover, the case was inspired by the success of a famous Dutch tort law case, *Urgenda*, in which the State of the Netherlands was ordered to formulate more ambitious greenhouse gases reduction targets.[33] A comparative law approach is thus required to contextualise this case. What ought to be done against climate change is an issue that is (geo-)politically very salient, and democratically challenging. It is against this background that one can understand (though not necessarily agree with) the Court's decision to declare the claim inadmissible.

It is with this lens that we asked a number of very well qualified authors to write chapters on various aspects of European private law. Not all of them include all of these aspects in their chapters, but most weave in at least a number of the above elements. The structure of the book is as follows.

The most important basics of European private law are treated in Part I of the book, entitled 'Foundations': the highly diversified concepts of justice in European private law (Chapter 2), negative integration (Chapter 3), positive integration (Chapter 4), and the constitutionalisation of European private law (Chapter 5).

The following parts of the book cover relevant topics of European private law, based on the expertise of the Amsterdam Centre for Transformative Private Law (ACT) affiliated collective of authors who wrote this book. In this sense, the book does not aim to be comprehensive and the collection of contributions is somewhat

32 For the purposes of this book, we understand *transdisciplinarity* as a method studying different legal disciplines, and *interdisciplinarity* as a method studying different scientific disciplines. The contextual approach taken in this book comes close to using an interdisciplinary method, but the scholars who contribute to this book are primarily legal scholars who borrow insights from other disciplines rather than engage themselves into those disciplines like sociology, economy, climate science etc.

33 Hoge Raad der Nederlanden (Dutch Supreme Court) *Urgenda v State of the Netherlands* [2019] Dutch original ECLI:NL:HR:2019:2006; English translation ECLI:NL:HR:2019:2007.

path-dependent: chapters do not cover the whole array of European private law, but a selection of topics based on the authors' expertise. Hence, Part II of the book moves to delve into some, but certainly not all, important 'Institutions' of European private law: the principle of good faith (Chapter 6), concepts of ownership or property (Chapter 7), limited liability (Chapter 8), as well as the consumer (Chapter 9). Other chapters may be added here in subsequent editions of this *Handbook*.

Part III of the book, entitled 'Transformations', studies recent or topical developments and their impact to European private law: the emergence of the so-called 'social enterprise' (Chapter 10), the financial crisis (Chapter 11), housing (Chapter 12), data subjects (Chapter 13), and sustainable finance (Chapter 14). This part also lends itself for expansion in subsequent editions of the handbook. Given the immanent challenges posed by both digitalisation as well as environmental sustainability issues, it is likely that we will devote more attention to topics related hereto in the future.

The final Part V of the book treats two methodologies that can be of use to students writing their master's thesis: political economy (Chapter 15) and comparative law (Chapter 16). Naturally, many other methodologies can be equally interesting, for example law and economics, law and literature, an empirical method, etc. The reason that we chose to highlight these two in the first edition are the following. A political economy lens has become very popular in European private law (EPL) scholarship more recently, in no small measure due to Katharina Pistor's groundbreaking 'private law' bestseller, *The Code of Capital*. Given the growing interest in this type of institutionalist analysis, we hope that the chapter will provide a set of helpful questions and tools. As for the comparative method, this evergreen in private law scholarship does not require much justification. Historically, as in the present, it is one of the most widely used methods in private law. In the upcoming editions, we aim to further expand this methodological section, as we believe that reading about methods helps students also to develop logical and critical thinking more generally.

We asked every author to include reflections on the legal context of their topic, i.e. to situate their topic in the multi-level legal order of national, European, and international law; to underline the societal relevance of their topic, i.e. to make the stakes behind it clear; and to raise some points for further reflection in the form of questions. When studying the chapters in this book, allow yourself some time to think about these questions, and where possible, discuss them with your fellow students.

5. Points for Reflection

Q1: The EU has grown from an international economic cooperation between nation-states into an organisation with its own parliament, fundamental rights document and bureaucracy. Given that the cooperation has become so intense, what do you think of the fact that the goal to establish an internal market remains the most important legal basis to enact secondary legislation in the area of private law in Europe?

Q2: Should the resolution of conflicts between private parties be guided by a different conception of justice than the resolution of conflicts between citizens and public authorities?

Q3: Should private law be coherent?

Q4: Is private law a form of public law?

Q5: What issues should absolutely be regulated by private law, and what issues by public law, if any? And what issues require European instead of national regulation?

Bibliography

Collins, H., *The European Civil Code: The Way Forward* (Cambridge: Cambridge University Press, 2014), https://doi.org/10.1017/CBO9780511620010

Collins, H., 'On the (In)compatibility of Human Rights Discourse and Private Law', in H.-W. Micklitz (ed.), *Constitutionalization of European Private Law* (Oxford: Oxford University Press, 2014), pp. 49–51, https://hdl.handle.net/1814/31533

Collins, H., 'The Vanishing Freedom to Choose a Contractual Partner', *Law and Contemporary Problems* 76.2 (2013), 71–88

Common-core, 'Welcome to The Common Core of European Private Law', *Common-core* (2020), https://common-core.org/

Hartkamp, A., 'The Effect of the EC Treaty in Private Law: On Direct and Indirect Horizontal Effects of Primary Community Law', *European Review of Private Law* 18.2 (2010), 527–548, https://doi.org/10.54648/erpl2010040

Hesselink, M., 'The Politics of a European Civil Code', *European Law Journal* 10.6 (2004), 675–697, https://doi.org/10.1111/j.1468-0386.2004.00238.x

Hoekema, A. J., *Legitimiteit door legaliteit, over het recht van de overheid* (Nijmegen: Ars Aequi Libri, 1991)

Honneth, A., *The Struggle for Recognition: The Moral Grammar of Social Conflicts* (Cambridge: John Wiley and Sons, 2018)

Kim, S. H., 'Max Weber', in E. N. Zalta (ed.), *The Stanford Encyclopedia of Philosophy* (*Summer 2021 Edition*), https://plato.stanford.edu/archives/sum2021/entries/weber/

Kochenov, D., G. de Búrca and A. Williams (eds), *Europe's Justice Deficit?* (Oxford: Hart Publishing, 2015)

Krans, B., and A. Nylund (eds), *Procedural Autonomy across Europe*, 1st edn (Antwerp: Intersentia, 2021), https://doi.org/10.1017/9781780689951

Legrand, P., 'Against a European Civil Code', *Modern Law Review* 66.1 (1997), 44–63

Mak, C., 'Rights and Remedies—Article 47 EUCFR and Effective Judicial Protection in European Private Law Matters', *Amsterdam Law School Legal Studies Research Paper* 2012.88 (2012), https://papers.ssrn.com/abstract=2126551

Pistor, K., *The Code of Capital; How the Law Creates Wealth and Inequality* (Princeton, NJ: Princeton University Press, 2019)

Parker, D., *The Official History of Privatisation Vol. I: The Formative Years 1970–1987* (London: Routledge, 2009), https://doi.org/10.4324/9780203881521

Schmid, C. U., 'The Instrumentalization Thesis in a Nutshell', in C. Joerges and T. Ralli (eds), *European Constitutionalism without Private Law; Private Law without Democracy* (Oslo: ARENA, 2011), pp. 17–27, https://reconproject.eu/files/main.php/reconreport1411-fileitem-50487361.pdf

Smits, J. M., *Advanced Introduction to Private Law* (Cheltenham: Edward Elgar Publishing, 2017)

Van Dam, C., 'Strict Liability', in *European Tort Law*, 2nd edn (Oxford: Oxford University Press, 2013), pp. 297–306

Weinbrib, E., *The Idea of Private Law* (Oxford: Oxford University Press, 1995)

Wilson, J., 'Gabriel Garcia Marquez—A Life, by Gerald Martin', *The Independent* (24 October 2008), https://www.independent.co.uk/arts-entertainment/books/reviews/gabriel-garc-237-a-m-225-rquez-a-life-by-gerald-martin-5358667.html

II. FOUNDATIONS

2. (In)justice in European Private Law

Martijn W. Hesselink

Abstract

This chapter explores the main justice dimensions of European private law (EPL). It distinguishes three different types of (in)justice—social (in)justice, interpersonal (in)justice, and epistemic (in)justice—and determines their relevance, first, for private law in general, and, then, specifically for the private law of the EU. Grounded in a discussion of the European Union's responsibility for private law justice, it considers several possible instances of EPL injustice.

1. Introduction

This chapter explores the main justice dimensions of European private law (EPL). Should EPL be an agent of justice? And in practice, is EPL sometimes—or maybe even often—a source of injustice? What would a minimally just EPL look like? Which reforms might be undertaken to overcome any existing justice deficit in EPL? These are some of the questions central to this chapter.

An important point to realise from the outset is that questions about justice are normative questions about the 'ought' (*Sollen*), as opposed to positive questions about the 'is' (*Sein*). This does not mean at all that the answers necessarily are a matter of mere opinion, as is sometimes thought. There is no reason to think (as an epistemic matter) that truth and plausibility are properties that can apply only to empirical claims. Similarly, the fact that we cannot observe it does not mean that justice and injustice are not real (ontologically speaking). Yet, justice will never be a matter of proof either, be it empirical or logical, but always of reasoning. Ultimately, in matters of justice (and in normative questions more generally) all we have—and what should be decisive—is the unforced force of the better argument, to use the Habermasian phrase.

Questions of justice have not received as much attention in the literature on EPL as one might expect, given the importance that people generally attach to justice. This lack of attention may be due, in part, to the acquis positivism that has characterised much of the discussion on EPL since the debate on a European civil code came to a sudden

 https://doi.org/10.11647/OBP.0448.02

end with the failure of the European Commission's proposal for a common European sales law in 2014. Until then, the debate had been much more about what EPL should become than about analysing the positive EU private law contained in EU legislation and the rulings of the Court of Justice.[1] Moreover, to the extent that the discussion on EPL today is not positivistic the focus is often predominantly economical (whether in the 'law and economics' or 'political economy' approach) or empirical, entirely ignoring the justice dimensions of EPL. The aim of this chapter is to foreground the importance of justice for EU private law.

The focus will not only be on justice and agents of justice, but also on injustice and its victims.[2] While contemporary justice theories tend to focus on what an ideally just society would look like and how it could be realised, we are confronted here and now with the pervasive reality of injustices, great and small, especially the experiences of victims of injustice, the intersecting nature of various injustices,[3] and their justified claims.

The inquiry will proceed as follows. First, we need to clarify what we mean by 'justice'. To that end, Section 2 will explore the main types of (in)justice, the contexts in which they may become pertinent, as well as the question of whether these different kinds of (in)justice can plausibly be grounded in one unitary concept of (in)justice. The following section discusses whether private law has any role to play in ensuring these various types of justice. Section 4 proceeds with the issue of the specific responsibility of the EU for justice in private law. With these three general questions settled, Section 5 will address salient instances of EU private law (in)justice.

2. The Idea of Justice

What do we mean when we speak of 'justice'? The first thing to note is that questions of justice may arise in quite different contexts. Relatedly, injustices can be done to a person in various capacities. Here, we will focus on three types of (in)justice and the contexts in which they typically arise, i.e. the (in)justice done to a person as a member of a society (social justice), as someone involved in an interpersonal relationship (interpersonal justice), and in their capacity as a knower (epistemic justice). The next question is how (if at all) these various types and contexts of justice (and others) are interrelated. Unsurprisingly, many quite diverse understandings of the idea of justice have been proposed. Here, we will discuss one such general idea of justice, i.e. justice as justifiability.

---

1 See e.g. the contributions to H.-W. Micklitz (ed.), *The Many Concepts of Social Justice in European Private Law* (Cheltenham: Edward Elgar, 2011).

2 J. N. Shklar, *The Faces of Injustice* (New Haven, CT: Yale University Press, 1990).

3 K. Crenshaw, 'Demarginalizing the Intersection of Race and Sex: A Black Feminist Critique of Antidiscrimination Doctrine, Feminist Theory and Antiracist Politics', *University of Chicago Legal Forum* 1.8, 139–167.

Social Justice

We can start our discussion of the idea of justice with the distinction between distributive and commutative justice, which was famously introduced by Aristotle.[4] Distributive justice means justice in the distribution of whichever divisible goods there are in a society. In political conversations nowadays, the relevant *distribuendum* is often reduced to wealth and income. However, questions of distributive justice can arise, in principle, with regard to any scarce resource that can make people's lives better.[5] As Aristotle pointed out, different standards can be considered for determining the justice of distributive shares, for example, distribution in proportion to merit, contribution, or need.

The shift in John Rawls' theory of justice from distributive towards social justice is significant in two respects. First, while Aristotle understood justice as a personal virtue of individuals (albeit of particular relevance in political contexts, given Aristotle's understanding of the person as first and foremost a political being and of ethics as especially pertinent in the exercise of a public office) and injustice as the corresponding personal vice of the unjust agent (i.e. taking more than one's due, a form of greed), in the Rawlsian frame the main focus comes to fall on the responsibility of societies to deliver justice through their institutions (leaving to individuals a duty to support just institutions). Indeed, Rawls regards social justice as the first virtue of social institutions.[6] Secondly, the notion of social justice is wider than distributive justice alone: societies can be unjust in different respects than the mere distribution of resources. Social justice, notably, also includes the right to a set of basic liberties (under Rawls' first principle of justice) and equal access to positions (under the first part of Rawls' second principle). Moreover, when it comes to the distribution of resources (under the difference principle, which is the second part of the second principle of justice) the focus is on 'primary goods', which include not only income and wealth but also, for example, the social bases of self-respect.

Yet, in the eyes of certain fellow liberal egalitarians this does not go far enough. In particular, Amartya Sen and Martha Nussbaum have argued that Rawls' approach concentrates too much on distributive outcomes (the number of certain goods one ends up with), thus paying insufficient attention to the importance of human agency. They also contend that Rawls mistakenly presumes the commensurability (expressed in the single currency of primary goods) of the main goods there can be in human life, while human values are plural and in most cases have no common denominator, which entails that they cannot be traded off against one another. Hence, their focus is on ensuring a wide range of human capabilities that allow individuals, through their own choices, to achieve the functions in life that matter to them. However, it

4 Aristotle, *Nicomachean Ethics*, trans. H. Rackham (Cambridge, MA: Harvard University Press, 1994), V, ii, 12. The terms derive from algebra. They refer to different properties of mathematical operations.

5 As David Hume pointed out, circumstances of justice are obtained whenever there is disagreement about the division of advantages and disadvantages of human cooperation.

6 J. Rawls, *A Theory of Justice* (Cambridge, MA: Belknap, 1999), p. 3.

was Rawls' explicit aim that the principles of social justice should depend as little as possible on any particular conception of the good life because in a pluralist society, people can reasonably disagree on what it means to live a good and meaningful life (the fact of reasonable pluralism). And arguably the capabilities approach, especially that of Martha Nussbaum, who proposes a tentative list of ten basic capabilities,[7] relies on too 'thick' a conception of the good life to ensure equal respect for every person, independent of their particular worldview. This brief discussion illustrates how social justice depends not only on how much inequality there is in a society but also on the prior question of what exactly it is that society should ensure equality of ('the equality of what'), and whether in determining the *distribuendum* it is acceptable to favour one conception of what is good and valuable in life over others.

Contrary to those engaged in the debate on the right standard for distributive and social justice, neoliberals and libertarians reject the very notion of social justice as a mere 'mirage', claiming that there is no society, that could be unjust or just, only individuals .[8] They emphatically dismiss the Rawlsian notion of social justice as a 'manna from heaven model', claiming that distributive justice is nothing more (or less) than the repeated operation of justice in transactions (understood purely formally).[9] Apart from being based on a very particular, atomic conception of the person, these views place the entire justificatory burden ultimately on the (Lockean) proviso of justice in original acquisition, which however, can no longer be established most of the time while many if not most cases were plainly unjust (think only of the 'discoveries' of 'new' territories made by European colonists).

Interpersonal Justice

By commutative justice Aristotle meant justice in transactions, which include both voluntary transactions, such as contracts, and involuntary transactions, for example, theft or causing personal injury. The focus here is on the restoration of equality after it was disturbed in a transaction that brought one party a gain and the other a corresponding loss. The determination of equality in exchange can be either substantive (e.g. the idea of a fair price)[10] or formal (e.g. grounded in consent: 'qui dit contractuel dit juste').[11]

The notion of commutative justice has also been widened by contemporary theorists, beyond the narrow sense of mere corrective justice, to a broader concept

---

7 M. C. Nussbaum, *Creating Capabilities: The Human Development Approach* (Cambridge, MA: Belknap Press, 2011), ch. 2.

8 F. A. Hayek, *Law, Legislation and Liberty, Vol 2: The Mirage of Social Justice* (London: Routledge, 2003).

9 R. Nozick, *Anarchy, State, and Utopia* (Oxford: Basic Books, 2013), p. 151.

10 J. Gordley, *The Philosophical Origins of Modern Contract Doctrine* (Oxford: Clarendon Press, 1991), pp. 109–111.

11 A. Fouillée, *La science sociale contemporaine* (Paris: Hachette, 1880), p. 410: 'qui dit contractuel dit juste'. See also T. Hobbes, *Leviathan* (London: Penguin, 1985), p. 208: 'The value of all things contracted for, is measured by the appetite of the contractors: and therefore the just value, is that which they be contented to give.'

of interpersonal justice. In these latter understandings, the focus comes to lie on just and unjust interpersonal conduct. Here, the question of whether interpersonal justice should be understood more substantively (taking into account certain personal characteristics of the parties) or more formally (ignoring all personal differences) has been the main battlefield. As we will see, much of this debate has focused on the appraisal of the materialisation (*Materialisierung*) of private law in the 20th century, i.e. the shift from a formal to a more substantive understanding of the freedom and equality of the parties to private transactions.[12]

Epistemic Injustice

A type of injustice, that transcends both the distributive/commutative and social/interpersonal justice dichotomies, and has attracted much attention recently (and quite rightly so), is epistemic injustice. This is the injustice done to a person in their capacity as a knower. Miranda Fricker distinguishes two main kinds of epistemic injustice.[13] A testimonial injustice is done to someone when they are credited less than others as a trustworthy source of knowledge on arbitrary grounds, for example along racialised or gendered lines. By contrast, hermeneutical injustice is the type of epistemic injustice where a person is inhibited in making sense of her own experience by dominant ways of looking at the world. Think for example, of hate speech or sexual harassment. Where such specific (legal) categories are unavailable, this constitutes an additional injustice for victims, through society's failure or unwillingness to recognise their experiences of these forms of violence. Contrary to certain poststructuralist critiques of the power structures at play in knowledge production, the idea of epistemic justice, vindicating reason (especially reasons for justified belief), understands epistemic injustices as cases where epistemic failure coincides with a moral wrong done to an epistemic agent.

The Right to Justification

Finally, as said, the question arises of whether these different types of justice (and others), that respond to claims and objections arising in different contexts, where persons stand in different types of relationships with each other, can meaningfully be understood as having something in common. This is the question of whether justice claims have a joint root in a single idea of justice. Rainer Forst proposes to understand human beings as justificatory subjects, with a basic right to the justification of decisions and acts affecting them, with reasons which they cannot reasonably reject.[14] Although the specific content of such reasons will depend on the context at hand, in order to

---

12 See M. Auer, *Der privatrechtliche Diskurs der Moderne* (Tübingen: Mohr Siebeck, 2014).

13 M. Fricker, *Epistemic Injustice: Power and the Ethics of Knowing* (Oxford: Oxford University Press, 2007).

14 See R. Forst, *The Right to Justification: Elements of a Constructivist Theory of Justice* (New York: Columbia University Press, 2013). He borrows the standard of non-rejectability from T. M. Scanlon, *What We Owe to Each Other* (Cambridge, MA: Belknap, 1998).

count as reasonably non-rejectable reasons, at a minimum, they will have to meet the two basic conditions of reciprocity and generality. Reciprocity means not claiming any privileges that one is not willing to grant also to others (reciprocity of content) and not projecting one's own values or worldviews onto others (reciprocity of reasons), while generality entails not excluding the arguments coming from anyone affected, given from their own respective points of view. On this view, societal, interpersonal, epistemic, and other justificatory relations are unjust to the extent that reasonably non-rejectable justifications are not available and forthcoming.

Justice Relativism and Justice Scepticism

Before moving on to the relationship between private law and justice it is important to point out that the ideas of social (and distributive) justice, interpersonal (and corrective) justice, epistemic justice, and indeed the right to justification are usually understood as universal. This does not exclude that their concrete implementation in different contexts (different societies, different interpersonal relationships, different epistemic communities) may allow for a margin of appreciation, which may lead to certain (prima facie) divergences in application. Yet, at root, these remain local variations of one and the same idea of justice—in a way quite similar to local interpretations and applications of the same, universal human right.[15]

However, there also exist more relativist conceptions of justice. These include, for example: views of justice as solidarity where justice demands arise out of—and their content and scope is determined by—the interaction between a specific set of individuals and the ensuing interdependence among them; understandings of justice as culture, where justice precepts are determined hermeneutically through the interpretation of a group's respective own traditions; welfarist views where justice is seen exclusively as a matter of (aggregate) subjective personal preferences for a just society (e.g. 'taste for fairness'); of systems theories that regard justice as the (contingent) outcome of functional differentiation; and of constructivist understandings where justice is considered a social construct. Such conceptions are relativist in that they consider the validity of justice claims to be always relative to a given society or group.

Justice scepticism (an instance of moral scepticism) goes further: it denies the reality of justice and the possible validity of justice claims. In this view, justice does not exist and the debate on the demands of justice is meaningless.[16] Notably, sceptics

15 The reference is of course to the 'margin of appreciation' doctrine developed by the European Court of Human Rights in Strasbourg in its interpretation of the European Convention on Human Rights.

16 Some of the most radical instances of social-constructivist relativism, especially the purportedly Foucauldian ones that understand the social construction of justice (and of truth, for that matter) as the mere product of power struggles, verge on scepticism. For example, constructivist views that regard any reference to justice merely as the hegemonic discourse produced by capitalism, patriarchy, or colonialism, aim to delegitimate, not merely to relativise, the idea of justice, thus renouncing the possibility to denounce capitalism, patriarchy, or colonialism as being fundamentally unjust. Moral (and epistemic) scepticism seems in contrast with Michel Foucault's own view about the historically contingent social preconditions for the validity of moral and epistemic claims (historical a priori),

regard justice as a mere label given by those in power to whatever corresponds to their interests (Thrasymachus),[17] as purely ideological, an expression of false consciousness (Marx), or, conversely, they reject the denunciation of injustice as (Christian) pity for the weak (Nietzsche).[18]

3. Private Law as an Agent of (In)justice

Justice is not merely a matter of determining who should have what (rights), but also of establishing who has a corresponding responsibility to ensure and protect these fair shares and entitlements (obligations). As Onora O'Neill points out, 'in the end obligations rather than rights are the active aspects of justice'.[19] Therefore, our next question in the present context concerns the relationship between justice and private law: can and should systems of private law be agents of justice? If so, does this equally hold for all types of justice or is it private law's task to ensure only specific types of justice? Let's consider the types of justice just introduced and ask ourselves whether private law ought to be an agent of distributive, interpersonal, and epistemic justice, respectively, followed by the question of whether a general right to justification of private law exists.

Distributive (In)justice through Private Law

Some theorists argue that private law has no role to play in achieving distributive justice. They offer different reasons for this claim.

The first set of reasons postulates a division of labour between private law, on the one hand, and the welfare state on the other. Welfare economists, for example, argue that the pursuit of distributive justice through private law is inefficient. The argument is straightforward, indeed definitional. If private law is used for other purposes than to maximise overall welfare in society, then, insofar, there is a potential welfare loss. Therefore, if distributive justice is a societal objective (i.e. when there exists an aggregate preference for distributive fairness), then the pie to be divided will be smaller if private law is made instrumental to achieving a fair distribution of income than it could be if private law limited itself to setting efficient incentives for private parties and redistribution was done exclusively through the system of tax and transfer (subsidies etc.). In other words, the argument goes, distributive justice through private law harms the poor.[20] As it has been pointed out, however, this

---

which is merely relativistic. See M. Foucault, *The Order of Things: An Archaeology of the Human Sciences* (New York: Vintage, 1994).

17 Plato, *The Republic* (London: Penguin, 2007).

18 F. Nietzsche, *On the Genealogy of Morals: A Polemic* (London: Penguin, 2013).

19 O. O'Neill, 'Agents of Justice', in O'Neill, *Justice Across Boundaries: Whose Obligations?* (Cambridge, UK: Cambridge University Press, 2016), pp. 177–192 (p. 183).

20 L. Kaplow and S. Shavell, 'Why the Legal System is Less Efficient than the Income Tax in Redistributing Income', *Journal of Legal Studies* 23.2 (1994), 667–681.

outcome-oriented economic idea of distributive justice as redistribution of money fails to consider the source-sensitive nature of justice. Money hand-outs by the State are not the same (not even on the welfarists' own terms of preference satisfaction, let alone in terms of human dignity) as preventing distributive injustice from arising (or being exacerbated) in the first place in relationships governed by private law.[21]

Rawls also thought that the law applicable to individual transactions should not be counted among the socio-economic institutions responsible for delivering social justice (what he called the 'basic structure of society'). His argument, which explicitly invokes the notion of a division of labour, is not strictly economical but relies on the notion of practicability. The idea is that it is not feasible for private parties—and can therefore not be expected from them—to foresee all the distributive ramifications of their private transactions.[22] However, this diagnosis fails to distinguish between the respective responsibilities of the private parties for their transactions and of society for its private law. Nobody argues that private transactions should be considered part of the basic structure of society, but private law (or at least its basic structure) may well be de facto among the main institutions responsible for distributive justice.[23] This has been the case especially since the socio-economic policies of privatisation, deregulation, and the dismantling of the welfare state (often referred to as 'neoliberalism') radically (re-)transformed private law's distributive role.

Finally, there is the argument relying on a moral division of labour, based on a moralist reading of private law (on which further below). If we understand private law as exclusively concerned with implementing interpersonal morality, formally understood, then (again, by definition) private law should not pursue distributive justice, because individual persons (as opposed to society) have no personal (positive) responsibility for how well other people's lives go; all they have to do is to refrain (negatively) from taking something that is not theirs and it is private law's only task to restore the status quo ante (corrective justice) after such 'boundary-crossing'.[24]

In contrast, other scholars are in favour of distributive justice through private law.[25] None of them claims, of course, that private law alone could achieve distributive justice. All they sustain is that the basic structure of private law has a legitimate

21 D. Lewinsohn-Zamir, 'In Defense of Redistribution Through Private Law', *Minnesota Law Review* 91 (2006), 326–397.

22 J. Rawls, *Political Liberalism* (New York: Columbia University Press, 2005), pp. 266–269.

23 In this sense, see e.g. K. A. Kordana and D. H. Tabachnick, 'Rawls and Contract Law', *George Washington Law Review* 73 (2005), 598–632; J. Klijnsma, *Contract Law as Fairness: A Rawlsian Perspective on the Position of SMEs in European Contract Law* (Amsterdam: University of Amsterdam, 2014); S. Scheffler, 'Distributive Justice, the Basic Structure and the Place of Private Law', *Oxford Journal of Legal Studies* 35.2 (2015), 213–235; M. W. Hesselink, 'Unjust Conduct in the Internal Market: On the Role of European Private Law in the Division of Moral Responsibility Between the EU, its Member States and Their Citizens', *Yearbook of European Law* 35 (2016), 410–452; L. K. L. Tjon Soei Len, *Minimum Contract Justice: A Capabilities Perspective on Sweatshops and Consumer Contracts* (Portland, OR: Hart Publishing, 2017).

24 E. J. Weinrib, *The Idea of Private Law* (Cambridge, MA: Harvard University Press, 1995); A. Ripstein, 'Private Order and Public Justice: Kant and Rawls', *Virginia Law Review* 92 (2006), 1391–1438. See also R. Dworkin, *Justice for Hedgehogs* (Cambridge, MA: Belknap Press, 2011), p. 287: 'swimming in your own lane'.

25 A. T. Kronman, 'Contract Law and Distributive Justice', *Yale Law Journal* 89 (1980), 472–511.

structural role to play in ensuring background justice for individual transactions. In particular, private law should determine rights and obligations in such a way that they do not 'exacerbate distributive injustice'.[26] As a general matter, from the point of view of distributive justice, it is much better to prevent distributive injustices from occurring (e.g. in the context of exploitative transactions) than to remedy them through redistribution via tax and transfer.[27] Put differently, private law has no legitimate role to play in making people unjustifiably become poorer. Moreover, it makes no sense—and at some point it becomes cynical—to keep referring to a redistribution through tax and transfer that realistically speaking will never come to pass. Therefore, as a matter of nonideal theory, given the absence of any realistic prospect for progressive reform, we should take into account the current state of the overall basic structure of society rather than merely its ideal version.[28] Perhaps in an ideal society, it would be possible to achieve full background social justice through other institutions than private law. However, that theoretical possibility does not relieve our private law as it exists today from preventing distributive injustices where it can, especially those that will not be prevented or remedied by any other institutions where these are lacking.[29]

Interpersonal (In)justice through Private Law

The role of interpersonal justice in private law is much less controversial. Of course, welfare fundamentalists will argue that private law should solely be a matter of economic efficiency, not also justice,[30] and radical Marxists will claim that all private transactions in a market economy are intrinsically exploitative.[31] However, beyond these extreme positions, there is wide agreement that interpersonal justice has an

26 A. Bagchi, 'Distributive Justice and Contract', in G. Klass, G. Letsas, and P. Saprai (eds), *Philosophical Foundations of Contract Law* (Oxford: Oxford University Press, 2014), pp. 193–212 (p. 199).

27 See S. V. Shiffrin, 'Paternalism, Unconscionability Doctrine, and Accommodation', *Philosophy and Public Affairs* 29 (2000), 205–250 (p. 224), who observes that the American contract law doctrine of unconscionability, for example, 'works directly to staunch the flow of resources from the disadvantaged to those who are better off, both by voiding exploitative contracts and by deterring their formation. These are some of the very effects that the redistributive transfers brought about by the tax system would aim in part to reverse'.

28 See A. Bagchi, 'Distributive Injustice and Private Law', *Hastings Law Journal* 60 (2008), 105–149.

29 The extreme version of this argument is the mirror image of Nozickean justice: in the total absence of any other institutions responsible for social justice, it will fall upon private law alone to ensure social justice. In that hypothetical scenario, private law alone would constitute the basic structure of society responsible for ensuring distributive justice. This nightmare scenario is sometimes celebrated by libertarians (in particular, ordoliberals) as the 'private law society'. See F. Böhm, 'Privatrechtsgesellschaft und Marktwirtschaft', ORDO*: Jahrbuch für die Ordnung von Wirtschaft und Gesellschaft* 17 (1966), 75–151, and with specific reference to European private law, S. Grundmann, 'The Concept of the Private Law Society: After 50 years of European and European Business Law', *European Review of Private Law* 16 (2008), 553–581.

30 L. Kaplow and S. Shavell, *Fairness Versus Welfare* (Cambridge, MA: Harvard University Press, 2002).

31 This is the case simply because they reproduce economically determined power relationships. Specifically with regard to labour contracts, see K. Marx, *Capital: An Abridged Edition*, ed. by D. McLellan (Oxford: Oxford University Press), p. 323. With regard to commercial contracts, see K. Marx, 'On James Mill', in D. McLellan (ed.), *Karl Marx: Selected Writings*, 2nd edn (Oxford University Press, 2000), pp. 124–133 (p. 130): 'mutual plundering'.

important role to play in private law, and conversely, that much of private law can be justified in terms of interpersonal justice.

This immediately raises the question of what exactly this entails. On the narrowest version of this (natural law) view, private rights, obligations, and remedies should be entirely formal. They should not distinguish between private parties in terms of, for instance, their power, vulnerability, experience, expertise, cognitive skills etc., because, according to this perspective, a more substantive approach would not constitute justice at all. It would already amount to the pursuit of objectives external to interpersonal justice.[32] By contrast, on a 'materialised' or substantive view of interpersonal justice, the equality between private parties and their private autonomy should indeed be understood in a more substantive sense.[33]

The next question is whether private law can legitimately pursue other aims than interpersonal justice. On one view, all that private law should do is implement interpersonal morality, nothing more and nothing less.[34] To be more precise, private law should be understood as giving rise to a system of interpersonal rights and corresponding obligations (whether merely formal or materialised). From this perspective, it is illegitimate to treat parties in private law transactions as mere means to achieve some end that is considered socially desirable. Ends that could be pursued by a teleological private law may relate to the private parties themselves, facilitating them in leading better lives by some objective standard, for example, autonomy understood as self-authorship ('writing the story of one's own life').[35] They may also be more collective, for example, economic growth,[36] or halting climate change.[37] On a

32 Weinrib, *The Idea of Private Law*; E. J. Weinrib, *Corrective Justice* (Oxford: Oxford University Press, 2012); A. Ripstein, *Force and Freedom: Kant's Legal and Political Philosophy* (Cambridge, MA: Harvard University Press, 2009).

33 C. Canaris, 'Wandlungen des Schuldvertragsrechts—Tendenzen zu seiner "Materialisierung"', *Archiv für die civilistische Praxis* 200 (2000), 273–364. The distinction between formal and substantive concepts of law goes back to Max Weber, who, however, identified formal legality with reason and was critical of substantive notions of contractual fairness. See M. Weber, *Economy and Society*, ed. by G. Roth and C. Wittich, 2 vols (Oakland, CA: University of California Press, 1978) II, p. 886.

34 See Weinrib, *The Idea of Private Law*, and Ripstein, *Force and Freedom*. In contrast, S. V. Shiffrin, 'The Divergence of Contract and Promise', *Harvard Law Review* 120 (2007), 708–753, makes the much more modest claim that private law should accommodate persons who understand their private law rights and obligations also as morally binding.

35 H. Dagan and M. Heller, *The Choice Theory of Contracts* (Cambridge, UK: Cambridge University Press, 2017). See also H. Dagan and A. Dorfman, 'Just Relationships', *Columbia Law Review* 116 (2016), 1395–1460, who focus more on self-determination (a deontological-republican concept), rather than on self-authorship (a teleological notion), but still understand interpersonal justice mostly in terms—and perhaps at the service—of (substantive) autonomy.

36 See Kaplow and Shavell, *Fairness Versus Welfare.*

37 To the extent that climate change can be understood as something for which certain private parties (e.g. shareholders in an international corporation engaged in massive emissions) are responsible towards other private parties (individuals whose human rights to life and health are affected) climate justice may be a case of interpersonal justice. However, this understanding involves several hurdles, including whether interpersonal justice applies to corporations (e.g. via joint responsibility of their shareholders, which include major pension funds) and whether the right to health gives rise to horizontal duties. Arguably a (bold) step in this direction, was the decision in the Dutch case, The Hague District Court, *Vereniging Milieudefensie and others v Royal Dutch Shell* [26 May 2021] ECLI:NL:RBDHA:2021:5339. Alternatively, the case can be read as concerned mainly with distributive

somewhat wider view, private law can pursue other ends but only to the extent that these do not undermine interpersonal justice (the priority of the right over the good). Finally, on the widest view, interpersonal justice is merely one value among many that the legitimate lawmaker may freely pursue. This question of the legitimacy of private law instrumentalism will be further addressed below.

Epistemic (In)justice through Private Law

Epistemic injustice in or through private law is still underexplored. However, there are certain obvious cases. For example, in civil litigation, a testimonial injustice is done whenever a party, legal counsel, a witness, or an expert is granted lower or higher authority than others based on prejudice, e.g. along gendered or racialised lines.[38] Another instance is cases where women (until far into the 20th century), as well as minors and persons with mental disabilities (still today), lack 'legal capacity' and, therefore, need legal representation in order to conclude a legally binding contract or similar juridical act.[39] As an example of hermeneutical injustice, Lyn Tjon Soei Len shows how contract law, by splitting of global value chains (GVCs) into discrete contractual transactions, obscures how these various contractual relations are interconnected and, thus, renders the nature and structure of exploitation in GVCs unintelligible even to those subjected to it.[40]

The Right to Justification of Private Law

Is there a general right to justification of private law?[41] Arguably there is, at least as far as the basic structure of private law is concerned, which, as we saw, may be a part of the basic structure of society. The basic structure consists of those structural elements

justice (fair shares in emission rights, given that that stopping climate change does not require zero emissions), or of subjective rights of other-than-human entities (animals, plants, Mother Nature). The judgment was overturned on appeal on the grounds that 'Shell cannot be bound by a 45% reduction standard (or any other percentage) agreed by climate science because this percentage does not apply to every country and every business sector individually' (The Hague Court of Appeal, Judgment of 12 November 2024, ECLI:NL:GHDHA:2024:2100). This seems a rejection in particular of the distributive justice argument.

38 M. Fricker, *Epistemic Injustice*, p. 23, discusses the example of the testimony given by the accused in the criminal trial central to H. Lee, *To Kill a Mockingbird* (1960).

39 UN Convention on the Rights of Persons with Disabilities (2006), Article 12 (equal recognition before the law). Cf. Committee on the Rights of Persons with Disabilities, 'General Comment No. 1' (2014), https://ukraine.un.org/en/133050-general-comment-no-1-article-12-equal-recognition-law, para. 3 and 9: '[T]here has been a general failure to understand that the human rights-based model of disability implies a shift from the substitute decision-making paradigm to one that is based on supported decision-making. ... [P]ersons with cognitive or psychosocial disabilities have been, and still are, disproportionately affected by substitute decision-making regimes and denial of legal capacity'.

40 L. K. L. Tjon Soei Len, 'Hermeneutical Injustice, Contract Law, and Global Value Chains', *European Review of Contract Law* 16.1 (2020), 139–159.

41 Specifically with regard to contract law, see M. W. Hesselink, 'The Right to Justification of Contract', *Ratio Juris* 33 (2020), 196–222.

and features of a system of private law that are most important in determining the rights and obligations of the persons to whom it applies. From a discourse-theoretical point of view, it is for the addressees of a legal system themselves to decide which of its aspects matters most in terms of social, interpersonal, epistemic, and other types of justice (and insofar as the definition of the basic structure is always circular to some extent). Having said that, the basic structure of private seems unlikely to coincide with its main doctrinal structure. For example, from a doctrinal point of view much of what Hans Micklitz has called 'regulatory private law' (such as the various rules and standards applying to privatised utilities) may seem rather peripheral and accidental (it will be hardly ever found in the civil code),[42] but from an (in)justice point of view it is likely to be much more central and fundamental.

4. The EU's Responsibility for Justice

The next question is whether the EU is responsible for private law justice. The answer is less straightforward—and more controversial—than it might seem. This has much to do with the controversial ontological question of the nature of the EU and its legal system(s), following from the fact that the EU's legislative competences are limited, instrumental, and (in the field of private law) shared with the Member States.

The European Society

So far, the debate on EU justice has concentrated mainly on social justice. Following Rawls, many theories of justice regard the basic structure of society as the first subject of justice.[43] This seems to suggest—if it does not already follow from the very idea of social justice—that there must be a society, whose basic structure it is, and which can be held responsible for justice. But is the EU a society? That question is akin to the questions of whether the EU is a state and whether the EU has a people, represented by the European Parliament. While the question about statehood is widely answered in the negative (the EU is not a state), the question of whether there is such a thing as a 'we the people' of the EU is more controversial.[44] Central to this debate is the no-demos thesis, as famously defended by the German Federal Constitutional Court and by one of its former justices Dieter Grimm and equally famously rejected by Jürgen Habermas, arguing that the thesis relies on an unduly ethical conception of a people (*Volk, demos*), understood as a community sharing thick cultural-historical bonds.[45]

---

42 See H.-W. Micklitz, Y. Svetiev, and G. Comparato (eds), 'European Regulatory Private Law—The Paradigm Tested', *EUI-ERC Working Paper* 4 (2014), 69–97; H.-W. Micklitz, *The Politics of Justice in European Private Law: Social Justice, Access Justice, Societal Justice* (Cambridge, UK: Cambridge University Press, 2018).

43 Rawls, *Political Liberalism*, p. 287. In the same sense, Nussbaum, *Creating Capabilities*, p. 166; Forst, The *Right to Justification*, p. 80.

44 Cf. the famous preamble of the US constitution: 'We the people of the United States, in order to form a more perfect union ...'.

45 See, respectively, BVerfG, *Judgment of the Second Senate of 30 June 2009—2 BvE 2/08—(Lisbon)*

However, arguably, the question of social justice should be addressed from the opposite end. The EU has set up an institutional structure with a pervasive impact on people's lives, not least on distributive shares. In other words, the facts of an EU basic structure and of EU citizens (and others) being subjected to it, demand, normatively speaking, the applicability of principles of social justice.[46]

Similarly, the question of sovereignty should not be decisive either. Even if it were true that Member States have retained sovereignty, as Grimm claims—maintaining *Kompetenz-Kompetenz* as 'lords of the treaties', with the sole authority to limit their own sovereign power (or not)—and Habermas denies, advocating instead for *pouvoir constituant mixte*, where citizens are sovereign in their dual capacity as both Member State and EU citizen,[47] then still the mere fact of pervasive EU competences (acknowledged also by Grimm) bars any generalised 'ought implies can' defence against the EU's moral responsibility (or that of its Members States jointly) for the justice of its basic structure.[48]

Attributed Competences

Having said that, the EU is clearly handicapped in delivering justice by the fact that a key feature of the EU's basic structure is that the EU has only a limited set of competences to legislate (principle of conferral), and that none of them constitutes the explicit competence to promote justice. Arguably, a legislative programme with justice as its explicit and only aim would lack a legal basis and therefore would be ultra vires. In other words, does not the moral maxim of 'ought implies can' absolve the EU after all from any responsibility for ensuring that the basic structure of EU law is sufficiently just? Again, arguably this line of arguing gets things backwards. As a series of treaty reforms culminating in the Lisbon Treaty (2007) has shown, the EU—or, on the sovereigntist view, its Member States—can change its basic structure at any time, even radically if it wants. Therefore, rather than exempting the EU from moral responsibility for social justice, arguably the structure of limited, functional competences is itself subject to principles of justice. And the EU (or its sovereign Member States) should take responsibility for any injustices deriving from it.

[2009] ECLI:DE:BVerfG:2009:es20090630.2bve000208, para. 280 ('the European Parliament is not a representative body of a sovereign European people'); D. Grimm, 'Does Europe Need a Constitution?', *European Law Journal* 1.3 (1995), 282–302; and J. Habermas, *Europe: The Faltering Project* (Cambridge, UK: Polity Press, 2009), p. 86.

46 There is the additional constitutional argument of the EU's commitment, in Article 3 Paragraph 3 TEU, to 'promote social justice'.

47 See respectively, D. Grimm, *The Constitution of European Democracy* (Oxford: Oxford University Press, 2017), esp. ch. 3; and J. Habermas, *The Crisis of the European Union: A Response* (Cambridge, UK: Polity Press, 2012); J. Habermas, 'Citizen and State Equality in a Supranational Political Community: Degressive Proportionality and the *pouvoir constituant mixte*', *Journal for Common Market Studies* 55 (2017), 171–182.

48 Grimm, *The Constitution of European Democracy*, p. 44: 'As far as the number of powers and the density of the organizational structure are concerned, the EU does not differ fundamentally from the central state in a federal system'.

Functional Competences

From a justice point of view, it is not clear that the European constitutionalisation of private law functionalism is acceptable, because it ignores the priority of the right over the good.[49] It may well have been acceptable and even desirable for the EU to 'adopt measures with the aim of establishing or ensuring the functioning of the internal market', comprising 'an area without internal frontiers in which the free movement of goods, persons, services and capital is ensured' (Article 26 TFEU). However, that objective and the related competence should remain subject to justice concerns rather than overriding them through the constitutionalisation of the market-building objective.[50]

Shared Competences

The presence of shared competences, notably with regard to the internal market (Article 4 Paragraph 2 TFEU), poses another puzzle. What does this mean for the EU's moral responsibility to ensure justice in the internal market?[51] Pursuant to Article 2 Paragraph 2 TFEU, when the treaties confer a competence in a specific area upon the EU shared with the Member States, then both the EU and the Member States are free to legislate in that area. But wherever the EU has already exercised its competence the Member States are pre-empted insofar from legislating in that area. In practice, pre-emption occurs with regard to potential national legislation within the scope of regulations and full harmonisation directives. Arguably, in those cases of pre-emption, the EU takes full responsibility for the proper functioning of the particular aspect or sector of the internal market at hand, including its justice dimensions, because there the Member States are prohibited from legislating, including with a view to ensuring justice. Ought implies can. This means that only in the cases of minimum harmonisation directives (still a vast proportion of EU private law) can the EU shift the blame for any injustices to the Member States.

5. EU Private Law as an Agent of (In)justice

The Failed Social Justice Agenda

A manifesto published by a group of legal scholars in 2004, in response to the European Commission's Action Plan on European Contract Law,[52] brought the issue of social

49 See Rawls, *Political Liberalism*, 173ff (Lecture V: 'The priority of right and ideas of the good').

50 Arguably, the establishment of a properly functioning internal market already requires the prevention of any injustices from occurring in that market, even when this entails, for example, a limitation to free movement. However, this reading of Article 114 TFEU is far from generally established.

51 See Hesselink, 'Unjust Conduct in the Internal Market'.

52 Commission Communication, 'A More Coherent European Contract Law: An Action Plan', COM (2003) 68 final, https://eur-lex.europa.eu/legal-content/EN/TXT/?uri=oj:JOC_2003_063_R_0001_01

justice in European private law to academic and political agendas.[53] One of the core claims in the manifesto was that:

> The rules of contract law shape the distribution of wealth and power in modern societies. To the extent that nation-states reduce their use of the direct re-distributive mechanisms of the welfare state, the distributive effects of the market become the determining force governing people's life chances. A modern statement of the principles of the private law of contract needs to recognise its increasingly pivotal role in establishing distributive fairness in society.[54]

Although the manifesto attracted quite some attention, it failed to make social justice concerns become an integral part of European private law-making. To give merely one striking example, the impact assessments that have accompanied legislative proposals ever since the adoption of the EU's Lisbon strategy,[55] including those in the area of private law, while emphasising economic growth, remain entirely silent as to the distribution of the wealth that new EU private law measures are expected to create. Meanwhile, new social justice concerns have arisen. Think, for example, of the uneven benefits Europeans located in Member States at the European periphery derive from free movement rights and consumer protection compared to those situated at its core.[56] A more recent social justice concern is how to decolonise European private law. Little is known at present, for example, about any differential impacts of EU private law between Europeans with different racial and ethnic backgrounds, which does not necessarily bode well. And if European private law, which claims general applicability in Europe (and beyond), is made nearly exclusively by white people (in the legislature, courts, and legal doctrine), then do the many Europeans of colour have good reason to expect that it will work equally well for them?

EU Consumer Law as Substantive Interpersonal Justice

The vast majority of EU private law consists of the consumer law acquis. The language used by the EU legislator in justifying consumer legislation has varied over time. During the first stage the focus was on the protection of consumers as the weaker parties in their relationships with professional sellers and service providers. Typical examples

53 Study Group on Social Justice in European Private Law, 'Social Justice in European Contract Law: A Manifesto', *European Law Journal* 10.6 (2004), 653–674. Two decades later, a new generation came together in Amsterdam to discuss a new manifesto on social justice in European private law. Cf the thirty-three blogposts published at Symposium Social Justice '44, Transformative Private Law Blog (https://transformativeprivatelaw.com/category/symposium-social-justice-44/).

54 Ibid., p. 665.

55 Council of the European Union, 'Presidency Conclusions, Lisbon European Council 23 and 24 March 2000', https://www.europarl.europa.eu/summits/lis1_en.htm, para. 5, 14. The aim of the strategy was for the internal market to become the most competitive economy in the world.

56 See D. Caruso, 'Qu'ils mangent des contrats: Rethinking Justice in EU Contract Law', in D. Kochenov, G. de Búrca, and A. Williams (eds), *Europe's Justice Deficit?* (Oxford: Hart Publishing, 2014), n.p. See more generally, D. Kukovec, 'Law and the Periphery', *European Law Journal* 21 (2015), 406–428.

include the Doorstep Selling Directive and the Unfair Terms Directive (1993).[57] Then, following the Lisbon Agenda (2000), the attention shifted towards efforts to increase consumer confidence in cross-border shopping and to create a level playing field for sellers with a view to boosting the European economy ('justice for growth' was the favourite slogan at the time).[58] The Consumer Rights Directive, in spite of its title, which speaks the language of rights, and especially the (failed) proposal for a common European sales law, were paradigmatic during this second stage.[59] Finally, in more recent years, starting with the New Deal for Consumers, the European Commission has shown a renewed interest in fairness ('building a fair single market for consumers and businesses').[60] It is too soon to tell whether this change of tune inaugurated an era of EU consumer law as interpersonal justice and fairness—a third in the development of EU private law.[61]

By contrast, the Court of Justice of the European Union (CJEU) has been consistent in its focus on weaker party protection and substantive equality, especially in its interpretation of the unfair terms directive. The exemplary case is *Mostaza Claro*.[62] There the Court held that the directive 'aims to replace the formal balance which the [contract] establishes between the rights and obligations of the parties with an effective balance which re-establishes equality between them'.[63] This focus on party inequality amounts in effect to reading consumer law in terms of substantive interpersonal justice. Note that it moves internal market instrumentalism entirely to the background. In sum, in spite of its legal basis in Article 114 TFEU and its usually explicitly stated legislative aim of the internal market building, much of the consumer law acquis can plausibly be read, nevertheless, as an attempt at promoting substantive interpersonal justice.[64]

---

57 See, respectively, Council Directive 85/577/EEC to protect the consumer in respect of contracts negotiated away from business premises [1985] OJ L372/31, and Council Directive 93/13/EEC on unfair terms in consumer contracts, in particular the preliminary recitals [1993] OJ L95/29.

58 See Commission Communication 'The EU Justice Agenda for 2020: Strengthening Trust, Mobility and Growth within the Union', COM (2014) 144 final, https://eur-lex.europa.eu/legal-content/EN/TXT/?uri=celex:52014DC0144, esp. para. 2, 7: 'justice for growth'.

59 See Directive 2011/83/EU of the European Parliament and of the Council on consumer rights [2011] OJ L304/69, and Commission Communication, 'Proposal for a Regulation of the European Parliament and of the Council on a Common European Sales Law', COM (2011) 635 final, https://eur-lex.europa.eu/legal-content/en/TXT/?uri=CELEX%3A32011L0083, respectively.

60 Commission Communication, 'A New Deal for Consumers', COM (2018) 183 final, https://eur-lex.europa.eu/legal-content/EN/TXT/?uri=celex:52018DC0183

61 For a somewhat differently articulated three-stage account, see Micklitz, The Politics of Justice, p. 257.

62 Case C-168/05 *Mostaza Claro* [2006] EU:C:2006:675, para. 36. In CJEU, 16 June 2011, *Gebr. Weber and Putz*, joined cases C-65/09 and C-87/09, EU:C:2011:396, para. 75, the Court held also with reference to the consumer sales directive 1999 that it 'aims to establish a fair balance between the interests of the consumer and the seller'.

63 This is consistently held by the CJEU. More recently, see e.g. Case C-266/18 *Aqua Med* [2019] ECLI:EU:C:2019:282, para. 27; Case C-383/18 *Lexitor* [2019] ECLI:EU:C:2019:702, para. 29.

64 See further Hesselink, 'Unjust Conduct in the Internal Market', esp. 436ff. In the same sense, for the unfair terms directive, see also C. Leone, *The Missing Stone in the Cathedral: Of Unfair Terms in Employment Contracts and Coexisting Rationalities in European Contract Law* (doctoral thesis, University of Amsterdam, 2020), whose analysis, however, is based on impersonal 'rationalities' rather than on political agency and on moral responsibility for justice.

Yet, there is a complication. The idea of substantive interpersonal justice is that, instead of ignoring, as formal corrective justice does, the relevant differences between the parties, such as their respective cognitive skills, experience, expertise, and bargaining power, it takes these into account where relevant. Put differently, while formal corrective justice adopts an entirely abstract conception of the person engaged in transactions governed by private law, a more substantive justice approach understands persons addressed by private law more fully as they are situated. In practice, this means, for example, that substantive interpersonal justice is not satisfied with merely formal freedom of contract (i.e. the mere absence of interference, without any realistic alternative options) or with mere formal party equality (i.e. the formally equal right to influence the terms of the contract, without the realistic possibility to do so). Therefore, substantive interpersonal justice demands a contextualised approach where the characteristics of the actual parties and their actual relationship are taken into account. A complicating factor, however, in understanding EU consumer law as in fact concerned with substantive interpersonal justice, is that consumer protection is entirely formal. It emphatically does *not* take into account the substantive characteristics of the parties. Instead, it treats them as belonging to one of two formal categories, i.e. consumers and sellers or professional service providers. From the point of view of EU consumer law, it is indifferent whether the professional is a small business (e.g. a shop-owner without employees), inexperienced (e.g. a start-up), in a weak bargaining position (e.g. on the verge of insolvency), or suffering from some cognitive bias (e.g. presence bias or path-dependence). Nor does it matter if the consumer is in fact a highly skilled and powerful billionaire. The result is that the categorical protection of consumers, based as it is on formal definitions of legal categories, is bound to be frequently off the mark (i.e. be over- and underinclusive) from the point of view of interpersonal justice.

However, arguably, what may thus be unacceptable from a point of view of interpersonal justice may perhaps be justified to some extent in terms of social justice. Insofar as access to justice for different social groups in society is a plausibly important aspect of social justice, this may in fact justify categorical consumer protection (and other instances of categorical protection in private law, e.g. the protection of employees and tenants). To try to fully ensure substantive interpersonal justice in all transactions, even the smallest ones, would probably be very expensive—indeed, so expensive that in some cases it might become available in reality only to the richest individuals (because poor consumers are priced out of the market for the relevant services or goods).[65] Therefore, arguably as a matter of non-ideal justice theory, it is acceptable for a society to distribute access to interpersonal justice through private law in such a way that it remains affordable, by keeping it less costly (formal rules are much cheaper to apply than more substantive ones), at the inevitable price, however, of being also more approximative in terms of interpersonal justice (the other side of the coin).[66]

---

65 See D. Kennedy, 'Distributive and Paternalist Motives in Contract and Tort Law, with Special Reference to Compulsory Terms and Unequal Bargaining Power', *Maryland Law Review* 41 (1982), 563–658.

66 See further M. W. Hesselink, 'Private Law, Regulation, and Justice', *European Law Journal* 22 (2016), 681–695.

Alienation through Consumer Law

More generally, the reading of EU consumer law as substantive interpersonal justice risks becoming apologetic when it slips from a critical normative assessment into acquis positivism and CJEU adulation. Remember that some justice conceptions focus on outcomes while for others the source, justificatory discourse, and epistemic dimensions may be equally important. To start with the latter. From the point of view of epistemic justice, it matters how one is addressed as a person. Being treated by the law as a consumer makes it more difficult to understand oneself—and the relationship one has with others—as a person involved in activities that have nothing to do with consumption. Indeed, more generally the transformation, through privatisation and liberalisation, of relationships between citizens (or residents) and the State into market transactions with a private firm, has had an undeniable impact on the self-understanding of individuals in the EU. How can one continue to understand oneself as availing oneself of public utilities if the EU relabels those as the provision of essential services, of which one now has become a consumer, that are provided on the internal market, and to which the EU ensures access?[67] Indeed, it has even been argued that guaranteeing market access has become the EU's own characteristic conception of justice: access justice.[68] However, arguably the transformations of public utilities into market services, of citizens and residents into consumers, and of social justice into market access justice, constitute an epistemic injustice (more specifically, a hermeneutical injustice) to the extent that these impede individuals in understanding themselves in vast areas of their lives as other than economic agents, in particular consumers of services on the internal market.

Agency

Finally, if we take the dignity and agency of human beings as justificatory subjects seriously, then clearly, legal scholars cannot determine the (in)justice of European private law over the heads of those subjected to it. Indeed, as Forst points out, the first demand of justice is for those subjected to a normative order to have standing as equal normative authorities within that order.[69] Therefore, the instances of potential cases of injustice in European private law presented here can only be tentative. It is likely to be both over and underinclusive, written as it is (inevitably) from a particular point of view. Indeed, also for European private law, it is true that its justice can only be determined discursively, in an inclusive democratic debate. However, as indicated

67 See Directive 2002/22/EC of the European Parliament and of the Council on universal service and users' rights relating to electronic communications networks and services ('Universal Service Directive') as amended by Directive 2009/136/EC [2002] OJ L108/51.

68 On access justice, see H.-W. Micklitz, 'Social Justice and Access Justice in Private Law', in H.-W. Micklitz (ed.), *The Many Concepts of Social Justice in European Private Law* (Cheltenham: Edward Elgar, 2011), pp. 3–60; Micklitz, *The Politics of Justice*.

69 R. Forst, *Normativity and Power: Analyzing Social Orders of Justification* (Oxford: Oxford University Press, 2017), p. 43.

at the beginning, that was also not the point of this chapter. Rather, its main objective has been to show how much justice matters for European private law—and vice versa.

Points for Reflection

Q1: Is private law an agent of justice?

Q2: Does EPL suffer from a justice deficit?

Q3: Can the (in)justice of EPL be objectively determined?

Q4: Is the internal market only properly functioning if it is free from any injustices?

Q5: Is consumer protection a matter of justice?

Q6: Is it a justice problem that EPL has been made nearly exclusively by white people (in the legislature, courts, and legal doctrine)?

Q7: Should justice have priority over all other considerations in EPL?

Q8: Is it time for a new social justice manifesto?

Bibliography

Aristotle, *Nicomachean Ethics*, trans. H. Rackham (Cambridge, MA: Harvard University Press, 1994)

Auer, M., *Der privatrechtliche Diskurs der Moderne* (Tübingen: Mohr Siebeck, 2014)

Bagchi, A., 'Distributive Justice and Contract', in G. Klass, G. Letsas, and P. Saprai (eds), *Philosophical Foundations of Contract Law* (Oxford: Oxford University Press, 2014), pp. 193–212, https://doi.org/10.1093/acprof:oso/9780198713012.003.0011

Bagchi, A., 'Distributive Injustice and Private Law', *Hastings Law Journal* 60 (2008), 105–149, https://doi.org/10.2139/ssrn.1012954

Böhm, F., 'Privatrechtsgesellschaft und Marktwirtschaft', ORDO*: Jahrbuch für die Ordnung von Wirtschaft und Gesellschaft* 17 (1966), 75–151

Canaris, C., 'Wandlungen des Schuldvertragsrechts—Tendenzen zu seiner "Materialisierung"', *Archiv für die civilistische Praxis* 200 (2000), 273–364

Caruso, D., 'Qu'ils mangent des contrats: Rethinking Justice in EU Contract Law', in D. Kochenov, G. de Búrca, and A. Williams (eds), *Europe's Justice Deficit?* (Oxford: Hart Publishing, 2014), n.p.

Commission Communication 'The EU Justice Agenda for 2020: Strengthening Trust, Mobility and Growth within the Union', COM (2014) 144 final, https://eur-lex.europa.eu/legal-content/EN/TXT/?uri=celex:52014DC0144

Commission Communication, 'A More Coherent European Contract Law: An Action Plan', COM (2003) 68 final, https://eur-lex.europa.eu/legal-content/EN/TXT/?uri=oj:JOC_2003_063_R_0001_01

Commission Communication, 'A New Deal for Consumers', COM (2018) 183 final, https://eur-lex.europa.eu/legal-content/EN/TXT/?uri=celex:52018DC0183

Commission Communication, 'Proposal for a Regulation of the European Parliament and of the Council on a Common European Sales Law', COM (2011) 635 final, https://eur-lex.europa.eu/legal-content/en/TXT/?uri=CELEX%3A32011L0083

Committee on the Rights of Persons with Disabilities, 'General Comment No. 1' (2014), https://ukraine.un.org/en/133050-general-comment-no-1-article-12-equal-recognition-law

Council of the European Union, 'Presidency Conclusions, Lisbon European Council 23 and 24 March 2000', https://www.europarl.europa.eu/summits/lis1_en.htm

Crenshaw, K., 'Demarginalizing the Intersection of Race and Sex: A Black Feminist Critique of Antidiscrimination Doctrine, Feminist Theory and Antiracist Politics', *University of Chicago Legal Forum* 1.8 (1989), 139–167

Dagan, H., and A. Dorfman, 'Just Relationships', *Columbia Law Review* 116 (2016), 1395–1460, https://doi.org/10.2139/ssrn.2463537

Dagan, H., and M. Heller, *The Choice Theory of Contracts* (Cambridge, UK: Cambridge University Press, 2017), https://doi.org/10.1017/9781316477045

Dworkin, R., *Justice for Hedgehogs* (Cambridge, MA: Belknap Press, 2011), https://doi.org/10.4159/9780674059337

Forst, R., *Normativity and Power: Analyzing Social Orders of Justification* (Oxford: Oxford University Press, 2017), https://doi.org/10.1093/oso/9780198798873.001.0001

Forst, R., *The Right to Justification: Elements of a Constructivist Theory of Justice* (New York: Columbia University Press, 2013)

Foucault, M., *The Order of Things: An Archaeology of the Human Sciences* (New York: Vintage, 1994)

Fouillée, A., *La science sociale contemporaine* (Paris: Hachette, 1880)

Fricker, F., *Epistemic Injustice: Power and the Ethics of Knowing* (Oxford: Oxford University Press, 2007)

Grundmann, S., 'The Concept of the Private Law Society: After 50 years of European and European Business Law', *European Review of Private Law* 16 (2008), 553–581, https://doi.org/10.54648/erpl2008046

Grimm, D., *The Constitution of European Democracy* (Oxford: Oxford University Press, 2017), https://doi.org/10.1093/oso/9780198805120.001.0001

Grimm, D., 'Does Europe Need a Constitution?', *European Law Journal* 1.3 (1995), 282–302, https://doi.org/10.1111/j.1468-0386.1995.tb00033.x

Habermas, J., 'Citizen and State Equality in a Supranational Political Community: Degressive Proportionality and the *pouvoir constituant mixte*', *Journal for Common Market Studies* 55 (2017), 171–182, https://doi.org/10.1111/jcms.12517

Habermas, J., *The Crisis of the European Union: A Response* (Cambridge, UK: Polity Press, 2012)

Habermas, J., *Europe: The Faltering Project* (Cambridge, UK: Polity Press, 2009)

Hayek, F. A., *Law, Legislation and Liberty, Vol 2: The Mirage of Social Justice* (London: Routledge, 2003)

Hesselink, M. W., 'Private Law, Regulation, and Justice', *European Law Journal* 22 (2016), 681–695, https://doi.org/10.1111/eulj.12195

Hesselink, M. W., 'The Right to Justification of Contract', *Ratio Juris* 33 (2020), 196–222, https://doi.org/10.1111/raju.12287

Hesselink, M. W., 'Unjust Conduct in the Internal Market: On the Role of European Private Law in the Division of Moral Responsibility Between the EU, its Member States and Their Citizens', *Yearbook of European Law* 35 (2016), 410–452, https://doi.org/10.1093/yel/yew014

Hobbes, T., *Leviathan* (London: Penguin, 1985)

Kaplow, L., and S. Shavell, *Fairness Versus Welfare* (Cambridge, MA: Harvard University Press, 2002)

Kaplow, L., and S. Shavell, 'Why the Legal System is Less Efficient than the Income Tax in Redistributing Income', *Journal of Legal Studies* 23.2 (1994), 667–681, https://doi.org/10.1086/467941

Kennedy, D., 'Distributive and Paternalist Motives in Contract and Tort Law, with Special Reference to Compulsory Terms and Unequal Bargaining Power', *Maryland Law Review* 41 (1982), 563–658

Klijnsma, J., *Contract Law as Fairness: A Rawlsian Perspective on the Position of SMEs in European Contract Law* (Amsterdam: University of Amsterdam, 2014)

Kordana, K. A., and D. H. Tabachnick, 'Rawls and Contract Law', *George Washington Law Review* 73 (2005), 598–632

Kronman, A. T., 'Contract Law and Distributive Justice', *Yale Law Journal* 89 (1980), 472–511

Kukovec, K., 'Law and the Periphery', *European Law Journal* 21 (2015), 406–428, https://doi.org/10.1111/eulj.12113

Leone, C., *The Missing Stone in the Cathedral: Of Unfair Terms in Employment Contracts and Coexisting Rationalities in European Contract Law* (doctoral thesis, University of Amsterdam, 2020)

Lewinsohn-Zamir, D., 'In Defense of Redistribution through Private Law', *Minnesota Law Review* 91 (2006), 326–397

Marx, K., *Capital: An Abridged Edition*, ed. by D. McLellan (Oxford: Oxford University Press)

Marx, K., 'On James Mill', in D. McLellan (ed.), *Karl Marx: Selected Writings*, 2nd edn (Oxford University Press, 2000), pp. 124–133

Micklitz, H.-W. (ed.), *The Many Concepts of Social Justice in European Private Law* (Cheltenham: Edward Elgar, 2011)

Micklitz, H.-W., *The Politics of Justice in European Private Law: Social Justice, Access Justice, Societal Justice* (Cambridge, UK: Cambridge University Press, 2018), https://doi.org/10.1017/9781108539777

Micklitz, H.-W., 'Social Justice and Access Justice in Private Law', in H.-W. Micklitz (ed.), *The Many Concepts of Social Justice in European Private Law* (Cheltenham: Edward Elgar, 2011), pp. 3–60

Micklitz, H.-W., Y. Svetiev, and G. Comparato (eds), 'European Regulatory Private Law—The Paradigm Tested', *EUI-ERC Working Paper* 4 (2014), 69–97, https://doi.org/10.2139/ssrn.2423306

Nietzsche, F., *On the Genealogy of Morals: A Polemic* (London: Penguin, 2013)

Nozick, R., *Anarchy, State, and Utopia* (Oxford: Basic Books, 2013)

Nussbaum, M. C., *Creating Capabilities: The Human Development Approach* (Cambridge, MA: Belknap Press, 2011)

O'Neill, O., 'Agents of Justice', in O. O'Neill, *Justice Across Boundaries: Whose Obligations?* (Cambridge, UK: Cambridge University Press, 2016), pp. 177–192, https://doi.org/10.1017/cbo9781316337103.012

Plato, *The Republic* (London: Penguin, 2007)

Rawls, J., *Political Liberalism* (New York: Columbia University Press, 2005)

Rawls, J., *A Theory of Justice* (Cambridge, MA: Belknap, 1999)

Ripstein, A., *Force and Freedom: Kant's Legal and Political Philosophy* (Cambridge, MA: Harvard University Press, 2009)

Ripstein, A., 'Private Order and Public Justice: Kant and Rawls', *Virginia Law Review* 92 (2006), 1391–1438

Scanlon, T. M., *What We Owe to Each Other* (Cambridge, MA: Belknap, 1998)

Scheffler, S., 'Distributive Justice, the Basic Structure and the Place of Private Law', *Oxford Journal of Legal Studies* 35.2 (2015), 213–235, https://doi.org/10.1093/ojls/gqu030

Shiffrin, S. V., 'The Divergence of Contract and Promise', *Harvard Law Review* 120 (2007), 708–753

Shiffrin, S. V., 'Paternalism, Unconscionability Doctrine, and Accommodation', *Philosophy and Public Affairs* 29 (2000), 205–250

Shklar, J. N., *The Faces of Injustice* (New Haven, CT: Yale University Press, 1990)

Study Group on Social Justice in European Private Law, 'Social Justice in European Contract Law: A Manifesto', *European Law Journal* 10.6 (2004), 653–674, https://doi.org/10.1111/j.1468-0386.2004.00237.x

Tjon Soei Len, L. K. L., 'Hermeneutical Injustice, Contract Law, and Global Value Chains', *European Review of Contract Law* 16.1 (2020), 139–159, https://doi.org/10.1515/ercl-2020-0008

Tjon Soei Len, L. K. L., *Minimum Contract Justice: A Capabilities Perspective on Sweatshops and Consumer Contracts* (Portland, OR: Hart Publishing, 2017)

Weber, M., *Economy and Society*, ed. by G. Roth and C. Wittich, 2 vols (Oakland, CA: University of California Press, 1978)

Weinrib, E. J., *Corrective Justice* (Oxford: Oxford University Press, 2012)

Weinrib, E. J., *The Idea of Private Law* (Cambridge, MA: Harvard University Press, 1995)

3. Negative Integration, European Private Law, and the Government's Role in the Marketplace

C. J. W. (Jaap) Baaij

Abstract

On the surface, the deregulatory character of Europe's initial use of negative legal integration in the 1950s appears to have little bearing on today's positive integration of consumer rights protection through European private law (EPL). This chapter argues to the contrary. On closer inspection, EPL is cut from the same political cloth as negative European integration. The reason is that both negative and positive legal integration permit the use of contract law as a tool of private market regulation for the sake of societal wealth maximisation. The chapter concludes, therefore, that describing, supporting, or criticising the current state or trajectory of EPL should consider these utilitarian underpinnings related to the government's regulatory role in the marketplace.

1. Introduction

One might wonder why a handbook on European private law would need a chapter on negative European integration. On the one hand, negative integration, ostensibly, appears to stand for the European Union's early days after the Second World War, when it was still centred around free trade, deregulation, and economic welfare. Negative integration has been a regulatory instrument the EU uses to remove obstacles or interferences in Europe's internal market. On the other hand, EPL, including the law on consumer contracts, exemplifies Europe's modern-day use of positive integration: introducing new, harmonised rules geared towards realising social and economic equality in the European single market. To underline the appearance of a binary distinction between Europe's traditional negative integration policies and its modern EPL, the word 'negative' expresses a policy that is geared towards *not* having something in place. In contrast, positive European integration is a method used to *have* something in place.

 https://doi.org/10.11647/OBP.0448.03

However, it is the object of this chapter to demonstrate that negative integration is not radically different from positive integration at all. In fact, a thorough understanding of EPL cannot go without recognising its intrinsic relationship with negative integration policies, that is to say, with its underlying philosophical conception concerning state intervention in the marketplace.

To explain how today's EPL rests on the same political foundations as Europe's early emphasis on negative integration, first, Section 2 offers a brief historical overview of the evolution of European integration to show that the EU, did not at some specific point switch from negative to positive integration policies. Instead, both integration techniques existed side by side from the outset. Still, over time, the European government's emphasis slowly moved from negative to positive integration policies without ever giving up either technique.

Then, Section 3 presents the argument that negative and positive integration are not merely concurrent policy instruments in the EU's toolkit, but that both approaches are the progeny of a single political philosophy. It explains that while negative integration is often associated with an autonomy-based, free-trade ideology, and its positive counterpart as adhering to principles of social distributive justice, it turns out that both integration techniques best fit a single justificatory framework: a utilitarian theory under which the European Union uses contract law as a private market regulatory tool to maximise societal wealth. The chapter will conclude that EPL's political foundations are interwoven with basic concepts underlying Europe's initial focus on negative integration. Consequently, any normative debate on the status quo or development of EPL should address its roots in a utilitarian justification of the government's role in the marketplace.

2. The Evolution from Negative to Positive European Integration

a. The Early Emphasis on Negative Integration

Historically, negative and positive integration always existed concurrently within the Europeanisation project. These two distinct techniques of national integration markets, negative and positive integration techniques, are neither inconsistent nor mutually exclusive within the European project.

When speaking of *negative* integration policies or the internal market in the negative sense, we refer to the policy objective of *not* having distortions in the common market.[1] The term 'negative integration' was first coined in 1954 by Dutch economist and Nobel-prize laureate Jan Tinbergen in his book *International Economic Integration*.[2] Tinbergen authored his book in the wake of the Treaty establishing the European Coal

1 J. Pinder, 'Positive Integration and Negative Integration: Some Problems of Economic Union in the EEC', *World Today* 24 (1968), 88–110 (p. 99); see also S. Weatherill, *The Internal Market as a Legal Concept*, 1st edn (Oxford: Oxford University Press, 2017), p. 4.

2 J. Tinbergen, *International Economic Integration*, 2nd edn (Amsterdam: Elsevier, 1954).

and Steel Community (ECSC), the European Treaty from which today's European Union originates, signed on 18 April 1951 and entered into force on 23 July 1952. Tinbergen described negative integration as 'removing artificial hindrances to the optimal operation' of the international economy[3] by the 'elimination of instruments of international economic policy'.[4]

Notwithstanding the historical importance of the ECSC Treaty, we begin our story of the European Union's negative integration approach with the subsequent Treaty, establishing the European Economic Community (EEC), which entered into force on 1 January 1958 alongside the Treaty establishing the European Atomic Energy Community (Euratom).[5] Besides setting up the European institutions that are still with us today (i.e., the Parliament, the Commission, and the Court of Justice),[6] the EEC also introduced a central objective. The goal was to lay the foundations for an ever-closer union between the European peoples, to work towards economic and social progress, and to strengthen peace and freedom.[7]

Before the dawn of the European Union, economic markets were bound within the geographical boundaries of individual countries.[8] National protective economic measures made cross-border business trading expensive relative to domestic trade.[9] In response to this economic nationalism,[10] the EEC Treaty sought to create a common European market by removing interferences and obstacles among its Member States' national markets.[11] The EEC Treaty aimed to realise this common market by introducing

3 Ibid., p. 95.

4 Ibid., p. 122.

5 Treaty Establishing the European Atomic Energy Community, 25 March 1957 (consolidated version in force: OJ C203, 7 June 2016). The EEC and Euratom Treaties are generally referred to as the 'Rome Treaties,' as it was Rome where both treaties were signed on 18 April 1951 by the then six Member States: Belgium, Germany, France, Italy, Luxembourg, and the Netherlands.

6 Articles 137–188 EEC. The EEC institutions were later merged with the Euratom and ECSC treaties by the Treaty establishing a Single Council and a Single Commission of the European Communities ('Merger Treaty' or 'Brussels Treaty'), which was signed on 8 April 1965 and entered into force on 1 July 1967. See Article 13(1) TEU.

7 See Preamble of EEC Treaty; see also H.-W. Micklitz, 'On the Intellectual History of Freedom of Contract and Regulation', *Penn State Journal of Law and International Affairs* 4 (2015), 1–32 (p. 29).

8 F. W. Scharpf, 'Negative and Positive Integration in the Political Economy of European Welfare State', in M. G. Marks, F. W. Scharpf, P. C. Schmitter, and W. Streeck (eds), *Governance in the European Union* (London: SAGE Publications, 1996), pp. 15–39 (p. 16).

9 See in this respect, F. W. Scharpf, 'Balancing Positive and Negative Integration: The Regulatory Options for Europe', *MPIfG Working Paper* 97.8 (1997), http://hdl.handle.net/10419/41672

10 R. Schütze, *European Union Law*, 2nd edn (Cambridge, UK: Cambridge University Press, 2018), p. 493.

11 Pinder, 'Positive Integration and Negative Integration', p. 90; see, e.g., Opinion of the Economic and Social Committee on the 'Communication from the Commission: Strategic Objectives 2000–2005—Shaping the New Europe' [2001] OJ C14/25, p. 139; M. P. Maduro and P. C. Sousa, 'The Free Movement of Goods', in D. M. Patterson and A. Södersten (eds), A Companion to *European Union Law and International Law* (Malden: Wiley Blackwell, 2016), pp. 205–216 (p. 212); K. A. Armstrong, 'Governing Goods: Content and Context', in A. Arnull and D. Chalmers (eds), *The Oxford Handbook of European Union Law*, 1st edn (Oxford: Oxford University Press, 2015), pp. 508–536 (p. 510); G. Majone, *Dilemmas of European Integration: The Ambiguities and Pitfalls of Integration by Stealth* (Oxford: Oxford University Press, 2005), p. 144; and Scharpf, 'Positive Integration and Negative Integration', p. 15; F. W. Scharpf, *Governing in Europe: Effective and Democratic?* (Oxford: Oxford University Press, 1999), p. 46.

four 'fundamental freedoms': the free movement of goods,[12] people,[13] services,[14] and capital[15] across the Member States' borders. These freedoms entailed, for example, that the Member States were prohibited from imposing national customs duties on imports and exports[16] or discriminating between workers based on nationality.[17] Member States were also expected to gradually reduce, and impose no new, restrictions on the performance of services by subjects of other Member States[18] and the cross-border movement of capital and payments.[19]

b. The Emergence of Positive Integration

As Marco Loos will address in greater detail in Chapter 4, the usual form of positive integration consists of EU institutions harmonising national laws and policies, including consumer contracts, through directives and regulations.[20] Like negative integration, positive integration is geared towards realising or advancing a single or common market. However, it seeks to do so not by *removing* national rules that hinder the market but by *introducing* new, harmonising rules through EU legislation.[21]

Positive integration in consumer protection gained traction at the Community level in the 1980s with the adoption of several directives, such as Directive 85/577, on contracts negotiated away from business premises.[22] Then, the Single European Act (SEA) arrived, signed on 28 February 1986, and entered into force on 1 July 1987. Moreover, the SEA shifted from pursuing a 'common' market to an 'internal' market. This new label was more than cosmetic, representing a more ambitious expansion of the European Community's competencies.[23] For example, a necessary modification of the

12 Articles 9–37 EEC.
13 Articles 48–58 EEC.
14 Articles 59–66 EEC.
15 Articles 67–73 EEC.
16 Articles 12 and 13 EEC.
17 Articles 48(2) EEC.
18 Articles 59 EEC.
19 Articles 67(1) EEC.
20 See also L. Azoulai, 'The Complex Weave of Harmonisation', in A. Arnull and D. Chalmers (eds), *The Oxford Handbook of European Union* Law, 1st edn (Oxford: Oxford University Press, 2015), pp. 589–611 (p. 591); M. Blauberger, 'From Negative to Positive Integration: European State Aid Control Through Soft and Hard Law', *MPIfG Discussion Paper* 08.4 (2008), p. 5, https://ssrn.com/abstract=1660981
21 Tinbergen, *International Economic Integration*, p. 97; see also Azoulai, 'The Complex Weave', p. 591; Armstrong, 'Governing Goods', p. 510; C. Barnard, 'The Construction of the Internal Market', in D. M Patterson and A. Södersten (eds), *A Companion to European Union Law and International Law* (Malden: Wiley Blackwell, 2016), pp. 195–204 (p. 196).
22 Council Directive 85/577/EEC of 20 December 1985 to protect the consumer in respect of contracts negotiated away from business premises [1985] OJ L372/31 (contracts negotiated away from business premises). Repealed by Directive 2011/83/EU of the European Parliament and of the Council of 25 October 2011 on consumer rights, amending Council Directive 93/13/EEC and Directive 1999/44/EC of the European Parliament and of the Council and repealing Council Directive 85/577/EEC and Directive 97/7/EC of the European Parliament and of the Council [2011] OJ L304/64 (Consumer Rights Directive, CRD).
23 Commission Communication, 'Towards a Single Market Act For a Highly Competitive Social Market Economy 50 Proposals for Improving our Work, Business and Exchanges With One Another', COM (2010) 609 final, https://eur-lex.europa.eu/legal-content/EN/TXT/?uri=celex:52010DC0608, p. 2.

EEC Treaty consisted of abolishing the unanimity requirement for Council decisions.[24] The Council could now make decisions by a qualified majority, instead of unanimity, making it easier for the European Community to take legislative measures relating to, among others, environmental protection and consumer protection.[25] Moreover, it was with the SEA that the EEC, for the first time, made mention of consumer rights protection, namely by requiring that when Commission proposals in pursuit of a common market involved health, safety, environmental protection, or consumer protection, it would take 'as a base a high level of protection'.[26]

Still, without an express expansion of competences, the EU's economic policy would fail to consider 'the social aspects of consumer policy', the Social and Economic Committee reasoned in 1991.[27] In the 1990s, the 1992 Treaty of Maastricht (Treaty on European Union)[28] and the 1999 Treaty of Amsterdam[29] solidified the European Union's competency to pursue a policy of positive integration in consumer law. The treaties authorised the Community, for the first time, to 'promote the interests of consumers and to ensure a high level of consumer protection', entailing the protection '[contributing] to protecting the health, safety and economic interests of consumers' in their own right.[30]

Fast forward to today, positive integration has become the predominant form of EU legal integration. The Treaty on the Functioning of the European Union (TFEU) created a competency for both EU institutions and the Member States to take positive action in a wide range of policy fields, from ensuring employment[31] and working conditions,[32] giving priority to the protection of human health,[33] contributing to the preserving, protecting, and improving the quality of the environment,[34] and, indeed, take action to promote the interests of consumers and ensure a high level of consumer protection.[35]

---

24 Article 100a(1) of the Single European Act [1987] OJ L169.

25 Article 100a(3) SEA. See, e.g., Scharpf, 'Balancing Positive and Negative Integration', p. 4; Blauberger, 'From Negative to Positive Integration', p. 5.

26 Article 100a(3) SEA.

27 Economic and Social Committee, 'Opinion on Consumer Protection and Completion of the Internal Market', 91/C 339/08, p. 19.

28 Treaty on European Union [1992] OJ C191 (Treaty of Maastricht). Signed on 7 February 1992 and entered into force on 1 November 1993.

29 Treaty of Amsterdam amending the Treaty on European Union, the treaties establishing the European Communities and certain related acts [1997] OJ C340 (Treaty on the European Union). Signed on 2 October 1997 and entered into force on 1 May 1999.

30 Article 129a Treaty on European Union ([1992] OJ C191), as amended by Article K.2(27) of the Treaty of Amsterdam ([1997] OJ C340).

31 Articles 145–147 of the Treaty of the Functioning of the European Union [1958] OJ L326/47 (TFEU).

32 Article 151 TFEU.

33 Article 168 TFEU.

34 Article 191 TFEU.

35 Article 169 TFEU.

c. The Concurrence of Negative and Positive Integration

While distinct techniques for integrating national markets, the EU has not used negative and positive integration techniques as mutually exclusive. On the contrary, in 1968, John Pinder observed that economic integration requires both positive and negative integration.[36] The reason is that negative integration had its limitations. First, the four freedoms left Member States some room to pursue their own domestic or regional policies and, within limits, impose discriminatory regulations on foreign goods on the grounds of public policy, security, and health.[37] Positive integration could thus harmonise areas that fell within the domain of the four freedoms but were not or not sufficiently negatively integrated yet.[38] The second explanation for the limited effect of negative integration was that national laws remained dissimilar beyond the eliminated discriminatory policies. Thus, the disparities among the Member States that negative integration aimed to remove were embedded within otherwise diverging national policies and practices.[39]

Indeed, the EEC Treaty did include positive integration methods along with negative ones.[40] Article 3, for example, stipulated positive actions in the common commercial, agricultural, and transport policy field, although the language was relatively broad and permissive.[41] In that respect, positive integration can be perceived to support or supplement negative integration objectives.[42]

Hence, positive integration techniques have been part of the EU legislative project from the outset. In fact, both negative and positive integration measures have been the fabric of the EU's common or internal market policies. The shift from a predominately negative to a predominately positive approach was gradual rather than radical The EU legislator initially placed the predominant weight on a negative integration approach.[43] Then, in the 1980s, the emphasis of EU lawmaking started to shift, however, from a negative, to gradually a more positive overall integration strategy.[44]

Even today, where positive integration policies in private law, and other areas,

36 Pinder, 'Positive Integration and Negative Integration', pp. 89, 90.

37 Ibid., p. 91. See also Barnard, 'Construction of the Internal Market'; A. Johnston, *EC Regulation of Corporate Governance* (Cambridge, UK: Cambridge University Press, 2009), p. 148.

38 Pinder, 'Positive Integration and Negative Integration', pp. 89, 90; see also Azoulai, 'Complex Weave of Harmonisation', p. 603.

39 See, on Directive 2014/54/EU of the European Parliament and of the Council of 16 April 2014 on measures facilitating the exercise of rights conferred on workers in the context of freedom of movement for workers [2014] OJ L128/8 and the barriers to the movement of migrant workers that it leaves in place, e.g., E. Spaventa, 'The Free Movement of Workers in the Twenty-first Century', in A. Arnull and D. Chalmers (eds), *The Oxford Handbook of European Union Law*, 1st edn (Oxford: Oxford University Press, 2015), pp. 456–476 (p. 469).

40 Azoulai, 'Complex Weave of Harmoniation', p. 591.

41 Pinder, 'Positive Integration and Negative Integration', p. 99.

42 Barnard, 'Construction of the Internal Market', p. 196; Azoulai, 'Complex Weave of Harmoniation', p. 603.

43 Pinder, 'Positive Integration and Negative Integration', p. 104; Majone, *Dilemmas of European Integration*, p. 145.

44 See also Opinion of the Economic and Social Committee, [2001] OJ C14/25, p. 139.

appear to dominate EU policy today, negative integration measures are still very much alive within the EU policy framework. Most importantly, the four freedoms introduced by the EEC Treaty of 1958 are central to the Treaty on the Functioning of the European Union (TFEU) in force today,[45] as is the prohibition of national customs duties on imports and exports and measures of equivalent effect.[46] The 'freedom' language in the preamble of TFEU is very similar to the EEC Treaty.[47] In this respect, the EU has continually pursued a dual negative and positive integration strategy.[48]

d. Negative Integration's Impact on European Private Law

One would be forgiven to think that the move from more negative towards more positive integration measures meant that, only gradually, European integration policies became relevant to EPL as the emphasis on positive integration grew. That inference would overlook the fact, however, that the EU's predominately negative approach to integration initially also impacted private law, particularly contract law. That is to say, the early negative integration policies may not have been focused on, but certainly had a bearing on, contractual relationships among European citizens and, thus, national contract laws.

On the one hand, it is true that, other than its rules on competition,[49] the EEC rules did not regulate, nor did they expressly authorise EU institutions to legislate, contractual relationships between private individuals—the subject of private law. Instead, the EEC Treaty laid down public law rules and rules on how the Member States should regulate their respective markets.

Nevertheless, the four freedoms did indirectly affect contractual relationships. After all, the four freedoms look to make cross-border trade less costly and cumbersome, which directly affects cross-border contracting. Because markets run on trade, and trade runs on contracts, integrating economic markets affects the contractual relationships between private individuals.[50] Therefore, the EU's early negative integration policies

---

45 TFEU, Article 26(2), and Articles 28–37 (goods), Articles 45–55 (persons), Articles 56–62 (services), Articles 63–59 (capital and payments).

46 Article 28(1), 30, and 34 TFEU.

47 TFEU, Preamble.

48 Schütze, *European Union Law*, p. 493. In fact, the Charter of Fundamental Rights of The European Union, adopted in 2012, uses negative integration in stipulating various negative freedoms (the freedom *from*). See, e.g., Article 2(2) ('No one shall be condemned to the death penalty, or executed'), Article 4 ('No one shall be subjected to torture or to inhuman or degrading treatment or punishment'), Article 5(1) ('No one shall be held in slavery or servitude'), Charter of Fundamental Rights of the European Union [2012] OJ C 326326/1 (Charter of Fundamental Rights of the European Union).

49 See in particular Article 85(2) EEC, currently embodied in Article 101(2) TFEU, which renders contracts that violate rules of competition legally null and void.

50 See for indications of the European Commission's recognition of the importance of (consumer) contract law for the internal market in, Commission Communication, 'GREEN PAPER FROM THE COMMISSION: On Policy Options for Progress Towards a European Contract Law for Consumers and Businesses', COM (2010) 348 final, https://eur-lex.europa.eu/LexUriServ/LexUriServ.do?uri=COM:2010:0348:FIN:en:PDF, p. 2; Commission Communication, 'Communication from the Commission to the European Parliament and the Council—A More Coherent European Contract Law—An Action Plan', COM (2003) 68 final, https://eur-lex.europa.eu/legal-content/EN/

sought to expand the quantity and value of contracts that European traders could enter into.

The effect of negative integration on contract law became more immediate when, in the 1970s, the European Court of Justice developed the rule of 'direct horizontal effect'. This doctrine entailed that, for the rules of free movement to be effective, private actors should be able to invoke these freedoms against their governments as well as in contract disputes against other, generally large or powerful, non-state actors.[51] The Court's case law further spawned the principle of 'indirect horizontal effect', which meant that national courts should set aside a national rule that affected the performance of private contracts and, thus, the outcome of contractual disputes.[52]

Consequently, while directed at policing Member States' economic market regulation, negative integration significantly did affect the legal relationships among private individuals,[53] indirectly at first but increasingly directly. Hence, besides positive integration being connected to negative integration from the outset, negative integration alone should be directly relevant to our comprehension of EPL and its history, status quo, and future pathways.

3. The Normative Link between Negative Integration and European Private Law

a. European Integration and State Intervention

So far, we have seen that negative and positive integration are not opposites, neither conceptually nor historically. EPL, an instance of the EU's positive integration policies, should, therefore, not be considered antithetical to the EU's negative integration. Instead, negative integration measures have always been part of the EU legislative project, even though, through time, the emphasis has increasingly, yet incrementally, shifted from negative to positive integration.

However, at a more fundamental level, from the viewpoint of political legitimacy, negative and positive integration policies still appear distinct and potentially

TXT/?uri=oj:JOC_2003_063_R_0001_01, pp. 6, 10–11, 14–15; and Commission Communication, 'Communication from the Commission to the Council and the European Parliament on European Contract Law', COM (2001) 398 final, https://eur-lex.europa.eu/LexUriServ/LexUriServ.do?uri=COM:2001:0398:FIN:EN:PDF, pp. 8–9.

51 See Case C-36/74 *Walrave and Koch v Union Cycliste Internationale and Others* [1974] ECLI:EU:C:1974:140. See for a detailed overview of the development of the direct horizontal effect of fundamental freedoms, C. Mak, 'Free Movement and Contract Law', in C. Twigg-Flesner (ed.), *Research Handbook on EU Consumer and Contract Law* (Cheltenham: Edward Elgar Publishing, 2016), pp. 182–196 (p. 185). Who observes that the applicability of this principle in relation to the free movement of goods is to date not undisputed.

52 See Case C-47/90 *Delhaize frères and Compagnie Le Lion SA v Promalvin SA and AGE Bodegas Unidas SA* [1992] ECLI:EU:C:1992:250.

53 See also A. Hartkamp et al. (eds), *Cases, Materials, and Text on European Law and Private Law* (Oxford: Hart Publishing, 2017), p. 3.

contradictory. Questions of political legitimacy include those relating to state intervention, i.e., the government's proper role in the marketplace. These questions ask what justifies using state power to support or control free individuals' private or commercial dealings. Such questions pertain to the appropriate balance between economic freedom and government economic intervention. Hence, politically, negative and political integration present an ostensive dichotomy of principles.

On the one hand, the negative integration policies at the outset of the European Union were commonly associated with a 'free-trade ideology' or trade liberalisation.[54] Indeed, Europe's negative integration was aimed at deregulation,[55] because it sought to eliminate national rules that made it more difficult for traders to do business across the Member States' borders. It focused essentially on the distribution and circulation of production.[56] In this respect, seemingly, the EEC primarily served the narrow business interest of traders.[57] Even though the EEC Treaty contained a chapter on 'social policy', that chapter was remarkably concise.[58] The EEC Treaty focused on realising *economic* welfare instead of, after all, seeking to advance a European 'economic' community. The primary aim, namely, to realise a common market, was an objective of *economic* policy. It sought to bring Member States' economic policies into line.[59] Indeed, the barriers that the Member States sought to remove between their countries primarily involved obstacles to trade between the Member States.[60] A liberal political climate was one reason—besides the French hesitancy to create a supranational authority[61]—why European integration was limited mainly to deregulation.[62] Traders were further empowered by two early landmark rulings by the European Court of Justice, *Van Gend en Loos* (1963) and *Costa v ENEL* (1964). Here, it decided that Community law had a direct effect at the national level and, under certain conditions, gave individuals a claim against the government of a Member State that violated said law.[63]

In contrast, positive integration has historically been associated with a proactive government that uses regulatory means to maximise social welfare.[64] Policies commonly

---

54 Tinbergen, *International Economic Integration*, p. 119; Pinder, 'Positive Integration and Negative Integration', p. 98; see also, e.g., Scharpf, 'Positive Integration and Negative Integration', p. 17.

55 Maduro and Sousa, 'Free Movement of Goods', p. 212.

56 Azoulai, 'Complex Weave of Harmonisation', p. 592.

57 Majone, *Dilemmas of European Integration*, p. 146.

58 EEC Treaty, Title II (Article 117–128).

59 For example, EEC Treaty, Article 2.

60 EEC Treaty, Preamble.

61 Pinder, 'Positive Integration and Negative Integration', p. 99.

62 Ibid., p. 108.

63 Case C-26/62 *NV Algemene Transport- en Expeditie Onderneming van Gend & Loos v Netherlands Inland Revenue Administration* [1963] ECLI:EU:C:1963:1, par. II(B) ('... [A]ccording to the spirit, the general scheme and the wording of the treaty, article 12 must be interpreted as producing direct effects and creating individual rights which national courts must protect.'), and Case C-6/64 *Flaminio Costa v E.N.E.L* [1964] ECLI:EU:C:1964:66. par. 7 ('A member state's obligation under the EEC treaty ... is legally complete and consequently capable of producing direct effects on the relations between member states and individuals. Such an obligation becomes an integral part of the legal system of the member states, and thus forms part of their own law, and directly concerns their nationals in whose favour it has created individual rights which national courts must protect.').

64 Pinder, 'Positive Integration and Negative Integration', p. 104.

pursued through positive integration tend to have economic or welfare objectives beyond removing obstacles to trade.[65] Positive integration is widely characterised by introducing or protecting positive social and economic rights, not merely of traders but the entire EU's citizenry.[66] It is not simply about advancing the market itself but about improving market conditions for its participants,[67] ultimately increasing their social conditions.[68] The SEA ushered in a concept of the internal market[69] that no longer served economic welfare alone but included 'raising the standard of living' more broadly.[70] As the Economic Social Committee expressed in 1991:

> [A]gainst the background of a European Community keen to establish economic and social cohesion among its members, it is important to give the institutions the legal powers they need to create equal opportunities for everyone and to restore balance through measures to protect the weakest sections of the community.[71]

Consequently, the free-trade connotation of negative integration and the social welfare association with positive integration suggests a philosophical dichotomy. One approach, the negative one, justifies a passive and standoffish government, in which interventions in the market are only appropriate to create the ideal market conditions benefitting free private agents, in this case, fostering a common or internal marketplace that permits unhindered trade across Europe. The other, positive approach to integration does not limit government action to merely getting out of the way and letting the market forces do their work. In contrast, it justifies further policies to combat market inequalities and uses private law rules to respect and improve all market participants' economic and social rights.

b. Theories of Contract Law and State Intervention

The preceding section showed that, at least on its face, negative and positive integration policies in the EU appear to spring from distinct or even inconsistent justificatory principles related to the appropriate government's role in the marketplace. That realisation raises the question of whether EPL, as a prominent example of positive integration, is irreconcilable with negative integration at this fundamental level.[72]

A classic polemic between two schools of thought in the theory of contract law

65 Ibid., p. 90; see also N. Walker, 'The Philosophy of European Union Law', in A. Arnull and D. Chalmers (eds), *The Oxford Handbook of European Union Law*, 1st edn (Oxford: Oxford University Press, 2015), pp. 3–27 (pp. 12–13).

66 Majone, *Dilemmas of European Integration*, p. 146.

67 Scharpf, 'Positive Integration and Negative Integration', p. 15.

68 See Azoulai, 'Complex Weave of Harmonisation', p. 592.

69 Article 81 SEA.

70 Article 2 SEA.

71 Economic and Social Committee, 'Opinion on Consumer Protection and Completion of the Internal Market', 91/C 339/08, p. 18.

72 See H. Unberatth and A. Johnston, 'The Double-Headed Approach of the ECJ Concerning Consumer Protection', *Common Market Law Review* 44.5 (2007), 1237–1284, who answer this question in the affirmative.

appears to answer this question in the affirmative. On the one hand, the free-trade philosophy associated with Europe's initial negative integration policy echoes theories of contract law that emphasise the autonomy of contract parties. Liberal theories of contract emphasise the individual autonomy of the contracting parties as free and equal persons.[73] Enforcing the parties' contract respects and facilitates the individual's right to self-determination, self-authorship,[74] self-guidance, or self-rule.[75] To this extent, liberal theories of contract find that contract law is, and should be, 'content-neutral';[76] it should avoid imposing on the parties substantive policy, principles, values, or considerations.[77] Under this view, the State is to assume a hands-off approach. In enforcing contracts, courts do not make (new) laws; they effectuate the parties' free will.[78] The only kind of justice that contract law is to achieve is 'corrective justice', to restore possible disturbances in the transactional equality inherent to the parties' contract.[79]

Indeed, earlier, we saw that the EU's early negative integration policies affected contractual relationships among market participants by removing obstacles to doing business across European borders and allowing contracting parties to invoke the four freedoms within their relationship. Negative integration's effect on contract law illustrates the close connection between the free-trade ideology associated with negative integration and liberal, autonomy-based contract theories, which typically protect negative liberty rights or the right to non-interference.[80]

On the other hand, the social welfare philosophy that seems to describe Europe's current positive integration policies recalls theories of contract law based on social distributive justice. Theories of this kind explain or justify contract law regarding its

73 P. Benson, Justice in Transactions: *A Theory of Contract Law* (Cambridge, MA: Harvard University Press, 2019), p. 26.

74 H. Dagan and M. Heller, *The Choice Theory of Contracts* (Cambridge, UK: Cambridge University Press, 2017), p. 1; A. S. Smith, *Contract Theory* (Oxford: Oxford University Press, 2004), p. 47.

75 L. L. Fuller, 'Considerations and Form', *Columbia Law Review* 41 (1941), 799–824 (p. 806: '[T]he principle of private autonomy ... simply means that the law views private individuals as possessing a power to effect, within certain limits, changes in their legal relations [through entering into contracts with others]'); J. Raz, *The Morality of Freedom* (Oxford: Oxford University Press, 1988), p. 370 ('The autonomous person is part author of his life ... An autonomous person's well-being consists in the successful pursuits of self-chosen goals and relationships'); See also B. Bix, *Contract Law. Rules, Theory, and Context* (Cambridge: Cambridge University Press, 2012), p. 133; Smith, *Contract Theory*, p. 47.

76 Benson, *Justice in Transactions*, p. 129.

77 Ibid., p. 303.

78 B. C. Zipursky, 'Philosophy of Private Law', in J. L. Colman et al. (eds), *The Oxford University Handbook of Jurisprudence and Philosophy of Law* (Oxford: Oxford University Press, 2004), pp. 623–630 (p. 629). See for criticism within the liberal theory of contract of such 'legal passivisity', Dagan and Heller, *Choice Theory of Contracts*, p. 6.

79 See E. J. Weinrib, 'Corrective Justice in a Nutshell', *The University of Toronto Law Journal* 52 (2002), 349–356 (p. 349); and, e.g., Benson, *Theory of Contract Law*, p. 30, Zipursky, 'Philosophy of Private Law', p. 629, and Smith, *Contract Theory*, p. 47.

80 See for a description of the liberal theories of contracts more generally, Smith, *Contract Theory*, p. 47. For a critical discussion of autonomy theories, see A. Schwartz and R. E. Scott, 'Contract Theory and the Limits of Contract Law', *Yale Law Review* 113 (2003), 541–619 (p. 569).

contribution to an equal distribution of wealth,[81] or the correction,[82] or at least not worsening of existing economic or social inequalities.[83] In contrast with autonomy-based theories, social distributive theories treat—or recognise—contract law or private law more generally as a policy instrument,[84] or a vehicle, for the State's promotion of a particular notion of what is good.[85] Social distributive justice theories, thus, allow contract law to constrain the parties' freedom to contract, namely when what the parties have consented to does not satisfy the needs of distributive justice.[86] This feature is why proponents of autonomy-based theories critique social distributive justice theories for allowing 'extra-transactional' values, or standards alien or external to the perceived domain of contract law, to influence or determine which contract terms are enforced.[87]

Hence, social distributive justice theories show striking similarities with the social welfare ideology associated with positive integration. Social distributive justice, through contracts, aims to equalise diverging starting positions of society's members.[88] Indeed, for example, EU legislation protects consumers, not their contracting partners, against unfair terms[89] and offers them—not their business counterparts—a cooling-off period within which they can rescind a contract without giving a reason.[90]

Understood through these two lenses of contract law theory, the political philosophies underpinning negative and positive integration seem difficult to reconcile. After all, the liberal autonomy-based theories advocate for a role for the government in the marketplace, that resists the role put forward by social distributive theories, and vice versa.

If the dicohtomy between said philosophical depictions of negative and positive

81 See, e.g., Smith, *Contract Theory*, pp. 46–47.

82 Benson, *Justice in Transactions*, p. 191.

83 A. Bagchi, 'Distributive Justice and Contract', in G. Klass et al. (eds), *Philosophical Foundations of Contract Law* (Oxford: Oxford University Press 2014), pp. 193–212 (p. 201).

84 As observed by Bagchi, 'Distributive Justice and Contract', pp. 195 and 201. See also G. Comparato, H.-W. Micklitz, and Y. Svetiev, 'The Regulatory Character of European Private Law', in C. Twigg-Flesner (ed.), *Research Handbook on EU Consumer and Contract Law* (Cheltenham: Edward Elgar Publishing, 2016), pp. 35–67 (p. 48), calling this instrumental use of private law, 'regulatory private law'.

85 Smith, *Contract Theory*, p. 47.

86 Bagchi, 'Distributive Justice and Contract', pp. 195 and 201. Bagchi herself presents an account of distributive justice that constrains contract law not instrumentally but as the social context or political justice background by which the morality of contracting is conditioned, see Bagchi, 'Distributive Justice and Contract', p. 201.

87 See for descriptions of this position, e.g., Benson, *Justice in Transactions*, p. 130, Dagan and Heller, *Choice Theory of Contracts*, p. 52, and Bagchi, 'Distributive Justice and Contract', p. 197.

88 Benson, *Justice in Transactions*, p. 191.

89 Article 3(1) Council Directive 93/13/EEC on unfair terms in consumer contracts [1993] OJ L95/29 (Unfair Terms Directive, UTD) ('A contractual term which has not been individually negotiated shall be regarded as unfair if, contrary to the requirement of good faith, it causes a significant imbalance in the parties' rights and obligations arising under the contract, to the detriment of the consumer').

90 Article 9(1) Directive 2011/83/EU of the European Parliament and of the Council of 25 October 2011 on consumer rights, amending Council Directive 93/13/EEC and Directive 1999/44/EC of the European Parliament and of the Council and repealing Council Directive 85/577/EEC and Directive 97/7/EC of the European Parliament and of the Council [2011] OJ L304/64 (Consumer Rights Directive, CRD)('...[T]he consumer shall have a period of 14 days to withdraw from a distance or off-premises contract, without giving any reason...').

European integration is correct, then the historical shift from one technique to the other since the 1980s gives the impression of presenting a radical realignment regarding the State's role in its citizens' private affairs. Hence, negative and positive legal integration appears to pose an inherent conflict between an anti-interventionist and an interventionist conception of the role of government in the marketplace.[91]

To be sure, not all would agree that the apparent opposition between negative and positive integration amounts to an inconstancy of contract law theories. For example, within the field of contract law theory, some scholars argue that European contract law is inherently pluralist in that it is justified not on a single principle but on multiple, sometimes contradicting, principles. To them, this feature does not make European contract law inherently unsound. It merely means that the unity of EPL across diverging national private law traditions is more procedural and less substantive.[92] Other theorists of contract law have proposed pluralist theories of contract law that can integrate potentially conflicting contract values into a coherent hierarchy.[93] Still, these theories tend to put forward a single ultimate or end value, limiting the other value in case of conflict.[94]

However, whether or not one considers the varying theories underpinning EPL and negative integration irreconcilable, the more pressing threshold question is whether the apparency of a contradiction between EPL and negative integration is accurate, to begin with. As we will see next, it is not.

c. A Utilitarian Justification of Negative Integration

In these final two sections, the argument will be presented that negative integration and EPL are not opposites in terms of their justificatory underpinnings but are part of the same political cloth. The reason is that a third non-pluralist theory of political legitimacy explains both negative integration and EPL better than the two schools of thought discussed so far. This theory is a utilitarian theory based on economic efficiency. It unites negative integration and EPL as part of a single theory on the proper role of government, because it offers a better fitting explanation than autonomy-based liberal theories and social distributive justice theories do.

First, regarding *negative* integration, recall that the EEC Treaty aimed to advance economic and social progress by realising a common market and removing national cross-border trade restrictions. The EEC aimed to improve market conditions.[95] So,

91 See also Scharpf, *Governing in Europe*, pp. 46–47.

92 See M. W. Hesselink, 'Contract Theory in EU Contract Law', in C. Twigg-Flesner (ed.), *Research Handbook on EU Consumer and Contract Law* (Cheltenham: Edward Elgar Publishing, 2016), pp. 508–534 (pp. 532–533).

93 See N. B. Oman, 'The Failure of Economic Interpretations of the Law of Contract Damages', *Washington and Lee Law Review* 64 (2007), pp. 829–875 (pp. 834 and 864) (proposing a hierarchical arrangement, a 'vertical integration strategy', for deontological and consequentialist theories of contract); and A. Bagchi, 'Distributive Injustice and Private Law', *Hastings Law Journal* 60 (2008), 105–149 (p. 146).

94 See Dagan and Heller, *Choice Theory of Contracts*, p. 80, naming autonomy the 'ultimate value.'

95 See also, Azoulai, 'Complex Weave of Harmonisation', p. 592.

it may have been true that this negative integration policy benefited traders and businesses who could enlarge their business beyond domestic borders for lower transaction costs. However, the economic benefits for individual traders may also be considered a means to an end—a separate end from individual autonomy. After all, the EEC's goal was to realise that the common market would bring the envisioned economic and social prosperity for the citizens of its Member States. In this respect, neither autonomy-based nor social distributive justice theories of contracts might best fit the European Union's early negative integration approach.

Instead, the utilitarian economic efficiency theory of contract law might offer the better fitting philosophical underpinnings of negative integration. Efficiency-based or economic theories of contract law are similar to social distributive theories. They can both take a 'utilitarian' approach to interpreting contract law, which is to say, an approach that explains or justifies contract law based on some independent criterion of the good.[96] Here, contract law is perceived in terms of the incentives it can provide market participants to behave in a manner that enhances the economic efficiency of their transactions[97] and, thus, both the individual and social gains from trade.[98] Hence, taken normatively, this theory states that contract law should achieve optimal performance for the lowest transaction costs.[99]

As with proponents of social distributive justice analysis, legal economists, too, may treat contract law as an instrument, or a 'regulatory enterprise of the state', to promote or maximise the welfare of society's members.[100] However, in contrast with social distributive justice, the economic efficiency theory then values individual and societal wealth maximisation particularly.[101] Critics claim that this economic take on contract law imposes extra-transactional norms on the parties' contractual relationship,[102] just as critics of social distributive justice theories argue. Naturally, contracting parties, especially traders, may wish their transaction to be efficient and maximise its gains. However, within an efficiency-based utilitarian theory, the law enforces the contract in

96 See M. Rosenfeld, 'Contract and Justice: The Relation between Classical Contract Law and Social Contract Theory', *Iowa Law Review* 70 (1985), 769–900 (p. 771); D. Markovits, 'Making and Keeping Contracts', *Virginia Law Review* 92 (2006), 1325–1332. Richard Posner famously rejected the common equation of the economic theory of law and utilitarianism, arguing it was no more than a 'restrained' form of utilitarianism, see R. A. Posner, 'Utilitarianism, Economics, and Legal Theory', *The Journal of Legal Studies* 8 (1979), 103–140; R. A. Posner, 'The Ethical and Political Basis of the Efficiency Norm in Common Law Adjudication', *Hofstra Law Review* 8 (1980), 487–507; cf. A. T. Kronman, 'Wealth Maximization as a Normative Principle', *The Journal of Legal Studies* 9 (1980), 227–229. Given the more general nature of our discussion, this issue does not need to be resolved here.

97 Benson, *Theory of Contract Law*, pp. 153 and 161; Dagan and Heller, *Choice Theory of Contracts*, p. 52; Zipursky, 'Philosophy of Private Law', p. 626.

98 Bix, *Contract Law*, p. 134; Schwartz and Scott, 'Contract Theory', p. 544.

99 Dagan and Heller, *Choice Theory of Contracts*, p. 52.

100 Smith, *Contract Theory*, p. 47.

101 Bix, *Contract Law*, p. 98; R. E. Barnett, 'A Consent Theory of Contract', *Columbia Law Review* 86 (1986), 269–321 (pp. 277–278); But, see Micklitz, 'Intellectual History', p. 29, who depicts EU's economic integration not merely as a means to achieve wealth, but also—or primarily—peace. See also Hesselink, 'Contract Theory', p. 530, underscoring pursuing social justice through offering also weaker citizens access to markets, while referencing concurrently the ideas put forward by Micklitz.

102 Dagan and Heller, *Choice Theory of Contracts*, p. 52.

that case, not because it seeks to enforce whatever the parties desire, as proponents of autonomy-based theories would have it, but because their contract happens to align with the public good that contract law is used to realise.[103] Hence, from the viewpoint of an economic or efficiency theory of contract, negative integration may indeed have favoured free-trade policies. Still, it did so because it served a higher-level objective: societal welfare.

d. A Utilitarian Justification of European Private Law

Second, when we look closer at today's *positive* integration policies pursued by the EU in consumer protection, an economic efficiency theory looks like a better fitting explanatory model than social distributive justice theories. The TFEU provides EU institutions a freestanding competence for measures protecting 'the health, safety and economic interests of consumers'.[104] While this might echo a sense of social distributive justice, this competency is still intricately connected to a higher-level internal market narrative. The Treaty instructs EU institutions to contribute to consumer protection *by* advancing the internal market through harmonisation measures.[105] The policy goal of establishing and ensuring the functioning of the internal market is still central to the TFEU.[106] To promote the internal market, the EU institutions shall adopt measures to harmonise national laws[107] and implement a high level of protection if such measures involve health, safety, environmental protection, and consumer protection.[108] Hence, the internal market language is the policy vehicle through which the European Union publicly justifies its consumer contract policies.

Indeed, recent EU harmonisation measures related to consumer contracts are not based on the EU's competency in consumer policy alone, but steadily invoke the premise that protecting consumers' interests benefits the internal market.[109] Specifically, the EU's

103 See for a similar reasoning, Zipursky, 'Philosophy of Private Law', p. 627.

104 Article 169(1) TFEU.

105 Article 169(2)(a) TFEU. One gets the sense from the TFEU that the protection of consumer interest has become a vital policy aim, yet one that is secondary or auxiliary to other policy fields, see, e.g., Article 12 ('Consumer protection requirements shall be taken into account in defining and implementing other Union policies and activities').

106 Article 26(1) TFEU.

107 Article 114(1) TFEU.

108 Article 114(3) TFEU and Article 38 Charter of Fundamental Rights of the European Union ([2012] OJ C 326326/1) ('Union policies shall ensure a high level of consumer protection').

109 Preamble under (2), Directive (EU) 2019/770 of the European Parliament and of the Council of 20 May 2019 on certain aspects concerning contracts for the supply of digital content and digital services [2019] OJ L139/1 (Directive on Contracts for the Supply of Digital Content and Digital Services); Preamble under (3) and (4) Consumer Rights Directive ([2011] OJ L304/64); Preamble under (2), Directive (EU) 2019/771 of the European Parliament and of the Council of 20 May 2019 on certain aspects concerning contracts for the sale of goods, amending Regulation (EU) 2017/2394 and Directive 2009/22/EC, and repealing Directive 1999/44/EC [2019] OJ L138/26 (Sale of Goods Directive, SGD); Preamble under (3) and (5), Directive (EU) 2015/2302 of the European Parliament and of the Council of 25 November 2015 on package travel and linked travel arrangements, amending Regulation (EC) No 2006/2004 and Directive 2011/83/EU of the European Parliament and of the Council and repealing Council Directive 90/314/EEC [2015] OJ L326/1 (Package Travel Directive);

competency in enacting consumer protection legislation, as embodied in Article 169 TFEU is supplementary to and must be combined with other EU competencies, such as the approximation of national laws in furthering the establishment and functioning of the internal market, as exemplified by Article 114(1) and (3). Subsequently, the EU institutions tend to justify consumer protection measures by explaining that the uniform protection of consumer rights remedies a lack of consumer confidence in the internal market, alongside reducing transaction costs for businesses,[110] making cross-border trade more appealing and thus removing at least two barriers to the functioning of the internal market.[111]

Additionally, the European Commission has repeatedly confirmed the economic value of consumer protection in its communications, claiming that increasing consumer confidence 'will benefit the European economy given the importance of consumer expenditure in maintaining a sustainable economic model'.[112] It has explained the need to address demographic, environmental, and social challenges to develop a 'continental single market',[113] as it has done concerning the mobility of citizens and businesses.[114] Moreover, it has explained the EU's strict rules on consumer protection through today's positive consumer rights by arguing that a healthy consumer environment is a critical factor for economic growth.[115]

Hence, the EU legal framework on consumer protection measures, including the bulk of EPL, is ultimately not based on notions of social justice but on the kind of societal wealth the internal market should realise. The same economic efficiency model that explains Europe's negative integration policies offers a convincing account of the positive integration that characterises EPL. As with negative integration, the positive integration of consumer contract laws seeks to build and improve the internal market and, thus, the social and economic prosperity that the EU expects from it.

Preamble under (1), Directive (EU) 2019/2161 of the European Parliament and of the Council of 27 November 2019 amending Council Directive 93/13/EEC and Directives 98/6/EC, 2005/29/EC and 2011/83/EU of the European Parliament and of the Council as regards the better enforcement and modernisation of Union consumer protection rules [2019] OJ L328/7 (Modernisation Directive).

110 Preamble under (3) and (4), Directive on Contracts for the Supply of Digital Content and Digital Services ([2019] OJ L139/1); Preamble under (6), Consumer Rights Directive ([2011] OJ L304/64); Preamble under (7), Sale of Goods Directive ([2019] OJ L138/26); Preamble under (4), Package Travel Directive ([2015] OJ L326/1).

111 See, e.g., Preamble under (5) and (8), Directive on Contracts for the Supply of Digital Content and Digital Services ([2019] OJ L139/1); Preamble under (6), Consumer Rights Directive ([2011] OJ L304/64); Preamble under (8), Sale of Goods Directive ([2019] OJ L138/26); Preamble under (6), Directive 2009/22/EC of the European Parliament and of the Council of 23 April 2009 on Injunctions for the Protection of Consumers' Interests [2009] OJ L110/30 (Injunctions Directive).

112 Commission Communication, 'A New Deal for Consumers (Green Paper)', COM (2018) 138 final, https://eur-lex.europa.eu/legal-content/EN/TXT/?uri=celex:52018DC0183, p. 3. See also Commission Communication, 'Better Governance of the Single Market', COM (2012) 259 final, https://eur-lex.europa.eu/LexUriServ/LexUriServ.do?uri=COM:2012:0259:FIN:EN:PDF, p. 3 (placing consumer and business confidence in the key of economic growth).

113 Commission Communication, 'Towards a Single Market Act', p. 7.

114 Commission Communication, 'Single Market Act II Together for New Growth', COM (2012) 573 final, https://eur-lex.europa.eu/legal-content/EN/TXT/?uri=celex:52012DC0573, p. 9.

115 Commission Communication, 'A New Deal for Consumers', p. 1.

Consequently, a utilitarian analysis of today's positive integration policies, at least related to consumer contracts, presents a more convincing explanatory model than social distributive justice.

It follows that positive integration, and to that extent, EPL, is part of the same political philosophy as negative integration. Negative integration is therefore intrinsically connected to EPL, not merely historically or in terms of regulatory coherency, but also in virtue of the principles they share concerning the justification of the state's use of state power through private law to regulate or control the economic activities within the EU's internal market.

4. Concluding Remarks

It turns out that the connection between negative and positive integration techniques in EU policy is not merely one of co-existence. Rather, the EU's early emphasis on negative integration policies and EPL stems from the same underlying principle justifying the European government's role in the marketplace. In other words, EPL is not only compatible with negative integration in a historical and regulatory sense; it is part of the same political makeup. A utilitarian, economic-efficiency philosophy underlies both Europe's early negative and contemporary positive integration techniques.

More than pursuing free trade or social justice, the EU presents both negative integration and EPL as examples of positive integration and an ongoing attempt to ease cross-border trade and, thus, advance Europe's internal market space. In this policy justification, both facilitating traders to expand their business across national borders and offering consumers confidence in being protected across Europe are mere means to the ultimate end of securing peace, freedom, and economic and social progress in the Union. The European integration project has always testified to a conception of a centralised government, that acts as a proactive regulatory force in the market space, willing to adjust the rules of trade and contract in furthering society's economic and social progress. Within this project, over time, the emphasis has shifted from seeking primarily economic progress to including social progress. Still, Europe's integration project has consistently displayed a utilitarian inclination since the beginning.

Consequently, the historical transition from the early negative integration policies to the positive integration of contract law in Europe's 'shared economic space'[116] signifies a movement on a single spectrum rather than a change of spectra. Put differently, the shift does not signal a qualitative paradigm switch but, instead, a quantitative expansion of the scope of societal utility that the EU pursued through private law.

If one accepts the conclusion of this chapter that a utilitarian theory best explains EPL, one is not also committed to saying that this theory *should* be invoked to justify the government's role in the marketplace through private law. For example, one might wish to argue that the proper regulatory role of government through EPL is less

116 See, e.g., Commission Communication, 'Better Governance of the Single Market', p. 2 ('The Single Market is a key driver for economic growth'); see also Azoulai, 'Complex Weave of Harmonisation', p. 603.

interventionist or, instead, even more than it is today. This type of normative question is explored by Martijn Hesselink in Chapter 2. Regardless of where one stands on these matters, this chapter aimed to demonstrate that defending or critiquing the rules and principles of EPL as an instance of positive European integration should not ignore EPL's intricate relationship to the current utilitarian normative underpinnings that it shares with the EU's history of legal integration policies.

5. Points for Reflection

Q1: Should consumer protection in EPL be a matter of wealth maximisation, or would the EU do better by taking a social distributive justice approach?

Q2: What difference would your answer to the previous question make to the scope and content of European consumer protection laws?

Q3: Do the European Union Institutions have competencies to that extent? Should they have such powers?

Q4: Is the European Union better to refrain from using private law, including contract law, as a regulatory tool to meet certain substantive notions of wealth or justice?

Q5: Is that even possible?

Q6: If so, would a negative integration approach and, thus, a more hands-off approach not present a more proper regulatory role of government in the market space?

Bibliography

Armstrong, K. A., 'Governing Goods: Content and Context', in A. Arnull and D. Chalmers (eds), *The Oxford Handbook of European Union Law*, 1st edn (Oxford: Oxford University Press, 2015), pp. 508–536, https://doi.org/10.1093/oxfordhb/9780199672646.001.0001

Azoulai, L., 'The Complex Weave of Harmonisation', in A. Arnull and D. Chalmers (eds), *The Oxford Handbook of European Union* Law, 1st edn (Oxford: Oxford University Press, 2015), pp. 589–611, https://doi.org/10.1093/oxfordhb/9780199672646.001.0001

Bagchi, A., 'Distributive Justice and Contract', in G. Klass et al. (eds), *Philosophical Foundations of Contract Law* (Oxford: Oxford University Press 2014), pp. 193–212, https://doi.org/10.1093/acprof:oso/9780198713012.001.0001

Bagchi, A., 'Distributive Injustice and Private Law', *Hastings Law Journal* 60 (2008), 105–149

Benson, P., Justice in Transactions: *A Theory of Contract Law* (Cambridge, MA: Harvard University Press, 2019), https://doi.org/10.2307/j.ctv2524z3h.13

Barnett, R. E., 'A Consent Theory of Contract', *Columbia Law Review* 86 (1986), 269–321 (pp. 277–278), doi:10.2307/1122705

Barnard, C., 'The Construction of the Internal Market', in D. M. Patterson and A. Södersten (eds), *A Companion to European Union Law and International Law* (Malden: Wiley Blackwell, 2016), pp. 195–204.

Blauberger, M., 'From Negative to Positive Integration: European State Aid Control Through Soft and Hard Law', *MPIfG Discussion Paper* 08.4 (2008), https://ssrn.com/abstract=1660981

Bix, B., *Contract Law. Rules, Theory, and Context* (Cambridge: Cambridge University Press, 2012), https://doi.org/10.1017/CBO9781139024877

Commission Communication, 'Better Governance of the Single Market', COM (2012) 259 final, https://eur-lex.europa.eu/LexUriServ/LexUriServ.do?uri=COM:2012:0259:FIN:EN:PDF

Commission Communication, 'Communication from the Commission to the Council and the European Parliament on European Contract Law', COM (2001) 398 final, https://eur-lex.europa.eu/LexUriServ/LexUriServ.do?uri=COM:2001:0398:FIN:EN:PDF,

Commission Communication, 'Communication from the Commission to the European Parliament and the Council—A More Coherent European Contract Law—An Action Plan', COM (2003) 68 final, https://eur-lex.europa.eu/legal-content/EN/TXT/?uri=oj:JOC_2003_063_R_0001_01

Commission Communication, 'GREEN PAPER FROM THE COMMISSION: On Policy Options for Progress Towards a European Contract Law for Consumers and Businesses', COM (2010) 348 final, https://eur-lex.europa.eu/LexUriServ/LexUriServ.do?uri=COM:2010:0348:FIN:en:PDF

Commission Communication, 'A New Deal for Consumers (Green Paper)', COM (2018) 138 final, https://eur-lex.europa.eu/legal-content/EN/TXT/?uri=celex:52018DC0183

Commission Communication, 'Single Market Act II Together for New Growth', COM (2012) 573 final, https://eur-lex.europa.eu/legal-content/EN/TXT/?uri=celex:52012DC0573

Commission Communication, 'Towards a Single Market Act for a Highly Competitive Social Market Economy 50 Proposals for Improving our Work, Business and Exchanges with One Another', COM (2010) 609 final, https://eur-lex.europa.eu/legal-content/EN/TXT/?uri=celex:52010DC0608

Comparato, G., H.-W. Micklitz, and Y. Svetiev, 'The Regulatory Character of European Private Law', in C. Twigg-Flesner (ed.), *Research Handbook on EU Consumer and Contract Law* (Cheltenham: Edward Elgar Publishing, 2016), pp. 35–67, https://doi.org/10.4337/9781782547372.00009

Dagan, H., and M. Heller, *The Choice Theory of Contracts* (Cambridge, UK: Cambridge University Press, 2017), https://doi.org/10.1017/9781316477045

Fuller, L. L., 'Considerations and Form', *Columbia Law Review* 41 (1941), 799–824, https://doi.org/10.2307/1117840

Hartkamp, A., et al. (eds), *Cases, Materials, and Text on European Law and Private Law* (Oxford: Hart Publishing, 2017).

Hesselink, M. W., 'Contract Theory in EU Contract Law', in C. Twigg-Flesner (ed.), *Research Handbook on EU Consumer and Contract Law* (Cheltenham: Edward Elgar Publishing, 2016), pp. 508–534, https://doi.org/10.4337/9781782547372.00031

Johnston, A., *EC Regulation of Corporate Governance* (Cambridge, UK: Cambridge University Press, 2009), https://doi.org/10.1017/CBO9780511770753

Kronman, A. T., 'Wealth Maximization as a Normative Principle', *The Journal of Legal Studies* 9 (1980), 227–229, https://doi.org/10.1086/467637

Maduro, M. P., and P. C. Sousa, 'The Free Movement of Goods', in D. M. Patterson and A. Södersten (eds), *A Companion to European Union Law and International Law* (Malden: Wiley Blackwell 2016), pp. 205–216

Majone, G., *Dilemmas of European Integration: The Ambiguities and Pitfalls of Integration by Stealth* (Oxford: Oxford University Press, 2005), https://doi.org/10.1093/0199274304.001.0001

Mak, C., 'Free Movement and Contract Law', in C. Twigg-Flesner (ed.), *Research Handbook on EU Consumer and Contract Law* (Cheltenham: Edward Elgar Publishing, 2016), pp. 182–196, https://doi.org/10.4337/9781782547372.00015

Markovits, D., 'Making and Keeping Contracts', *Virginia Law Review* 92 (2006), 1325–1332

Micklitz, H.-W., 'On the Intellectual History of Freedom of Contract and Regulation', *Penn State Journal of Law and International Affairs* 4 (2015), 1–32

Oman, N. B., 'The Failure of Economic Interpretations of the Law of Contract Damages', *Washington and Lee Law Review* 64 (2007), pp. 829–875

Pinder, J., 'Positive Integration and Negative Integration: Some Problems of Economic Union in the EEC', *World Today* 24 (1968), 88–110

Posner, R. A., 'The Ethical and Political Basis of the Efficiency Norm in Common Law Adjudication', *Hofstra Law Review* 8 (1980), 487–507

Posner, R. A., 'Utilitarianism, Economics, and Legal Theory', *The Journal of Legal Studies* 8 (1979), 103–140

Raz, J., *The Morality of Freedom* (Oxford: Oxford University Press, 1988), https://doi.org/10.1093/0198248075.001.0001

Rosenfeld, M., 'Contract and Justice: The Relation between Classical Contract Law and Social Contract Theory', *Iowa Law Review* 70 (1985), 769–900

Scharpf, F. W., 'Balancing Positive and Negative Integration: The Regulatory Options for Europe', *MPIfG Working Paper* 97.8 (1997), http://hdl.handle.net/10419/41672

Scharpf, F. W., *Governing in Europe: Effective and Democratic?* (Oxford: Oxford University Press, 1999).

Scharpf, F. W., 'Negative and Positive Integration in the Political Economy of European Welfare State', in M. G. Marks, F. W. Scharpf, P. C. Schmitter, and W. Streeck (eds), *Governance in the European Union* (London: SAGE Publications, 1996), pp. 15–39, https://doi.org/10.4135/9781446279328.n2

Schütze, R., *European Union Law*, 2nd edn (Cambridge, UK: Cambridge University Press 2018), https://doi.org/10.1017/9781108555913

Schwartz, A., and R. E. Scott, 'Contract Theory and the Limits of Contract Law', *Yale Law Review* 113 (2003), 541–619, https://doi.org/10.2307/3657531

Smith, A. S., *Contract Theory* (Oxford: Oxford University Press, 2004)

Spaventa, E., 'The Free Movement of Workers in the Twenty-first Century', in A. Arnull and D. Chalmers (eds), *The Oxford Handbook of European Union Law*, 1st edn (Oxford: Oxford University Press, 2015), pp. 456–476, https://doi.org/10.1093/oxfordhb/9780199672646.013.20

Tinbergen, J., *International Economic Integration*, 2nd edn (Amsterdam: Elsevier, 1954)

Unberatth, H., and A. Johnston, 'The Double-Headed Approach of the ECJ Concerning Consumer Protection', *Common Market Law Review* 44.5 (2007), 1237–1284

Walker, N., 'The Philosophy of European Union Law', in A. Arnull and D. Chalmers (eds), *The Oxford Handbook of European Union Law*, 1st edn (Oxford: Oxford University Press, 2015), pp. 3–27, https://doi.org/10.1093/oxfordhb/9780199672646.013.2

Weatherill, S., *The Internal Market as a Legal Concept*, 1st edn (Oxford: Oxford University Press, 2017), https://doi.org/10.1093/acprof:oso/9780198794806.001.0001

Weinrib, E. J., 'Corrective Justice in a Nutshell', *The University of Toronto Law Journal* 52 (2002), 349–356

Zipursky, B. C., 'Philosophy of Private Law', in J. L. Colman et al. (eds), *The Oxford University Handbook of Jurisprudence and Philosophy of Law* (Oxford: Oxford University Press, 2004), pp. 623–630, https://doi.org/10.1093/oxfordhb/9780199270972.013.0016

4. Positive Integration: Harmonisation of National Law through Directives and Regulations[1]

Marco B. M. Loos

Abstract

This chapter discusses 'positive integration' (i.e. the EU promulgating legislation in the form of directives and regulations to create a common market for its Member States) and its impact on the national private laws of EU Member States. The chapter discusses the differences between regulations and directives, highlighting advantages and disadvantages of both. Whilst regulations and so-called 'maximum harmonisation' directives seem to harmonise the laws of the Member States, they can be difficult to fit into the national legal system, threatening the latter's coherence. Minimum harmonisation directives, on the other hand, seem easier to fit in, but in practice this is not always the case. Furthermore, it is questioned whether positive integration is actually helping to create an internal market—other factors, such as language or physical distance might be bigger obstacles than different legal regimes. At the same time, an online market is emerging, and the EU has perhaps a better case for harmonisation of private law applying there. The chapter also touches upon other pressing questions, including: should only consumers be protected as weaker parties or should small business be regarded as in need of special protection as well? And should the EU maintain its focus on sales or also harmonise service contract law, especially in light of the call for a more sustainable private law and the upcoming servitisation?

1 An earlier version of this chapter was published under the title 'Harmonization of Private Law in the 2020s: Targeted Full Harmonization 2.0?', in A. Janssen, M. Lehmann, and R. Schulze, *The Future of European Private Law* (Baden-Baden/München/Oxford: Beck/Nomos/Hart, 2023), pp. 403–427.

 https://doi.org/10.11647/OBP.0448.04

1. Introduction

According to Article 26(2) of the Treaty on the Functioning of the European Union (TFEU),[2] the European Union's internal market consists of an area, without internal frontiers, in which the free movement of goods, persons, services, and capital is ensured in accordance with the provisions of the Treaties. Under EU law, negative integration pertains to the absence of barriers to the exercise of these four fundamental freedoms. Negative integration thus aims to ensure that consumers and businesses may

- purchase and provide goods and services in another EU Member State,
- move for such purpose to such other EU Member State, and
- move capital to such country, e.g. to invest in that country,

without either the consumers' or businesses' home state or the receiving state preventing or restricting the exercise of these fundamental freedoms in any other way than by measures applied equally to domestic cases. This implies that consumers and businesses entering into cross-border contracts may not be discriminated against when compared to parties concluding domestic contracts.[3]

However, as the Member States have in principle retained the freedom to regulate their markets in any way that seems best to them, differences between national laws may continue to exist. Such differences may then hinder the proper functioning of the internal market, as consumers and businesses cannot rely on their knowledge of the law of their Member States when concluding a cross-border contract, since the law applicable to the contract may contain rather different rules. This implies that in a cross-border contract at least one of the parties may not know which rights and obligations stem from the contract, or how these rights and obligations can be enforced. This in turn may prevent parties from concluding cross-border contracts and, thus, from taking advantage of the internal market. Negative integration fails to remove these barriers to trade.

For this reason, Article 26(1) TFEU authorises the European Union to adopt measures with the aim of establishing or ensuring the functioning of the internal market. Under Article 114(1) TFEU, the European Parliament and the Council are allowed to adopt 'measures for the approximation of the provisions laid down by law, regulation or administrative action in Member States which have as their object the establishment and functioning of the internal market'. The measures taken on the basis of Article 114(1) TFEU lead to positive integration, i.e. at removing barriers to trade resulting from differences in the national laws of the Member States. The same applies of course to measures based on other provisions of the Treaty. To give some examples:

1. Article 50 TFEU constitutes a legal basis to enact directives in the area of company law, establishing the abolition of restrictions on the freedom of establishment.[4]

---

2 Consolidated version of the Treaty on the Functioning of the European Union [2008] OJ L115/47 (TFEU).

3 Cf. Chapter 3 by Jaap Baaij in this volume.

4 See for instance Directive (EU) 2017/1132 of the European Parliament and of the Council of 14 June

2. Article 59 TFEU contains a legal basis for directives in the area of services.[5]
3. Article 100 TFEU is the legal basis for legislative measures in the area of transport, which has given rise to a number of regulations pertaining to the rights of passengers.[6]
4. Articles 102 and 103 TFEU constitute a legal basis for the enactment of regulations or directives giving effect to the principles of competition law.[7]
5. Article 153 TFEU offers the possibility to create directives pertaining to social policy.[8]
6. Article 194 TFEU provides a legal basis for directives pertaining to the energy market.[9]

2017 relating to certain aspects of company law [2017] OJ L169/46; Directive (EU) 2019/2121 of the European Parliament and of the Council of 27 November 2019 amending Directive (EU) 2017/1132 as regards cross-border conversions, mergers and divisions [2019] OJ L321/1.

5 See for instance Directive 2006/123/EC of the European Parliament and of the Council of 12 December 2006 on services in the internal market [2006] OJ L376/36; Directive 2014/24/EU of the European Parliament and of the Council of 26 February 2014 on public procurement and repealing Directive 2004/18/EC [2014] OJ L94/65.

6 Regulations regarding passenger rights exist in the area of transport by airline, boat, bus, and train: Regulation (EC) No 261/2004 of the European Parliament and of the Council of 11 February 2004 establishing common rules on compensation and assistance to passengers in the event of denied boarding and of cancellation or long delay of flights, and repealing Regulation (EEC) No 295/91 [2004] OJ L46/1 (Denied Boarding Regulation, DBR); Regulation (EC) No 1107/2006 of the European Parliament and of the Council of 5 July 2006 concerning the rights of disabled persons and persons with reduced mobility when travelling by air [2006] OJ L204/1; Regulation (EC) No 392/2009 of the European Parliament and of the Council of 23 April 2009 on the liability of carriers of passengers by sea in the event of accidents [2009] OJ L131/24; Regulation (EU) No 1177/2010 of the European Parliament and of the Council of 24 November 2010 concerning the rights of passengers when travelling by sea and inland waterway and amending Regulation (EC) No 2006/2004 [2010] OJ L334/1; Regulation (EU) No 181/2011 of the European Parliament and of the Council of 16 February 2011 concerning the rights of passengers in bus and coach transport and amending Regulation (EC) No 2006/2004 [2011] OJ L55/1; Regulation (EU) No 2021/782 of the European Parliament and of the Council of 29 April 2021 on rail passengers' rights and obligations (recast) [2021] OJ L172/1. On 29 November 2023, a Proposal for a Regulation of the European Parliament and of the Council on passenger rights in the context of multimodal journeys, COM (2023) 752 final, was submitted to the Parliament and the Council, together with a Proposal for a Regulation of the European Parliament and of the Council amending Regulations (EC) No 261/2004, (EC) No 1107/2006, (EU) No 1177/2010, (EU) No 181/2011, and (EU) 2021/782 as regards enforcement of passenger rights in the Union, COM (2023) 753 final.

7 See for instance Directive 2014/104/EU of the European Parliament and of the Council of 26 November 2014 on certain rules governing actions for damages under national law for infringements of the competition law provisions of the Member States and of the European Union [2014] OJ L349/1; Directive (EU) 2019/1 of the European Parliament and of the Council of 11 December 2018 to empower the competition authorities of the Member States to be more effective enforcers and to ensure the proper functioning of the internal market [2018] OJ L11/3.

8 See for instance Directive (EU) 2019/1152 of the European Parliament and of the Council of 20 June 2019 on transparent and predictable working conditions in the European Union [2019] OJ L186/105; Directive (EU) 2019/1158 of the European Parliament and of the Council of 20 June 2019 on work-life balance for parents and carers and repealing Council Directive 2010/18/EU [2019] OJ L188/79.

9 See for instance Directive 2009/72/EC of the European Parliament and of the Council of 13 July 2009 concerning common rules for the internal market in electricity and repealing Directive 2003/54/EC [2009] OJ L211/55; Directive 2009/73/EC of the European Parliament and of the Council of 13 July 2009 concerning common rules for the internal market in natural gas and repealing Directive

In many cases, however, legal instruments in fact have several legal bases. For instance, the Commercial Agency Directive[10] is based on (what currently are) Articles 50 and 53 TFEU as well as Article 114 TFEU.

In practice, Article 114 TFEU offers the European Commission the possibility to develop proposals in very many different areas, ranging from payment services,[11] copyright,[12] late payments of commercial transactions,[13] and advertising.[14] Moreover, Article 114 TFEU also constitutes the main legal basis for directives and regulations in the area of consumer law.[15] In this chapter, I will primarily draw on examples taken from consumer (contract) law.[16]

2. Legal Architecture

a. Harmonisation Measures

Article 114(1) TFEU thus entitles the European Commission to propose 'harmonisation measures' aiming to remove differences between the laws of the Member States, and the European Parliament and the Council to jointly adopt such measures 'in accordance with the ordinary legislative procedure'. This procedure is defined in Article 294 TFEU. Typically, the European Parliament adopts its position by ordinary majority of the votes of the Members of Parliament, whereas the Council acts by a qualified majority of at least 55% of the members of the Council representing the participating Member States, comprising at least 65% of the population of EU States.[17] The fact that a (qualified) majority suffices at the level of the Council implies that Member States may be forced to accept harmonising measures against their will, provided that a large enough majority is obtained for the proposals of the European Commission (as amended by the Council and the European Parliament).

2003/55/EC [2009] OJ L221/94.

10 Council Directive 86/653/EEC of 18 December 1986 on the coordination of the laws of the Member States relating to self-employed commercial agents [1986] OJ L382/17.

11 Directive (EU) 2015/2366 of the European Parliament and of the Council of 25 November 2015 on payment services in the internal market, amending Directives 2002/65/EC, 2009/110/EC and 2013/36/EU and Regulation (EU) No 1093/2010, and repealing Directive 2007/64/EC [2015] OJ L337/35.

12 Directive (EU) 2019/790 of the European Parliament and of the Council of 17 April 2019 on copyright and related rights in the Digital Single Market and amending Directives 96/9/EC and 2001/29/EC [2019] OJ L130/92.

13 Directive 2011/7/EU of the European Parliament and of the Council of 16 February 2011 on combating late payment in commercial transactions [2011] OJ L48/1.

14 See for instance Directive 2003/33/EC of the European Parliament and of the Council of 26 May 2003 on the approximation of the laws, regulations and administrative provisions of the Member States relating to the advertising and sponsorship of tobacco products [2003] OJ L152/16; Directive 2006/114/EC of the European Parliament and of the Council of 12 December 2006 concerning misleading and comparative advertising [2006] OJ L376/21.

15 Article 169 TFEU provides for an additional legal basis to enact measures which support, supplement, and monitor the policy pursued by the Member States

16 On the relevance of consumer law in the harmonisation of European private law in more detail, see Chapter 9 in this volume.

17 Cf. Article 238(3) TFEU.

The measures, taken on the basis of Article 114(1) TFEU, may not relate to tax law, the free movement of persons or the rights and interests of employed persons.[18] This implies that harmonisation measures on the basis of this Article pertain primarily to the establishment and the functioning of the internal market for goods and services. Translated into private law terms, this means that Article 114(1) TFEU primarily facilitates the creation of common European rules in the area of contract law and, to a lesser extent, of tort law.[19]

When proposing harmonisation measures that relate to health, safety, environmental protection, and consumer protection, the European Commission is required to 'take as a base a high level of protection, taking account, in particular of, any new development based on scientific facts'. Similarly, when adopting these measures, both the European Parliament and the Council are required to take a high level of consumer protection as a base.[20] This implies, for instance, that when the European Commission proposes a directive to further the internal market of goods and services offered to consumers, the directive must contribute to the protection of the health, safety and economic interests of consumers, as well as to promoting their right to information, education and to organise themselves in order to safeguard their interests.[21] The Treaty, however, does not indicate when the level of consumer protection (or health, safety, and environmental protection) offered by a regulation or directive may be considered 'high', as required by Article 114(1) TFEU. It is therefore, first of all, a matter of negotiations within and between the institutions of the European Union whether the protection offered meets the requirements of the Treaty, and ultimately, it is up to the Court of Justice of the European Union (CJEU) to determine whether the achieved level of protection indeed meets these requirements. If the Court finds that it does not, it will invalidate (the relevant part of) the regulation or directive.[22]

Notwithstanding the demands set by the adoption of a regulation or directive, under Article 114(4) TFEU, a Member State is entitled to maintain national provisions

---

18 Cf. Article 114(2) TFEU.

19 Examples in the area of tort law are Council Directive 85/374/EEC of 25 July 1985 on the approximation of the laws, regulations and administrative provisions of the Member States concerning liability for defective products [1985] OJ L210/29 (Product Liability Directive, PLD), Directive 2005/29/EC of the European Parliament and of the Council of 11 May 2005 concerning unfair business-to-consumer commercial practices in the internal market and amending Council Directive 84/450/EEC, Directives 97/7/EC, 98/27/EC, and 2002/65/EC of the European Parliament and of the Council and Regulation (EC) No 2006/2004 of the European Parliament and of the Council [2005] OJ L149/22 (Unfair Commercial Practices Directive, UCPD), and Directive 2006/114/EC of the European Parliament and of the Council of 12 December 2006 concerning misleading and comparative advertising [2006] OJ L376/21 (Misleading Advertisement Directive). In 2024, the Product Liability Directive was replaced by Directive (EU) 2024/2853 of the European Parliament and of the Council of 23 October 2024 on liability for defective products and repealing Council Directive 85/374/EEC. This Directive (henceforth, PLD2), will take effect as of 9 December 2026.

20 Cf. Article 114(3) TFEU.

21 Cf. Article 1691(1) and (2) TFEU.

22 For an example where a national court (in vain) called for the invalidation of a provision of the PLD, see Case C-83/22 *Tuk Tuk Travel* [2023] ECLI:EU:C:2023:664.

that exist on the date of adoption of the regulation or directive.[23] The Member State may, however, only do so on the grounds identified in Article 36 TFEU and provided that these provisions do not constitute a means of arbitrary discrimination or a disguised restriction on trade between Member States. Therefore, where there are grounds pertaining to

- public morality, public policy, or public security,
- the protection of health and life of humans, animals, or plants,
- the protection of national treasures possessing artistic, historic, or archaeological value, or
- the protection of industrial and commercial property,

that Member State may continue to apply these provisions even if they contradict the provisions of the adopted regulation or directive. The same holds true, Article 114(4) TFEU adds, where these grounds relate to the protection of the environment or the working environment. In addition, Article 114(5) TFEU allows for the introduction of national provisions derogating from a regulation or directive,[24] provided that the introduction of such provision is deemed necessary for the protection of the environment or the working environment and is based on new scientific evidence. The grounds mentioned in Article 36 TFEU, therefore, cannot be invoked to justify the introduction of new derogations from EU law. In both cases, the Member State must notify the European Commission of these provisions as well as the grounds for maintaining them.[25] A failure to do so implies that these provisions may not be relied on.[26] The European Commission then decides whether it accepts or rejects the derogation from the harmonisation measure and whether it shall propose an amendment of the harmonisation measure.[27] In both cases, the derogation from the directive or regulation only allows for an increase of protection and not for a decrease thereof.[28] Moreover, Article 114(5) TFEU may be relied on only in case a particular problem arises (only) in the Member State that wishes to introduce such new legislation or in some Member States: if the same problem occurs throughout the European Union, action may be undertaken only at the EU level, i.e. by amending the existing directive or regulation or adopting a new one.[29]

---

23 Cf. J. Osiejewicz, 'The Opt-out-Clause of Article 114 TFEU: Remarks on the Judgment of the General Court of 7 March 2013—*Republic of Poland v. European Commission* (CaseT-370/11)', *Studia IURIDICA AUCTORITATE Universitatis Pecs PUBLICATA* 154 (2016), 161–177 (pp. 167–168). Osiejewicz, at p. 169, indicates that Article 114(4) TFEU applies to legislation that is and remains unaltered at and after the time of the adoption of the directive or regulation, or is amended only slightly.

24 This provision also applies to substantive amendments to pre-existing legislation, cf. ibid., p. 169.

25 Cf. Article 114(4) and (5) TFEU.

26 Cf. Case C-194/94 *CIA Security International v Signalson and Securitel* [1996] ECLI:EU:C:1996:172.

27 Cf. Article 114(6) and (7) TFEU.

28 Cf. Osiejewicz, 'The Opt-out-Clause', pp. 169–170.

29 Cf. ibid., pp. 172–173.

Under Article 12(3) Package Travel Directive (PTD),[30] the organiser of a package travel (the tour organiser) may terminate the package travel contract before departure if it is prevented from performing the contract because of 'unavoidable and extraordinary circumstances'. Similarly, under Article 12(2) PTD, the traveller may also terminate the contract under such conditions if these occur at the place of destination, or its immediate vicinity, and significantly affecting the performance of the package, or if they significantly affect the carriage of passengers to the destination. In both cases, the tour organiser must provide the traveller with a full refund of any payments made for the package, but is not liable to pay damages. Para. (4) adds that the reimbursements must be made to the traveller not later than fourteen days after the package travel contract is terminated.

At the outbreak of the Covid-19 pandemic in March 2020, both tour organisers and travellers terminated package travel contracts, and new contracts were no longer concluded. At the same time, travellers that were already *en route* had to be repatriated at no extra cost for the traveller and had to be offered an appropriate price reduction under Articles 13(6) and 14(1) PTD. For tour organisers, this meant that overnight income streams dried up, while operating costs largely continued. By issuing vouchers instead of cash as the form of repayment, but in clear violation of their obligations under the PTD, tour organisers could prevent immediate insolvency. In several Member States, the legislator intervened to provide a legal basis for the forced acceptance of vouchers instead of reimbursement of payments made by travellers. However, as the Covid-19 pandemic was not a particular problem arising (only) in these Member States, but throughout the European Union, these interventions did not meet the requirements of Article 114(5) TFEU, which meant that such measures could only be taken at the EU level by amending the PTD—which process was not followed. For this reason, the European Commission launched infringement procedures against ten Member States.[31] In 2023, in a case where Article 114(5) TFEU was not invoked, the CJEU held that such voucher schemes were indeed not allowed under the PTD.[32]

b. Regulations and Directives

The harmonisation measures adopted on the basis of Article 114 TFEU may consist in the adoption of a regulation or a directive, or of any other decision.

According to Article 288 TFEU, a regulation binds in its entirety and is directly applicable in all Member States. This implies that the provisions of a regulation, in the same manner as the treaty provisions themselves, are a direct source of rights and obligations of parties, without any need for the Member State to first transpose

30 Directive (EU) 2015/2302 of the European Parliament and of the Council of 25 November 2015 on package travel and linked travel arrangements, amending Regulation (EC) No 2006/2004 and Directive 2011/83/EU of the European Parliament and of the Council and repealing Council Directive 90/314/EEC [2015] OJ L326/1.

31 See European Commission, 'July Infringement Package: Key Decisions', *European Commission* (2 July 2022), https://ec.europa.eu/commission/presscorner/detail/en/INF_20_1212. Most of these procedures were soon afterwards terminated as the respective Member States had either corrected their legislation, or the legislation they introduced had expired. On this, see M. B. M. Loos, 'One Day I'll Fly Away... Voucher Schemes for Cancelled Package Travel Contracts After the Outbreak of the Covid-19 Pandemic', *Journal of European Consumer and Market Law* 10 (2021), 122–124.

32 Case C-407/21 *UFC-Que-choisir* [2023] ECLI:EU:C:2023:449.

the provisions of the regulation into national law.[33] Moreover, as European Union law takes precedence over national law, the provisions of a regulation cannot be set aside by a later national provision unless European law expressly allows for that.[34]

As a regulation may create rights and obligations of individuals and no transposition into national law is needed, the instrument of a regulation appears to be the most efficient means to introduce uniform rules in all Member States. However, as the provisions of such a regulation are not fit into the national legal system into which they are to be applied, and therefore are not well-connected to national law, the question may arise how the rights and obligations stemming from a regulation relate to private law concepts.

Articles 4, 5, and 7 of the 2004 Denied Boarding Regulation (DBR) provide that, under certain conditions, passengers who are denied boarding the aircraft for which they have a valid ticket or who are confronted with cancellation of their flight are entitled to compensation. According to standing case law, the same holds true for passengers that suffer from delays of more than three hours.[35] The CJEU made clear that the compensation referred to in Article 7 DBR does not pertain to the individual damage sustained by each individual passenger, for which an individual case-by-case assessment must take place of the extent of the damage caused and the existence of a causal link between being denied boarding, the cancellation, or the delay, and the damage sustained. Instead, the CJEU held, the compensation pertains to the damage consisting of the inconvenience caused by being denied boarding, by the cancellation, or by the excessive delay. As this inconvenience is almost identical for every passenger, redress for this inconvenience may take the form of standardised and immediate assistance or care for everybody concerned.[36] In other words, the rules on compensation under the DBR may not to be seen as resulting in a claim for damages under national law of contractual or non-contractual liability, but constitute a *sui generis* claim.

Moreover, as the concepts of a regulation differ from those used under national law, courts may find it difficult to determine whether or not the conditions for granting a right or a remedy are fulfilled, and whether or not an exception to such a right or remedy applies. As a consequence, a multitude of questions may be referred to the CJEU for preliminary ruling.

An exception to the right to claim compensation under the DBR in case of cancellation or delay applies where the cancellation or delay is caused by 'extraordinary circumstances which could not have been avoided even if all reasonable measures had been taken'.[37] Airlines suffer from the amount of compensation they are required to pay to all passengers that have sustained, for instance, a long delay, and therefore frequently invoke the exception. The exception may look similar to national legal concepts such as

33 Case C-106/77 *Amministrazione delle finanze dello Stato v Simmenthal* [1978] ECLI:EU:C:1978:49, para 15.

34 Ibid., para. 17.

35 Joined Cases C-402/07 and C-432/07 *Sturgeon and Others* [2009] ECLI:EU:C:2009:716; Joined Cases C-581/10 and C-610/10 *Nelson and Others* [2012] ECLI:EU:C:2012:657 (*Nelson and Others*).

36 Case C-344/04 *IATA and ELFAA* [2006] ECLI:EU:C:2006:10, para 43; *Nelson and Others*, para. 48–53.

37 Cf. Article 5(3) DBR regarding cancellation, which according to *Sturgeon and Others*, para. 43, is also to be applied in case of delay.

force majeure, Höhere Gewalt, and frustration of contract, but does not coincide with any of these concepts. As a result, the CJEU has rendered a decision (i.e. a judgment or an order) in which this concept has played a role in no less than ninety-two cases decided between the original Sturgeon judgment of 19 November 2009 and 21 February 2024.[38]

This suggests that the use of regulation may not be as efficient for the European legislator as one would at first glance expect.

By contrast, a directive is binding only as to the result to be achieved, but leaves to the Member States the choice of form and method. Moreover, whereas a regulation may be relied upon by individuals, also in relations between private parties, a directive only binds the Member States to which it is addressed. This implies that in principle, private parties do not directly derive rights and obligations from a directive.[39] Member States are therefore required to transpose (or implement) the directive into national law and to 'fit' the directive into the legal system of that Member State. Rules of contract law may, for instance, be transposed by adding new provisions to the national civil code or by amending existing provisions, but also by adding new provisions to a commercial or consumer code and amending provisions thereof, or by introducing or amending a self-standing act.

The 2007 Shareholders Rights Directive[40] sets out certain rights for shareholders in listed companies. This directive was amended in 2017 in order to encourage more long-term engagement of shareholders.[41] The 2017 directive is transposed through an amendment of the civil code (and some other laws) in the Netherlands[42] and by a self-standing act in Ireland.[43]

For Member States, the use of a directive, instead of a regulation, offers the advantage that the coherence of national law is disturbed to a lesser extent, as the Member State may draft the transposing provisions rules in accordance with national terminology.

Article 6 of the Unfair Contract Terms Directive (UCTD)[44] provides that unfair terms do

38 Another seventy-six cases were removed from the register of the CJEU before a decision was taken, e.g. because the underlying case had been settled by the parties.

39 Cf. Case C-271/91 *Marshall v Southampton and South West Hampshire Area Health Authority* [1993] ECLI:EU:1993:335; Case C-91/92 *Faccini Dori v Racreb* [1994] ECLI:EU:1994:292.

40 Directive 2007/36/EC of the European Parliament and of the Council of 11 July 2007 on the exercise of certain rights of shareholders in listed companies [2007] OJ L184/17.

41 Directive (EU) 2017/828 of the European Parliament and of the Council of 17 May 2017 amending Directive 2007/36/EC as regards the encouragement of long-term shareholder engagement [2017] OJ L132/1.

42 Act of 6 November 2019 amending Book 2 of the Civil Code, the Law on Financial Supervision and the Law on book-entry securities implementing Directive (EU) 2017/828 of the European Parliament and of the Council of 17 May 2017 amending Directive 2007/36/EC as regards the encouragement of long-term shareholder engagement (OJ L2017/132) [Wet van 6 november 2019 tot wijziging van Boek 2 van het Burgerlijk Wetboek, de Wet op het financieel toezicht en de Wet giraal effectenverkeer ter uitvoering van Richtlijn 2017/828/EU van het Europees Parlement en de Raad van 17 mei 2017 tot wijziging van Richtlijn 2007/36/EG wat het bevorderen van de langetermijnbetrokkenheid van aandeelhouders betreft (PbEU 2017, L 132)], Stb. 2019, 423.

43 European Union (Shareholders' Rights) Regulations 2020, S.I. No. 81, which are to be read as one with the Companies Act 2014, S.I. No. 38, as section 1(2) of the Regulations provide.

44 Council Directive 93/13/EEC of 5 April 1993 on unfair terms in consumer contracts [1993] OJ L95/29

not bind consumers. The directive does not qualify whether this means that an unfair term is null and void, or that the term may be binding on the seller or supplier making use of the term, but voidable by consumers. As a result, Member States are free to apply existing private law notions to achieve the required result.

There are also drawbacks to the use of directives. At the national level, in particular when the provisions of a directive are implemented in an existing code or act, it may be difficult to see which provisions of the law have a European background and must therefore be interpreted in light of the directive, and which do not. There is a substantive risk that both courts and lawyers overlook the European origin and therefore interpret the transposed provisions in line with national rules of interpretation of legal provisions instead of adopting an autonomous (EU) interpretation of the notions included in the transposing provisions.

To come back to the example of Article 6 UCTD: if under national law an unfair term is voidable, this typically means that the term is valid and thus binding upon the parties until the aggrieved party avoids the term. If a consumer is unaware of the unfairness of the term or the possibility to avoid the term, they may continue to be bound by the term. Under the national contract laws of many Member States, courts typically do not avoid unfair terms of their own motion, and would, therefore, uphold the term if the consumer had not avoided it. This would mean, however, that the term effectively would bind the consumer, contrary to Article 6 UTCD, and thus that the aim set by the European legislator would not be met. Moreover, if the consumer would have avoided the term, the normal course of action would be that the term would be replaced by the default rule that would have applied if the term had not been incorporated into the contract.

In standing case law, the CJEU has clarified that Article 6 UCTD requires national courts to test the possible unfairness of a term of their own motion and not to apply the term if it is found to be unfair, i.e. to actively intervene on behalf of the consumer.[45] Moreover, the Court has also indicated that the national court is not allowed to replace the term by the otherwise applicable default rule, unless this would mean that the contract, as a whole, would become invalid.[46] This implies that where a contractual interest clause is unfair, it may not be replaced by the otherwise applicable statutory interest.

At the European level, it is clear that the use of directives instead of regulations leads to less convergence between the laws of the Member States, as Member States may transpose a directive in diverging ways, which in practice may lead to diverging interpretations. As these directives are embedded in national law and discussed primarily in national literature, these interpretations may not come to the fore and may continue to exist, without the need for clarification at the European level becoming (sufficiently) apparent to the national courts.

Articles 1 and 9 under (b) Product Liability Directive (PLD) provide that the producer of a defective product is liable, i.e. for damage to, or destruction of, any item of property other than the defective product itself, 'with a lower threshold of' €500, provided that

(Unfair Contract Terms Directive, UCTD).

45 See for instance Case C-243/08 *Pannon GSM* [2009] ECLI:EU:2009:350.

46 Joined Cases C-229/19 and C-289/19 *Dexia Nederland* [2021] ECLI:EU:2021:68.

the item of property is ordinarily intended for private use or consumption, and was in fact used for such consumption by the injured person. In Dutch law, in line with the parliamentary proceedings pertaining to the transposition of the directive,[47] the common opinion among scholars is that this threshold implies that when the damage sustained exceeds €500, the producer is liable for the full damage caused by the defective product,[48] even though it is acknowledged that in other Member States the threshold is interpreted as the amount that is to be deducted from the damage that must be compensated.[49] Whereas the Dutch translation of the PLD is unclear as to the meaning of the threshold, the German ('unter Selbstbeteiligung von', i.e. 'under a deductible of') and French ('sous deduction de', i.e. 'under deduction of') text versions of the Directive leave no doubt that the threshold is indeed meant as an amount that need not be compensated by the producer of the defective product even when the damage sustained exceeds the threshold. However, the Dutch courts are in practice not called upon to decide the matter—so no need for the courts to refer a question for preliminary ruling to the CJEU—as Article 13 PLD leaves open the possibility for victims to invoke national rules on non-contractual liability, and these (in any case) offer the possibility to claim compensation of the full damage sustained by the victim. The threshold does not appear anymore in the new Product Liability Directive from 2024 (PLD2), which takes effect from 9 December 2026. In the near future, this particular problem therefore will no longer exist.

3. Societal Relevance: Stakes and Challenges

As regulations apply directly in all Member States and are a direct source for rights and obligations of individuals, for an individual benefitting from the rights that derive from the regulation, the use of a regulation may seem to be more advantageous as that individual need not wait for the Member State to transpose the provisions creating the individual's rights. In contrast, the individual that is burdened with the corresponding obligation would, for the same reason, favour the use of a directive instead of a regulation.

Yet, the idea that individuals cannot rely on the provisions of a directive that has not been timely transposed into national law, must be nuanced. First of all, even though an individual may not rely directly on a directive towards another individual, they may do so in case the other party to the contract is (part of) the Member State.[50] Secondly, where national private law makes use of open norms such as 'good faith and fair dealing', 'reasonable, 'unfair', etc., courts are required to interpret these notions in

47 Kamerstukken II 1987/88, 19636, No 6, pp. 27–28.

48 Cf. C. H. Sieburgh, *Mr. C. Assers Handleiding tot de beoefening van het Nederlands Burgerlijk Recht. 6. Verbintenissenrecht. Deel IV. De verbintenis uit de wet*, 15th edn (Deventer: Wolters Kluwer, 2019), note 267: 'Voor zaakschade geldt wel een franchise van € 500, hetgeen naar de Nederlandse opvatting wil zeggen dat schade die niet méér bedraagt niet moet worden vergoed, maar schade die wel meer bedraagt voor het geheel moet worden vergoed' ('For property damage, a threshold of €500 applies, which according to the Dutch view means that damage that does not exceed this amount must not be compensated, but damage that does exceed this amount must be compensated in full'; translated by the author).

49 Ibid.

50 Case C-41/74 *Van Duyn v Home Office* [1974] ECLI:EU:C:1974:133.

the light of the wording and purpose of a directive,[51] also in relations between private parties.[52] Thirdly, where national law does not leave room for such interpretation in line with the directive, and an individual therefore misses out on a right, a remedy or a defense they should have had under EU law, they may under certain conditions claim damages from the Member State on the basis of state liability for failure to (properly) transpose the directive.[53]

In addition, even though regulations apply directly in all Member States, without the need for transposition, and private parties may rely directly on the rights awarded to them by the regulation, in practice, these regulations still need to be embedded in national law, in particular in national procedural law. For this reason, often national law needs to be amended or added to by specific legislation, e.g. by identifying which court is competent to decide on a claim based on the regulation and by defining the procedural rules for such a case to be decided. The absence of such accompanying national legislation is, however, not a prerequisite for private parties to be able to rely on the provisions of the regulation.

Next, even though, in theory, Member States remain free to 'fit' a directive into their national legal system when transposing its provisions, in practice often little room is left to the Member States when doing so. This is true in particular with full harmonisation, as Member States may not maintain or introduce in their national law, provisions diverging from those laid down in the full harmonisation directive even if these national provisions would offer better protection to weaker parties.[54]

Traditionally, in areas where weaker parties, such as consumers, employees, and tenants, conclude contracts with stronger parties, such as traders, employers, and landlords, national contract law offers mandatory protection to these weaker parties. In these areas, the laws of the Member States may differ to a large extent, reflecting different national preferences and policies. In such—typically politically sensitive—areas, directives used to contain a so-called minimum harmonisation clause.[55] On the basis of such a minimum harmonisation clause, Member States are allowed to introduce or maintain consumer protection rules that exceed the level of protection offered by these directives. A minimum harmonisation clause makes it easier for Member States

---

51 Case C-14/93 *Von Colson and Kamann v Land Nordrhein-Westfalen* [1984] ECLI:EU:1984:153, para. 26 and 28.

52 Case C-106/89 *Marleasing v Comercial Internacional de Alimentación* [1990] ECLI:EU:1990:395, para. 8–9.

53 Joined Cases C-6/90 and C-9/90 *Francovich and Bonifaci v Italy* [1991] ECLI:EU:1991:428; *Faccini Dori*.

54 See for instance Article 4 of Directive 2011/83/EU of the European Parliament and of the Council of 25 October 2011 on consumer rights, amending Council Directive 93/13/EEC and Directive 1999/44/EC of the European Parliament and of the Council and repealing Council Directive 85/577/EEC and Directive 97/7/EC of the European Parliament and of the Council [2011] OJ L304/64 (Consumer Rights Directive, CRD).

55 Cf. also N. Reich, 'Von der Minimal- zur Voll- zur "Halbharmonisierung". Ein europäisches Privatrechtsdrama in fünf Akten', *Zeitschrift für Europäisches Privatrecht* 1 (2010), 7–39 (pp. 8–9); H.-W. Micklitz, 'The Targeted Full Harmonisation Approach: Looking Behind the Curtain', in G. Howells and R. Schulze (eds), *Modernising and Harmonising Consumer Contract Law* (Munich: Sellier European Law Publisher 2009), pp. 47–86 (p. 48); P. Rott, 'Minimum Harmonization for the Completion of the Internal Market? The Example of Consumer Sales Law', *Common Market Law Review* 50 (2003), 1107–1135 (pp. 1107–1108).

to absorb a directive into their legislation as only the minimum requirements of the directive must be met.[56]

However, this necessarily implies that the effect of the harmonisation measure is limited: whereas the aim of harmonisation is to approximate the laws of the Member States, these laws in fact still differ when Member States make use of the minimum harmonisation clause.[57] In theory, the differences between the laws of the Member States could even increase if in one or more legal systems the implementation of the directive is accompanied by 'goldplating', i.e. by introducing extra protection in areas where the directive is silent. The minimum harmonisation approach therefore entails the risk that traders that offer their goods or services across the border may still face different rules that apply to their contracts than they are accustomed to in their home country.[58] The need to investigate whether this is the case or not and the subsequent need to amend the sales method and the contract terms used may make it more difficult for traders to trade cross-border than would be the case if all rules were the same.[59] As a result, cross-border trade is more expensive for traders than purely domestic trade, which implies that the conditions for competition are not the same throughout Europe, and in fact worse for foreign traders than for domestic traders.

Consumers, on the other hand, cannot be sure that they will receive the same level of protection they are used to in their home country when they shop cross-border.[60] This would, in particular, discourage small and medium-sized businesses (SMEs) and consumers to contract cross-border, as the costs of legal diversity are particularly deterrent to them.[61] In this sense, minimum harmonisation is thought not to remove the barriers to the internal market in a sufficient manner. If, by contrast, the EU were to take legislative measures on the basis of (targeted)[62] full harmonisation, Member

56 Cf. also C. Twigg-Flesner, 'Introduction: Key Features of European Union Private Law', in C. Twigg-Flesner (ed.), *European Union Private Law* (Cambridge, UK: Cambridge University Press, 2010), pp. 1–19 (p. 4).

57 Ibid. This would be different if minimum harmonisation would stand in the way of Member States adopting or maintaining more stringent consumer protection rules with regard to the core provisions of a directive based on Article 114 TFEU, as is argued by P. Rott, 'Minimum Harmonization', pp. 1115–1117.

58 Cf. also M. Artz, 'Die "vollständige Harmonisierung" des Europäischen Verbraucherprivatrechts', *Zeitschrift für Gemeinschaftsprivatrecht* 6.4 (2009), 171–177 (pp. 171, 172).

59 Cf. E. H. Hondius, 'The Proposal for a European Directive on Consumer Rights: A Step Forward', *European Review of Private Law* 18 (2010), 103–127 (pp. 109–110).

60 Cf. Commission Communication, 'GREEN PAPER on the Review of the Consumer Aquis', COM (2006) 744 final, https://eur-lex.europa.eu/LexUriServ/LexUriServ.do?uri=COM:2006:0744:FIN:en:PDF, p. 10.

61 Ibid.; see on this argument G. Low, 'The (Ir)relevance of Harmonization and Legal Diversity to European Contract Law: A Perspective from Psychology', *European Review of Private Law* 18 (2010), 285–305 (pp. 288–289). In the rest of his paper, Low convincingly demonstrates that these perceived reasons not to trade cross-border are in fact hardly relevant, or of such nature that they can't be taken away by any kind of harmonisation measure.

62 'Targeted', as the legislative measure respects the existence of national law in areas that have not been the subject of regulation in the legislative measure. For instance, Article 3(10) of Directive (EU) 2019/770 of the European Parliament and of the Council of 20 May 2019 on certain aspects concerning contracts for the supply of digital content and digital services [2019] OJ L136/1 (Digital Content Directive) specifically provides that the directive 'shall not affect the freedom of Member States to

States would be required to abrogate national legislation that is not in conformity with the European level of consumer protection, irrespective of whether the existing national level of consumer protection is higher or lower than the new European level. As a consequence, full harmonisation would cause consumers and traders to be able to rely on the fact that in the whole of the European Union one uniform set of rules applies to the rights and obligations of the parties. Full harmonisation is therefore seen to lead to a uniform level of consumer protection throughout the European Union, and therefore to a 'level playing field' for all traders and consumers.[63] That in turn should make it easier for both businesses and consumers to conclude cross-border contracts and should ultimately lead to an increase in the use of the internal market. From the perspective of the functioning of the internal market, one could therefore argue that full harmonisation of 'key concepts' of European consumer law is necessary in order to create legal certainty for both consumers and businesses.

4. Points for Reflection

It seems rather doubtful whether the arguments in favour of full harmonisation hold much truth[64]—if only because goldplating is not restricted to the transposition of minimum harmonisation directives, because recitals in full harmonisation directives invite Member States to extend the scope of directives to contracts not directly covered, and because the accompanying national legal infrastructure (the national rules of general contract law and general tort law) apply with regard to matters not covered, and these rules still differ. Nevertheless, whereas the original directives in the area of, for instance, consumer protection law were based on minimum harmonisation, currently almost all European directives in this area are based on full harmonisation—with the notable exception of the Unfair Contract Terms Directive, which dates back to 1993. Moreover, many directives contain very detailed provisions, thus leaving little room for the Member States to retain existing legislation. In fact, where the European legislator has opted for full harmonisation, Member States are more or less required to copy out the directive into their national legal system, thus incorporating foreign notions into their legal systems, which may or may not derogate from the rules applicable to other contracts. As regards practical effect, there seems to be little difference between a full harmonisation directive and a regulation.

From the perspective of national law, problems may arise, in particular, where

---

regulate aspects of general contract law, such as rules on the formation, validity, nullity or effects of contracts, including the consequences of the termination of a contract in so far as they are not regulated in this Directive, or the right to damages'.

63 Remarkably, the argument of the creation of a level playing field originally was invoked to justify minimum harmonisation, cf. Reich, 'Von der Minimal- zur Voll- zur "Halbharmonisierung"', p. 17.

64 See extensively M. B. M. Loos, 'Full Harmonisation as a Regulatory Concept and its Consequences for the National Legal Orders. The Example of the Consumer Rights Directive', in M. Stürner (ed.), *Vollharmonisierung im Europäischen Verbraucherrecht?* (Munich: Sellier European Law Publisher, 2010), pp. 47–98. This section as well as the next is largely based on that paper.

similar provisions already exist at the national level that apply not only in B2C-contracts (business-to-consumer contracts) but also in B2B-contracts (business-to-business contracts) and, as the case may be, in contracts between two consumers (C2C-contracts). The national legislator must then choose to either introduce specific, slightly different, rules for B2C-contracts, or to amend the general rules also for contracts not regulated within the scope of the directive. The first alternative has the disadvantage of creating disparities at the national level, thus endangering the coherence of national contract law. The second alternative may be problematic as the consequences of such an amendment may not always be anticipated, particularly not given the short time for transposing a directive in the first place. This means that, whereas full harmonisation may lead to more convergence at European level in the area regulated, it may lead to less coherence of law at national level.

This is problematic as the justification for legislation in the area of contract law on the basis of Article 114 TFEU is shaky, to say the least. Harmonisation of contract law rules can only do so much in order to create an internal market for goods and services where traders and consumers may benefit from. As a directive can only regulate what is within its scope, much will still be left to the Member States to regulate. Consequentially, (consumer) contract law legislation in the Member States will continue to differ.[65] This means that the need for traders to take legal advice when contracting cross-border, and therefore the need for traders to incur costs, may be diminished by the adoption of a full harmonisation directive, but will not be taken away completely. Moreover, it is not clear why the argument that the internal market requires full harmonisation should focus on consumer contracts and not also—or primarily—apply to B2B-contracts, in particular to allow SMEs to profit from the benefits of the internal market. Obviously, SMEs may just as easily be prevented from concluding cross-border (commercial or consumer) contracts by differences in legislation as consumers supposedly are from concluding cross-border consumer contracts.

More importantly, from the perspective of psychology, it is doubtful whether harmonisation, let alone full harmonisation, is even all that relevant to the question whether consumers and businesses are willing or interested to contract cross-border.[66] As Low puts it: to most consumers and businesses, 'harmonization is a solution to an irrelevant or non-existent problem'.[67] That consumers and businesses do not make optimal use of the internal market is most likely not so much a consequence of differences in the consumer contract law legislation of the Member States, but rather of differences in language and culture, of different national customs and preferences, of different taxation regimes, and, most importantly, of the mere geographical distance

65 Cf. B. Gsell and H. M. Schellhase, 'Vollharmonisiertes Verbraucherkreditrecht—ein Vorbild für die weitere europäische Angleichung des Verbrauchervertragsrechts?', *JuristenZeitung* 64 (2009), 20–29 (22–23).

66 In this sense, see T. Wilhelmsson, 'The Abuse of the "Confident Consumer" as a Justification for EC Consumer Law', *Journal of Consumer Policy* 27 (2004), 317–337 (pp. 325, 328).

67 Cf. Low, 'The (Ir)relevance of Harmonization', p. 303; compare also Reich, 'Von der Minimal- zur Voll- zur "Halbharmonisierung"', p. 10.

between trader and consumer.[68] Others point to different technical standards, which in fact may mean that electronic equipment bought in one country cannot be used in another because the second country uses different plugs,[69] to the fear that consumers may have of not being able to enforce any contractual claims they may have (be it under the law of country X or Y) and problems of access to justice,[70] to positive experiences with and trust in the local seller or service provider, and to the 'after sales services', which may be expected of such a trader located in the same local community.[71] For instance, as regards the possibility to enforce contractual claims, it matters greatly whether a consumer may terminate a contract for non-performance himself or whether the contract may only be dissolved by a court. However, this is explicitly left to the Member States' general contract law.

It seems almost as if the harmonisation of private law at the EU level—be it through a directive or through a regulation—is a solution looking for a problem instead of the other way around.

Q1: Can harmonisation of private law be justified on the basis of the need to create and improve the internal market?

Q2: In case harmonisation is justified, should harmonisation take place on the basis of (targeted) full harmonisation or on the basis of minimum harmonisation?

However, with the emergence of electronic commerce since the early 2000s, and particularly with the development of the Digital Single Market strategy since 2015,[72] the case for harmonisation may have changed. In this strategy, the European Commission set out that the internet as well as information and communication technology have led to rapid changes of the economy and to legal challenges for all Member States. According to the Commission, the European level is the right framework to deal with these challenges, offering better access for consumers and businesses to online goods and services across Europe, creating the right conditions for digital networks and services to flourish, and maximising the growth potential of the European digital economy.[73] In executing this policy, several legislative reforms have been adopted, including, for instance,

68 Cf. Wilhelmsson, 'Abuse of the "Confident Consumer"', pp. 329–330; Low, 'The (Ir)relevance of Harmonization', p. 303; Twigg-Flesner, 'Introduction', p. 15.

69 M. Faure, 'Towards a Maximum Harmonization of Consumer Contract Law?', *Maastricht Journal of European and Comparative Law* 15 (2008), 433–445 (p. 438).

70 Cf. Wilhelmsson, 'Abuse of the "Confident Consumer"', p. 329.

71 Cf. Artz, 'Die "vollständige Harmonisierung"', p. 172; see also Faure, 'Towards a Maximum Harmonization', p. 437, who points to other factors that are relevant for competition, such as environmental legislation, differences in infrastructure, amount of wages, productivity, and development of the labour market.

72 Commission, 'A Digital Single Market Strategy for Europe' (Communication) COM (2015) 192 final.

73 Ibid., p. 3.

- a regulation banning unjustified geoblocking,[74]
- a regulation promoting fairness and transparency in contracts between a business and the provider of online intermediation services,[75]
- a directive on copyright and related rights in the Digital Single Market,[76]
- a directive introducing information obligations for online platforms in B2C-situations,[77]
- directives pertaining to the sale of goods[78] and to the supply of digital content and digital services,[79] and
- regulations pertaining to digital services[80] and digital markets.[81]

Q3: Can harmonisation of private law be justified with a view to the Digital Single Market?

The question, of course, is whether the emergence of the Digital Single Market indeed justifies legislation at the European level, and whether the advantages of regulation the matter in part on a European level outweigh the disadvantages at national level. For instance, the original proposal for the Sale of Goods Directive was restricted to online sales contracts.[82] If implemented in that way, the directive would have led to difference at the national level between online and offline sales contracts, which

74 Regulation (EU) No 2018/302 of the European Parliament and of the Council of 28 February 2018 on addressing unjustified geoblocking and other forms of discrimination based on customers' nationality, place of residence, or place of establishment within the internal market and amending Regulations (EC) No 2006/2004 and (EU) 2017/2394 and Directive 2009/22/EC [2018] OJ LI60/1.

75 Regulation (EU) No 2019/1150 of the European Parliament and of the Council of 20 June 2019 on promoting fairness and transparency for business users of online intermediation services [2019] OJ L186/57.

76 Directive (EU) 2019/790 of the European Parliament and of the Council of 17 April 2019 on copyright and related rights in the Digital Single Market and amending Directives 96/9/EC and 2001/29/EC [2019] OJ L130/92.

77 Directive (EU) 2019/2161 of the European Parliament and of the Council of 27 November 2019 amending Council Directive 93/13/EEC and Directives 98/6/EC, 2005/29/EC and 2011/83/EU of the European Parliament and of the Council as regards the better enforcement and modernisation of Union consumer protection rules [2019] OJ L328/7 (Modernisation Directive).

78 Directive (EU) 2019/771 of the European Parliament and of the Council of 20 May 2019 on certain aspects concerning contracts for the sale of goods, amending Regulation (EU) 2017/2394 and Directive 2009/22/EC, and repealing Directive 1999/44/EC [2019] OJ L136/28 (Sale of Goods Directive).

79 Digital Content Directive.

80 Regulation (EU) No 2022/2065 of the European Parliament and of the Council of 19 October 2022 on a Single Market for Digital Services and amending Directive 2000/31/EC [2022] OJ L277/1 (Digital Services Act).

81 Regulation (EU) No 2022/1925 of the European Parliament and of the Council of 14 September 2022on contestable and fair markets in the digital sector and amending Directives (EU) 2019/1937 and (EU) 2020/1828 [2022] OJ L265/1 (Digital Markets Act).

82 Commission Communication, 'Proposal for a Directive of the European Parliament and of the Council on certain aspects concerning contracts for the online and other distance sales of goods', COM (2015) 635 final, https://eur-lex.europa.eu/legal-content/EN/HIS/?uri=celex:52015PC0635.

would have been very problematic in legal practice.[83] For this reason, ultimately, the scope of the directive was enlarged to include all consumer sales contracts. However, consumers are not the only parties that are 'weaker' than sellers—the same is true for many SMEs. Do they not deserve protection similar to consumers?[84] And if so, can it be justified that some weaker parties do obtain protection at EU level, whereas others do not? The matter is not completely overlooked by the European legislator. In fact, recital (21) of the preamble to the Sale of Goods Directive expressly mentions that Member States could 'extend the protection afforded to consumers also to natural or legal persons that are not consumers within the meaning of this Directive, such as non-governmental organisations, start-ups or SMEs'. But if one Member State does so and another does not, does that not create new barriers to trade? And is harmonisation of non-consumer sales contracts then not necessary in order to realise and improve the internal market? And, assuming that one would answer these questions affirmatively, what justification would there be for harmonising sales law for B2SME (business-to-SME) sales contracts, and not for harmonising other B2B sales contracts? In addition, with its focus on contracts under which a trader sells goods to a consumer, consumer law legislation ignores the fact that consumers may also be the seller in a contract with the trader being the buyer. In such a C2B (consumer-to-business) sales contract, the consumer is largely unprotected by EU consumer law.[85] This is all the more problematic, since consumers offering goods to traders often are in a problematic situation—either because they sell their inheritance, often in a period of grief, or they are in a dire financial position—and traders may be tempted to take advantage thereof. One may wonder why the European Commission does not take action to offer relief to these particularly vulnerable consumers.

Q4: Should 'weaker party protection' be awarded as well in contractual relations other than B2C-situations?

Another question is why harmonisation—at least with regard to consumer contracts—to a large extent (still) focuses on sales contracts, whereas—already in 2006—

83 See on this extensively M. B. M. Loos, 'Not Good but Certainly Content. The Proposals for European Harmonisation of Online and Distance Selling of Goods and the Supply of Digital Content', in I. Claeys and E. Terryn (eds), *Digital Contents & Distance Sales. New Developments at EU Level* (Cambridge, UK: Intersentia, 2017), pp. 3–53.

84 Cf. J. G. Klijnsma, *Contract Law as Fairness. A Rawlsian Perspective on the Position of SMEs in European Contract Law* (doctoral thesis, University of Amsterdam, 2014), https://pure.uva.nl/ws/files/2071551/142288_thesis.pdf

85 Not only the former Directive 1999/44/EC of the European Parliament and of the Council of 25 May 1999 on certain aspects of the sale of consumer goods and associated guarantees [1999] OJ L171/12 (Consumer Sales Directive) and its successor, the Sale of Goods Directive, but also the Consumer Rights Directive and the Digital Content Directive only apply to a contract whereby the trader provides goods and services to the consumer, and therefore do not apply in the case of a C2B-contract. Some protection may, however, be offered by the Unfair Contract Terms Directive and the Unfair Commercial Practices Directive.

services make up for more than two thirds of the EU economy?[86] According to EU Commissioner Bieńkowska, who in 2017 was the EU Commissioner responsible for Internal Market, Industry, Entrepreneurship, and SMEs, the internal market does not function properly for services.[87] But if that is the case, should the European legislator not prioritise the harmonisation of service contract law? Indeed, the Services Directive aims at removing barriers to the development of services, but it focuses primarily on simplification of administrative rules, freedom of establishment and movement of service providers. It therefore contains many provisions enabling service providers to access markets in other countries, but hardly provides for substantive rules governing the contracts they conclude with their customers—whether these are businesses or consumers.[88] Yet, insofar as harmonisation of law contributes to the conclusion of cross-border contracts, there seems to be a strong case for the development of European rules on service contracts. Whereas both the 1980 Vienna Sales Convention,[89] ratified by all current EU Member States, except Ireland and Malta, and the 1999 Consumer Sales Directive[90] have had a strong harmonising effect on sales law in the Member States,[91] such instruments do not exist in the area of service contract law. Moreover, even on a national level, a clear legal framework for service contract law often does not exist. In most Member States only a rudimentary set of 'general provisions' for service contracts exist, which often apply only insofar as the specific service has not been regulated elsewhere in the legislation. Specific rules for specific categories of services have been developed in one country, but not in another. Familiar-looking notions at the national level such as the Dutch 'opdracht', the German 'Auftrag', and the French 'mandat' in fact represent different and incoherent sets of legal rules, which do not particularly lend themselves for generalisation, even more so because their scope differs considerably and contracts that are included in one set of legal rules are governed by another set of rules in the next country. In short, the legislation on service contracts generally is a patchwork of rules that were developed by legislators or courts on an ad hoc basis without taking into account similar or opposite rules developed for other services, let alone similar developments in other legal systems.[92] So, if one wants to foster the conclusion of (cross-border) service contracts, should service contract law

86 Cf. recital (4) of the preamble to Directive 2006/123/EC of the European Parliament and of the Council of 12 December 2006 on services in the internal market [2006] OJ L376/36 (Services Directive); cf. also European Commission, 'A Services Economy that Works for Europeans: Questions and Answers', *European Commission* (10 January 2017), https://ec.europa.eu/commission/presscorner/detail/en/MEMO_17_11

87 Ibid.

88 Cf. M. Schauer, 'Contract Law of the Services Directive', *European Review of Contract Law* 4 (2008), 1–14.

89 United Nations Convention on Contracts for the International Sale of Goods (CISG) (adopted 11 April 1980, entered into force 1 January 1988) 1489 UNTS 3.

90 Consumer Sales Directive.

91 It should be noted that the Consumer Sales Directive itself was heavily influenced by the Vienna Sales Convention, cf. M. J. Bonell, 'The CISG, European Contract Law and the Development of a World Contract Law', *American Journal of Comparative Law* 56 (2008), 1–28 (5–7).

92 On this, see M. B. M. Loos, 'Service Contracts', in A. S. Hartkamp et al. (eds), *Towards a European Civil Code*, 4th edn (Alphen aan den Rijn: Kluwer Law International, 2010), pp. 757–785.

not be harmonised in order for the internal market to prosper?[93]

Q5: Should service contract law be harmonised?

A different matter is coherence at EU level. Whether the European legislator makes use of directives or regulations, consistency of terminology is important. Unfortunately, the EU does not have a good track record in this respect.

> Just to give one example: Article 5(3) DBR indicates that there is no right to claim compensation where the cancellation or delay is caused by 'extraordinary circumstances which could not have been avoided even if all reasonable measures had been taken'.[94] How does this notion relate to the—seemingly similar—notion of 'unavoidable and extraordinary circumstances' under the Package Travel Directive?[95] As regards to the latter notion, the Court of Justice already has established that it 'is akin to the concept of "force majeure" as defined in well-established case-law' and 'gives concrete expression to' that concept in the context of the Package Travel Directive.[96] Is the same true for the Denied Boarding Regulation? And do the two notions mean (exactly) the same, or is there a difference between the two? And if so: what is that difference?

Yet three other developments need to be mentioned here. First, the distinction between goods and services—underlying the Treaty on the Functioning of the European Union and the fundamental freedoms enshrined in it—is not as clear cut as it used to be. In particular since the development of the Digital Single Market, digital content and digital services have developed into a category of their own, somewhere in-between goods and services—in the same way as energy not stored in a movable container is treated differently from goods and services. This was reflected already in the 2011 Consumer Rights Directive, where a specific provision was introduced regarding the moment when the withdrawal period starts,[97] and is re-enforced in the 2019 Digital Content Directive, which applies to both digital content and digital services, irrespective of the manner in which the digital content or service is made available to the consumer. The directive therefore applies to a contract for the supply of digital content consisting of a game stored on a DVD, but also to that file being made available for a download, or for providing access to the game in the cloud or for storing the downloaded file there.

93 A draft for such a general set of rules for service contracts was prepared by a working group in which I participated: J. M. Barendrecht et al., *Principles of European Law on Service Contracts* (Oxford: Oxford University Press, 2007). This draft was later incorporated in Chr. von Bar et al. (eds), *Principles, Definitions and Model Rules of European Private Law. Draft Common Frame of Reference (DCFR)* (Oxford: Oxford University Press, 2009). The DCFR is available online, including explanatory comments and comparative notes, at https://www.law.kuleuven.be/personal/mstorme/european-private-law_en.pdf. On the DCFR and its relevance for the development of European private law, see P. Giliker, 'The Draft Common Frame of Reference and European contract law: Moving from the "Academic" to the "Political"', in J. Devenney and M. Kenny (eds), *The Transformation of European Private Law* (Cambridge, UK: Cambridge University Press, 2013), pp. 23–44.

94 Cf. Article 5(3) DBR.

95 Cf. Article 12(2) and (3) PTD.

96 Cf. Case C-407/21 *UFC-Que-choisir* [2023] ECLI:EU:C:2023:449, para. 54.

97 Cf. Article 9(2)(c) Consumer Rights Directive.

Moreover, as this directive was developed in close connection with the Sale of Goods Directive, conformity rules and rules on contractual remedies in the two directives are rather similar. There is a good reason for the strong relation between these two directives, since more and more 'traditional' goods will be replaced by smart goods, i.e. goods with digital elements. For this reason, it is not surprising that not only the Digital Content Directive, but also the Sale of Goods Directive, contains an obligation for the trader to provide updates of the provided digital content in order to keep the digital content and the goods, respectively, in conformity with the contract.[98]

A second development that deserves attention is the ideal of more sustainable production. Business models are being developed that, on the one hand, embrace the concept of cradle-to-grave (or cradle-to-cradle) production aiming at minimising the ecological impact of goods and services, and the possibility of renewing and recycling. In addition, companies increasingly adopt and implement policies regarding corporate social responsibility, placing emphasis on the labour and other social conditions under which goods are produced, and potentially leading to better respect for the human rights of the persons involved in the production process.

Both these processes may call for further legislation stimulating these developments, but also require vigilance in order to prevent greenwashing. In this respect, the recent strengthening of the tools for the enforcement of the Unfair Commercial Practices Directive may provide the right incentive.[99] Whereas in the meantime company law has responded,[100] it is yet unclear at this point whether contract law may have something to offer as well.[101]

Finally, a shift from 'owning' towards 'leasing' may be observed. In case of this so-called servitisation, the consumer or business no longer obtains ownership, but merely the right to use a good owned by their contractual counterparty, often combined with repair and maintenance of that good by the lessor during the lease.[102] Whereas a sales contract leads to a one-time payment, a lease contract produces a returning and steady income to the trader leasing out the good. In that sense, servitisation constitutes a relatively new business model. Servitisation may lead to more sustainable consumption, in particular, if goods are being more heavily used, if consumers pay per use, and if goods are re-used by another consumer after the original lease has ended. However, if consumers are less careful with the goods supplied to them as they 'merely' lease them, these goods may be damaged more easily, resulting in earlier replacement. In

98 See Article 8(2) Digital Content Directive and Article 7(3) Sale of Goods Directive.

99 Cf. also V. Mak and E. Terryn, 'Circular Economy and Consumer Protection: The Consumer as a Citizen and the Limits of Empowerment Through Consumer Law', *Journal of Consumer Policy* 43 (2020), 227–248 (p. 232).

100 Directive (EU) 2022/2464 of the European Parliament and of the Council of 14 December 2022 amending Regulation (EU) No 537/2014, Directive 2004/109/EC, Directive 2006/43/EC and Directive 2013/34/EU, as regards corporate sustainability reporting [2022] OJ L322/15. See also the Proposal for a Directive of the European Parliament and of the Council of 23 February 2022 on Corporate Sustainability Due Diligence and amending Directive (EU) 2019/1937, COM (2022) 71 final.

101 Cf. V. Ulfbeck and O. Hansen, 'Sustainability Clauses in an Unsustainable Contract Law?', *European Review of Contract Law* 16 (2020), 186–205.

102 Cf. Mak and Terryn, 'Circular Economy', p. 239.

this case, servitisation may in fact lead to less sustainability. The same is true if after the original lease has ended, the goods are not cleaned and repaired for re-use, but destroyed. From a private law perspective, the shift towards servitisation also implies a shift from heavily regulated sales contract law towards much less regulated service contract law, with significantly less mandatory legislation protecting the consumer.[103] This development re-enforces the plea for the development of rules governing service contracts—either on the basis of a general set of rules as suggested above or on the basis of sector-specific legislation.[104]

Q6: Is the distinction in EU law between goods and services tenable in the 2020s?

Q7: Is specific EU legislation needed to regulate (contract law aspects of) servitisation?

Q8: Should the development of sustainable consumption and production and of corporate social responsibility lead to the introduction of uniform or harmonised rules of private law?

Bibliography

Artz, M., 'Die "vollständige Harmonisierung" des Europäischen Verbraucherprivatrechts', *Zeitschrift für Gemeinschaftsprivatrecht* 6.4 (2009), 171–177

Barendrecht, M., et al., *Principles of European Law on Service Contracts* (Oxford: Oxford University Press, 2007)

Bonell, M. J., 'The CISG, European Contract Law and the Development of a World Contract Law', *American Journal of Comparative Law* 56 (2008), 1–28, https://doi.org/10.5131/ajcl.2007.0001

Commission Communication, 'GREEN PAPER on the Review of the Consumer Aquis', COM (2006) 744 final, https://eur-lex.europa.eu/LexUriServ/LexUriServ.do?uri=COM:2006:0744:FIN:en:PDF

Commission Communication, 'Proposal for a Directive of the European Parliament and of the Council on Certain Aspects Concerning Contracts for the Online and Other Distance Sales of Goods', COM (2015) 635 final, https://eur-lex.europa.eu/legal-content/EN/HIS/?uri=celex:52015PC0635

European Commission, 'July Infringement Package: Key Decisions', *European Commission* (2 July 2022), https://ec.europa.eu/commission/presscorner/detail/en/INF_20_1212

European Commission, 'A Services Economy that Works for Europeans: Questions and Answers', *European Commission* (10 January 2017), https://ec.europa.eu/commission/presscorner/detail/en/MEMO_17_11

Faure, M., 'Towards a Maximum Harmonization of Consumer Contract Law?', *Maastricht Journal of European and Comparative Law* 15 (2008), 433–445, https://doi.org/10.1177/1023263x0801500401

103 Ibid., p. 239.
104 Ibid., p. 241.

Giliker, P., 'The Draft Common Frame of Reference and European Contract Law: Moving from the "Academic" to the "Political"', in J. Devenney and M. Kenny (eds), *The Transformation of European Private Law* (Cambridge, UK: Cambridge University Press, 2013), pp. 23–44, https://doi.org/10.1017/cbo9781139870559.004

Gsell, B., and H. M. Schellhase, 'Vollharmonisiertes Verbraucherkreditrecht—ein Vorbild für die weitere europäische Angleichung des Verbrauchervertragsrechts?', *JuristenZeitung* 64 (2009), 20–29

Hondius, E. H., 'The Proposal for a European Directive on Consumer Rights: A Step Forward', *European Review of Private Law* 18 (2010), 103–127, https://doi.org/10.54648/erpl2010005

Klijnsma, J. G., *Contract Law as Fairness. A Rawlsian Perspective on the Position of SMEs in European Contract Law* (doctoral thesis, University of Amsterdam, 2014), https://pure.uva.nl/ws/files/2071551/142288_thesis.pdf

Loos, M. B. M., 'Full Harmonisation as a Regulatory Concept and its Consequences for the National Legal Orders. The Example of the Consumer Rights Directive', in M. Stürner (ed.), *Vollharmonisierung im Europäischen Verbraucherrecht?* (Munich: Sellier European Law Publisher, 2010), pp. 47–98

Loos, M. B. M., 'Not Good but Certainly Content. The Proposals for European Harmonisation of Online and Distance Selling of Goods and the Supply of Digital Content', in I. Claeys and E. Terryn (eds), *Digital Contents & Distance Sales. New Developments at EU Level* (Cambridge, UK: Intersentia, 2017), pp. 3–53, https://doi.org/10.1017/9781780686035.002

Loos, M. B. M., 'One Day I'll Fly Away… Voucher Schemes for Cancelled Package Travel Contracts After the Outbreak of the Covid-19 Pandemic', *Journal of European Consumer and Market Law* 10 (2021), 122–124

Loos, M. B. M., 'Service Contracts', in A. S. Hartkamp et al. (eds), *Towards a European Civil Code*, 4th edn (Alphen aan den Rijn: Kluwer Law International, 2010), pp. 757–785

Low, G., 'The (Ir)relevance of Harmonization and Legal Diversity to European Contract Law: A Perspective from Psychology', *European Review of Private Law* 18 (2010), 285–305, https://doi.org/10.54648/erpl2010018

Mak, V., and E. Terryn, 'Circular Economy and Consumer Protection: The Consumer as a Citizen and the Limits of Empowerment through Consumer Law', *Journal of Consumer Policy* 43 (2020), 227–248, https://doi.org/10.1007/s10603-019-09435-y

Micklitz, H.-W., 'The Targeted Full Harmonisation Approach: Looking Behind the Curtain', in G. Howells and R. Schulze (eds), *Modernising and Harmonising Consumer Contract Law* (Munich: Sellier European Law Publisher 2009), pp. 47–86, https://doi.org/10.1515/9783866538603.2.47

Osiejewicz, J., 'The Opt-out-Clause of Article 114 TFEU: Remarks on the Judgment of the General Court of 7 March 2013—*Republic of Poland v. European Commission* (CaseT-370/11)', *Studia IURIDICA AUCTORITATE Universitatis Pecs PUBLICATA* 154 (2016), 161–177

Reich, N., 'Von der Minimal- zur Voll- zur "Halbharmonisierung". Ein europäisches Privatrechtsdrama in fünf Akten', *Zeitschrift für Europäisches Privatrecht* 1 (2010), 7–39

Rott, P. 'Minimum Harmonization for the Completion of the Internal Market? The Example of Consumer Sales Law', *Common Market Law Review* 50 (2003), 1107–1135, https://doi.org/10.54648/cola2003053

Schauer, M., 'Contract Law of the Services Directive', *European Review of Contract Law* 4 (2008), 1–14, https://doi.org/10.1515/ercl.4.1.1

Sieburgh, C. H., *Mr. C. Assers Handleiding tot de beoefening van het Nederlands Burgerlijk Recht. 6. Verbintenissenrecht. Deel IV. De verbintenis uit de wet*, 15th edn (Deventer: Wolters Kluwer, 2019)

Twigg-Flesner, C., *European Union Private Law* (Cambridge, UK: Cambridge University Press, 2010), https://doi.org/10.1017/cco9780511777714

Ulfbeck, V., and O. Hansen, 'Sustainability Clauses in an Unsustainable Contract Law?', *European Review of Contract Law* 16 (2020), 186–205, https://doi.org/10.1515/ercl-2020-0010

von Bar, Chr., et al. (eds), *Principles, Definitions and Model Rules of European Private Law. Draft Common Frame of Reference (DCFR)* (Oxford: Oxford University Press, 2009), https://doi.org/10.1515/9783866537279.131

Wilhelmsson, T., 'The Abuse of the "Confident Consumer" as a Justification for EC Consumer Law', *Journal of Consumer Policy* 27 (2004), 317–337, https://doi.org/10.1023/b:copo.0000040517.34781.7d

5. Human Rights in Private Law[1]

Chantal Mak

Abstract

This chapter introduces the academic debate on the role of human rights in private law for an audience of master students in transnational and European private law. It first explores the ways in which dignity may provide a foundation for extending human rights protection to private legal relations and sets out the legal context in which the 'constitutionalisation of private law' has developed, both nationally and under European law. Subsequently, the societal relevance of these legal developments is analysed and mapped according to three strands in the academic discourse in the field: one that holds that constitutionalisation does not provide a new view on private law, a second that sees a role for human rights in pursuing social justice in private law, and a third that considers private law to contribute to the constitutional imagination of Europe.

1. Introduction: Private Actors and the Public Interest

Although the combination of the notions of 'human rights' and 'private law' at first glance may seem to be at odds with existing systemic divisions, the impact of human rights on private legal relationships has become a part of both national[2] and European[3]

1 An expanded version of this chapter has been published in L. Antoniolli and P. Iamiceli (eds), *The Making of European Private Law: Changes and Challenges* (Trento: Università degli Studi di Trento, 2024), pp. 37–61.

2 G. Brüggemeier, A. Colombi Ciacchi, and G. Comandé (eds), *Fundamental Rights and Private Law in the European Union*, 2 vols (Cambridge, UK: Cambridge University Press, 2010); O. O. Cherednychenko, *Fundamental Rights, Contract Law and the Protection of the Weaker Party: A Comparative Analysis of the Constitutionalisation of Contract Law, with Emphasis on Risky Financial Transactions* (Munich: Sellier, 2007); C. Mak, *Fundamental Rights in European Contract Law: A Comparison of the Impact of Fundamental Rights on Contractual Relationships in Germany, the Netherlands, Italy and England* (Alphen a/d Rijn: Kluwer Law International, 2008); C. Busch and H. Schulte-Nölke, *EU Compendium—Fundamental Rights and Private Law* (Munich: Sellier, 2011); S. Walkila, *Horizontal Effect of Fundamental Rights in the EU* (Groningen: Europa Law Publishing, 2016).

3 H. Collins (ed.), *European Contract Law and the Charter of Fundamental Rights* (Cambridge/Antwerp: Intersentia, 2017); H.-W. Micklitz (ed.), *Constitutionalization of European Private Law* (Oxford: Oxford University Press, 2014); S. Grundmann (ed.), *Constitutional Values and European Contract Law* (Deventer: Kluwer Law International, 2008).

 https://doi.org/10.11647/OBP.0448.05

developments. While human rights are often located in the sphere of public law, where they protect citizens against public authorities, they have been recognised also to affect private legal matters.[4] National courts have, for instance, extended human rights reasoning to topics as diverse as access to goods and services, mortgage contracts,[5] and climate change liability.[6] The Court of Justice of the European Union (CJEU) and European Court of Human Rights (ECtHR) have contributed to the extension of human rights to such private legal questions by establishing the potential for the EU Charter of Fundamental Rights (EUCFR)[7] and European Convention on Human Rights (ECHR)[8] to pose obligations on private parties.

These developments raise the question as to what extent private actors should heed the public interest that is reflected in human rights reasoning. Although the principles of private autonomy and freedom of contract provide individuals and companies with space to make their own decisions on their legal relationships, their freedom is not absolute.[9] This is inherent in the idea of autonomy, since one person's freedom finds its limits in the freedom of others,[10] who deserve equal concern and respect.[11] Taking into account societal concerns may even go further and require parties to consider the consequences of their conduct on, for instance, equal access to employment[12] and

4 H. Collins, 'On the (In)compatibility of Human Rights Discourse and Private Law', in Micklitz (ed.), *Constitutionalization of European Private Law*, pp. 26–60, who discusses both doctrinal and theoretical questions that these developments raise.

5 J. M. L. van Duin, *Effective Judicial Protection in Consumer Litigation: Article 47 of the EU Charter in Practice* (Cambridge, UK: Intersentia, 2022).

6 L. E. Burgers, *Justitia, the People's Power and Mother Earth: Democratic Legitimacy of Judicial Law-making in European Private Law Cases on Climate Change* (doctoral thesis, University of Amsterdam, 2020), https://hdl.handle.net/11245.1/0e6437b7-399d-483a-9fc1-b18ca926fdb5

7 Case C-176/12 *Association de Médiation Sociale v Union locale des syndicats CGT and Others* [2014] ECLI:EU:C:2014:2; Joined Cases C-569/16 and C-570/16 *Stadt Wuppertal v Maria Elisabeth Bauer and Volker Wilmeroth v Martina Broßonn* [2018] ECLI:EU:C:2018:871. See also E. Frantziou, '(Most of) the Charter of Fundamental Rights is Horizontally Applicable', *European Constitutional Law Review* 15.2 (2019), 306–323 (p. 306).

8 E.g. *Pla and Puncernau v Andorra* ECtHR 13 July 2004, application no. 69498/01, [2004] ECLI:CE:ECHR:2004:0713JUD006949801. It may be noted that the ECtHR does not rule in private legal disputes itself. Its case law has, nevertheless, impacted private legal relations indirectly, through the assessment of the compliance of national private laws with the Convention; A. S. Hartkamp, *European Law and National Private Law* (Cambridge/Antwerp: Intersentia, 2016), pp. 188–192.

9 M. R. Marella, 'The Old and the New Limits to Freedom of Contract in Europe', *European Review of Contract Law* 2.2 (2006), 257–274(p. 258). It is important to add that different legal traditions in Europe draw limits to freedom of contract in different manners; on the French, German and English traditions, and what a comparative perspective may offer, see H.-W. Micklitz, 'On the Intellectual History of Freedom of Contract and Regulation', *Penn State Journal of Law & International Affairs* 4 (2015), 100–131, http://elibrary.law.psu.edu/jlia/vol4/iss1/3

10 I. Berlin, 'Two Concepts of Liberty', in I. Berlin, *Four Essays on Liberty* (Oxford: Oxford University Press, 1969), pp. 171–173.

11 R. Dworkin, *Sovereign Virtue: The Theory and Practice of Equality* (Cambridge, MA: Harvard University Press, 2000), pp. 121–122, 182–183, and *Justice for Hedgehogs* (Cambridge, MA: Harvard University Press, 2011), pp. 364–371.

12 H. Collins, 'Discrimination, Equality and Social Inclusion', *The Modern Law Review* 66.1 (2003), 16–43 (p. 16).

housing,[13] the protection of the environment,[14] or the safety of the digital sphere.[15] In the past decades, these concerns have more and more often been recognised as interests that are so fundamental that they should also be protected in private legal relationships.[16] Human rights provide an inroad for such concerns in private legal cases. As individual rights, they may offer protection against one-sided balances of interests in private law.[17] At the same time, the societal interests that human rights represent may induce a more fundamental rethinking of the legal responsibilities of private actors.[18] Still, it remains the topic of debate how far private actors' responsibility for human rights goes.

This chapter explores the legal framework and traces the legal-political debates on the impact of human rights in European private law. 'Human rights' are understood broadly, including both national constitutional norms and international rights protecting the basic needs of people. The main question is which factors determine whether and to what extent private legal relations should be rethought in constitutional terms. In order to answer this question, first, a brief description will be given of the history of the gradual extension of human rights to the realm of private law, in national laws, and under the ECHR and EUCFR. Subsequently, the legal-political implications of human rights reasoning in private law will be further explored. While my view on the potential influence of human rights in private law is mostly favourable, the contrast with more sceptical voices presents an overview of the nuances in the debates. In line with this reflective attitude, the chapter will conclude with some points for further reflection on what may be called 'the public dimension of private law'.

2. Legal Context: Constitutionalising Private Law

a. Dignity as Basis

From a legal and philosophical perspective, a basis for human rights protection is often found in human dignity.[19] Article 1 of the UN's Universal Declaration of Human Rights (1948) determines that 'All human beings are born free and equal in dignity

13 I. Domurath, *Consumer Vulnerability and Welfare in Mortgage Contracts* (Oxford: Hart Publishing, 2017).

14 Burgers, *Justitia.*

15 A. Davola, 'Fostering Consumer Protection in the Granular Market: The Role of Rules on Consent, Misrepresentation and Fraud in Regulating Personalized Practice', *Technology And Regulation (Techreg)* 2021 (2021), 76–86 (p. 76).

16 For an overview of fact patterns of cases in which such effects of human rights have been recognised, see A. Colombi Ciacchi, 'European Fundamental Rights, Private Law, and Judicial Governance', in Micklitz (ed.), *Constitutionalization of European Private Law*, pp. 102–136.

17 A. Colombi Ciacchi, 'The Constitutionalization of European Contract Law: Judicial Convergence and Social Justice', *European Review of Contract Law* 2.2 (2006), 167–180 (p. 178).

18 Mak, *Fundamental Rights* , pp. 294–295, building on the idea that (fundamental) rights mediate between law and politics, as elaborated by D. Kennedy, *A Critique of Adjudication {fin de siècle}* (Cambridge, MA: Harvard University Press, 1997), pp. 125, 305, 319–320.

19 J. Habermas, 'The Concept of Human Dignity and the Realistic Utopia of Human Rights', in Habermas, *The Crisis of the European Union: A Response* (Cambridge, UK: Polity Press, 2012), pp. 71–100.

and rights'. The reference to dignity is repeated in the preambles of such binding instruments as the International Covenant on Civil and Political Rights (1966) and the International Covenant on Economic, Social and Cultural Rights (1966). The EUCFR, as well as many European Constitutions, recognise dignity as an underlying principle or sometimes even a self-standing human right.[20] In private legal cases with a strong moral dimension, such as those on prostitution, surrogate motherhood, or unfair exploitation, it does therefore not seem surprising that this concept is often referred to.[21] The increasing impact of human rights on the legal relations between private actors might, accordingly, be seen as inspired by the wish to protect human dignity.

The matter is, however, more complex. In the first place, as put forward by Maria Marella, there may be a tension between ideals of human dignity and social dignity.[22] Cases on controversial forms of employment illustrate this well. In the famous case of *Wackenheim v France*,[23] for instance, the idea of human dignity was in tension with a more social reading of dignity. The case concerned the prohibition of so-called 'dwarf-tossing events', in which strong men would compete at throwing a person with dwarfism through a bar onto an airbed. Several municipalities in France had prohibited such games since they would infringe upon human dignity. Mr Wackenheim, who had dwarfism and wished to participate in the events, challenged these decisions. One of his arguments was that these activities would allow him to make a living and would, thus, actually be beneficial to him.[24] While Mr Wackenheim's claim remained unsuccessful, his reliance on social dignity deserves further thought on the possibility of finding diversified solutions for morally controversial contracts.

In the second place, new developments in, for instance, cases on climate change liability may not easily be explained on the basis of human dignity. In a groundbreaking judgment of 26 May 2021, the District Court of The Hague ordered the multinational oil company Royal Dutch Shell to reduce its greenhouse gas emissions by 45% by the year 2030 in respect to 2019.[25] The decision was based on Shell's duty of care under Dutch tort law, which had been invoked by the NGO Milieudefensie in a public interest action.[26] Similar to the well-known *Urgenda* case,[27] the court embedded the duty of care in the right to life and the right to respect for private and family life,

---

20 For an overview, see https://fra.europa.eu/en/eu-charter/article/1-human-dignity#TabNational

21 A. Colombi Ciacchi, C. Mak, and Z. Mansoor (eds), *Immoral Contracts in Europe*, The Common Core of European Private Law Series (Cambridge, UK: Intersentia, 2020).

22 Marella, 'The Old and the New Limits', pp. 272–274.

23 UN Human Rights Committee 15 July 2002, Communication No. 854/1999, *Manuel Wackenheim v France*, http://hrlibrary.umn.edu/undocs/854–1999.html

24 Ibid., under 4) *Legal arguments*.

25 Rb. (district court) The Hague 26 May 2021, ECLI:NL:RBDHA:2021:5339 (*Milieudefensie/Shell*). For an early comment on the cases, see this blogpost by Laura Burgers, 'Friends of the Earth Netherlands Versus Royal Dutch Shell: All Companies Must Act Against Climate Change', *Transformative Private Law Blog* (29 May 2021), https://transformativeprivatelaw.com/friends-of-the-earth-netherlands-versus-royal-dutch-shell-all-companies-must-act-against-climate-change/

26 Article 3:305a of the Dutch Civil Code allows foundations or associations that represent public interests to bring such actions.

27 Hoge Raad (Dutch Supreme Court) 20 December 2019, ECLI:NL:HR:2019:2007 (*The State of The Netherlands/Urgenda*).

which are protected under Articles 2 and 8 of the ECHR respectively. Where *Urgenda* established unprecedented environmental obligations of the Dutch government, the judgment in the *Shell* case extends such obligations to businesses.[28] It might seem difficult to explain cases like *Urgenda* and *Milieudefensie v Shell* solely on the basis of human dignity. Although the basis of these judgments was found in human rights, the protection of these rights very much depends on the preservation of the (clean) environment in which people live. Accordingly, Burgers rightly raises the question as to if and how to include the interests and possibly rights of non-human entities, like animals, plants, rivers, and mountains—either through human rights protection or private legal mechanisms such as legal personhood.[29] One way to solve the conundrum, proposed by Dina Townsend, would be to include the protection of these entities within the notion of human dignity, holding that people would harm their own dignity if they showed a lack of respect for non-human entities.[30] A further-reaching solution might be to extend rights to nature itself.[31] These developments do not only require a fundamental rethinking of the scope of human rights protection, but will also impact the enforcement of such rights through private legal mechanisms such as tort law.[32]

In the third place, and slightly shifting the perspective, human dignity can be understood as a status concept, which defines dignity in relation to people's agency under the law. This view has been elaborated by Jeremy Waldron, who holds that both substantive and procedural aspects of law may be understood to allow people to make their own choices and be recognised as equals in society.[33] For example, the law provides safeguards of a procedural nature (e.g. the right to be heard) as well as ceremonies or rituals that acknowledge the equality and agency of those subjected to the law.[34] In private law, the right to effective judicial protection may be read in this light, as it forms a basis for access to justice and a fair remedy.[35]

While human dignity, thus, seems to provide a convincing basis for human rights protection, the previous observations do not fully answer the question as to why

---

28 It should be noted that an appeal against the judgment of the district court is currently pending. Nevertheless, Shell is already obliged to comply with this judgment in first instance, as the court declared the order to be provisionally enforceable ('uitvoerbaar bij voorraad'); see para. 4.5.7 of the judgment.

29 Burgers, *Justitia*, pp. 283–297; C. D. Stone, *Should Trees Have Standing? Law, Morality and the Environment*, 3rd edn (Oxford: Oxford University Press, 2010).

30 D. Townsend, 'Taking Dignity Seriously? A Dignity Approach to Environmental Disputes before Human Rights Courts', *Journal of Human Rights and the Environment* 6.2 (2015), 218–242 (pp. 220–221).

31 N. Naffine, 'Legal Personality and the Natural World: on the Persistence of the Human Measure of Value', *Journal of Human Rights and the Environment* 3 (2012), 68–83. See also Burgers, *Justitia*, pp. 291–294, referring, inter alia, to the Belgian *Klimaatzaak* (climate case), in which the lawyers included a complaint on behalf of eighty-two trees. On 17 June 2021, the claim against the Belgian State was awarded by the court of first instance, but it did not grant standing to the trees; Tribunal de première instance francophone de Bruxelles, Section Civile-2015/4585/A.

32 M. Hinteregger, 'Civil Liability and the Challenges of Climate Change: A Functional Analysis', *Journal of European Tort Law* 8.2 (2017), 238–260.

33 J. Waldron, 'How Law Protects Dignity', *Cambridge Law Journal* 71.1 (2012), 200–222 (p. 202).

34 Waldron speaks of 'moral orthopaedics', ibid., p. 219.

35 Van Duin, *Effective Judicial Protection*, pp. 15 and 202.

these rights should extend to private legal relations at all. Why should private actors be concerned with societal ideals of human dignity in contractual relations, cases of possible tort liability, or claims concerning property rights? We need to turn to the development of the 'constitutionalisation of private law' in order to get a better understanding of the reasons for relating human rights to private law.

b. Constitutionalisation of Private Law

From a doctrinal legal perspective, the impact of human rights on private legal relationships can be discerned in direct and more indirect ways. In national legal systems in Europe, courts have interpreted some constitutional rights in the sense that they do not only address the relationship between the State and its citizens, but to a certain extent also the relations of citizens among each other.[36] A direct horizontal effect of human rights is said to occur when courts in private legal relationships attach legal consequences to the breach of human rights as such.[37] An indirect horizontal effect of human rights takes place when provisions of private law are read in the light of the principles and values expressed in such rights.[38]

A German case on personal suretyships very well illustrates how the constitutionalisation of private law has taken shape. This *Bürgschaft* case[39] concerned a young woman who had agreed to provide security for her father's business loan at a bank. At the time of signing the suretyship contract, she was twenty-one years old, did not have any higher education, and was often unemployed.[40] When the father's company got into financial difficulties, the bank requested the daughter to pay the amount of the surety. She was not able to do so and given her financial circumstances it was unlikely that she would ever be able to resolve the debt.[41] In ensuing civil proceedings that went up to the highest German court in civil cases, the *Bundesgerichtshof*, the suretyship contract was, nevertheless, upheld. Since the daughter had reached the age of majority when entering into the contract, the Court considered that she should have been aware of the risks attached to the contract.[42] According to the rules of private law that governed the contract, thus, there seemed to be no remedy for her. At this point, the case took a constitutional turn, as the daughter brought an individual complaint to the German Constitutional Court, the *Bundesverfassungsgericht*, claiming that the judgments of the civil courts infringed her constitutional rights. In

36 For country reports on England, France, Germany, Italy, the Netherlands, Poland, Portugal, Spain, and Sweden, see Brüggemeier, Colombi Ciacchi, and Comandé, *Fundamental Rights and Private Law*, I.

37 Collins, 'On the (In)compatibility of Human Rights Discourse and Private Law', p. 38. For an overview of the development of the conceptual distinction between direct and indirect horizontal effects in German case law and literature, see Mak, *Fundamental Rights in European Contract Law*, pp. 47–50; and Cherednychenko, *Fundamental Rights, Contract Law and the Protection of the Weaker Party*, pp. 58–63.

38 Collins, 'On the (In)compatibility of Human Rights Discourse and Private Law', p. 38.

39 BVerfG 19 October 1993, BVerfGE 89, 214 (*Bürgschaft*).

40 BVerfGE 89, 214, 218.

41 BVerfGE 89, 214, 220–221.

42 BVerfGE 89, 214, 219.

a now famous judgment, the *Bundesverfassungsgericht* found that the judgment of the *Bundesgerichtshof* had indeed violated the daughter's private autonomy, which was protected under Article 2(1) of the German Constitution, the *Grundgesetz* (*GG*), in combination with the principle of the social state safeguarded by Articles 20(1) and 28(1) *GG*.[43] In particular, the civil courts had failed to address the structural imbalance of power between the parties, which should have been redressed through the interpretation of the open norm of 'good morals and public policy' of § 138 of the German Civil Code, the *Bürgerliches Gesetzbuch* (*BGB*).[44] The complexity of the contract was difficult to assess even for more experienced clients than the twenty-one-year-old daughter and the bank employee who had concluded the contract had downplayed the risk rather than informing her well.[45] Therefore, the *Bundesverfassungsgericht* found that the civil courts had not correctly interpreted and applied § 138 *BGB* in light of the Constitution. Following this judgment, the *Bundesgerichtshof* established the nullity of the contract. The constitutional reading of the Civil Code, thus, changed the legal framework for personal suretyships.

Although the protection of weaker parties like the unfortunate daughter in the *Bürgschaft* case is often not challenged, judgments like these do require further thought on the extent to which private legal relations are and should be governed by basic constitutional rights that have been written for the State/citizen relation. In the German national academic debate concerning the *Bürgschaft* judgment, it was asserted that clearer boundaries needed to be defined for the scope of the substantive review of contracts in light of the Constitution.[46] Almost thirty years after the decision, it is still questioned whether the law is sufficiently clear on when and how to apply the principles defined in the *Bürgschaft* case.[47] Similar doubts on the possibility of constitutional and human rights to guide the interpretation of private law have been expressed in the international academic debate.[48] Yet, the potential for human rights reasoning to enrich the range of private legal remedies has also been recognised.[49] The *Bürgschaft* case, thus, remains an important point of reference, as it provides an opening for human rights in private law, but does not fully establish the conditions for the application of these rights in actual cases.

---

43 BVerfGE 89, 214, 234–235.

44 BVerfGE 89, 214, 234.

45 BVerfGE 89, 214, 234, 235.

46 H. Wiedemann, 'BVerfG, 19.10.1993—1 BvR 567 u. 1044/89. Zur verfassungsrechtlichen Inhaltskontrolle von Verträgen', *JuristenZeitung* 49 (1994), 412–413; J. Schapp, 'Privatautonomie und Verfassungsrecht', *Zeitschrift für Bankrecht und Bankwirtschaft* 11.1 (1998), 30–42 (p. 33). For an overview of the debate, see also Mak *Fundamental Rights in European Contract Law* pp. 75–82, with further references.

47 L. Kähler, 'Case 12: Immoral Suretyships—Germany', in Colombi Ciacchi, Mak, and Mansoor (eds), *Immoral Contracts*, p. 677.

48 O. O. Cherednychenko, 'Subordinating Contract Law to Fundamental Rights: Towards a Major Breakthrough or towards Walking in Circles?', in S. Grundmann (ed.), *Constitutional Values and European Contract Law* (Deventer: Kluwer Law International, 2008), pp. 35–60; H. Collins, 'Cosmopolitanism and Transnational Private Law', *European Review of Contract Law* 8.3 (2012), 311–325 (p. 316).

49 Mak, *Fundamental Rights in European Contract Law*, pp. 294–295, 311.

c. Europeanisation and Transnationalisation of Private Law

The influence of European law on national systems of private law has introduced another human rights strand, which is becoming more and more important.[50] The main sources for this development are the ECHR and EUCFR, which both have found application in private legal relationships.[51] Although the institutional structures surrounding the two instruments are very different, the extension of the European Convention and the EU Charter to private law raises similar questions on the interaction between public and private law and the intensity of effects of human rights between private actors.

An example is found in the case law on housing, where privatisation has raised the question as to what extent tenants and homeowners may rely on equal protection in the 'horizontal' relation to private landlords and banks as they would in the 'vertical' relation to (semi-)public housing providers and the State.[52] Consider, for instance, a homeowner who has obtained a mortgage loan at a bank, for which the house provides security. If the bank has imposed standard terms that allow it to invoke the security under conditions that rather one-sidedly favour its interest, to what extent can such terms be challenged on the basis of a human right to housing? On the basis of a case law analysis, Irina Domurath and I found that under the ECHR, in contrast to the EUCFR, the answer very much depends on the balance struck in national laws.[53] Although an eviction based on the mortgage contract falls within the broad scope of the notion of the 'home' protected under Article 8 ECHR,[54] the ECtHR's scrutiny of legislation that legitimately limits the right to housing does not involve a proportionality test if the regulation of the privatised housing market is concerned.[55] The reason for this is that the national legislature has already struck a balance between contracting parties' interests, with which the EctHR does not wish to interfere.[56] As a consequence, ECHR protection does not fully extend to private housing provision. Under EU law, such restrictions do not exist since the policing of unfair terms has been harmonised throughout Member States by the Unfair Terms Directive. The right to housing (Article 7 EUCFR) and the right to effective judicial protection (Article 47 EUCFR) have implicitly[57] and explicitly[58] affected the application of the directive to

50 Collins, 'Cosmopolitanism and Transnational Private Law', pp. 315–316, 318–319.

51 For an overview, see Hartkamp, *European Law and National Private Law*, chapter 6.

52 I. Domurath and C. Mak, 'Private Law and Housing Justice in Europe', *The Modern Law Review* 83 (2020), 1188–1220. See also Irina Domurath's contribution to this volume.

53 Ibid., pp. 1204–1206.

54 ECtHR 24 April 2012, application no. 25446/06, ECLI:CE:ECHR:2012:0424JUD002544606, *Yordanova and others v Bulgaria.*

55 ECtHR 12 July 2016, application no. 43777/13, ECLI:CE:ECHR:2016:0712JUD004377713, *Vrzić v Croatia.*

56 ECtHR *Vrzić*, para. 107; ECtHR 6 November 2018, application no. 76202/16, ECLI:CE:ECHR:2018:1106DEC007620216, *F.J.M. v the United Kingdom*, para. 42–46.

57 Case C-415/11 *Mohamed Aziz v Caixa d'Estalvis de Catalunya, Tarragona i Manresa (Catalunyacaixa)* [2013] ECLI:EU:C:2013:164, para. 60–61, where the Court underlines the importance of protecting the family home.

58 Case C-169/14 *Sánchez Morcillo and Abril García v Banco Bilbao* [2014] ECLI:EU:C:2014:2099, para. 48–50; Case C-34/13, *Monika Kušionová v SMART Capital* [2014] ECLI:EU:C:2014:2189, para. 65–66.

standard terms of banks in mortgage enforcement proceedings. Accordingly, human rights reasoning may reshape the substantive review of mortgage contracts through EU law.[59] At the same time, the question remains whether the framework of EU consumer law will provide sufficient protection, as it relies on a relatively high standard of the 'average consumer'.[60]

The contrast between the approaches to privatised housing provision under the ECHR and under EU law, thus, in a nutshell, contains two big questions on human rights reasoning in private law. Similar to national debates, the division between public and private legal spheres is challenged: to what extent may one rely on equal human rights protection (be it on employment, financial products, housing, or climate change) with respect to a private actor as one may in relation to public authorities? Furthermore, the European dimension creates different spheres of substance and competence: to what extent may European human rights guide the development of national private laws? Developments in case law further specify these questions for different substantive matters, thus contributing to the constitutionalisation of private law as well as exploring its limits.

3. Societal Relevance: The Imaginative Power of Private Law

a. Legal-Political Stakes in Private Law

It is likely not a coincidence that human rights reasoning in private law mostly occurs in cases with a sensitive legal-political dimension, given the fundamental values that these rights refer to. Therefore, despite the doctrinal difficulties of integrating this type of reasoning in private law, human rights have the potential to contribute to solutions for societal issues, ranging from access to (mortgage) credit under fair conditions to measures needed to prevent climate change.

The political stakes are not always immediately visible, especially in cases that concern technical questions on, for instance, the validity of contract terms.[61] In the *Bürgschaft* case, for example, in the initial dispute, any concerns regarding the validity of the suretyship were dismissed as the formal requirements for concluding a contract had been fulfilled. Only when the case was referred to constitutional review, did the tension become clearer between the interests of banks and prospective sureties with a personal relationship to the principal debtor. The judgment of the *Bundesverfassungsgericht*, thus, allowed for a rebalancing of underlying interests under § 138 of the German Civil Code. These and other examples from case law show how

59 The potential influence of the EUCFR has been further increased by the CJEU's judgment that Charter rights may entail obligations for private actors, insofar as these rights are 'mandatory and unconditional in nature'; CJEU *Bauer and Broßonn*, para. 85, 87.

60 J. W. Rutgers, 'The Right to Housing (Article 7 of the Charter) and Unfair Terms in General Conditions', in Collins (ed.), *European Contract Law*, pp. 136–137.

61 D. Kennedy, 'The Political Stakes in "Merely Technical" Issues of Contract Law', *European Review of Private Law* 10 (2001), 7–28.

human rights have the capacity to make explicit the more fundamental legal-political considerations underlying the balance that in private legal rules has been struck between the parties' interests.[62]

The question is still open, however, as to how and to what extent this repoliticisation of private legal doctrines in light of human rights may serve the solution of societal issues. In the academic debate, a diverse range of views can be found. Without attempting to give an exhaustive overview, at least three distinct perspectives may be discerned.

b. First Perspective: Nothing New?

In the first place, a relatively sceptical strand of literature maintains that human rights reasoning does not add much to existing frameworks and principles of private law. Olha Cherednychenko has, for instance, submitted that human rights are too vague to give guidance to balancing processes in private law.[63] The well-established general clauses of private law would be substituted or even subordinated to vague standards of a public legal nature, if fundamental rights were applied.[64] The handling of societally sensitive questions would, thus, not be made easier, but would rather become more complicated.

What is more, insofar as both parties to a dispute may rely on human rights, courts face a very difficult task in establishing which one should prevail.[65] In this context, Hugh Collins has submitted that civil courts are requested to conduct a 'double proportionality test' to strike the balance between conflicting rights.[66] In line with the proportionality test developed in public law, courts then have to assess to what extent a restriction of a human right may be justified. The balance becomes a double one in private legal cases in which both parties may rely on human rights.[67] The difficulty of conducting such an 'ultimate balancing test' provides another argument against the (direct) effect of human rights in private legal relationships and for remaining within established doctrines and principles of private law.[68]

62 Mak, *Fundamental Rights in European Contract Law*, pp. 220 and 229, building on Kennedy, *Critique of Adjudication*, p. 305. See also D. Kennedy, 'Form and Substance in Private Law Adjudication', *Harvard Law Review* 88 (1976), 1685–1778 (pp. 1724, 1766–1767).

63 Cherednychenko, 'Subordinating Contract Law'. In a similar sense, B. De Vos, *Horizontale werking van grondrechten: een kritiek* (Apeldoorn: Maklu, 2010). In more recent work, Cherednychenko indicates some potential for human rights to define individual, private law remedies under EU Directives; 'Rediscovering the Public/Private Divide in EU Private Law', *European Law Journal* 26 (2019), 27–47 (p. 29).

64 Cherednychenko, 'Subordinating Contract Law', p. 44.

65 Ibid., pp. 43–44.

66 Collins, *European Contract Law*, pp. 50–51.

67 Ibid., p. 50.

68 Ibid., p. 51.

c. Second Perspective: Social Justice in European Private Law

In the second place, and partly in response to sceptical views on constitutionalisation of private legal questions, a justice perspective has been put forward.[69] This view is based on the idea that, despite its technical intricacies, human rights reasoning in private law may contribute to the elaboration of a social justice agenda for Europe. In a 2004 Manifesto, the Study Group on Social Justice in European Private Law highlighted this justice dimension as one of the 'real issues' that the European legislature should focus on in regard to the further harmonisation of contract law.[70] The work of one of the authors of the Manifesto, Aurelia Colombi Ciacchi, finds inspiration for the elaboration of this social justice dimension in a comparative analysis of case law of national civil courts in Europe. She observes that the application of human rights in contract law is not politically neutral:[71] courts rely on these rights to protect weaker contracting parties against stronger ones (e.g. consumer versus business, employee versus employer) and to safeguard basic democratic values (e.g. equality, freedom of speech, freedom of religion).[72] More recently, in the context of the reform of the French Civil Code, Muriel Fabre-Magnan has added that a modern law of contracts should extend human rights reasoning to cases of discrimination on the basis of social and financial resources[73] and sustainable contracting.[74]

This justice view does, however, not fully escape the difficulties highlighted by those who are sceptical of the application of human rights in private law. In particular, the question remains which goals are pursued. Evaluating the effects of the Social Justice Manifesto, Daniela Caruso observes that it has certainly affected the discourse on the social dimension of European contract law.[75] Still, since no clear definition of

69 Study Group on Social Justice in European Private Law, 'Social Justice in European Contract Law: a Manifesto' *European Law Journal* 10.6 (2004), 653–674; Colombi Ciacchi, 'The Constitutionalization of European Contract Law', p. 178; B. Lurger, 'The "Social" Side of Contract Law and the New Principle of Regard and Fairness', in A. S. Hartkamp, M. W. Hesselink, E. H. Hondius, C. Mak, and C. E. du Perron (eds), *Towards a European Civil Code*, 4th edn (Nijmegen/Alphen aan den Rijn: Ars Aequi Libri/ Kluwer Law International, 2011), pp. 353–386.

70 Study Group on Social Justice in European Private Law, 'Social Justice in European Contract Law', p. 656.

71 In this sense, see also M. W. Hesselink, 'The Justice Dimension of the Relationship between Fundamental Rights and Private Law', in Collins (ed.), *European Contract Law*, pp. 167–196.

72 Colombi Ciacchi, 'The Constitutionalization of European Contract Law', p. 177. See also Brüggemeier, Colombi Ciacchi, and Comandé, *Fundamental Rights and Private Law*, II, 12.

73 M. Fabre-Magnan, 'What is a Modern Law of Contracts? Elements for a New Manifesto for Social Justice in European Contract Law', *European Review of Contract Law* 13.4 (2017), 376–388 (p. 381). On the potential for human rights to foster social inclusion in horizontal legal relationships, see also Collins, 'Discrimination, Equality and Social Inclusion'; E. Frantziou, *The Horizontal Effect of Fundamental Rights in the European Union* (Oxford: Oxford University Press, 2019), p. 167; B. Kas, 'Transforming the European "Legal Field" by Strategic Litigation', in L. de Almeida, M. Cantero Gamito, M. Djurovic, and K. Purnhagen (eds), *The Transformation of Economic Law* (Oxford: Hart Publishing, 2019), pp. 347–366 (p. 366).

74 Fabre-Magnan, 'What is a Modern Law of Contracts?', p. 385. See also D. Caruso, '*Qu'ils mangent des contrats*: Rethinking Justice in EU Contract Law', in D. Kochenov, G. de Búrca, and A. Williams (eds), *Europe's Justice Deficit?* (Oxford: Hart Publishing, 2015), pp. 367–378 (p. 375).

75 Caruso, '*Qu'ils mangent des contrats*', p. 370.

distributive goals was established, much of the Manifesto's ambitions have failed to materialise into conclusive effects.[76] Although Caruso's critique mostly concerns the development of legislative instruments, her analysis may easily be extended to the case law in which human rights have been invoked to protect social, distributive interests. While Colombi Ciacchi's examination of national case law provides some common starting points for the conceptualisation of social justice, these have not yet found an undisputed translation on the European level. In fact, the CJEU's predominantly market-oriented interpretation of EU (private) law is perceived as a risk in regard to the constitutionalisation of private law: where the *Aziz* judgment raised some hope for the development of a social dimension to European private law, the Court's business-friendly approach in cases like *Alemo-Herron* showed that human rights reasoning might also go the other way.[77]

d. Third Perspective: Reimagining Europe through Private Law

In the third place, then, the repoliticisation of private law may be related to the debate on the constitutional foundations of Europe.[78] From this point of view, the focus no longer primarily rests on what human rights contribute to private legal reasoning—'the constitutionalisation of private law'—but rather shifts to what private law may contribute to the shaping of a European society or even a political community—what I would call 'the Europe-making capacity of private law'[79]. This development is still at a relatively early stage, compared to national ideas on the relationship between human rights and private law.[80] Yet, a number of observations in the academic literature on the theme show glimpses of this imaginative power of private law in Europe.

The origins of this perspective on the societal relevance of private law may be found in the connection that was forged between citizenship and private legal relations in the development of EU law.[81] Consumer law provides an illustration. In this field, the EU's

76 Ibid., p. 371.

77 M. Bartl and C. Leone, 'Minimum Harmonisation and Article 16 of the CFREU. Difficult Times Ahead for Social Legislation?', in Collins (ed.), *European Contract Law*, pp. 113–124; H. Collins, 'Introduction', in Collins (ed.), *European Contract Law*, p. 20; M. W. Hesselink, in Collins (ed.), *European Contract Law* pp. 188–189, considering this interpretation of Article 16 to be 'partisan and therefore illegitimate from the perspective of the principles of justice that should prevail in a pluralist society'.

78 E.g. J. H. H. Weiler, *The Constitution of Europe: 'Do the New Clothes Have an Emperor?' and Other Essays on European Integration* (Cambridge, UK: Cambridge University Press, 1999); the contributions to G. De Búrca and J. H. H. Weiler (eds), *The Worlds of European Constitutionalism* (Cambridge, UK: Cambridge University Press, 2012); K. Tuori, *European Constitutionalism* (Cambridge, UK: Cambridge University Press, 2015).

79 Reminiscent of M. Loughlin, 'The Constitutional Imagination', *The Modern Law Review* 78.1 (2015), 1–25. This idea is further elaborated in C. Mak, 'Reimagining Europe through Private Law Adjudication', in C. Mak and B. Kas (eds), *Civil Courts and the European Polity: The Constitutional Role of Private Law Adjudication in Europe* (Oxford: Hart Publishing, 2023), pp. 63–77.

80 H.-W. Micklitz, 'The Consumer: Marketised, Fragmentised, Constitutionalised', in D. Leczykiewicz and S. Weatherill (eds), *The Images of the Consumer in EU Law: Legislation, Free Movement and Competition Law* (Oxford: Hart Publishing, 2016), pp. 25–26.

81 H.-W. Micklitz, *The Politics of Justice in European Private Law: Social Justice, Access Justice, Societal Justice* (Cambridge, UK: Cambridge University Press, 2018), pp. 392–393.

instrumental use of private law to enhance the functioning of the European market resulted in the hybrid idea of the 'consumer citizen'.[82] This conceptualisation of market participants received considerable criticism for its marginalisation of social concerns, insofar as EU law mainly understands consumption in economic terms.[83] As a response, in part inspired by ideals of social justice, consumers started to rely on human rights to counterbalance the detrimental effects of a too far-reaching marketisation of their legal position.[84] The Spanish mortgage cases, with *Aziz* as their flagship, attest to this trend. While consumers, thus, have to 'fight for their rights',[85] the constitutionalisation of European private law in consumer cases has started to provide constitutive elements of a developing European society.[86]

A variety of views on the contribution of private law to the (re)imagination of a European community may be categorised under this heading. They all place considerable emphasis on the role of courts in this process. Colombi Ciacchi, for instance, considers private law adjudication to contribute to 'societal policy-making', insofar as it balances interests and policy objectives through the application of human rights.[87] Giovanni Comandé discerns the emergence of a 'shadow citizenship' in the CJEU's case law on private legal matters, submitting that a European private law may serve to develop a European social model.[88] And Oliver Gerstenberg reads the case law in light of a theory of democratic experimentalism, proposing that adjudication can provide a forum for the deliberation of legal-political questions.[89]

None of these views is uncontested, as they require new ways of understanding the role of courts and political deliberation.[90] In my view, however, they provide an important theoretical contribution to the understanding of the process of reimagining Europe through deliberation on the legal-political stakes reflected in high-profile cases. Human rights protection in private legal relations as diverse as those concerning housing, non-discrimination, or climate change may serve to include those whose voices are less prominent in private legal frameworks.[91]

---

82 On this development, see I. Benöhr, *EU Consumer Law and Human Rights* (Oxford: Oxford University Press, 2013), pp. 37–39.

83 See e.g. G. Davies, 'The Consumer, the Citizen and the Human Being', in in D. Leczykiewicz and S. Weatherill (eds), *The Images of the Consumer in EU Law: Legislation, Free Movement and Competition Law* (Oxford: Hart Publishing, 2016), pp. 325–338; Benöhr, *EU Consumer Law*, p. 38.

84 Micklitz, 'The Consumer', pp. 35–37.

85 Micklitz, *Politics of Justice in European* p. 393.

86 Ibid., p. 392.

87 A. Colombi Ciacchi, 'Judicial Governance in European Private Law: Three Judicial Cultures of Fundamental Rights Horizontality', *European Review of Private Law* 28 (2020), 931–952 (p. 935).

88 G. Comandé, 'The Fifth European Union Freedom: Aggregating Citizenship...around Private Law', in Micklitz (ed.), *Constitutionalization of European Private Law*, pp. 61–101.

89 O. Gerstenberg, *Euroconstitutionalism and its Discontents* (Oxford: Oxford University Press, 2018).

90 Eg O. O. Cherednychenko and N. Reich, 'The Constitutionalization of European Private Law: Gateways, Constraints, and Challenges', *European Review of Private Law* 23.5 (2015), 797–827 (p. 827), who observe that the adjudication of sensitive legal-political issues may undermine the legitimacy of the CJEU.

91 Frantziou, '(Most of) the Charter of Fundamental Rights is Horizontally Applicable', p. 167; Mak, 'Reimagining Europe through Private Law Adjudication'.

4. Points for Reflection

This chapter traced the debate on the impact of human rights in private law along three lines: the basis in human dignity of an extension of human rights protection to private legal relationships; the constitutionalisation of private law on the national and European levels; and the legal-political dimensions of these developments, including the role of courts in elaborating human rights reasoning in private law. Surveying the general tendencies, the question no longer is whether human rights should have a place in private law. Both national and European courts have embedded the possibility to rely on such overarching or background rights in doctrines of private law, slowly but steadily expanding the reach of human rights. Current questions, thus, regard the understanding of the substantive, transformative effects that result from these dynamics: on the one hand, the reimagination of private law in light of human rights and, on the other hand, societal transformations to which private law may contribute.

Q1: To what extent should private actors be considered to be bound to human rights? And on what basis?

Q2: Can human rights be applied in private legal relationships in a similar manner as in public legal relationships between citizens and public authorities?

Q3: Which theoretical view on human rights and private law do you find most convincing and why?

Q4: Can you think of an example in which human rights reasoning offers a solution to a societal problem involving private actors that cannot be reached through private law alone?

Q5: What are the limits of human rights reasoning in private law?

Bibliography

Benöhr, I., *EU Consumer Law and Human Rights* (Oxford: Oxford University Press, 2013), https://doi.org/10.1093/acprof:oso/9780199651979.001.0001

Berlin, I., *Four Essays on Liberty* (Oxford: Oxford University Press, 1969)

Brüggemeier, G., A. Colombi Ciacchi, and G. Comandé (eds), *Fundamental Rights and Private Law in the European Union*, 2 vols (Cambridge, UK: Cambridge University Press, 2010)

Burgers, L., 'Friends of the Earth Netherlands Versus Royal Dutch Shell: All Companies Must Act Against Climate Change', *Transformative Private Law Blog* (29 May 2021) https://transformativeprivatelaw.com/friends-of-the-earth-netherlands-versus-royal-dutch-shell-all-companies-must-act-against-climate-change/

Burgers, L. E., *Justitia, the People's Power and Mother Earth: Democratic Legitimacy of Judicial Law-making in European Private Law Cases on Climate Change* (doctoral thesis, University of Amsterdam, 2020), https://hdl.handle.net/11245.1/0e6437b7-399d-483a-9fc1-b18ca926fdb5

Busch, C., and H. Schulte-Nölke, *EU Compendium—Fundamental Rights and Private Law* (Munich: Sellier, 2011)

Caruso, D., '*Qu'ils mangent des contrats*: Rethinking Justice in EU Contract Law', in D. Kochenov, G. de Búrca, and A. Williams (eds), *Europe's Justice Deficit?* (Oxford: Hart Publishing, 2015), pp. 367–378, https://doi.org/10.5040/9781474201193.ch-025

Cherednychenko, O. O., *Fundamental Rights, Contract Law and the Protection of the Weaker Party: A Comparative Analysis of the Constitutionalisation of Contract Law, with Emphasis on Risky Financial Transactions* (Munich: Sellier, 2007)

Cherednychenko, O. O., 'Rediscovering the Public/Private Divide in EU Private Law', *European Law Journal* 26 (2019), 27–47

Cherednychenko, O. O., 'Subordinating Contract Law to Fundamental Rights: Towards a Major Breakthrough or towards Walking in Circles?', in S. Grundmann (ed.), *Constitutional Values and European Contract Law* (Deventer: Kluwer Law International, 2008), pp. 35–60

Cherednychenko, O. O., and N. Reich, 'The Constitutionalization of European Private Law: Gateways, Constraints, and Challenges', *European Review of Private Law* 23.5 (2015), 797–827, https://doi.org/10.54648/erpl2015049

Collins, H., 'Cosmopolitanism and Transnational Private Law', *European Review of Contract Law* 8.3 (2012), 311–325, https://doi.org/10.1515/ercl-2012-0311

Collins, H., 'Discrimination, Equality and Social Inclusion', *The Modern Law Review* 66.1 (2003), 16–43, https://doi.org/10.1111/1468-2230.6601002

Collins, H. (ed.), *European Contract Law and the Charter of Fundamental Rights* (Cambridge/Antwerp: Intersentia, 2017), https://doi.org/10.1017/9781780684963

Colombi Ciacchi, A., 'The Constitutionalization of European Contract Law: Judicial Convergence and Social Justice', *European Review of Contract Law* 2.2 (2006), 167–180, https://doi.org/10.1515/ercl.2006.013

Colombi Ciacchi, A., 'Judicial Governance in European Private Law: Three Judicial Cultures of Fundamental Rights Horizontality', *European Review of Private Law* 28 (2020), 931–952, https://doi.org/10.54648/erpl2020055

Colombi Ciacchi, A., C. Mak, and Z. Mansoor (eds), *Immoral Contracts in Europe*, The Common Core of European Private Law Series (Cambridge, UK: Intersentia, 2020), https://doi.org/10.1017/9781839701153.003

Davies, G., 'The Consumer, the Citizen and the Human Being', in D. Leczykiewicz and S. Weatherill (eds), *The Images of the Consumer in EU Law: Legislation, Free Movement and Competition Law* (Oxford: Hart Publishing, 2016), pp. 325–338, https://doi.org/10.5040/9781474202510

Davola, A., 'Fostering Consumer Protection in the Granular Market: The Role of Rules on Consent, Misrepresentation and Fraud in Regulating Personalized Practice', *Technology and Regulation (Techreg)* 2021 (2021), 76–86, https://doi.org/10.71265/w34brs50

De Búrca, G., and J. H. H. Weiler (eds), *The Worlds of European Constitutionalism* (Cambridge, UK: Cambridge University Press, 2012), https://doi.org/10.1017/CBO9781139026734

Domurath, I., *Consumer Vulnerability and Welfare in Mortgage Contracts* (Oxford: Hart Publishing, 2017)

Domurath, I., and C. Mak, 'Private Law and Housing Justice in Europe', *The Modern Law Review* 83 (2020), 1188–1220, https://doi.org/10.1111/1468-2230.12557

Dworkin, R., *Justice for Hedgehogs* (Cambridge, MA: Harvard University Press, 2011), https://doi.org/10.4159/9780674059337

Dworkin, R., *Sovereign Virtue: The Theory and Practice of Equality* (Cambridge, MA: Harvard University Press, 2000)

Fabre-Magnan, M., 'What is a Modern Law of Contracts? Elements for a New Manifesto for Social Justice in European Contract Law', *European Review of Contract Law* 13.4 (2017), 376–388, https://doi.org/10.1515/ercl-2017-0020

Frantziou, E., *The Horizontal Effect of Fundamental Rights in the European Union* (Oxford: Oxford University Press, 2019)

Frantziou, E., '(Most of) the Charter of Fundamental Rights is Horizontally Applicable', *European Constitutional Law Review* 15.2 (2019), 306–323, https://doi.org/10.1017/S1574019619000166

Gerstenberg, O., *Euroconstitutionalism and its Discontents* (Oxford: Oxford University Press, 2018), https://doi.org/10.1093/oso/9780198834335.001.0001

Grundmann, S. (ed.), *Constitutional Values and European Contract Law* (Deventer: Kluwer Law International, 2008)

Habermas, J., *The Crisis of the European Union: A Response* (Cambridge, UK: Polity Press, 2012)

Hartkamp, A. S., *European Law and National Private Law* (Cambridge/Antwerp: Intersentia, 2016), https://doi.org/10.1017/9781780687513

Hinteregger, M., 'Civil Liability and the Challenges of Climate Change: A Functional Analysis', *Journal of European Tort Law* 8.2 (2017), 238–260, https://doi.org/10.1017/9781780687513

Kas, B., 'Transforming the European "Legal Field" by Strategic Litigation', in L. de Almeida, M. Cantero Gamito, M. Djurovic, K. Purnhagen (eds), *The Transformation of Economic Law* (Oxford: Hart Publishing, 2019), pp. 347–366

Kennedy, D., *A Critique of Adjudication {fin de siècle}* (Cambridge, MA: Harvard University Press, 1997)

Kennedy, D., 'Form and Substance in Private Law Adjudication', *Harvard Law Review* 88 (1976), 1685–1778, https://doi.org/10.1515/9780691186429-018

Kennedy, D., 'The Political Stakes in "Merely Technical" Issues of Contract Law', *European Review of Private Law* 10 (2001), 7–28, https://doi.org/10.54648/399190

Loughlin, M., 'The Constitutional Imagination', *The Modern Law Review* 78.1 (2015), 1–25, https://doi.org/10.1111/1468-2230.12114

Lurger, B., 'The "Social" Side of Contract Law and the New Principle of Regard and Fairness', in A. S. Hartkamp, M. W. Hesselink, E. H. Hondius, C. Mak, and C. E. du Perron (eds), *Towards a European Civil Code*, 4th edn (Nijmegen/Alphen aan den Rijn: Ars Aequi Libri/Kluwer Law International, 2011), pp. 353–386

Mak, C., *Fundamental Rights in European Contract Law: A Comparison of the Impact of Fundamental Rights on Contractual Relationships in Germany, the Netherlands, Italy and England* (Alphen a/d Rijn: Kluwer Law International, 2008)

Mak, C., 'Reimagining Europe through Private Law Adjudication', in C. Mak and B. Kas (eds), *Civil Courts and the European Polity: The Constitutional Role of Private Law Adjudication in Europe* (Oxford: Hart Publishing, 2023), pp. 63–77, https://doi.org/10.5040/9781509941704.ch-004

Marella, M. R., 'The Old and the New Limits to Freedom of Contract in Europe', *European Review of Contract Law* 2.2 (2006), 257–274, https://doi.org/10.1515/ercl.2006.019

Micklitz, H.-W. (ed.), *Constitutionalization of European Private Law* (Oxford: Oxford University Press, 2014), https://doi.org/10.1093/acprof:oso/9780198712107.001.0001

Micklitz, H.-W., 'The Consumer: Marketised, Fragmentised, Constitutionalised', in D. Leczykiewicz and S. Weatherill (eds), *The Images of the Consumer in EU Law: Legislation, Free Movement and Competition Law* (Oxford: Hart Publishing, 2016), pp. 25–26, https://doi.org/10.5040/9781474202510.ch-002

Micklitz, H.-W., 'On the Intellectual History of Freedom of Contract and Regulation', *Penn State Journal of Law & International Affairs* 4 (2015), 100–131, http://elibrary.law.psu.edu/jlia/vol4/iss1/3

Micklitz, H.-W., *The Politics of Justice in European Private Law: Social Justice, Access Justice, Societal Justice* (Cambridge, UK: Cambridge University Press, 2018), https://doi.org/10.1017/9781108539777

Naffine, N., 'Legal Personality and the Natural World: on the Persistence of the Human Measure of Value', *Journal of Human Rights and the Environment* 3 (2012), 68–83, https://doi.org/10.4337/jhre.2012.02.04

Schapp, J., 'Privatautonomie und Verfassungsrecht', *Zeitschrift für Bankrecht und Bankwirtschaft* 11.1 (1998), 30–42, https://doi.org/10.15375/zbb-1999-0105

Stone, C. D., *Should Trees Have Standing? Law, Morality and the Environment*, 3rd edn (Oxford: Oxford University Press, 2010)

Study Group on Social Justice in European Private Law, 'Social Justice in European Contract Law: A Manifesto' *European Law Journal* 10.6 (2004), 653–674, https://doi.org/10.1111/j.1468-0386.2004.00237.x

Townsend, D., 'Taking Dignity Seriously? A Dignity Approach to Environmental Disputes before Human Rights Courts', *Journal of Human Rights and the Environment* 6.2 (2015), 218–242, https://doi.org/10.4337/jhre.2015.02.04

Tuori, K., *European Constitutionalism* (Cambridge, UK: Cambridge University Press, 2015), https://doi.org/10.1017/CBO9781316091883

van Duin, J. M. L., *Effective Judicial Protection in Consumer Litigation: Article 47 of the EU Charter in Practice* (Cambridge, UK: Intersentia, 2022), https://doi.org/10.1017/9781839702501

Waldron, J., 'How Law Protects Dignity', *Cambridge Law Journal* 71.1 (2012), 200–222, https://doi.org/10.1017/S0008197312000256

Walkila, S., *Horizontal Effect of Fundamental Rights in the EU* (Groningen: Europa Law Publishing, 2016)

Weiler, J. H. H., *The Constitution of Europe: 'Do the New Clothes Have an Emperor?' and Other Essays on European Integration* (Cambridge, UK: Cambridge University Press, 1999), https://doi.org/10.1017/CBO9780511606119

Wiedemann, H., 'BVerfG, 19.10.1993—1 BvR 567 u. 1044/89. Zur verfassungsrechtlichen Inhaltskontrolle von Verträgen', *JuristenZeitung* 49 (1994), 412–413

III. INSTITUTIONS

6. *Bona fides* (Good Faith) in European Private Law

Talya Deibel

Abstract

This chapter introduces good faith as a fundamental principle of European private law. It proposes to reconsider its inner logic and future potential through exploring how it has emerged and how it has been recontextualised across different periods of European private law. Good faith refers to loyalty to promises, honesty, and expediency in contractual relations. As an essential pillar in the development of European private law, it predates both the EU and even nation states. The legal evolution of good faith reveals a remarkable continuity, forming a transhistorical pattern from its Roman law origins through medieval developments, early modern civil codes, and into contemporary EU legal frameworks. Yet, good faith has not remained static; it has evolved alongside changing markets and various conceptions of contractual fairness and justice. This chapter analyses good faith from a broader perspective to highlight its pluralistic and evolving nature, with the aim of fostering further dialogue on its reimagination in European private law.

Introduction

Even though good faith is a moral principle, its application poses legal challenges. In contract law, good faith refers to a standard of conduct which requires the parties to act in an honest, loyal, and reasonable manner. It emphasises the trust relation between private parties, and as such it provides mechanisms to secure the protection of legitimate interests and the re-calibration of the contractual balance. However, its vague character is controversial. It is widely disputed whether it is a fundamental principle of law, an open norm, a general rule with direct application, or an empty concept which refers nothing but the power of discretion of the judge in civil law

 https://doi.org/10.11647/OBP.0448.06

tradition.[1] This chapter proposes to re-examine the historical and cultural roots of good faith in order to better understand its relevance for European private law.

Good faith is the contemporary reflection of the Roman law principle *bona fides* which already signified loyalty to promises and honesty in the performance of obligations. Its transformation happened in the long course of history, beginning with classical Roman law, medieval *ius commune* (common law), and as part of the effect of natural law on the codifications of law in Europe. Medieval jurists referred to good faith primarily to determine the scope of obligations and the modes of performance. Sharing this common history, many European civil codes contain a specific good faith provision and adopt the duty of good faith in the performance of obligations to moralise contract laws (e.g. German Civil Code (BGB) § 242, French Civil Code 1104, Italian Civil Code 1375, Swiss Civil Code (ZGB) 2, etc.).

Bona fides flourished in Roman *ius gentium* (law of nations), a quasi-cosmopolitan set of private law rules applicable in trade relations between citizens and foreigners. It was a compromise: a natural law principle which gained momentum throughout Roman jurisprudential law to accommodate different interests of parties with different legal and social backgrounds. This gave *bona fides* a 'transnational character'. This is mirrored today in how global value networks operate on the outside of nation states.[2]

Hence, good faith played an essential role in the European trade culture that shaped European legal systems. The flexibility of *bona fides* inevitably revealed its fertility. Throughout European legal history, different manifestations of good faith gained gravity and became fundamental contract law doctrines, independent from their source. Nevertheless, modernity came with more complex contractual relationships, which stripped good faith of much of its practical relevance. For a long time now, good faith has operated through the sub-doctrines it created in response to a wide variety of social contexts.

Today the role of good faith is increasing in the global commercial scene where flexible contract law principles are needed to accommodate different social systems, in and outside of the court. This chapter follows the legal-theoretical line which takes good faith as a fundamental principle of contract law and as well-equipped to provide flexibility, communication, and responsiveness in global private legal relations.[3] This observation is more than simply erudite ornamentation; such a perspective is not only relevant for understanding the harmonisation and even unification of European

---

1 P. Tercier, *Traité de Droit Privé Suisse: II/1* (Basel: Helbing Lichtenhahn, 2008), pp. 177–179; M. W. Hesselink, 'The Concept of Good Faith', in A. S. Hartkamp, M. W. Hesselink, E. Hondius, C. Mak, and E. Du Perron (eds), *Towards a European Civil Code* (Alphen aan den Rijn: Kluwer Law International, 2011), pp. 619–650 (p. 645).

2 T. U. Deibel, 'Corporate Social Responsibility in the Legal Framework of Global Value Chains', *Law and Development Review* 15.2 (2022), 329–356.

3 P. Schlechtriem, *Good Faith in German Law and International Uniform Laws* (Rome: Centro di studi e ricerche di diritto comparato e straniero, 1997); R. Brownsword, 'Individualism, Cooperativism and an Ethic for European Contract Law', *Modern Law Review* 64.4 (2001), 628–642; R. Zimmermann and S. Whittaker (eds), *Good Faith in European Contract Law* (Cambridge, UK: Cambridge University Press, 2006); also see Hesselink, 'The Concept of Good Faith'.

private law around a 'European legal culture' but also for understanding private law theory at a global level. In other words, it allows us to critically reflect on what private law means today for both EU and non-EU countries.

As such this article takes European private law as a legal field and as a method of studying private law. It first examines the wide reception of the European legal tradition all over the world. This continues today as a Romanist legal identity formed around a shared culture of commerce. Second, it explains the legal evolution of Roman *bona fides* to analyse its contemporary relevance in private law. Last, it examines its social and political significance by discussing how global trade networks are inevitably forcing us to adopt flexible and shared legal mechanisms. As a result, it is once again necessary to channel an old tradition and renew our general understanding of private law.

Legal Context

1. Good Faith and the European Legal Culture

The term 'legal culture' refers to a relatively stable pattern of legal behaviour, common techniques to deal with legal problems, shared values, and intellectual roots.[4] As such, it does not only refer to continental Europe but also England, North America, large parts of Central and South America, Northern Asia, and the British commonwealth.[5] European legal culture has never existed in a homogenous unitary form as Europe has always been polyjural.[6] Therefore a pragmatic stance would be based on the observation that their similarities outweigh their differences.

This is relatively easier to observe for the civilian tradition, yet to some extent applicable to the common law orbit as well. English law methodologically shares the tradition of Roman law which was also developed as case law.[7] The Anglo-American legal system has always contained special legal techniques and doctrinal sources to provide honesty, loyalty, and reasonableness in contractual relations to overcome the rigidities of the formal law on an *ad hoc* basis.

Many European legal systems adopt good faith as a general duty imposed on the judge and the parties.[8] Although it has been highly disputed whether English law

4 F. Wieacker, 'Foundations of Legal Culture', trans. by Edgar Bodenheimer, *American Journal of Comparative Law* 38 (1990), 1–29 (p. 4).

5 Ibid., pp. 4–6.

6 R. Zimmermann, 'Civil Code and Civil Law: The "Europeanisation" of Private Law within the European Community and the Re-Emergence of a European Legal Science', *ColumJEurL* 63 (1994–95), 73–80; P. Legrand, 'Against a European Civil Code', *Modern Law Review* 60 (1997), 44–63 (p. 45).

7 Wieacker, 'Foundations of Legal Culture', p. 6.

8 *Bona fides* has two dimensions. On the one hand, it reflects loyalty and honesty from an objective standpoint. On the other hand, it protects reliance and trust which are inherently subjective concepts. Starting from the medieval age, its different dimensions evolved into two distinct private law doctrines and modern codifications adopted good faith both in its objective and subjective sense. While some systems kept the same terminology (*bonne foi objective/subjective* in French law, *buona fede oggettiva/soggettiva* in Italian law etc.) some others adopted different terms to address objective good faith (*Treu und Glauben* in German law, *redelijkheid en billijkheid* in Dutch law, fair dealing in *lex mercatoria*

recognises a general duty of good faith in contracts, it is today accepted that good faith is required in the performance of the contractual obligations. The role of good faith in common law sustained its normative value due to the adoption of 'reasonable commercial standards of fair dealing in the trade' and the developments in consumer law. In EU consumer law good faith is particularly relevant as it lies behind the rules that ensure fairness in consumer contracts and functions as a private law tool against discrimination and unfair treatments.[9] For example under Article 3(1) of the Unfair Contract Terms Directive, 'a contractual term which has not been individually negotiated shall be regarded as unfair if, contrary to the requirement of good faith, it causes a significant imbalance in the parties' rights and obligations arising under the contract, to the detriment of the consumer'.[10]

Accordingly, former harmonisation and unification projects primarily concerned with the European legal space refer to Roman *bona fides* in their multiplicity.[11] Examples are Principles of European Contract Law (PECL), the Draft Common Frame of Reference (DCFR), the Restatement of Nordic Contract Law, as well as other *lex mercatoria* (international trade law) tools that aim for a more harmonious legal system at the global level.[12] Specifically, PECL Article 1(201) imposes a general duty of good faith on the parties. The article reads as: (1) Each party must act in accordance with good faith and fair dealing. (2) The parties may not exclude or limit this duty. It has two major implications: First, good faith is a general principle of European contract law and second, it is non-derogable.

---

etc.). Subjective good faith refers to the state of mind of an individual in not knowing and not being reasonably expected to know a certain event or phenomenon. This lack of knowledge plays a major role in the acquisition of rights, and therefore mainly demonstrates itself in property relations. Yet, it is historically and functionally intertwined with the ethos of objective good faith which primarily operates within the contractual realm. O. Lando, 'Salient Features of the Principles of European Contract Law: A Comparison with the UCC', *Pace Int. Law Rev* 13 (2001), 339–369; Hesselink, 'The Concept of Good Faith', pp. 620–621.

9 See Case C-415/11 *Mohamed Aziz v Caixa d´Estalvis de Catalunya, Tarragona i Manresa* (*Catalunyacaixa*) [2013] ECLI:EU:C:2013:164; Case C-349/18 *Nationale Maatschappij der Belgische Spoorwegen* (*NMBS*) *v Mbutuku Kanyeba* ECLI:EU:C:2019:936; Case C-350/18 *Larissa Nijs*, Case C-351/18 *Jean-Louis Anita Dedroog*, Joined Cases C-349/18 to C-351/18 [2019] ECLI:EU:C:2019:936 and ECLI:EU:C:2019:726.

10 See Case C-186/16 *Ruxandra Paula Andriciuc and Others v Banca Românească SA* [2017] ECLI:EU:C:2017:703.

11 Also see Translex principles No. i.1.1 available at https://www.trans-lex.org/901000 and UNIDROIT Principles Article 1(7) available at https://www.unidroit.org/wp-content/uploads/2021/06/Unidroit-Principles-2016-English-bl.pdf. R. Michaels, 'The UNIDROIT Principles as Global Background Law', *Uniform Law Review* 19 (2014), 643–668. Whether the United Nations Convention on Contracts for the International Sale of Goods (CISG) imposes a general duty of good faith on the contracting parties is open to discussion. It is generally accepted that CISG Article 7(1) refers to good faith as a general principle of law directed to the parties as it is the underlying concept of the duties laid by the convention. Schlechtriem, *Good Faith in German Law*; I. Schwenzer and P. Hachem, 'Article 7 of the CISG', in P. Schlechtriem and I. Schwenzer (eds), *Commentary on the UN Convention on the Sale of Goods* (*CISG*) (Oxford: Oxford University Press, 2016), 129–137.

12 Discussions in the comparative law field on whether the uniformisation of European private law is useful or even possible falls outside of the scope of this chapter. For more information see A. Watson, *Legal Transplants*, 2nd edn (Athens, GA: University of Georgia Press, 1993); G. Teubner, 'Legal Irritants: Good Faith in British Law or How Unifying Law Ends Up in New Differences', *Modern Law Review* 61 (1998), 11–32; A. S. Hartkamp, M. W. Hesselink, E. Hondius, C. Mak, and E. Du Perron (eds), *Towards a European Civil Code* (Alphen aan den Rijn: Kluwer Law International, 2011).

Alongside its relevance to European law, good faith is also crucial for non-European legal systems which have been heavily influenced by Europe or have adopted the same principles. This is part of the history of colonialism, but its implication is simultaneously that Europe has no monopoly over global legal culture. Indeed, good faith is found in many countries that remained fully or partially free from colonisation. To some extent, however, Europe retains its primary position, with a world-wide influence of its laws, due to the history of colonialism, the requirements of neoliberalism, and today's global commercial relations. While we can interpret this development in various ways, the large scale adoption, codification, and application of the general duty of good faith is an example of how European states share a long legal history and culture derived from Roman law, and how it ends up being extended to the global legal sphere.

Today the primary unit where laws are reflected is not only the nation but also the global economic sphere where good faith acts as an organising principle.[13] The pluralistic legal order highlights the role of good faith not only because it is an expression of the predominant continental legal culture but also because it evolved as a well-equipped principle to communicate through a multiplicity of legal discourses as it is closely tied to global economy and production regimes.[14] The contemporary value of *bona fides* lies in its history stemming from Roman imperialism and trade, which gives it its transformative and transnational character.

2. From *Fides* to *Bona Fides:* The Legal Evolution of Good Faith

Analysing good faith raises the question of why we should invest ourselves in a tautological idiom. *Bona fides* derives from *Fides*, the name of the Roman goddess of loyalty to promises and honesty. In ancient Rome, it signified one's commitment to one's own words, and was believed to reside on the right hands of individuals as a mark of trustworthiness. Having *Iuppiter* as her patron, *Fides* was highly respected in the Roman world.[15] The word *fides* was derived from the international law concept *foedus* that referred to the alliances between two nations. In parallel *bona fides* represented minimum cooperation in social relations; not necessarily amicable, but civilised and pragmatic.

Stoic philosophy gave its secular character to *Fides* which later transformed into a legal concept in the Republican era.[16] According to Cicero, *bona fides* was fundamental for justice.[17] The legal evolution of good faith happened through the application of Roman procedural law, namely the revolutionary *ex fide bona* clauses in the Roman

---

13 Teubner, 'Legal Irritants: Good Faith in British Law or How Unifying Law Ends Up in New Differences', p. 25.

14 Ibid.

15 *Iuppiter* signified the supreme religious entity. The word *ius* (law) is also derived from *Iuppiter*. G. Freyburger, *Fides: Étude Sémantique et Religieuse Depuis les Origines jusqu'à l'Époque Augustéenne* (Paris: Collection d'Études Anciennes, 1986), p. 228.

16 M. Villey, *La Formation de la Pensée Juridique Moderne: Cours d'Histoire et de la Philosophie du Droit* (Paris: Montchrestien, 1975), p. 66.

17 Cicero, *De Officiis*, 1.23.

formulary procedure.[18] They referred to special clauses added in the formularies of special actions—later to be named *iudicia bonae fidei*—which ordered the judge to oblige the parties to all the requirements of good faith. *Fides* transformed the formal and strict law of contract into a system adapted to a developed 'international' economy whereby it provided law's recourse to social morality.[19]

The reason why equity and *bona fides* became central in Roman jurisprudence was the formal and strict characteristic of civil law. In Roman law, actions were one of the praetorian remedies to provide equity in private law matters. Initially in the majority of the actions the judge had to decide according to the strict legal rules and facts of the case. However, the special actions with *ex fide bona* clauses gave the judge the power of discretion when deciding the requirements of good faith and as such, it provided legal elasticity.

Iudicia bonae fidei let value judgments enter into the legal realm. This might be understood as Roman judges created 'an ideal behavioural model' based on good faith to determine the scope of the obligations of the parties. This behavioural standard was based on a good man (*bonus vir*) who is prudent, careful, loyal, and honest.[20] It required the protection of the legitimate interests of the other party in contractual relationships, and provided legal foreseeability which was necessary for the development of trade relations as the Roman empire expanded.

Therefore, *bona fides* blossomed out of the commercial relations between foreigners and citizens of Rome.[21] Roman law of nations (*ius gentium*) contained flexible legal rules with universal character which were derived from the Roman conception of natural reason. These rules were mostly developed to accommodate trade relations among people with different legal and social backgrounds. As the Roman empire valued trade and approached it pragmatically, the inherent elasticity of *bona fides* made it the founding stone of commerce between different groups for centuries.[22]

Roman *bona fides* was an example of how mutual trust and respecting legitimate

18 The formulary system referred to the civil procedure which started in the Republican era and lasted until the third century, when it was replaced by a quasi-modern litigation system. According to the formulary procedure, each cause of action had a special formula which signified formal statements issued by the praetors (Roman high magistrate concerned with legal matters), and addressed to the judge. The formulary procedure made Roman law a quasi-judge made law. W. W. Buckland, *A Text Book of Roman Law from Augustus to Justinian* (Cambridge, UK: Cambridge University Press, 1950), p. 629; F. Wieacker, 'Zum Ursprung der Bonae Fidei Iudicia', *ZSS* 80 (1963), 1–41.

19 Teubner, 'Legal Irritants: Good Faith in British Law or How Unifying Law Ends Up in New Differences', p. 23.

20 M. J. Schermaier, 'Bona fides in Roman Contract Law', in R. Zimmermann and S. Whittaker (eds), *Good Faith in European Contract Law* (Cambridge, UK: Cambridge University Press, 2006), pp. 63–92 (p. 87).

21 About *ius gentium* see P. Jörs, W. Kunkel, and L. Wenger, *Römisches Recht*, 3. Auflage (Berlin: Springer, 1949), p. 58; A. Burdese, *Manuale di Diritto Privato Romano* (Turin: UTET, 1969), p. 26. M. Kaser, R. Knütel, and S. Lohsse, *Römisches Privatrecht*, 22. Auflage (Munich: Beck, 2021), p. 36; Burdese, *Manuale di Diritto Privato Romano*, p. 26.

22 F. Gallo, 'Bona Fides e Ius Gentium', in A. Burdese and L. Garofalo (eds), *Il Ruolo della Buona Fede Oggettiva nell'Esperienza Giuridica Storica e Contemporanea. Atti del Convegno Internazionale di Studi in Onore di Alberto Burdes, Vol II* (Milan: CEDAM, 2003), p. 131.

expectations were essential components in honouring promises especially in long-term contractual relations.[23] Throughout history the nature of each private relationship required a different understanding of *bona fides* and its jurisprudential development motivated the legal systems to harmonise the moral requirements of private legal relations. Today, loyalty and the protection of legitimate expectations in contractual relations are of particular importance in relational contracts based on trust and long-term business practices where good faith becomes a self-imposed constraint by the parties guided by their self-interests.[24]

Due to its strong connection with *ius gentium* and natural law, *bona fides* has always bound different societies and times together, giving the legal system a dynamic stability and a moral standard for business relations. In other words, good faith is historically associated with natural law, universality of private law norms and practicality of the daily life. It has demonstrated that *ius* is more than *lex*. This is particularly important today as globalism and the transnationality of production mechanisms brings ethical and flexible legal mechanisms into the spotlight again.

3. Good Faith, Abuse of Rights, and Equity

Roman legal tradition defines law as *ars boni et aequi* (the art of knowing what is good and equitable).[25] Classical and medieval legal scholarship attributed great importance to *aequitas* (equity) and defined it as the concrete reflection of justice on a case-by-case basis.[26] As such, two requirements of *bona fides* were set as follows: the absence of *dolus* (deceit) and the obligation to behave according to *aequitas naturalis* (natural equity).[27]

Its organic relation with *dolus* (deceit) was another milestone in the evolution of good faith. Since the classical era, *bona fides* has been understood as the conceptual antonym of *dolus*.[28] Initially a praetorian delict, *dolus* referred to the fraudulent intent

23 In the Anglo-American legal sphere the shortcomings of traditional contract theory are sometimes addressed by the doctrine of 'relational contract', characterised by the 'trust' relation between parties. The common examples of relational contracts include joint venture agreements, franchise agreements, and long-term distributorship agreements. In the civilian tradition, long-term contracts (*contrats à execution succesives* and *dauernde Schuldverhältnisse*) are examples of contracts with relational nature which require flexible extra-legal mechanisms such as the risk of exclusion or losing reputation. Such mechanisms were also pillars of *lex mercatoria* in the middle ages. S. Macaulay, 'Non-Contractual Relations in Business: A Preliminary Study', *Am. Soc. Rev.* 28 (1963), 55–67; I. Macneil, 'Reflections on Relational Contract', *Journal of Institutional and Theoretical Economics* 141 (1985), 541–546; L. Hawthorne, 'Relational Contract Theory, Principles of European Contract Law—Long-term Contracts, and the Impact of Implicit Dimensions', *Tydskrif vir Hedendaagse Romeins-Hollandse Reg* 70 (2007), 371–390; S. Grundmann, 'Between Market and Hierarchy', in S. Grundmann et al. (ed.), *New Private Law Theory: A Pluralist Approach* (Cambridge, UK: Cambridge University Press, 2021), pp. 315–338.

24 R. Brownsword, 'Two Concepts of Good Faith', *J. Contract Law* 7 (1994), 197–204 (p. 200).

25 Celsus. D. 1.1.1 pr.

26 Buckland, *A Text Book of Roman Law from Augustus to Justinian*, p. 55.

27 N. Horn, *Aequitas in den Lehren des Baldus* (Köln: Böhlau, 1968), p. 103; J. Gordley, *The Philosophical Origins of Modern Contract Doctrine* (Oxford: Clarendon, 1993).

28 R. Monier, *Manuel Élémentaire de Droit Romain, Tome II* (Paris: Montchrestien, 1947), p. 69; G. Pugliese, *Istituzioni Di Diritto Romano* (Turin: Giappichelli, 1992), p. 265; J. Gordley, 'Good Faith in Contract Law in the Medieval Ius Commune', in R. Zimmermann and S. Whittaker (eds), *Good Faith in European*

to trick the other party for one's own benefits.[29] One judicial remedy was *exceptio doli* (plea of deceit) which was granted against the party who abuses his contractual rights.[30] In the medieval era it became a general mechanism to dispel all the claims that are contrary to good faith. This reflected the exclusionary nature of *bona fides*. Being an ambiguous concept, *bona fides* started to be determined by excluding and prohibiting all *mala fide* (bad faith) behaviour in contracts.[31]

Exceptio doli was not a plea in a technical sense. Rather, it provided *ipso iure* (by the law itself) sanctions to the fraudulent party whereby depriving him from the right of action. This legal measure has evolved into the prohibition of abuse of rights in European law. In the civilian tradition *mala fide* exercise of a right is prohibited if it causes harm or danger of harm to another.[32] In this case, examples of *mala fide* behaviour are the inexpedient, contradictory, and unreasonable exercise of rights or having an excessive imbalance between the expected benefits of the exercise of a right and the inconvenience caused to the other party. This shows that good faith and the prohibition of abuse of rights are functionally and historically intertwined and the line between them is blurred.[33] The primary difference between the general duty of good faith and the prohibition of abuse of rights is that the former is a direct obligation to the parties, while the latter is an assessment standard for the judge.[34]

The prohibition of deceit was a requirement of equity which was considered as 'the natural law interpreted by the judge'. Through the *ex fide bona* clauses, good faith helped to overcome the firmness and formalism of the law and internalised the risk of unfairness in contractual settings.[35] As such, the observance of equity and requirements of good faith have been historically entangled with judicial discretion.[36] The behavioural standard provided by good faith would have been an empty promise without individual value judgments. This is also clear considering how *bona fides* emerged: it was an instrument for equity, applied through the discretion given to the judge.

Contract Law (Cambridge, UK: Cambridge University Press, 2000), pp. 93–117 (p. 93).

29 R. Zimmermann, *The Law of Obligations Roman Foundations of the Civilian Tradition* (Oxford: Oxford University Press, 1996), p. 665; Gordley, 'Good Faith in Contract Law in the Medieval Ius Commune', p. 101.

30 Pugliese, *Istituzioni Di Diritto Romano*, p. 297; Buckland, *A Text Book of Roman Law from Augustus to Justinian*, p. 652.

31 For a similar understanding in American law, see R. S. Summers, 'Good Faith in General Contract Law and the Sales Provision of the Uniform Commercial Code', *Virginia Law Review* 54, (1968), 199–206 (p. 206).

32 H. Honsell, Article 2, No 24, P. Tercier and P. Pichonnaz, *Le Droit des Obligations* (Zurich: Schultess, 2012), p. 27.

33 For example, German *Treu und Glauben* (objective good faith, BGB § 242) is seen as the modern application of *bona fides* and *exceptio doli*. Swiss law and Spanish law regulate these two concepts within the same article (ZGB 2 and Spanish Civil Code Article 7), under general provisions. G. Roth, § 242, No 177; D. Medicus and J. Petersen, *Allgemeiner Teil des BGB* (Heidelberg: C. F. Müller, 2016), p. 51.

34 H. Honsell, Article 2, No 9–10, A. Egger, Article 2, No. 23; H. Deschenaux, *Schweizerisches Privarecht II* (Basel: Helbing Lichtenhahn, 1988), p. 147.

35 Horn, *Aequitas in den Lehren des Baldus*, p. 103; F. Pringsheim, 'Aequitas und Bona Fides', *Conferenze per il XIV Centenario delle Pandette* 33 (1931), 183.

36 Hesselink, 'The Concept of Good Faith', p. 637.

Good faith in European legal tradition primarily aims at creating equitable outcomes in private law relations, whether as a guiding principle, a source of obligation or an instrument of interpretation. Its close connection to equity is visible in many European codifications. For example, Articles 6(2) and 6(248) of the new Dutch Civil Code (BW) refer to 'reasonableness and fairness' (*redelijkheid en billijkheid*). This emphasises the objective characteristic of good faith and its relationship with equity and general principles of law. That is to say, good faith is employed as a legal technique for dealing with cases where a strict application of a rule would cause injustice.[37]

However, understanding good faith merely as equity implies that we cannot easily differentiate the technical applications of the principle from its wide moral connotations. Roman judges took equity as justice, and used good faith as insurance against overly strict and uniform application of legal norms that might harm individuals. Today, some jurisdictions (e.g. Swiss law) regulate the general duty of good faith and the power of discretion under different provisions rather than seeing them as interchangeable. Swiss law has particular importance in comparative studies as the Swiss Civil Code contains multiple conscious legal gaps to accommodate different cantonal legal practices. This makes it a well-equipped model for legal receptions and harmonisation projects, as it gives a bigger role to the judge and the normativity of extra-legal systems.

In other words, good faith is important when there is heterogeneity. Its practical importance reminds us that judges follow reality rather than creating it. It emphasises the accommodation of social reality to policy-making without giving the courts too much autonomy. The intricate relationship between equity, the prohibition of abuse of rights, the power of discretion, and good faith illustrates that law sits in social life, inside and outside the court. Ideally, good faith is personified by the whole society, rather than being merely a moral idea of fairness interpreted by the judge.

4. (Old and New) Functions of Good Faith

The contemporary relevance of good faith lies not only in its ability to moralise contractual relations, but also in how it shaped European contract laws. Good faith is like dark matter: invisible, hard to measure, yet everywhere. For the majority of the cases, good faith only functions through its sub-doctrines which have become independent in the complexity of contemporary relations. They are sometimes regulated in special provisions, and sometimes seen as included in the coherent inner system of *bona fides*. For example, German law adopts the general duty of good faith which is applied through a systematic analysis of the categories and sub-categories of its *de facto* applications.[38]

The examples of specific applications of good faith are the prohibition of contradictory behaviour (*venire contra factum proprium*), adaptation of contracts to

37 R. Zimmermann and S. Whittaker, 'Coming to Terms with Good Faith', in Reinhard Zimmermann and Simon Whittaker (eds), *Good Faith in European Contract Law* (Cambridge, UK:Cambridge University Press, 2000), pp. 653–702 (pp. 677–678).

38 Roth, § 242, No 97.

unforeseen circumstances (e.g. doctrines of hardship, *imprévision Wegfall/Störung der Geschäftsgrundlage*), *laesio enormis* (*unfair advantage, lesion/übervorteilung*), obligations of information, clarification, and co-operation, *culpa post pactum perfectum* (post-contractual breach of duties) and so on. One reason of evaluating good faith as a general principle is to establish its connection with its sub-doctrines, to understand and apply them to contemporary questions which requires a higher legal consciousness.

Good faith has been making contract laws evolutive, expansive, dynamic, and universal. But its dynamism had also created shortcomings. Deriving from a subjective value system, history is full of examples of how good faith was instrumentally used to justify decisions taken in specific eras. The wide power of discretion of judges makes it open to personal biases, as in the end it is the judge who has to evaluate honesty, loyalty, and reasonableness, which are psychological and social phenomena. Its dynamism is favourable especially when there is constant change in the techno-social paradigm which requires us to re-calibrate contract laws.[39] This is particularly important today where the global market place pragmatically needs special tools to stabilise transactions and help solving problems posed by this pluralistic and complex atmosphere.[40] Good faith is about balance, and expediency is required when and if it is directly applied. Such direct application can only be *ultima ratio* (the last resort), where there is a manifest, gross, and intolerable breach of the requirements of equity and contractual fairness.

Again, this goes back to Roman praetorian law which had three distinct functions. Its purpose was to clarify vague statutory norms, to supplement them in case of a need, and to adjust them to the necessities of the time.[41] *Bona fides* played a major role in fulfilling these functions in the classical era. The contemporary reflections of good faith mirrors Roman law once again. Good faith is used in interpretation, supplementation, and correction of law. As they are inevitably interlinked, they sometimes overlap.[42] Good faith either determines the content of the obligations of the parties or guides the judge in the interpretation of such obligations. It might even impose new obligations that are not laid down in the contract.

First, since medieval Europe *bona fides* has been acknowledged as a principle of interpretation above all. Today the principle of good faith is applied in the interpretation of the contracts either by statutory provisions (e.g. German BGB §157 and Italian

39 This is especially relevant in the era of digitalisation as the role of good faith and justice are important pillars of market building. On the change of the classical conception of private law see E. J. Weinrib, *The Idea of Private Law* (Oxford: Oxford University Press, 1995); C. U. Schmid, 'The Thesis of the Instrumentalisation of Private Law by the EU in a Nutshell', in C. Joerges and T. Ralli (eds), *European Constitutionalism without Private Law, Private Law without Democracy*, ARENA Report No 3/11, RECON Report No 14 (Oslo: Arena, 2011), pp. 17–27.

40 F. G. Sourgens, *Good Faith in Transnational Law: A Pluralist Account* (Leiden: Brill, 2022), p. 1; Teubner, 'Legal Irritants: Good Faith in British Law or How Unifying Law Ends Up in New Differences'.

41 Papinian suggests that *ius praetorium* operates with *iuris civilis iuvandi, supplendi or corrigendi* causes. D.1.1.7.1.

42 As M. Hesselink argues, applying abstract law to concrete cases necessarily implies creating the law. Hesselink, 'The Concept of Good Faith', pp. 630, 636.

Civil Code Article 1366) or judicial practice (e.g. the Netherlands).[43] In case there is ambiguity, the common intention of the parties is determined based on the meaning that a reasonable party of the same kind would ascribe to it in the same circumstances and whereby to do this, special regard should be given to good faith.[44] In case of a doubt about the meaning of a contractual term which was not individually negotiated, the interpretation is done *contra proferentem*, against the party who supplied the terms.[45]

Second, *bona fides* has been used in supplementing contractual terms. In contractual relationships, parties are not expected to foresee all possible situations and regulate every legal consequence. When the parties do not negotiate on subjective essential points of the contract or negotiate but do not agree on their effect, the contractual gap is filled according to good faith.[46]

Third, *bona fides* aims at rectifying inequitable outcomes caused by the strict application of law. The corrective function of good faith is primarily visible in the historical and modern applications of *exceptio doli*.[47] Good faith acts as a safeguard of party autonomy and contractual fairness. As such, another example of correcting *strictum ius* is the adaptation of the contract to changing circumstances.

In Roman law contractual relationships were seen as *vincula iuris* (legal chains). Yet, the requirements of good faith could sometimes override the explicit will of the parties for the sake of rectifying injustices. In the medieval era, fidelity to contractual relationships and loyalty to promises were theorised under *pacta sunt servanda* (agreements must be kept) as a result of the Christianised reconceptualisation of Roman law. This required the contract to be binding providing the conditions remain same (*clausula rebus sic stantibus*).[48] Following this tradition it is accepted that in case of a disturbance of the contractual equilibrium by the unforeseen change of circumstances which could not reasonably have been taken into account at the time of the conclusion of the contract and which make the performance excessively onerous, the contract is either to be terminated or adapted to new circumstances.[49] In such a case the parties

43 Hesselink, 'The Concept of Good Faith', p. 630.

44 See DCFR II-8:101 and PECL Article 5.101. Available at https://www.trans-lex.org/400725/_/outline-edition-/ and https://www.trans-lex.org/400200/_/pecl/. In Swiss law, this particular application of good faith is known as the doctrinal principle of trust (*Vertrauensprinzip, principe de la confiance*). P. Gauch, W. R. Schluep, and J. Schmid, *Schweizerisches Obligationenrecht Allgemeiner Teil* (Zurich: Schultess, 2003).

45 See DCFR II-8:103; French Civil Code Article 1190; Article 5 Unfair Terms Directive.

46 Gordley, *The Philosophical Origins of Modern Contract Doctrine*, p. 101; V. Arangio-Ruiz, *Istiuzioni Dei Dritto Romano* (Naples: Jovene, 2012), p. 83; DCFR II-9:101.

47 Many European legal systems (e.g. Germany, France, Italy, the Netherlands, Belgium, Switzerland, Spain) consider the prohibition of abuse of rights within the corrective function of good faith. However, in German law it is sometimes considered within the supplementary function of *bona fides* since it only provides negative protection. Hesselink, 'The Concept of Good Faith', pp. 626–627; G. Roth, § 242, No 177; A. Lenaerts, 'The General Principle of the Prohibition of Abuse of Rights: A Critical Position on Its Role in a Codified European Contract Law', *European Review of Private Law* 18 (2010), 1121–1154.

48 Zimmermann, *The Law of Obligations Roman Foundations of the Civilian Tradition*, p. 579. P. Pichonnaz, 'From *clausula rebus sic stantibus* to Hardship: Aspects of the Evolution of the Judge's Role', *Fundamina* 17 (2011), 125–143; Medicus and Petersen, *Allgemeiner Teil des BGB*, p. 20; Roth, § 242, No 431.

49 See PECL 6.111.

are either bound to enter into negotiations or the judge is given the discretion to adapt the contract to new circumstances.[50] The negotiations and adaptation are based on good faith.[51]

The corrective and supplementing functions of good faith directly determine the content of the party obligations derived from the contractual relationship. However, since Roman law *bona fides* has sometimes been an independent source of obligation. It can impose additional and implicit obligations on the parties that are neither explicitly addressed in the contract nor laid down in law.[52] A secondary trust relation between parties emerges when the parties enter into social contact with the intent to enter into a contractual relationship. Ancillary duties such as duties of conduct or protection derive from this relationship.[53]

Such duties might also arise in the pre-contractual stage. For example, the doctrine of *culpa in contrahendo* (breach of post-contractual duties) requires the parties to act in good faith during the bargaining stage, or else they face pre-contractual liability.[54] Even though some national laws do not explicitly regulate pre-contractual liability, it is generally accepted that the party who negotiates or breaks off negotiations contrary to good faith is liable for the losses incurred by the other party.[55] This is usually referred as a *sui generis* legal liability which is independent from the obligations of performance. The moral ground of the doctrine prevents parties from relying on their dishonest, contradictory, and unreasonable conduct. Especially when there is an asymmetrical relationship between parties, the need to secure contractual fairness becomes more prevalent, inside and outside of the court.[56] This is relevant for the duty to negotiate in good faith, as well as for its interpretative, supplementary, and corrective functions.

---

50 E.g. German BGB § 313, Italian Civil Code Article 1467.

51 Under which conditions a pure relationship of trust might override a contractual provision is open to discussion. It is sometimes accepted that good faith imposes a behavioral standard which can override even the clearest provisions of the contract because it is about contractual morality and public order. Nonetheless its effects are still to be considered from the perspective of the freedom of the will. For example, good faith cannot correct nullity. M. J. Bonell, *The Unidroit Principles in Practice* (Leiden: Brill, 2002), p. 60.

52 For example, about an implied duty of honesty in insurance contracts in English law see *HIH Casualty and General Insurance Ltd v Chase Manhattan Bank* [2003] UKHL 6.

53 C. W. Canaris, *Die Vertrauenshaftung im Deutschen Privatrecht* (Munich: Beck, 1971); see also PECL 6.102.

54 R. von Jhering, *Culpa in Contrahendo* (Jena: Friedrich Mauke, 1860).

55 For example, Swiss law considers pre-contractual liability as a requirement of the general duty of good faith. Also see German BGB § 311, Italian Civil Code 1337, Greek Civil Code 197, PECL Article 2. 301, DCFR II 3: 301 and so on. About the nature of the liability see Case C-334/00 *Fonderie Officine Meccaniche Tacconi SpA and Heinrich Wagner Sinto Maschinenfabrik GmbH (HWS)* [2002] ECLI:EU:C:2002:499.

56 Contrary to the civilian tradition, the duty to negotiate in good faith in the pre-contractual stage is still open to discussion in common law tradition. See P. Giliker, 'Pre-contractual Good Faith and the Common European Sales Law: A Compromise Too Far?', *European Review of Private Law* 21.1 (2013), 79–104.

Societal Implications

Seeing Good Faith as a Bundle of Values

The societal importance of good faith lies in its ability to facilitate communication in a pluralistic atmosphere by allowing parties to develop expectations and trust. Its communicative characteristic has driven it further away from being a unified doctrine. In European law good faith has not reflected a unitary concept, rather it has been seen as a bundle of values. In a pragmatic sense, a tripartite classification regarding its major components can be proposed. *Bona fides* requires loyalty, honesty, and reasonableness in contractual relations. Loyalty refers to the fulfilment of promises, whereas honesty as an objectified value requires disclosure of the necessary information that would harm the other party if withheld. For instance, the general duty of disclosure in European contract law derives from good faith.[57] Good faith neither refers to honesty nor loyalty in a strict moral sense. Rather, it is an agent of equity in private relations that should be considered through the lens of reason. Reasonableness is a necessary tool used by the courts to test breaches of good faith.[58] It bridges the gap between ethics and social expectations in contractual relationships. It also refers to expediency and avoidance from contradictory behaviour.

In contractual relationships the time and vision of the parties are limited. They might not foresee or cover all the possibilities that can arise during the exercise of the contract. Intents might not be clear, conditions can change, legitimate expectations can be created and then violated. Moreover, these are not isolated from various types of injustices with a social and epistemic nature. The general duty of good faith aims at securing the investment of trust of the parties on each other's actions.[59] It is efficient, as it decreases information, negotiation, drafting, and litigation costs of the parties. In other words, good faith mostly matters before going to the court. As a general principle of European private law good faith may or may not apply to a specific situation, yet it is helpful in the creation of an environment of trust in business relations both in national and transnational settings.[60]

Good faith is sometimes argued to have a purely cooperative nature, imposing an altruistic model of contracting. However, individualism is one of the distinctive characteristics of the European legal thought as heritage of Roman *ius gentium*. As such,

---

57 See DCFR Article II-3:101 (1): 'Duty to disclose information about goods and services (1) Before the conclusion of a contract for the supply of goods or services by a business to another person, the business has a duty to disclose to the other person such information concerning the goods or services to be supplied as the other person can reasonably expect, taking into account the standards of quality and performance which would be normal under the circumstances'. In common law tradition, the general duty of disclosure is usually seen as incompatible with the logic of contract law. See J. Cartwright, *Misrepresentation, Mistake and Non-Disclosure* (London: Sweet and Maxwell, 2019). However particular duties of disclosure such as in fiduciary relationships derive from good faith.

58 See *Yam Seng Pte Limited v. International Trade Corporation Limited* [2013] EWHC 111 (QB).

59 Canaris, *Die Vertrauenshaftung im Deutschen Privatrecht*.

60 Sourgens, *Good Faith in Transnational Law: A Pluralist Account*, p. 225.

Roman *bona fides* has been about setting a moral standard for the rival parties which are expected to act with profit maximisation concerns.[61] Good faith helps find a reasonable balance between rivalry and social cooperation in business and it does so without contradicting Western individualism. Taking good faith as a general principle moves it one step further in this direction today. Its emphasis on trust makes it a matter of public policy as well as linking it to solidarity within the frame of constitutionalisation of private law.[62]

Bona fides is a good example of how European legal history has produced special corrective mechanisms that exist in-between moral and legal realms as antidotes to formalised rule-bound justice. Classical natural law theory (e.g. Grotius, Pufendorf, Locke) did not decouple legal rules from moral goals. Only with the over-emphasised Kantian separation of morals and law, such antinomies started to transform the European legal thought.[63] As such, the moral standards in contract law are reflected in modern statutory positivism as open norms. [64]

In most civil codes *bona fides* is formulated in open norms, which are composed of uncertain phenomenal elements which change over time, space, and across different techno-social paradigms. They require the judge to determine the content of those elements by considering extra-legal disciplines such as economics, sociology, or ethics. Open norms create legal gaps either to be filled by judicial interpretation or by the general duty of research of the judge. They also require a holistic approach towards good faith. However sometimes it is argued that open norm means no norm at all. According to Martijn Hesselink, good faith ceased to be a norm since it assumed a completely open character.[65] In other words, it is vague as a theoretical norm and only becomes concrete as a practical rule system. Nonetheless, the open norm characteristic accommodates good faith to various social relationships and prevents the legal case from being seen as an abstraction from social reality. It opens up space for extra-legal elements and enriches the broader ecology of law. Although its vagueness is the Achilles heel of good faith, it is also why it should remain as an open norm from a historical and philosophical standpoint.

In sum, good faith operates in two forms. When dealing with concrete legal disputes its practical application is secondary and requires a pragmatic case-by-case approach.[66] However, it is societally relevant as a general principle that guides parties through long-term contractual relations in today's complex reality. Such distinction

---

61 Wieacker, 'Foundations of Legal Culture', p. 21, 23.

62 L. A. Barroso and L. P. Sthel, 'The Role of Objective Good Faith in Current Contract Law: For a General Duty of Inter Partes Cooperation and Solidarity', *Journal of Civil Law Studies* 8 (2015), 187–207. About the constitutional role of European private law see C. Mak and B. Kas (eds), *Civil Courts and the European Polity: The Constitutional Role of Private Law Adjudication in Europe* (Oxford: Bloomsbury, 2023).

63 Wieacker, 'Foundations of Legal Culture', p. 24, 25.

64 Ibid.

65 Hesselink, 'The Concept of Good Faith', p. 640.

66 Brownsword, 'Two Concepts of Good Faith', p. 213.

is a result of what good faith is capable of providing and what good faith aims for.[67] Good faith reminds us of the non-binary relationship between the parties, the court, the lawgiver, and society. It is re-contextualised within the internal logic of business relations inside and outside the court. In sum, good faith is still crucial in avoiding the conflicts. This is particularly visible in trade as its vagueness becomes an asset which motivates business actors to avoid entering into disputes in the first place.[68]

Conclusion and Points for Reflection

This chapter argues that it is crucial to analyse good faith in European private law for two primary reasons. First *bona fides* has been the building block of private laws in Europe. This makes a deeper analysis of the application of good faith important both for the national and supranational legislators. As good faith mainly operates through its sub-principles, its ongoing significance is sometimes not visible to the naked eye. Understanding the ethos and historical development of good faith is important in analysing its relation to the discretion of the judge, to equity, and to its sub-doctrines that already became individual and independent principles themselves. This helps us develop a new perspective on the inconsistencies within national legal systems and European private law as a whole.

Second, good faith is flexible enough to give the European legal space the dynamism it needs. It provides a useful way of engagement with different values. A *Digest* fragment attributed to Ulpian states: 'Justice is the constant and perpetual will to give each his own. The rules are these: to live honestly, not to injure others, and to give each other his due'.[69] This fragment summarises *bona fides* well. Discussing how good faith has emerged and been applied in Roman law of contracts requires a retrospective analysis with a modern lens. Otherwise, one could simply deduct the essential elements of good faith throughout European legal history. Good faith refers to honesty, loyalty, and reasonableness. But if we accept this formulation without its complexities, we underestimate why it has been alive for centuries and its relevance for today's challenges. Good faith is a transhistorical example of what social and technological trends shape and are shaped by contract laws.

Roman remedies were crucial in the development of European law because they introduced flexibility in law. As an ethical pathway *bona fides* enabled Roman law to be an open system: letting the jurists respond to the demands of the extra-legal elements such as cross-border trade, social relations, morality, and so on. Today globalism and emerging technologies highlight the role of flexible and general legal principles. This suggests that good faith should be formulated in response to the questions posed by the global legal scene which needs communicative tools that could translate between

67 R. A. Eisenberg, 'Good Faith under the Uniform Commercial Code—A New Look at an Old Problem', *Marquette Law Review* 54 (1971), 1–18 (p. 17); Brownsword, 'Two Concepts of Good Faith', p. 211.

68 Sourgens, *Good Faith in Transnational Law: A Pluralist Account*, p. 10.

69 D.1.1.10.pr.

different interests, values, and discourses. This would make its role visible in the daily life of complex contractual relations, specifically outside of the court, whenever and wherever reality resists law.

Bibliography

Arangio-Ruiz, V., *Istiuzioni Dei Dritto Romano* (Naples: Jovene, 2012)

Barroso, L. A., and L. P. Sthel, 'The Role of Objective Good Faith in Current Contract Law: For a General Duty of Inter Partes Cooperation and Solidarity', *Journal of Civil Law Studies* 8 (2015), 187–207

Bonell, M. J., *The Unidroit Principles in Practice* (Leiden: Brill, 2002)

Brownsword, R., 'Individualism, Cooperativism and an Ethic for European Contract Law', *Modern Law Review* 64.4 (2001), 628–642, http://doi.org/10.1111/1468-2230.00343

Brownsword, R., 'Two Concepts of Good Faith', *J. Contract Law* 7 (1994), 197–208

Buckland, W. W., *A Text Book of Roman Law from Augustus to Justinian* (Cambridge, UK: Cambridge University Press, 1950)

Burdese, A., *Manuale di Diritto Privato Romano* (Turin: UTET, 1969)

Canaris, C. W., *Die Vertrauenshaftung im Deutschen Privatrecht* (Munich: Beck, 1971)

Cartwright, J., *Misrepresentation, Mistake and Non-Disclosure* (London: Sweet and Maxwell, 2019)

Deibel, T. U., 'Corporate Social Responsibility in the Legal Framework of Global Value Chains', *Law and Development Review* 15.2 (2022), 329–356, https://doi.org/10.1515/ldr-2021-0098

Deschenaux, H., *Schweizerisches Privarecht II* (Basel: Helbing Lichtenhahn, 1988)

Eisenberg, R. A., 'Good Faith under the Uniform Commercial Code—A New Look at an Old Problem', *Marquette Law Review* 54 (1971), 1–18

Freyburger, G., *Fides: Étude Sémantique et Religieuse Depuis les Origines jusqu'à l'Époque Augustéenne* (Paris: Collection d'Études Anciennes, 1986)

Gallo, F., 'Bona Fides e Ius Gentium', in A. Burdese and L. Garofalo (eds), *Il Ruolo della Buona Fede Oggettiva nell'Esperienza Giuridica Storica e Contemporanea. Atti del Convegno Internazionale di Studi in Onore di Alberto Burdes, Vol II* (Milan: CEDAM, 2003), p. 131

Gauch, P., W. R. Schluep, and J. Schmid, *Schweizerisches Obligationenrecht Allgemeiner Teil* (Zurich: Schultess, 2003)

Giliker, P., 'Pre-contractual Good Faith and the Common European Sales Law: A Compromise Too Far?', *European Review of Private Law* 21.1 (2013), 79–104, https://doi.org/10.54648/ERPL2013003

Gordley, J. 'Good Faith in Contract Law in the Medieval Ius Commune', in R. Zimmermann and S. Whittaker (eds), *Good Faith in European Contract Law* (Cambridge, UK: Cambridge University Press, 2000), pp. 93–117

Gordley, J., *The Philosophical Origins of Modern Contract Doctrine* (Oxford: Clarendon, 1993)

Grundmann, S., 'Between Market and Hierarchy', in S. Grundmann et al. (ed.), *New Private Law Theory: A Pluralist Approach* (Cambridge, UK: Cambridge University Press, 2021), pp. 315–338, https://doi.org/10.1017/9781108760089.019

Hartkamp, A. S., M. W. Hesselink, E. Hondius, C. Mak, and E. Du Perron (eds), *Towards a European Civil Code* (Alphen aan den Rijn: Kluwer Law International, 2011)

Hawthorne, L., 'Relational Contract Theory, Principles of European Contract Law—Long-term Contracts, and the Impact of Implicit Dimensions', *Tydskrif vir Hedendaagse Romeins-Hollandse Reg* 70 (2007), 371–390

Hesselink, M. W., 'The Concept of Good Faith', in A. S. Hartkamp, M. W. Hesselink, E. Hondius, C. Mak, and E. Du Perron (eds), *Towards a European Civil Code* (Alphen aan den Rijn: Kluwer Law International, 2011), pp. 619–650

Horn, N., *Aequitas in den Lehren des Baldus* (Köln: Böhlau, 1968)

Jörs, P., W. Kunkel, and L. Wenger, *Römisches Recht*, 3. Auflage (Berlin: Springer, 1949)

Kaser, M., R. Knütel, and S. Lohsse, *Römisches Privatrecht*, 22. Auflage (Munich: Beck, 2021)

Lando, O., 'Salient Features of the Principles of European Contract Law: A Comparison with the UCC', *Pace Int. Law Rev* 13 (2001), 339–369

Legrand, P., 'Against a European Civil Code', *Modern Law Review* 60 (1997), 44–63

Lenaerts, A., 'The General Principle of the Prohibition of Abuse of Rights: A Critical Position on Its Role in a Codified European Contract Law', *European Review of Private Law* 18 (2010), 1121–1154, https://doi.org/10.54648/erpl2010082

Macaulay, S., 'Non-Contractual Relations in Business: A Preliminary Study', *Am. Soc. Rev.* 28 (1963), 55–67

Macneil, I., 'Reflections on Relational Contract', *Journal of Institutional and Theoretical Economics* 141 (1985), 541–546

Mak, C., and B. Kas (eds), *Civil Courts and the European Polity: The Constitutional Role of Private Law Adjudication in Europe* (Oxford: Bloomsbury, 2023)

Medicus, D., and J. Petersen, *Allgemeiner Teil des BGB* (Heidelberg: C. F. Müller, 2016)

Michaels, R., 'The UNIDROIT Principles as Global Background Law', *Uniform Law Review* 19 (2014), 643–668, https://doi.org/10.1093/ulr/unu033

Monier, R., *Manuel Élémentaire de Droit Romain, Tome II* (Paris: Montchrestien, 1947)

Pichonnaz, P., 'From *clausula rebus sic stantibus* to Hardship: Aspects of the Evolution of the Judge's Role', *Fundamina* 17 (2011), 125–143

Pringsheim, F., 'Aequitas und Bona Fides', *Conferenze per il XIV Centenario delle Pandette* 33 (1931), 183

Pugliese, G., *Istituzioni Di Diritto Romano* (Turin: Giappichelli, 1992)

Schermaier, M. J., 'Bona fides in Roman Contract Law', in R. Zimmermann and S. Whittaker (eds), *Good Faith in European Contract Law* (Cambridge, UK: Cambridge University Press, 2006), pp. 63–92

Schlechtriem, P., *Good Faith in German Law and International Uniform Laws* (Rome: Centro di studi e ricerche di diritto comparato e straniero, 1997)

Schmid, C. U., 'The Thesis of the Instrumentalisation of Private Law by the EU in a Nutshell', in C. Joerges and T. Ralli (eds), *European Constitutionalism without Private Law, Private Law without Democracy*, ARENA Report No 3/11, RECON Report No 14 (Oslo: Arena, 2011), pp. 17–27

Schwenzer, I., and P. Hachem, 'Article 7 of the CISG', in P. Schlechtriem and I. Schwenzer (eds), *Commentary on the UN Convention on the Sale of Goods (CISG)* (Oxford: Oxford University Press, 2016), n.p.

Sourgens, F. G., *Good Faith in Transnational Law: A Pluralist Account* (Leiden: Brill, 2022)

Summers, R. S., 'Good Faith in General Contract Law and the Sales Provision of the Uniform Commercial Code', *Virginia Law Review* 54, (1968), 199–206

Tercier, P., *Traité de Droit Privé Suisse: II/1* (Basel: Helbing Lichtenhahn, 2008)

Tercier, P., and P. Pichonnaz, *Le Droit des Obligations* (Zurich: Schultess, 2012)

Teubner, G., 'Legal Irritants: Good Faith in British Law or How Unifying Law Ends Up in New Differences', *Modern Law Review* 61 (1998), 11–32

Villey, M., *La Formation de la Pensée Juridique Moderne: Cours d'Histoire et de la Philosophie du Droit* (Paris: Montchrestien, 1975)

Watson, A., *Legal Transplants*, 2nd edn (Athens, GA: University of Georgia Press, 1993)

Weinrib, E. J., *The Idea of Private Law* (Oxford: Oxford University Press, 1995)

Wieacker, F., 'Foundations of Legal Culture', trans. by Edgar Bodenheimer, *American Journal of Comparative Law* 38 (1990), 1–29

Wieacker, F., 'Zum Ursprung der Bonae Fidei Iudicia', *ZSS* 80 (1963), 1–41

Zimmermann, R., 'Civil Code and Civil Law: The "Europeanisation" of Private Law within the European Community and the Re-Emergence of a European Legal Science', *ColumJEurL* 63 (1994–95), 73–80

Zimmermann, R., *The Law of Obligations Roman Foundations of the Civilian Tradition* (Oxford: Oxford University Press, 1996), https://doi.org/10.1093/acprof:oso/9780198764267.001.0001

Zimmermann, R., and S. Whittaker, 'Coming to Terms with Good Faith', in Reinhard Zimmermann and Simon Whittaker (eds), *Good Faith in European Contract Law* (Cambridge, UK: Cambridge University Press, 2000), pp. 653–702

Zimmermann, R., and S. Whittaker (eds), *Good Faith in European Contract Law* (Cambridge, UK: Cambridge University Press, 2006)

7. Concepts of Ownership in European Property Law: Centralising the Social Function of Ownership

Eva Vermeulen

Abstract

This chapter delves into European property law, explaining its meaning and fundamentals. It demonstrates how three key legal concepts of ownership coexist in European property law: 'dominium ownership' rooted in classical liberalism, 'economic ownership' that stems from the law and economics movement, and 'social ownership', which embodies the social function of property and aligns with communitarian thought. The chapter identifies that dominium and economic ownership concepts are currently prevalent in European property law, even though they contribute to societal challenges like rising inequality and ecological disaster. In contrast, it posits the ownership concept of social ownership as a less harmful starting point, which could even help in mitigating some of the societal harms at play in Europe. A more central role for social ownership in European property law would align private interests better with societal needs and environmental well-being. The chapter therefore advocates for European property lawyers to integrate the social ownership concept, as well as the broader principles of social property, into their practice, to create a more just European property law.

1. Introduction: What Is European Property Law?

Property law is that part of the law that governs the rights that people have vis-à-vis each other over goods. A defining feature of property rights is that they are absolute, which means that they can be enforced against anyone else.[1] This can be contrasted

1 G. S. Alexander and E. M. Peñalver, *An Introduction to Property Theory* (Cambridge, UK: Cambridge University Press, 2012), p. 2. 'Everyone else' is not completely adequate, as it can be the case that

 https://doi.org/10.11647/OBP.0448.07

with relative rights, which are rights held against specific persons, such as rights out of contract. The absolute character of property law means that there are high stakes at play: it is the law of property that decides who can deploy which powers over goods in the outside world. Because of this distributive and constitutive power, property law is considered to be a controversial, or political topic: it is commonplace that the design, structure, and distribution of property are for national democracies to decide on, and not for the EU or any other supranational organ or Court. This is illustrated by the explicit exclusion of property law matters from the authority of the EU in Article 345 TFEU (Treaty on the Functioning of the European Union), and the wide margin of appreciation that Member States are granted by the European Court of Human Rights in deciding on property matters.[2] Other traditional private law areas, such as contract law, labour law and consumer law, are therefore harmonised to a greater extent at the European level than property law, which is still largely considered to be a domestic matter.[3]

The most important instruments of property law in Europe are thus domestic civil codes and property acts containing rules about goods. Indeed, every European legal system has its own version of property law and ownership, based on a unique mix of political, historical, cultural, and environmental factors.[4] Within Europe, there are two main types of property law: the property law of common law systems on the one hand, and civil law systems on the other. Although both systems can be traced back to Roman law, they have developed rather differently.[5] Because civil law systems mainly have written law in civil codes, their property rules are drafted top-down, in a systematic and structured way. The property law in these countries is often close to exhaustive, structured with the intention to capture all legitimate property relations and conflicts in one legal code. In contrast, common law property systems are primarily based on

---

certain property rights are granted in one legal system and not acknowledged towards the people of that other system. More precise would be to say that property rights can be enforced against most of the other people on the world. NB: not everyone would agree with property rights being absolute as opposed to relative rights. There are strands of property theory that do not really see the difference between property and relative rights, mainly in the economic and realist tradition. T. W. Merrill and H. E. Smith, 'What Happened to Property in Law and Economics?', *The Yale Law Journal* 111.2 (2001), 357–398.

2 See the Consolidated Version of the Treaty on the Functioning of the European Union Article 345 [2008] OJ C115/47. The wide margin of appreciation in the area of property law has been reiterated in many cases brought before the supra-national European Court of Human Rights (ECtHR), such as the relatively recent cases: ECtHR, Grand Chamber, *Béláné Nagy v. Hungary* [13 December 2016] § 113; ECtHR, *Papachela and AMAZON S.A. v. Greece* [3 December 2020] §56.

3 Sjef van Erp recently wrote the following about the domestic attitude towards European property law rules: 'EU law, so it looks like, is not seen by Member States as a tool to effectively protect property rights, but as undesirable interference in their national systems of property law'. S. van Erp, A. Salomons, and B. Akkermans, *The Future of European Property Law* (Munich: Otto Schmidt/De Gruyter European Law Publishers, 2012), pp. 204–205.

4 S. van Erp, 'European Property Law: A Methodology for the Future', in Reiner Schulze and Hans Schulte-Nölke (eds), *European Private Law—Current Status and Perspectives* (Munich: Otto Schmidt/De Gruyter European Law Publishers, 2011), pp. 227–248; B. Akkermans, 'The Use of the Functional Method in European Union Property Law', *European Property Law Journal* 2.1, 95–118.

5 S. van Erp, 'A Numerus Quasi-Clausus of Property Rights as a Constitutive Element of a Future European Property Law?', *Electronic Journal of Comparative Law* 7.2 (2003), p. 3.

judge-made case law, and have formed their property rules, principles, and concepts bottom-up, on a case-by-case basis.[6]

> This different preference with regards to law-making manifests itself in different structures of property law: whilst in civil law countries the law of property is one unitary system that is applicable to all types of objects (such as land, movable objects, animals and claims), it is split into different categories in common law systems.[7] The common law thus has a more fragmented and flexible approach: there is not one 'property law', but a dynamic set of rules that regulate the relation between goods and humans.

Nonetheless, these common and civil law systems are united in one continent; they are governed not only by their own national property rules but also by supra-national treaties, directives, and human rights documents. The European Convention on Human Rights and Fundamental Freedoms (ECHR) has even ventured to define ownership autonomously from domestic definitions, in Article 1 of its First Protocol, a fact that might seem trivial to us Europeans, but is an extraordinary achievement in the eyes of property lawyers in other parts of the world.[8] Since the human rights of the ECHR need to interact with both common and civil law property regimes in order to be able to create legal effects for European citizens, an abstract and functional concept of ownership was chosen ('possessions').[9] This means that differently defined—but functionally comparable—property rights over goods in European states receive the same fundamental protection. Moreover, states influence one another through legal transplants, harmonisation of legal areas related to property law, and the increasing scope of European human rights law.[10] Hence, even if European countries all have their own property laws and systems, they share commonalities and interconnections.

What, then, is 'European property law'? Posing this question has led to the study and discovering of interesting functional similarities and differences between different property law systems in Europe, but it has not resulted in broader harmonisation of property rules or a comprehensive binding legal instrument on property at the EU

6 It is useful to acknowledge the distinction between common law and civil law systems for clarity. However, the perceived differences between these two legal systems are not as pronounced as commonly thought. For example, judges in civil law jurisdictions frequently engage in law-making through interpretation, and many common law systems possess established written codes, blending characteristics of both systems.

7 Land law in the United Kingdom, for example, is seen as a different category than the category of personal property, which entails consumer goods and claims.

8 A. Lehavi, *Property Law in a Globalizing World* (Cambridge, UK: Cambridge University Press, 2019), pp. 10–12, 27–28

9 The official definition of possessions is often said to be 'covering both "existing possessions" and "assets", including claims, in respect of which the applicant can argue that he or she has at least a "legitimate expectation". "Possessions" include rights "in rem" and "in personam". The term encompasses immovable and movable property and other proprietary interests.' See Registry of the Council of Europe, 'Guide on Article 1 of Protocol No. 1—Protection of Property', *European Court of Human Rights* (31 August 2022), p. 7.

10 There are only three articles of the ECHR invoked more often since 1959 than Article 1 of the First Protocol to the ECHR. See 'Statistics ECHR—Violations by Article and by State 1959–2022', https://www.echr.coe.int/documents/d/echr/stats_violation_1959_2022_eng

level.[11] This is not to say that the field stands still: because the EU has extensive powers with respect to the free movement of goods, services, capital, and persons, all of which necessarily interact with national property laws in important ways, there are quite a few EU law rules that indirectly affect national property laws.[12] A solid 'common core' of 'European property law' is, however, lacking to date. European property law can therefore be defined, for now, as the interplay of national, supra-national, and international laws that govern the relation between individuals over goods in Europe. A family of property systems that show resemblances and share some rules, but also have a strong independent core.

What most European property systems have in common, is that they have instituted one 'most complete' or 'primary' title over a good, which will be referred to as ownership.[13] The right to own, or ownership, is often regarded as the keystone right of property law: it grants the rights holder(s) more powers or authority over a good than all other types of property right. The concept of ownership seems easy to grasp; as a basic social idea it can even be called universal.[14] All over the world, human, but also non-human animals tend to formally or informally categorise things as 'mine', 'yours', and 'ours'.[15] In this more basic sense, ownership is clear and speaks well to the imagination: even in situations that involve no law, one can have a rough sense of what does and should belong to whom.[16]

However, this simple intuition does not always inform one too well with regard to more complex questions. Should land be held in common, or does this lead to wasteful overuse? Is it just if one person privately owns the means of production of a company when only other people are working for it? Can owners legitimately abandon their property? Is it possible to own your own body? On the basis of which principles should property be distributed? These and other normative questions have been the subject

11 B. Akkermans, *The Principle of Numerus Clausus in European Property Law* (doctoral thesis, Maastricht University, 2008), pp. 7–13, https://cris.maastrichtuniversity.nl/en/publications/5f05ac50-733d-45c8-b230-6ff1d83aa8fd; C. von Bar and U. Drobnig, *The Interaction of Contract Law and Tort and Property Law in Europe* (New York: Otto Schmidt/De Gruyter European Law Publishers, 2009).

12 Some examples of EU laws indirectly affecting national property laws include: Article 63 TFEU on Freedom of Movement of Capital, impacting real estate transactions; EU State Aid Rules under Articles 107–109 TFEU, influencing property transactions involving state subsidies; and directives like the Anti-Money Laundering Directive (EU 2015/849) and Mortgage Credit Directive (2014/17/EU), which set standards and requirements in property-related financial transactions.

13 Although there are several other names for the same legal concept (such as 'freehold' or 'fee simple' in common law), ownership has the most universal meaning. Van Erp, 'European Property Law', p. 235.

14 M. Graziadei, 'The Structure of Property Ownership and the Common Law/Civil Law Divide', in M. Graziadei and L. Smit (eds), *Comparative Property Law: Global Perspectives*, Research Handbooks in Comparative Law (Cheltenham: Edward Elgar Publishing, 2017), pp. 71–99 (p. 73).

15 L. C. Becker, 'The Moral Basis of Property Rights', *Nomos* 22 (1980), 187–220 (p. 199, 212); A. I. Hallowell, 'The Nature and Function of Property as a Social Institution', in Hallowell, *Culture and Experience* (Philadelphia, PN: University of Pennsylvania Press, 1955), pp. 236–249.

16 Illustrative is the large and old body of psychological literature, proving that all types of species have possessive customs. E. Beaglehole, *Property: A Study in Social Psychology* (London: Psychology Press, 2015); L. W. Kline and C. J. France, 'The Psychology of Ownership', *The Pedagogical Seminary* 6.4 (1899), 421–470.

of ongoing political-philosophical and legal-theoretical debate, and they continue to be relevant, especially in periods that are characterised by technological progress or social and environmental challenges.

The following section provides a broad introduction to three different concepts of ownership that are used in European property law.[17] To do so, it first delves into the property theories that underly them. It then shows how they are reflected in current European property law. It will be argued that these concepts of ownership co-exist: European legal systems, and the EU legal system as a whole, have a mix of all three concepts of ownership incorporated at the same time.

2. Legal Context: Three Concepts of Ownership and their Coexistence in European Property Law

Property theory is a sub-category of legal theory that aims to justify and conceptually clarify property rights. It holds the middle ground between (political)-philosophical theories of property and pure property doctrine in that it aims to connect philosophical and normative arguments to legal practice.

> Property theory tends to discuss 'property' as a broad institution, rather than discussing it as a narrow legal area in a purely doctrinal sense. While property law is often a clearly delineated part of private law that—especially in civil law countries—can be found in a specific part of the civil code, property as a legal institution is a broader category, that concerns the allocation of material resources more generally, a function that clearly transcends the private law alone. Property as an institution is thus established and shaped just as much by constitutional property clauses as it is in public law limitations to private entitlements and government or European policy.

I will discuss three strands of property theory.[18] To give a brief and comprehensible introduction to the different property theories, I will contrast and discuss them in their archetypal form.[19] Because this chapter focuses on concepts of ownership, I will focus on their account of that one, most-encompassing keystone right in particular. Three features will be addressed. The first one is their justification of ownership. How does the property theory justify having a system that grants some people ownership over goods, what values are at its foundation and which form should this system take to be justified? The second step delves into the ontology of ownership: how does the property theory explain or define property, of which building blocks does it think ownership exists? Note that these two questions are interrelated: the reason for

17 There are also large internal differences within the property theories that will be discussed below, especially when looking at a more detailed level.

18 These three property concepts are based on the three property theories I discuss in my dissertation, which is forthcoming. See E. Vermeulen, *Dimensions of Inequality and Legal Property Design: The Case of Dutch Housing* (doctoral thesis, University of Amsterdam, forthcoming).

19 In reality, these movements frequently emerged as responses to each other, and the distinctions between them are more nuanced and interconnected than this portrayal suggests, indicating a less clear-cut, black-and-white differentiation.

granting ownership rights will often also dictate the form that the ownership concept has. Also note that these two modes of inquiry are both philosophical and thus external to the law: they do not look at what the law is, but they try to understand the ideas that led to the incorporation of the law. The last and third step moves away from the external angle and looks at how the property theory is implemented in current European property law.

a. Ownership as *Dominium*

Justification: Liberty and Autonomy

The dominium property theory emphasises the importance of having absolute freedom of control over goods. It focuses on private ownership, as opposed to other forms of ownership like collective and public ownership. It justifies property on the basis of the relationship between the holder and a thing: because the entitlement over the thing provides a holder with (more) autonomy and freedom, it must be justified. This line of thinking sprung from classical liberalism, which is the political philosophy promoting individual liberty, property rights, and the rule of law that dominated the West between the eighteenth and twentieth centuries. Well-known philosophers in this line of thinking are John Locke and Immanuel Kant, who both argued that private property can be justified on the basis of the freedom and autonomy it affords to the property holder.[20]

Dominium theory has been the most prominent concept of ownership in Europe since the sixteenth century.[21] It has its origins in Roman law; it owes its name to the Latin word dominium, meaning 'control' or 'ownership'. In Roman law, *dominium* had many forms and types: it did not refer to only one type of ownership. Yet dominium ownership has come to be known as a particular absolute form of ownership: an all-encompassing right to full control.

> The notion of dominium most likely derives its meaning from a famous phrase that William Blackstone, an important English seventeenth-century jurist wrote: '... the right of property; or that sole and despotic dominion[22] which one man claims and exercises over the external things of the world, in total exclusion of the right of any other individual in the universe'.[23]

---

20 Both Locke and Kant argue that the right to property is important because of its contribution to and protection of a pre-existing innate or natural right to liberty or freedom. See J. Locke, *Two Treatises of Government* (Cambridge, UK: Cambridge University Press, 1988); I. Kant, *Kant: The Metaphysics of Morals* (Cambridge, UK: Cambridge University Press, 1996).

21 A. di Robilant, 'Property and Democratic Deliberation: The "Numerus Clausus" Principle and Democratic Experimentalism in Property Law', *The American Journal of Comparative Law* 62.2 (2014), 367–416; A. di Robilant, *The Making of Modern Property: Reinventing Roman Law in Nineteenth Century Europe and Its Periphery* (Cambridge, UK: Cambridge University Press, 2022).

22 *Dominium* and *dominion* share the same meaning: *dominium* is the Latin version of the English *dominion*, which both mean 'lordship'.

23 Sir W. Blackstone, *Commentaries on the Laws of England: Book II: Of the Rights of Things* (Altenmünster:

Ontology: Choice and Full Control

The dominium concept of ownership can best be defined as an indivisible whole of decentralised power. What is conferred upon an owner is a monolithic set of rights that should all be present, together representing the right of choice and full control over a good.[24] Notable is that dominion thinkers mainly take efforts to justify full private ownership and express themselves more rarely about other types of property rights. Since dominium thinkers follow the classical-liberal idea that property is an instrument to protect individuals from interference from both others and the collective, they simply have less interest in discussing other forms. Even though this property theory treats ownership legally as an indivisible whole, to better understand what dominium property theory conceptually makes of ownership, they have elaborated on the elements that should be present for full liberal ownership to exist. In the dominium tradition, often the rights to exclude, use, and transfer are seen as indispensable elements of property. Typical for the dominium school of thought is that it tends to treat ownership over all types of goods as conceptually similar. Being the owner of a bunch of bananas thus in principle comes with the same (broad) set of rights and powers as being the owner of a large corporation, a large dataset, or an apartment complex.[25]

Dominium Ownership in European Property Law

Dominium property theory is probably closest to most lay people's intuition of what property is.[26] This is illustrated by the wording of many of the provisions that institute ownership in European legal systems. Article 903 of the German Civil Code, for instance, states that 'the owner of a thing may, unless the law or the rights of third parties conflict therewith, deal with the thing as he pleases and exclude others from any interference'. Also France and the Netherlands have such 'catch-all' phrases instituting ownership.[27]

In a way, the dominium concept might be said to be the 'default ownership concept' of European legal systems: they start from this rather absolute form of ownership, and then 'undress' or limit that right according to need, type of good, and situation. Yet if

---

Jazzybee Verlag, 2017), p. 1.

24 J. Christman, 'Reinterpreting Property by Margaret Jane Radin', *Ethics* 106.3 (1996), 648; M. J. Radin, 'The Liberal Conception of Property: Cross Currents in the Jurisprudence of Takings', *Columbia Law Review* 88.8 (1988), 1668–1671.

25 E. Rossi, 'Reconsidering the Dual Nature of Property Rights: Personal Property and Capital in the Law and Economics of Property Rights', *SSRN Scholarly Paper* (2020), 19–20

26 This could further explain its prominent representation in the laws of European legal systems. Conversely, it might be that the era of vigorous advocacy for the dominium concept in Europe resulted in contemporary societies perceiving it as the most instinctive approach to understanding ownership. See footnote 20 above.

27 The provision that institutes ownership in the Netherlands (Article 5(1) Civil Code), translates to 'property, in the sense of this section, is the most comprehensive right that a person can have in a thing'.

such an absolute right leads to harmful effects with regard to a specific type of good, or if external political or economic events occur, the government of a state can and will place limitations on the powers of private owners. They can choose to redistribute or choose an alternative type of ownership, like public ownership, but more often they choose to regulate. The more a state limits what owners can do with the goods they own via regulation, the further they move away from dominium ownership. The extent to which ownership over goods is actually regulated in reality in European legal systems is often a matter of politics, and therefore differs highly from country to country.

Another way in which dominium property theory is reflected in European property law is in the protection of property and ownership on the human rights level. In human rights documents, ownership is often protected as a 'first-generation', or 'civil and political' human right. These rights were implemented in human rights documents long before socio-economic rights (which is why they are called first generation rights) and have as their overarching aim to protect citizens from interferences by the government. The human right to property, laid down in Article 1 of Protocol 1 to the ECHR (A1P1), is thus also 'framed' as a right to have one's possession protected from one's government. Instead of protecting or promoting the positive provision of a certain right, such as the socio-economic rights to education, water or housing, ownership is protected only in a 'negative' sense.[28] It does not contain a positive right to acquire property, but only protects existing holdings.[29] The pre-existing relation between a particular property holder and the thing stands central, as opposed to the relation between the holder and other people in its society.

b. Ownership as a Bundle of Efficient Rights

Justification: Welfare Maximisation

Economic property theories instrumentally justify property based on its contribution to the maximisation of total 'welfare' in the world. It finds its roots in the law and economics movement, which, in turn, sprung from the utilitarianism of philosophers like Jeremy Bentham and John Stuart Mill.[30] Utilitarianism is a broad-based philosophical movement that states that rules are morally good if they produce the highest amount of welfare.[31] For utilitarians, welfare is not a notion that we should

28 K. Casla, 'The Right to Property Taking Economic, Social, and Cultural Rights Seriously', *Human Rights Quarterly* 45.2 (2023), 178–180.

29 See the cases ECtHR (Grand Chamber), *Marckx v Belgium* and ECtHR (Grand Chamber), *Anheuser-Busch Inc. v Portugal.*

30 C. Donahue and G. Alexander, 'Property Law', *Encyclopedia Britannica* (27 November 2023), https://www.britannica.com/topic/property-law

31 This type of utilitarianism is called rule-utilitarianism. It addresses the consequences of rules and should not be confused with act utilitarianism, which focuses on the welfare that certain individual acts create. See also Chapter 2 by Martijn Hesselink in this volume.

rationalise objectively, but it is the sum of all people's subjective individual preferences. Economic property proponents therefore find markets a very convenient system, as markets are designed to let people satisfy their own preferences. It is commonplace in the law and economics movement to argue that the maximum amount of welfare can best be reached if the most efficient rules are set.[32] The most efficient rules are the rules with the lowest transaction costs. Transaction costs are necessary costs that parties need to make to be able to trade.[33] By minimising those costs, more wealth remains in total—wealth that whichever party can use to achieve their own subjective form of welfare.

Economic property theorists argue that well-defined or strong private property rights have the best ability to minimise transaction costs by internalising the consequences of the decisions of owners.[34] Contrary to that, other property institutions, such as public and collective property rights, lead to inefficient behaviour. Examples of such behaviour are freeriding and overconsumption; because no one feels personally responsible for an asset or resource, people tend to take less effort and care.[35] This process of internalising externalities can be done by means of instituting ownership, but it does not have to be full ownership per se; as long as it is clear for all the parties on the market what their precise entitlements and ensuing responsibilities are, the internalisation of efficiency effects can take place through various forms of private property.

Ontology: A Bundle of Rights

The economic theory of property conceptualises ownership as a 'bundle of rights' or a 'bundle of sticks'.[36] Nobody knows for sure who coined that now famous notion, but its intellectual history started in the beginning of the twentieth century, when Wesley Hohfeld 'unpacked' legal rights into smaller components that he called correlatives and opposites.[37] The economic property version of the bundle of rights reads that property is nothing more than the right to 'carry out a circumscribed list of actions'.[38] Property rights do not have a predetermined form and meaning but are ad hoc collections of powers and rights. Ownership is just one of the optional collections, albeit the most complete one.

This concept of property is convenient for trade and investment: the possibility to create all kinds of different assemblies over goods on the spot leaves more room for

32 R. Cooter and T. Ulen, *Law and Economics*, 6th edn (Berkeley, CA: Berkeley Law Books, 2016), pp. 4–7.
33 R. H. Coase, 'The Problem of Social Cost', *The Journal of Law and Economics* 56.4 (2013), 837–877.
34 H. Demsetz, 'Toward a Theory of Property Rights', *The American Economic Review* 57.2 (1967), 347–359.
35 Also known as 'the tragedy of the commons'. G. Hardin, 'The Tragedy of the Commons', *Science* 162.3859 (13 December 1968), 1243–1248.
36 Merrill and Smith, 'What Happened to Property in Law and Economics?', p. 359.
37 W. N. Hohfeld, 'Some Fundamental Legal Conceptions as Applied in Judicial Reasoning', *The Yale Law Journal* 23.1 (1913), 16–59.
38 Coase, 'The Problem of Social Cost', p. 44.

'engineering' with entitlements that could lead to more efficient resource allocation. Typical examples of this type of engineering are securitisation, which is the process of taking an illiquid asset, such as a mortgage, and transforming it into tradable securities. Following the economic property rationale, property rights holders should not be barred from creatively disassembling their property rights if that fosters trade possibilities or leads to higher profits.

Just like dominium theorists, economic property theorists will generally favour a relatively free market, as they argue that free markets often spur competition, efficiency, and economic growth.[39] Nevertheless, most economic property theorists will be less averse to governmental regulation or limitation of ownership than dominium theorists are. After all, completely free markets can lead to market failures and other inefficiencies, in which case it can make economic sense to limit ownership in an effort to decrease such inefficiencies.

Economic Ownership in European Property Law

It has been said that economic property has had a bigger influence on common property law than it has had on the civil law.[40] The bundle of rights approach to property law is indeed most explicitly reflected in the national law, legal education, and legal practice of Great Britain, where it can be found in the fragmented structure of property law that was mentioned before, but also in the mentality of common lawyers: common lawyers and judges are attracted more to efficiency argumentation than civil lawyers, who tend to be more inclined towards moral or principled legal arguments.[41]

Nevertheless, economic thinking has also had a major influence on European private law—including European property law. The use of the efficiency criterion can be found in governmental policies that promote the functioning and growth of their domestic economic markets, but also in policies that foster the European internal market. The basic idea that is incorporated here is one that springs from the economic property concept of ownership, namely the idea that limitations to ownership hinder trade—and will therefore lead to less economic growth.[42] The idea is that regulating or limiting ownership will distort the owner's behaviour on the market, making it harder for them and other market actors to satisfy their own preferences. Creating all kinds of limitations to ownership also makes trading more complex for market participants, which will increase transaction costs: potential buyers need more information to be sure about the best deal or purchase, for which they have to invest time or incur costs.[43]

39 Cooter and Ulen, *Law and Economics*, p. 103.

40 U. Mattei and R. Pardolesi, 'Law and Economics in Civil Law Countries: A Comparative Approach', *International Review of Law and Economics* 11.3 (1991), 265–275.

41 van Erp, 'European Property Law: A Methodology for the Future.'

42 The background rationale of law and economics is that people should be able to trade as freely as possible and that this will cause the economy to grow. Limitation to the ownership is often related to the transferability of objects, which will make it harder to trade and thus will lead to a decline in economic growth.

43 T. W. Merrill and H. E. Smith, 'Optimal Standardization in the Law of Property: The Numerus Clausus

Governments should therefore aim to regulate ownership as little as possible, and if they do there is a strong preference for only regulating via taxes, a measure which is seen to distort relatively little.[44] This idea can be found in the design of many national welfare states that are based on free markets and progressive taxation, but also in the broader design of the EU, which is committed to minimising barriers to markets for goods, people, capital, and services in order to promote welfare across the EU.

The economic concept of ownership is also reflected in the case law of the ECtHR. The Court identifies interests as property (or 'possessions', in their terminology) not necessarily based on their inclusion in a legal Act or Code, but primarily if they hold significant economic value.[45] This interpretation of ownership, encompassing any reasonably secure right over an asset with value, resonates with the broader understanding of property rights espoused by economic property scholars, often referred to as random use rights. The broad interpretation has even led to the recognition of economically valuable interests as private property, which many countries might not traditionally classify as property, such as the 'legitimate expectation' to obtain an asset.[46] The broadening of the scope of what can be considered eligible for property protection is a strategic move that not only acknowledges but also incentivises trade and the pursuit of welfare.

c. Ownership as a Social Function

Justification: Community and Solidarity

There is a third property theory, that emphasises that property rights are not just about the individual's control and use of their assets, but also about the responsibilities and the impact that the ownership and use of property rights have on society as a whole.[47] This property theory, that I will call social property theory here, argues that property rights like ownership should fulfil, above all, a social function. Ownership in this property theory is social ownership: it is not merely about freedom or efficiency, but also about thinking about others. Social owners carry a responsibility to use their

---

Principle', *The Yale Law Journal* 110.1 (2000), 1–70 (p. 5); Merrill and Smith, 'What Happened to Property in Law and Economics?', 385–388. For a counterclaim to this argument, see: L. S. Underkuffler et al., *The Idea of Property: Its Meaning and Power* (Oxford: Oxford University Press, 2003), pp. 37–51.

44 L. Kaplow and S. Shavell, 'Why the Legal System Is Less Efficient than the Income Tax in Redistributing Income', *The Journal of Legal Studies* 23.2 (1994), 667–681.

45 See, for instance, the case ECtHR (Grand Chamber), *Anheuser-Busch Inc. v Portugal*, 73049/01 [11 January 2007], §§ 72, 76, and 78. T. Allen, 'Liberalism, Social Democracy and the Value of Property under de European Convention of Human Rights', *International and Comparative Law Quarterly* 59.4 (2010), 1055–1078.

46 This happened in the case ECtHR, *Pine Valley Developments Ltd and Others v Ireland*.

47 P. Babie and J. Viven-Wilksch, 'Léon Duguit and the Propriété Function Sociale', in P. Babie and J. Viven-Wilksch (eds), *Léon Duguit and the Social Obligation Norm of Property: A Translation and Global Exploration* (Singapore: Springer, 2019), pp. 1–32; A. Cordeiro Santos and R. Ribeiro, 'Bringing the Concept of Property as a Social Function into the Housing Debate: The Case of Portugal', *Housing, Theory and Society* 39.4 (2022), 464–483.

property in ways that are beneficial, or at least not harmful, to the community and society.[48]

Seeing property as a social function is often traced back to Leon Duguit, the Frenchman who coined the concept in the early 20th century.[49] Instead of simply focusing on the protection of property titles (because of their contribution to freedom of wealth), the social function of property movement understood property as shaping and reflecting social relationships.[50] The theory of the social function of property argued that individual property rights must be balanced against the rights and needs of the community. This can involve considerations like environmental protection, urban planning, and a just distribution of resources.

Duguit's ideas did not align strictly with one single political-philosophical movement. His theories were rooted in a form of social positivism and were influenced by the French sociological jurisprudence movement in his time.[51] His emphasis was on social solidarity in actual law, which placed him somewhat outside the conventional categories of more abstract political-philosophical movements. Nevertheless, one could say that social property theory is closely associated with various political-philosophical movements, particularly those that emphasise the interconnectedness of individual rights and social responsibilities, such as communitarianism and Aristotelian philosophy based on human flourishing.[52]

---

48 The movement known as progressive property theory in Anglo-American legal circles serves as a functional counterpart to the social function of property theory. Emerging in the United States shortly after the turn of the century, this school of thought views property as a dynamic institution. It is anchored in the belief that property should uphold and advance a range of fundamental human values. These include the right to life, the safeguarding of physical security, the freedom to acquire knowledge, the power to make choices, control over one's life, and the pursuit of wealth, happiness, and broader aspects of individual and communal well-being. In the United States, property theory has traditionally been a more prominent area of academic inquiry compared to Europe. Consequently, the literature from this region offers a richer and more elaborate theoretical exploration of these concepts. G. S. Alexander et al., 'A Statement of Progressive Property', *Cornell Law Review* 94 (2008), 743.

49 L. Duguit, 'Objective Law', *Columbia Law Review* 20.8 (1920), 817–831; L. Duguit, 'Objective Law. II', *Columbia Law Review* 21.1 (1921), 17–34.

50 Alexander et al., 'A Statement of Social Property', p. 743.

51 R. Kolb, 'Politis and Sociological Jurisprudence of Inter-War International Law', *European Journal of International Law* 23.1 (2012), 237–240; See, for an old but still relevant introduction into this school of thought: R. Pound, 'The Scope and Purpose of Sociological Jurisprudence. [Concluded.] III. Sociological Jurisprudence', *Harvard Law Review* 25.6 (1912), 489–516.

52 Progressive property scholars, drawing inspiration from Aristotle's philosophy, often justify the institution of ownership they advocate for through the lens of human flourishing. They argue that to thrive and actively engage in societal life, individuals require ownership of certain (scarce) resources. However, echoing Aristotle's view of humans as inherently social and political beings, these scholars emphasise the necessity of considering the community's needs alongside the value property holds for its owners. This approach advocates for a broader perspective on property use, one that extends beyond individual ownership and includes its contribution to the welfare of the community at large. See G. S. Alexander, 'The Human Flourishing Theory', *Cornell Legal Studies Research Paper Series* 20.2 (2020), n.p.; E. M. Penalver, 'Land Virtues', *Cornell Law Review* 94.4 (2009), 821–888; G. S. Alexander and E. M. Peñalver, 'Properties of Community', *Theoretical Inquiries in Law* 10.1 (2009), 127–160.

Ontology: Social Obligations and Contextuality

The most outstanding feature of the concept of ownership in the social function theory is the emphasis on the duties of the owner next to their rights. Property rights—and private ownership in particular—have social obligations towards the community ingrained.[53] These social obligations can be rather broad, for instance in the form of general redistributive demands or duties for owners to act in accordance with the needs of the community or the collective. But they can also be formulated more narrowly, for instance when they come in the form of duties to accept people roaming over one's private land or to take (extra) care of cultural objects.[54] Depending on the needs of the individual and the community, the scope of the social obligation ingrained in an ownership right can be interpreted as being more general or specific.[55]

On a more general level, it can be said that the social ownership concept is more contextual than dominium and economic ownership: instead of protecting individual formal titles—either because formal ownership titles are seen as relatively inviolable because they are seen as lowering transaction costs, the ownership concept that is promoted by the social function of property movement changes shape and form according to the type of good, the relevant interests and actors, and the community.[56] Ownership that has a social function thus has to take account of many more—and often competing—values. Which entitlement should be protected and to what extent, can thus only be assessed in direct context. This also means that an owner's social duties may be different in different states, communities, and situations.

Social Ownership in European Property Law

The ownership concept of social property theory has been less dominant in European property law and legal literature than dominium and economic ownership.[57] Particularly notable is that property as a social function often manifests itself through public law rules that limit private property rules, rather than being directly incorporated into property law as a private law area. This is owing to the more traditional foundations of European private law, which has long asserted that the principal aim of private property law is to safeguard individual rights and interests, focusing on autonomy and personal choice.[58] As a result, the incorporation of social responsibilities and wider societal considerations into property law typically takes place

---

53 G. S. Alexander, 'The Social-Obligation Norm in American Property Law', *Cornell Law Review* 94 (2008), 760–761.

54 The scope of these social obligations tend to be stronger in Europe compared to the United States. R. Lubens, 'The Social Obligation of Property Ownership: A Comparison of German and U.S. Law', *Arizona Journal of International and Comparative Law* 24.2 (2007), 389–449 (p. 426).

55 G. S. Alexander, *Property and Human Flourishing* (Oxford: Oxford University Press, 2018), pp. 55–62.

56 J. W. Singer, *Entitlement: The Paradoxes of Property* (London: Yale University Press, 2000), p. 147.

57 Despite the European roots of the social function theory of property, the core ideas of social ownership has been more influential in South-America than in Europe. Santos and Ribeiro, 'Bringing the Concept of Property as a Social Function into the Housing Debate'.

58 See also Chapter 1 in this volume.

through public law measures, aimed at striking a balance between individual liberties that are protected by one of the other two ownership concepts and the common good.

Still, the concept of property as a social function is also represented in black-letter European property law. The social obligation norm can, for instance, almost literally be found in Germany's constitution, which reads in Article 14 *GG* (*Grundgesetz*): 'Property entails obligations. Its use shall also serve the common good'.[59] This provision lies at the foundation of several social regulations with regard to goods in Germany, for example in the context of housing. In some municipalities, there are requirements for property developers to include a certain percentage of social housing in new developments or contribute to municipal housing funds.[60] Ownership over housing in Germany has traditionally been regulated in favour of tenants: the majority of owned German houses are rent-controlled, and Germany has instituted a tax system that favours long-term property ownership and discourages speculation. This treatment of homeownership is more social as it increases the chances of non-owners to find housing.[61]

A second more historical example of the integration of social ownership into European property law can be found in Italy's mid-20th century reforms of agrarian property rights.[62] These reforms addressed the imbalanced power dynamics between landlords and agricultural tenants. The traditional *mezzadria* system, where tenants paid rent with a portion of their produce, evolved into a more equitable monetary rent structure, significantly reducing the financial burden on tenants. This burden was henceforth—and rightly so—borne partly by the owner, who was reminded of the social function of their landownership through the reform. This transition thus nicely exemplifies the embedding of social principles into past Italian property law, ensuring fairer agricultural leases.[63]

---

59 *Grundgesetz* [GG], Article 14(2) (F.R.C.).

60 One example of this is Munich's Socially Equitable Land Use Model (SoBoN), a model in which developers who want to build on land zoned for increased density or changed use must allocate a portion of the new living space for social housing. Alternatively, they can make financial contributions to the city's social housing funds. Another example is Stuttgart's model for Affordable Housing, where the city provides land to developers at below-market prices on the condition that they build a certain percentage of social housing units. R. Cucca and C. Ranci, *Unequal Cities: The Challenge of Post-Industrial Transition in Times of Austerity* (Abingdon: Taylor and Francis, 2016), pp. 209–227; A. G. Hansson, 'Inclusionary Housing Policies in Gothenburg, Sweden, and Stuttgart, Germany: The Importance of Norms and Institutions', *Nordic Journal of Surveying and Real Estate Research* 14.1 (2019), 17–24.

61 It is important to contextualise the connection between social housing regulations and Germany's constitutional property clause. Numerous countries have implemented extensive social regulations despite lacking a clause explicitly mandating social obligations for owners. Additionally, it has been argued that the symbolic strength of the German constitutional property right may surpass its practical impact, underlining differences between the U.S. and German property regimes. Lubens, 'The Social Obligation of Property Ownership: A Comparison of German and U.S. Law', p. 448.

62 It is not by chance that these reforms are a good example of social ownership. The group of Italian property scholars who drew them up had adopted much of Duguit's thinking. However, the Italian property law reforms, on the other hand, were driven more by specific socio-economic conditions in Italy, particularly post-World War II. A. di Robilant, 'Property: A Bundle of Sticks or a Tree?', *Vanderbilt Law Review* 66 (n.d.), 908–912.

63 Ibid., pp. 912–14.

3. Prevalent Ownership Concepts and Their Effects on Rising Inequality and Ecological Disaster

The foregoing section gave a brief introduction into three property theories and their concepts of ownership. It revealed how ownership in European property law can be traced back to several political philosophies and legal theories that coexist with each other in contemporary European property law. European property law thus has incorporated a mix of all three concepts.[64] That being said, dominium and economic property theory are prevalent in European property law. That is to say that overall, property provisions and notions of ownership align better with the legal-theoretical backdrops of dominium and economic property theory than they do with property as a social function. This especially holds for the legal property provisions that can be found in the private law domain, as opposed to regulations and policies in the public law domain.

> This is not to suggest that every European legal system shares an identical blend of property ideas and concept of ownership. Indeed, some European systems lean markedly more towards one archetypal interpretation of property, while others veer towards another. Such variation is hardly surprising: over time, diverse social, economic, and (geo)political issues and ideologies have necessitated differing approaches to the notion of ownership, influencing European legal systems in myriad ways. A pivotal moment in shaping an ownership system, for instance, is the shift from a communist to a capitalist framework, a change that has left conspicuous imprints in several Eastern European nations such as Hungary, Bulgaria, Romania, and Ukraine. Other times, certain property concepts stem from historical coincidences or arbitrary legal-theoretical preferences. For instance, the Scandinavian approach to the transfer of ownership in property law differs significantly from that of many other European countries, primarily due to distinct historical and legal events. Unlike unitary systems found in some European nations, such as the United Kingdom and Germany, Scandinavian countries like Sweden, Norway, Denmark, and Finland have developed a functional approach over centuries.[65]

As highlighted in the introduction of this chapter, the concept and structure of ownership wields considerable influence: its design directly impacts both the natural and social environment. In recent years, the concept of private ownership has come under increasing scrutiny for its role in exacerbating certain societal harms. In particular, it is argued that the current design of ownership in European property law is implicated in two major societal challenges of our era: rising inequality and the exacerbation of climate change and ecological disaster.[66]

In the following discussion, I will argue that it is primarily the prevailing ownership

---

64 R. M. Ballardini, J. Kaisto, and J. Similä, 'Developing Novel Property Concepts in Private Law to Foster the Circular Economy', *Journal of Cleaner Production* 279 (2021), 123747, p. 4.

65 K. R. Haug, *Transfer of Movables: A Comparison of the Unitary Approach and the Scandinavian Functional Approach* (doctoral thesis, University of Amsterdam, 2021), https://dare.uva.nl/search?identifier=f24a58e9-e335-4c45-bd23-753caf6670d3

66 K. Pistor, *The Code of Capital; How the Law Creates Wealth and Inequality* (Princeton, NJ: Princeton University Press, 2019); H. Doremus, 'Climate Change and the Evolution of Property Rights', *UC Irvine Law Review* 1.4 (2011), 1092, https://escholarship.org/uc/item/20x9r9hx

concepts that play a significant role in these two prominent societal challenges, rather than the concept of social ownership as advocated in social property theory. I will demonstrate how the dominant notions of ownership in European property law have contributed to these two major social problems precisely by overlooking the social dimension of property.

a. Rising Inequality

The predominant ownership concepts within European property law result in increasing inequality, marked by the extreme concentration of power and wealth. The recent work of Thomas Piketty and Katharina Pistor offers valuable perspectives on the role of property law in perpetuating inequality.

In his first influential book, *Capital in the Twenty-First Century*, Piketty argues that economic inequality, particularly wealth inequality, tends to increase over time due to the rate of return on capital (such as investments and property) exceeding the rate of economic growth.[67] He introduces the concept of the 'r > g' formula, where 'r' represents the rate of return on capital and 'g' represents the rate of economic growth, to explain how wealth accumulates in the hands of a few.[68] This in turn means that wealth is growing faster than income, which leads to high and threatening levels of economic inequality. In his second book, *Capital and Ideology*, he argues that ideologies, including those related to property, influence the distribution of wealth and income.[69] He explores how different ideologies, from feudalism to communism and social democracy, have affected economic structures and inequality.[70] In essence, Piketty thus highlights how the structure of private property rights leads to a disproportionate accumulation of wealth, particularly when protecting capital.[71]

Pistor's work, focusing on the role of private law in wealth accumulation, further elucidates this point. She demonstrates how private law not only protects assets but also actively facilitates their transformation into capital. This was already discussed in Marija Bartl's chapter on European private law and political economy: private actors use the modules of private law to 'code' assets and turn them into capital.[72] Private law provides a lot of space for 'legal engineering', i.e. for cleverly using legal institutions to increase profit and reduce risk.[73] This legal structure benefits existing property holders, creating an entrenched inequality in European societies. The advantage conferred to

67 T. Piketty, *Capital in the Twenty-First Century*, trans. A. Goldhammer (Cambridge, MA: Harvard University Press, 2014).

68 Ibid., p. 571.

69 T. Piketty, *Capital and Ideology* (Cambridge, MA: Harvard University Press, 2020).

70 Piketty also calls these institutions 'property regimes', because at their core they are about how property rights are distributed among a country's various public and private actors. Ibid., pp. 5–6.

71 Piketty himself calls these levels of economic inequality unsustainable, because they tend to correlate with inequality of power and at some point threaten democracy. Piketty, *Capital in the Twenty-First Century*, p. 1.

72 See Chapter 15 in this volume.

73 Pistor, *The Code of Capital; How the Law Creates Wealth and Inequality*, p. 11.

property owners through these legal mechanisms is a key factor in the perpetuation of economic disparities. In a way, one could argue that Katharina Pistor has specified Piketty's claim by explaining how private law, including property law, plays a key role in creating and exacerbating inequality by instituting the rules and entitlements that can be used to create capital.

Property law is one of the most important modules. Ownership of assets provides substantial opportunities for legal engineering, particularly in the context of financial markets.[74] A prime example of this is seen in the handling of mortgage loans by banks. These financial institutions often pool together numerous mortgage loans and then fragment this pool into smaller, distinct entitlements.[75] This process effectively transforms the original asset—the mortgage loans—into a new type of asset, commonly referred to as mortgage-backed securities. These securities offer holders diverse opportunities for capital accumulation. By repackaging and redistributing the ownership rights in this way, banks can create new financial products that appeal to different investors, thereby facilitating the flow of capital and potentially amplifying wealth generation. The process of fragmenting and reassembling entitlements tends to make banks richer—and mortgage holders more at risk. The problem with legal engineering is thus that the unlimited fragmentation of ownership can lead to a loss of control for governments and vulnerable parties. This argument shows how the economic ownership concept, which states that property may be freely 'chopped up into pieces' as long as it benefits the involved private parties' personal preferences, can lead to inequality of power and wealth.

The adherence to traditional ownership concepts such as dominium and the economic property theory in European law thus fuels the processes that Piketty and Pistor describe.[76] Dominium ownership prioritises the freedom and interests of property owners over broader societal needs. Together with the ownership concept of economic property theory, which views property primarily as a tool for wealth generation and accumulation, it stimulates the quest for economic gain, creating a legal environment where wealth begets wealth. Moreover, economic ownership actively promotes the fragmentation of the rights in the property bundle to create more efficient or profitable results. As a result, those already possessing property and capital have a significant advantage, leading to a cycle where wealth and resources are increasingly concentrated in the hands of a few.

One could read into the insights of Piketty and Pistor a call for a critical re-examination of the dominant ownership concepts in European property law.[77] They

74 Ibid., pp. ix–x, 3–5, 23–46, 160.

75 Ibid., pp. 38–45.

76 Especially in his second book Piketty explicitly reflects on the concept of ownership ('property regimes') and argues that the process of wealth accumulation has much to do with our monolithic and absolutist concept of ownership accompanied by an aversion to inheritance and wealth taxes. Piketty, *Capital and Ideology*.

77 That Pistor's book could be a good starting point to rethink EPL has also been suggested by another author of this book, Martijn Hesselink. See M. W. Hesselink, 'Reconstituting the Code of Capital: Could a Progressive European Code of Private Law Help Us Reduce Inequality and Regain Democratic

suggest that the current legal frameworks do not merely reflect socio-economic disparities but also amplify them, calling for legal reforms that reassess the impact of current private law frameworks on wider societal inequality.[78] Since property law is one of the fundamental components of private law and the one that most clearly protects capital and the status quo, the work of Piketty and Pistor thus points to rethinking the structure and implementation of property laws and the regimes in which they are placed, to find a better balance between the interests of property owners with broader social and economic equity. In addition, their findings provide a compelling case for re-evaluating the prevalent ownership concepts used in European property law, as this is necessary to address the underlying causes of inequality in Europe.

b. Ecological Disaster

It is also increasingly recognised that ownership in European property law plays a major role in the creation and sustenance of ecological disaster, like pollution, loss of biodiversity and climate change.[79] The overarching argument is that the current structure and enforcement of European property law, with its focus on exclusive ownership rights and limited accountability, significantly contributes to environmental issues by promoting practices that are ecologically detrimental and resistant to sustainable regulation.

In particular the dominium concept in European property law, with its emphasis on private property and its focus on owners' rights rather than on their duties, has led to significant environmental concerns. This approach grants private natural and legal persons as property owners' considerable autonomy in how they use their land and resources, often resulting in ecologically harmful practices like deforestation and land degradation. Additionally, the framework of dominium tends to limit the accountability of property owners for environmental damage, as the law typically prioritises their rights over broader ecological responsibilities. This legal stance tacitly allows practices that contribute to pollution and climate change.

Examples of harmful consequences of private property rights leading to environmental issues in Europe are plentiful. In the Netherlands, the Tata Steel plant in IJmuiden exemplifies this. Despite environmental regulations, the plant's

---

Control?', *European Law Open* 1 (2022), 316–433.

78 Piketty is the most explicit about which legal reforms are necessary. He suggests that progressive taxation and wealth redistribution policies are necessary to mitigate rising inequality and promote a more equitable society. In his first book he proposes a global wealth tax as a potential solution. In his second book he suggests a participatory form of social democracy, where wealth and political power are more evenly distributed. Pistor discusses some 'roll-back strategies' in her book, in which the power that private actors have creatively appropriated is generally taken back by (international) governments.

79 F. Capra and U. Mattei, *The Ecology of Law: Toward a Legal System in Tune with Nature and Community* (Oakland, CA: Berrett-Koehler Publishers, Inc, 2015); N. Graham, *Lawscape: Property, Environment, Law* (London: Routledge-Cavendish, 2010); K. Bosselmann, 'Property Rights and Sustainability: Can They Be Reconciled?', in D. Grinlinton and P. Taylor (eds), *Property Rights and Sustainability* (The Hague: Brill, 2011), pp. 21–42.

operations, protected under industrial property rights, have significantly polluted the air with fine particulate matter and heavy metals, impacting local air quality and public health.[80] This case highlights the challenges in balancing industrial property rights with environmental and health concerns. Another example is seen in Poland with the Białowieża Forest, one of Europe's last primeval forests. Starting from 2017, property owners in Poland are allowed to cut down trees and shrubs on their land without permits, unless the vegetation is connected to business activities or has special protection status. This change was made to emphasise and expand property owners' rights, eliminating the previous requirement for permits for tree removal, which was seen as excessive interference with private property rights.[81] The increased logging activities have led to notable habitat destruction and biodiversity loss.[82] This situation illustrates the tension between forestry management and environmental conservation, showing how property rights can contribute to deforestation and ecological imbalance when not aligned with sustainable practices.[83]

The economic conception of ownership, if anything, has exacerbated this tension. The possibility to legally engineer one's bundle of private property rights in land tends to lead to land fragmentation. The fragmentation of rights over land, executed via fences, water, and different land use and management can disrupt ecosystems and harm biodiversity, as it may restrict the movement of species, reduce genetic diversity, and hinder natural processes essential for ecological health. In addition, it makes it much harder to coherently environmentally regulate land that ecologically and biologically speaking belong together. The ownership concept of economic property theory moreover prioritises short-term financial gains, which incentivises environmentally unsustainable practices, such as intensive agriculture or unchecked industrial development.[84]

Moreover, (legal) resistance to environmental regulation is ingrained in both ownership concepts. Strong property rights often clash with necessary environmental conservation measures. This means that property owners are hindered in their freedom or profit opportunities, which might lead property owners to oppose restrictions placed on their land use, to which they are legally entitled in European property law, either via Article 1P1 or via a national constitutional property provision. Governments may obviously regulate and limit these harmful uses of land and resources if it is in the public interest, but they will have to consider and balance the public interest with

80 A. Keys, M. Van Hout, and B. Daniels, 'Decarbonisation Options for the Dutch Steel Industry', *PBL Netherlands Environmental Assessment Agency* (2019).

81 Piotr Żuk and Paweł Żuk, 'Between Private Property, Authoritarian State and Democracy: Clearing Trees in Cities and Destroying the Białowieża Forest in Poland', *Capitalism Nature Socialism* 32.2 (2021), 56–60.

82 M. Blicharska and A. Van Herzele, 'What a Forest? Whose Forest? Struggles over Concepts and Meanings in the Debate about the Conservation of the Białowieża Forest in Poland', *Forest Policy and Economics* 57 (2015), 24–25.

83 Żuk and Żuk, 'Between Private Property, Authoritarian State and Democracy', pp. 59–65.

84 Terry W. Frazier, 'The Green Alternative to Classical Liberal Property Theory', *Vermont Law Review* 20 (1996), 299–371.

the strong property rights of the owner.[85] This means that they must always consider whether it is proportionate to restrict a use of property and cannot simply prevent all harmful uses. Unbridled ownership, then, not only contributes to ecological disasters, but also practically hinders possible solutions to it.[86]

The above dynamics between ownership and ecological disaster highlight the need for a re-evaluation of the prevalent concept of ownership in European property law to ensure a balance between property rights and environmental duties for the sake of sustainability.[87] In light of these shortcomings, (property) theorists have critiqued the dominium and economic ownership models for failing to recognise the intrinsic rights of nature.[88] They argue that parts of nature, such as rivers, forests, and ecosystems, should not be viewed as commodities under private or public ownership but should be considered as possessing their own rights, independent of their utility to human interests.[89] Their critique underscores a fundamental flaw in the dominium and economic ownership concepts: their anthropocentric focus and neglect of the natural world's inherent value and the necessity of its protection. Alternative to the concept of granting rights to nature include the idea of 'stewardship', where property owners act as guardians of their land, focusing on sustainable resource use and a responsibility-driven environmental relationship.[90] The 'commons' approach, contests private resource ownership, promoting their communal management for shared and intergenerational benefits. Additionally, integrating sustainability considerations directly into (European) property law is proposed, aiming for the incorporation of social obligations in ownership and legal limits on resource exploitation.[91]

---

85 V. Petersen, 'Constitutional Property Law', in Bram Akkermans (ed.), *Research Agenda in Property Law* (Northampton: Edward Elgar, 2023), pp. 1–3.

86 The point here is not that ecological circumstances are not considered at all in relation to property law. Quite the opposite: ecological circumstances have always been a relevant factor in shaping property law now and in history as they have always been implied in policy choices on (the regulation of) property law. Nevertheless, the principle of private ownership over land or resources still comes with quite a set of inviolable rights, leading to too much space to pollute and harm, and too little to regulate. See J. Robbie and E. van der Sijde, 'Assembling a Sustainable System: Exploring the Systemic Constitutional Approach to Property in the Context of Sustainability', *Loy. L. Rev.* 66 (2020), 553–616; J. Robbie, 'The Nature of Comparing', in B. Akkermans and A. Berlee (eds), *Sjef-Sache 'Essays in Honour of Prof. Mr. Dr. JHM (Sjef) van Erp on the Occasion of His Retirement* (The Hague: Eleven International Publishing, 2021), pp. 17–27; N. Graham, 'Owning the Earth', in P. Burdon (ed.), *Exploring Wild Law: The Philosophy of Earth Jurisprudence* (Cambridge, MA: Wakefield Press: 2011), pp. 259–269; Graham, *Lawscape*.

87 B. Akkermans, 'Sustainable Ownership–New Obligations towards Achieving a Sustainable Society', *European Property Law Journal* 10.2–3 (2021), 277–303; Y. R. Lifshitz, M. Gilboa, and Y. Kaplan, 'The Future of Property', *Cardozo L. Rev.* 44 (2022), 1443; Petersen, 'Constitutional Property Law'.

88 T. Berry (ed.), *The Great Work: Our Way into the Future* (New York: Harmony, 1999), pp. 80–100; M. Maloney, 'Building an Alternative Jurisprudence for the Earth: The International Rights of Nature Tribunal', *Vermont Law Review* 41.1 (2017), 132–133; L. Burgers, 'Private Rights of Nature', *Transnational Environmental Law* 11.3 (2022), 463–474.

89 B. Hoops, 'What If the Black Forest Owned Itself? A Constitutional Property Law Perspective on Rights of Nature', *Transnational Environmental Law* 11.3 (2022), 498–500

90 C. M. Raymond et al., 'The Farmer as a Landscape Steward: Comparing Local Understandings of Landscape Stewardship, Landscape Values, and Land Management Actions', *Ambio* 45 (2016), 173–184.

91 B. Akkermans, 'Sustainable Property Law: Towards a Revaluation of Our System of Property Law', *SSRN Scholarly Paper* (2020), https://doi.org/10.2139/ssrn.3645983; Akkermans, 'Sustainable

4. Conclusion: Time for a More Central Role for Social Ownership?

As the foregoing sector exemplified, the harmful effects in the two examples discussed are mainly caused by the more absolutist or economist interpretations of ownership, and not so much by the ownership conception that is held onto in the social function theory of property. This is no surprise, as I already mentioned that dominium and economic ownership are prevalent conceptions of ownership in European property law, implying that they were better able to shape social reality. This does not mean that social property has not played a role at all; for both the case of rising inequality and ecological disaster, the idea of the social function of property is strongly embedded as a counterweight. It manifests itself in the form of extensive and expanding fields of public law: tax law and environmental law.[92] These fields of law are external to the concept of ownership as such. This means that the concept of social ownership, which makes the social side of property an internal part of (private) property, has been pushed into the background.

This is problematic, as such an approach inherently segregates the responsibility for the human and non-human collective from the rights of ownership, often leading to a dichotomy where private interests can supersede the public good. Indeed, most social ownership theorists are critical of the current societal effects of ownership in European property law and argue that the distributive and sustainability dimension of property should be emphasised more in property law itself.[93] Ownership detached from social responsibilities can foster a narrow pursuit of individual gain, at times to the detriment of wider societal needs, such as environmental conservation and social equity. Hence, by not integrating social obligations into the legal concept of ownership in European property law, a regulatory framework is created that is reactive rather than preventative, addressing issues only after they emerge rather than embedding a sense of collective responsibility from the outset.

Reorienting ownership in European property law towards social ownership would offer viable counterweight to the issues previously discussed. By integrating social responsibilities into the core of property ownership, private interests are aligned with public well-being and will no longer be regarded as interferences with ownership. Therefore, a more central role for social ownership would represent a shift from the dominant individualistic, profit-focused model to a community-centred approach, which will likely lead to more just and sustainable resource management from the

Ownership–New Obligations towards Achieving a Sustainable Society'.

92 This aligns with my earlier remark that an important difference between social property theory and the other two property theories is that social property theory is reflected much more firmly in public law and is therefore mainly framed in terms of *limitations and exceptions to* domination and economic ownership. See above, Section 2.c.

93 Alexander et al., 'A Statement of Social property'; Mulvaney, 'Social property Moving Forward'; L. L. Butler, 'The Pathology of Property Norms: Living Within Nature's Boundaries', *Southern California Law Review* 73 (1999), 927–1015; Underkuffler et al., *The Idea of Property: Its Meaning and Power*.

start. Such a transformation would not only address the limitations of current reactive regulations, but also holds promise to actively steer property use towards prioritising societal and environmental well-being.

Concretely this would mean that the private law of property is changed internally rather than through the public law rules that are externally shaping it. This can be done in a myriad of ways. One is to exclude certain goods that are of high collective importance from private property rights altogether. With regard to rising inequality, one could focus on property law-based redistributive remedies, such as transfer restrictions or choosing different property forms, like common property and lease systems for certain goods. These change the distribution of power and rights, and thus of economic means and opportunities more broadly from the start, as opposed to (public law-based) taxes. A great example of what this could mean in terms of ecological disaster is the idea of rights of nature discussed in Section 3.b. By acknowledging the self-ownership of nature, the legal system can really shift from a paradigm of exploitation to one of stewardship and conservation.[94]

The importance of making changes to the property law system, rather than solely relying on regulatory measures such as tax or environmental laws, stems from the constitutive role property law plays in shaping societal structures and individual rights. Regulatory measures like taxation or environmental regulation, while useful, primarily address the symptoms rather than the root causes of these societal harms. For instance, tax laws can redistribute income but cannot redistribute power or change the basic rules of property ownership. And environmental laws may prescribe how property can be used to protect the environment, but they will not change the fundamental power dynamics and rights associated with property ownership. This preservation of power dynamics allows property owners to continually devise methods that perpetuate societal and environmental harms, stemming from the unchecked drive for self-gain and accumulation inherent in current ownership models. Consequently, regulation remains perpetually reactive, struggling to mitigate these evolving challenges. Moreover, regulatory laws like tax and environmental legislation operate within the framework set by property law and therefore have limited capacity to drive systemic change in these areas.

Social ownership provides a valuable theoretical basis and some important legal-analytical tools for rethinking the role of property law in addressing inequality and climate change. Yet to effectively update the complex, multi-layered, and longstanding European property law system, a thorough, context-aware, and nuanced theoretical framework is essential. Social ownership alone does not provide a detailed blueprint for legal reform. To really centralise the role of social ownership in European property law, it is crucial for both existing and emerging European property lawyers to actively incorporate its principles in their thinking and legal practice. This integration is key to reshaping property law in a way that better aligns with societal needs and environmental sustainability.

---

94 Burgers, 'Private Rights of Nature', p. 474.

5. Points for Reflection

Q1: Is there a 'neutral' way to shape property law and/or ownership? What would that be?

Q2: Which of the three ownership concepts is most intuitive to you? Can you explain why?

Q3: Would it be good if all European countries would have the same ownership concept? If so, why? If not, why not?

Q4: Think of an example of a legal incorporation of the social ownership concept in your own jurisdiction. What do you think of that rule?

Q5: Does it make sense to treat property rights over different goods differently? If so, on the basis of what should we decide that a property right over a certain object should be treated differently?

Q6: Which rights should be held in common? And which rights are better held in private?

Q7: Can you think of disadvantages of giving a more central role to social ownership in European property law?

Q8: How should we govern goods that are now unowned, perhaps even uncovered yet, such as resources in outer space and 'nobody's lands'?

Bibliography

Akkermans, B., 'The Use of the Functional Method in European Union Property Law', *European Property Law Journal* 2.1, 95–118, https://doi.org/10.1515/eplj-2013-0007

Akkermans, B., *The Principle of Numerus Clausus in European Property Law* (doctoral thesis, Maastricht University, 2008), https://cris.maastrichtuniversity.nl/en/publications/5f05ac50-733d-45c8-b230-6ff1d83aa8fd

Akkermans, B., 'Sustainable Property Law: Towards a Revaluation of Our System of Property Law', *SSRN Scholarly Paper* (2020), https://doi.org/10.2139/ssrn.3645983

Akkermans, B., 'Sustainable Ownership–New Obligations towards Achieving a Sustainable Society', *European Property Law Journal* 10.2–3 (2021), 277–303, https://doi.org/10.1515/eplj-2021-0014

Alexander, G. S., 'The Human Flourishing Theory', *Cornell Legal Studies Research Paper Series* 20.2 (2020), n.p., https://dx.doi.org/10.2139/ssrn.3536381

Alexander, G. S., *Property and Human Flourishing* (Oxford: Oxford University Press, 2018), https://doi.org/10.1093/oso/9780190860745.001.0001

Alexander, G. S., 'The Social-Obligation Norm in American Property Law', *Cornell Law Review* 94 (2008), 760–761

Alexander, G. S., et al., 'A Statement of Progressive Property', *Cornell Law Review* 94 (2008), 743

Alexander, G. S., and E. M. Peñalver, *An Introduction to Property Theory* (Cambridge, UK: Cambridge University Press, 2012), https://doi.org/10.1017/CBO9780511978548

Alexander, G. S., and E. M. Peñalver, 'Properties of Community', *Theoretical Inquiries in Law* 10.1 (2009), 127–160

Allen, T., 'Liberalism, Social Democracy and the Value of Property under de European Convention of Human Rights', *International and Comparative Law Quarterly* 59.4 (2010), 1055–1078, https://doi.org/10.1017/S0020589310000448

Babie, P., and J. Viven-Wilksch, 'Léon Duguit and the Propriété Function Sociale', in P. Babie and J. Viven-Wilksch (eds), *Léon Duguit and the Social Obligation Norm of Property: A Translation and Global Exploration* (Singapore: Springer, 2019), pp. 1–32, https://doi.org/10.1007/978-981-13-7189-9_1

Ballardini, R. M., J. Kaisto, and J. Similä, 'Developing Novel Property Concepts in Private Law to Foster the Circular Economy', *Journal of Cleaner Production* 279 (2021), 123747, p. 4, https://doi.org/10.1016/j.jclepro.2020.123747

Beaglehole, E., *Property: A Study in Social Psychology* (London: Psychology Press, 2015), https://doi.org/10.4324/9781315730349

Becker, L. C., 'The Moral Basis of Property Rights', *Nomos* 22 (1980), 187–220,

Berry, T. (ed.), *The Great Work: Our Way into the Future* (New York: Harmony, 1999)

Blackstone, Sir W., *Commentaries on the Laws of England: Book II: Of the Rights of Things* (Altenmünster: Jazzybee Verlag, 2017)

Blicharska, M., and A. Van Herzele, 'What a Forest? Whose Forest? Struggles over Concepts and Meanings in the Debate about the Conservation of the Białowieża Forest in Poland', *Forest Policy and Economics* 57 (2015), 24–25, https://doi.org/10.1016/j.forpol.2015.04.003

Bosselmann, K., 'Property Rights and Sustainability: Can They Be Reconciled?', in D. Grinlinton and P. Taylor (eds), *Property Rights and Sustainability* (The Hague: Brill, 2011), pp. 21–42, https://doi.org/10.1163/ej.9789004182646.i-415

Burgers, L., 'Private Rights of Nature', *Transnational Environmental Law* 11.3 (2022), 463–474, https://doi.org/10.1017/S2047102522000401

Butler, L. L., 'The Pathology of Property Norms: Living Within Nature's Boundaries', *Southern California Law Review* 73 (1999), 927–1015

Capra, F., and U. Mattei, *The Ecology of Law: Toward a Legal System in Tune with Nature and Community* (Oakland, CA: Berrett-Koehler Publishers, Inc, 2015)

Casla, K., 'The Right to Property Taking Economic, Social, and Cultural Rights Seriously', *Human Rights Quarterly* 45.2 (2023), 178–180, https://doi.org/10.1353/hrq.2023.0010

Christman, J., 'Reinterpreting Property by Margaret Jane Radin', *Ethics* 106.3 (1996), 648, https://doi.org/10.1086/233657

Coase, R. H., 'The Problem of Social Cost', *The Journal of Law and Economics* 56.4 (2013), 837–877, http://dx.doi.org/10.1086/674872

Cooter, R., and T. Ulen, *Law and Economics*, 6th edn (Berkeley, CA: Berkeley Law Books, 2016)

Cordeiro Santos, A., and R. Ribeiro, 'Bringing the Concept of Property as a Social Function into the Housing Debate: The Case of Portugal', *Housing, Theory and Society* 39.4 (2022), 464–483, https://doi.org/10.1080/14036096.2021.1998218

Cucca, R., and C. Ranci, *Unequal Cities: The Challenge of Post-Industrial Transition in Times of Austerity* (Abingdon: Taylor and Francis, 2016), https://doi.org/10.1080/02723638.2017.1381537

Demsetz, H., 'Toward a Theory of Property Rights', *The American Economic Review* 57.2 (1967), 347–359

Donahue, C., and G. Alexander, 'Property Law', *Encyclopedia Britannica* (27 November 2023), https://www.britannica.com/topic/property-law

Doremus, H., 'Climate Change and the Evolution of Property Rights', *UC Irvine Law Review* 1.4 (2011), 1092, https://escholarship.org/uc/item/20x9r9hx

Duguit, L., 'Objective Law', *Columbia Law Review* 20.8 (1920), 817–831

Duguit, 'Objective Law. II', *Columbia Law Review* 21.1 (1921), 17–34

Frazier, Terry W., 'The Green Alternative to Classical Liberal Property Theory', *Vermont Law Review* 20 (1996), 299–371

Graham, N., *Lawscape: Property, Environment, Law* (London: Routledge-Cavendish, 2010), https://doi.org/10.4324/9780203847169

Graham, N., 'Owning the Earth', in P. Burdon (ed.), *Exploring Wild Law: The Philosophy of Earth Jurisprudence* (Cambridge, MA: Wakefield Press: 2011), pp. 259–269

Graziadei, M., 'The Structure of Property Ownership and the Common Law/Civil Law Divide', in M. Graziadei and L. Smit (eds), *Comparative Property Law: Global Perspectives*, Research Handbooks in Comparative Law (Cheltenham: Edward Elgar Publishing, 2017), pp. 71–99, https://doi.org/10.4337/9781785369162.00012

Hallowell, A. I., 'The Nature and Function of Property as a Social Institution', in Hallowell, *Culture and Experience* (Philadelphia, PN: University of Pennsylvania Press, 1955), pp. 236–249,

Hansson, A. G., 'Inclusionary Housing Policies in Gothenburg, Sweden, and Stuttgart, Germany: The Importance of Norms and Institutions', *Nordic Journal of Surveying and Real Estate Research* 14.1 (2019), 17–24, https://doi.org/10.30672/njsr.75140

Hardin, G., 'The Tragedy of the Commons', *Science* 162.3859 (13 December 1968), 1243–1248, https://doi.org/10.1126/science.162.3859.1243

Haug, K. R., *Transfer of Movables: A Comparison of the Unitary Approach and the Scandinavian Functional Approach* (doctoral thesis, University of Amsterdam, 2021), https://dare.uva.nl/search?identifier=f24a58e9-e335-4c45-bd23-753caf6670d3

Hesselink, M. W., 'Reconstituting the Code of Capital: Could a Progressive European Code of Private Law Help Us Reduce Inequality and Regain Democratic Control?', *European Law Open* 1 (2022), 316–433, https://doi.org/10.1017/elo.2022.16

Hohfeld, W. N., 'Some Fundamental Legal Conceptions as Applied in Judicial Reasoning', *The Yale Law Journal* 23.1 (1913), 16–59, https://doi.org/10.2307/785533

Hoops, B., 'What If the Black Forest Owned Itself? A Constitutional Property Law Perspective on Rights of Nature', *Transnational Environmental Law* 11.3 (2022), 498–500, https://doi.org/10.1017/S2047102522000322

Kant, *Kant: The Metaphysics of Morals* (Cambridge, UK: Cambridge University Press, 1996), https://doi.org/10.1017/CBO9780511809644

Kaplow, L., and S. Shavell, 'Why the Legal System Is Less Efficient than the Income Tax in Redistributing Income', *The Journal of Legal Studies* 23.2 (1994), 667–681

Keys, A., M. Van Hout, and B. Daniels, 'Decarbonisation Options for the Dutch Steel Industry', *PBL Netherlands Environmental Assessment Agency* (2019)

Kline, L. W., and C. J. France, 'The Psychology of Ownership', *The Pedagogical Seminary* 6.4 (1899), 421–470

Kolb, R., 'Politis and Sociological Jurisprudence of Inter-War International Law', *European Journal of International Law* 23.1 (2012), 237–240, https://doi.org/10.1093/ejil/chs012

Lehavi, A., *Property Law in a Globalizing World* (Cambridge, UK: Cambridge University Press, 2019), https://doi.org/10.1017/9781108595391

Lifshitz, Y. R., M. Gilboa, and Y. Kaplan, 'The Future of Property', *Cardozo L. Rev.* 44 (2022), 1443

Locke, J., *Two Treatises of Government* (Cambridge, UK: Cambridge University Press, 1988)

Lubens, R., 'The Social Obligation of Property Ownership: A Comparison of German and U.S. Law', *Arizona Journal of International and Comparative Law* 24.2 (2007), 389–449

Maloney, M., 'Building an Alternative Jurisprudence for the Earth: The International Rights of Nature Tribunal', *Vermont Law Review* 41.1 (2017), 132–133

Mattei, U., and R. Pardolesi, 'Law and Economics in Civil Law Countries: A Comparative Approach', *International Review of Law and Economics* 11.3 (1991), 265–275, https://doi.org/10.1016/0144-8188(91)90004-W

Merrill, T. W., and H. E. Smith, 'Optimal Standardization in the Law of Property: The Numerus Clausus Principle', *The Yale Law Journal* 110.1 (2000), 1–70, https://doi.org/10.2307/797586

Merrill, T. W., and H. E. Smith, 'What Happened to Property in Law and Economics?', *The Yale Law Journal* 111.2 (2001), 357–398, https://doi.org/10.2307/797592

Penalver, E. M., 'Land Virtues', *Cornell Law Review* 94.4 (2009), 821–888

Petersen, V., 'Constitutional Property Law', in Bram Akkermans (ed.), *Research Agenda in Property Law* (Northampton: Edward Elgar, 2023), pp. 1–3, https://doi.org/10.4337/9781803924816.00008

Piketty, T., *Capital and Ideology* (Cambridge, MA: Harvard University Press, 2020), https://doi.org/10.2307/j.ctv3405w0k

Piketty, T., *Capital in the Twenty-First Century*, trans. A. Goldhammer (Cambridge, MA: Harvard University Press, 2014), https://doi.org/10.2307/j.ctvjnrvx9

Pistor, K., *The Code of Capital; How the Law Creates Wealth and Inequality* (Princeton, NJ: Princeton University Press, 2019), https://doi.org/10.2307/j.ctvc777c1

Pound, R., 'The Scope and Purpose of Sociological Jurisprudence. [Concluded.] III. Sociological Jurisprudence', *Harvard Law Review* 25.6 (1912), 489–516, https://doi.org/10.2307/1324775

Radin, M. J., 'The Liberal Conception of Property: Cross Currents in the Jurisprudence of Takings', *Columbia Law Review* 88.8 (1988), 1668–1671, https://doi.org/10.2307/1122597

Raymond, C. M., et al., 'The Farmer as a Landscape Steward: Comparing Local Understandings of Landscape Stewardship, Landscape Values, and Land Management Actions', *Ambio* 45 (2016), 173–184, https://doi.org/10.1007/s13280-015-0694-0

Registry of the Council of Europe, 'Guide on Article 1 of Protocol No. 1—Protection of Property', *European Court of Human Rights* (31 August 2022)

Robbie, J., 'The Nature of Comparing', in B. Akkermans and A. Berlee (eds), *Sjef-Sache 'Essays in Honour of Prof. Mr. Dr. JHM (Sjef) van Erp on the Occasion of His Retirement* (The Hague: Eleven International Publishing, 2021), pp. 17–27

Robbie, J., and E. van der Sijde, 'Assembling a Sustainable System: Exploring the Systemic Constitutional Approach to Property in the Context of Sustainability', *Loy. L. Rev.* 66 (2020), 553–616

Robilant, A. di, *The Making of Modern Property: Reinventing Roman Law in Nineteenth Century Europe and Its Periphery* (Cambridge, UK: Cambridge University Press, 2022), https://doi.org/10.1017/9781108859844

Robilant, A. di, 'Property: A Bundle of Sticks or a Tree?', *Vanderbilt Law Review* 66 (n.d.), 908–912

Robilant, A. di, 'Property and Democratic Deliberation: The "Numerus Clausus" Principle and Democratic Experimentalism in Property Law', *The American Journal of Comparative Law* 62.2 (2014), 367–416

Rossi, E., 'Reconsidering the Dual Nature of Property Rights: Personal Property and Capital in the Law and Economics of Property Rights', *SSRN Scholarly Paper* (2020), 19–20, https://doi.org/10.2139/ssrn.3659193

Singer, J. W., *Entitlement: The Paradoxes of Property* (London: Yale University Press, 2000)

Underkuffler, L. S., et al., *The Idea of Property: Its Meaning and Power* (Oxford: Oxford University Press, 2003), https://doi.org/10.1093/acprof:oso/9780199254187.001.0001

van Erp, S., 'European Property Law: A Methodology for the Future', in Reiner Schulze and Hans Schulte-Nölke (eds), *European Private Law—Current Status and Perspectives* (Munich: Otto Schmidt/De Gruyter European Law Publishers, 2011), pp. 227–248, https://doi.org/10.1515/9783866539334.227

van Erp, S., 'A Numerus Quasi-Clausus of Property Rights as a Constitutive Element of a Future European Property Law?', *Electronic Journal of Comparative Law* 7.2 (2003)

van Erp, S., A. Salomons, and B. Akkermans, *The Future of European Property Law* (Munich: Otto Schmidt/De Gruyter European Law Publishers, 2012), https://doi.org/10.1515/9783866539310

Vermeulen, E., *Doing Justice to Property: A Capability Theory for Legal Property Design* (doctoral thesis, University of Amsterdam, forthcoming)

von Bar, C., and U. Drobnig, *The Interaction of Contract Law and Tort and Property Law in Europe* (New York: Otto Schmidt/De Gruyter European Law Publishers, 2009), https://doi.org/10.1515/9783866537316

Żuk, Piotr, and Paweł Żuk, 'Between Private Property, Authoritarian State and Democracy: Clearing Trees in Cities and Destroying the Białowieża Forest in Poland', *Capitalism Nature Socialism* 32.2 (2021), 56–60, https://doi.org/10.1080/10455752.2020.1849335

8. Limited Liability through the Lens of Expected Value Analysis[1]

Michael Bakker and Rolef de Weijs

Abstract

The aim of this chapter is to illustrate how limited liability rules enable the transfer of risks and costs away from the shareholders of a corporation to other parties, such as creditors. We illustrate this inherent feature of limited liability by applying expected value analysis, a simple and intuitive analytical framework, to two stylised numerical examples. Subsequently, we briefly discuss several legal strategies that seek to address the externalisation of risks and costs through the corporate form.

1. Introduction: The Limited Liability Corporation

Corporations are omnipresent and their impacts on society are profound in many ways. For one, they are an important driver for wealth creation.[2] The significance of (the 'invention' of) the corporation in this respect was articulated over one hundred years ago by Nicolas Murray Butler:

> [...] the limited liability corporation is the greatest single discovery of modern times [...] Even steam and electricity are far less important than the limited liability corporation, and they would be reduced to comparative impotence without it.[3]

Note that Butler refers to 'the limited liability corporation'. Limited liability is one of the key characteristics of 'the corporate form' in most jurisdictions.[4] The term 'limited

1 Sections of this chapter are based on M. H. C. Bakker and R. J. de Weijs, 'Basic Introduction to Expected Value Analyses and Investments through the Corporate Form', *Amsterdam Law School Research Paper* 2019.4 (2019), https://papers.ssrn.com/abstract_id=3329268

2 I. H.-Y. Chiu, 'Operationalising a Stakeholder Conception in Company Law', *Law and Financial Markets Review* 10.4 (2016), 173–192.

3 N. M. Butler, 'Politics and Business' (The 143rd Annual Banquet of the Chamber of Commerce of the State of New York, New York, 16 November 1911), cited in S. M. Bainbridge, 'Abolishing Veil Piercing', *The Journal of Corporation Law* 26.3 (2001), 479–535.

4 J. Armour et al., 'What Is Corporate Law?', in R. Kraakman and others (eds), *The Anatomy of Corporate*

 https://doi.org/10.11647/OBP.0448.08

liability' is somewhat confusing since it does not refer to any party being only partially liable. In fact, the corporation itself carries full liability, while the directors and shareholders are shielded from direct liability. Instead, this legal concept primarily relates to the position of creditors of the corporation. The most accurate explanation of the concept is that limited liability provides that claims of creditors of the corporation are limited to assets that are owned by the corporation.[5] As such, shareholders (and directors) of the corporation are shielded against claims of creditors of the corporation. In the event of corporate bankruptcy, shareholders, in principle, stand to lose only their initial investments and no more.[6]

Another key characteristic of the corporate form in most jurisdictions is that shares in the corporation are owned by investors who contribute equity capital and receive several rights (and some duties) in return.[7] Importantly, these shareholders are legally entitled to the corporation's residual earnings (i.e. any profits).[8] The position of shareholders as residual claimants in combination with the limited liability rules facilitates and kindles entrepreneurship, which helps explain why the limited liability corporation has been heralded as 'the greatest single discovery of modern times'.[9]

At the same time, however, the privileged position of shareholders can result in an asymmetric pay-off for the shareholders, in the sense that their economic rights vis-à-vis the corporation allow them to profit if the company fares well, while limited liability rules ensure that their losses are capped if the corporation does not survive.[10] This position can potentially give rise to the opportunistic use of corporations.[11] The problem, in essence, is that companies may at the behest of shareholders take excessive

---

Law: A Comparative and Functional Approach (Oxford: Oxford University Press, 2017), pp. 1–28. The other four characteristics are legal personality, shares that are transferable, the management of the organisation being delegated to professional managers, and shares owned by investors that contribute equity capital and receive several rights (and duties) in return.

5 Ibid., p. 8.

6 For example, Articles 2(164) and 2(275) of the Dutch Civil Code (*Burgerlijk Wetboek*), §1 of the German Stock Corporation Act (*Aktiengesetz*), and §13 of the German Limited Liability Company Act (*Gesetz betreffend die Gesellschaften mit beschränkter Haftung*), and Articles L223–1 and L225–1 of the French Commercial Code (*Code de Commerce*).

7 J. Armour et al., 'What Is Corporate Law?', pp. 13–14.

8 See, for instance, Articles 2(105) and 2(216) of the Dutch Civil Code (*Burgerlijk Wetboek*), §58 of the German Stock Corporation Act (*Aktiengesetz*), and §29 of the German Limited Liability Company Act (*Gesetz betreffend die Gesellschaften mit beschränkter Haftung*), and Articles L232–11 and L232–12 of the French Commercial Code (*Code de Commerce*).

9 For a discussion of the rationale for and benefits of limited liability, see *inter alia* F. H. Easterbrook and D. R. Fischel, 'Limited Liability and the Corporation', *The University of Chicago Law Review* 52.1 (1985), 89–117 and S. M. Bainbridge and M. T. Henderson, *Limited Liability: A Legal and Economic Analysis* (Cheltenham: Edward Elgar Publishing, 2016), pp. 47–51.

10 M. Simkovic, 'Limited Liability and the Known Unknown', *Duke Law Journal* 68.2 (2018), 275–332; C. M. Bruner, 'Corporate Governance Reform and the Sustainability Imperative', *Yale Law Journal* 131.4 (2022), 1217–1278.

11 H. Hansmann and R. Kraakman, 'Toward Unlimited Shareholder Liability for Corporate Torts', *Yale Law Journal* 100.7 (1991), 1918; M. G. Faure, 'Environmental Liability of Companies in Europe', *Arizona Journal of International and Comparative Law* 39.1 (2022), 1–152; D. Bruloot, L. De Meulemeester, and C. Van der Elst, 'Veil Piercing and Abuse of the Corporate Form', in H. S. Birkmose, M. Neville, and K. Engsig Sørensen (eds), *Abuse of Companies* (Alphen aan den Rijn: Kluwer Law International, 2019), pp. 159–178.

risks (or too few precautionary measures) or shift (social) costs at the expense of third parties, such as creditors or society more broadly.[12] In this chapter, we numerically illustrate that limited liability rules, by their design, allow for or exacerbate such externalisation of risk and costs. For that purpose, we use expected value analysis (EVA), which is a simple and intuitive analytical tool.

The remainder of this chapter is organised as follows. In Section 2, we will introduce our analytical framework and apply it to the game of roulette by way of an example. Subsequently, in Section 3, we will apply the analytical framework to two stylised numerical examples to illustrate how limited liability rules create a setting where risks and costs may be externalised. In Section 4, we will touch upon several legal strategies that are used to address risk and cost-externalisation through corporations. Finally, we offer some points for reflection in Section 5.

2. Expected Value, Expected Return, and Expected Rate of Return

a. Introduction to the Analytical Framework: EVA

EVA can be employed as a tool to inform decision-making, using probabilities of various potential outcomes. In a financial context, EVA can be employed as a tool to determine the attractiveness of investment opportunities. Three interrelated concepts are important to this analytic framework: expected value, expected return, and expected rate of return. In this section, we provide a brief explanation of these concepts and outline the calculation process. Do not be put off by the formulas. As you read on, the example of a game of roulette will clarify these concepts and formulas.

Expected value, denoted as 'E[V]', is a fundamental but rather simple and intuitive statistical concept. Intuitively and put somewhat crudely, it is what one is expected to get on average. It can be defined as the 'weighted average of the possible outcomes [...], where the weights are the probabilities of that outcome'.[13] Expected value is thus conceptually equivalent to the average, or mean.[14] In the context of investment decision-making, the expected value can be calculated to determine how much an investment will be worth, taking multiple potential states of the world into account.

12 Easterbrook and Fischel, 'Limited Liability'; D. W. Leebron, 'Limited Liability, Tort Victims, and Creditors', *Columbia Law Review* 91.7 (1991), 1565–1650; Bainbridge and Henderson, *Limited Liability*, pp. 47–51; A. M. Pacces, 'Civil Liability in the EU Corporate Sustainability Due Diligence Directive Proposal: A Law and Economics Analysis', *Ondernemingsrecht* 5(2023), 268–276. Furthermore, different conditions and circumstances may exacerbate the externalisation problems. See *inter alia*, Hansmann and Kraakman, 'Toward Unlimited Shareholder Liability for Corporate Torts'; M. K. Polborn, 'Mandatory Insurance and the Judgment-proof Problem', *International Review of Law and Economics* 18.2 (1998), 141–146; J. Armour, G. Hertig, and H. Kanda, 'Transactions with Creditors', in R. Kraakman et al. (eds), *The Anatomy of Corporate Law: A Comparative and Functional Approach* (Oxford: Oxford University Press, 2017), pp. 110–119; Simkovic, 'Limited Liability and the Known Unknown', pp. 289–293; Faure, 'Environmental Liability', p. 1.

13 G. Keller, *Managerial Statistics*, 9th edn (Mason, OH: South-Western Cengage Learning, 2012), p. 65.

14 Ibid., pp. 878–881.

To illustrate, consider a straightforward scenario with two possible future outcomes: one where the investment succeeds and another where it fails. In this context, we can calculate the expected value of the investment using Formula (1):

1. $E[V] = (\text{payoff if success} \times \text{chance of success}) + (\text{payoff if failure} \times \text{chance of failure})$

The formula demonstrates that the outcomes in both scenarios are considered in proportion to the probabilities of their occurrence (i.e. they are weighted). To arrive at the overall expected value of the investment, we sum the values of these two outcomes. The expected value reflects the anticipated future worth of the investment in gross terms, without factoring in the initial investment costs.

The expected return ('E[R]') takes the costs associated with the initial investment into account. The expected return, thus, relates to the anticipated net proceeds (i.e. break-even, profit, or loss) from an investment. Formula (2) shows that it can be calculated by subtracting the initial investment from the expected value of the investment:[15]

2. $E[R] = E[V] - \text{initial investment}$

The expected return is an absolute value,[16] which can make it tricky to compare across various investment opportunities. To enable a more meaningful comparison between different investments, the expected rate of return ('E[RoR]') of an investment can be calculated. Formula (3) demonstrates how this is done: the expected return of the investment is weighted against its initial costs. The expected rate of return is generally presented as a percentage value, hence the multiplication by 100% in this formula.

3. $E[RoR] = \dfrac{E[R]}{\text{initial investment}} \times 100\%$

To get a better grasp of expected value, expected return, and expected rate of return we now illustrate how these concepts work by applying them to the game of roulette.

> Note that *expected* value and *expected* return represent the values which the investor receives *on average* if the investment is made a large number of times, with exactly the same payoffs and probabilities. In other words, it is the long-run average value.[17] However, this is not to say that E[V] or E[R] lose their relevance for individual investment decisions.[18] Also note that in these examples we ignore the time value of money,[19] which is generally an important part of these calculations if an investment has a time horizon of several years.[20] In other words, we do not calculate the net present value ('NPV') of the investment but the expected (future) value of the investment. Furthermore, note that it

15 There is also a quicker manner to calculate the expected return. See Bakker and De Weijs, 'Basic Introduction'.

16 As in: non-relative (we are not referring to modulus).

17 J. H. Stock and M. W. Watson, *Introduction to Econometrics* (New York: Pearson, 2020), p. 65.

18 Keller, *Managerial Statistics*, p. 881.

19 See J. B. Berk and P. M. DeMarzo, *Corporate Finance* (New York: Pearson, 2020).

20 Cf. R. Shapira and L. Zingales, 'Is Pollution Value-Maximizing? The DuPont Case', *ECGI Working Paper Series in Law* 723 (2023).

is possible to work with more than two outcomes/states of the world. In fact, expected value analyses can be rather sophisticated.

b. The Game of Roulette as a Concrete Application of EVA

We now turn to the game of roulette to give a concrete example of the application of EVA. A European roulette wheel consists of 37 compartments that each have a colour and a number. A small ball is launched which can land in any of these compartments. Of the 37 compartments, 18 compartments are black and another 18 compartments are red. The final compartment is green and is labelled '0' (zero). Players have several options when they place a bet. A straightforward course of action is to place a bet on either black or red.

For example, if you were to place a bet of €100 on red. The rules provide that if you win (i.e. the ball lands on any of the 18 red compartments), you double your investment—resulting in €200 in this case—and if you lose (i.e. the ball lands on any of the black compartments *or* the single green compartment), you lose your initial bet of €100. The question then is: is this a good investment, a bad investment, or is a risk-neutral individual indifferent? To answer this question, we can employ EVA. First, we calculate the expected value of the bet (see Formula (1)):

$$\begin{aligned}
&E[V] \text{ of a bet of €100 on red}\\
&= (€200 \times \frac{18}{37}) + (€0 \times \frac{19}{37})\\
&= (€97.30) + (€0)\\
&= €97.30
\end{aligned}$$

Thus, the expected value of the bet is the payoff if the roulette ball lands on any of the 18 red compartments (€200) times the probability that it lands on a red compartment (18 out of 37), plus the payoff if the ball does not land on a red compartment (€0) times the probability that it does not land on a red compartment (19 out of 37). As such, the expected value of the €100 bet on red is €97.30. The expected value, however, does not yet account for the initial investment; it is simply the expected gross future value of the bet. To arrive at the expected return we need to subtract the initial investment from the expected value (see Formula (2)):

$$\begin{aligned}
&E[R] \text{ of a bet of €100 on red}\\
&= €97.30 - €100\\
&= -€2.70
\end{aligned}$$

Thus, the expected return of a bet of €100 on red is minus €2.70. In other words, on average you will lose €2.70 each time you place a €100 bet on red (or black for that matter). Finally, we can calculate the expected rate of return of the bet in question (see Formula (3)):

$$E[RoR] \text{ of a bet of €100 on red} = \frac{-€2.70}{€100} \times 100\% = -2.70\%$$

The expected rate of return is – 2.70%. Placing a bet of €100 on red is an investment with a negative expected (rate of) return. So, in principle, it is not a good investment from the perspective of the player. Put differently and phrased as a rule of thumb, 'the house always wins'. Note that this does not mean that the house wins each time. But in the long run, the house wins.

3. Limited Liability through the Lens of Expected Value Analysis

Now that we have introduced the analytical framework, we will apply it to two simple and stylised numerical examples in order to illustrate that limited liability rules, by their design, create a setting that allows for the externalisation of risk and costs. In the first example, we illustrate that limited liability rules can lead to risk-shifting from shareholders to third parties, most often creditors. The second example illustrates that limited liability rules can exacerbate the externalisation of costs to society.

a. First Example: Externalisation of Risk to Creditors

One way in which risks can be shifted to third parties through the corporate form is if excessive risks are taken at the expense of the corporation's creditors.[21] We will illustrate this dynamic using our first example. For that purpose, we have to compare two scenarios. First, we have to examine a stand-alone investment opportunity, where we ignore limited liability and assume the project is entirely funded by an investor through equity contributions. Second, we look at the same investment opportunity but with two key modifications: the introduction of limited liability and the inclusion of debt financing from external creditors.

The key characteristics of the investment opportunity are as follows. An investor has the option to invest in the development of a solar park. The project requires an investment of €5,000,000. The solar park will be sold upon completion.[22] In case of favourable (market) conditions, the completed solar park is projected to be valued at €6,000,000. However, if (market) conditions are unfavourable, the project will be worth €2,000,000. Due to various factors, including uncertainty surrounding energy prices, the likelihood of success is 70% (and, as such, the expected likelihood of failure is 30%). Using these numbers, we can calculate the expected value of the project itself:

---

21 This is sometimes also characterised as an agency problem. See Hansmann and Kraakman, 'Toward Unlimited Shareholder Liability'; J. Armour, H. Hansmann, and R. Kraakman, 'Agency Problems and Legal Strategies', in R. Kraakman et al. (eds), *The Anatomy of Corporate Law: A Comparative and Functional Approach* (Oxford: Oxford University Press, 2017), pp. 29–48 (p. 30).

22 Note that, as stated previously, we will not be considering the time value of money for this analysis.

$$
\begin{aligned}
&\text{E[V] of the project} \\
&= (\text{value in favourable conditions} \times \text{chance of favourable conditions}) \\
&+ (\text{value in unfavourable conditions} \times \text{chance of unfavourable conditions}) \\
&= (€6{,}000{,}000 \times 70\%) + (€2{,}000{,}000 \times 30\%) \\
&= €4{,}200{,}000 + €600{,}000 \\
&= €4{,}800{,}000
\end{aligned}
$$

So, the project is expected to be worth €4,800,000 upon its completion. However, it is more informative to include the initial investment. In other words, we calculate the expected return of the project:

$$
\begin{aligned}
\text{E[R] of the project} &= \text{E[V] of the project} - \text{initial investment} \\
&= €4{,}800{,}000 - €5{,}000{,}000 \\
&= -€200{,}000
\end{aligned}
$$

Or expressed in percentages:

$$
\begin{aligned}
\text{E[RoR] of the project} &= \text{E[R]} / \text{initial investment} \times 100\% \\
&= \frac{-€200{,}000}{€5{,}000{,}000} \times 100\% \\
&= -4\%
\end{aligned}
$$

Since the expected rate of return of the project is negative (–4%), we can assume that the investor will not invest in this project. However, by altering two key parameters, we come to see that the investor may actually want to invest in this project. Firstly, we incorporate the project. So, there is a legal entity with limited liability, in which case the investor, as a shareholder, is not liable for debts of the corporation. Secondly, we introduce creditors to the capital structure of the corporation. In practice, most corporations are indeed financed by a mix of equity and debt. Creditors of the corporation in question could be *inter alia* suppliers of the solar panels, contractors, or banks.

We now return to the same investment opportunity, but this time, we consider the situation where the project is undertaken through a limited liability corporation, which is partly financed by a loan of €4,000,000 against 10% interest. The remaining required funding for the project is provided by the investor (i.e., the shareholder), amounting to €1,000,000 in equity. Thus, in this setup, the shareholder's investment is lower. But, at the same time, a portion of the revenues is allocated towards servicing interest payments on the loan, and as a result, the investor will receive a smaller share of the project's proceeds. To be more specific, in case of favourable (market) conditions, the value of the corporation's equity, to which the shareholder is entitled, would amount to €1,600,000. The value of the equity under favourable conditions is calculated by taking the value of the project in this case and subtracting the money that needs to be paid to the creditors, being the principal amount as well as the interest:

$$\begin{aligned}&\text{Value of equity in favourable conditions}\\&= \text{project value in favourable conditions} - \text{principal of the loan}\\&\quad - \text{interest payment } (10\%)\\&= €6{,}000{,}000 - €4{,}000{,}000 - €400{,}000\\&= €1{,}600{,}000.\end{aligned}$$

In the event of unfavourable conditions, the equity value of the corporation will be – €2,400,000:

$$\begin{aligned}&\text{Value of equity in unfavourable conditions}\\&= \text{project value in unfavourable conditions} - \text{principal of the loan}\\&\quad - \text{interest payment } (10\%)\\&= €2{,}000{,}000 - €4{,}000{,}000 - €400{,}000\\&= -€2{,}400{,}000.\end{aligned}$$

With limited liability rules in place, the shareholder is in principle not obligated to compensate for negative equity. Therefore, in the event of unfavourable conditions, the shareholder's perspective of the corporation's value is effectively capped at €0. Put differently, if adverse conditions materialise, the shareholder will receive nothing, but it also will not have to bear the negative value of the project (totalling – €2,400,000 in this situation). Using these equity values of the corporation under both scenarios, we can employ EVA to illustrate that limited liability rules and the inclusion of debt financing can reshape the investment decision-making process from the shareholder's perspective. More specifically, we now calculate the E[V], E[R], and E[RoR] for the shareholder:

$$\begin{aligned}&E[V] \text{ for shareholder}\\&= (\text{equity value in favourable conditions} \times \text{chance of favourable conditions})\\&\quad + (\text{equity value in unfavourable conditions} \times \text{chance of unfavourable conditions})\\&= (€1{,}600{,}000 \times 70\%) + (€0 \times 30\%)\\&= €1{,}120{,}000 + €0\\&= €1{,}120{,}000\end{aligned}$$

$$\begin{aligned}E[R] \text{ for shareholder} &= E[V] \text{ for shareholder} - \text{initial investment}\\&= €1{,}120{,}000 - €1{,}000{,}000\\&= €120{,}000\end{aligned}$$

$$\begin{aligned}E[RoR] \text{ for shareholder} &= \frac{E[R] \text{ for shareholder}}{\text{initial investment}} \times 100\%\\&= \frac{€120{,}000}{€1{,}000{,}000} \times 100\%\\&= 6\%\end{aligned}$$

Thus, the expected value, expected return, and expected rate of return of the investment from the shareholder's perspective all shift to positive values. For instance, the expected rate of return is now 6%; an improvement from the initial – 4% in the stand-alone project that we considered first. But it should be emphasised that these figures relate to the investment from the shareholder's perspective. By introducing limited liability rules and including debt in the capital structure, we have neither eliminated any inherent risks from the project nor have we increased its intrinsic value.[23] Instead, there has been a transfer of risk from the shareholder to the creditors of the corporation. To illustrate this, we can calculate the expected value, expected return, and expected rate of return from the perspective of the creditors:

$$
\begin{aligned}
&\text{E[V] for creditors} = \\
&(\text{value of debt in favourable conditions} \times \text{chance of favourable conditions}) \\
&+ (\text{value of debt in unfavourable conditions} \times \text{chance of unfavourable conditions}) \\
&= [(€4{,}000{,}000 + €400{,}000) \times 70\%] + (€2{,}000{,}000^{24} \times 30\%) \\
&= €3{,}080{,}000 + €600{,}000 \\
&= €3{,}680{,}000
\end{aligned}
$$

$$
\begin{aligned}
\text{E[R] for creditors} &= \text{E[V] for creditors} - \text{initial loans} \\
&= €3{,}680{,}000 - €4{,}000{,}000^{25} \\
&= -\,€320{,}000
\end{aligned}
$$

$$
\begin{aligned}
\text{E[RoR] for creditors} &= \frac{\text{E[R] for creditors}}{\text{initial loans}} \times 100\% \\
&= \frac{-\,€320{,}000}{€4{,}000{,}000} \times 100\% \\
&= -\,8\%
\end{aligned}
$$

This stylised example illustrates that limited liability rules by their design allow for a transfer of risk from shareholder to creditor in cases where a corporation faces insolvency in at least one scenario.[26]

b. Second Example: Externalisation of Costs to Society

Another manifestation of the problem that is inherent to limited liability rules is that they can allow for cost-shifting from a corporation to society. The basic idea here is that companies may have an opportunity to impose (social) costs on society—such as polluting a river, emitting greenhouse gases, or benefiting from low-cost child labour—*inter alia* when liability for such harmful action exceeds the corporation's equity.[27] In this case, the corporation is 'judgment-proof'.[28] We illustrate this by way of another

23 Cf. F. Modigliani and M. H. Miller, 'The Cost of Capital, Corporation Finance and the Theory of Investment', *American Economic Review* 48.3 (1958), 261–297.

24 If the project fails, the creditors will be entitled to the assets. Recall shareholders are residual claimants.

25 We do not include the interest here but a case could be made to include it in the calculations.

26 See also Simkovic, 'Limited Liability', p. 306.

27 A. M. Pacces, 'Supply Chain Liability in the Corporate Sustainability Due Diligence Directive Proposal', *Oxford Business Law Blog* (22 April 2022), https://blogs.law.ox.ac.uk/business-law-blog/blog/2022/04/supply-chain-liability-corporate-sustainability-due-diligence. See Shapira and Zingales, 'Is Pollution Value-Maximizing?', for an in-depth study in respect of a specific case of externalisation.

28 Ibid., making reference to S. Shavell, 'The Judgment Proof Problem', *International Review of Law and Economics* 6.1 (1986), 45–58.

stylised numerical example.[29]

A clothing company plans to construct a new factory to produce jeans. Building and operating the factory requires an investment of €10,000,000. For the sake of simplicity, we first assume the project is fully equity financed. The value of the project is expected to amount to €20,000,000. As part of the production process, chemicals are discharged into a river, resulting in environmental and societal damage. This harm is estimated to amount to €30,000,000, which includes clean-up costs and the impact of the released chemicals on the livelihoods and health of the downstream population. The clothing company does not bear and thus internalises these costs unless the affected individuals successfully claim compensation. We assume a 40% likelihood that such claims against the polluter will be instituted and will be successful.

Furthermore, the clothing company has to decide whether to undertake the project within the existing corporation or establish a new subsidiary corporation to carry out the project.[30] We will utilise EVA to compare these two alternatives, which helps us shed light on the potential influence of limited liability rules on investment decisions that involve social costs. We will first calculate the expected value, expected return, and expected rate of return of the project if the clothing company executes the project within the current corporation.

$$
\begin{aligned}
E[V] \text{ of the project} &= \text{value if claim is successful} + \text{value if claim fails} \\
&= [(€20{,}000{,}000 - €30{,}000{,}000) \times 40\%] + (€20{,}000{,}000 \times 60\%) \\
&= -\,€4{,}000{,}000 + €12{,}000{,}000 \\
&= €8{,}000{,}000
\end{aligned}
$$

The expected value of the project is €8,000,000. But this does not yet include the costs associated with building and operating the factory:

$$
\begin{aligned}
E[R] \text{ of the project} &= E[V] \text{ of the project} - \text{investment costs} \\
&= €8{,}000{,}000 - €10{,}000{,}000 \\
&= -\,€2{,}000{,}000
\end{aligned}
$$

Or, expressed as a percentage value:

$$
\begin{aligned}
E[RoR] \text{ of the project} &= \frac{E[R] \text{ of the project}}{\text{investment costs}} \times 100\% \\
&= \frac{-\,€2{,}000{,}000}{€10{,}000{,}000} \times 100\% \\
&= -\,20\%
\end{aligned}
$$

With an expected rate of return of – 20%, the clothing company would typically refrain from pursuing the project. If, however, the clothing company establishes a subsidiary corporation to undertake the project, it will, in its capacity as shareholder of that subsidiary, benefit from limited liability vis-à-vis any creditors of that subsidiary,

---

29 Even though we do not necessarily need EVA to show this numerically, we will employ it to provide another opportunity for practising the application of the analytical framework.

30 In practice, it may also be outsourced to companies entirely separate from the group. Thereby, creating even more (legal) distance from any harmful activities.

including tort creditors. We will now illustrate that the act of incorporating the project itself has the potential to alter the dynamics of the investment decision.

$$
\begin{aligned}
&E[V] \text{ for the shareholder if project is } \textit{incorporated separately}\\
&= \text{value if claim is successful} + \text{value if claims fails}\\
&= (0 \times 40\%) + (€20{,}000{,}000 \times 60\%)\\
&= €0 + €12{,}000{,}000\\
&= €12{,}000{,}000
\end{aligned}
$$

Thus, the total expected value of the project is €12,000,000. We can calculate the expected return by including the initial investment:

$$
\begin{aligned}
&E[R] \text{ for the shareholder if the project is } \textit{incorporated separately}\\
&= E[V] \text{ of the project} - \text{investment costs}\\
&= €12{,}000{,}000 - €10{,}000{,}000\\
&= €2{,}000{,}000
\end{aligned}
$$

Finally, we can calculate the expected rate of return:

$$
\begin{aligned}
&E[RoR] \text{ for the shareholder if the project is } \textit{incorporated separately}\\
&= \frac{E[R] \text{ of the project}}{\text{investment costs}} \times 100\%\\
&= \frac{€2{,}000{,}000}{€10{,}000{,}000} \times 100\%\\
&= 20\%
\end{aligned}
$$

Thus, by creating a subsidiary corporation, the clothing company has turned a project with an expected rate of return of – 20% into a potentially profitable investment, with a positive expected rate of return of 20%. The numerical example, thus, illustrates that an overall negative-value and socially harmful project can be turned into a privately beneficial one by executing the project through a (judgment-proof) subsidiary with limited liability.[31]

4. Legal Strategies to Address Externalisation through the Corporate Form

The stylised examples in the previous section illustrate that limited liability rules create a setting where it can be profitable to use corporations to take excessive risks or to shift costs.[32] In these

31 See for an example of the application of expected value analysis to a real-world case, including time-effects, Shapira and Zingales, 'Is Pollution Value-Maximizing?'. See also Pacces, 'Civil Liability', p. 272.

32 'May' because in practice, a great many other factors are at play. For instance, these problems are more likely to manifest in closely held companies than in publicly listed companies. See Easterbrook and Fischel, 'Limited Liability and the Corporation', pp. 110–111; Armour, Hertig, and Kanda, 'Transactions with Creditors', p. 112. There is some empirical evidence that suggests that limited

instances, liability of the corporation itself is insufficient to deter such behaviour, especially when insolvency looms.[33] In this section, we briefly cover certain company law-based legal strategies that can be employed to address the consequences of limited liability rules that we have illustrated in the preceding section.[34] Our aim is to explore and touch upon how these legal strategies could ensure that costs and risks are internalised. We distinguish between *ex ante* and *ex post* rules as well as who is targeted by these rules. The *ex ante* rules we consider include legal capital rules and mandatory due diligence requirements. The legal strategies relying on *ex post* mechanisms that we discuss involve the liability of shareholders and directors.

a. Legal Capital Requirements

Legal capital rules ensure that shareholders contribute a specified amount of capital which must remain available to the corporation.[35] In essence, such rules establish that there is a financial cushion available to meet the corporation's obligations to third parties. Rules on legal capital can be in the form of minimum capital requirements,[36] constraints on distributions to shareholders (e.g. dividends and share repurchases), and obligations following a serious loss in capital.[37] Legal capital rules can serve as a deterrent to externalising risks through the corporate form since the shareholders' mandatory minimum subscription means that they have more to lose if the company fails.[38] In other words, they have more skin in the game. In current practice, legal capital rules play a very limited role in deterring externalisation. In many jurisdictions, mandatory capital subscriptions are set at relatively low values.[39] Furthermore, the effectiveness of legal capital rules, which are generally bright-line rules, can be diminished if companies engage in financial engineering to circumvent them, such as through complex financial transactions or restructurings.[40]

---

liability does increase an appetite for risk. See P. Akey and I. Appel, 'The Limits of Limited Liability: Evidence from Industrial Pollution', *Journal of Finance* 76.1 (2021), 5–55; Y. Koskinen, N. Nguyen, and J. Ari Pandes, 'Does Limited Liability Matter? Evidence from a Quasi-Natural Experiment', *ECGI Working Paper Series in Finance* 740 (2021), https://papers.ssrn.com/abstract_id=3554101

33 Pacces, 'Civil Liability', p. 271.

34 Traditionally, the argument is—or at least was—that corporate law should not deal with externalities; it should be left to other fields of law such as environmental law or human rights law. Cf. L. Enriques et al., 'The Basic Governance Structure: Minority Shareholders and Non-Shareholder Constituencies', in R. Kraakman et al. (eds), *The Anatomy of Corporate Law: A Comparative and Functional Approach* (Oxford: Oxford University Press, 2017), pp. 79–108 (p. 93). We should mention that, in addition to direct regulation, the two other core solutions to externalities are taxes and the allocation of property rights. See for contractual tools to mitigate the externalisation of risks or costs Armour, Hertig, and Kanda, 'Transactions with Creditors', pp. 112–114.

35 Faure, 'Environmental Liability', p. 47. See more generally on legal capital rules in the EU, M. Gelter and L. Vicente, 'Abuse of Companies through Choice of Incorporation?', in H. S. Birkmose, M. Neville, and K. Engsig Sørensen (eds), *Abuse of Companies* (Alphen aan den Rijn: Kluwer Law International, 2019), pp. 13–33. Some parts of the legal capital rules for public limited companies (not in relation to private limited companies) have been harmonised within the EU.

36 See Faure, 'Environmental Liability', p. 47.

37 Armour, Hertig, and Kanda, 'Transactions with Creditors', pp. 124–127.

38 In addition, some critics argue that these rules may hinder corporate flexibility and entrepreneurial activities. For more detail, see ibid., pp. 125–126, with references.

39 Actually, the current trend is that jurisdictions are doing away with minimum legal capital rules. See ibid., p. 124.

40 Gelter and Vicente, 'Abuse of Companies'.

b. Mandatory Sustainability-Related Due Diligence Requirements

Recently, several jurisdictions, including the European Union,[41] have introduced or are in the process of introducing laws that require companies of certain sizes to conduct due diligence throughout their value chains.[42] Essentially, these regulations mandate in-scope companies to identify, address, and mitigate adverse impacts on the environment and human rights that result from their policies, practices, and products.[43] These requirements can, in the words of Alessio Pacces, 'be interpreted as an attempt to cope with the under deterrence of negative externalities on human rights and the environment depending on the strategic use of limited liability by corporate groups'.[44] As such, these requirements relate to the second example that we discussed in Section 3.b. The exact shape that the enforcement of the due diligence requirements should take is a topic of debate.[45]

c. Liability of Shareholders and Directors of the Corporation

Another method to address or deter (potential) risk- or cost-shifting, particularly when viewed from an economic perspective, is through liability.[46] Apart from the company itself, two actors that may be held accountable are the shareholders and the directors of the corporation.[47] This potential liability becomes acute when the company is insolvent.

Shareholder liability, sometimes referred to as veil piercing, is a legal doctrine that allows courts, under specific circumstances, to essentially and effectively disregard the separate legal identity of a corporation and hold its shareholders personally liable for the corporation's actions or debts.[48] In many jurisdictions, legislators or courts have, in one form or another, developed doctrines that make it possible to pierce the corporate veil if certain conditions are met.[49] Successful veil piercing means that shareholders will, at least to some extent, *ex post* internalise the costs caused by the corporation. However, a difficulty associated with shareholder liability is that it may be challenging for injured parties to successfully prove the necessary conditions for veil piercing, as it generally requires demonstrating a certain standard of knowledge or intent on the part of the shareholder.[50]

---

41 However, at the time of writing, the fate of the European Union initiative in this respect, the proposed Corporate Sustainability Due Diligence Directive (CSDDD), is hanging in the balance.

42 H.-J. de Kluiver, 'Towards a Framework for Effective Regulatory Supervision of Sustainability Governance in Accordance with the EU CSDD Directive. A Comparative Study', *European Company and Financial Law Review* 1 (2023), 203–239.

43 Ibid., p. 221; Pacces, 'Civil Liability', p. 269.

44 Pacces, 'Civil Liability', pp. 268, 271.

45 See, for instance, De Kluiver, 'Towards a Framework', and Pacces, 'Civil Liability'.

46 Pacces (n 11) at p. 270.

47 In relation to directors, we primarily refer to executive directors, who manage the company.

48 Bruloot, De Meulemeester, and Van der Elst, 'Veil Piercing and Abuse', p. 159.

49 See also B. Sjåfjell, A. Johnston, L. Anker-Sørensen, and D. Millon, 'Shareholder Primacy: The Main Barrier to Sustainable Companies', in B. Sjåfjell and B. J. Richardson (eds), *Company Law and Sustainability: Legal Barriers and Opportunities* (Cambridge, UK: Cambridge University Press, 2015), pp. 79–147 (p. 138).

50 See Bruloot, De Meulemeester, and Van der Elst, 'Veil Piercing and Abuse', p. 175, who note that

Directors, too, can be liable for actions or debts of a (bankrupt) corporation under certain circumstances.[51] However, from a conceptual viewpoint, shareholder liability and director liability operate differently in the context of the externalisation of risks and costs through corporations. Directors do not benefit from externalisation through limited liability corporations in the same way or to the same extent as shareholders. So, in the case of director liability, risks and costs are not internalised *per se*. As such, this mechanism simply relies on deterring externalisation through liability risk, without a (substantial) element of internalisation. In essence, by imposing personal liability on directors for breaches of their fiduciary duties or unlawful conduct, the law seeks to discourage them from making decisions that could harm third parties or shift the financial burden to external parties.

5. Conclusion and Points for Reflection

In the introduction to this chapter, we started with a quote that described the limited liability corporation as the greatest invention of modern times. In this chapter, we have used the lens of expected value analysis to illustrate a side-effect of this impactful innovation: the ability to shift risks and costs through limited liability corporations.[52] In a more general sense, the type of analysis used in this chapter to study limited liability facilitates a critical yet nuanced reflection on limited liability rules, as well as the legal strategies that can be employed in order to address externalisation through the corporate form. It allows us to consider how these rules can influence the balance between the distribution of costs and risks on the one hand and rewards on the other.[53] This may be especially helpful given the heightened cognisance of, and concern about, externalities and their ultimate consequences. In conclusion, we offer some points for reflection:

Q1: What are the benefits of limited liability, and for whom?

Q2: If you were to tackle externalities and externalisation of risks and costs through company law, what are the benefits and drawbacks of targeting either the shareholders or directors of corporations?

Q3: If we want to address externalities and externalisation of risks and costs through company law, should we differentiate between publicly listed and closely held (private) companies?

---

jurisdictions diverge as regards the specific standards in this respect, with some jurisdictions requiring other elements.

51 See in more detail, for instance, M. Iannaccone and A. Rosa Adiutori, 'The Liability of Directors and the Abuse of Companies', in H. S. Birkmose, M. Neville, and K. Engsig Sørensen (eds), *Abuse of Companies* (Alphen aan den Rijn: Kluwer Law International, 2019), pp. 141–157.

52 See too G. Dari-Mattiacci, O. Gelderblom, J. Jonkers, and E. C. Perotti, 'The Emergence of the Corporate Form', *Journal of Law, Economics, and Organization* 33.2 (2017), 193–236 (p. 226).

53 See H.-J. de Kluiver, 'Het einde van de rechtspersoonlijkheid: een rechtseconomisch perspectief', in G. van Solinge and others (eds), *Relativering van rechtspersoonlijkheid* (Deventer: Wolters Kluwer, 2013), pp. 87–98.

Q4: How do mandatory sustainability-related due diligence requirements address externalities, and how should these rules be enforced?

Q5: What legal strategies other than the ones discussed in this chapter exist in order to address risk and cost-shifting through limited liability corporations?

Bibliography

Akey, P., and I. Appel, 'The Limits of Limited Liability: Evidence from Industrial Pollution', *Journal of Finance* 76.1 (2021), 5–55, https://doi.org/10.1111/jofi.12978

Armour, J., H. Hansmann, and R. Kraakman, 'Agency Problems and Legal Strategies', in R. Kraakman et al. (eds), *The Anatomy of Corporate Law: A Comparative and Functional Approach* (Oxford: Oxford University Press, 2017), pp. 29–48, https://doi.org/10.1093/acprof:oso/9780198739630.003.0002

Armour, J., G. Hertig, and H. Kanda, 'Transactions with Creditors', in R. Kraakman et al. (eds), *The Anatomy of Corporate Law: A Comparative and Functional Approach* (Oxford: Oxford University Press, 2017), pp. 110–119, https://doi.org/10.1093/acprof:oso/9780198739630.003.0005

Armour, J., et al., 'What Is Corporate Law?', in R. Kraakman and others (eds), *The Anatomy of Corporate Law: A Comparative and Functional Approach* (Oxford: Oxford University Press, 2017), pp. 1–28, https://doi.org/10.1093/acprof:oso/9780198739630.003.0001

Bainbridge, S. M., 'Abolishing Veil Piercing', *The Journal of Corporation Law* 26.3 (2001), 479–535

Bainbridge, S. M., and M. T. Henderson, *Limited Liability: A Legal and Economic Analysis* (Cheltenham: Edward Elgar Publishing, 2016)

Bakker, M. H. C., and R. J. de Weijs, 'Basic Introduction to Expected Value Analyses and Investments through the Corporate Form', *Amsterdam Law School Research Paper* 2019.4 (2019), https://papers.ssrn.com/abstract_id=3329268

Berk, J. B., and P. M. DeMarzo, *Corporate Finance* (New York: Pearson, 2020)

Bruloot, D., L. De Meulemeester, and C. Van der Elst, 'Veil Piercing and Abuse of the Corporate Form', in H. S. Birkmose, M. Neville, and K. Engsig Sørensen (eds), *Abuse of Companies* (Alphen aan den Rijn: Kluwer Law International, 2019), pp. 159–178

Bruner, C. M., 'Corporate Governance Reform and the Sustainability Imperative', *Yale Law Journal* 131.4 (2022), 1217–1278

Chiu, I. H.-Y., 'Operationalising a Stakeholder Conception in Company Law', *Law and Financial Markets Review* 10.4 (2016), 173–192, https://doi.org/10.1080/17521440.2017.1309161

Dari-Mattiacci, G., O. Gelderblom, J. Jonkers, and E. C. Perotti, 'The Emergence of the Corporate Form', *Journal of Law, Economics, and Organization* 33.2 (2017), 193–236, https://doi.org/10.1093/jleo/ewx002

Easterbrook, F. H., and D. R. Fischel, 'Limited Liability and the Corporation', *The University of Chicago Law Review* 52.1 (1985), 89–117

Enriques, L., et al., 'The Basic Governance Structure: Minority Shareholders and Non-Shareholder Constituencies', in R. Kraakman et al. (eds), *The Anatomy of Corporate Law: A Comparative and Functional Approach* (Oxford: Oxford University Press, 2017), pp. 79–108, https://doi.org/10.1093/acprof:oso/9780198739630.003.0004

Faure, M. G., 'Environmental Liability of Companies in Europe', *Arizona Journal of International and Comparative Law* 39.1 (2022), 1–152

Gelter, M., and L. Vicente, 'Abuse of Companies through Choice of Incorporation?', in H. S. Birkmose, M. Neville, and K. Engsig Sørensen (eds), *Abuse of Companies* (Alphen aan den Rijn: Kluwer Law International, 2019), pp. 13–33

Hansmann, H., and R. Kraakman, 'Toward Unlimited Shareholder Liability for Corporate Torts', *Yale Law Journal* 100.7 (1991), 1918

Iannaccone, M., and A. Rosa Adiutori, 'The Liability of Directors and the Abuse of Companies', in H. S. Birkmose, M. Neville, and K. Engsig Sørensen (eds), *Abuse of Companies* (Alphen aan den Rijn: Kluwer Law International, 2019), pp. 141–157

Keller, G., *Managerial Statistics*, 9th edn (Mason, OH: South-Western Cengage Learning, 2012)

Kluiver, H.-J. De, 'Het einde van de rechtspersoonlijkheid: een rechtseconomisch perspectief', in G. van Solinge et al. (eds), *Relativering van rechtspersoonlijkheid* (Deventer: Wolters Kluwer, 2013), pp. 87–98

Kluiver, H.-J. de, 'Towards a Framework for Effective Regulatory Supervision of Sustainability Governance in Accordance with the EU CSDD Directive. A Comparative Study', *European Company and Financial Law Review* 1 (2023), 203–239, https://doi.org/10.1515/ecfr-2023-0010

Koskinen, Y., N. Nguyen, and J. Ari Pandes, 'Does Limited Liability Matter? Evidence from a Quasi-Natural Experiment', *ECGI Working Paper Series in Finance* 740 (2021), https://papers.ssrn.com/abstract_id=3554101

Leebron, D. W., 'Limited Liability, Tort Victims, and Creditors', *Columbia Law Review* 91.7 (1991), 1565–1650

Modigliani, F., and M. H. Miller, 'The Cost of Capital, Corporation Finance and the Theory of Investment', *American Economic Review* 48.3 (1958), 261–297

Pacces, A. M., 'Civil Liability in the EU Corporate Sustainability Due Diligence Directive Proposal: A Law and Economics Analysis', *Ondernemingsrecht* 5 (2023), 268–276, https://doi.org/10.2139/ssrn.4391121

Pacces, A. M., 'Supply Chain Liability in the Corporate Sustainability Due Diligence Directive Proposal', *Oxford Business Law Blog* (22 April 2022), https://blogs.law.ox.ac.uk/business-law-blog/blog/2022/04/supply-chain-liability-corporate-sustainability-due-diligence

Polborn, M. K., 'Mandatory Insurance and the Judgment-proof Problem', *International Review of Law and Economics* 18.2 (1998), 141–146

Shapira, R., and L. Zingales, 'Is Pollution Value-Maximizing? The DuPont Case', *ECGI Working Paper Series in Law* 723 (2023)

Shavell, S., 'The Judgment Proof Problem', *International Review of Law and Economics* 6.1 (1986), 45–58

Simkovic, M., 'Limited Liability and the Known Unknown', *Duke Law Journal* 68.2 (2018), 275–332, https://doi.org/10.2139/ssrn.3121519

Sjåfjell, B., A. Johnston, L. Anker-Sørensen, and D. Millon, 'Shareholder Primacy: The Main Barrier to Sustainable Companies', in B. Sjåfjell and B. J. Richardson (eds), *Company Law and Sustainability: Legal Barriers and Opportunities* (Cambridge, UK: Cambridge University Press, 2015), pp. 79–147, https://doi.org/10.1017/cbo9781107337978.005

Stock, J. H., and M. W. Watson, *Introduction to Econometrics* (New York: Pearson, 2020)

9. Consumers in European Private Law

Joasia Luzak

Abstract

This is an introduction for future students of (European) consumer law to its main concepts, such as average and vulnerable consumers, unfairness, and product risks. Upon reading you may expect to start being able to place this research area within the legal architecture of European private law. You are encouraged to think about the impact of selected issues on consumer protection, including such issues as consumer apathy in enforcing rights, digitalisation, and climate change. Throughout, you are given points for reflection to encourage further reading and help with understanding the content.

1. Introduction: 'Ordinary People'

We're just ordinary people,
We don't know which way to go... (John Legend, 'Ordinary People', 2005)

John Legend's song could describe consumers, at least how scholars perceive them. The perception that consumers are the weaker party in transactions they conclude with traders, that they do not have sufficient access to information or capacities to process the relevant information, persists.[1] It is not unfounded, as a breadth of scholarship on consumer behaviour documents various consumer biases and disadvantages.[2] These studies provide us with ample evidence of the consumers' lack of attention or comprehension, (financial) illiteracy, and gullibility. Such consumer traits could justify deviating from the standards of protection offered in general contract law rules

1 See e.g. H. Luth, *Behavioural Economics in Consumer Policy* (Brussels: Intersentia, 2010); W. Wagner and W. Walker, *Incomprehensible!* (Cambridge, UK: Cambridge University Press, 2019).

2 See e.g. O. Bar-Gill, *Seduction by Contract* (Oxford: Oxford University Press, 2012); O. Ben-Shahar and C. E. Schneider, *More Than You Wanted to Know* (Princeton, NJ: Princeton University Press, 2014); G. Helleringer and A.-L. Sibony, 'European Consumer Protection through the Behavorial Lens', *The Columbia Journal of European Law* 23 (2017), 607–646. Interestingly, consumers tend to think of themselves as smarter than they are, see e.g. CLICKON, 'How Crucial is a Consumer's Self-Concept in Advertising', *CLICKON* (13 August 2019), https://news.clickon.co/how-crucial-is-a-consumers-self-concept-in-advertising

 https://doi.org/10.11647/OBP.0448.09

and adding another layer thereof, applicable to consumer transactions.

Importantly, the internal characteristics of a person do not determine who is a consumer in European private law (EPL). EPL mainly defines consumers as natural persons who are acting for purposes unrelated to their business, craft, or profession.[3] The consumer status is, therefore, attached to the reason behind the conclusion of a particular transaction, rather than the internal characteristics of a person involved therein. In practice, it may not always be easy to differentiate between a purchase of goods or services for private versus professional purposes. A smartphone could be used for private and professional calls, a person could travel for business purposes, but easily extend their trip to include holidays, too. Such mixed purpose contracts tended to be excluded from the scope of consumer protection, unless the professional purpose was negligible at the moment of the contract's conclusion.[4] Recently, the Court of Justice of the European Union (CJEU) extended the scope of consumer protection to mixed purpose contracts by declaring that only when consumers acted exclusively for professional purposes when concluding them, the protections would not apply.[5] Overall, we could question the suitability of the consumer notion adopted in EPL, and its scope of application, if the only purpose of consumer protection measures in EPL was to assure weaker party protection. After all, the actual imbalance of power remains irrelevant, if we do not consider whether consumers are rich or poor, well or poorly educated.[6]

Instead, we find the origins of many of the EPL consumer protection measures in the need to assure a harmonised, well-functioning, cross-border marketplace in the EU.[7] For example, mandatory pre-contractual information obligations could facilitate consumers easier accessing and obtaining that information, and consequently making better-informed transactional decisions. However, such obligations also facilitate comparing offers amongst competitors on the market. This is especially relevant when promoting cross-border transactions, as foreign traders may be less familiar to consumers in a given Member State but may present them with better offers.[8] This double-edged objective of consumer protection measures in EPL is worth considering, when critically assessing their effectiveness.[9]

We could question whether it is at all feasible to grant effective consumer protection, considering how heterogenous consumers in various Member States are and how

3 See e.g. Article 2(1) Directive 2011/83/EU of the European Parliament and of the Council on Consumer Rights [2011] OJ L304/64 (Consumer Rights Directive, CRD).

4 See e.g. Recital 17 CRD; Case C-464/01 *Johann Grubber v Bay WA AG* [2005] ECLI:EU:C:2005:32, paras. 41–50.

5 Case C-485/21 *S.V. (Immeuble en copropriété)* [2022] ECLI:EU:C:2022:839.

6 See e.g. E. Terryn, 'Consumers, by Definition, Include Us All... But Not for Every Transaction', *European Review of Private Law* 24 (2016), 271–286.

7 This can be achieved either by negative or positive integration in the EU. To read further, see Chapter 3 and Chapter 4 in this volume.

8 See Recitals 5–7 CRD.

9 See further e.g. S. de Vries, 'Consumer Protection and the EU Single Market Rules—The Search for the "Paradigm Consumer"', *Journal of European Consumer and Market Law* 4 (2012), 228–242.

many different transactions they conclude.[10] If the protection standard were set at the level of the individual needs of every consumer, this would significantly increase the level of uncertainty for traders. They would then need to examine every consumer's expectation in-depth, before, for example, issuing the pre-contractual information to them. This explains why EPL uses a certain consumer benchmark instead.

Whilst regulating unfair commercial practices, the European legislator introduced the benchmark of an average consumer.[11] This benchmark refers to a reasonably well-informed, observant, and circumspect consumer.[12] Traders may then expect consumers to pay attention to the information they disclose. They may also assume that consumers will ask for any additional explanations. Intuitively, the average consumer benchmark seems reasonable, especially since it may account for national, cultural differences.[13] What leads to questions about its use is the prevalence of research showing consumers suffering from the information overload and highlighting their limited information-processing capabilities (*Point for reflection 1*).[14] This is particularly applicable in the online environment.

The digitalisation of consumer transactions has contributed to the change in the perception of consumer vulnerability.[15] Traditionally, legislators introduced additional protection for vulnerable consumers by determining characteristics that make groups of consumers more susceptible to commercial exploitation, for instance, their mental or physical infirmity, age, or credulity.[16] For example, marketing and selling restrictions may be imposed on consumer products that are harmful to children. Yet, we could also assess vulnerability in a more contextual way. We could identify which external factors expose weaknesses and vulnerabilities in all consumers, instead of focusing on consumers' internal characteristics, which seem to weaken them only compared to

---

10 See e.g. C. Sunstein, *Free Markets and Social Justice* (Oxford: Oxford University Press 1997), p. 284; O. Ben-Shahar and O. Bar-Gill, 'Regulatory Techniques in Consumer Protection: A Critique of European Consumer Contract Law', *Common Market Law Review* 50 (2013), 109–126 (pp. 113–114).

11 Recital 18 Directive 2005/29/EC of the European Parliament and of the Council concerning unfair business-to-consumer commercial practices [2005] OJ L149/22 (Unfair Commercial Practices Directive, UCPD). This benchmark has in practice been applied to other areas of European consumer protection, see e.g. J. Luzak, 'The Steady Creep of an Average Consumer as a Reference Consumer in the Assessment of the Transparent Provision of Mandatory Information', *Tijdschrift voor Consumentenrecht en handelspraktijken* 5 (2020), 265–274.

12 See e.g. Case C-210/96 *Gut Springenheide and Tusky v Oberkreisdirektor des Kreises Steinfurt* [1998] ECLI:EU:C:1998:369, para 31.

13 See e.g. Case C-220/98 *Estée Lauder* [2000] ECLI:EU:C:2000:8, para 29.

14 See e.g. V. Mak, 'Standards of Protection: In Search of the 'Average Consumer' of EU Law in the Proposal for a Consumer Rights Directive', *European Review of Private Law* 19.1 (2011), 25–42; B. Duivenvoorde, *The Consumer Benchmarks in the Unfair Commercial Practices Directive* (Cham: Springer, 2015); H. Schebesta and K. Purnhagen, 'Island or Ocean: Empirical Evidence on the Average Consumer Concept in the UCPD', *European Review of Private Law* 28.2 (2020), 293–310.

15 See e.g. J. Luzak, 'Vulnerable Travellers in the Digital Age', *Journal of European Consumer and Market Law* 3 (2016), 130–135; N. Bol et al., 'Vulnerability in a Tracked Society: Combining Tracking and Survey Data to Understand who gets Targeted with what Content', *New Media and Society* 22 (2020), 1996–2017. See also Chapter 13 in this volume.

16 Article 5(3) UCPD.

other consumers.[17] This approach would follow Fineman's vulnerability theory.[18] For example, online traders tend to have more information about their customers than ever previously, due to the prevalence of algorithm-use and Big Data collection. Hence, the asymmetry in transactional power and balance between traders and consumers is exacerbated online. Consequently, scholars argue that we should perceive all online consumers as vulnerable regardless of their internal characteristics (*Point for reflection* 2).[19]

This short introduction to the notion of 'consumers' in EPL precedes the discussion on issues consumers commonly experience and measures that EPL adopted to remedy the situation (Section 2). Section 3 then illustrates changes that consumers have had to face in the modern market and elaborates on EPL's response to this new societal context.

2. Legal Architecture

The European legislator has competences to enact various consumer protection measures. Article 114 TFEU (Treaty on the Functioning of the European Union) allows adopting consumer protection measures in the ordinary legislative procedure to approximate national rules, harmonising the internal market. Article 169 TFEU further emphasises the need to promote consumers' health, safety, and economic interests, as well as their right to information, education, and to organise themselves to protect their interests. Article 12 TFEU reminds the European legislature to keep consumer protection in mind when drafting various EU policies.

European consumer protection reflects a pointillistic approach to regulation.[20] The European legislator drafted consumer protection measures to address specific issues, usually related to a conclusion of a particular type of a consumer contract. This led to separate pieces of legislation governing, e.g. contracts for: the sale of goods, the supply of digital content, consumer credit or package travel. However, EPL contains also certain horizontal measures, applying to various types of consumer contracts, and this part focuses on such measures. The following sections illustrate how various EPL measures address issues that consumers commonly experience: information asymmetry, unfairness, product risks, and apathy when enforcing their rights.

---

17 See e.g. N. Helberger et al., 'EU Consumer Protection 2.0. Structural Asymmetries in Digital Consumer Markets', BEUC Study (March 2021), paras 24–27, 12–14, https://www.beuc.eu/sites/default/files/publications/beuc-x-2021-018_eu_consumer_protection_2.0.pdf

18 M. A. Fineman, 'The Vulnerable Subject: Anchoring Equality in the Human Condition', *Yale Journal of Law and Feminism* 20 (2008), 1–23.

19 See e.g. Helberger et al., 'EU Consumer Protection 2.0.', paras 57–63, 24–27.

20 See e.g. W.-H. Roth, 'Transposing 'Pointillist' EC Guidelines into Systematic National Codes—Problems and Consequences', *European Review of Private Law* 6 (2002), 761–776.

a. Information Asymmetry: 'One Step Closer'

> All these words they make no sense
> I find bliss in ignorance
> Less I hear the less you'll say (Linkin Park, 'One Step Closer', 2000)

How often have you ticked a box indicating 'I have read the terms and conditions' (T&Cs) when concluding an online contract, without having opened the link leading to them? Most consumers ignore (pre-)contractual disclosures, partially because even if they attempt reading them, they struggle to understand them.[21] There are other reasons for staying blissfully ignorant. First, even if consumers read T&Cs, they are unlikely to influence terms they disagree with. Second, the sheer number and length of disclosures they need to read are overwhelming.[22] Researchers estimated that just reading privacy policies, which is only one type of T&Cs, could cost consumers around 201 hours a year.[23] Law and economics analysis indicates that it may be a perfectly rational solution for consumers not to read T&Cs (*Point for reflection 3*).[24]

Why then did the European legislator adopt mandatory information obligations as one of the main consumer protection mechanisms in EPL (*Point for reflection 4*)?[25] The rationale for this lies on the one hand in the information paradigm, and on the other hand, in the need to harmonise the regulatory practices across the EU.

The information paradigm recognises that consumers suffer from information asymmetry, as traders have many more resources to collect and process information.[26] By obliging traders to share the information with consumers, EPL aims to minimise consumer costs in searching for the relevant data, ultimately enabling them to make an informed transactional decision.[27] This objective also led to the adoption of the principle of transparency, as only the information that is accessible (formally transparent) and comprehensible (substantively transparent) could actually impact the consumer's decision-making.[28] Moreover, traders must provide a reasonable opportunity for consumers to read the relevant information.[29]

---

21 E.g. Furnell and Phippen reported that half the working adults in the UK have a reading age of eleven or lower, whilst most of the online privacy policies they examined are drafted at the level of twelve and higher: S. Furnell and A. Phippen, 'Online Privacy: A Matter of Policy', *Computer Fraud and Security* 8 (2012), 12–18.

22 See e.g. Ben-Shahar and Schneider, *More Than You Wanted to Know.*

23 A. M. McDonald and L. F. Cranor, 'The Cost of Reading Privacy Policies', *A Journal of Law and Policy for the Information Society* 4 (2008), 540–565.

24 See e.g. Ben-Shahar and Schneider, *More Than You Wanted to Know.*

25 See e.g. Articles 5–6 CRD; Articles 8–11, 21–23 Directive (EU) 2023/2225 of the European Parliament and of the Council on credit agreements for consumers [2023] OJ L2023/2225 (Consumer Credit Directive, CCD); Article 9 Regulation (EU) 2023/988 of the European Parliament and of the Council on general product safety [2023] OJ L135/1 (General Product Safety Regulation, GPSR).

26 See e.g. G. Straetmans, *Information Obligations and Disinformation of Consumers* (Cham: Springer, 2019).

27 See e.g. Recitals 5–7 CRD.

28 See e.g. J. Luzak and M. Junuzović, 'Blurred Lines: Between Formal and Substantive Transparency in Consumer Credit Contracts', *Journal of European Consumer and Market Law* 8 (2019), 97–107.

29 See e.g. M. Loos, 'Art. 70–71: Incorporation and Making Available of Standard Contract Terms', in A. Colombi Ciacchi (ed.), *Contents and Effects of Contracts—Lessons to Learn from the Common European Sales Law* (Cham: Springer, 2016), pp. 179–202.

Yet, we could question the effectiveness of mandatory information obligations in alleviating information asymmetry.[30] Even if traders only provide consumers with the mandatory information, there are still so many pieces thereof that consumers are unlikely to pay attention to all of it. For example, the Consumer Rights Directive aimed to harmonise information obligations for various consumer sales contracts, which led to the adoption of a list of twenty mandatory information requirements for distance and off-premises sales contracts.[31] Further, even if traders attempt to make this information transparent, the consumers' levels of (financial) literacy vary, leading to the consumers' struggle with comprehending disclosures.[32] Consequently, placing such obligations on traders is unlikely to actually improve the consumers' transactional position, not allowing them to make an 'informed' decision.

To fully assess the (lack of) effectiveness of mandatory information obligations, it is, however, crucial that the information is first provided transparently. Most current research on disclosures focuses on this aspect of their regulation.[33] Further, researchers started emphasising the usefulness of these disclosures at the post-contractual stage.[34] If the mandatory information does not facilitate the consumers' decision-making in a pre-contractual phase, it could be useful when consumers attempt to identify their rights and obligations when they find themselves in a dispute with traders. Transparent mandatory disclosures could then be more effective in helping consumers enforcing their rights (see Section 2.d).

We could also criticise mandatory information obligations as a regulatory tool aimed at harmonising market practices across the EU, which aim at lowering compliance costs for cross-border traders. Usually, information obligations in EPL are non-exhaustive and the Member States could add further information requirements for traders, which undermines the harmonisation objective. There is also no common toolbox for drafting mandatory information obligations. Consequently, for example, if a consumer purchases a package travel on credit, different information obligations apply to the provision of these two services, even if the same provider facilitates both of them.[35] As some information obligations overlap, but have been designed separately and formulated differently, this may hinder noticing either duplication or variances in

---

30 See e.g. O. Seizov, A. J. Wulf, and J. Luzak, 'The Transparent Trap: A Multidisciplinary Perspective on the Design of Transparent Online Disclosures in the EU', *Journal of Consumer Policy* 42 (2019), 149–173; A. Rossi et al., 'When Design Met Law: Design Patterns for Information Transparency', *Droit de la consummation* 122 (2019), 79–121.

31 This list was recently further extended by Directive (EU) 2019/2161 of the European Parliament and of the Council as regards the better enforcement and modernisation of Union consumer protection rules [2019] OJ L328/7 (Modernisation Directive).

32 See e.g. V. Mak, 'The Myth of the "Empowered Consumer"—Lessons from Financial Literacy Studies', *Zeitschrift für Europäisches Unternehmens- und Verbraucherrecht (euvr)* 1 (2012), 254–263.

33 Researchers even claim that we should stop discussing information asymmetry and instead focus on comprehensibility asymmetry, see Wagner and Walker, *Incomprehensible!* See also footnote 31, above.

34 See e.g. G. Straetmans, 'Misleading Practices, the Consumer Information Model and Consumer Protection', *Journal of European Common Market Law* 5 (2016), 199–210 (p. 207); Seizov, Wulf, and Luzak, 'The Transparent Trap', p. 152.

35 Following information requirements in CCD and in Directive 2015/2302 of the European Parliament and of the Council on package travel and linked travel arrangements [2015] OJ L326/1.

them. This leads to inefficiencies and may raise compliance costs for traders. Finally, we should note that even if the information obligations were fully harmonised, this could only benefit consumers indirectly, with goods and services' costs being lowered. We could then question whether the mandatory information obligations ultimately help improving the consumers' position on the market.

b. Unfairness: 'Mastermind'

What if I told you none of it was accidental...
...I laid the groundwork and then, just like clockwork
The dominoes cascaded in a line...
 ...It was all by design
'Cause I'm a mastermind (Taylor Swift, 'Mastermind', 2022)

The power imbalance between traders and consumers may expose consumers, not only to information asymmetry, but also unfair commercial practices and unfair contract terms. For example, consumers may fall for such unfair practices of online traders as the use of dark patterns, also called deceptive design, which pushes consumers into making transactional decisions they otherwise would not have made.[36] Consumers will also likely not have an option to negotiate T&Cs, instead receiving pre-drafted, standardised terms that they could only decide to accept or reject.[37] If market actors were perfectly rational, competitors would exert control over each other's practices and terms, ensuring their fairness. As real-life market behaviour is far from rational, the European legislature decided to intervene. To protect consumers and prevent further abuse of the power imbalance, two main horizontal instruments of consumer protection were adopted in EPL: the Unfair Commercial Practices Directive (UCPD) and the Unfair Contract Terms Directive (UCTD).[38] They both aim at assuring that traders conduct honest business practices, prohibiting unfair conduct, including specifically the drafting of unfair contract terms, regardless of the type of contract being concluded. Despite their harmonious overarching goals, these two EPL instruments differ as to the test for unfairness they apply.

Consumers may be exposed to various types of unfair commercial practices. The UCPD adopts a tiered system of prohibitions, starting with blacklisted practices of its Annex, followed by the test of one of its three unfairness clauses. If a practice is listed in the Annex, consumers may simply invoke this fact and national courts should declare it to be a blacklisted (and thereby prohibited) practice. Amongst the blacklisted

36 See e.g. Norwegian Consumer Council, 'You Can Log Out, But You Can Never Leave', *Forbrukerraadet* (14 January 2021), https://storage02.forbrukerradet.no/media/2021/01/2021-01-14-you-can-log-out-but-you-can-never-leave-final.pdf. The term 'dark patterns' was first coined by Harry Brignull. Recently, it has started being replaced with the term 'deceptive design'. See e.g. 'Deceptive Patterns' (*Testimonium*), https://www.deceptive.design/

37 See e.g. F. Kessler, 'Contracts of Adhesion: Some Thoughts about Freedom of Contract', *Columbia Law Review* 43 (1943), 629–642.

38 Council Directive 93/13/EEC on unfair terms in consumer contracts [1993] OJ L95/29 (Unfair Contract Terms Directive, UCTD).

practices are, e.g. offering 'free' products if consumers have to pay more than delivery costs, persistent and unwanted solicitations by phone or e-mail, and recently also commissioning false consumer product reviews or endorsements.[39] Such practices are unfair in all circumstances (*Point for reflection 5*).[40]

The two small unfairness clauses prohibit misleading (Articles 6 and 7 UCPD) and aggressive (Article 8 UCPD) commercial practices. They determine that a practice is unfair by examining the impact that it has on the consumers' decision-making.[41] A practice is then unfair if consumers would have taken a different transactional decision, if they had not received false or deceiving information (misleading action), or if the trader neglected to provide them with material information (misleading omission), or if consumers had not been subjected to harassment, coercion or undue influence (aggressive practice).[42] Despite the broad interpretation of the notion of a transactional decision, consumers may struggle to prove that they would have taken a different decision without the influence of the unfair commercial practice (*Point for reflection 6*).

Finally, the general unfairness clause aims to cover all other situations, in which unfairness may arise (Article 5 UCPD). It also tests the impact of a commercial practice on the consumers' decision-making, but it adds the requirement of a practice needing to be contrary to professional diligence, e.g. codes of conduct.[43]

Unfairness is tested at the moment, in which the practice influences the decision-making of a consumer, whether it occurs in the pre-, post- or contractual context. Further, a commercial practice could still be unfair when consumers do not conclude a contract or when they suffer no losses,[44] and when it could be a one-off circumstance.[45]

The unfairness test is different under the provisions of the UCTD, perhaps owing to the minimum harmonisation character of this directive. To prevent traders from abusing their position as drafters of T&Cs, Article 3 UCTD states that terms that have not been individually negotiated are unfair if they fulfil three conditions: 1) contrary to good faith,[46] 2) they cause a significant imbalance in parties' rights and obligations, 3) to the detriment of the consumer.[47]

The UCTD also includes an Annex, however, it is not a list of prohibited terms that would be unfair in all circumstances. Instead, it indicates, which terms could be considered by national courts as potentially unfair. The Annex does not even amount

39 See points 20 and 26 in Annex to UCPD and new point 23c introduced by Modernisation Directive.

40 Article 5(5) UCPD.

41 Case C-281/12 *Trento Sviluppo and Centrale Adriattica* [2013] ECLI:EU:C:2013:859, para. 29.

42 See further e.g. G. Howells, H.-W. Micklitz and T. Wilhelmsson, 'Towards a Better Understanding of Unfair Commercial Practices', *International Journal of Law and Management* 51 (2009), 69–90; B. Duivenvoorde, 'The Upcoming Changes in the Unfair Commercial Practices Directive: A Better Deal for Consumers?', *Journal of European Common Market Law* 6 (2019), 219–228.

43 Case C-435/11 *CHS Tour Services* [2013] ECLI:EU:C:2013:574, para. 36.

44 See *Trento Sviluppo*, para. 36 and Article 11(2) UCPD.

45 Case C-388/13 *UPC Magyarország* [2015] ECLI:EU:C:2015:225, para. 60.

46 You can read more on the role that good faith plays in EPL in Chapter 6 in this volume.

47 See further e.g. M. Loos and J. Luzak, 'Wanted: A Bigger Stick. On Unfair Terms in Consumer Contracts with Online Service Providers', Journal of Consumer Policy 2016.1 (2016), 63–90.

to a grey list, of terms presumed to be unfair until proven otherwise.[48]

Unfairness is assessed at the moment the contract was concluded, considering all circumstances surrounding the contract's conclusion. The post-contractual context should then not impact that assessment.[49]

A comparison of these unfairness tests raises a question of whether EPL should aim to develop more synergies between them. This could occur, for instance, by adopting a more general unfairness test; EPL could simply stipulate that an unfair commercial practice and an unfair contract term are contrary to good faith. Alternatively, EPL could accept that a commercial practice based on a term found to be unfair is automatically unfair,[50] and that an unfair commercial practice leading to the adoption of T&Cs, makes them unfair, in turn. Such links have not yet, however, been made. The CJEU only stipulated that a recognition that an unfair commercial practice had led to the conclusion of a contract with unfair terms should be weighed by national courts as part of the circumstances surrounding the contract's conclusion that could lead to the determination of a term's unfairness.[51]

c. Product Risks: 'Poison'

> One look, could kill
> My pain, your thrill (Alice Cooper, 'Poison', 1989)

Consumers purchase products for their utility but also for fun, the thrill. It is important to realise that despite the EPL's objectives of ensuring the health and safety of consumers,[52] no product is 100% safe. Contrarily, consumer products generate certain risks, and the technological progress complicates both production and supply process of consumer products, as well as hinders the consumers' ability to observe defects in them.[53] As EU law promotes the freedom of movement of goods, it became crucial to not only adopt strict but also harmonised EPL product safety standards. The system of *ex ante* controls aims to reduce the possibility of the consumers' harm occurring. Therefore, the EU legislature has advanced from only regulating product liability to prioritising product safety rules.[54]

48 Such grey lists have often been adopted in national laws of various Member States, see Commission, Guidance on the interpretation and application of Council Directive 93/13/EEC on unfair terms in consumer contracts [2019] Case C-323/4, paras 35–36.

49 Ibid., para. 33.

50 Reference to Article 47 of the Charter of Fundamental Rights of the EU could perhaps further substantiate this claim, as mentioned by H-W. Micklitz and N. Reich, 'AGB-Recht und UWG—(endlich) ein Ende des Kästchendenkens nach Pereničova und Invitel?', *Europäisches Wirtschafts- und Steuerrecht* 23 (2012), 257–264 (p. 263).

51 Case C-453/10 *Pereničová and Perenič* [2012] ECLI:EU:C2012:144, para. 47.

52 Recital 4 GPSR.

53 See further e.g. C. Ullrich, 'New Approach Meets New Economy: Enforcing EU Product Safety in E-Commerce', *Maastricht Journal of European and Comparative Law* 26 (2019), 558–584; Recital 2 GPSR.

54 See further e.g. G. Howells, 'The Relationship between Product Liability and Product Safety—Understanding a Necessary Element in European Product Liability through a Comparison with the US Position', *Washburn Law Journal* 39 (2000), 305–346.

There are two important, horizontal sets of rules in this area that aim to be complimentary: the General Product Safety Regulation (GPSR) and the Product Liability Directive (PLD).[55] The GPSR sets general product safety rules that producers of consumer goods need to comply with when introducing their products to the EU market. This general product safety framework works as a net, applying to any consumer products that are not separately regulated.[56] Economic operators are exempt from the liability for defective products if they can prove that a defect in their products is due to compliance with these EPL product safety rules.[57]

The PLD aims to ensure that consumers receive compensation for damage suffered due to unsafe products, by introducing strict liability of various economic operators in such cases, with manufacturers of defective products or of defective components liable in the first place.[58] When a manufacturer is established outside of the EU, the liability shifts to either an importer or an authorised representative of the manufacturer in the EU, and in their absence to the fulfilment service provider.[59] Only if neither of the above-mentioned parties can be identified, consumers could turn to the defective product's distributor or an online platform.[60]

The burden of proof consists of consumers evidencing specific damage (either to their person or to other consumer products or to data not used for professional purposes) that occurred due to a defect in a consumer product.[61] Economic operators have then only a limited number of defences available to them.[62] Moreover, the CJEU has been lenient in accepting that national courts may deduce either the existence of the damage or of a defect from circumstances of the case, despite consumers not being able to prove it conclusively.[63] The causal link between damage and defect may also be inferred,[64] and these presumptions have been codified in the recent revision of the PLD.[65]

Interestingly, the GPSR and the PLD vary in their use of the notion of 'product safety'. Article 3(2) GPSR defines safe products as:

> [A]ny product which, under normal or reasonably foreseeable conditions of use [...] does not present any risk or only the minimum risks compatible with the product's use, considered acceptable and consistent with a high level of protection of the health and safety of consumers [...]

55 Directive (EU) 2024/2853 on liability for defective products [2024] OJ L2024/2853 (Product Liability Directive, PLD).

56 For example, there are sector-specific safety rules for such consumer products as toys (Directive 2009/48/EC of the European Parliament and of the Council on the safety of toys [2009] OJ L170/1) or cosmetics (Regulation (EC) No 1223/2009 of the European Parliament and of the Council of 30 November 2009 on cosmetic products [2009] OJ L342/59).

57 Article 11 (1)(d) PLD.

58 Article 8 PLD.

59 Article 8 (1) (c) PLD.

60 Article 8 (3) and (4) PLD.

61 Articles 6 and 10 PLD

62 Article 11 PLD.

63 Joined Cases C-503/13 and C-504/13 *Boston Scientific Medizintechnik* [2015] ECLI:EU:C:2015:148, paras 43 and 55.

64 Case C-621/15 *N.W. and others* [2017] ECLI:EU:C:2017:484, para. 55.

65 Article 10 (2)-(5) PLD.

Article 7(1) PLD, however, emphasises that products are defective and unsafe when they do not provide 'the safety which a person is entitled to expect or that is required under Union or national law'. Therefore, the GPSR determines safety through risk assessments, whilst the PLD relies on reasonable societal expectations as to safety (*Point for reflection 7*).

The recent revision of the EPL's product safety and liability frameworks did not harmonise the approach determining product safety between these two instruments. Further points that the revision aimed to address were: 1) the concept of 'covered product risks'; 2) the notion of a 'product' itself; 3) the moment at which safety of a product should be assessed; 4) the parties bearing liability for unsafe products.

Regarding the first point of covered product risks, traditionally, product safety was related to physical health and the safety of consumers.[66] This focus may then exclude the need to assure consumers' wellbeing and mental health and ignore the fact that consumer products may also be a hazard to the environment or cybersecurity, which indirectly would also negatively impact consumers. The new Article 6(1) PLD recognises now that consumers may suffer a 'medically recognised damage to psychological health', as well as experience damage by 'destruction or corruption of data that are not used for professional purposes'. These two new types of damages will, however, only address a small portion of risks that consumers encounter in digital environments.[67]

On the second point we should note that Internet of Things (IoT) technologies blurred the lines between physical consumer products, (digital) services, and digital content. Therefore, the Commission examined whether leaving the product safety framework only applicable to narrowly defined 'products' would sufficiently protect consumers in the modern economy. The expansion of the product notion to cover integrated or interconnected digital content and digital services in the PLD will lead to certain legal uncertainties as to the exact application scope of the new product notion[68] (*Point for reflection 8*).

Moreover, as to the third point, the assessment of the products' safety currently only occurs at the moment consumer products are put into circulation. However, many modern consumer products may be, even substantially, changed by their subsequent modifications (e.g. via software, also provided by third parties, or through a learning process of algorithms) and new risks may emerge from the interconnectivity between various consumer products. Consequently, new Article 8(2) PLD introduces liability of any person that substantially modifies a product outside the manufacturer's control.

Finally, on the last point, digitalisation also changed roles that many actors play in consumer goods' production, supply, and marketing.[69] Should manufacturers remain

66 See e.g. BEUC, 'Why the EU Needs to Improve Its Product Safety Law', *BEUC* (26 August 2020).

67 See e.g. J. Luzak, 'Protecting Consumers against Their Poison: Defects in Digital Content and Digital Services', in S. Martinelli, C. Poncibo, and P. Perri (eds.), *EU Product Liability: Platforms, Internet of Things, and Artificial Intelligence* (Routledge, 2025, forthcoming).

68 Ibid.

69 See further e.g. J. Luzak, 'A Broken Notion: Impact of Modern Technologies on Product Liability',

liable for harms caused by defective products even if these clearly occurred due to the interference of third parties (e.g. digital content providers) in their products?[70] Strict liability does not need to be too burdensome for manufacturers, if they have proper redress measures and insurance options. It would also simplify consumers' claims for compensation for the damage suffered, thus it comes as a welcomed addition that the extension of strict product liability to multiple economic operators comes together with the recognition of their joint and several liability.[71] This brings us to the issues consumers have with claiming their rights.

d. Apathy in Enforcement of Consumer Rights: 'Texas Hold 'Em'

This ain't Texas, ain't no hold 'em
So lay your cards down, down, down (Beyoncé, 'Texas Hold 'Em', 2024)

Consumer protection cannot be effective if EPL only awards substantive consumer rights.[72] Traders also need to know that their lack of compliance with substantive consumer protection rules will have negative consequences for them.[73] Therefore, it is important to have robust enforcement of consumer protection measures, investigation of traders infringing consumer rights, whether by negligence or intent, and sanctions thereof.

Interestingly, EPL mainly focused on preventing further infringements of consumer rights by traders (making them lay down their cards) in the injunctions procedure.[74] This enforcement measure only works for the future and does not provide already harmed consumers with remedies. Its prominence in the framework of consumer protection enforcement emphasises the importance that public enforcement can play alongside the private one.[75]

A few EPL consumer protection rules specified sanctions for their breach, awarding consumers with remedies. For example, the Consumer Sales Directive determines remedies for consumers receiving non-conforming goods.[76] Many sanctions, however,

---

European Journal of Risk Regulation 11.3 (2020), 630–649; C. Twigg-Flesner, 'Guiding Principles for Updating the Product Liability Directive for the Digital Age', *ELI Innovation Paper Series* (January 2021), https://papers.ssrn.com/sol3/papers.cfm?abstract_id=3770796

70 Compare with the solution adopted for non-conforming consumer goods with embedded software in the Directive (EU) 2019/771 of the European Parliament and of the Council on certain aspects concerning contracts for the sale of goods [2019] OJ L136/28.

71 Article 12 (1) PLD.

72 Emphasis has been placed on the need to educate consumers more about their rights as the first step towards the enforcement thereof. See e.g. J. Luzak, 'Who Calls the Tune? Stock Taking of Behavioural Consumer Protection in Europe', in H.-W. Micklitz, A.-L. Sibony, and F. Esposito (eds), *Research Methods in Consumer Law* (Cheltenham: Edward Elgar, 2018), pp. 239–275 (para. 4).

73 See further e.g. H.-W. Micklitz and G. Saumier, *Enforcement and Effectiveness of Consumer Law* (Cham: Springer, 2018).

74 Directive 2009/22/EC of the European Parliament and of the Council on injunctions for the protection of consumers' interests [2009] OJ L110/30.

75 See e.g. R. Steennot, 'Public and Private Enforcement in the Field of Unfair Contract Terms', *European Review of Private Law* 23 (2015), 589–614.

76 Article 3 Directive 1999/44/EC of the European Parliament and of the Council on certain aspects of

were left to the discretion of the Member States, with the added caveat of the European legislature that they needed to be effective, dissuasive, and proportionate (*Point for reflection 9*).[77] Cross-border traders may then be exposed to different sanctions in different Member States for following the same commercial practice. Moreover, EPL could even neglect to require the Member States to adopt a sanction, e.g. for the breach of the principle of transparency in the UCTD. Therefore, the first weakness of EPL in enforcing consumer protection is its lack of a harmonised and strict approach to adopting sanctions for infringements of substantive consumer protection rules. Recently, EPL tried to address this weakness through the introduction of more harmonised sanctions in the Modernisation Directive.[78]

The second weakness follows from the findings on consumer behaviour in disputes. As consumers often suffer only a small harm, they may lack incentives to pursue redress options, especially if costs of enforcing a claim could exceed the potential redress benefit.[79] Enforcement costs cover not only direct costs of the dispute resolution, e.g. court fees or costs of hiring a lawyer, but also indirect costs generated by the need to invest time in a dispute and by the uncertainty of its resolution. Especially the latter could discourage consumers from taking an action until someone else's similar claim is successfully resolved, creating a precedent (so-called 'free-rider behaviour').[80] Consequently, EPL must account for the consumers' apathy in enforcing their rights.

EPL adopted various solutions to address the above-mentioned issues. Of note here should be the promotion of the alternative dispute resolution (ADR) mechanisms to judicial enforcement.[81] Arbitration and mediation could be faster and cheaper than court proceedings. However, scholars have indicated various weaknesses of the current ADR framework,[82] for instance, a continued uncertainty about the procedure's outcome, which results amongst others from the lack of a public record on previous ADR cases. As ADR bodies do not need to follow EPL rules in their procedures, this also decreases the likelihood of fair outcomes and provides traders—as repeat-players—with an advantage (*Point for reflection 10*).[83]

---

the sale of consumer goods and associated guarantees [1999] OJ L171/12 (Consumer Sales Directive).

77 E.g. Article 13 UCPD.

78 E.g. Article 13 UCPD will soon be changed by Article 3 Modernisation Directive, further specifying sanctions that the Member States should introduce in their legal systems for traders engaging in unfair commercial practices.

79 See e.g. R. Van den Bergh, 'Should Consumer Protection Law Be Publicly Enforced?', in W. van Boom and M. Loos (eds), *Collective Enforcement of Consumer Law* (Groningen: Europe Law Publishing, 2007), pp. 179–203 (p. 184); C. Hodges, 'Mass Collective Redress: Consumer ADR and Regulatory Techniques', *European Review of Private Law* 5 (2015), 829–874 (p. 832).

80 See e.g. I. Benöhr, 'Consumer Dispute Resolution after The Lisbon Treaty: Collective Actions and Alternative Procedures', *Journal of Consumer Policy* 36 (2013), 87–110 (p. 97).

81 Directive 2013/11/EU of the European Parliament and of the Council on alternative dispute resolution for consumer disputes [2013] OJ L165/63.

82 See e.g. F. Weber, 'Is ADR the Superior Mechanism for Consumer Contractual Disputes?—an Assessment of Incentivizing Effects of the ADR Directive', *Journal of Consumer Policy* 38 (2015), 265–285; J. Luzak, 'The ADR Directive: Designed to Fail? A Hole-Ridden Stairway to Consumer Justice', *European Review of Private Law* 24.1 (2016), 81–101.

83 See e.g. S. Talesh, 'How Dispute Resolution System Design Matters: An Organizational Analysis of

The newest development in this field is the adoption of the Representative Actions Directive.[84] To an extent, this new measure addresses the lack of the collective enforcement options in the EU.[85] However, this directive did not adopt a class action option for European consumers. Instead, it provides so-called qualified entities, likely national consumer protection authorities and organisations, with a right to claim a collective redress remedy on behalf of consumers. It also does not assure harmonising of the representative actions' procedure. Despite the adoption of EPL rules in this area, a lot has been left to the discretion of the Member States, including important issues such as: whether to adopt an opt-in or opt-out procedure for registering consumer claims; what rules apply to adverse costs or to the certification stage. Overall, the recent adoption of the first ever European collective redress mechanism could still only be called a work-in-progress.[86]

3. Societal Context: 'Where Is the Love?'

> It just ain't the same, old ways have changed,
> New days are strange, is the world insane? (Black Eyed Peas, 'Where Is the Love?', 2003)

To observe the drastic change that has occurred in the consumer markets, just talk to your older relatives—about the ways they used to shop, products they had available to them, and relationships they had with traders. Old ways have changed. Instead of shopping at a local supermarket, where the shopkeeper could have recognised you and remembered your shopping patterns, consumers shop now more often online, and let their preferences be registered by anonymous algorithms. The recent Covid-19 pandemic further exacerbated the rate of growth of the online trade.[87] Our consumption patterns have also shifted. Consumers more often choose now to lease consumer products, rather than owning them, moving away from the product-economy to service-economy.[88] Digitalisation and servitisation are two of the new trends on the consumer marketplace. The above-mentioned trends revealed a gap in the market for intermediaries who could link consumers and service providers. This gap was quickly

---

Dispute Resolution Structures and Consumer Lemon Laws', *Law and Society Review* 46 (2012), 463–496 (p. 468).

84 Directive (EU) 2020/1828 of the European Parliament and of the Council on representative actions for the protection of the collective interests of consumers [2020] OJ L409/1.

85 See e.g. C. Hodges and S. Voet, *Delivering Collective Redress: New Technologies* (Oxford: Hart Publishing, 2018).

86 See further e.g. J. M. L. van Duin and C. Leone, 'The Real (New) Deal: Levelling the Odds for Consumer-Litigants: On the Need for Modernization. Part II', *European Review of Private Law* 27 (2019), 1227–1250; C. Pavillon, 'Private Enforcement as a Deterrence Tool: A Blind Spot in the Omnibus-Directive', *European Review of Private Law* 27 (2019), 2397–1328.

87 See e.g. UNCTAD, 'How Covid-19 Triggered the Digital and E-Commerce Turning Point', *UNCTAD* (15 March 2021), https://unctad.org/news/how-covid-19-triggered-digital-and-e-commerce-turning-point

88 See e.g. M. P. Fritze et al., 'From Goods to Services Consumption: A Social Network Analysis on Sharing Economy and Servitization Research', *Journal of Service Management Research* 2 (2018), 3–16.

filled by online platforms, which led to the development of the sharing economy.[89]

In the past decade of consumer policymaking, the European legislature focused on adjusting existing rules to the digitalisation of consumer markets. This led to the adoption of the Digital Single Market strategy,[90] which led, amongst others, to modernising sales law to include rules for non-conforming digital content or goods with embedded digital content.[91] Further, as the growth of online trade contributed to the increase in the collection and processing of consumer data, this provided an added impulse to the revision of data protection rules—through the General Data Protection Regulation.[92] Recently, the focus shifted to drafting new obligations for online platform operators, e.g. in the Digital Services Act.[93]

At the summit in Brussels in 2020, the Commission announced its plans to focus the New Consumer Agenda around the Green Deal.[94] Climate change is a concern for policymakers, irrespective of their expertise area, which means that also in consumer protection we should explore how to contribute to a greener economy.[95] Therefore, the focus of the forthcoming EPL rules is likely to shift to the promotion of sustainable consumption. This could be achieved in many ways. For example, EPL could oblige traders ensuring the repairability of their products and could promote the consumers' right to repair over replacement of defective consumer products.[96] Further improvement of the consumers' sustainable decision-making could follow from ensuring that they receive factual and informative data on the impact of their purchases on the environment.[97] This could go hand-in-hand with the prohibition of greenwashing as an unfair commercial practice, i.e. a practice where traders present themselves as environmentally-friendly, without supporting such claims with evidence.[98] This area

89 See e.g. L. Lessig, *Remix: Making Art and Commerce Thrive in the Hybrid Economy* (London: Penguin, 2008); K. Frenken and J. Schor, 'Putting the Sharing Economy into Perspective', *Environmental Innovation and Societal Transitions* 23 (2017), 3–10.

90 European Council, 'Digital Single Market for Europe', *European Council*, https://www.consilium.europa.eu/en/policies/digital-single-market/

91 See footnote 73 above, and Directive (EU) 2019/770 of the European Parliament and of the Council on certain aspects concerning contracts for the supply of digital content and digital services [2019] OJ L136/1.

92 Regulation (EU) 2016/679 of the European Parliament and of the Council on the protection of natural persons with regard to the processing of personal data and on the free movement of such data [2016] OJ L119/1.

93 See e.g. Regulation (EU) 2022/2065 of the European Parliament and of the Council of 19 October 2022 on a Single Market for Digital Services [2022] OJ L277/1 (Digital Services Act, DSA).

94 European Commission, 'A European Green Deal', *European Commission*, https://ec.europa.eu/info/strategy/priorities-2019–2024/european-green-deal_en

95 See further e.g. V. Mak and E. Terryn, 'Circular Economy and Consumer Protection: The Consumer as a Citizen and the Limits of Empowerment Through Consumer Law', *Journal of Consumer Policy* 43 (2020), 227–248.

96 See e.g. E. Terryn, 'A Right to Repair? Towards Sustainable Remedies in Consumer Law', *European Review of Private Law* 27 (2019), 851–873.

97 See e.g. A. Ní Choisdealbha and P. D. Lunn, 'Green and Simple: Disclosures on Eco-labels Interact with Situational Constraints in Consumer Choice', *Journal of Consumer Policy* 43 (2020), 699–722.

98 See e.g. European Commission, 'Screening of Websites for "Greenwashing": Half of Green Claims Lack Evidence', *European Commission* (28 January 2021) https://ec.europa.eu/commission/presscorner/detail/en/ip_21_269. See also Proposal for a Directive of the European Parliament and

of consumer protection in EPL is still new and undoubtedly more achievements will be made therein in the coming years.

4. Points for Reflection: 'Try Again'

If at first you don't succeed
Then dust yourself off and try again (Aaliyah, 'Try Again', 2000)

Q1: Compare the benchmark of an average consumer to the concept of consumers as weaker parties. Do you think they are compatible?

Q2: If we assessed the consumers' vulnerability considering its external rather than internal causes, what consequences could this have for the enforcement of consumer protection measures across the EU?

Q3: Have you read all T&Cs of online contracts you have concluded, e.g. when you subscribed to a TikTok, an Instagram or a Gmail account? If you have read them, did you understand them? What would you say stands in the consumers' way of reading and understanding T&Cs? Could EPL tackle such obstacles?

Q4: Develop an argument against adopting many different mandatory information obligations in EPL. You could base it either on the reasoning related to legal design, economic analysis or insights from consumer behaviour.

Q5: Read the Annex to the UCPD to check whether you might have been exposed to a practice that has already been blacklisted. Why do you think traders still employ such practices in the EU?

Q6: Imagine consumers finding out that, say, Amazon used dark patterns to have them join their Amazon Prime subscription or that Facebook did not inform them about the full use they will make of the consumers' data. If consumers were aware of these potentially unfair commercial practices, do you think they would not have concluded a contract with these service providers?

Q7: Can you imagine a scenario when a product would meet the requirements of one of these safety tests, but not the other? What consequences could this difference in the assessment of the product safety have?

Q8: Imagine a defective drone injuring someone. What consequences do you foresee of having two product safety and two product liability frameworks applicable in this scenario: one set—when a defect in the drone occurred due to a fault in its

---

of the Council amending Directives 2005/29/EC and 2011/83/EU as regards empowering consumers for the green transition through better protection against unfair practices and better information (Commission Communication, 'Proposal for a DIRECTIVE OF THE EUROPEAN PARLIAMENT AND OF THE COUNCIL', COM (2022) 143 final, https://eur-lex.europa.eu/legal-content/EN/TXT/?uri=celex:52022PC0143).

physical design, and the second set—in its software?

Q9: Could you explain what is 1) an effective, 2) a dissuasive, and 3) a proportionate sanction and give examples thereof?

Q10: What advantages could traders have as repeat-players in ADR procedures in your opinion?

Bibliography

Bar-Gill, O., *Seduction by Contract* (Oxford: Oxford University Press, 2012), https://doi.org/10.1093/acprof:oso/9780199663361.001.0001

Ben-Shahar, O., and O. Bar-Gill, 'Regulatory Techniques in Consumer Protection: A Critique of European Consumer Contract Law', *Common Market Law Review* 50 (2013), 109–126, https://doi-org.uoelibrary.idm.oclc.org/10.54648/cola2013039

Ben-Shahar, O., and C. E. Schneider, *More Than You Wanted to Know* (Princeton, NJ: Princeton University Press, 2014)

Benöhr, I., 'Consumer Dispute Resolution after The Lisbon Treaty: Collective Actions and Alternative Procedures', *Journal of Consumer Policy* 36 (2013), 87–110, https://doi.org/10.1007/s10603-012-9202-0

BEUC, 'Why the EU Needs to Improve Its Product Safety Law', *BEUC* (26 August 2020)

Bol, N., et al., 'Vulnerability in a Tracked Society: Combining Tracking and Survey Data to Understand who gets Targeted with what Content', *New Media and Society* 22 (2020), 1996–2017, https://doi-org.uoelibrary.idm.oclc.org/10.1177/1461444820924631

CLICKON, 'How Crucial is a Consumer's Self-Concept in Advertising', *CLICKON* (13 August 2019), https://news.clickon.co/how-crucial-is-a-consumers-self-concept-in-advertising

Commission Communication, 'Proposal for a DIRECTIVE OF THE EUROPEAN PARLIAMENT AND OF THE COUNCIL', COM (2022) 143 final, https://eur-lex.europa.eu/legal-content/EN/TXT/?uri=celex:52022PC0143

Duivenvoorde, B., *The Consumer Benchmarks in the Unfair Commercial Practices Directive* (Cham: Springer, 2015), https://doi.org/10.1007/978-3-319–13924–1

Duivenvoorde, B., 'The Upcoming Changes in the Unfair Commercial Practices Directive: A Better Deal for Consumers?', *Journal of European Common Market Law* 6 (2019), 219–228

European Commission, 'A European Green Deal', *European Commission*, https://ec.europa.eu/info/strategy/priorities-2019-2024/european-green-deal_en

European Commission, 'Screening of Websites for "Greenwashing": Half of Green Claims Lack Evidence', *European Commission* (28 January 2021) https://ec.europa.eu/commission/presscorner/detail/en/ip_21_269

European Council, 'Digital Single Market for Europe', *European Council*, https://www.consilium.europa.eu/en/policies/digital-single-market/

Fineman, M. A., 'The Vulnerable Subject: Anchoring Equality in the Human Condition', *Yale Journal of Law and Feminism* 20 (2008), 1–23

Frenken, K., and J. Schor, 'Putting the Sharing Economy into Perspective', *Environmental Innovation and Societal Transitions* 23 (2017), 3–10, https://doi.org/10.1016/j.eist.2017.01.003

Fritze, M. P., et al., 'From Goods to Services Consumption: A Social Network Analysis on Sharing Economy and Servitization Research', *Journal of Service Management Research* 2 (2018), 3–16, http://10.15358/2511-8676-2018-3-3

Furnell, S., and A. Phippen, 'Online Privacy: A Matter of Policy', *Computer Fraud and Security* 8 (2012), 12–18, https://doi.org/10.1016/S1361-3723(12)70083-0

Helberger, N., et al., 'EU Consumer Protection 2.0. Structural Asymmetries in Digital Consumer Markets', BEUC Study (March 2021), https://www.beuc.eu/sites/default/files/publications/beuc-x-2021-018_eu_consumer_protection_2.0.pdf

Helleringer, G., and A.-L. Sibony, 'European Consumer Protection through the Behavorial Lens', *The Columbia Journal of European Law* 23 (2017), 607–646

Hodges, C., 'Mass Collective Redress: Consumer ADR and Regulatory Techniques', *European Review of Private Law* 5 (2015), 829–874, https://doi-org.uoelibrary.idm.oclc.org/10.54648/erpl2015050

Hodges, C., and S. Voet, *Delivering Collective Redress: New Technologies* (Oxford: Hart Publishing, 2018)

Howells, G., 'The Relationship between Product Liability and Product Safety—Understanding a Necessary Element in European Product Liability through a Comparison with the US Position', *Washburn Law Journal* 39 (2000), 305–346

Howells, G., H.-W. Micklitz and T. Wilhelmsson, 'Towards a Better Understanding of Unfair Commercial Practices', *International Journal of Law and Management* 51 (2009), 69–90, https://doi-org.uoelibrary.idm.oclc.org/10.1108/17542430910947103

Kessler, F., 'Contracts of Adhesion: Some Thoughts about Freedom of Contract', *Columbia Law Review* 43 (1943), 629–642

Lessig, L., *Remix: Making Art and Commerce Thrive in the Hybrid Economy* (London: Penguin, 2008)

Loos, M., 'Art. 70–71: Incorporation and Making Available of Standard Contract Terms', in A. Colombi Ciacchi (ed.), *Contents and Effects of Contracts—Lessons to Learn from the Common European Sales Law* (Cham: Springer, 2016), pp. 179–202, https://doi.org/10.1007/978–3-319–28074–5

Loos, M., and J. Luzak, 'Wanted: A Bigger Stick. On Unfair Terms in Consumer Contracts with Online Service Providers', Journal of Consumer Policy 2016.1 (2016), 63–90, https://doi-org.uoelibrary.idm.oclc.org/10.1007/s10603-015-9303-7

Luth, H., *Behavioural Economics in Consumer Policy* (Brussels: Intersentia, 2010)

Luzak, J., 'The ADR Directive: Designed to Fail? A Hole-Ridden Stairway to Consumer Justice', *European Review of Private Law* 24.1 (2016), 81–101, https://doi-org.uoelibrary.idm.oclc.org/10.54648/erpl2016005

Luzak, J., 'A Broken Notion: Impact of Modern Technologies on Product Liability', *European Journal of Risk Regulation* 11.3 (2020), 630–649, https://doi.org/10.1017/err.2020.13

Luzak, J., 'Protecting Consumers against Their Poison: Defects in Digital Content and Digital Services', in S. Martinelli, C. Poncibo, and P. Perri (eds.), *EU Product Liability: Platforms, Internet of Things, and Artificial Intelligence* (Routledge, 2025, forthcoming)

Luzak, J., 'The Steady Creep of an Average Consumer as a Reference Consumer in the Assessment of the Transparent Provision of Mandatory Information', *Tijdschrift voor Consumentenrecht en handelspraktijken* 5 (2020), 265–274

Luzak, J., 'Vulnerable Travellers in the Digital Age', *Journal of European Consumer and Market Law* 3 (2016), 130–135

Luzak, J., 'Who Calls the Tune? Stock Taking of Behavioural Consumer Protection in Europe', in H.-W. Micklitz, A.-L. Sibony, and F. Esposito (eds), *Research Methods in Consumer Law* (Cheltenham: Edward Elgar, 2018), pp. 239–275, https://doi-org.uoelibrary.idm.oclc.org/10.4337/9781785366611.00013

Luzak, J., and M. Junuzović, 'Blurred Lines: Between Formal and Substantive Transparency in Consumer Credit Contracts', *Journal of European Consumer and Market Law* 8 (2019), 97–107

Mak, V., 'The Myth of the "Empowered Consumer"—Lessons from Financial Literacy Studies', *Zeitschrift für Europäisches Unternehmens- und Verbraucherrecht* (*euvr*) 1 (2012), 254–263

Mak, V., 'Standards of Protection: In Search of the 'Average Consumer' of EU Law in the Proposal for a Consumer Rights Directive', *European Review of Private* Law 19.1 (2011), 25–42, https://doi-org.uoelibrary.idm.oclc.org/10.54648/erpl2011003

Mak, V., and E. Terryn, 'Circular Economy and Consumer Protection: The Consumer as a Citizen and the Limits of Empowerment Through Consumer Law', *Journal of Consumer Policy* 43 (2020), 227–248, https://doi-org.uoelibrary.idm.oclc.org/10.1007/s10603-019-09435-y

McDonald, A. M., and L. F. Cranor, 'The Cost of Reading Privacy Policies', *A Journal of Law and Policy for the Information Society* 4 (2008), 540–565

Micklitz, H.-W., and N. Reich, 'AGB-Recht und UWG—(endlich) ein Ende des Kästchendenkens nach Pereničova und Invitel?', *Europäisches Wirtschafts- und Steuerrecht* 23 (2012), 257–264

Micklitz, H.-W., and G. Saumier, *Enforcement and Effectiveness of Consumer Law* (Cham: Springer, 2018), https://doi.org/10.1007/978–3-319–78431–1

Ní Choisdealbha, A., and P. D. Lunn, 'Green and Simple: Disclosures on Eco-labels Interact with Situational Constraints in Consumer Choice', *Journal of Consumer Policy* 43 (2020), 699–722, https://doi-org.uoelibrary.idm.oclc.org/10.1007/s10603-020-09465-x

Norwegian Consumer Council, 'You Can Log Out, But You Can Never Leave', *Forbrukerraadet* (14 January 2021), https://storage02.forbrukerradet.no/media/2021/01/2021-01-14-you-can-log-out-but-you-can-never-leave-final.pdf

Pavillon, C., 'Private Enforcement as a Deterrence Tool: A Blind Spot in the Omnibus-Directive', *European Review of Private Law* 27 (2019), 2397–1328, https://doi-org.uoelibrary.idm.oclc.org/10.54648/erpl2019072

Rossi, A., et al., 'When Design Met Law: Design Patterns for Information Transparency', *Droit de la consummation* 122 (2019), 79–121

Roth, W.-H., 'Transposing 'Pointillist' EC Guidelines into Systematic National Codes—Problems and Consequences', *European Review of Private Law* 6 (2002), 761–776, https://doi-org.uoelibrary.idm.oclc.org/10.54648/5114788

Schebesta, H., and K. Purnhagen, 'Island or Ocean: Empirical Evidence on the Average Consumer Concept in the UCPD', *European Review of Private Law* 28.2 (2020), 293–310, https://doi-org.uoelibrary.idm.oclc.org/10.54648/erpl2020015

Seizov, O., A. J. Wulf, and J. Luzak, 'The Transparent Trap: A Multidisciplinary Perspective on the Design of Transparent Online Disclosures in the EU', *Journal of Consumer Policy* 42 (2019), 149–173, https://doi-org.uoelibrary.idm.oclc.org/10.1007/s10603-018-9393-0

Straetmans, G., *Information Obligations and Disinformation of Consumers* (Cham: Springer, 2019), https://doi.org/10.1007/978–3-030–18054–6

Straetmans, G., 'Misleading Practices, the Consumer Information Model and Consumer Protection', *Journal of European Consumer and Market Law* 5 (2016), 199–210

Steennot, R., 'Public and Private Enforcement in the Field of Unfair Contract Terms', *European Review of Private Law* 23 (2015), 589–614, https://doi-org.uoelibrary.idm.oclc.org/10.54648/erpl2015039

Sunstein, C., *Free Markets and Social Justice* (Oxford: Oxford University Press 1997), https://doi.org/10.1093/oso/9780195102727.001.0001

Talesh, S., 'How Dispute Resolution System Design Matters: An Organizational Analysis of Dispute Resolution Structures and Consumer Lemon Laws', *Law and Society Review* 46 (2012), 463–496, https://doi-org.uoelibrary.idm.oclc.org/10.1111/j.1540-5893.2012.00503.x

Terryn, E., 'Consumers, by Definition, Include Us All... But Not for Every Transaction', *European Review of Private Law* 24 (2016), 271–286, https://doi-org.uoelibrary.idm.oclc.org/10.54648/erpl2016017

Terryn, E., 'A Right to Repair? Towards Sustainable Remedies in Consumer Law', *European Review of Private Law* 27 (2019), 851–873, https://doi-org.uoelibrary.idm.oclc.org/10.54648/erpl2019044

Twigg-Flesner, C., 'Guiding Principles for Updating the Product Liability Directive for the Digital Age', *ELI Innovation Paper Series* (January 2021), https://papers.ssrn.com/sol3/papers.cfm?abstract_id=3770796

Ullrich, C., 'New Approach Meets New Economy: Enforcing EU Product Safety in E-Commerce', *Maastricht Journal of European and Comparative Law* 26 (2019), 558–584, https://doi-org.uoelibrary.idm.oclc.org/10.1177/1023263X1985

UNCTAD, 'How Covid-19 Triggered the Digital and E-Commerce Turning Point', *UNCTAD* (15 March 2021), https://unctad.org/news/how-covid-19-triggered-digital-and-e-commerce-turning-point

Van den Bergh, R., 'Should Consumer Protection Law Be Publicly Enforced?', in W. van Boom and M. Loos (eds), *Collective Enforcement of Consumer Law* (Groningen: Europe Law Publishing, 2007), pp. 179–203

Van Duin, J. M. L., and C. Leone, 'The Real (New) Deal: Levelling the Odds for Consumer-Litigants: On the Need for Modernization. Part II', *European Review of Private Law* 27 (2019), 1227–1250, https://doi-org.uoelibrary.idm.oclc.org/10.54648/erpl2019069

Vries, S. de, 'Consumer Protection and the EU Single Market Rules—The Search for the "Paradigm Consumer"', *Journal of European Consumer and Market Law* 4 (2012), 228–242

Wagner, W., and W. Walker, *Incomprehensible!* (Cambridge, UK: Cambridge University Press, 2019), https://doi-org.uoelibrary.idm.oclc.org/10.1017/9781139051774

Weber, F., 'Is ADR the Superior Mechanism for Consumer Contractual Disputes?—an Assessment of Incentivizing Effects of the ADR Directive', *Journal of Consumer Policy* 38 (2015), 265–285, https://doi-org.uoelibrary.idm.oclc.org/10.1007/s10603-015-9291-7

IV. TRANSFORMATIONS

10. Social Enterprises and the Role of Profit in Company Law

Nena van der Horst and Marleen van Uchelen

Abstract

All over the world, social enterprises are actively contributing to solve societal problems. To ensure that these enterprises prioritise their 'social purpose' over other goals, these enterprises can make use of a variety of legal forms and legal structures. The chapter sets out that transparency requirements, rules on supervision, and enforcement mechanisms all play an important role in securing the social purpose of the social enterprise. Then, the chapter focuses on profit distributions and the possibilities to limit these as a very important mechanism for securing a social purpose. The chapter outlines the legal rules for profit distribution that apply to social enterprises in Europe with a focus on the Netherlands. Furthermore, it demonstrates that social enterprises have space within these legal rules to design their own limitations on profit distributions. This may be helpful in securing their social purpose, not only because it leaves more reserves available for reinvestments in the social purpose, but also because it may be of influence to certain incentives in the enterprise such as involvement of employees and beneficiaries. Finally, the chapter points out that it is important for social enterprises to have access to sufficient financial resources, in particular to attract capital investors. An important question is how this can be combined with limiting profit distributions. All these topics will undoubtedly be central in company law discussions in Europe in the coming years. In the conclusion, some points for reflection are posed that may contribute to these discussions.

1. Introduction

All over the world, scholars and legislators are discussing the role of business organisations ('enterprises') in relation to environmental and social problems. Some enterprises fail to address these problems effectively or even exacerbate them. At the same time, and on a more positive note, some enterprises do the opposite: they are

 https://doi.org/10.11647/OBP.0448.10

incorporated and have as their mission to actively contribute to solve these societal problems. Many of them do so from the conviction that their 'social mission' should be their central purpose.[1] Their main objective is to have a positive social impact, rather than make profit. This view on the purpose of enterprises differentiates itself from the idea that enterprises, first and foremost, exist to make profits and distribute them to their shareholders.[2] Enterprises with a social objective are often referred to as 'social enterprises'. Social enterprises serve a range of impact areas like circular economy,[3] renewable energy,[4] and job market participation.[5] Social enterprises can acquire private labels, of which the most well-known is the B-Corp label. B-Corp is an international label of which there are currently over 7,000 B-Corp certified companies worldwide and the number is rapidly increasing.[6] In order to acquire the label, companies need to achieve a minimum score on an impact assessment.[7] Next to labels such as B-Corp, various European countries have also created specific legal frameworks for social enterprises or organisations with a social purpose. Such initiatives include the *Società Benefit* in Italy, the *Société à Mission* in France, the *Société d'Impact Societal* (SIS) in Luxembourg, and the recent Dutch proposal for the BVm. BV stands for *besloten vennootschap met beperkte aansprakelijkheid* (private limited liability company) and the addition '*m*' stands for *maatschappellijk*, which means social. In the UK, the Community Interest Company (CIC) is a legal form for a social enterprise that has become rather popular.

One important element of having a social purpose is making sure that this social purpose is actually prioritised, and that it is not merely a nice marketing statement. Social enterprises therefore sometimes put certain structures in place with which they commit themselves to reinvesting a substantial part of their profits in the social purpose of the enterprise. Profit is the money that an enterprise earns above what it costs to produce and sell goods and services. The alternative for reinvestment of profits would be to distribute these profits to shareholders (or members in case of a cooperative), for example in the form of dividends. These profit distributions are sometimes perceived to

---

1 On social purpose, see e.g. C. Mayer, 'Governance of Corporate Purpose', *European Corporate Governance Institute—Law Working Paper* 609.2021 (2021), https://dx.doi.org/10.2139/ssrn.3928613; N.-H. Hsieh et al., 'The Social Purpose of Corporations', *Journal of the British Academy* 6 (2018), 49–73.

2 The most well-known expression of this idea was made by Milton Friedman. See M. Friedman, 'A Friedman Doctrine—The Social Responsibility of Business Is to Increase Its Profits', *The New York Times* (13 September 1970), https://www.nytimes.com/1970/09/13/archives/a-friedman-doctrine-the-social-responsibility-of-business-is-to.html

3 An example is Dopper, the producer of sustainable drink bottles (*Dopper*, www.dopper.com).

4 An example is Vandebron, an energy company that delivers energy from sustainable sources in the Netherlands (*Vandebron*, www.vandebron.nl).

5 An example is Het Goed, a Dutch thrift store that works together with municipalities and other partners to employ people at a distance to the job market (*Het Goed*, www.hetgoed.nl).

6 Also, large enterprises that do not primarily serve social objectives, but do have a social purpose, obtain the B-Corp label.

7 Companies like the American outdoor clothing company Patagonia, the French multinational food company Danone, and Dutch chocolate producer Tony's Chocolonely all have acquired the B-Corp label. See respectively: *Patagonia*, www.patagonia.com; *Tony's Chocolonely*, www.tonyschocolonely.com; *Danone*, www.danone.com

stand in the way for social enterprises to achieve their social purpose, not only because profit distributions leave less funds available for reinvestment in the social purpose, but also because they create incentives in the organisation to focus on maximising profit instead of trying to achieve the social purpose.

Therefore, more and more social enterprises use the options of limiting profit distributions. The idea behind this is that it creates a more circular flow of funds and ensures that incentives in the organisation are in line with the organisations' social purpose. Examples of such organisations include computer security consultant Radically Open Security, which is a 100% not-for-profit organisation, and soup seller Oma's Soep, which has set a limit on profit distributions of 50%. Both of these organisations will be addressed later in this chapter. On the other hand, there are also many social enterprises that have no specific limitations on profit distributions to shareholders but have other ways to achieve their social purpose. For example, the Dutch chocolate company Tony's Chocolonely recently implemented a 'mission-lock'. This means that they have appointed three 'mission guardians' who hold a golden share in Tony's Chocolonely that they can use to protect the social mission of Tony's when they would fear that a certain business decision in the future would endanger that mission.[8]

The aim of this chapter is to show how enterprises in the EU can use legal rules to secure their social purpose, with a focus on the limitation and reinvestment of profits. In Section 2 of this chapter the EU initiatives, definition of social enterprise by the European Commission, and mechanisms to legally secure the social objectives are set out. Subsequently, three existing legal forms with different variants of profit distribution rules, transparency requirements, and supervision are touched upon: the CIC in the UK, the SIS in Luxembourg, and the *Société à Mission* in France. Thereafter, the Netherlands is zoomed in on as an interesting case where the legal form for social enterprises is still under development, but enterprises themselves are already experimenting with limiting their profit distributions within the existing legal framework. First, the chapter outlines the proposal for the BVm in the Netherlands, which is in the process of being prepared by the Dutch Ministry of Economic Affairs and Climate. Subsequently, the default rules for profit distribution of the BV are described. Although social enterprises are not bound to a certain legal form in the Netherlands, they usually structure themselves as a BV because this legal form is generally most attractive to investors. Within these default rules for the BV, there is also space for social enterprises to create constraints on profit distributions by themselves. Section 3 explains why it makes a difference for society how organisations distribute their profits. Finally, Section 4 will conclude with some points for reflection.

8 Tony's Chocolonely, 'We lanceren Tony's Mission Lock—om onze missie voor altijd te borgen', *Tony's Chocolonely* (31 May 2023), www.tonyschocolonely.com/nl/nl/onze-missie/nieuws/we-lanceren-tonys-mission-lock-om-onze-missie-voor-altijd-te-borgen

2. Legal Framework for Profit Distribution in Social Enterprises in Europe

This section sets out the legal framework for social enterprises in the EU and the UK, and the rules that apply to them in terms of profit distribution. First, attention is paid to the definition, characteristics, and legal forms that are created for social enterprises, and to the rules for profit distribution in these legal forms. Thereafter, the chapter zooms in on the Netherlands and explains the Dutch rules for profit distribution in the BV—the legal form that is most often used by social enterprises in the Netherlands. These rules are similar in many other European countries. In the final part of this section, it is explained how social enterprises with the legal form of a BV can themselves create limitations on profit distribution, in order to put their social purpose central.

a. EU Initiatives, Definition, and Mechanisms to Secure the Social Objectives

In 2021, the European Union launched its Social Economy Action Plan, which builds further on the Social Business Initiative which was launched ten years earlier in 2011. With this Action Plan, the EU aims to help the European social economy thrive, for instance, by creating favourable tax, state aid, and public procurement conditions, by helping them to start and scale up, and by increasing their visibility in the European Union.[9] Social enterprises form an important part of this social economy the EU is aiming to support, together with cooperatives, mutual benefit societies, associations, and foundations. Social enterprises are defined by the European Commission as the following types of businesses:

- Those for who the social or societal objective of the common good is the reason for the commercial activity, often in the form of a high level of social innovation;
- Those whose profits are mainly reinvested to achieve this social objective;
- Those where the method of organization or the ownership system reflects the enterprise's mission, using democratic or participatory principles or focusing on social justice.[10]

Although the EU social economy action plan covers enterprises that fulfil these three criteria, the EU has not created its own legal framework or form for social enterprises. In 2018, the European Parliament proposed a resolution for a 'European Social Enterprise' label, which would facilitate social enterprise's cross-border activities. The resolution

9 Commission Communication, 'Building an Economy that Works for People: An Action Plan for the Social Economy', COM (2021) 778 final, https://eur-lex.europa.eu/legal-content/EN/TXT/?uri=celex:52021DC0778

10 Commission Communication, 'Social Business Initiative: Creating a Favourable Climate for Social Enterprises, Key Stakeholders in the Social Economy and Innovation', COM (2011) 682 final, https://eur-lex.europa.eu/LexUriServ/LexUriServ.do?uri=COM:2011:0682:FIN:en:PDF

was rejected by the European Commission, because of differences in Member States' national legal traditions and contexts.[11] Until today, the Social Economy Action Plan does not include any intention for creating a legal framework on the European level. However, many European countries have introduced special legislation and even special legal forms for social enterprises. In this section, three of those legal forms will be discussed, which have all implemented different rules on profit distribution. The forms that will be discussed are the CIC in the UK, the SIS in Luxembourg, and the *Société à Mission* in France.

The European Commission recognises that it is important for the achievement of a social purpose to (re)invest most of the profits that the enterprise makes into the social purpose of the enterprise. Limiting profit distributions is not the only way to legally secure a social purpose. There are also other legal mechanisms that social enterprises can—or must—adopt. An important characteristic of a social enterprise is transparency. In many cases, the management board of a social enterprise voluntarily publishes information regarding its objectives, mission, and the policy plans to achieve its social objectives. In addition, the governance structure, restrictions on profit distribution, yearly donations, and even dividend policy may be published on the website of the social enterprise. Transparency increases the possibilities for stakeholders to hold the management board of a social enterprise accountable for non-compliance with the social purpose. Another way to secure the social mission is by instituting a form of internal and/or external supervision. The social enterprise legal forms in European countries have various solutions for this.

b. Legal Forms in Europe

The CIC in the UK was designed as a special type of limited company and was introduced in 2005.[12] A CIC is created for the use of people who want to conduct a business or other activity for community benefit, and not purely for private advantage. The CIC Regulator is a special external supervisor for the CIC. A CIC is allowed to make profits and even deliver returns to investors (including dividend payments on shares) but these must be balanced and reasonable.[13] The legal provisions for CICs include an asset lock.[14] A CIC must issue a statement that its assets, including its profits or other surpluses generated by its activities, shall only be used for its social objective

11 Commission Communication, 'Statute for Social and Solidarity-Based Enterprises', *European Commission* (2018) https://www.europarl.europa.eu/legislative-train/theme-deeper-and-fairer-internal-market-with-a-strengthened-industrial-base-services-including-transport/file-statute-for-social-and-solidarity-based-enterprises

12 The Community Interest Company Regulations were brought into force in 2005 by the Companies (Audit, Investigations and Community Enterprise) Act 2004 and the Companies Act 1989 (Commencement No 18) Order 2004 (SI 2004/3322) (CIC Regulations).

13 Office of the Regulator of Community Interest Companies, 'Community Interest Companies Guidance', gov.uk (2013), https://www.gov.uk/government/publications/community-interest-companies-how-to-form-a-cic

14 Chapter 6 of the CIC Regulations.

and it must set limits to the payments to shareholders. The CIC must either retain its assets within the CIC or transfer its assets under strict requirements, including the requirement that the transfer is made for full market value so that the CIC retains the value of the assets transferred.[15] A CIC with a share capital may pay dividends to its shareholders but this payment is subject to a dividend cap of 35%.[16] This ensures that 65% of the CICs profits are reinvested back into the CIC or used for the community (social purpose) it was set up to serve.

Luxembourg has created the public label SIS. Commercial companies that comply with certain principles may be accredited as societal impact companies (SIS's) by the minister that is responsible for the regulation of the social and solidarity economy.[17] The SIS must annually publish a report certifying that it has fulfilled its legal obligations, and this must be approved by an (internal or external) auditor. Furthermore, all SISs must produce an annual non-financial impact report for their shareholders.[18] The share capital of an SIS-accredited company must be made up of at least 50% impact shares, which confer no entitlement to dividends, and no more than 50% distribution shares, which confer entitlement to dividends provided that the corporate purposes, as assessed using performance indicators, have been achieved. Profits allocated to impact shares may only be used to achieve the corporate purpose and are reinvested in full towards maintaining and developing the activity of the SIS-accredited company.

In France, the Law on the Social and Solidarity Economy (SSE) adopted in 2014 provides a regulatory framework for French social enterprises that fulfil certain conditions, including the establishment of a mandatory reserve which cannot be distributed.[19] Special legislation was introduced in 2019[20] on the basis of which commercial enterprises with social or environmental objectives can obtain the label *Société à Mission*.[21] The French legislation does not include an asset lock or dividend cap but requires disclosure and publication of certain information regarding the activities and ways to achieve the company's objectives. According to the rules for the French *Société à Mission* internal supervision is mandatory in the form of a separate legal body: the *Comité à Mission*. The *Comité à Mission* consists of at least one employee of the *Société à Mission*. Each year the *Comité à Mission* produces a report on how the *Société à Mission* has executed its social and environmental objectives. The *Comité* has access to all relevant information to perform its tasks. One of the legal requirements is that the company periodically seeks verification by an independent expert of the

15 6.1.1. CIC Regulations.

16 6.3.3. CIC Regulations.

17 The basis of the SIS is the Loi du 12 décembre 2016 portant création des sociétés d'impact sociétal.

18 'Societal Impact Company (SIS)', *Guichet* (3 August 2021), https://guichet.public.lu/en/entreprises/creation-developpement/forme-juridique/societe-capitaux/societe-impact-societal.html

19 Loi No. 2014–856 du 31 juillet 2014 relative à l'économie sociale et solidaire. European Social Enterprise Monitor 2021–2022, p. 23, https://euclidnetwork.eu/portfolio-posts/european-social-enterprise-monitor-esem/

20 Loi No. 2019–486 du 22 mai 2019 relative à la croissance et la transformation des entreprises (Loi Pacte).

21 L.2.10.10-L.2.10.12 Code de Commerce.

(report on) proper execution of the social and environmental objectives. This expert opinion is published on the company's website.[22]

c. The BVm: A New Legal Form in the Netherlands?

At present social enterprises in the Netherlands generally use as a legal form a BV or a foundation (*stichting*), or a combination of these two forms. A special corporate legal form or legislation for social enterprises does not exist in the Netherlands yet. However, in March 2021 the outlines for a special type of BV, the BVm, was published for public consultation by the Dutch Ministry of Economic Affairs and Climate ('BVm Outlines').[23] According to the BVm Outlines, a BV may opt to become a BVm by a notarial deed which includes certain elements and which is registered in the Dutch trade register. One of the conditions is that the articles of association include objectives that benefit society. The BVm Outlines do not mention a dividend cap but include a duty for the management board. The management board of the BVm may only approve a distribution (including a dividend payment) if it does not have reasonable doubt that the distribution will prevent the BVm from achieving its societal purpose and objectives. Although the BVm Outlines do not prescribe strict dividend restrictions (a dividend cap), they mention a reference point that at least 50% of the profit made in any financial year will be allocated to the social purpose of the BVm. Moreover, the management board must describe in its annual report how the BVm is benefiting society.

A more detailed draft act (bill) for the BVm has not been made available yet. Some shareholders will prioritise the social purpose of the enterprise, while many others will find it, at least, equally as important to receive a solid financial return on their investment. Therefore, for the BVm, some legal scholars have suggested that a larger group of stakeholders must be granted the right to go to court and/or the Enterprise Chamber if the BVm is not compliant with its social objectives.[24] The most important questions still are: who will qualify as stakeholders and on which legal grounds can stakeholders go to court? The BVm Outlines state that the rules for the BVm will provide that a foundation or association with collective interests will be granted the right to start inquiry proceedings with the Enterprise Chamber. One of the conditions is that the foundation or association must promote similar social interests as the BVm pursuant to its articles of association.

---

22 L.2.10.10 Code de Commerce.

23 'Besloten vennootschap met een maatschappelijk doel', *Dutch Ministry of Economic Affairs and Climate* (9 March 2021), https://www.internetconsultatie.nl/bvm

24 M. J. van Uchelen-Schipper, 'Sociale ondernemingen in Nederland: is het BV-recht nog flexibel genoeg?', WPNR 7298 (2020), 713–726, https://www.houthoff.com/-/media/houthoff/publications/mvanuchelen/wpnr-10-oktober-2020.pdf

d. Rules for Profit Distributions for BVs in the Netherlands

A BV has shareholders and is allowed to distribute (a part of) the profits that it makes to these shareholders. The yearly profit distributions, on the basis of the annual accounts, are called dividends. Usually, shareholders receive dividends at the end of the financial year, after the amount of profit is calculated. A management board can however also decide to pay out interim-dividends during the year. Profit that is not paid out to shareholders is usually transferred to the company's reserves. In later years, dividends can now also be paid out from these reserves.

For all BVs the same default rules for profit distribution apply. First of all, the general meeting of shareholders is empowered to decide to make any distribution to shareholders, but only to the extent the BV's equity is larger than the reserves that must be maintained by the law or the BV's articles of association.[25]

Such a shareholders resolution requires the approval of the BV's management board. The management board shall withhold such approval if it knows or should reasonably expect that, as a result of this distribution, the BV will no longer be able to continue to pay its debts when they fall due.[26] The purpose of this so called 'solvency test' is to protect creditors. When the profit distribution is approved and afterwards it turns out that the BV is no longer able to pay its debts, and the management board knew or should have reasonably foreseen it, then the board can be held personally liable for the deficit caused by the distribution. Shareholders that have received dividend distributions while they knew or should have reasonably foreseen that the BV would no longer be able to pay its debts, can also be held personally liable for the deficit, up until the height of the distribution they received.[27]

There are also disguised forms of dividend payments, in which shareholders receive money from the company in different ways other than through dividends. The most important form is share buybacks. With share buybacks, corporations buy back shares that are held by shareholders, by which the BV pays money to shareholders, which causes a decrease in the company's equity capital, similar as with dividend payments. Therefore, the same rules apply to share buybacks as to dividend payments.[28]

e. Limiting Profit Distribution by the BV Itself; Combination of a BV and a Foundation

Within these default rules, there is also space for social enterprises that are structured as a BV to voluntarily create constraints on profit distributions. One way in which they can do this is by creating a special reserve in the BV's articles of association that may only be used to achieve the BV's societal objectives.[29] As has been pointed out earlier,

25 Article 2(216) Paragraph 1 Dutch Civil Code.
26 Article 2(216) Paragraph 2 Dutch Civil Code.
27 Article 2(216) Paragraph 3 Dutch Civil Code.
28 Article 2(207) Paragraph 2 Dutch Civil Code.
29 Article 2(373) Paragraph 1(e) Dutch Civil Code.

reserves that must be maintained by the articles of association cannot be distributed to shareholders. The articles of association could for instance require that a certain part of the profits should be transferred to this reserve each financial year.

Another possibility is to create two different types of shares: profit-sharing and non-profit or limited profit sharing.[30] Hereby, certain shareholders can be excluded from receiving profits or the situation can be created in which certain shareholders are entitled to a larger share of profit than others.

After its incorporation, the BV's articles of association can only be amended in this respect and create such a special reserve or shares without rights to profits pursuant to a shareholder's resolution. In other words: the general meeting of shareholders must cooperate in order to achieve this.

In practice, many Dutch social enterprises use a combination of a BV and a foundation. In some combinations, the foundation can hold one, multiple or even all of the BV's shares. The foundation is set up by the BV and incorporates the social objective. As a shareholder, the foundation receives distributions on its shares, including dividends. As a foundation, it in turn cannot distribute profits to shareholders, dividends and other amounts received from the BV, rather such can solely be allocated to the social objectives.[31] An example is TBI, which is a construction company with a social purpose of which all the shares are held by a foundation, that uses part of the dividends they receive for the preservation of cultural heritage in the Netherlands.[32]

An example of a limited liability corporation that has put limitation of profit distribution into practice in a slightly different way is the Dutch Radically Open Security BV. Radically Open Security describes itself as 'an idealistic bunch of security researchers, networking/forensics geeks, and Capture The Flag winners that are passionate about making the world more secure'. They deliver all kinds of computer security consultancy services like ethical hacking, threat detection, workshops, and training. Radically Open Security transfers 100% of its profits as a donation to a charitable foundation, namely Stichting Nlnet. This foundation supports open-source, Internet research, and digital rights organisations.[33] The foundation does not hold shares and does not receive these funds as dividends, but rather as a donation. Yet another example is the Dutch private limited liability company Oma's Soep BV. The social purpose of Oma's Soep is to promote social involvement of the elderly and fight loneliness among the elderly. The social enterprise sells soups and stews based on the recipes of our grandparents. Oma's Soep is not entirely not-for-profit, but it did limit the possibility to pay out dividends to shareholders to 50% of the freely distributable profits, according to the statutes of the corporation. The other 50% is reserved and

30 Article 2(216) Paragraph 7 Dutch Civil Code.

31 Article 2(285) Dutch Civil Code.

32 *TBI*, www.tbi.nl

33 *Radically Open Security*, www.radicallyopensecurity.com. Radically Open Security also has a foundation as its sole shareholder for the sake of securing the social purpose and the not-for-profit form, but this foundation does not receive the profits of the enterprise. This is another variant of steward ownership.

donated to the foundation Oma's Soep, that organises cooking days, at which elderly people cook together with young people.[34]

Some enterprises with a foundation as their shareholder and 'responsible owner' call themselves 'steward owned'. Steward ownership is a relatively new concept which aims to rethink business based on two principles. First, the control over the enterprise is exercised by people who are committed to the enterprise's mission in the long term, and who have no economic interest in the enterprise's profits. And second, profits serve the mission of the enterprise. The foundation model that is well-known in the Netherlands is an example of how enterprises can put these principles into practice.

3. Profit Distribution in Social Enterprises in a Societal Context

This section puts the legal framework with limitations on profit distributions in a societal context, in order to make clear why it matters for society what happens with an organisation's profits. First addressed is why organisations distribute profits to shareholders in the first place. Second, it is discussed whether and how limiting profit distributions can help put a social purpose central. Finally, in Section 3 an important problem with limiting profit distribution is discussed—namely the difficulties with attracting finance.

a. The Rationale behind Profit Distribution

Profit distribution is considered to be important for investors as a return on their investment. Corporations issue shares to attract finance. In private limited liability corporations, such as BVs, there are typically one or a few shareholders, who provide the capital to the corporation. In return, these shareholders get voting rights and the right to share in the profits. One way in which shareholders share in the profits is that they are entitled to a share in the assets upon the dissolution of the company. The other way in which they share in the profits is capital distributions, especially dividends. Shareholders can calculate their 'dividend yield' as a measure of the financial success of their investment by dividing the dividends paid per share by the share value. A last way in which shareholders can benefit from their investment is when they make a profit with selling their shares to other shareholders. In private limited liability companies, this usually happens at a business acquisition.

b. Limiting Profit Distribution in order to Secure Social Purpose

Social enterprises may limit their profit distributions in order to secure their social purpose. Nevertheless, it is equally important that while doing business and making profits (distributable or not), enterprises observe that they protect and mitigate the impact of their activities on the

34 *Oma's Soep*, www.omassoep.nl/de-organisatie

environment and on human rights abuses. When profits are distributed to shareholders, less funds are left available for reinvestment in the social purpose of the enterprise. Reinvestment means that profits are redirected into the enterprise, and allocated in such a way that the board believes will foster the purpose of the enterprise. Hence, reinvestments are crucial in striving for a social purpose. Instead of reinvesting the profits immediately in the next year, profits can also be reserved for the future, for example for long-term investments or simply as a buffer for bad times. Next to reinvesting in the enterprise itself, the percentage of profits that is not paid out to shareholders can also be donated to a cause that furthers the social purpose of the enterprise. An even larger percentage of profits can be allocated to charitable causes when profits do not have to be distributed to individual shareholders.

Another way in which limiting profit distribution may help to secure social purpose is by changing incentives. After all, the possibility to unlimitedly distribute dividends to the shareholders creates incentives in the organisation to maximise the profit that is available for these dividends' distributions. Whereas it is generally the board that is responsible for the strategy and the day-to-day operations of the company,[35] shareholders do have some influence on the board. Their most important lever of power is that they can decide over the appointment and dismissal of board members. Therefore, board members will usually, to some extent, try to promote the interests of shareholders—and thus try to create high profits. The most obvious way in which enterprises can maximise their profits, is by minimising their expenses. Important expenses for enterprises that they can try to minimise include salaries, procurement costs, and costs of materials. This aim to maximise profits can be harmful, because it can lead to underpaying the employees of the company, exploitation of employees in supply chains, or the usage of materials that are cheap but have large CO2 emissions. Enterprises can also try to avoid taxes in order to cut on expenses. This system of incentives focused on profit distribution is often called 'shareholder primacy'.[36]

In enterprises where we see this shareholder primacy and, accordingly, a strong focus on profit distributions, people working in the enterprise are often evaluated based on financial criteria that are based on the maximisation of profit. This can be demotivating. It has been argued by several scholars that in an organisation where maximising profits for shareholders is the main goal, it is difficult to find meaning in your work.[37] Therefore, limiting profit distributions, and thereby putting a social purpose more central, may spark the intrinsic motivation of employees. Eliminating the possibility for paying out dividends takes away these incentives. While in theory this only applies to enterprises that become 100% not-for-profit, significantly capping the dividend distributions can already reinforce the social purpose by signalling that profit distribution is not the main goal. This may attract more long-term focused shareholders and board members, as well as more intrinsically motivated and involved employees.

35 P. L. Davies and K. J. Hopt, 'Corporate Boards in Europe—Accountability and Convergence', *American Journal of Comparative Law* 61 (1 April 2013), 301–376.

36 L. Stout, 'The Toxic Side Effects of Shareholder Primacy', University of Pennsylvania Law Review 161 (2013), 2003–2023.

37 B. Schwartz, 'There Must Be an Alternative', *Psychological Inquiry* 18 (2007), 48–51; J. Winter, 'Ontmenselijking van de grote onderneming', *Ondernemingsrecht* 2 (2019), 3–9.

This shareholder primacy is driven by more than merely the existence of the possibility for the distribution of profit. The incentives in the enterprise depend on multiple factors including the things shareholders find important, the relation between the board and shareholders, and the structure of the organisation. It reaches too far for this chapter to discuss this dynamic system of drivers in the enterprise. The main point is that, although the possibility of paying out dividends brings with it the risk of a focus on these profits, this is certainly not the reality in all enterprises that distribute dividends, especially not social enterprises with a strong focus on the social purpose. Many social enterprises are transparent, not only about their financial accounts, profits and amount of profit distribution, but also regarding the salaries of management.

c. Attracting Finance with Limitations on Profit Distribution

If we return to the rationale behind profit distributions, the question arises how these organisations with limitations on profit distributions attract (enough) finance from capital investors. If there is no, or only limited, return on investment it may be more difficult to attract these investors. This can be especially problematic in the start-up phase. In this phase a social enterprise generally needs (venture) capital next to bank loans, private donations, and other forms, such as crowd funding. Once the corporation has proved its growth potential it is easier to have access to different forms of finance.

This return-on-investment requirement is likely an important reason why organisations such as Tony's Chocolonely and Rituals have no limitations on shareholder distributions. Both of these organisations are B-Corps, and although becoming not-for-profit or low-profit are mentioned as options to secure the social mission of the B-Corp, it is only mentioned as an alternative to securing the mission via the articles of association and accountability mechanisms.[38] The reason for this is probably again the difficulty with attracting finance when profit distributions are limited.

Recently, social impact investing has been gaining traction. This notion refers to investments being made with the purpose to generate a positive impact on society. Although most impact investors still also require a sufficiently high return on their investment, there are also increasingly more impact investors that see financial gain not as the primary motive for investing, and thus it is not problematic if the financial returns are lower because of limitations to profit distribution. The impact investor seeks for measurable social and environmental impact alongside a financial return. Moreover, new ways of investing are being developed in the world of impact investing. For example, some impact investors do not invest by buying shares but by giving out loans, on which they only receive interest payments.[39] Another way of impact investing in not-for-profit organisations is by doing donations.[40] Other alternative ways of attracting financing can also be imagined. For example, organisations that are affiliated with the Dutch Stichting Sleipnir move (part of) their profits into the Sleipnir liquidity fund, which is used for financing needs of like-minded organisations.[41]

---

38 'The Basics of Mission-Aligned Governance', *B-Lab*, https://kb.bimpactassessment.net/support/solutions/articles/43000046071-the-basics-of-mission-aligned-governance

39 See for example *Actiam*, https://www.actiam.com/nl/impact-case/

40 See for example *DIIF*, https://diif.foundation/

41 *Sleipnir*, https://sleipnir.nl/

4. Conclusions

This chapter has outlined the rules for profit distribution in social enterprises, and explained why limitations on profit distributions can contribute to solving societal challenges by making the social purpose of social enterprises more central. We have however also seen that creating limitations on profit distributions may not be sufficient in order to secure the social purpose of the social enterprise. Other legal rules with regard to transparency, enforcement, and supervision also play a role in this regard. This may be even more important because of the difficulty for social enterprises with limitations on profit distributions to attract finance. Although innovations in impact investing are rapidly developing, limitations on profit distributions may still present a hurdle in the search for (equity) investors.

Undoubtedly, the topics discussed in this chapter will be an important part of the discussions in company law in the coming years. Some questions that are interesting for these discussions are laid down in the following section as points of reflection.

5. Points for Reflection

Q1: Can limited liability companies, like the Dutch BV, (fully) limit profit distribution altogether in their articles of association?

Q2: Would limiting profit distribution have the potential to change the incentives for employees in enterprises?

Q3: What is the importance of (internal and external) supervision for social enterprises?

Q4: What is the importance of transparency for social enterprises?

Q5: Should the Dutch legislation for the BVm include a dividend cap?

Q6: Should the Dutch legislation for the BVm include a form of external supervision?

Q7: Would it be a good idea for the EU to create a legal form for social enterprises or another type of harmonisation, and if yes, what rules should it contain?

Q8: Are the possibilities for attracting finance for social enterprises with limitations on profit distributions sufficient? What are other solutions to this problem?

Q9: What about a 'not-for-profit' world: a world with only not-for-profit enterprises. Would such a world be realistic? What would be the benefits and downsides of such a world?

Bibliography

'The Basics of Mission-Aligned Governance', *B-Lab*, https://kb.bimpactassessment.net/support/solutions/articles/43000046071-the-basics-of-mission-aligned-governance

'Besloten vennootschap met een maatschappelijk doel', *Dutch Ministry of Economic Affairs and Climate* (9 March 2021), https://www.internetconsultatie.nl/bvm

Commission Communication, 'Building an Economy that Works for People: An Action Plan for the Social Economy', COM (2021) 778 final, https://eur-lex.europa.eu/legal-content/EN/TXT/?uri=celex:52021DC0778

Commission Communication, 'Social Business Initiative: Creating a Favourable Climate for Social Enterprises, Key Stakeholders in the Social Economy and Innovation', COM (2011) 682 final, https://eur-lex.europa.eu/LexUriServ/LexUriServ.do?uri=COM:2011:0682:FIN:en:PDF

Commission Communication, 'Statute for Social and Solidarity-Based Enterprises', *European Commission* (2018) https://www.europarl.europa.eu/legislative-train/theme-deeper-and-fairer-internal-market-with-a-strengthened-industrial-base-services-including-transport/file-statute-for-social-and-solidarity-based-enterprises

Davies, P. L., and K. J. Hopt, 'Corporate Boards in Europe—Accountability and Convergence', *American Journal of Comparative Law* 61 (1 April 2013), 301–376, https://doi.org/10.5131/AJCL.2012.0020

Friedman, M., 'A Friedman Doctrine—The Social Responsibility of Business Is to Increase Its Profits', *The New York Times* (13 September 1970), https://www.nytimes.com/1970/09/13/archives/a-friedman-doctrine-the-social-responsibility-of-business-is-to.html

Hsieh, N.-H., et al., 'The Social Purpose of Corporations', *Journal of the British Academy* 6 (2018), 49–73, https://doi.org/10.5871/jba/006s1.049

Mayer, C., 'Governance of Corporate Purpose', *European Corporate Governance Institute—Law Working Paper* 609.2021 (2021), https://dx.doi.org/10.2139/ssrn.3928613

Office of the Regulator of Community Interest Companies, 'Community Interest Companies Guidance', *gov.uk* (2013), https://www.gov.uk/government/publications/community-interest-companies-how-to-form-a-cic

Schwartz, B., 'There Must Be an Alternative', *Psychological Inquiry* 18 (2007), 48–51, https://doi.org/10.1080/10478400701389086

'Societal Impact Company (SIS)', *Guichet* (3 August 2021), https://guichet.public.lu/en/entreprises/creation-developpement/forme-juridique/societe-capitaux/societe-impact-societal.html

Stout, L., 'The Toxic Side Effects of Shareholder Primacy', *University of Pennsylvania Law Review* 161 (2013), 2003–2023

Tony's Chocolonely, 'We lanceren Tony's Mission Lock—om onze missie voor altijd te borgen', *Tony's Chocolonely* (31 May 2023), www.tonyschocolonely.com/nl/nl/onze-missie/nieuws/we-lanceren-tonys-mission-lock-om-onze-missie-voor-altijd-te-borgen

Uchelen-Schipper, M. J. van, 'Sociale ondernemingen in Nederland: is het BV-recht nog flexibel genoeg?', WPNR 7298 (2020), 713–726, https://www.houthoff.com/-/media/houthoff/publications/mvanuchelen/wpnr-10-oktober-2020.pdf

Winter, J., 'Ontmenselijking van de grote onderneming', *Ondernemingsrecht* 2 (2019), 3–9

11. Financial Crises and European Private Law

Guido Comparato

Abstract

Does private law play a role in the occurrence of financial crises, and how does it react and change in response to them? The chapter illustrates the relationship between private law and financial crises by looking at the constitutive role of law for finance, the impact of crises on private law relations, the ways in which the law can be used to mitigate the impact of crises on consumers, the relationship between financial regulation and contract, the reform of private law to achieve financial stability and, more fundamentally, the societal significance of financial crises for European private law itself: what do we expect from private law in a financialised society and how has the European private law project evolved since the last global crisis?

1. Introduction

One of the events that had the greatest impact on the development of European law in the new millennium was the Global Financial Crisis (GFC) of 2007–2008. Starting in the US as a subprime mortgage crisis, it soon spread internationally and turned into the eurozone crisis in the EU, which at its peak seemed to threaten the entire European integration process as it had been pursued so far. The crisis highlighted the need for better regulation of the banking and financial system, but its profound effects have also called into question the societal role of private law and EU law, leading us to look more critically at aspects such as the political economy of private debt, the relationship between law and finance, the interplay between financial regulation and contract law, as well as the perspectives of further Europeanisation of private law. This chapter undertakes to introduce the interrelationship between financial crises and European private law considering the socio-economic context in which the law operates.

It is well known that regulatory frameworks are highly relevant to the stability or instability of financial institutions and, as a consequence, of financial systems

 https://doi.org/10.11647/OBP.0448.11

more broadly: if supervision and regulation did not limit the possibility of engaging in excessively risky or unsustainable practices, investors, depositors or banks could suffer economic losses and the viability of a financial institution, or, in particularly dramatic cases, the economy of a country, could be jeopardised. Indeed, some private institutions are 'systemically important' enough—or, in the usual parlance, 'too big to fail'—to the point that they could drag the whole economy into disaster if they were to run into serious difficulties. Conversely, reducing supervision and regulation could increase systemic risk: it has been noted that many relatively recent crises have occurred after financial deregulation.[1] It is therefore common for financial crises to be followed by reforms of the regulatory and supervisory infrastructure intended to address practices that are seen as having caused previous economic disasters, with the expectation that re-regulation will prevent such events from recurring.[2]

> The GFC was followed by a plethora of institutional reforms at various levels: notably, the creation of the Financial Stability Board at the international level, the establishment of new European Supervisory Authorities[3] and the attempt to complete a Banking Union in the EU,[4] as well as several reforms of the domestic regulatory infrastructure in countries such as the United Kingdom and, on the other side of the Atlantic, the United States of America.

While financial crises routinely lead to a re-discussion of the architecture of financial regulation and supervision, the role of private law must also be considered.[5] In fact, private law in general, and contract law in particular, is extremely relevant to the financial sector and, consequently, to financial crises. The basic institutions of private law—property, contract, tort—enable the creation and maintenance of capital and tradable commodities.[6] Financial products are contracts. In this sense, there is a natural link between contract law and finance.[7] An efficient and fair contract law therefore appears to be crucial to the well-functioning of the financial system as much as institutional reforms. But what should the role of private law, and contract law in particular, be?

---

1 J. Furman and J. E. Stiglitz, 'Economic Crises: Evidence and Insights from East Asia', *Brookings Papers on Economic Activity* 29.2 (1998), 1–136; A. Musacchio, 'Mexican Financial Crisis of 1994–1995', in G. Caprio (ed.), *The Evidence and Impact of Financial Globalization* (London: Elsevier, 2012), pp. 657–667; S. Jönsson, *A Comparative History of Bank Failures. From Medici to Barings* (London: Routledge, 2021), p. 118.

2 F. S. Mishkin, 'Lessons from the Asian crisis', *Journal of International Money and Finance* 18 (1999), 709–723.

3 Regulations No 1093/2010, No 1094/2010, and No 1095/2010 establishing the European Securities and Markets Authority, European Banking Authority, European Insurance and Occupational Pensions Authority.

4 See the contributions in D. Busch and G. Ferrarini (eds), *European Banking Union*, 2nd edn (Oxford: Oxford University Press, 2020).

5 M. Bridge and J. Braithwaite, 'Private Law and Financial Crises', *Journal of Corporate Law Studies* 13 (2013), 361–399.

6 K. Pistor, *The Code of Capital. How the Law Creates Wealth and Inequality* (Princeton, NJ: Princeton University Press, 2019).

7 J. Black, 'Reconceiving Financial Markets. From the Economic to the Social', *Journal of Corporate Law Studies* 13 (2001), 401–442.

Traditionally, the role of private law in this context is understood as being concerned with the interpretation and enforcement of contracts as freely agreed by the parties, in the light of the most basic principles of freedom of contract and sanctity of contract. The role of regulation, on the other hand, would be to set the framework within which these interactions take place and to intervene prudently in the limited number of situations where externalities or market failures might arise. However, while it may be functional to ensure economic certainty and financial innovation, a view that limits the role of private law to one of safeguarding the sanctity and freedom of contract does not seem to be appropriate to counter the risk of instability and to offer viable solutions in times of crises. In other words, this view would be 'a theory for good times in finance, not for bad times'.[8] How, then, should European private law operate in the 'bad times' of a crisis?

In the next part on the 'legal context', three instances of the more complex interaction between private law and financial crises will be considered: the question whether binding contracts can be amended following a crisis, the interaction of contract law and financial regulation, and the reform of contract law in light of the goals of financial stability and consumer protection. The remaining part will broaden the perspective and discuss the 'societal relevance' of European private law in this context.

2. Legal Context

The financial market is legally constructed and relies on the enforcement of freely concluded contracts, but a strict adherence to the principle of sanctity of contract might exacerbate the effects of a crisis. Paradoxically, as Katharina Pistor noted, there are 'bad times' in which the full enforcement of legal commitments might lead to the financial system's demise and the full force of the law will need to be suspended in the interest of the financial market itself.[9] This does not mean that a hypothetical state of emergency allows to disregard the law—although the question whether public authorities did follow the law when they attempted to govern the effects of the GFC has indeed been raised[10]—but, when stability at large is under threat, the law might have to respond in an 'elastic' way. In this sense, the sanctity of the contract principle in private law too could be loosened. At the same time, Pistor critically noted that the financial system tends to be elastic at the top but rigid at the periphery: in other words, insolvent banks might expect to be rescued (through bailouts or other procedures which have also been introduced or improved in recent years), but defaulting mortgage borrowers are

8 K. Pistor, 'A Legal Theory of Finance', *Journal of Comparative Economics* 41 (2013), 315–330.

9 Ibid., p. 315. In the perspective of system theory, this can be regarded as a crisis of the distinction between cognitive and normative expectation structures: M. Renner, 'Death by Complexity. The Financial Crisis and the Crisis of Law in World Society', in P. F. Kjaer, G. Teubner, and A. Febbrajo (eds), *The Financial Crisis in Constitutional Perspective. The Dark Side of Functional Differentiation* (Oxford: Hart, 2011), pp. 93–111.

10 In the US: E. A. Posner, *Last Resort. The Financial Crisis and the Future of Bailouts* (Chicago, IL: University of Chicago Press, 2018).

more likely to be held responsible for their debts. To what extent is European private law insensible to financial, and consequently, social crises?

a. Between *pacta sunt servanda* and *rebus sic stantibus*

To introduce this multifaceted topic, let us first consider the question of the effects of worsened financial conditions on the ability of parties to perform their obligations. A contract obliges parties to keep their promises, but performance might unexpectedly become excessively onerous or perhaps even impossible in the context of a severe economic crisis. Should non-performance of monetary obligations be excused in that case, or should we instead assume that one contract party must always have the money to perform (in fact, the performance of a monetary obligation can technically never become impossible because money can never perish)? To make a few concrete examples involving both financial and non-financial contracts, should a commercial tenant be entitled to a rent reduction if, because of economic recession, his or her business is no longer profitable to the point that the tenant is unable to meet his or her obligations? Should a mortgage borrower be relieved of his or her payment obligations if he or she can no longer pay the instalments due to extraordinary inflation or due to losing his or her job because of an economic crisis? This dilemma keeps reoccurring in 'bad times' and underlies contract law in all its manifestations: in B2C (business-to-consumer), B2B (business-to-business), as well as even in relationships between private investors and sovereigns.

In that latter regard, even States facing severe economic crises might have to restructure their debt avoiding repaying in full the holders of government bonds, which raises the question whether those investors are entitled to payment.

> The Argentine default of 2001, the largest sovereign default ever recorded in history,[11] resulted in a wave of lawsuits brought by dissatisfied bondholders who opposed the restructuring of Argentine debt, insisting on full repayment. The dispute raised a plurality of questions at the interface between contract and public international law, [12] involving issues of immunity, international investment law, and state of necessity. In Europe, the German Federal Constitutional Court was called to pronounce itself on the question whether Argentina could avail itself of a possible exception based on a state of necessity rooted in international law, but ultimately answered the question in the negative, finding that no general rule of international law entitles a State to 'temporarily refuse to meet private-law payments claims due towards private individuals by invoking state necessity declared because of inability to pay'.[13]

In private B2B and B2C disputes, the question whether a worsened financial situation

---

11 S. Takagi, 'Argentina's Default of 2001', in G. Caprio (ed.), *The Evidence and Impact of Financial Globalization* (London: Elsevier, 2012), pp. 709–719.

12 For an analysis, see S. Grund, 'Restructuring Argentina's Sovereign Debts. Navigating the Legal Labyrinth', (2019), https://ssrn.com/abstract=3485370

13 German Federal Constitutional Court, 2 BvM 1/03, 2 BvM 2/03, 2 BvM 3/03, 2 BvM 4/03, 2 BvM 5/03, 2 BvM 1/06, 2 BvM 2/06, 8 May 2007.

due to the macroeconomic scenario might excuse debtors from performing their obligations is a vexed one. The starting point—although by no means the only principle—of contract law is that promises should be kept, which is often referred to with the Latin phrase *pacta sunt servanda*. This is nonetheless counterbalanced by a plurality of other doctrines with different denominations and characteristics in various jurisdictions,[14] expressions of the *rebus sic stantibus* principle, which on the contrary may allow one party to be excused for non-performance when a fundamental and unexpected change of circumstances has occurred.

> Despite its extensive and illustrious historical origins, the *rebus sic stantibus* principle was not initially recognised in most codifications, as it conflicted with ideals of legal certainty and sanctity that were predominant in codes inspired by more formalistic and individualistic values. Nonetheless, it developed mostly through legal scholarship and judicial practice in the face of the increased complexity of modern times. Even if the German Civil Code (BGB) did not explicitly recognise the doctrine, German courts in the 1920s accepted that some events, such as the dramatic hyperinflation of those years, could affect the foundation of the contract.[15] That doctrine was later codified through a reform of the BGB. More recently, a doctrine allowing the revision of a contract that has become excessively onerous, as opposed to impossible, was also included in the reform of the French Civil Code.

Could such an approach be employed to offer relief to customers who have become over-indebted due to a crisis?[16] In fact, as exceptions to the binding force of the agreement, these doctrines are formulated and interpreted in a narrow way, which makes it difficult to rescind, terminate, or revise transactions. Courts in various European jurisdictions might reach different conclusions based on the application of different general contract law doctrines[17] but, in the aftermath of the GFC, they have overall been cautious when it comes to invalidating or terminating agreements.[18]

> It has been argued that the different approaches by various national judges might be explained by 'the different frequency and intensity of financial crises' in each country.[19] For instance, in austerity-plagued Greece, Courts have occasionally and exceptionally

14 Frustration, *Störung der Geschäftsgrundlage*, *imprévision*, *eccessiva onerosità sopravvenuta*, etc. It's important to note that each of these possesses distinct meanings and application criteria, yet they all have in common the objective of acknowledging the effects of a fundamental change of circumstances on the contract.

15 See the case studies in E. Hondius and E.C. Grigoleit (eds), *Unexpected Circumstances in European Contract Law* (Cambridge, UK: Cambridge University Press, 2011), p. 218 ff.

16 J. Pulgar, 'A Contractual Approach to Overindebtedness: rebus sic stantibus Instead of Bankruptcy', in L. Nogler and U. Reifner (eds), *Life Time Contracts. Social Long-Term Contracts in Labour, Tenancy and Consumer Credit Law* (The Hague: Eleven International Publishing, 2014), p. 534.

17 R. Momberg Uribe, 'Beyond the Risk: Swaps, Financial Crisis and Change of Circumstances. Comparative Case Note. Supreme Court of Portugal—10.10.2013. Conclusions', *European Review of Private Law* 23 (2015), 149–151.

18 For an overview of the legal doctrines which could at least theoretically be used in a few jurisdictions, see B. Başoğlu (ed.), *The Effects of Financial Crises on the Binding Force of Contracts—Renegotiation, Rescission or Revision* (Cham: Springer, 2016).

19 R. Serozan, 'General Report on the Effects of Financial Crises on the Binding Force of Contracts: Renegotiation, Rescission or Revision', in Başoğlu (ed.), *The Effects of Financial Crises*, pp. 3–32 (p. 28).

resorted to the general principle of good faith to revise the price of private commercial leases.[20] A point worth further consideration involves contemplating how significant socio-economic events within a country affect the interpretation of legal rules.

The possibility of being released from an unfavourable transaction in the aftermath of a crisis relying on general doctrines such as *rebus sic stantibus* thus exists but is particularly limited. It might thus appear at first glance that the sanctity of contract principle remains the rule and *rebus sic stantibus* the narrow exception, indicating an inelasticity of the system at its periphery. Other legal strategies might nonetheless prove appropriate to navigate the effects of a crisis.

1) Contractual Approach to Crises

Attention can be paid first to the precise terms of the contract. The agreement might in fact include terms which, appropriately construed, offer a solution to some of the described issues.

With regard to the above-mentioned sovereign debt contracts, comparable problems to those seen during the Argentine default occurred during the eurozone crisis with regard to the Greek government-debt crisis. In order to restructure its debt, Greece could retrospectively insert Collective Action Clauses in its Greek-law-governed sovereign debt contracts. These are terms which establish that a supermajority of bondholders can agree to a 'haircut' which then becomes binding on all investors. That approach was challenged by some investors who lamented the violation of their fundamental right to property. However, the Greek approach was deemed lawful by courts in Europe, notably including the European Court of Human Rights, which placed particular emphasis on the exceptional background of the measures.[21]

In B2B transactions—where strong forms of statutory controls on the contents of the contract are generally lacking—contract terms could allow renegotiation or termination due to exceptional circumstances. For instance, so-called '*force majeure* clauses' can be included in long-term contracts to relieve a party from an obligation when something beyond the party's reasonable control prevents them from performing. However, it must be noted that, in line with the *rebus sic stantibus* principle, these terms too tend to be interpreted in a particularly restrictive way and, consequently, they are not always likely to apply to situations in which performance was made impracticable due to the effects of a financial crisis.

In a 2010 English case involving the sale of a jet aircraft, one party tried to claim that the 'unanticipated, unforeseeable, and cataclysmic downward spiral of the world's financial markets'[22] of that period triggered a *force majeure* clause which excused their

---

20 N. A. Davrados, 'Financial Turmoil as a Change of Circumstances Under Greek Contract Law', in Başoğlu (ed.), *The Effects of Financial Crises*, pp. 145–162 (p. 154).

21 ECtHR, *Mamatas and Others v Greece*, Appl. Nos. 63066/14, 64297/14 and 66106/14, judgment of 21 July 2016.

22 *Tandrin Aviation Holdings Ltd v Aero Toy Store LLC* [2010] EWHC 40 (Comm), para. 38.

non-performance. The Court noted that '[i]t is well established under English law that a change in economic / market circumstances, affecting the profitability of a contract or the ease with which the parties' obligations can be performed, is not regarded as being a *force majeure* event. Thus a failure of performance due to the provision of insufficient financial resources has been held not to amount to *force majeure*'.[23] As a point for further reflection: in explaining the correct interpretation of the clause, the Court mentioned that 'matters relevant to the delivery of the aircraft [...] would be caught by that clause, such as the seller being unable to deliver the aircraft on time due to a pandemic causing a dearth of delivery pilots';[24] one can reflect on the similarities and differences between events such as a global financial crisis and a pandemic crisis in terms of their possible effects on the binding force of a contract.

2) Unfair Terms in Consumer Contracts

The existence of legislation creating statutory rights for consumers is relevant for the invalidation of contract terms which might be responsible for the onerousness of financial transactions. Specific contract terms in B2C relationships have in fact been tested for unfairness and declared to be non-binding on the consumer applying the 1993 Unfair Contract Terms Directive.[25] The importance of this instrument is demonstrated by a wave of cases which in the wake of the GFC reached the Court of Justice of the European Union (CJEU) and that demonstrate the relevance of contract law to cope with social problems, as consumers in countries facing severe socio-economic crisis used that legislation to challenge terms in their now unsustainable loan agreements.[26] Unfair terms legislation—with particular emphasis on its transparency requirements[27] and occasionally read in light of fundamental rights[28]—has been used to test foreign-currency-indexation clauses,[29] floor clauses,[30] and acceleration clauses[31] in mortgage loan agreements.

One interesting aspect to note in this respect is that in those instances the instrument employed by the courts was indeed the Unfair Contract Terms Directive—thus a relatively old instrument designed to apply to all consumer contracts instead of being specifically intended to regulate financial transactions: why was 'general' consumer law more effective in coping with this issue than the supposedly more detailed rules of financial regulation? Is this a sign of the inadequacy of EU rules on consumer credit

23 Ibid., para. 40.

24 Ibid., para. 46.

25 Council Directive 93/13/EEC of 5 April 1993 on unfair terms in consumer contracts.

26 H. W. Micklitz and N. Reich, 'The Court and Sleeping Beauty: The Revival of the Unfair Contract Terms Directive (UCTD)', *Common Market Law Review* 51 (2014), 771–808.

27 C. Leone, 'Transparency Revisited—On the Role of Information in the Recent Case-Law of the CJEU', *European Review of Contract Law* 10.2 (2014), 312–325.

28 CJEU, Case C-34/13, *Monika Kušionová v SMART Capital a.s.* [2014] ECLI:EU:C:2014:2189.

29 CJEU, Case C-26/13, *Kásler and Káslerné Rábai* [2014] ECLI:EU:C:2014:282; C-260/18, *Kamil Dziubak and Justyna Dziubak v Raiffeisen Bank International AG* [2019] ECLI:EU:C:2019:819.

30 CJEU, Joined Cases C-154, 307, and 308/15, *Gutiérrez Naranjo.*

31 CJEU, Case C-415/11, *Mohamed Aziz v Caixa d'Estalvis de Catalunya, Tarragona i Manresa (Catalunyacaixa)* [2013] ECLI:EU:C:2013:164.

and mortgage credit to deal with such burning social issues? To address this question, let us now move on to consider European financial contract law.

b. Contract Law and Financial Regulation

In the aftermath of the GFC, investors have occasionally claimed that they had been mis-sold financial products without being properly informed about the risks involved in the transactions. Such a claim can be based on the violation of a private law duty of care but has often been based on the alleged violation of the information duties imposed by financial regulation. This leads to a question: to what extent do contract law principles interact with financial regulation?

When interpreting general private law concepts, we could in theory look for guidance in financial regulation, where precise rules of conduct detail certain behaviours to be expected from financial service providers, outlining the way in which they must behave towards their customers. Contract law creates rights and obligations between parties providing remedies for the non-breaching party, whereas financial regulation mandates specific rules of conduct that financial service providers must adhere to when offering their services. In this sense, regulation overlaps with notions to be found in general contract law with the result of intersections between contract law and financial supervision[32] and regulation.[33] This relationship has mostly been explored in relation to the implications of financial supervision and regulation for civil liability:[34] could the violation of a regulatory rule of conduct lead to the recognition of a private law remedy—such as contract avoidance or damages either in contract or tort—for the investor or consumer who has suffered a loss? In this regard, there is no clear-cut answer in European private law, as different jurisdictions adopt different approaches: in some cases, regulation and private law are kept separate, in other cases they interact more clearly.[35]

> The 2014 Markets in Financial Instruments Directive—known as MiFID II—is an important piece of EU legislation intended to provide a framework for the regulation of investment services[36] and that imposes relevant obligations on financial service providers, such as the duty to act in the best interest of the client and so called 'know your customer' and 'know your product' obligations. While some of these duties seem to echo existing private law duties, are such rules of conduct capable of creating contractual rights for investors? Interpreting the 2004 version of MiFID, the CJEU had already accepted that

32 Y. Svetiev and A. Ottow, 'Financial Supervision in the Interstices Between Private and Public Law', *European Review of Contract Law* 10.4 (2014), 496–544.

33 O. Cherednychenko, 'Two Sides of the Same Coin: EU Financial Regulation and Private Law', *European Business Organization Law Review* 22.2 (2021), 147–172.

34 See contributions in O. Cherednychenko and M. Andenas (eds), *Financial Regulation and Civil Liability in European Law* (Cheltenham: Elgar, 2020).

35 M. Wallinga, *EU Investor Protection Regulation and Liability for Investment Losses. A Comparative Analysis of the Interplay between MiFID & MiFID II and Private Law* (Cham: Springer, 2020).

36 On the evolution of the EU regime of investment services regulation, see N. Moloney, *EU Securities and Financial Markets Regulation* (Oxford: Oxford University Press, 2014), pp. 327 ff.

> Member States could reinforce financial regulation with private law remedies.[37] An explicit intersection of the two domains of financial regulation and private law is visible in instruments such as the amended Credit Rating Agencies Regulation, which now gives investors or issuers a right to claim damages from a credit rating agency that committed an infringement intentionally or with gross negligence.[38]

This might all sound a bit technical, perhaps. However, the blurring of the line between regulation and private law is not just a matter of technics, but rather tells us something about the rationale of the rules. In fact, regulation is inspired by a number of sometimes competing goals—market integrity, financial stability, competition, sustainability, and so on—which might be different from those—freedom of contract, commutative justice, efficiency, and so on—which are traditionally said to inspire private law. Yet it is not always useful nor possible to clearly distinguish between those, with the result of considerable intersections at the level of both technics and values. The next section illustrates this with regard to consumer credit and mortgage law.

c. The Reform of Private Law in Light of Financial Stability

The regulation of contracts can be inspired by policy objectives explicitly aimed at ensuring investor protection or even financial stability[39] instead of simply giving effectiveness to the will of the parties. This is particularly clear in the case of EU private law which, as various scholars have highlighted either in critical or in approving terms, has a strong 'instrumentalist' dimension. This is well-illustrated by the case of consumer credit.

It should be noted that a contract law which places emphasis on freedom of contract may facilitate over-lending: on the one hand, lenders are not constrained in their freedom to offer loans to consumers who on the other hand have the necessity to access finance. In 'good times' lenders tend to lower the lending standards so that more customers will have access to credit. This is further facilitated by financial practices which allow the lender to minimise the credit risk—as in the case of securitisation—or to make an immediate profit by selling additional and possibly unnecessary financial products to the consumer—as in the case of cross-selling and mis-selling[40] of services (for instance, a bank might agree to grant a loan only on condition that the consumer additionally purchases a payment protection insurance).

Access to credit is of course crucial for the economy and consumer welfare, but when lenders have an incentive to lend easy money to borrowers in financial need regardless

37 CJEU, Case C-604/11, *Genil v Bankinter* [2013] ECLI:EU:C:2013:344.

38 Regulation (EC) No 1060/2009 of the European Parliament and of the Council of 16 September 2009 on credit rating agencies, Title IIIA, Article 35a.

39 G. Comparato, 'Financial Stability in Private Law: Intersections, Conflicts, Choices', *Common Market Law Review* 58.2 (2021), 391–430.

40 See Better Finance, 'A Major Enforcement Issue. The Mis-selling of Financial Products', Briefing Paper (April 2017), https://betterfinance.eu/wp-content/uploads/publications/Misselling_of_Financial_Products_in_the_EU_-_Briefing_Paper_2017.pdf

of the possible inability of the latter to repay—i.e. their so-called 'credit-worthiness'—the problem of over-indebtedness might emerge.[41] Such excessive accumulation of household debt is likely to increase consumers' vulnerability to external shocks[42] and is even regarded by various economists as one of the reasons behind financial crises.[43]

> Should private law encourage consumers' access to finance, or should it be more cautious in order to avoid over-indebtedness? Where is the line to be drawn? In EU law, the 2008 Consumer Credit Directive[44] did follow at least in part a freedom of contract approach since, as the culmination of a complex legislative history, it ended up including a rather toothless principle of responsible lending.[45] The Directive, which did not also apply to mortgage loans, provided in one of its recitals that Member States 'should take appropriate measures' to ensure responsible practices and 'determine the necessary means to sanction creditors' engaging in irresponsible lending,[46] but failed to outline the consequences of a violation of that principle. Later, the CJEU pushed for giving such obligations more teeth, ensuring that penalties are effective, proportionate and dissuasive as requested by the Directive.[47] The ineffectiveness of that Directive later led to a new and more detailed Consumer Credit Directive in 2023.

A possible deficiency of a private law design predicated on the freedom of contract and sanctity of contract approach emerges here; those principles allow for loosely restrained lending, while not also offering the instruments to cope with the resulting debt problems: as you remember from a previous section, contract law does not easily allow a debtor to be excused for non-performance of his or her obligations. Post-GFC reforms have attempted to address this mismatch in two ways.

On the one hand, there is an attenuation of freedom of contract. Newer reforms have attempted to restrain the freedom to provide loans when there is a risk that debt might become unsustainable for the customer. This includes stricter responsible lending rules[48] in the area of mortgage loans, as included in the 2014 Mortgage Credit Directive.[49] Considering that the GFC is rooted (at least in part) in the US subprime

---

41 H. W. Micklitz, 'Access to and Exclusion from Financial Markets after the Global Financial Crisis', in T. Wilson (ed.), *International Responses to Issues of Credit and Over-Indebtedness in the Wake of the Crisis* (Burlington, VT: Ashgate, 2013), pp. 47–75.

42 I. Domurath, *Consumer Vulnerability and Welfare in Mortgage Contracts* (Oxford: Hart, 2020).

43 S. Claessens, G. Dell'Ariccia, and D. Igan, L. Laeven, 'A Cross-Country Perspective on the Causes of the Global Financial Crisis', in Caprio (ed.), *The Evidence and Impact of Financial Globalization*, pp. 737–752; A. Mian and A. Sufi, *House of Debt. How They (and You) Caused the Great Recession, and How We Can Prevent It from Happening Again* (Chicago, IL: University of Chicago Press, 2015).

44 Directive 2008/48/EC of the European Parliament and of the Council on credit agreements for consumers and repealing Council Directive 87/102/EEC.

45 See Y. M. Atamer, 'Duty of Responsible Lending. Should the European Union Take Action?', in S. Grundmann and Y. M. Atamer (eds), *Financial Services, Financial Crisis and General European Contract Law: Failure and Challenges of Contracting* (Alphen aan den Rijn: Kluwer, 2011), pp. 179–202 (p. 179).

46 CCD, Recital 26.

47 CJEU, C-388/11, *Le Crédit Lyonnais* [2013] ECLI:EU:C:2013:120; C-449/13, *CA Consumer Finance SA v Ingrid Bakkaus* [2014] ECLI:EU:C:2014:2464; more recently: C-303/20, *Ultimo Portfolio Investment SA v KM* [2021] ECLI:EU:C:2021:479.

48 T. Wilson, 'The Responsible Lending Response', in T. Wilson (ed.), *International Responses to Issues of Credit and Over-indebtedness in the Wake of Crisis* (Farnham: Ashgate, 2013), pp. 109–134.

49 Directive 2014/17/EU of the European Parliament and of the Council on credit agreements for consumers relating to residential immovable property.

mortgage crisis, the importance of rules on consumer mortgages clearly appears. The CJEU has had an occasion to reflect upon these rules explaining that their rationale is in fact rooted in the GFC and reveals the intention of the EU legislator to make lenders accountable, so that possibly more restrictive interpretations of consumer credit laws even outside the area of residential mortgages are consistent with EU law.[50] Moreover, the Mortgage Credit Directive (MCD) sets limits to the possibility of bundling and tying mortgages and additional financial services,[51] while obliging Member States to promote the financial education of consumers.[52]

> While EU directives oblige traders to provide consumers with detailed information, in practice this information might be of limited use if it is excessively abundant and complicated.[53] This problem is particularly evident in the case of financial contracts which might involve exceptionally complex details and jargon. The idea of financial education thus aims at ensuring that consumers have sufficient knowledge to understand the information they are presented with.[54] It should be noted that while European courts have often shown a willingness to protect vulnerable uninformed parties through the application of various contract law doctrines, the CJEU has more recently clarified that the fact that a consumer possesses a certain level of knowledge and expertise is not enough to take them outside the scope of the definition of 'consumer'—which is traditionally understood objectively by the Court[55]—and thus deprive them of the protection offered by EU law.[56] In other words: even if you are financially literate and have a perfect understanding of finance, you are still a consumer.

The MCD was then the blueprint for the reform of the Consumer Credit Directive (CCD): considering the shortcomings highlighted above, the EU undertook a reform of consumer credit law. The new CCD[57] shows continuity with the approach of the MCD instead and includes more precise rules on responsible lending, bundling and tying, and forbearance, explicitly aiming at counteracting the risk of consumer over-indebtedness.

On the other hand, a partial attenuation of the sanctity of contract principle should be noted. It has become apparent that insisting on debt repayment from vulnerable consumers who are struggling financially and at risk of social exclusion is not only unjust but might end up posing a threat to stability itself. Therefore, procedural forms of consumer debt restructuring similar to those already available to businesses[58]

---

50 CJEU, Case C-58/18, *Schyns* [2019] ECLI:EU:C:2019:467.

51 MCD, Article 12. CJEU, C-778/18, *Association française des usagers de banques* [2020] ECLI:EU:C:2020:831.

52 MCD, Article 6.

53 O. Ben-Shahar and C. E. Schneider, *More Than You Wanted to Know: The Failure of Mandated Disclosure* (Princeton, NJ: Princeton University Press, 2014).

54 On financial literacy, V. Mak and J. Braspenning, 'Errare humanum est. Financial Literacy in European Consumer Credit Law', *Journal of Consumer Policy* 35 (2012), 307–332.

55 CJEU, Case C-110/14, *Horațiu Ovidiu Costea v SC Volksbank România SA* [2015] ECLI:EU:C:2015:538.

56 CJEU, Case C-208/18, *Jana Petruchová v FIBO Group Holdings Limited* [2019] ECLI:EU:C:2019:825.

57 Directive (EU) 2023/2225 of the European Parliament and of the Council of 18 October 2023 on credit agreements for consumers and repealing Directive 2008/48/EC.

58 In fact, when a business becomes insolvent, i.e. unable to pay all its debts, the law creates various procedures which are intended to ensure that most creditors get at least part of the sums they are due, also to minimise the risk that one debtor's insolvency might have a domino effect and lead to the

become necessary and most countries have introduced mechanisms of consumer insolvency.[59] In European law, while the EU has traditionally been less active in this area leaving that aspect to Member States under the auspices of the Council of Europe,[60] a renewed interest in the issue has emerged recently with EU law, which now explicitly encourages Member States to apply new rules on debt discharge to consumers.[61]

1) *Criticisms*

One should not hastily conclude, however, that the current reforms have somewhat 'fixed' the law and averted the possibility of new crises. Criticisms can be articulated at different levels. For example, the new approach to responsible lending raises doubts as to whether the new measures did have any impact at all or even contributed to the opposite problem of financial exclusion: contract law facilitated over-extension of credit in times of credit boom and restricted access in times of credit squeeze. Thus, it appears to have been pro-cyclical and mimicking already existing market dynamics[62] rather than steering them in a meaningful way.

> The inherent tension between ensuring access to credit and the need to avoid overlending has always been present in the regulation of financial services and keeps reappearing: if consumers do not have access to financial services offered by legitimate providers, will they more easily become victim of unregulated predatory lenders? In the UK, the regulator Financial Conduct Authority imposed limits to high-cost short-term credit, more commonly known as 'payday loans', which had become a problematic source of over-indebtedness for many vulnerable consumers.[63] This raised the question where those consumers could now gain access to finance. The answer of the FCA is that '[a]part from a short initial period we believe these customers will be better off not having taken out a loan',[64] on the basis of the consideration that '[o]ur research indicates that it is unlikely that these customers will turn to illegal money lending'.[65]

Furthermore, a certain moral overtone characterising debt as the result of individual fault or even guilt, and thus the indebted consumer as irresponsible, still appears

---

collapse of other businesses. Incidentally, after the GFC, the laws relating to the insolvency of banks were also reformed.

59 I. Ramsay, *Personal Insolvency in the 21st Century. A Comparative Analysis of the US and Europe* (London: Bloomsbury, 2017).

60 Council of Europe, Recommendation CM/Rec (2007) 8.

61 Directive (EU) 2019/1023 of the European Parliament and of the Council of 20 June 2019 on preventive restructuring frameworks, on discharge of debt and disqualifications, and on measures to increase the efficiency of procedures concerning restructuring, insolvency and discharge of debt, Recital 21.

62 It should be recalled that, as C. P. Kindleberger, *Manias, Panics and Crashes: A History of Financial Crises* (London: Wiley, 2005), p. 10, notes discussing the common pattern of financial crises, 'the credit supply increases relatively rapidly in good times, and then when economic growth slackens, the rate of growth of credit has often declined sharply'.

63 On the topic, see J. Gardner, *The Future of High-Cost Credit. Rethinking Payday Lending* (London: Hart Bloomsbury, 2022).

64 The Financial Conduct Authority, 'Proposals for a Price Cap on High-Cost Short-Term Credit', CP14/10 (15 July 2014), https://www.fca.org.uk/publications/consultation-papers/cp14-10-proposals-price-cap-high-cost-short-term-credit, para. 1.27.

65 Ibid., para 1.28.

to permeate consumer credit and mortgage law. In the case of the restructuring of consumer debts, one can debate whether the above-mentioned reforms aimed at offering relief to debtors, occasionally even introduced in the context of international obligations, are in fact excessively skewed towards the interests of the creditors instead of being an instrument to offer actual relief to the debtor.[66]

> To demonstrate how deeply ingrained the moral conception of debt is, an interesting linguistic consideration is often proposed:[67] in German (as well as in Dutch) the word *Schuld* means both 'debt' and 'guilt'. If debtors are guilty, then they can only be *forgiven* if they atone for their guilt, possibly going through an expiatory path of punishment and rehabilitation, to partially regain their (credit-)*worthiness*. Insolvency procedures—even acknowledging a considerable plurality of approaches in comparative terms[68]—have traditionally shown a somewhat punitive approach towards debtors, becoming over time more focused on rehabilitation instead.

More radical criticisms may further question whether those interventions tackle the real socio-economic causes of financial crises in the first place rather than just their manifestations. To understand some of these broader criticisms, we will need to widen our view and consider the societal relevance of law.

3. Societal Relevance

While it is obviously important to look at the way in which specific rules might have facilitated laying down the conditions for crises and how reforms might make the financial system more stable or resilient, adopting a bird's-eye socio-legal view can also shed light on the role of private law in general in relation to the political economy of financial crises. It should be recalled in fact that 'finance is a social system like many others, and financial relations are socially and culturally embedded'.[69] It is useful to place private law within an economic sociology of law,[70] discussing the societal relevance of the rules discussed so far, and also to invite more critical reflections on European private law.

a. The Political Economy of Financial Crises

As the economists Carmen Reinhart and Kenneth Rogoff wrote at the start of an influential study of financial crises, 'excessive debt accumulation, whether it be by the government, banks, corporations, or consumers, often poses greater systemic risks

66 J. Spooner, 'The Quiet-Loud-Quiet Politics of Post-Crisis Consumer Bankruptcy Law: The Case of Ireland and the Troika', Modern Law Review 81 (2018), 790–824.

67 See already the discussion of guilt and debt in F. Nietzsche, *Zur Genealogie der Moral. Eine Streitschrift* (Leipzig: Naumann, 1887).

68 I. Ramsay, *Personal Insolvency*.

69 K. Pistor, 'A Legal Theory of Finance', p. 315.

70 See R. Swedberg, 'The Case for an Economic Sociology of Law', Theory and Society 32.1 (2003), 1–37. S. Frerichs, 'The Legal Constitution of Market Society: Probing the Economic Sociology of Law', *Economic Sociology European Electronic Newsletter* 10.3 (2009), 20–25.

than it seems during a boom'.[71] If it is true that systemic risk is associated with debt accumulation, most notably including private debt, one could ask what are the reasons behind such accumulation and why it is so that credit bubbles appear to have become more frequent in recent decades. Does private law play a role in those dynamics as well?

One among many possible answers to this question has to do with the political economy of finance. Over the last few decades, financial services have become increasingly important for corporations, consumers, and the economy of entire countries—a phenomenon which is generally described with the evocative although somewhat unclear term 'financialisation'. The development has occurred because of innovations endogenous to the financial system itself but also as part of societal changes and a deliberate redefinition of the role of the State, in line with a view suggesting that the State should retreat as far as possible from direct interventions in the economy and leave ample market freedoms to private entities through privatisation and so-called deregulation.

With the development of a consumer society centred on mass production and consumption, there is on the one hand a societal expectation that citizens have access to the increased number of goods and services available on the market, and on the other hand a necessity of fostering consumer demand by offering them sufficient economic resources, thus sustaining production and economic growth. But how can this be achieved? Simplifying, one can say that in a possibly Keynesian model[72] such consumer demand could be fostered by increasing the labour force's bargaining power, recognising social rights and through public spending, which includes the consolidation of a welfare state that actively provides certain services and social benefits to citizens.

> In various countries, legislations and constitutions of the second post-war period show traces of this inspiration, as they portray an active role for the State in the economy. Such active role was the founding characteristic of the historical period, following the destruction caused by the war, that is known in France as the 'glorious thirty'[73] and that was generally characterised by economic growth and low unemployment. The same period, roughly from the mid 1940s to the mid 1970s, was also marked by the absence of major banking crises in the world (although the same cannot always be said of currency crises).[74]

This model was challenged by the development of monetarist and neoliberal theories which, intending to reverse phenomena of high inflation unexpectedly coupled with high unemployment, on the one hand put emphasis on price stability as the main

71 C. M. Reinhart and K. S. Rogoff, *This Time is Different. Eight Centuries of Financial Folly* (Princeton, NJ: Princeton University Press, 2009), p. xxv.

72 Keynesianism, based on the ideas of John Maynard Keynes (1883–1946), is an economic theory which places emphasis on aggregate demand and on the need for public spending in order to boost economic growth under certain circumstances.

73 J. Fourastié, *Les trente glorieuses ou la révolution invisible de 1946 à 1975* (Paris: Fayard: 1979).

74 F. Allen and D. Gale, *Understanding Financial Crises* (Oxford: Oxford University Press, 2007), p. 2. M. J. Oliver, 'Financial Crises', in M. J. Oliver and D. H. Aldcroft (eds), *Economic Disasters of the Twentieth Century* (Cheltenham: Elgar, 2007), p. 205.

objective of central banks[75] and on the other hand attempted to free the private sector from excessive government interference.

Deregulation and financial innovation would thus ensure that the market itself can make an increasing number of essential services available to citizens. Against that backdrop, it was private credit that started performing the task of fostering demand in capitalist economies. Citizens became financial citizens.[76] The shift from the public to the private sector,[77] which began in the 1970s in Europe and even earlier in the US, relied on the availability of credit to provide basic social needs satisfaction to individuals, but paid little attention to the possible negative consequences that might have followed a default.

Governing those market relations, private law had to perform an indirect macroeconomic function for which it was not necessarily well-equipped. It should be kept in mind that general private law is to a large extent inspired by individualist principles, as the question of the social function of private law has remained an open issue since at least the nineteenth century.[78]

> These tendencies, which in hindsight became apparent in Europe only during the GFC, had already manifested themselves elsewhere and before. Even the Great Depression in the US can be linked to an overextension of the financial sector which developed to take into account consumer needs not directly dealt with by the State: for several years US American courts, as notoriously seen at the start of the twentieth century in the Supreme Court's *Lochner* case,[79] had crippled the public powers to produce social legislation by way of outlining an unrestrained and constitutionally protected freedom of contract.[80] The notorious 'Lochner era' came to an end in the 1930s, but the idea of a constitutionalisation of freedom of contract has remained a subject of controversy in legal scholarship since then.

b. European and Comparative Law after the Crisis

The legal implications of financial crises as socio-legal phenomena far exceed those which are immediately visible when looking at the reforms of financial law. The GFC, and its European ramifications in the form of the eurozone crisis, led to a reconsideration of the European economic constitution[81] but also had repercussions on the European

---

75 Maintaining price stability is the primary objective of the European Central Bank as well; the general objectives of the Union are secondary goals.

76 D. Kingsford-Smith and O. Dixon, 'The Consumer Interest and the Financial Markets', in N. Moloney, E. Ferran, and J. Payne (eds), *The Oxford Handbook of Financial Regulation* (Oxford: Oxford University Press, 2015), pp. 697–735.

77 C. Crouch, 'Privatised Keynesianism: An Unacknowledged Policy Regime', *The British Journal of Politics and International Relations* 11.3 (2009), 382–399.

78 See O. von Gierke, *Die soziale Aufgabe des Privatrechts* (Berlin: Springer, 1889).

79 *Lochner v New York*, 198 U.S. 45 (1905).

80 E. McGaughey, 'Introduction: A Social Law Beyond Public v Private, English translation of Otto von Gierke, The Social Role of Private Law', *German Law Journal* 19.4 (2018), 1017–1116.

81 C. Joerges, 'The European Economic Constitution and its Transformation through the Financial Crisis', in D. Patterson and Södersten (eds), *A Companion to European Union Law and International Law* (Oxford: Wiley, 2016), pp. 242–261.

polity itself: after years in which, following the events described above, the general understanding was that the benefits of the financial markets could and should be democratised, thus extended to consumers who could rely on finance to improve their welfare, the GFC damaged citizens' trust in the financial sector and, to an extent, in the political institutions which appeared to have failed at regulating the markets and to have taken inadequate corrective measures. As the crisis appeared to be international in nature and rooted in dynamics seemingly beyond the reach of national political institutions, the ever-present appeal of the nation and re-nationalisation increased. At first glance, this reaction seems counterintuitive: after all, addressing a phenomenon by definition international such as a GFC appears to require an internationally coordinated rather than an isolationist response. In fact, most reforms have envisioned a more coherent international approach to finance and as already mentioned new international bodies have been created to that purpose. Yet, one should consider the role that the national State, in contrast to transnational private networks rooted in an economic rationality, is still expected to play in ensuring some form of protection in 'bad times': an attempt, often prone to failure, to re-embed the economy in society in line with what Karl Polanyi described in the 1940s as a double-movement.[82] For example, over-indebted consumers primarily expect assistance from their welfare state. This scenario might be paradoxical, since on the one hand internationalisation appears to reduce the room for regulatory manoeuvre of the State (or at least some States) while on the other hand, it puts increased pressure on it.

This political climate further changed the priorities of the EU legislator and, consequently, of European legal scholarship. It is worth recalling that still in the first half of the 2000s, European legal scholarship was mainly occupied with the two political 'grand-projects' of the time: the European constitution and the European Civil Code.[83] The first project had already failed the test of democratic acceptance in two national referenda although it substantially survived in the reformed EU treaties. The ambitions of EU private law were even more clearly downplayed: the agenda in European private law continuously deflated in grandeur, moving from an ambitious conversation about something resembling a civil codification for Europe, to the idea of a common European sales law, and eventually to initiatives for the regulation of the digital market, which became the new main research focus of European private law scholarship. At the same time, the GFC seemed to inaugurate a promising new age of consumer law which now appeared to be more open to substantive social considerations.[84]

Against this backdrop, the aftermath of financial crises raises fundamental questions for comparative law. Many regard the post-GFC scenario of general re-

---

82 K. Polanyi, *The Great Transformation. The Political and Economic Origins of Our Time* (Boston, MA: Beacon Press, 2001).

83 H. W. Micklitz, 'Failure or Ideological Preconceptions? Thought on Two Grand Projects: The European Constitution and the European Civil Code', in K. Tuori and S. Sankari (eds), *The Many Constitutions of Europe* (Farnham: Ashgate, 2010), pp. 109–142 (p. 109).

84 V. Mak, *Legal Pluralism in European Contract Law* (Oxford: Oxford University Press, 2020), p. 78.

nationalisation as one of the key themes that, exacerbating pre-existing sentiments, led to the most theatrical drawback in the history of EU integration, i.e. the withdrawal of the United Kingdom from the EU. In comparative law terms, this might breathe new life into the old distinction between English common law and continental civil law. While that opposition had been downplayed by comparative lawyers on the basis of the functionalist method and of historical considerations occasionally instrumental to the European integration project, that very distinction was on the contrary central to some comparative law and finance accounts which problematically predicated the superiority of one of those families in terms of economic efficiency.

> The common law appears to be a highly relevant legal regime for finance. As a telling example, the vast majority of over-the-counter derivative contracts worldwide are subject to either English law or the law of the State of New York. This is because those contracts incorporate a set of standard terms, drafted by an international association of financial institutions, which include a 'choice of law' and 'choice of forum' clause in favour of those jurisdictions. Disputes around the interpretation of those contracts, possibly even in seemingly domestic settings,[85] are therefore likely to end up being adjudicated by Anglo-American courts applying the common law of contract.

Yet that view might paradoxically be challenged by the reality of Brexit itself, as at least some financial service providers start relocating from London to other destinations in continental Europe to keep full access to the EU financial markets.

c. Is the Financial System Safe Now?

While different and possibly contrasting readings can be offered of the political-economic developments described so far, this simplified overview of events spanning over three centuries across two continents rather suggests that inquiring about the role of private law within financial crises cannot be reduced to a merely technical exercise in evaluating the economic efficiency of given rules, possibly inspired by the neo-positivist idea that there is one 'right' approach. Neither can contract law ignore the overall systemic rather than purely interpersonal implications of contractual relations. Consideration of the wider context is necessary instead, also in the interest of effective economic regulation as well as social cohesion. In fact, an exclusive emphasis on the current regulatory reforms risks overlooking further possibly relevant societal issues or underlying contradictions in the socio-economic system which might then constitute the trigger for new catastrophic developments. Just as financial crises are historically followed by re-regulation, re-regulation is followed by a general perception that because of the introduction of new rules issues have been solved.[86] In particular,

85 For a notable English case involving a swap contract concluded by two Italian parties, see *Dexia Crediop S.p.A. v Comune di Prato* [2017] EWCA Civ 428.

86 Reinhart and Rogoff, *This Time is Different*. Moreover, 'as soon as memories of the past crisis have faded, advocates of free markets will raise their heads again and demand the dismantling of regulatory structures that stand in the way of the private sectors' unconstrained debt minting', K. Pistor, *The Code of Capital*, p. 106.

the reforms which have been introduced in the last decade have been produced with an eye to the triggers of the GFC, which might make them appropriate to deal with a possibly similar new event, but might not be sufficient to avoid crises rooted in different causes—or even the same causes if one adopts a more pessimistic perspective on the effectiveness of the new rules. In that regard, current economic models still appear inadequate to predict when and how financial crises will occur: while economists learn from each crisis, the previous generation of models suddenly appears inadequate as soon as a new crisis occurs.[87] This holds true keeping in mind the wave of European re-regulation following the GFC: the financial system can be said to be safer but still not safe.[88]

More fundamentally and sceptically, crises may also be thought to be endogenous to the market itself.[89] The instability of capitalist economies has been highlighted by a long list of economic thinkers, from Marx to Keynes, pointing out the inherent contradictions of the economic system, and is now being more accepted in mainstream economics as well. The post-Keynesian economist Hyman Minsky, whose work enjoyed a renewed popularity after the GFC, stressed the innovative characteristic of banking and finance as profit-seeking activities and explained that 'over periods of prolonged prosperity, the economy transits from financial relations that make for a stable system to financial relations that make for an unstable system'.[90] This suggests that periods characterised by financial innovations have a tendency to destabilise the market, possibly triggering that sequence of 'manias, panics, and crashes' mentioned in the explicative title of Charles Kindleberger's influential work on financial crises.[91]

If this is true, it could be noted that the times we live in, characterised by unprecedented levels of innovation in a plurality of often under-regulated areas, seem particularly fertile for new unfavourable events. In this context, the law will at least need to ensure that episodes of instability are governed so as to make their consequences socially sustainable, through the recognition of the necessity of pursuing financial as well as more broadly social stability.

4. Points for Reflection

Q1: One of the key tensions within contract law is the one between the principle that promises must be kept and the one that non-performance of an obligation might be excused in exceptional circumstances. How should the right balance between

87 D. Rodrik, 'Who Needs Capital-Account Convertibility?', *Princeton Essays in International Finance* 207 (1998).

88 M. Hellwig, 'Twelve Years after the Financial Crisis—Too-big-to-fail is still with us' (2021) 7(1) Journal of Financial Regulation 175–187.

89 As well as more fundamentally to modernity itself, see H. Brunkhorst, 'The Return of Crisis', in Kjaer, Teubner, and Febbrajo (eds), *The Financial Crisis in Constitutional Perspective*, pp. 133–171.

90 H. P. Minsky, 'The Financial Instability Hypothesis', in Ph. Arestis and M. Sawyer (eds), *The Elgar Companion to Radical Political Economy* (Cheltenham: Elgar, 1994), pp. 153–158 (p. 157).

91 Kindleberger, *Manias, Panics and Crashes*.

the two be struck in the context of a financial crisis? More generally, is a crisis such an exceptional event which justifies a suspension of the normal application of the law?

Q2: To what extent should the line between regulation and private law be blurred? Is a closer relation between the two desirable, or can we think of good reasons why the two domains should instead be kept separate?

Q3: To what extent should contract law itself be concerned with further issues such as ensuring the stability of the financial system? Would this challenge the alleged inner rationality of contract law?

Q4: What are the long-term consequences of financial crises on the European private law project itself?

Bibliography

Allen, F., and D. Gale, *Understanding Financial Crises* (Oxford: Oxford University Press, 2007), https://doi.org/10.4337/9781785366468

Atamer, Y. M., 'Duty of Responsible Lending. Should the European Union Take Action?', in S. Grundmann and Y. M. Atamer (eds), *Financial Services, Financial Crisis and General European Contract Law: Failure and Challenges of Contracting* (Alphen aan den Rijn: Kluwer, 2011), pp. 179–202

Başoğlu, B. (ed.), *The Effects of Financial Crises on the Binding Force of Contracts—Renegotiation, Rescission or Revision* (Cham: Springer, 2016), https://doi.org/10.1007/978-3-319-27256-6

Ben-Shahar, O., and C. E. Schneider, *More Than You Wanted to Know: The Failure of Mandated Disclosure* (Princeton, NJ: Princeton University Press, 2014)

Better Finance, 'A Major Enforcement Issue. The Mis-selling of Financial Products', Briefing Paper (April 2017), https://betterfinance.eu/wp-content/uploads/publications/Misselling_of_Financial_Products_in_the_EU_-_Briefing_Paper_2017.pdf

Black, J., 'Reconceiving Financial Markets. From the Economic to the Social', *Journal of Corporate Law Studies* 13 (2001), 401–442, https://doi.org/10.5235/14735970.13.2.401

Bridge, M., and J. Braithwaite, 'Private Law and Financial Crises', *Journal of Corporate Law Studies* 13 (2013), 361–399, http://dx.doi.org/10.5235/14735970.13.2.361

Brunkhorst, H., 'The Return of Crisis', in P. F. Kjaer, G. Teubner, and A. Febbrajo (eds), *The Financial Crisis in Constitutional Perspective. The Dark Side of Functional Differentiation* (Oxford: Hart, 2011), pp. 133–171.

Busch, D., and G. Ferrarini (eds), *European Banking Union*, 2nd edn (Oxford: Oxford University Press, 2020)

Cherednychenko, O., 'Two Sides of the Same Coin: EU Financial Regulation and Private Law', *European Business Organization Law Review* 22.2 (2021), 147–172, https://doi.org/10.1007/s40804-020-00202-y

Cherednychenko, O., and M. Andenas (eds), *Financial Regulation and Civil Liability in European Law* (Cheltenham: Elgar, 2020)

Claessens, S., G. Dell'Ariccia, and D. Igan, L. Laeven, 'A Cross-Country Perspective on the Causes of the Global Financial Crisis', in G. Caprio (ed.), *The Evidence and Impact of Financial Globalization* (London: Elsevier, 2012), pp. 737–752

Comparato, G., 'Financial Stability in Private Law: Intersections, Conflicts, Choices', *Common Market Law Review* 58.2 (2021), 391–430, https://doi.org/10.54648/cola2021024

Crouch, C., 'Privatised Keynesianism: An Unacknowledged Policy Regime', *The British Journal of Politics and International Relations* 11.3 (2009), 382–399, https://doi.org/10.1111/j.1467–856X.2009.00377.x

Davrados, 'Financial Turmoil as a Change of Circumstances Under Greek Contract Law', in B. Başoğlu (ed.), *The Effects of Financial Crises on the Binding Force of Contracts—Renegotiation, Rescission or Revision* (Cham: Springer, 2016), pp. 145–162

Domurath, I., *Consumer Vulnerability and Welfare in Mortgage Contracts* (Oxford: Hart, 2020)

Financial Conduct Authority, 'Proposals for a Price Cap on High-Cost Short-Term Credit', CP14/10 (15 July 2014), https://www.fca.org.uk/publications/consultation-papers/cp14-10-proposals-price-cap-high-cost-short-term-credit

Fourastié, J., *Les trente glorieuses ou la révolution invisible de 1946 à 1975* (Paris: Fayard: 1979)

Frerichs, S., 'The Legal Constitution of Market Society: Probing the Economic Sociology of Law', *Economic Sociology European Electronic Newsletter* 10.3 (2009), 20–25

Furman, J., and J. E. Stiglitz, 'Economic Crises: Evidence and Insights from East Asia', *Brookings Papers on Economic Activity* 29.2 (1998), 1–136

Gardner, J., *The Future of High-Cost Credit. Rethinking Payday Lending* (London: Hart Bloomsbury, 2022)

Gierke, O. von, *Die soziale Aufgabe des Privatrechts* (Berlin: Springer, 1889)

Grund, S., 'Restructuring Argentina's Sovereign Debts. Navigating the Legal Labyrinth' (2019), https://ssrn.com/abstract=3485370

Hondius, E., and E. C. Grigoleit (eds), *Unexpected Circumstances in European Contract Law* (Cambridge, UK: Cambridge University Press, 2011), https://doi.org/10.1017/CBO9780511763335

Joerges, C., 'The European Economic Constitution and its Transformation through the Financial Crisis', in D. Patterson and Södersten (eds), *A Companion to European Union Law and International Law* (Oxford: Wiley, 2016), pp. 242–261

Jönsson, S., *A Comparative History of Bank Failures. From Medici to Barings* (London: Routledge, 2021)

Kindleberger, C. P., *Manias, Panics and Crashes: A History of Financial Crises* (London: Wiley, 2005)

Kingsford-Smith, D., and O. Dixon, 'The Consumer Interest and the Financial Markets', in N. Moloney, E. Ferran, and J. Payne (eds), *The Oxford Handbook of Financial Regulation* (Oxford: Oxford University Press, 2015), pp. 697–735, https://doi.org/10.1093/OXFORDHB/9780199687206.013.25

Leone, C., 'Transparency Revisited—On the Role of Information in the Recent Case-Law of the CJEU', *European Review of Contract Law* 10.2 (2014), 312–325, https://doi.org/10.1515/ercl-2014-0012

Mak, V., *Legal Pluralism in European Contract Law* (Oxford: Oxford University Press, 2020)

Mak, V., and J. Braspenning, 'Errare humanum est. Financial Literacy in European Consumer Credit Law', *Journal of Consumer Policy* 35 (2012), 307–332, https://doi.org/10.1007/s10603-012-9194-0

McGaughey, E., 'Introduction: A Social Law Beyond Public v Private, English translation of Otto von Gierke, The Social Role of Private Law', *German Law Journal* 19.4 (2018), 1017–1116, https://doi.org/10.1017/S207183220002294X

Mian, A., and A. Sufi, *House of Debt. How They (and You) Caused the Great Recession, and How We Can Prevent It from Happening Again* (Chicago, IL: University of Chicago Press, 2015)

Micklitz, H. W., 'Access to and Exclusion from Financial Markets after the Global Financial Crisis', in T. Wilson (ed.), *International Responses to Issues of Credit and Over-Indebtedness in the Wake of the Crisis* (Burlington, VT: Ashgate, 2013), pp. 47–75

Micklitz, H. W., 'Failure or Ideological Preconceptions? Thought on Two Grand Projects: The European Constitution and the European Civil Code', in K. Tuori and S. Sankari (eds), *The Many Constitutions of Europe* (Farnham: Ashgate, 2010), pp. 109–142

Micklitz, H. W., and N. Reich, 'The Court and Sleeping Beauty: The Revival of the Unfair Contract Terms Directive (UCTD)', *Common Market Law Review* 51 (2014), 771–808, https://doi.org/10.54648/cola2014061

Minsky, H. P., 'The Financial Instability Hypothesis', in Ph. Arestis and M. Sawyer (eds), *The Elgar Companion to Radical Political Economy* (Cheltenham: Elgar, 1994), pp. 153–158

Mishkin, F. S., 'Lessons from the Asian crisis', *Journal of International Money and Finance* 18 (1999), 709–723

Moloney, N., *EU Securities and Financial Markets Regulation* (Oxford: Oxford University Press, 2014)

Momberg Uribe, R., 'Beyond the Risk: Swaps, Financial Crisis and Change of Circumstances. Comparative Case Note. Supreme Court of Portugal—10.10.2013. Conclusions', *European Review of Private Law* 23 (2015), 149–151, https://doi.org/10.54648/erpl2015005

Musacchio, A., 'Mexican Financial Crisis of 1994–1995', in G. Caprio (ed.), *The Evidence and Impact of Financial Globalization* (London: Elsevier, 2012), pp. 657–667

Nietzsche, F., *Zur Genealogie der Moral. Eine Streitschrift* (Leipzig: Naumann, 1887)

Oliver, M. J., 'Financial Crises', in M. J. Oliver and D. H. Aldcroft (eds), *Economic Disasters of the Twentieth Century* (Cheltenham: Elgar, 2007), p. 205

Pistor, K., *The Code of Capital. How the Law Creates Wealth and Inequality* (Princeton, NJ: Princeton University Press, 2019)

Pistor, K., 'A Legal Theory of Finance', *Journal of Comparative Economics* 41 (2013), 315–330, http://dx.doi.org/10.2139/ssrn.2262936

Polanyi, K., *The Great Transformation. The Political and Economic Origins of Our Time* (Boston, MA: Beacon Press, 2001)

Posner, E. A., *Last Resort. The Financial Crisis and the Future of Bailouts* (Chicago, IL: University of Chicago Press, 2018)

Pulgar, J., 'A Contractual Approach to Overindebtedness: rebus sic stantibus Instead of Bankruptcy', in L. Nogler and U. Reifner (eds), *Life Time Contracts. Social Long-Term Contracts in Labour, Tenancy and Consumer Credit Law* (The Hague: Eleven International Publishing, 2014), p. 534

Ramsay, I., *Personal Insolvency in the 21st Century. A Comparative Analysis of the US and Europe* (London: Bloomsbury, 2017)

Reinhart, C. M., and K. S. Rogoff, *This Time is Different. Eight Centuries of Financial Folly* (Princeton, NJ: Princeton University Press, 2009)

Renner, M., 'Death by Complexity. The Financial Crisis and the Crisis of Law in World Society', in P. F. Kjaer, G. Teubner, and A. Febbrajo (eds), *The Financial Crisis in Constitutional Perspective. The Dark Side of Functional Differentiation* (Oxford: Hart, 2011), pp. 93–111

Rodrik, D., 'Who Needs Capital-Account Convertibility?', *Princeton Essays in International Finance* 207 (1998)

Serozan, R., 'General Report on the Effects of Financial Crises on the Binding Force of Contracts: Renegotiation, Rescission or Revision', in B. Başoğlu (ed.), *The Effects of Financial Crises on the Binding Force of Contracts—Renegotiation, Rescission or Revision* (Cham: Springer, 2016), pp. 3–32

Spooner, J., 'The Quiet-Loud-Quiet Politics of Post-Crisis Consumer Bankruptcy Law: The Case of Ireland and the Troika', Modern Law Review 81 (2018), 790–824, https://doi.org/10.1111/1468-2230.12365

Svetiev, Y., and A. Ottow, 'Financial Supervision in the Interstices Between Private and Public Law', *European Review of Contract Law* 10.4 (2014), 496–544, https://doi.org/10.1515/ercl-2014-0023

Swedberg, R., 'The Case for an Economic Sociology of Law', Theory and Society 32.1 (2003), 1–37, https://doi.org/10.1023/A:1023005905397

Takagi, S., 'Argentina's Default of 2001', in G. Caprio (ed.), *The Evidence and Impact of Financial Globalization* (London: Elsevier, 2012), pp. 709–719

Wallinga, M., *EU Investor Protection Regulation and Liability for Investment Losses. A Comparative Analysis of the Interplay between MiFID & MiFID II and Private Law* (Cham: Springer, 2020), https://doi.org/10.1007/978-3-030-54001-2

Wilson, T., 'The Responsible Lending Response', in T. Wilson (ed.), *International Responses to Issues of Credit and Over-indebtedness in the Wake of Crisis* (Farnham: Ashgate, 2013), pp. 109–134

12. The Construction of European Housing Markets through European Private Law

Irina Domurath

Abstract

This chapter highlights the constitutive role of European private law (EPL) in the construction of housing sectors in Europe. It identifies the different layers of housing regulation in the EU, broadly understood, while focusing on the EU law that affects housing relations in three dimensions: access to housing, adequacy of housing, and protection from evictions. It will become clear that EU law permeates all these dimensions to different degrees and always with a focus on building and fostering the internal market. This goal is achieved through the prohibition of market barriers, transparency requirements for contracts, and enforcement that respects the procedural rights of consumers. At the same time, EU law neglects social concerns related to the quality and affordability of housing, as well as material protection from eviction. The chapter raises questions about the role of EPL in the political economy of housing, in which housing is increasingly privatised, commodified, and financialised.

1. Introduction

Europe is faced with what Housing Europe has called an 'alarming housing challenge'.[1] There is less and less provision of public or social housing; less social housing is constructed and existing social housing stock is sold to and increasingly managed by private parties; private rental markets are expanding. Homelessness is rising, tenants are increasingly unable to service market rents and hundreds of thousands of mortgagors have lost their homes in the aftermath of the financial crisis of 2008.

1 Housing Europe, 'The State of Housing in the EU 2017' (2017), https://web.archive.org/web/20190708235116/ https://www.housingeurope.eu/file/614/download

 https://doi.org/10.11647/OBP.0448.12

There is a considerable market failure in housing markets: on the one hand, there are vacancies, and on the other, there is rising homelessness and over-indebtedness. Housing costs have risen significantly—rental costs by 19% on average in the EU and house prices by 47%.[2] This means that the trend of housing becoming increasingly unaffordable is not coming to an end.

Most housing problems concern access to affordable housing and protection from eviction. Addressing these problems cuts across different legal fields and layers of competences. Supranational, national, and local regulation intertwine, both concerning market regulation and private law. When buying a house, national property law is relevant. Contract law applies to rental and loan agreements. The rules in place for credit contracts impact the way in which credit information is being provided to the home-buyers and which rights they have in case of failure to repay. The construction of housing units depends on regional zoning regulations and construction licenses, but also on the freedom of capital and services under EU law which facilitate investment into the housing sectors. Moreover, local authorities—especially in cities where access to affordable housing is difficult—are trying to address the lack of affordability in their housing sectors through administrative law. Many cities have changed the application of the prohibition-of-misuse rules in order to enable fines for short-term offers (on Airbnb, for example) beyond a certain time threshold.[3] Some regions even have their own private laws, such as in Catalunya. In EU law—as in international law—the right to housing is a human and fundamental right. It is included in Article 7 Charter of Fundamental Rights (CFREU), forming part of the 'respect for private and family life'. This prompts the classical question as to the effect of fundamental rights in private law (see Chapter 5 in this volume). Can a tenant invoke the right to housing when being evicted after failing to pay rent? Finally, because housing has become an important investment to absorb surplus capital, it is impacted by the rules designed to reach stability of the financial system.

The meshing of housing with capital and financial markets through mortgage credit has received considerable scholarly and policy attention, especially since the financial crisis of 2008.[4] Also, the right to housing and the right to property in the housing context are the focus of in-depth analyses.[5] Similarly, the EU regulation of platforms

2 Housing Europe, 'The State of Housing in Europe 2023' (2023), https://www.stateofhousing.eu/#p=1, p. 7.

3 For example in Berlin: Gesetz über die Zweckentfremdung von Wohnraum (ZwVbG), 29 November 2013.

4 For example: R. J. Shiller, *The Subprime Solution: How Today's Global Financial Crisis Happened, and What to Do about It*, I (Princeton, NJ: Princeton University Press, 2008); Financial Services Authority, 'Mortgage Market Review: Responsible Lending', *Consultation Paper* 10.16 (2010), https://www.fca.org.uk/publication/consultation/fsa-cp10-16.pdf; OECD, 'Economic Policy Reforms 2011: Going for Growth' (2011), https://www.oecd.org/content/dam/oecd/en/publications/reports/2011/04/economic-policy-reforms-2011_g1g11692/growth-2011-en.pdf; I. Domurath, G. Comparato, and H.-W Micklitz (eds), 'The Over-Indebtedness of European Consumers: A View from Six Countries', *EUI Working Paper Series Law* 2014/10 (2014).

5 For example: P. Kenna, 'Globalization and Housing Rights', *Indiana Journal of Global Legal Studies* 15 (2008), 397–469; A. Kenna, 'Housing Rights: Positive Duties and Enforceable Rights at the European

in the so-called 'collaborative economy'[6] concerning the regulation of Airbnb has attracted much academic commentary,[7] not least because of its impact on the housing shortage. In contrast, the private law aspects of housing have been neglected in EU law.[8] This might be because housing is mostly regarded either as a social policy belonging to the realm of public law or as a national policy and therefore falling outside of the scope of EU law.[9] The focus of EU policy in the field of housing lies on cooperation, the exchange of best practices, and more indirect funding programmes.[10]

Nevertheless, EU law does impact the horizontal housing relations between contract parties, both for purchase and rent. These effects might be indirect or incidental but are nonetheless substantial. The aim of this chapter is to identify these effects and put them into a political economy context. The term 'housing regulation' is used broadly as encompassing legislation that impacts three dimensions of housing: access to housing, housing quality and affordability, and security of tenure and evictions also

---

Court of Human Rights', *European Human Rights Law Review* 13 (2008), 193–208; P. Kenna and H. Simón-Moreno, 'Towards a Common Standard of Protection of the Right to Housing in Europe through the Charter of Fundamental Rights', *European Law Journal* 25 (2019), 608–622; J. Hohmann, *The Right to Housing—Law, Concepts, Possibilities* (Oxford: Hart Publishing, 2013); B. Bengtsson, 'Housing as a Social Right: Implications for Welfare State Theory', *Scandinavian Political Studies* 24 (2001), 255–275; A. Remiche, 'Yordanova and Others v Bulgaria: The Influence of the Social Right to Adequate Housing on the Interpretation of the Civil Right to Respect for One's Home', *Human Rights Law Review* 12 (2012), 787–800; Y. Donders, 'Protecting the Home and Adequate Housing—Living in a Caravan or Trailer as a Human Right', *International Human Rights Law Review* 5 (2016), 1–25.

6 See for example: Commission Communication, 'Upgrading the Single Market: More Opportunities for People and Business', COM (2015) 550 final, https://eur-lex.europa.eu/legal-content/EN/TXT/?uri=CELEX%3A52015DC0550

7 V. Mak, 'Private Law Perspectives on Platform Services. Airbnb: Home Rentals between AYOR and NIMBY', *Journal of European Consumer and Market Law* 5.1 (2016), 19–25; C. Busch et al., 'The Rise of the Platform Economy: A New Challenge for EU Consumer Law?', *Journal of European Consumer and Market Law* 5.1 (2016), 3–10.

8 Discussions on the right to housing in private law have started however: J. Rutgers, 'The Right to Housing (Article 47 of the Charter) and Unfair Terms in General Conditions', in H. Collins (ed.), *European Contract Law and the Charter of Fundamental Rights* (Cambridge, UK: Intersentia, 2017), pp. 125–137; L. E. Perriello, 'Right to Housing and Unfair Contract Terms', *Journal of European Consumer and Market Law* 7 (2018), 96–103; K. Lilleholt, 'The Right to Housing and Its Impact on Contract Law', in K. Ketscher (ed.), *Velferd og rettferd : Festskrift til Asbjørn Kjønstad 70 år* (Oslo: University of Oslo, 2013), pp. 363–374; I. Domurath and C. Mak, 'Private Law and Housing Justice in Europe', *Modern Law Review* 83 (2020), 1188–1220.

9 It is not part of the enumerated competences of the EU, see Articles 5(2) and 3 TEU (Treaty on the European Union).

10 The European Structural Funds (European Regional Development Fund and the European Social Fund) can have effects on the funding of projects and initiatives that impact housing sectors; moreover, there are initiatives concerning energy efficiency, assistance for the elderly and disabled, see European Parliament, 'Overview of Housing Policies, Report No W-14' (1996), https://www.europarl.europa.eu/workingpapers/soci/w14/summary_en.htm. Moreover, the 2018 Action Plan of the Housing Partnership sets out, *inter alia*, guidance on EU regulation and public support for housing, the revision of the Services of General Economic Interest (SGEI) decision in order to include (social) housing, monitoring systems for good practices on affordable housing, and recommendations on EU funding of affordable housing. Also, the European Commission has also, as part of its regional policy agenda, launched the EU Urban Agenda with the Pact of Amsterdam in 2016, a coordinated approach to priority themes with dedicated partnerships with the goal to improve the quality of life in urban areas, see European Commission, 'Urban Agenda for the EU', *European Commission*, https://ec.europa.eu/regional_policy/policy/themes/urban-development/agenda_en

in horizontal relations. These dimensions are inspired by the content of the right to housing in Article 8 ECHR (European Convention on Human Rights). Even though the horizontal effect of this right is disputed, these dimensions still form a useful analytical grid with which to display laws and regulations that have an impact on housing relations. After identifying the effects of EPL in these dimensions, I discuss the political economy in which housing is embedded in order to shed light on the political and economic problems involved in housing.

2. EU 'Housing Regulation' with Impact on Contract Law

a. Access to Housing and Access to Mortgages

Access to housing has two dimensions: the access to housing for sale and rent and the access to credit in order to buy a home. The EU has intervened in both dimensions, albeit to different degrees.

1) Access to Housing Markets

Under EU law, access to housing can be protected via the fundamental market freedoms in Articles 45, 49, 56, and 64 TFEU when individuals want to access housing markets in other Member States—either for living or investment purposes.

> The most famous case in this regard is *Libert,*[11] concerning a provision in the Decree of the Flemish Region on land and real estate property. The Decree, aiming to combat gentrification and soaring housing prices, made the authorisation for land development and building projects dependent on a 'sufficient connection' with the commune. The Flemish Decree also imposed a 'social obligation' on the developer to ensure the supply of social housing units. The Court of Justice of the European Union (CJEU) considered the supply of social housing an overriding public interest which, in the end, however, disproportionately restricted the four market freedoms because it deterred all nationals of other Member States to move to the Flemish region, irrespective of their financial means. The CJEU considered that less restrictive means would have been available, such as purchase subsidies or other subsidy mechanisms designed to assist less affluent persons.[12]

As always in EU law, the benchmark is the functioning of the free market. Any regulation of a 'social obligation' such as in the *Libert* case is regarded as a possible limitation of the internal market rules that needs to be justified. What is more, there are evident differences in the requirement for proof: when claiming a hindrance of free movement, a merely hypothetic hindrance is enough to establish a violation of EU

11 Case C-197/11 and C-203/11 *Eric Libert and Others v Gouvernement flamand* (C-197/11) *and All Projects & Developments NV* and *Others v Vlaamse Regering* (C-203/11) (*Libert*) [2013] ECLI:EU:C:2013:288.

12 Ibid., para. 56.

law,[13] whereas other concerns, such as local housing needs, face the higher evidentiary burden of having to prove proportionality.[14] *Libert* reinforces this structural bias in favour of free movement rules,[15] because the CJEU considered all four fundamental market freedoms to be violated at once, without a detailed examination and legal subsumption of the facts; it only spent a few sentences on establishing a violation on the freedom of capital.[16] The potentially low impact of the *Living-in-your-own-region* policy was irrelevant to the CJEU,[17] as was the number of target communities; no evaluation of the impact on businesses in practices was made.[18] As any other national or regional policy, housing policy is regarded as a potential hindrance to the internal market that needs to be justified.

There is also EU secondary legislation with an impact on access to housing. Directive 2003/09/EC, laying down minimum standards for the reception of asylum seekers[19] also applies to housing. In *Saciri*,[20] where an asylum-seeking family who could not be provided with public accommodation was unable to afford private housing, the CJEU clarified that if a Member State has decided to provide material reception conditions in the form of financial allowances, those allowances must enable the recipient to obtain housing, if necessary, also on private rental markets.[21]

Hence, access to housing markets in EU law means the abolishment of barriers to (cross-border) housing investment and construction and that states have to either provide public accommodation to asylum seekers or enable them to access private housing markets.

2) Access to Housing Finance

An important pillar of EU law in the field of housing is the fostering of access to credit for the acquisition of housing. The Mortgage Credit Directive 2014/17/EU[22] (MCD) aims at

13 Case C-8/74 *Procureur du Roi v Benoît and Gustave Dassonville* (*Dassonville*) [1974] ECLI:EU:C:1974:82.

14 S. Reynolds, 'Housing Policy as a Restriction of Free Movement and Member States' Discretion to Design Programmes of Social Protection: Libert', *Common Market Law Review* 52 (2015), 259–280.

15 The forceful imposition of those rules on Member States, mainly through the doctrines of supremacy and direct effect is called constitutionalisation. See W. Sauter and H. Schepel, *State and Market in European Union Law* (Cambridge, UK: Cambridge University Press, 2009); see also: F. W. Scharpf, 'The European Social Model: Coping with the Challenges of Diversity', *Journal of Common Market Studies* 40 (2002), 645–670; and Chapter 1 by Laura Burgers, Chantal Mak, and Marija Bartl in this volume.

16 *Libert*, paras 41–48.

17 A *de minimis* rule does not apply to violations of the fundamental market freedoms, see Joined Cases C-177 and 178/82 *Criminal proceedings against Jan van de Haar and Kaveka de Meern BV* [1984] ECLI:EU:C:1984:144; also Case C-49/89 *Corsica France v Direction générale des douanes* [1989] ECLI:EU:C:1989:649.

18 Reynolds, 'Housing Policy as a Restriction of Free Movement', p. 272.

19 Council Directive 2003/9/EC of 27 January 2003 laying down minimum standards for the reception of asylum seekers, OJ L31/18, 6 February 2003.

20 Case C-79/13 *Federaal agentschap voor de opvang van asielzoekers* v *Selver Saciri and Others* [2014] ECLI:EU:C:2014:103 (*Saciri*).

21 Ibid., para. 42; at the same time, the CJEU confirmed that it was not up to the recipients to make their own choice of housing, para. 43.

22 Directive 2014/17/EU of the European Parliament and of the Council of 4 February 2014 on credit

stimulating the development of a 'supply-driven' EU mortgage market.[23] It is an instrument of market regulation (regulatory character),[24] but also establishes rules on pre-contractual information, standardised information to be provided at the time of the conclusion of the contract or rules on the creditworthiness assessment. MCD cases on contractual obligations of mortgage credit providers concern bundling, calculation practices, and the connection of contract law with financial regulation. For example, based on Article 12(2) MCD, the CJEU prohibited the bundling practice of obliging the borrower to deposit all his or her salary or similar income on a payment account opened with that lender.[25] Other cases concern the accuracy of the annual percentage of rate (APR, total yearly cost of borrowing money, expressed as a percentage of the principal loan amount),[26] or the possibility to annul a credit agreement if the bank is not authorised by the Member State authorities of which the borrower is a national; higher variable interest rate for non-nationals; and the language of pre-contractual information.[27] Guido Comparato (see Chapter 11 in this volume), addresses the further question of how market regulation especially in the aftermath of the Global Financial Crisis (GFC) also impacts contract law.

A salient question for the concrete housing relation—rather than the precise contractual obligations under the mortgage agreement—is the legal effect of an unfair contract term. Possibilities are the annulment of terms/whole contracts, re-negotiation, or replacement of the terms by statutory rules. In general, the annulment of the contract *ex tunc* would lead to the obligation of consumers to pay back the loan in its entirety, which they will often be unable to do without selling their home, often at a loss on top of that. Thus, the interpretation of Article 6(1) UCTD (Unfair Contract Terms Directive), according to which Member States must ensure that consumers are not 'bound' by the unfair provision, is vital. The CJEU states that national courts have to exclude the application of an unfair term.[28] Modification of the contract by revising the content of that term is, as a general rule, not allowed.[29] However, there are exceptions to this rule.

---

agreements for consumers relating to residential immovable property and amending Directives 2008/48/EC and 2013/36/EU and Regulation (EU) No 1093/2010, OJ L60/34.

23 European Commission, 'White Paper on the Integration of EU Mortgage Credit Markets', COM (2007) 807 final, https://eur-lex.europa.eu/legal-content/hr/LSU/?uri=CELEX:52007DC0807, p. 3.

24 Dispute over the relation between MC and MiFID II, see Opinion of AG Bobek in Case C-911/17 *Fédération bancaire française (FBF) v Autorité de contrôle prudentiel et de résolution (ACPR)* [2021] ECLI:EU:C:2021:294; also Case C-312/14 *Banif Plus Bank Zrt V Márton Lantos and Mártonné Lantos* [2015] ECLI:EU:C:2015:794.

25 Case C-778/18 *Association française des usagers de banques v Ministre de l'Économie et des Finances* [2020] ECLI:EU:C:2020:831, para. 58.

26 Request for a preliminary ruling, Case C-865/19 *Caisse de Crédit Mutuelle Le mans Pontlieue v OG* [2020] ECLI:EU:C:2020:1025.

27 In the end, the CJEU denied competence, see Order of the Court (Sixth Chamber) in Case C-277/19 *R. D. and A. D. v Raiffeisenbank St. Stefan-Jagerberg-Wolfsberg eGen* [2019] ECLI:EU:C:2019:791.

28 See Case C-243/08 *Pannon GSM* [2009] ECLI:EU:C:2009:350, para. 35; Case C-618/10 *Banco Español de Crédito* [2012] ECLI:EU:C:2012:349, para. 65; Cases C-70/17 and C-179/17, *Abanca Corporación Bancaria and Bankia* [2019] ECLI:EU:C:2019:250, para. 52.

29 Case C-618/10 *Banco Español de Crédito* [2012] ECLI:EU:C:2012:349, para. 73; Case C-26/13 *Kásler and Káslerné Rábai* [2014] ECLI:EU:C:2014:282, para. 77; and Cases C-70/17 and C-179/17 *Abanca Corporación Bancaria and Bankia* [2019] ECLI:EU:C:2019:250, para. 53.

> In a case, which was ultimately not decided on the merits, AG Kokott summarised that Article 6(1) UCTD can enable a national court to substitute the unfair terms with a supplementary rule if the contract cannot be maintained without the unfair term, the annulment of the contract would have unfavourable consequences for the consumer, and the parties have not opted for a supplementary provision under national law as a substitute for the removed term.[30]

First, if the contract cannot continue to exist without the unfair term—the national court has to assess this—the courts can replace it with a supplementary provision of national law instead of annulling the contract in its entirety.[31] This is reasonable because otherwise the borrower would have to repay the received sum and, most likely, lose their home. Second, if the validity of the contract is 'particularly unfavourable' for a consumer, the national court can replace this term, for example, with a reference to a statutory index.[32] Substitution can therefore be justified in order to restore the formal balance between the rights and obligations of the parties. An absolute limit for substitution is however the prohibition of substitution for general clauses.[33] Here, the national court must provide a framework for re-negotiation of the contract by the parties.[34] At any rate, there is the tendency to let the contract continue if possible.

b. Adequacy: Quality and Affordability

Adequacy of housing lies within the core of the right to housing.[35] This is because the right to housing means more than mere shelter; it relates to the place where one can simply 'be' and develop. Obviously, the home needs to be adequate to those needs and be habitable and affordability. The latter concerns both the affordability of rental housing and the cost of mortgage credit.

30 Opinion of Advocate General Kokott in Case C-81/19 *NG, OH v SC Banca Transilvania SA* [2020] ECLI:EU:C:2020:532, xi, para. 87.

31 See to that effect, Case C-26/13 *Kásler and Káslerné Rábai* [2014] ECLI:EU:C:2014:282, paras 80 to 84;, Cases C-70/17 and C-179/17 *Abanca Corporación Bancaria and Bankia* [2019] ECLI:EU:C:2019:250, paras 56 and 64; however replacement of contract terms with general clauses is not possible, see Case C-260/18 *Dziubak* [2019] ECLI:EU:C:2019:819, para. 48.

32 Case C-125/18 *Gómez del Moral Guasch v Bankia* [2020] ECLI:EU:C:2020:138, para. 62; also Case C-26/13 (*Kásler*), paras 81 and 82, and C-70/17 and C-179/17 (*Abanca Corporación Bancaria and Bankia*), para. 57.

33 *Dziubak*.

34 Case C-269/19 *Banca B* [2020] ECLI:EU:C:2020:954.

35 High Commissioner for Human Rights, 'The Right to Adequate Housing', *Fact Sheet* 21.1 (2009), https://unhabitat.org/sites/default/files/documents/2019-05/fact_sheet_21_adequate_housing_final_2010.pdf; UN Special Rapporteur on Adequate Housing, 'Report of the Special Rapporteur on Adequate Housing as a Component of the Right to an Adequate Standard of Living, and on the Right to Non-Discrimination in This Context' (2017), https://www.prosper.org.au/wp-content/uploads/2017/03/Report-of-the-Special-Rapporteur-on-finaincialisation-of-housing.pdf

1) *Quality of Housing*

As regards rental property, national civil codes contain rules on the quality and state of apartments or houses especially in rental agreements. For instance, Paragraph 536 of the German Civil Code or Article 7(207) Dutch Civil Code give the tenant the right to reduce the amount of rent to the owner in case of 'defects' that affect the possibility of normal usage. Similarly, Article 1576 Italian Civil Code contains the obligation of the landlord to undertake necessary repairs during the rental period. In EU law, tenancy agreements fall under the framework of consumer law, specifically the UCTD.[36] However, since the scope of the UCTD relates to the unfairness of contract terms, bad conditions or dilapidation of a residence would only be relevant if the bad quality of housing was reflected in an 'unfair' term in the tenancy agreement. This is highly unlikely.

The quality of housing property acquired by mortgage-secured credit agreements was dealt with in EU law in one line of German cases—the so-called *Schrottimmobilien* cases. In those cases, German consumers had fallen victim to a junk-property scheme. They ended up buying overpriced property and the rental income did not suffice to cover the mortgage payment, as initially promised by the sellers. In *Heininger*, the CJEU interpreted the old Doorstep Selling Directive 86/577/EC so as to grant consumers an 'eternal' right to withdrawal from the purchase agreement if they were not properly informed about their right to withdrawal.[37] The right to withdrawal here serves to protect the consumers' right to property and the protection of legitimate economic expectations. However, its concern with the quality of housing is indirect, to say the least. The profitability of property does not necessarily become apparent within a short period of time that coincides with the right to withdrawal. The consumers were, in a way, lucky that they had not been informed of the right to withdrawal because in this way they were able to cancel the purchase after they found out that the property was 'junk'. Had they been informed of their right to withdrawal, this would not have been possible.

2) *Affordability*

Rent Prices

Affordability issues are emblematic of the tensions tenancy law causes between a socially oriented private law, on the one hand, and urban planning or conflicting economic interests, on the other. In fact, Member States and cities have tried to control rental prices in order to address the problem of unaffordability.

36 Case C-488/11 *Asbeek Brusse & Katarina de Man Garabito v Jahani* [2013] ECLI:EU:C:2013:341.

37 Case C-481/99 *Georg Heininger and Helga Heininger v Bayerische Hypo- und Vereinsbank AG* [2001] ECLI:EU:C:2001:684; with regard to the consequences of cancellation for the obligations to immediately pay back the loan: Case C-229/04 *Crailsheimer Volksbank eG v Klaus Conrads and Others* [2005] ECLI:EU:C:2005:640.

Several countries have introduced caps on rent increases for new and renewed leases in 'high-pressure' areas.[38] In addition, local authorities are fighting for caps on rent.[39] National courts have dealt with the legality of such caps, especially with regard to the contested competences of the local authorities in the matter. A case in point is the rejection of the German Constitutional Court of the competence of the Berlin Senate to introduce rent caps.[40] Previously, Berlin had introduced such caps in its local Law on Rent Restriction in the Housing Sector in 2020, citing its constitutional competence in the housing sector. Instead, the German Constitutional Court interpreted broadly the federal competence for 'private law' contained in Article 74 Abs. 1 Nr. 1 *GG* (*Grundgesetz*), thus precluding local competence for the housing sector.

Rent control has also played a role as a restriction of the right to property. The European Court of Human Rights (ECtHR) has decided that the restriction of the right to property through rent caps can be justified under certain circumstances, taking into account the aim of fostering social justice and combatting housing shortages and soaring prices.[41]

The CJEU will probably not be asked to examine the legality of caps on rent because EU law is not designed to deal with this problem. Unfairness assessment under the UCTD 'does not relate to' the price as a main subject matter of the contract, Article 4(2) UCTD, as long as the respective contract term is drafted in plain, intelligible language.[42] The quality-price-ratio can only be taken into account when analysing other terms in the contract, Recital 19 UCTD. This emphasis on transparency and freedom of contract is a fundamental pillar of EU consumer law.

> For example, in *Gutiérrez Naranjo*, a case concerning a mortgage agreement, the CJEU stated that the 'substantive transparency' of so-called 'floor clauses' must be reviewed under Article 4(2) UCTD because the consumer needs to have all the necessary information on the contractual conditions and the consequences of entering into a contract.[43]

The UCTD's focus on transparency could, however, be used to assess the possible unfairness of rental price increase clauses. The issue is starting to come up in national court proceedings. While, for example, in Germany, increases in rent are only

38 In Germany, paras 556d to 556g BGB set out new rules for the calculation of rental increases. In France, a new law sets out caps on rent increases for new and renewed leases in 'zones tendues'. In Ireland, the Irish government introduced restrictions in 'Rent Pressure Zones' in Dublin and other more than twenty electoral areas, where private landlord rents cannot be increased by more than 4% per annum.

39 In Paris, new leases cannot set rents higher than reference rents plus supplementary charges. The Berlin Senate had introduced a cap for rents, based on the reference rent of previous years, paras 4, 5 MietenWoG Berlin.

40 BVerfG Order of 25 March 2021, 2 BvF 1/20, 2 BvL 5/20, 2 BvL 4/20.

41 *Mellacher v Austria* ECtHR 19 December 1989; *Lindheim & others v Norway* ECtHR 12 June 2012; *Nobel v The Netherlands* ECtHR 2 July 2013.

42 Case C-484/08 *Caja de Ahorros y Monte de Piedad de Madrid v Asociación de Usuarios de Servicios Bancarios (Ausbanc)* [2010] ECLI:EU:C:2010:309 at para. 32.

43 See Joined Cases C-154/15, C-307/15, and C-308/15 *Francisco Gutiérrez Naranjo v Cajasur Banco SAU* [2016] ECLI:EU:C:2016:980 at para. 73; further discussion in: C. Mak, 'Gutierrez Naranjo: On Limits in Law and Limits of Law', *European Law Review* 43 (2018), 447–459.

permissible for adjustment to the local comparative rent (§577 German Civil Code (BGB)), the Netherlands has introduced a rental cap in 2023 at inflation + 1%, meaning that adjustment due to inflation is possible. In contrast, another possibility to raise the rent was recently declared unfair by the District Court of Amsterdam. In two cases from 2023, the local court held that a term in standard terms for not rent-controlled housing was unfair because it provided (on top of the rise of the rent to accommodate for compensation of inflation) that the landlord had the right to further increase the rent by a certain maximum percentage, without making it clear to the tenant in advance on the basis of which the (further) rent increase was to be determined or why that increase would be necessary.[44] The judgments seem to be in line with EU law, which demands price increase clauses need to set out the calculation mechanisms in a transparent way.[45]

Cost of Mortgage Credit

In mortgage credit, an affordability issue arises with regard to the cost of credit. The MCD contains rules on how the total cost of credit shall be calculated (for example in Article 17) and how it shall be presented (in advertising, Article 11 and in Number 3 'main features of the loan' in the ESIS, the European Standard Information Sheet) in order to improve the comparability of credit offers (Recital 37). However, it focuses on transparency requirements, not the actual control of the cost of credit.

While Article 4(2) UCTD excludes the revision of price clauses in unfairness assessments, the CJEU made it clear that this is only the case for 'transparent' price clauses and carved out further requirements for this transparency, especially concerning variable interest rates and foreign-currency loans. Articles 4(1), 4(2), and 5 UCTD require that contract terms must not only be formally and grammatically intelligible but must also enable the 'reasonably circumspect' consumer to understand the specific functioning of the calculation methods and that the consumer be placed in a position to understand the economic consequences of clauses, for example concerning variable interest rates,[46] variable interest rates with a 'floor clause'[47] or concerning conversion mechanisms for foreign-currency loans.[48] Consumers must be able at any time to determine the exchange rate applied by the bank.[49] Transparency requirements

44 District Court Amsterdam [21 April 2023] ECLI:NL:RBAMS:2023:2420, and District Court Amsterdam [12 May 2023] ECLI:NL:RBAMS:2023:3124. Appeal by the landlords is expected. I thank Marco Loos for bringing these cases to my attention.

45 Case C-92/11 *RWE Vertrieb AG v Verbraucherzentrale Nordrhein-Westfalen eV* (*RWE*) [2013] ECLI:EU:C:2013:180, para. 55.

46 Case C-125/18 *Gómez del Moral Guasch v Bankia* [2020] ECLI:EU:C:2020:138, para. 56.

47 Case C-452/18 *XZ v Ibercaja Banco SA* [2020] ECLI:EU:C:2020:536, para. 56; *Gutiérrez Naranjo* Joined Cases C-154/15, C-307/15, and C-308/15 [2016] ECLI:EU:C:2016:980. The CJEU was less protective for consumers in Case C-452/18 *Ibercaja Banco* [2020] ECLI:EU:C:2020:536.

48 Case C-26/13 Á*rpád Kásler Hajnalka Káslerné Rábai v OTP Jelzálogbank Zrt* [2014] ECLI:EU:C:2014:282, para. 75.

49 Case C-212/20 *M.P. and B.P. v „A."* prowadzący działalność za pośrednictwem „A." S.A. (A.S.A) [2021] ECLI:EU:C:2021:934.

ensure that consumers are informed in plain and intelligible language of the inherent exchange rate risk in such foreign-currency agreements, especially since consumers do not usually receive their income in that currency.[50] This arguably implies that the lender needs to inform consumers comprehensively of the possible financial impact of such a term on their financial obligations, irrespective of whether the actual fall of the currency could have been predicted at the time of the signature of the agreement.[51]

c. Protection from Evictions

The third dimension of European private housing law concerns evictions. Eviction proceedings are initiated by landlords against tenants or by creditors against debtors when they fall behind with the repayment of mortgage credit or their monthly rental payments.[52] In EU law, evictions have only been dealt with in cases of outstanding mortgage payments. Despite Article 28 I MCD, which states that Member States shall adopt measures to encourage creditors to 'exercise reasonable forbearance' before initiating eviction proceedings, it is once again the UCTD that has come to fame in a line of seminal cases.

> The connection between enforcement of the mortgage agreement and unfairness control under the UCTD was made in the ground-breaking *Aziz* case, where the CJEU stated that the control of unfair terms under the UCTD could not be separated from the mortgage enforcement proceedings, because—even if separate proceedings found the terms of the mortgage contract to be unfair—the eviction could not be stopped. As monetary compensation would not prevent the loss of the family home,[53] consumer protection afforded under the UCTD would be ineffective. Therefore, the eviction proceedings must be halted while a court controls the underlying mortgage agreement for unfair terms.

Aziz triggered a substantial reform of Spanish procedural law, which was also challenged before the CJEU, for example concerning the extent of the procedural protection of mortgage debtors during evictions. This procedural dimension encompasses everything from ceilings on the default interest rates,[54] time limits for

50 See also: Case C-186/16 *Andriciuc and Others* [2017] ECLI:EU:C:2017:703, para. 50), and Case C-119/17 *Lupean* (not published) [2018] ECLI:EU:C:2018:103, para. 25. This holds true also if the Member States have not transposed Article 4(2) UCTD into national law, see *Gómez del Moral Guasch v Bankia*, para. 47.

51 Opinion of Advocate General Kokott, *NG, OH v SC Banca Transilvania SA*, para. 59.

52 ECtHR case law concerning outstanding rents: *Scollo v Italy* ECtHR 28 August 1995 and *Immobiliare Saffi v Italy* [2000] 30 EHRR 756; in both cases, Italian law violated Article 1 Protocol 1 and Article 6 ECHR. Concerning mortgage debt: *Vrzic v Croatia* ECtHR 13 July 2016; *FJM v UK* ECtHR 6 November 2018.

53 Case C-415/11 *Aziz v Catalunyacaixa* [2013] ECLI:EU:C:2013:164 (Aziz) at para. 60.

54 A provision imposing a ceiling on the default interest three times higher than the statutory rate is compatible with the UCTD under certain conditions, Cases C-482/13, C-484/13, C-485/13, and C-487/13 *Unicaja Banco, SA v José Hidalgo Rueda and Others and Caixabank SA v Manuel María Rueda Ledesma and Others* (Unicaja Banco and Caiixabank) [2015] ECLI:EU:C:2015:21.

bringing unfairness claims,[55] equality of legal remedies,[56] and the fact that *res judicata* in national law cannot impede the effectiveness of EU law.[57]

> In *Kušionová*, where there was no judge who could review *ex officio* the unfairness of contract terms, the CJEU ruled that interim measures must be in place to suspend or terminate unlawful mortgage enforcement proceedings if those measures are necessary to ensure effective legal protection under EU law.[58]

In these cases, national procedural remedies are 'upgraded' with the help of Article 47 CFREU, the EU's fundamental right to an effective remedy.[59] The CJEU makes it clear that the consumer rights derived from the UCTD are to be mirrored in national remedies and procedures.[60] In this way, Article 47 CFREU is used by the CJEU to make effective the prohibition of unfair consumer contract terms.

Connecting national procedural remedies with unfair terms control under the UCTD is called 'proceduralisation'.[61] Some view the success of this approach as a

---

55 Case C-8/14 *BBVA SA v Gabarro et al* [2015] ECLI:EU:C:2015:731: Individual consumers have to be able to take 'reasonable advantage' of a one-month time-limit (from the publication of the new law) for alleging unfairness of a contract term in mortgage enforcement proceedings (para. 39).

56 Case C-169/14 *Juan Carlos Sánchez Morcillo and María del Carmen Abril García v Banco Bilbao Vizcaya Argentaria SA* (*Sánchez Morcillo*) [2014] ECLI:EU:C:2014:2099: giving the creditor the right stay enforcement proceedings without giving the same right to the debtor is contrary to Article 47 ChFR and, thus, jeopardises the effectiveness of the UCTD, paras 48–50.

57 Case C-421/14 *Banco Primus SA v Jesús Gutiérrez García* [2017] ECLI:EU:C:2017:60: while the UCTD does not require 'continuous review of unfair terms' (paras 47–48), the national court still has to examine of its own motion the potential unfairness of previously not examined contract clauses (para. 52); in Case C-600/19 *MA v Ibercaja Banco, SA* [2022] ECLI:EU:C:2022:394, the CJEU made it clear that the judicial decision authorising mortgage enforcement must attest to an undertaken ex officio control of the underlying contract; otherwise *res judicata* would violate the UCTD.

58 Case C-34/13 *Monika Kušionová v SMART Capital* [2014] ECLI:EU:C:2014:2189, para. 66. In the end, because the term was based on a statutory provision according to Article 1(2) UCTD, whereby creditors could enforce in an extra-judicial procedure determining the amount owed and selling the property, the CJEU did not see a principled contradiction with EU law, para. 80.

59 N. Reich, *General Principles of EU Civil Law* (Cambridge, UK: Intersentia 2014), pp. 98–99; for an analysis of the role of Article 47 ChFR, see A. van Duin, *Effective Judicial Protection in Consumer Litigation—Article 47 of the EU Charter in Practice* (Cambridge, UK: Intersentia, 2022).

60 V. Trstenjak and E. Beysen, 'European Consumer Protection Law: Curia Semper Dabit Remedium?', *Common Market Law Review* 48.1 (2011), 95–125.

61 In its broadest sense, *proceduralisation* means the replacement of substantive decision by a legally established process, K. H. Ladeur, 'Proceduralization and Its Use in Post-Modern Legal Theory', *EUI Working Paper LAW* 96.5 (1996). It can be seen as an inherent—and therefore unproblematic—procedural dimension of law as a construct (Ladeur), or as a critically understood response to the crisis of the Welfare State, see J. Habermas, *Faktizität Und Geltung—Beiträge Zur Duskurstheorie Des Rechts Und Des Demokratischen Rechtsstaats* (Berlin: Suhrkamp, 1994). Rudolf Wiethölter uses it as referring to the justification for collision rules in 'Materialization and Proceduralization in Modern Law', in G. Teubner (ed.), *Dilemmas of Law in the Welfare State* (Berlin: De Gruyter, 1988), pp. 221–249; the term is also used in order describe the emphasis of procedures over material outcomes of the law, see F. Della Negra, 'The Uncertain Development of the Case Law on Consumer Protection in Mortgage Enforcement Proceedings: Sánchez Morcilla and Kusionová', *Common Market Law Review* 52 (2015), 1009–1032 (p. 1010).

'social activism' of the CJEU[62] or 'materialisation'[63] of EU law. Especially because of the attempt of the CJEU to include the purpose of the loan into the unfairness assessment, which alludes to some kind of proportionality assessment, Norbert Reich and Hans-W. Micklitz see *Aziz* and the reference to the debtor's home as a reflection of 'hidden constitutionalisation'.[64] Others have been more sceptical, emphasising the lack of an actual proportionality assessment as well as the missing balancing of two fundamental rights.[65]

To be sure, despite their importance in CJEU jurisprudence, there are inherent limits of the UCTD and of Article 47 CFREU in housing cases. First, Article 47 CFREU, as a procedural fundamental right, is not concerned with any material dimension of individual rights.[66] It is telling that the CJEU refers to the right to housing explicitly only in *Kušionová*, where the CJEU noted that 'the loss of a home is one of the most serious breaches of the right to respect for the home' and that the affected person must have the right to have the proportionality of the underlying enforcement measure reviewed.[67] In other cases, the CJEU mentions the special attention to be given when enforcement concerns the primary home of the debtor,[68] however without giving guidance as to the precise legal consequences. Second, Article 4(2) UCTD excludes from its scope *transparent* clauses concerning the definition of the main subject matter or the adequacy of remuneration. This aims at facilitating the establishment of the internal market through the abolishment of unfair terms from standard consumer contracts which stand in the way of shopping around for goods and services in different Member States with different contract law rules (Recitals 4–6 UCTD). EU consumer law focuses on transparency and is therefore conceptually ill-suited to accommodate any substantive fairness concerns.

---

62 G. Comparato, 'The Rationales of Financial Inclusion in the Changing European Private Law', *European Review of Contract Law* 11 (2015), 22–45; Perriello, 'Right to Housing'; S. I. Sánchez, 'Unfair Terms in Mortgage Loans and Protection of Housing in Times of Economic Crisis: Aziz c. Catalunyacaixa', *Common Market Law Review* 51 (2014), 955–974; differentiated: H.-W. Micklitz, 'Unfair Contract Terms—Public Interest Litigation before European Courts. Case C-415/11 Mohammed Aziz', in V. Colaert and E. Terryn (eds), *Landmark Cases of EU Consumer Law—in Honour of Jules Stuyck* (Cambridge, UK: Hart, 2013), pp. 615–634.

63 The term 'materialisation' comes from Max Weber's distinction between formal rationality and material justice, M. Weber, *Grundriss der Sozialökonomik—Wirtschaft und Gesellschaft* (Tübingen: Mohr and Siebeck, 1922), p. 664, https://archive.org/details/wirtschaftundges00webeuoft/page/664/mode/2up. For a discussion: Habermas, *Faktizität Und Geltung*, pp. 541 et seq.

64 H.-W. Micklitz and N. Reich, 'The Court and the Sleeping Beauty: The Revival of the Unfair Contract Terms Directive (UCTD)', *Common Market Law Review* 51 (2014), 771–808 (p. 801).

65 I. Domurath, *Consumer Vulnerability and Welfare in Mortgage Contracts* (Cambridge, UK: Hart Publishing, 2017); Perriello, 'Right to Housing'; Domurath and Mak, 'Private Law and Housing Justice'. As to the effect of human rights in private law, see Chapter 5 in this volume.

66 For a thorough analysis of the role of Article 47 ChFR under the UCTD, see van Duin, *Effective Judicial Protection in Consumer Litigation.*

67 Case C-34/13 *Monika Kušionová* v *SMART Capital* [2014] ECLI:EU:C:2014:2189 (*Kušionová*) at paras 63–64; confirmed in Case C-598/21 *SP and CI v Všeobecná úverová banka a.s.* (*VÚB*), ECLI:EU:C:2023:845.

68 Most famously: Case C-415/11 *Mohamed Aziz v Caixa d'Estalvis de Catalunya, Tarragona i Manresa* (*Catalunyacaixa*) [2013] ECLI:EU:C:2013:164.

3. Beyond the Law: Welfare, Commodities, and Finance

Housing and housing problems lie at the intersection of different social, political, and economic interests, policies, and developments. While some decades ago housing was considered a social good benefitting from social protection mechanisms of the welfare state, it is now a 'consumerised' commodity. Both classical market regulation and private law have played a constitutive role in the process of privatisation, commodification, and financialisation.[69]

a. Privatisation and Marketisation: The Change/Loss of Fundamental Rights

Housing is increasingly provided by private parties. Subsidised rental housing is either abolished or privatised.[70] While states had different degrees of public ownership of housing until the 1980s/1990s—often as part of welfare policies—there is a converging trend towards the expansion of private housing markets. In line with neo-liberal political and economic ideology, states have re-conceptualised housing not as a social good and as a means of re-distribution of wealth, but as a means to accumulate economic wealth.[71] Many acquire housing property for the purposes of reducing living costs at old age, when income is usually drastically reduced and many social security systems struggle to keep up with pension payments. Housing is now asset-based welfare[72] and a means to accumulate wealth.[73] Colin Crouch has called this 'privatised Keynesianism', referring to a policy regime where markets exist alongside housing and other debt among low- and medium-income people—different from public demand management (welfare).[74] Here, homeownership has become an ideology in itself.[75]

In order to enable privatisation—the sale of housing units to private parties, be it private individuals or investors or companies—the law needs to ensure open markets. Here, EU law comes in. Individuals and companies from one Member State are to have unrestricted access to housing markets in other Member States, as the *Libert* case shows. Unrestricted access enables the entering into contracts for construction, purchase, or rent in other Member States. Other issues, such as the material dimension of access

69 With regard to the role of private law generally in processes of market ordering, see Chapter 15 in this volume.

70 M. B. Aalbers, *The Financialization of Housing—A Political Economy Approach* (London: Routledge, 2016).

71 R. Rolnik, 'Late Neoliberalism: The Financialization of Homeownership and Housing Rights', *International Journal of Urban and Regional Research* 24.1 (2013), 95–104.

72 J. Doling and R. Ronald, 'Home Ownership and Asset-Based Welfare', *Journal of Housing and the Built Environment* 25 (2010), 165–173; M. Watson, 'Planning for a Future of Asset-Based Welfare? New Labour, Financialized Economic Agency and the Housing Market', *Planning Practice and Research* 24 (2009), 41–56.

73 OECD, 'Economic Policy Reform'.

74 C. Crouch, 'Privatised Keynesianism: An Unacknowledged Policy Regime', *British Journal of Politics and International Relations* 11 (2009), 382–399.

75 R. Ronald, *The Ideology of Home Ownership-Homeowner Societies and the Role of Housing* (London: Palgrave Macmillan, 2008).

to housing and affordability,[76] are outside of the scope of EU law. And considering that tenants renting accommodation at market rents are more affected by housing overburden costs,[77] the fact that there is no legal control of market rents leads to a considerable gap of protection under EU law; it is up to national and local authorities to respond to the problems entailed by this market opening.

This political economy has important effects on the nature and exercise of rights in the housing sector, for both the housing provider and the resident.[78] In fact, privatisation and marketisation also entail a shift in the character of housing-related rights. On the provider side, obligations to provide affordable housing are replaced by property and property-like rights. The right to make a profit is inherent in the right to property,[79] implying the right to leave a property empty if it is more profitable than renting it out to tenants.[80] The approach of the UCTD reflects and allows this: the owner of the housing property has the right to demand a profitable rental price from the tenant who can—theoretically—negotiate the price or find another accommodation. There is no price control. As long as the rental price is set out in a transparent manner and there is no obvious disproportion between the service (the provision of habitable living space) and the rental price, EU law has no concerns.

On the resident side, housing rights are replaced by consumer rights. It can be argued that public or social citizenship rights are 'subverted' or 'impoverished'[81] in a political economy of privatisation. The more housing is provided by private parties instead of states or state-owned companies, the more housing relations are governed by the workings of the market of supply and demand and customer relations (application of consumer law) rather than need and vulnerability (protection through human rights). It may be that Article 47 CFREU shifts the focus from the effective enforcement of EU law towards individual rights protection.[82] But, in EPL, where housing is treated under the EU consumer law framework, there are no parameters other than the effectiveness of EU law to conceptualise housing interests. Consumer

76 Once again we witness *access justice* instead of *social justice*, H.-W. Micklitz, 'Social Justice and Access Justice in Private Law', EUI Working Paper LAW 2011.02 (2011), https://cadmus.eui.eu/handle/1814/15706.

77 Housing Europe, 'The State of Housing in the EU 2019' (2019), https://www.housingeurope.eu/the-state-of-housing-in-the-eu-2019/

78 For a fundamental discussion, see C. Mak, *Fundamental Rights in European Contract Law: A Comparison of the Impact of Fundamental Rights on Contractual Relationships in Germany, the Netherlands, Italy and England* (Alphen aan den Rijn: Wolters Kluwer, 2008); H. Collins, *European Contract Law and the Charter of Fundamental Rights* (Cambridge, UK: Intersentia, 2017).

79 See the expansive case law of the ECtHR, for example: Application No 11179/84 *Langborger v Sweden*, Applications Nos 13221/08 and 2139/10, *Lindheim & others v Norway*, Application No 2–11/2013, *Nobel v The Netherlands*.

80 E. L. Moreno, 'Ghost Cities and Empty Houses: Wasted Prosperity', *American International Journal of Social Science* 3 (2014), 207–216; M. Gentili and J. Hoekstra, 'Houses without People and People without Houses: A Cultural and Institutional Exploration of an Italian Paradox', *Housing Studies* 34 (2019), 425–447.

81 M. Freedland, 'The Marketization of Public Services', in C. Crouch, K. Eder, and D. Tambini (eds), *Citizenship, Markets, and the State* (Oxford: Oxford University Press, 2001), pp. 90–110.

82 van Duin, *Effective Judicial Protection in Consumer Litigation*.

law in the EU is mainly concerned with market transparency and is, thus, an ill fit for any housing (or other social) interests.

b. Commodification and Financialisation

The privatisation of housing would be impossible without financialisation. Financialisation is the increasing importance of financial markets, financial motives, financial institutions, and financial elites in the operations of the economy and its governing institutions.[83] In the field of housing, the term denotes the transformation of housing into a financial asset or a commodity, increasingly dependent on financial markets.[84] Commodification means turning housing into an economic good that can be exchanged on markets. For the housing sector, financialisation enables more and more actors to acquire housing for different purposes —including investment. As a consequence, housing nowadays occupies a central role in the workings of global financial markets.

As housing has become an important absorber for international over-accumulated capital and excess liquidity,[85] its character changes from a good fulfilling the social purpose of providing shelter to an economic good with financial objectives. The interests of the parties involved in the housing relation do not concern housing as such: while for the resident, housing still plays a role of providing shelter, the interests of investors are the security of investment and profit-maximisation. As a result, individual owners are competing with multinational corporations for 'locations' of (not 'housing' but) 'real estate' property, generating centrifugal effects on land appreciation especially in highly sought-after metropolitan areas. This forces the less wealthy to live in areas with poor basic services, inadequate housing, and far away from their workplaces.[86] In fact, financialisation and commodification are considered the root causes of the lack of affordable housing.[87]

Housing is also an important collateral for debt. This has a significant impact on

---

83 G. Epstein, 'Financialization, Rentier Interests, and Central Bank Policy' (2002), https://peri.umass.edu/wp-content/uploads/joomla/images/publication/fin_Epstein.pdf. For housing, financialization can be defined as 'the increasing dominance of financial actors, markets, practices, measurements and narratives, at various scales, resulting in a structural transformation of economies, firms (including financial institutions), states and households', Aalbers, *The Financialization of Housing*, p. 2.

84 D. Caturianas, 'Policies to Ensure Access to Affordable Housing', Publication for the Committee on Employment and Social Affairs, Policy Department for Economic, Scientific and Quality of Life Policies (European Parliament, Luxembourg) (2020), https://www.europarl.europa.eu/RegData/etudes/STUD/2020/652729/IPOL_STU(2020)652729_EN.pdf

85 R. Fernandez and M. B. Aalbers, 'Housing and Capital in the Twenty-First Century: Realigning Housing Studies and Political Economy', *Housing, Theory and Society* 34 (2017), 151–158.

86 Rolnik, 'Late Neoliberalism', p. 1063.

87 H. Schwartz and L. Seabrooke, *The Politics of Housing Booms and Busts* (London: Palgrave Macmillan, 2009); Rolnik, 'Late Neoliberalism'; S. Sassen, 'Who Owns Our Cities—and Why This Urban Takeover Should Concern Us All', *The Guardian* (24 November 2015), https://www.theguardian.com/cities/2015/nov/24/who-owns-our-cities-and-why-this-urban-takeover-should-concern-us-all; D. Fields and S. Uffer, 'The Financialisation of Rental Housing: A Comparative Analysis of New York City and Berlin', *Urban Studies* 63 (2016), 1486–1502.

housing relations because, as we have seen in the field of mortgage-secured private housing property, the interest in having a roof over one's head—maybe coupled with the interest in saving at old age—clashes with the interest of a new actor, the creditor. There is a legal difference between an individual who is regarded as a citizen in a vulnerable position vis-á-vis the mortgage seller or whether the consumer is regarded as a normal debtor.[88] In case of repayment difficulties, the house becomes the object of a tugging war between the mortgagor who has an interest of not losing her home and the creditor with an interest in demanding the maturation of the security accessory to the principal debt. Residents are not seen as occupiers with social needs but as debtors who should not stand in the way of value-creation and financial and economic growth. When they lag behind with the payment of rent or the repayment of a mortgage credit, the creditor has all rights to evict. We have seen in the CJEU cases that there is no space for proportionality assessments that could directly take into account the social circumstances and needs of the occupiers.

There is a second level of abstraction: even mortgage debt is a commodified investment outlet. It is considered high-quality collateral, especially for global players like pension funds.[89] The sale of mortgage-backed securities (MBS) is a global market. It turns housing property—an immobile asset with long turnover times—into a product that can be converted easily into liquid capital. Securitisation was the key financial innovation that enabled the integration of global financial markets,[90] focusing on the profitability of the global circulation of mortgage pools, not the profitability of granting credit to individual borrowers. Similarly, the EU is now creating a market for non-performing loans. With the Credit Servicers and Credit Purchasers Directive 2021/2167 (CSD),[91] which regulates more specifically the sale, purchase, and servicing of non-performing loans, the EU completes the aim of establishing a market for NPLs, which is to facilitate 'private cross-border risk-sharing, while at the same time reducing the need to public risk sharing'. This basically means that banks can take non-performing loans off their balance sheets and instead sell them to third parties, which are then to deal with the recovery of the outstanding payments. It's a kind of securitization ex post.

88 Della Negra, 'Uncertain Development', p. 1011.

89 R. Fernandez and M. B. Aalbers, 'Financialization and Housing: Between Globalization and Varieties of Capitalism', *Competition and Change* 20 (2016), 71–88; M. B. Aalbers, 'The Variegated Financialization of Housing', *International Journal of Urban and Regional Research* 41.4 (2017), 542–554.

90 N. Fligstein and J. Habinek, 'Sucker Punched by the Invisible Hand: The World Financial Markets and the Globalization of the US Mortgage Crisis', *Socio-Economic Review* 12 (2014), 637–665 (p. 641).

91 Directive (EU) 2021/2167 of the European Parliament and of the Council of 24 November 2021 on credit servicers and credit purchasers and amending Directives 2008/48/EC and 2014/17/EU, OJ L 438/1 (CSD).

c. Financial Stability

Being bound up in a financial system,[92] housing and housing finance are tied to financial stability. The political interest in lending is not just one of welfare policy; it is also an important means for the creation of money[93] and economic growth. The expansion of mortgage credit leads to mortgage credit growth, which in turn exacerbates housing prices and leads to housing price booms. This again nurtures the expansion of mortgage credit and higher loan-to-value ratios.[94] However, this is inherently unsustainable.[95] In 2008, when the global financial crisis caused widespread economic and social decline, it became clear that the massive expansion of household debt through securitisation was highly fragile because it includes low-income households in financial markets even though they are not necessarily in a position to repay their debt. As those households started defaulting on their loans, they caused a global chain reaction that led to widespread corporate and private bankruptcy. Millions of people lost their homes, which they had often just acquired a short while ago by indebting themselves.

Against this backdrop, Recital 58 of the MCD links the availability of credit to the larger context of financial stability by referring to the principles of the Financial Stability Board, which, in turn, sees weak residential mortgage practices as a risk factor for global financial instability.[96] The centrality of mortgage debt to the financial system also explains the interest of financial institutions such as the International Monetary Fund (IMF) or the European Banking Authority (EBA) in mortgages. Both institutions are concerned with the connection of irresponsible mortgage lending and risks to financial stability. For example, the EBA issued 'Guidelines on arrears and foreclosure' in line with the EBA's objective of achieving a convergence of supervisory practices for Article 28 I MCD.[97] Because of the 'significant consequences for creditors, consumers and potentially financial stability of foreclosure' (Recital 27 MCD), these guidelines acknowledge the systemic importance of mortgages.[98]

> The CJEU also made the connection between financial stability and the importance of giving credit only in cases of positive creditworthiness assessments in *Schyns*, where it

92 Also rental markets are now considered a 'macroeconomic challenge', see C. Cuerpo, S. Kalantaryan, and P. Pontuch, 'Rental Market Regulation in the European Union', *Economic Papers* 515 (2014), https://ec.europa.eu/economy_finance/publications/economic_paper/2014/ecp515_en.htm, p. 17.

93 M. McLeay, A. Radia and R. Thomas, 'Money Creation in the Modern Economy', *Quarterly Bulletin* 14 (2014), https://www.bankofengland.co.uk/quarterly-bulletin/2014/q1/money-creation-in-the-modern-economy

94 International Monetary Fund, 'Housing Finance and Financial Stability—Back to Basics?' (2011), Chapter 3, https://www.imf.org/-/media/Websites/IMF/imported-flagship-issues/external/pubs/ft/GFSR/2011/01/pdf/_chap3pdf.ashx

95 A. Mian and A. Sufi, *House of Debt—How They (and You) Caused the Great Recession, and How We Can Prevent It from Happening Again* (Chicago, IL: University of Chicago Press, 2014); A. Mian, A. Sufi, and F. Trebbi, 'The Political Economy of the Subprime Mortgage Credit Expansion', *NBER Working Paper* (2010), 16107, https://www.nber.org/papers/w16107

96 FSB, 'Principles for Sound Residential Mortgage Underwriting Practices', *FSB* (18 April 2012), https://www.fsb.org/2012/04/r_120418/, p. 1.

97 Ibid., p. 4.

98 Ibid., p. 5.

> acknowledged that 'irresponsible behaviour by market participants can undermine the foundations of the financial system'.[99]

This connection of housing finance with financial stability is problematic. From a regulatory perspective, it is difficult to serve both aims—consumer protection and financial stability—at the same time.

> The *Gutiérrez Naranjo* case exposes the lack of their interchangeability.[100] In that case, the Spanish Supreme Court had put a temporal limitation on the retroactive effect of the unfair floor clauses given the effect it would have on the financial stability if banks had to repay the overpaid amounts. The CJEU stated that Article 6 UCTD ruled out the temporal restriction by national courts.[101]

In any case, Comparato shows that references to financial stability in the CJEU case law are more successfully invoked by public entities when justifying a restriction of private rights than in cases between private parties, such as banks and debtors.[102] While his—rather cautious—conclusion is that the concept of financial stability is not clearly cut out,[103] one could also be reminded of the discrepancy between public and private relations when it comes to invoking the fundamental right to housing.

Whether the connection between mortgagor protection and financial stability will prevent housing bubbles or the next financial crisis is doubtful. Almost a century ago, the Austrian-Hungarian scholar Polanyi argued that the problem of major crisis lies in the marketisation of 'fictitious commodities' itself (here: housing as relating to land).[104] This would mean that the housing sector will remain in crisis unless dissociated from commodification and financialisation. It also implies that law cannot do much in order to prevent crises unless it is used for the de-commodification of housing.[105]

4. Conclusions and Points for Reflection

EU law and EPL impact horizontal housing relations in different ways. Their focus is on facilitating cross-border access to housing markets and access to transparent and 'fair' mortgage credit, with the cost of credit being subject to transparency and legibility requirements. As regards evictions, the UCTD has had a substantial impact

99 Case C-58/18 *Schyns* [2019] ECLI:EU:C:2019:467, para. 46.

100 For a discussion, see: G. Comparato, 'Financial Stability in Private Law: Intersections, Conflicts, Choices', *Common Market Law Review* 58 (2021), 391–430, especially pp. 242–249. Comparato refers to the Opinion of AG Mengozzi in *Gutiérrez Naranjo*, where the latter argued that financial stability takes precedence over the retroactive resolution of unfair consumer mortgage contracts, versus the CJEU ruling in the same case, where the effectiveness of EU law was the determining legal concept.

101 *Gutiérrez Naranjo*, para. 70. The Spanish Supreme has since then confirmed the full retroactivity of unfairness, see Sánchez, 'Unfair Terms'.

102 Comparato, 'Financial Stability in Private Law'.

103 Ibid., p. 427.

104 K. Polanyi, *The Great Transformation* (Boston, MA: Beacon Press, 1944); F. Block and M. Somers, *The Power of Market Fundamentalism: Karl Polanyi's Critique* (Cambridge, MA: HUP, 2016).

105 For a broad framework, see I. Domurath and D. Gil McCawley, 'Re-Imagining Housing Provision from Markets to Welfare', *German Law Journal* 29.5 (2024), 1525–1544, https://doi.org/10.1017/glj.2024.69

not only on national contract law but also on procedural law. Combined with Article 47 CFREU, it has proven more apt than the MCD to deal with procedural problems impairing the effectiveness of EU consumer rights. However, the UCTD is not actually designed to deal with securing access to affordable housing or preventing evictions. It, thus, sits awkwardly with the right to housing. As a consequence, we can ask ourselves the question:

Q1: Should fundamental and human rights, such as the right to housing, have a direct horizontal effect? What would be the advantages and disadvantages?

In the current political economy, housing issues have become part of the consumer law framework of EU law, which works so as to support and enable privatisation, commodification, and financialisation. In this way, EU law has intertwined housing issues with financial regulation, raising questions of how contract law can and should react to macro-economic problems such as large-scale financial crises.[106] Against this backdrop, it must also be debated whether political institutions—on state and EU level—are still in a legal position to manage housing sectors. Privatising housing sectors takes the management out of the hands of states and public authorities and—in times of financialisation—relinquishes housing sectors to the workings of global investment and financial markets. It can be argued that by privatising housing sectors, states are actively relinquishing responsibility and power to respond to the needs of their citizens in this field.

It remains to be seen if increased investment programmes for social housing[107] will be sufficient to address housing problems in Europe. For EU law, I have discussed the possibility of treating housing as a universal service, aiming at putting housing sectors under the regulatory framework of Services of General (Economic) Interest.[108] While not turning around the current political economy, this approach would at least give some leeway to national and local authorities to address housing problems while benefitting from exemptions to the internal market rules. There is also discussion on submitting mortgage contracts to the idea of 'life-time contracts'.[109] Rental agreements could become part of the EU open method of coordination (OMC).[110] It remains to be seen to what extent any of these proposals can help to address the structural problems in housing markets. It is vital, therefore, to reflect on the questions:

106 See Chapter 11 in this volume.

107 Housing Europe, 'The State of Housing in the EU 2019'.

108 I. Domurath, 'Housing as a "Double Irritant" in EU Law: Towards an SGEI between Markets and Local Needs', *Yearbook of European Law* 38 (2019), 400–447; P. Kenna, 'Supporting the Irish Housing System to Address Housing Market Failure: Cost Rental Housing and Services of General Economic Interest (SGEI)', Irish Council for Social Housing (2021), https://www.universityofgalway.ie/media/housinglawrightsandpolicy/files/ICSH-NUI-Galway-_Report_Cost-Rental-and-SGEI-Full-Report-.pdf

109 L. Nogler and U. Reifner (eds), *Life Time Contracts—Social Long-Term Contracts in Labour, Tenancy and Consumer Credit Law* (The Hague: Eleven International Publishing, 2014).

110 C. U. Schmid, 'TENLAW: Tenancy Law and Housing Policy in Multi-Level Europe Analysis of EUs Role Towards a European Role in Tenancy Law and Housing Policy?' (2015), https://www.uni-bremen.de/fileadmin/user_upload/fachbereiche/fb6/fb6/Forschung/ZERP/TENLAW/EuropeanRole.pdf

Q2: Which role does (private) law play in the political economy of housing?

Q3: Which role does it play in commodifying housing and how could it serve its de-commodification?

Bibliography

Aalbers, M. B., *The Financialization of Housing—A Political Economy Approach* (London: Routledge, 2016), https://doi.org/10.4324/9781315668666

Aalbers, M. B., 'The Variegated Financialization of Housing', *International Journal of Urban and Regional Research* 41.4 (2017), 542–554, https://doi.org/10.1111/1468-2427.12522

Bengtsson, B., 'Housing as a Social Right: Implications for Welfare State Theory', *Scandinavian Political Studies* 24 (2001), 255–275, https://doi.org/10.1111/1467-9477.00056

Block, F., and M. Somers, *The Power of Market Fundamentalism: Karl Polanyi's Critique* (Cambridge, MA: HUP, 2016), https://doi.org/10.4159/harvard.9780674416345

Busch, C., et al., 'The Rise of the Platform Economy: A New Challenge for EU Consumer Law?', *Journal of European Consumer and Market Law* 5.1 (2016), 3–10, https://doi.org/10.2139/ssrn.2754100

Caturianas, D., 'Policies to Ensure Access to Affordable Housing', Publication for the Committee on Employment and Social Affairs, Policy Department for Economic, Scientific and Quality of Life Policies (European Parliament, Luxembourg) (2020), https://www.europarl.europa.eu/RegData/etudes/STUD/2020/652729/IPOL_STU(2020)652729_EN.pdf

Collins, H., *European Contract Law and the Charter of Fundamental Rights* (Cambridge, UK: Intersentia 2017), https://doi.org/10.1017/9781780684963

Commission Communication, 'Upgrading the Single Market: More Opportunities for People and Business', COM (2015) 550 final, https://eur-lex.europa.eu/legal-content/EN/TXT/?uri=CELEX%3A52015DC0550

Comparato, G., 'The Rationales of Financial Inclusion in the Changing European Private Law', *European Review of Contract Law* 11 (2015), 22–45, https://doi.org/10.1515/ercl-2015-0002

Comparato, G., 'Financial Stability in Private Law: Intersections, Conflicts, Choices', *Common Market Law Review* 58 (2021), 391–430

Crouch, C., 'Privatised Keynesianism: An Unacknowledged Policy Regime', *British Journal of Politics and International Relations* 11 (2009), 382–399, https://doi.org/10.1111/j.1467-856X.2009.00377.x

Cuerpo, C., S. Kalantaryan, and P. Pontuch, 'Rental Market Regulation in the European Union', *Economic Papers* 515 (2014), https://ec.europa.eu/economy_finance/publications/economic_paper/2014/ecp515_en.htm

Della Negra, F., 'The Uncertain Development of the Case Law on Consumer Protection in Mortgage Enforcement Proceedings: Sánchez Morcilla and Kusionová', *Common Market Law Review* 52 (2015), 1009–1032

Doling, J., and R. Ronald, 'Home Ownership and Asset-Based Welfare', *Journal of Housing and the Built Environment* 25 (2010), 165–173, https://doi.org/10.1007/s10901-009-9177-6

Domurath, I., *Consumer Vulnerability and Welfare in Mortgage Contracts* (Cambridge, UK: Hart Publishing, 2017)

Domurath, I., 'Housing as a "Double Irritant" in EU Law: Towards an SGEI between Markets and Local Needs', *Yearbook of European Law* 38 (2019), 400–447, https://doi.org/10.1093/yel/yez012

Domurath, I., and C. Mak, 'Private Law and Housing Justice in Europe', *Modern Law Review* 83 (2020), 1188–1220, https://doi.org/10.1111/1468-2230.12557

Domurath, I., and D. Gil McCawley, 'Re-Imagining Housing Provision from Markets to Welfare', *German Law Journal* 29.5 (2024), 1525–1544, https://doi.org/10.1017/glj.2024.69

Domurath, I., G. Comparato, and H.-W. Micklitz (eds), 'The Over-Indebtedness of European Consumers: A View from Six Countries', *EUI Working Paper Series Law* 2014.10 (2014)

Donders, Y., 'Protecting the Home and Adequate Housing—Living in a Caravan or Trailer as a Human Right', *International Human Rights Law Review* 5 (2016), 1–25, https://doi.org/10.1163/22131035-00501002

Epstein, G., 'Financialization, Rentier Interests, and Central Bank Policy' (2002), https://peri.umass.edu/wp-content/uploads/joomla/images/publication/fin_Epstein.pdf

European Commission, 'Urban Agenda for the EU', *European Commission*, https://ec.europa.eu/regional_policy/policy/themes/urban-development/agenda_en

European Commission, 'White Paper on the Integration of EU Mortgage Credit Markets', COM (2007) 807 final, https://eur-lex.europa.eu/legal-content/hr/LSU/?uri=CELEX:52007DC0807

European Parliament, 'Overview of Housing Policies, Report No W-14' (1996), https://www.europarl.europa.eu/workingpapers/soci/w14/summary_en.htm

Fernandez, R., and M. B. Aalbers, 'Financialization and Housing: Between Globalization and Varieties of Capitalism', *Competition and Change* 20 (2016), 71–88, https://doi.org/10.1177/1024529415623916

Fernandez, R., and M. B. Aalbers, 'Housing and Capital in the Twenty-First Century: Realigning Housing Studies and Political Economy', *Housing, Theory and Society* 34 (2017), 151–158, https://doi.org/10.1080/14036096.2017.1293379

Fields, D., and S. Uffer, 'The Financialisation of Rental Housing: A Comparative Analysis of New York City and Berlin', *Urban Studies* 63 (2016), 1486–1502, https://doi.org/10.1177/0042098014543704

Financial Services Authority, 'Mortgage Market Review: Responsible Lending', *Consultation Paper* 10.16 (2010), https://www.fca.org.uk/publication/consultation/fsa-cp10–16.pdf

Fligstein, N., and J. Habinek, 'Sucker Punched by the Invisible Hand: The World Financial Markets and the Globalization of the US Mortgage Crisis', *Socio-Economic Review* 12 (2014), 637–665, https://doi.org/10.1093/ser/mwu004

Freedland, M., 'The Marketization of Public Services', in C. Crouch, K. Eder, and D. Tambini (eds), *Citizenship, Markets, and the State* (Oxford: Oxford University Press, 2001), pp. 90–110, https://doi.org/10.1093/oso/9780199241217.003.0005

FSB, 'Principles for Sound Residential Mortgage Underwriting Practices', *FSB* (18 April 2012), https://www.fsb.org/2012/04/r_120418/

Gentili, M., and J. Hoekstra, 'Houses without People and People without Houses: A Cultural and Institutional Exploration of an Italian Paradox', *Housing Studies* 34 (2019), 425–447, https://doi.org/10.1080/02673037.2018.1447093

Habermas, J., *Faktizität Und Geltung—Beiträge Zur Duskurstheorie Des Rechts Und Des Demokratischen Rechtsstaats* (Berlin: Suhrkamp, 1994)

High Commissioner for Human Rights, 'The Right to Adequate Housing', *Fact Sheet* 21.1 (2009), https://unhabitat.org/sites/default/files/documents/2019-05/fact_sheet_21_adequate_housing_final_2010.pdf

Hohmann, J., *The Right to Housing—Law, Concepts, Possibilities* (Oxford: Hart Publishing, 2013)

Housing Europe, 'The State of Housing in the EU 2017' (2017), https://web.archive.org/web/20190708235116/ https://www.housingeurope.eu/file/614/download

Housing Europe, 'The State of Housing in the EU 2019' (2019), https://www.housingeurope.eu/the-state-of-housing-in-the-eu-2019/

Housing Europe, 'The State of Housing in Europe 2023' (2023), https://www.stateofhousing.eu/#p=1

International Monetary Fund, 'Housing Finance and Financial Stability—Back to Basics?' (2011), Chapter 3, https://www.imf.org/-/media/Websites/IMF/imported-flagship-issues/external/pubs/ft/GFSR/2011/01/pdf/_chap3pdf.ashx

Kenna, A., 'Housing Rights: Positive Duties and Enforceable Rights at the European Court of Human Rights', *European Human Rights Law Review* 13 (2008), 193–208

Kenna, P. 'Globalization and Housing Rights', *Indiana Journal of Global Legal Studies* 15 (2008), 397–469

Kenna, P., 'Supporting the Irish Housing System to Address Housing Market Failure: Cost Rental Housing and Services of General Economic Interest (SGEI)', Irish Council for Social Housing (2021), https://www.universityofgalway.ie/media/housinglawrightsandpolicy/files/ICSH-NUI-Galway-_Report_Cost-Rental-and-SGEI-Full-Report-.pdf

Kenna, P., and H. Simón-Moreno, 'Towards a Common Standard of Protection of the Right to Housing in Europe through the Charter of Fundamental Rights', *European Law Journal* 25 (2019), 608–622, https://doi.org/10.1111/eulj.12348

Ladeur, K. H., 'Proceduralization and Its Use in Post-Modern Legal Theory', *EUI Working Paper LAW* 96.5 (1996)

Lilleholt, K., 'The Right to Housing and Its Impact on Contract Law', in K. Ketscher (ed.), *Velferd og rettferd: Festskrift til Asbjørn Kjønstad 70 år* (Oslo: University of Oslo, 2013), pp. 363–374

Mak, C., *Fundamental Rights in European Contract Law: A Comparison of the Impact of Fundamental Rights on Contractual Relationships in Germany, the Netherlands, Italy and England* (Alphen aan den Rijn: Wolters Kluwer, 2008)

Mak, C., 'Gutierrez Naranjo: On Limits in Law and Limits of Law', *European Law Review* 43 (2018), 447–459

Mak, V., 'Private Law Perspectives on Platform Services. Airbnb: Home Rentals between AYOR and NIMBY', *Journal of European Consumer and Market Law* 5.1 (2016), 19–25

McLeay, M., A. Radia and R. Thomas, 'Money Creation in the Modern Economy', *Quarterly Bulletin* 14 (2014), https://www.bankofengland.co.uk/quarterly-bulletin/2014/q1/money-creation-in-the-modern-economy

Mian, A., and A. Sufi, *House of Debt—How They (and You) Caused the Great Recession, and How We Can Prevent It from Happening Again* (Chicago, IL: University of Chicago Press, 2014), https://doi.org/10.7208/chicago/9780226277509.001.0001

Mian, A., A. Sufi, and F. Trebbi, 'The Political Economy of the Subprime Mortgage Credit Expansion', *NBER Working Paper* (2010), 16107, https://www.nber.org/papers/w16107

Micklitz, H.-W., 'Social Justice and Access Justice in Private Law', EUI Working Paper LAW 2011.02 (2011), https://cadmus.eui.eu/handle/1814/15706

Micklitz, H.-W., 'Unfair Contract Terms—Public Interest Litigation before European Courts. Case C-415/11 Mohammed Aziz', in V. Colaert and E. Terryn (eds), *Landmark Cases of EU Consumer Law—in Honour of Jules Stuyck* (Cambridge, UK: Hart, 2013), pp. 615–634

Micklitz, H.-W., and N. Reich, 'The Court and the Sleeping Beauty: The Revival of the Unfair Contract Terms Directive (UCTD)', *Common Market Law Review* 51 (2014), 771–808

Moreno, E. L., 'Ghost Cities and Empty Houses: Wasted Prosperity', *American International Journal of Social Science* 3 (2014), 207–216

Nogler, L., and U. Reifner (eds), *Life Time Contracts—Social Long-Term Contracts in Labour, Tenancy and Consumer Credit Law* (The Hague: Eleven International Publishing, 2014)

OECD, 'Economic Policy Reforms 2011: Going for Growth' (2011), https://www.oecd.org/content/dam/oecd/en/publications/reports/2011/04/economic-policy-reforms-2011_g1g11692/growth-2011-en.pdf

Perriello, L. E., 'Right to Housing and Unfair Contract Terms', *Journal of European Consumer and Market Law* 7 (2018), 96–103

Polanyi, K., *The Great Transformation* (Boston, MA: Beacon Press, 1944)

Reich, N., *General Principles of EU Civil Law* (Cambridge, UK: Intersentia 2014), https://doi.org/10.1017/9781780685304

Remiche, A., 'Yordanova and Others v Bulgaria: The Influence of the Social Right to Adequate Housing on the Interpretation of the Civil Right to Respect for One's Home', *Human Rights Law Review* 12 (2012), 787–800, https://doi.org/10.1093/hrlr/ngs033

S. Reynolds, 'Housing Policy as a Restriction of Free Movement and Member States' Discretion to Design Programmes of Social Protection: Libert', *Common Market Law Review* 52 (2015), 259–280

R. Rolnik, 'Late Neoliberalism: The Financialization of Homeownership and Housing Rights', *International Journal of Urban and Regional Research* 24.1 (2013), 95–104, https://doi.org/10.1111/1468-2427.12062

Ronald, R., *The Ideology of Home Ownership-Homeowner Societies and the Role of Housing* (London: Palgrave Macmillan, 2008)

Rutgers, J., 'The Right to Housing (Article 47 of the Charter) and Unfair Terms in General Conditions', in H. Collins (ed.), *European Contract Law and the Charter of Fundamental Rights* (Cambridge, UK: Intersentia, 2017), pp. 125–137, https://doi.org/10.1017/9781780684963.006

Sánchez, S. I., 'Unfair Terms in Mortgage Loans and Protection of Housing in Times of Economic Crisis: Aziz c. Catalunyacaixa', *Common Market Law Review* 51 (2014), 955–974

Sassen, S., 'Who Owns Our Cities—and Why This Urban Takeover Should Concern Us All', *The Guardian* (24 November 2015), https://www.theguardian.com/cities/2015/nov/24/who-owns-our-cities-and-why-this-urban-takeover-should-concern-us-all

Sauter, W., and H. Schepel, *State and Market in European Union Law* (Cambridge, UK: Cambridge University Press, 2009), https://doi.org/10.1017/CBO9780511626647

Scharpf, F. W., 'The European Social Model: Coping with the Challenges of Diversity', *Journal of Common Market Studies* 40 (2002), 645–670, https://doi.org/10.1111/1468-5965.00392

Schmid, C. U., 'TENLAW: Tenancy Law and Housing Policy in Multi-Level Europe Analysis of EUs Role Towards a European Role in Tenancy Law and Housing Policy?' (2015), https://www.uni-bremen.de/fileadmin/user_upload/fachbereiche/fb6/fb6/Forschung/ZERP/TENLAW/EuropeanRole.pdf

Schwartz, H., and Seabrooke, L., *The Politics of Housing Booms and Busts* (London: Palgrave Macmillan, 2009)

Shiller, R. J., *The Subprime Solution: How Today's Global Financial Crisis Happened, and What to Do about It*, I (Princeton, NJ: Princeton University Press, 2008)

Teubner, G. (ed.), *Dilemmas of Law in the Welfare State* (Berlin: De Gruyter, 1988)

Trstenjak, V., and E. Beysen, 'European Consumer Protection Law: Curia Semper Dabit Remedium?', *Common Market Law Review* 48.1 (2011), 95–125

UN Special Rapporteur on Adequate Housing, 'Report of the Special Rapporteur on Adequate Housing as a Component of the Right to an Adequate Standard of Living, and on the Right to Non-Discrimination in This Context' (2017), https://www.prosper.org.au/wp-content/uploads/2017/03/Report-of-the-Special-Rapporteur-on-finaincialisation-of-housing.pdf

van Duin, A., *Effective Judicial Protection in Consumer Litigation—Article 47 of the EU Charter in Practice* (Cambridge, UK: Intersentia, 2022)

Watson, M., 'Planning for a Future of Asset-Based Welfare? New Labour, Financialized Economic Agency and the Housing Market', *Planning Practice and Research* 24 (2009), 41–56, https://doi.org/10.1080/02697450902742148

Weber, M., *Grundriss der Sozialökonomik—Wirtschaft und Gesellschaft* (Tübingen: Mohr and Siebeck, 1922), https://archive.org/details/wirtschaftundges00webeuoft/page/664/mode/2up

Wiethölter, R., 'Materialization and Proceduralization in Modern Law', in G. Teubner (ed.), *Dilemmas of Law in the Welfare State* (Berlin: De Gruyter, 1988), pp. 221–249

13. Data Subjects in European Private Law

Antonio Davola

Abstract

This chapter seeks to examine the discourse surrounding the involvement of private law in promoting the rights of data subjects, particularly within the evolving landscape of digital environments. To achieve this, it initially delves into the existing regulations within the European Union, exploring their foundational principles. Subsequently, it provides an overview of the key provisions of the General Data Protection Regulation, elucidating how the regulation currently recognises control over data as a significant—arguably, the primary—mechanism for safeguarding individuals when participating in digital interactions. However, as the far-reaching impact of data analyses on human lives suggests a need for a broader viewpoint, the chapter scrutinises the potential role of private law in complementing and enhancing the traditional stance of data protection law.

1. Introduction

The advent of digitalisation, together with the increasing interaction between individuals and virtual environments characterising the information society,[1] entails a growing risk, that citizens are deprived of control and lack awareness regarding which information about them is available on the web, as an inner corollary of the computerisation of interactions.

Nowadays, the industry accumulates knowledge about individuals, which is mined from interactions occurring online—and oftentimes offline as well, mainly by means of interactions occurring between users and Information and Communication Technologies (ICTs).

Through data acquisition, companies can innovate their strategies to gain a

1 L. Floridi, *The Onlife Manifesto. Being Human in a Hyperconnected Era* (Berlin: Springer, 2014).

 https://doi.org/10.11647/OBP.0448.13

competitive edge, deliver services, and market their products by engaging in comprehensive analyses of their target audience, allowing for the customisation of each user's experience.[2] The execution of these processes relies on automated algorithms that operate across various dimensions, employing a diverse range of techniques. For instance, companies may utilise artificial intelligence (AI) models to process user information and generate 'persuasion profiles',[3] enabling the creation of personalised content that serves the functional needs of product and service provision and, more broadly, the establishment of contracts and relationships.[4]

Amidst the pervasive sense of disorientation and disempowerment resulting from the structural changes and imbalances fostered by digital infrastructures,[5] privacy and data protection laws are increasingly viewed as pivotal instruments for enhancing individual protection. These regulations aim to ensure that individuals have meaningful oversight over information held by third parties. While privacy has traditionally been construed as the 'right to let alone',[6] functioning as a deterrent against unwarranted intrusions into personal space and as a prerequisite for exercising fundamental rights,[7] data protection laws seek to bolster individuals' effective (and, to some extent, proactive) control over the collection and utilisation of the information. In essence, these laws emphasise the right of individuals to have complete control over their analogical and digital identities.[8]

This progression can be traced, reaching at least as far back as the early 1970s. During this period, an initial strand of legal scholarship emerged, highlighting the potential new risks associated with data processing for citizens, particularly in the context of computers and large databases. In Europe, this concern led to the formulation of early sets of national laws and court decisions that established an individual right to informational self-determination,[9] building on the idea that a society, in which citizens remain unaware of who possesses information about them, is not acceptable.

Simultaneously, international agreements began to recognise a set of obligations for those involved in data processing, along with corresponding rights for individuals:

---

2 I. Domurath, 'Technological Totalitarianism: Data, Consumer Profiling, and the Law', in L. de Almeida, M. Cantero Gamito, M. Durovic, and K. P. Purnhagen (eds), *The Transformation of Economic Law: Essays in Honour of Hans-W. Micklitz* (Oxford: Hart Publishing, 2019), pp. 65–90.

3 B. J. Fogg, *Persuasive Technology: Using Computers to Change What We Think and Do* (Burlington: Morgan Kaufmann, 2002).

4 S. C. Boerman, S. Kruikemeier, and F. J. Z. Borgesius, 'Online Behavioural Advertising: A Literature Review and Research Agenda', *Journal of Advertisings* 46.3 (2017), 363–376; R. Walker, *From Big Data to Big Profits: Success with Data and Analytics* (Oxford: Oxford University Press, 2015).

5 See L. A. Bygrave, *Data Protection Law: Approaching Its Rationale, Logic and Limit* (Alphen aan den Rijn: Kluwer, 2002), p. 117.

6 S. D. Warren and L. D. Brandeis, 'The Right to Privacy', *Harvard Law Review* 4.5 (1890), 193–220.

7 W. L. Prosser, 'Privacy', *California Law Review* 48.3 (1960), 383–423; E. J. Bloustein, 'Privacy as an Aspect of Human Dignity: An Answer to Dean Prosser', *New York University Law Review* 39 (1964), 962–1007.

8 A. Westin, *Privacy and Freedom* (New York: Athenum, 1967); G. J. Stigler, 'An Introduction to Privacy in Economics and Politics', *Journal of Legal Studies* 9.4 (1980), 623–644.

9 Bundesverfassungsgericht 15 December 1983, 1 BvR 209/83, ECLI:DE:BVerfG:1983:rs19831215.1bvr020983.

the 1980 Guidelines on the Protection of Privacy and Transborder Flows of Personal Data, established by the Organisation for Economic Co-operation and Development (OECD; guided by the principle of openness shaping data treatment), clarified that individuals should have the ability to ascertain the existence and nature of their personal data undergoing processing, and that they should also be informed about the main purposes of data use, the identity of data controllers, and how to engage with them.[10] The openness principle evolved alongside and as a prerequisite to the principle of individual participation, granting individuals the right to access information about data concerning them held by others. This principle also aligned with the collection limitation principle, emphasising that the collection of data should generally occur with the knowledge of the individuals to whom the data pertains.[11]

A year later, these principles received additional reinforcement through the 1981 Council of Europe's Convention for the Protection of Individuals with regard to Automatic Processing of Personal Data.[12] The Convention mandated that individuals should have the ability to confirm the existence of any automated data files containing information about them, understand the primary purposes of these files, and know the residence or place of business of the file's controller.

Contemporary technological advancements have further intensified the imperative for data protection. In today's context, individuals function as 'informative agents', consistently sharing information through online activities and interactions with IoT (Internet of Things) products and wearable devices. Consequently, the scale of personal data collection and sharing has significantly expanded, with technology playing a crucial role in facilitating the seamless flow of personal data.

As a consequence, a discernible shift occurred in contemporary legal practice: the right to the protection of personal data was enshrined as a fundamental right under Article 8 of the Charter of Fundamental Rights of the European Union (CFREU) (2000/C 364/01),[13] and individuals were endowed with specific rights pertaining to the legal safeguarding of their personal data and information, being designated as 'data subjects' in this context.

The concept of 'data subject' was further defined in the now-repealed Directive 95/46/EC on the protection of individuals concerning the processing of personal data.[14] According to the directive (Article 2), a data subject is an identified or identifiable

---

10 OECD, *Recommendation of the Council of 23 September 1980: OECD Guidelines Governing the Protection of Privacy and Transborder Flows of Personal Data* (Paris: OECD Publishing, 1980), https://legalinstruments.oecd.org/en/instruments/OECD-LEGAL-0188, para. 12.

11 *OECD Guidelines*, paras 13 and 27.

12 Council of Europe, 'Convention for the Protection of Individuals with regards to Automatic Processing of Personal Data', Strasburg (28 January 1981), https://rm.coe.int/1680078b37

13 (1) Everyone has the right to the protection of personal data concerning him or her. (2) Such data must be processed fairly for specified purposes and on the basis of the consent of the person concerned or some other legitimate basis laid down by law. Everyone has the right of access to data which has been collected concerning him or her, and the right to have it rectified.

14 Directive 95/46/EC of the European parliament and of the Council of 24 October 1995 on the protection of individuals with regard to the processing of personal data and on the free movement of such data.

natural person whose personal data is processed by a controller or processor. This definition remained unaltered following the adoption of the EU General Data Protection Regulation (GDPR) in 2016,[15] where the term 'data subject' is qualified in identical terms under Article 4 within the broader definition of 'personal data'.[16]

It should be noted that the term 'data subjects' specifically refers to individuals, excluding non-physical entities such as corporations and public authorities from this classification—and hence excluding them from the normative coverage provided by the GDPR. Within the category of natural persons, the GDPR generally avoids differentiation based on specific characteristics, be it European Union citizenship or residency. This broad and inclusive approach aligns with the universal scope outlined in the GDPR's Recital 14, emphasising its application to any natural person within the EU's territory regarding the processing of their personal data, without discrimination.

The notion of a data subject is intricately tied to the notion of personal data, wherein information pertaining to individuals receives protection only if it either directly identifies the person or renders them identifiable.[17] Consequently, the processing of anonymous data falls outside the purview of data protection law. To determine the identifiability of a person, a test of reasonable likelihood must be conducted, taking into consideration the prevailing state-of-the-art technology pertaining to the processing, its foreseeable advancements, and various objective factors, including the costs and time required for identification.[18] This definition is intentionally broad and adaptable to technological advancements, with the sole stipulation that the data in question pertains to a specific individual.[19]

Even if, among data subjects, there is no explicit differentiation based on individual characteristics at the rule level—in order for everyone to be afforded equal protection—it is noteworthy that certain features, such as the public interest associated with a person, may be considered in assessing the fairness of data processing.[20] A notable exception to this uniform approach pertains to children: the General Data Protection Regulation specifically addresses the situation of children by imposing special requirements for consent[21] and transparency obligations.[22] Data related to children is deemed particularly crucial, given their presumed lack of awareness and

15 Regulation (EU) 2016/679 of the European parliament and of the Council of 27 April 2016 on the protection of natural persons with regard to the processing of personal data and on the free movement of such data, and repealing Directive 95/46/EC (GDPR).

16 Article 4 GDPR: 'personal data' means any information relating to an identified or identifiable natural person ('data subject'); an identifiable natural person is one who can be identified, directly or indirectly, in particular by reference to an identifier such as a name, an identification number, location data, an online identifier or to one or more factors specific to the physical, physiological, genetic, mental, economic, cultural or social identity of that natural person.

17 See P. Blume, 'The Data Subject', *European Data Protection Law Review* 4 (2015), 258–264.

18 Recital 26 GDPR.

19 See N. Purtova, 'The Law of Everything. Broad Concept of Personal Data and Future of EU Data Protection Law', *Law, Innovation and Technology* 10 (2018), 40–81.

20 See ECJ Case C-131/12 *Google Spain SL and Google Inc v. Agencia Española de Protecciòn de Datos (AEPD) e Mario Costeja Gonzàles* [2014] ECLI:EU:C:2014:317.

21 GDPR Article 8.

22 GDPR Article 12(1).

understanding regarding the consequences of data processing and their legal rights, which results in a diminished decision-making capability.[23]

The categorisation of an individual as a data subject serves as the normative foundation for the award and enforcement of a set of rights established by the General Data Protection Regulation. Despite their diverse structures, these rights share a common premise: the acknowledgement that, during digital interactions, data subjects often lack sufficient knowledge about the collection and processing of their data. Consequently, there is a need for substantial rectification of the information asymmetry between data subjects and their counterparts. This rectification is crucial to empower data subjects to make informed decisions about consenting to data-related practices[24] and to oversee that data processing aligns with their preferences.

2. Legal Context: Data Subjects and Their Rights in the European Normative Framework

In accordance with the structure outlined by the GDPR, measures to empower data subjects encompass both *ex ante* and *ex post* processing rights, that afford individuals a range of powers to be exercised both before and after the execution of data processing. This dual approach is designed to facilitate individuals' control over information across the entire lifecycle of personal data. Granting data subjects rights that can be asserted after data acquisition provides them with a meaningful opportunity to reassess the utilisation of their data in evolving contexts. This recognises the inherent challenge that individuals may not be able to anticipate all the consequences that may arise from the use of their personal data in advance.[25] Hence, *ex post* rights play a crucial role in guaranteeing the substantive fairness of data processing activities. Moreover, it is important to note that certain rights bestowed upon data subjects serve as prerequisites to others. For instance, the right to access information is a necessary precursor to exercising the distinct right to rectify incomplete or inaccurate data.[26] Ultimately, all data subject rights must be interpreted within the overarching framework of the general principles of transparency and fairness embedded in the GDPR.[27] These rights are operationalised through the observations and considerations made by the Court of Justice of the European Union (CJEU).

---

23 See Recital 38 GDPR, with regards to the special protection accorded to children under the GDPR see, among others, A. Mantelero, 'Children Online and the Future of EU Data Protection Framework: Empirical Evidences and Legal Analysis', *International Journal of Technology Policy and Law* 2 (2016), 169–181; E. Lievens and V. Verdoodt, 'Looking for Needles in a Haystack: Key Issues Affecting Children's Rights in the General Data Protection Regulation', *Computer Law and Security Review* 34.2 (2018), 269–278.

24 See G. G. Fuster, 'How Uninformed is the Average Data Subject? A Quest for Benchmarks in EU Personal Data Protection', *Revista de Internet, Derecho y Política* 9 (2014), 92–104.

25 J. Ausloos and P. Dewitte, 'Shattering One-Way Mirrors. Data Subject Access Rights in Practice', *International Data Privacy Law* 8.1 (2018), 4–28.

26 See ECJ Case C-454/16 *Peter Nowak v Data Protection Commissioner* [2014] ECLI:EU:C:2014:317; Case C-73/16 *College van burgemeester en wethouders van Rotterdam v Mee Rijkeboer* [2009] ECLI:EU:C:2009:293.

27 ECJ Case C-49/17 *Fashion ID GmbH & CoKG v Verbraucherzentrale NRW eV* [2019] ECLI:EU:C:2019:629, p. 102.

Data subject rights are mostly communication-based and inspired by an overall duty to enhance transparency and comprehensibility: accordingly, the General Data Protection Regulation requires information to be concise, transparent, intelligible, and expressed in an easily accessible form, using clear and plain language.[28]

The primary and foundational mechanism for safeguarding data subjects and establishing the initial legality of data-related activities is obtaining their aware consent for data processing. According to Article 4(11), this consent must be freely given, specific, informed, unambiguous, and involve an affirmative indication that the data subject agrees to the processing of personal data related to them. Even after consent is granted, data subjects retain a set of rights that they can exercise in their interactions with the involved party.

Such rights can be organised into five categories: a) right of access; b) right to rectification and erasure; c) data portability; d) right to be forgotten; and e) rights about profiling.

The entitlement of each data subject to access their personal data, as articulated in Article 15 of the GDPR, finds its roots in the Charter of Fundamental Rights of the European Union (Article 8, Paragraph 2) and is an offshoot of the broader right to the protection of personal data. As per Article 15 GDPR, a data subject has the right to receive confirmation from the controller regarding whether personal data concerning them are undergoing processing. In cases where processing is occurring, the data subject has the right to access that personal data, along with information concerning various aspects of the processing. This includes details such as the purposes of the processing, the recipients, or categories of recipients to whom the personal data have been or will be disclosed, the expected duration for which the personal data will be retained, and the existence of the right to request rectification, erasure, or restriction of the processing activity from the controller. It is imperative that all this information be presented to the data subject in a comprehensible format. Consequently, any technical abbreviations, codifications, or acronyms in the data format are unacceptable unless their meanings are adequately clarified for the recipient.

The right to rectification—as outlined in Article 16—serves as a crucial complement to the right to access, as the accuracy of stored data is paramount in maintaining the integrity of the data subject's identity. Consequently, the data subject holds the right to request the controller to modify, correct, or update the data concerning them at any time. This includes the ability to supplement incomplete personal data. This mechanism is designed to safeguard the personal identity of individuals, ensuring that statements pertaining to them are truthful and do not compromise the personal identity they have cultivated throughout their lifetime.

Closely tied to the right of access is the right to data portability, as articulated in Article 20 of the GDPR: this right empowers the data subject to receive all the personal data previously provided to the controller, with the purpose of having that

28 GDPR Article 12.

data transmitted to another data controller. For example, individuals have the right to retrieve their contact list from a webmail application for transfer to a cloud service provided by a different operator.

Additionally, the right to be forgotten, as specified in Article 17 of the GDPR, addresses the enduring presence of data on the internet and is a direct outcome of the conclusions drawn by the Court of Justice of the European Union in the landmark *Google Spain* case.[29] In its ruling, the Court affirmed the data subject's right to request the de-indication of a link associated with news about them when that information no longer holds public interest.

Lastly, the GDPR provides data subjects with a set of rights pertaining to profiling and automated decision-making. According to Article 22, data subjects have a general entitlement not to be subject to decisions based solely on the automated processing of their data. Exceptions to this rule include cases where the processing is necessary for the conclusion or execution of a contract (e.g. automatically sending an email to all participants in a mailing list), when the treatment is based on the data subject's explicit consent, or when required by EU or Member State law.

It is important to note that, in addition to the explicit provisions in the GDPR, the specifics of all data subjects' rights are further elucidated by guidelines developed by European authorities and agencies, such as the Article 29 Data Protection Working Party and the European Data Protection Supervisor.[30]

3. Societal Relevance: Control over Data as a Core Concept for Individuals' Freedom

The establishment of a comprehensive set of rights for each data subject, coupled with the principle that consent should serve as the primary condition for lawful data processing in the absence of other legal bases,[31] originates from the acknowledgement that control over data is crucial for the self-determination and free will of data subjects.[32] This notion of control primarily encompasses the right to determine the utilisation of

29 Case C-131/12 *Google Spain SL*.

30 Amongst the most relevant documents drafted by these entities, see Article 29 Working Party, 'Guidelines on Data Protection Impact Assessment (DPIA) and Determining Whether Processing Is "Likely to Result in a High Risk" for the Purposes of Regulation 2016/679' (2017), https://ec.europa.eu/newsroom/article29/items/611236, p. 10; European Data Protection Supervisor, 'Preliminary Opinion "Privacy and Competitiveness in the Age of Big Data"' (2014), https://edps.europa.eu/data-protection/our-work/publications/opinions/privacy-and-competitiveness-age-big-data_en; European Data Protection Supervisor, 'Opinion 8/2016 "On the Coherent Enforcement of Fundamental Rights in the Age of Big Data"' (2016), https://edps.europa.eu/sites/edp/files/publication/16-09-23_bigdata_opinion_en.pdf; Article 29 Working Party, 'Guidelines on Consent under Regulation 2016/679 WP259 rev.01' (2018), https://ec.europa.eu/newsroom/article29/item-detail.cfm?item_id=623051

31 See Article 6 GDPR.

32 D. J. Solove, *The Digital Person* (New York: New York University Press, 2004), p. 77; A. F. Westin, *Privacy and Freedom*.

personal information, including decisions regarding its collection and disclosure.[33]

Over time, both national and European courts have scrutinised the concept of control to provide a functional interpretation of the provisions outlined in the GDPR in favour of data subjects. Even before the European framework for data protection was established, the German Constitutional Court underscored the idea that individuals' control over their data is indispensable to enable the freedom of individuals to make plans or decisions relying on their personal self-determination.[34] In a recent judgment involving the regulation of data monitoring through cookies, the CJEU clarified that expressing consent through a pre-selected checkbox does not constitute active behaviour, as it would 'appear impossible' to objectively ascertain whether a user has given informed consent by not deselecting a pre-ticked checkbox.[35]

As a result, it is reasonable to assert that the rights and entitlements granted by the GDPR shall be interpreted to provide substantial protection to users, in line with a perspective that views privacy and data protection as fundamentally serving to shield individuals from imbalances created by data-driven technologies.[36]

a. The Role of Information in Defining and Exercising Control over Data Processing

In consideration of the abovementioned aspects, and of the prominent focus of data protection and privacy law on principles such as informational self-determination and autonomy,[37] it is not surprising that decision-making studies, following the neoclassical approach,[38] have been playing a crucial role in shaping the application of data subjects' rights, with the 'information paradigm' operating as a key focal point in shaping data subjects' rights.[39] Drawing on the established concept of individuals as *homini oeconomici* and building upon the expected utility theory for decisions made under uncertainty, data protection traditionally presents individuals as rational actors capable of processing available information to make logical decisions aligned with their priorities. Consequently, user empowerment heavily depends on the use of disclosures and information rights (as seen in Article 15 GDPR), recognised as a fundamental tool in addressing the information asymmetry operating at the core of their vulnerability. While disclosures are not the exclusive means of protecting users, coexisting with supervisory and structural obligations like privacy by design and

33 H. Ursic, 'The Failure of Control Rights in the Big Data Era: Does a Holistic Approach Offer a Solution?', in M. Bakhoum et al. (eds), *Personal Data in Competition, Consumer Protection and Intellectual Property Law* (Berlin: Springer, 2018), pp. 55–83.

34 Bundesverfassungsgericht 15 December 1983.

35 ECJ Case C-673/17, *Planet49* [2019] ECLI:EU:C:2019:801.

36 R. Calo, 'Privacy, Vulnerability, and Affordance', *DePaul Law Review* 66 (2017), 592–593.

37 D. Solove, *Understanding Privacy* (Cambridge, MA: Harvard University Press, 2008).

38 See, among others, A. Acquisti, C. Taylor, and L. Wagman, 'The Economics of Privacy', *Journal of Economic Literature* 54.2 (2016), 442–492.

39 See A. L. Allen, 'Privacy-as-Data Control: Conceptual, Practical, and Moral Limits of the Paradigm', *Faculty Scholarship at Penn Carey Law* 32 (2000), 861–875.

by default principles, informational duties still remain a primary, if not the primary, normative resource to advance the protection of data subjects.

Additionally, it should be mentioned that, beyond the influence of the neoclassical theory, several other reasons have been adduced to support the prominence of the information paradigm as a benchmark for developing regulatory tools and disclosure duties. For instance, disclosure is observed to be a relatively low-cost form of intervention and one that is transparent for all parties involved. *Ex-ante* disclosure rules are efficiently enforceable for supervisory authorities and simultaneously provide companies with a clear means of determining compliance with relevant provisions. Finally, it is often argued that disclosure obligations garner a form of 'bi-partisan' support, striking a favourable balance between paternalistic and liberalist approaches to market regulation.[40]

b. Critiques to the Information Paradigm and to Data Protection as the Main Resource to Advance Users' Protection in Digital Environments

Against this background, it is widely recognised that a considerable body of research, particularly in behavioural studies, contends that individual decision-making frequently diverges from the neoclassical paradigm.[41] These studies present evidence of interaction dynamics—including the ones pertaining to data processing and online relations more in general—that contradict the rigidity of conventional economic theories of individual behaviour, particularly in scenarios involving standard-form contracts.

Consequently, research on topics such as information overload, the impact and consequences of the no-reading problem, and the framing and saliency bias in information provision sheds light on the inherent limitations of traditionally conceived information duties.[42] These limitations pertain to the ability of disclosure-related rights to instil genuine awareness and, more specifically, to serve as effective strategies for preserving users' control over the collection and processing of their data.

Data protection law has not remained unaffected by these developments, prompting regulatory initiatives to integrate behavioural findings into the structure of the GDPR. This is primarily achieved by reconsidering the conventional approach to the principle of transparency and advocating for a substantive approach to disclosure as a means to foster informational self-determination. This shift is evident, for instance, in GDPR provisions mandating that information and communications regarding data processing

40 O. Ben-Shahar and C. E. Schneider, 'The Failure of Mandated Disclosure', *University of Pennsylvania Law Review* 159 (2011), 647–749 (pp. 681–684).

41 See, among others, C. Sunstein, *Behavioural Law & Economics* (Cambridge, UK: Cambridge University Press, 2000).

42 I. Ayres and A. Schwartz, 'The No-Reading Problem in Consumer Contract Law', *Stanford Law Review* 66.3 (2014), 545–609; Ben-Shahar and Schneider, 'The Failure of Mandated Disclosure'; F. Cheng and C. Wu, 'Debiasing the Framing Effect: The Effect of Warning and Involvement', *Decision Support Systems* 49.3 (2010), 328–334.

be easily accessible and comprehensible, employing clear and plain language for such disclosures.[43]

The increasing emphasis on ensuring awareness of consent, as evident in express statutory provisions[44] and judicial decisions from Member States and the European Commission,[45] lends further support to these considerations. Similar concerns have been raised regarding the effectiveness of consent and its associated rights in enhancing user protection: despite being equipped with the aforementioned rights, data subjects often find it challenging to exert practical control over data processing activities; limitations arise from the fact that terms and conditions are typically drafted unilaterally, offering only partially negotiable terms.[46] Consequently, the current conceptualisation of consent has been criticised as an inherently flawed mechanism,[47] unable to operate in practice.

In addition to criticisms directed at the information paradigm and consent as the primary means for advancing user protection in the digital environment, further doubts have been raised regarding the structural capacity of data protection law to provide a meaningful basis for protecting users' self-determination when subject to decisions based on data processing.

In particular, a competing narrative asserts that the concept of a data subject should primarily be interpreted as identifying a power imbalance, extending its scope beyond qualifying merely an informational imbalance between the parties and viewing information asymmetry as just one aspect of a much broader context. This alternative perspective has garnered increasing attention in recent legal scholarship. Scholars such as Daniel Solove have theorised privacy as a tool to address power imbalances—particularly between individuals and public administration.[48] Similarly, Julie Cohen has analysed privacy, surveillance, and self-exposure through the lens of relational power.[49]

---

43 Article 5(1)(a) and Recital 58 GDPR.

44 See Article 7 GDPR.

45 See, A. G. della Concorrenza e del Mercato, 'Sanzioni per 20 milioni a Google e ad Apple per uso dei dati degli utenti a fini commerciali (PS11147)', *AGCM* (16 November 2021), https://www.agcm.it/media/comunicati-stampa/2021/11/PS11147-PS11150; Bundeskartellamt, Decision No B6–22/16 [6 February 2019]; OLGDüsseldorf, VI-Kart 1/19 (V), Bundeskartellamt c. [Facebook 26 August 2019]; Bundesgerichtshof, KVR69/19 [23 June 2020]; Datatilsynet, 'Grindr LLC (Administrative Fine)' (2021), https://www.datatilsynet.no/contentassets/8ad827efefcb489ab1c7ba129609edb5/administrative-fine---grindr-llc.pdf; ECJ Case 673/17 *Bundesverband der Verbraucherzentralen und Verbraucherverbände - Verbraucherzentrale Bundesverband eV v Planet49 GmbH* [2019] ECLI:EU:C:2019:801. For a comparative analysis of these decisions and their implications, see A. Davola and G. Malgieri, 'Data-Powerful' (2022), https://papers.ssrn.com/sol3/papers.cfm?abstract_id=4027370

46 ECJ Cases C-240/98 to C-244/98 *Océano Grupo Editorial and Salvat Editores* [2000] ECLI:EU:C:2000:346, para. 25: 'the consumer is in a weak position vis-à-vis the seller or supplier, as regards both his bargaining power and his level of knowledge. This leads to the consumer agreeing to terms drawn up in advance by the seller or supplier without being able to influence the content of the terms'.

47 M. Durovic and F. Lech, 'A Consumer Law Perspective on the Commercialization of Data', *European Review of Private Law* 29 (2021), 701–732 (p. 712).

48 D. J. Solove, 'Privacy and Power: Computer Databases and Metaphors for Information Privacy', *Stanford Law Review* 53 (2001), 1393–1462 (p. 1399).

49 J. E. Cohen, *Configuring the Networked Self* (New Haven, CT: Yale University Press, 2012), Chapter 6; on

These studies have been advancing an increasing argument that the characteristics of the data subject—and therefore the meaningful application of the rights provided by the GDPR—can be accurately understood only by considering the corresponding capabilities of the 'counterparty' or the powerful entities, specifically digital companies utilising their data. In essence, user protection should be scrutinised and customised based on the interplay between individual characteristics and the capabilities or power of the digital companies using their data. Ideally, one could suggest that data subjects could be more appropriately identified as 'individuals subject to data processing'.

In addition, from a structural perspective, it has been noted that the primary limitations in applying data protection law arise because, by definition, the GDPR only applies when personal data is processed to deliver interactions in digital environments. Therefore, the rules of the GDPR do not extend to data that is anonymised or to techniques that do not involve personal data processing, such as gamification strategies. Additionally, in cases where personal data is used after being subjected to pseudonymisation, obtaining the data subject's explicit consent, or establishing the necessity of data processing for contract performance serves as a legal basis for the treatment. This approach reflects a focus, consistent with the goals of data protection law, on ensuring the lawfulness of the structural requirement for shaping the digital environment around users (i.e. the acquisition of data) rather than on regulating its impact on self-determination,[50] which is often regarded as offering only partial protection to individuals.

c. Data Subjects, or Subject to Data? Framing the Debate under the Lens of European Private Law

While recognising that the implementation of the GDPR has notably enhanced the position of data subjects in digital markets, it is currently questioned whether the existing framework provides individuals with sufficient protection, especially considering the pervasive impact of data-based techniques on people's lives. The deployment of ICTs, AI, and their integration into society has brought about significant changes to the human condition, resulting in transformations that profoundly alter our ways of acting and decision-making: this often leads to a blurring of distinctions between reality and virtuality—sometimes referred to as the 'onlife paradigm'.[51]

In this context, data protection law is frequently viewed as providing only a partial perspective on a much broader and more complex issue:[52] in particular, as digital technologies deeply influence various aspects of individuals' lives, with data processing

---

the relation between privacy and power in the work of the same author, see also J. E. Cohen, 'Turning Privacy Inside Out', *Theoretical Inquiries in Law* 20 (2019), 1–32 (p. 22).

50 Ursic, 'The Failure of Control Rights in the Big Data Era'.

51 Floridi, *The Onlife Manifesto*.

52 C. Koolen, 'Consumer Protection in the Age of Artificial Intelligence: Breaking Down the Silo Mentality Between Consumer, Competition, and Data', *European Review of Private Law* 31.2(2023), 427–468.

being the main conceptual antecedent for occurrences in digital environments, there is an ongoing debate about whether the discussion should be explored from a broader perspective under the purview of European private law.

Within this strand of analysis, growing attention is directed toward examining whether a set of contractual provisions or general clauses could be effectively applied to digital interactions to safeguard self-determination. For instance, provisions regulating defective consent are considered a temporary response to risks stemming from discriminatory processing.[53] More broadly, rules on fraud and misrepresentation are being explored as potentially applicable to situations where a party misunderstands the nature of an interaction due to conditions affecting their perception of the functioning or characteristics of the offered product or services, developed based on data processing and profiling strategies.

Building on similar conceptual foundations, some authors propose the use of general private law clauses to scrutinise manipulations of the digital environment that could impair users' rights. Specifically, departing from a critical evaluation of theories centred on digital operators as information fiduciaries, it has been suggested that the principle of good faith could serve as a tool to supplement and enhance existing legal standards not originally designed for digital economies.[54] This approach tailors the scope of parties' obligations based on their expectations and, ultimately, the characteristics of the online environment. More broadly, there is an ongoing debate about whether the current shortcomings observed in data protection law for protecting individuals in the digital environment could be addressed by referring to general principles rooted in private law. In this context, significant attention is given to two key concepts: vulnerability and self-determination (oftentimes coupled with autonomy).

Regarding the first aspect, the notion of digital vulnerability is currently being explored as a potential unified framework capable of establishing a comprehensive normative theory for individuals' protection.[55] This perspective aims to shift the focus from the technical activity of data processing to the societal implications of digital interactions. Accordingly, the characteristics of digital environments are seen as able to create conditions—whether contingent or structural—that expose users to exploitation by their counterparties. Consequently, the objective of private law is seen as dynamically identifying and rectifying these conditions by categorising them as unlawful or non-compliant with protection standards. In addition, in the context of peculiar contractual

---

53 C. Poncibò, 'Remedies for Artificial Intelligence', in C. Poncibò, M. Ebers, and M. Zou (eds), *Contracting and Contract Law in the Age of Artificial Intelligence* (London: Bloomsbury, 2022), pp. 201–220.

54 C. Goanta, 'The Ancient Alien: Good Faith as the Facilitator of Personalized Law', *The University of Chicago Law Review Online* (2022), https://lawreviewblog.uchicago.edu/2022/03/09/bp-goanta/. On the role of good faith in European Private Law, see also Chapter 6 by Talya Deibel in this volume.

55 With vulnerability being generally defined as a state of defencelessness and susceptibility to power imbalances as arising from structural inequalities, and other market or social conditions. S. Ranchordas and M. Beck 'Vulnerability', in M. Kaufmann and H. Lomell (eds) *Handbook of Digital Criminology* (Berlin: De Gruyter, 2024), pp. 509–518; G. Malgieri, *Vulnerability and Data Protection Law* (Oxford: Oxford University Press, 2023).

relations, such as business-to-consumer transactions, this approach may also involve referring to sector-specific bodies of law, such as consumer law.[56] Digital vulnerability is thus conceptualised as a pathological condition, potentially affecting individuals in their digital existence, leading to deviations from aware and self-conscious behaviours.

In parallel, digital techniques are scrutinised for their potential to undermine individuals' self-determination and autonomy, where these concepts are commonly perceived as the right of users to make meaningful choices about their lives without coercion.[57] This perspective encourages a re-interpretation of traditional legal notions rooted in self-determination. These notions, such as agency, unfairness, and good faith, are reconsidered in the context of the distinctive characteristics of contemporary online environments. Indeed, as data processing strategies isolate individuals' characteristics, transforming them into 'dividuals' (i.e. sets of categories)[58] used as predictors for the design of provided content, and establishing connections among the shared characteristics of various data subjects, the difficulty of comprehending the dynamics of such a process is seen as compromising individuals' capacity to make genuine decisions and fully exercise their autonomy, which constitutes a core value of private law.

4. Points for Reflection

This chapter aims at tracing the debate on the role of private law in advancing data subjects' rights, with a specific focus on the dynamics of processing occurring in contemporary digital environments. In order to do so, it provides a first insight into the relevant rules in the European Union, inspecting their conceptual underpinnings; then, it offers an overview of the main contents of the GDPR, so as to clarify how control over data is currently identified as a major—if not the major—resource to protect individuals engaging in digital interactions. Against this background, though, criticisms suggest that there is wide consensus that the field is not sufficiently robust to ensure a high level of user protection and that the pervasive impact of data analyses on human lives suggests embracing a wider perspective. Hence, private law could be inspected as potentially able to complement and enrich the traditional standpoint of data protection law. Current questions, though, still animate the debate and should inspire further reflections: first and foremost, given the absence of a structural unification of private law in the EU, solutions moving from the extension of its general clauses always encompass a major element of uncertainty within the discourse on the regulation of digital interactions, also considering its intrinsic transnational dimension.[59]

---

56 In this regard, see Chapter 9 in this volume.

57 H. Dagan and M. Heller, *The Choice Theory of Contracts* (Cambridge, UK: Cambridge University Press, 2017).

58 M. Hildebrandt, 'Privacy as Protection of the Incomputable Self. From Agnostic to Agonistic Machine Learning', *Theoretical Inquiries in Law* 20.1 (2019), 83–121.

59 S. Grundmann (ed.), *European Contract Law in the Digital Age* (Cambridge, UK: Intersentia, 2018); M. Bartl, 'Socio-Economic Imaginaries and European Private Law', in P. F. Kjaer (ed.), *The Law of Political*

In addition, the transformative effects—especially in terms of conceptualisation of self-determination—that could arise from a more substantive application of private law to digital techniques based on data processing are still largely unexplored: in particular, it is worth evaluating if, as self-determination in contemporary digital ecosystems emerges as a structural byproduct of the exposition of users to the unique characteristics of such environments, this could further reshape our understanding of self-determination itself, establishing ways for re-conceptualising its role within private law theory and moving beyond the primary qualification of users as 'data subjects' in the digital realm.

Q1: How might we reconceptualise the notion of 'data subject' to better capture the broader power dynamics at play in digital environments?

Q2: What specific limitations of the regulatory approach based on information and control have emerged in practice, and what alternative frameworks might better safeguard individuals' rights?

Q3: What advantages and challenges might arise from applying traditional private law doctrines to digital interactions?

Q4: How might this concept of 'digital vulnerability' be operationalised in legal practice, and what specific protections might it offer that current approaches do not?

Q5: How might consent mechanisms be redesigned to better align with the realities of digital interactions? Or should we move beyond consent-based models entirely?

Q6: What might a reconceptualised notion of self-determination look like in the digital age?

Bibliography

A. G. della Concorrenza e del Mercato, 'Sanzioni per 20 milioni a Google e ad Apple per uso dei dati degli utenti a fini commerciali (PS11147)', *AGCM* (16 November 2021), https://www.agcm.it/media/comunicati-stampa/2021/11/PS11147-PS11150

Acquisti, A., C. Taylor, and L. Wagman, 'The Economics of Privacy', *Journal of Economic Literature*54.2 (2016), 442–492, https://doi.org/10.1257/jel.54.2.442

Allen, A. L., 'Privacy-as-Data Control: Conceptual, Practical, and Moral Limits of the Paradigm', *Faculty Scholarship at Penn Carey Law* 32 (2000), 861–875

Article 29 Working Party, 'Guidelines on Consent under Regulation 2016/679 WP259 rev.01' (2018), https://ec.europa.eu/newsroom/article29/item-detail.cfm?item_id=623051

Economy: Transformations in the Function of Law (Cambridge, UK: Cambridge University Press, 2029), pp. 228–253.

Article 29 Working Party, 'Guidelines on Data Protection Impact Assessment (DPIA) and Determining Whether Processing Is "Likely to Result in a High Risk" for the Purposes of Regulation 2016/679' (2017), https://ec.europa.eu/newsroom/article29/items/611236

Ausloos, J., and P. Dewitte, 'Shattering One-Way Mirrors. Data Subject Access Rights in Practice', *International Data Privacy Law* 8.1 (2018), 4–28, https://doi.org/10.1093/idpl/ipy001

Ayres, I., and A. Schwartz, 'The No-Reading Problem in Consumer Contract Law', *Stanford Law Review* 66.3 (2014), 545–609

Bartl, M., 'Socio-Economic Imaginaries and European Private Law', in P. F. Kjaer (ed.), *The Law of Political Economy: Transformations in the Function of Law* (Cambridge, UK: Cambridge University Press, 2029), pp. 228–253, https://doi.org/10.1017/9781108675635

Ben-Shahar, O., and C. E. Schneider, 'The Failure of Mandated Disclosure', *University of Pennsylvania Law Review* 159 (2011), 647–749

Bloustein, E. J., 'Privacy as an Aspect of Human Dignity: An Answer to Dean Prosser', *New York University Law Review* 39 (1964), 962–1007

Blume, P., 'The Data Subject', *European Data Protection Law Review* 4 (2015), 258–264, https://doi.org/10.21552/EDPL/2015/4/4

Boerman, S. C., S. Kruikemeier, and F. J. Z. Borgesius, 'Online Behavioural Advertising: A Literature Review and Research Agenda', *Journal of Advertisings* 46.3 (2017), 363–376, https://doi.org/10.1080/00913367.2017.1339368

Bygrave, L. A., *Data Protection Law: Approaching Its Rationale, Logic and Limit* (Alphen aan den Rijn: Kluwer, 2002)

Calo, R., 'Privacy, Vulnerability, and Affordance', *DePaul Law Review* 66 (2017), 592–593

Cheng, F., and C. Wu, 'Debiasing the Framing Effect: The Effect of Warning and Involvement', *Decision Support Systems* 49.3 (2010), 328–334, https://doi.org/10.1016/j.dss.2010.04.002

Cohen, J. E., *Configuring the Networked Self* (New Haven, CT: Yale University Press, 2012)

Cohen, J. E., 'Turning Privacy Inside Out', *Theoretical Inquiries in Law* 20 (2019), 1–32

Council of Europe, 'Convention for the Protection of Individuals with regards to Automatic Processing of Personal Data', Strasburg (28 January 1981), https://rm.coe.int/1680078b37

Dagan, H., and M. Heller, *The Choice Theory of Contracts* (Cambridge, UK: Cambridge University Press, 2017)

Datatilsynet, 'Grindr LLC (Administrative Fine)' (2021), https://www.datatilsynet.no/contentassets/8ad827efefcb489ab1c7ba129609edb5/administrative-fine---grindr-llc.pdf

Davola, A., and G. Malgieri, 'Data-Powerful' (2022), https://papers.ssrn.com/sol3/papers.cfm?abstract_id=4027370

Domurath, I., 'Technological Totalitarianism: Data, Consumer Profiling, and the Law', in L. de Almeida, M. Cantero Gamito, M. Durovic, and K. P. Purnhagen (eds), *The Transformation of Economic Law: Essays in Honour of Hans-W. Micklitz* (Oxford: Hart Publishing, 2019), pp. 65–90

Durovic, M., and F. Lech, 'A Consumer Law Perspective on the Commercialization of Data', *European Review of Private Law* 29 (2021), 701–732

European Data Protection Supervisor, 'Opinion 8/2016 "On the Coherent Enforcement of Fundamental Rights in the Age of Big Data"' (2016), https://edps.europa.eu/sites/edp/files/publication/16-09-23_bigdata_opinion_en.pdf

European Data Protection Supervisor, 'Preliminary Opinion "Privacy and Competitiveness in the Age of Big Data"' (2014), https://edps.europa.eu/data-protection/our-work/publications/opinions/privacy-and-competitiveness-age-big-data_en

Floridi, B., *The Onlife Manifesto. Being Human in a Hyperconnected Era* (Berlin: Springer, 2014)

Fogg, B. J., *Persuasive Technology: Using Computers to Change What We Think and Do* (Burlington: Morgan Kaufmann, 2002)

Fuster, G. G., 'How Uninformed is the Average Data Subject? A Quest for Benchmarks in EU Personal Data Protection', *Revista de Internet, Derecho y Política* 9 (2014), 92–104

Goanta, C., 'The Ancient Alien: Good Faith as the Facilitator of Personalized Law', *The University of Chicago Law Review Online* (2022), https://lawreviewblog.uchicago.edu/2022/03/09/bp-goanta/

Grundmann, S. (ed.), *European Contract Law in the Digital Age* (Cambridge, UK: Intersentia, 2018)

Hildebrandt, M., 'Privacy as Protection of the Incomputable Self. From Agnostic to Agonistic Machine Learning', *Theoretical Inquiries in Law* 20.1 (2019), 83–121, https://doi.org/10.1515/til-2019-0004

Koolen, C., 'Consumer Protection in the Age of Artificial Intelligence: Breaking Down the Silo Mentality Between Consumer, Competition, and Data', *European Review of Private Law* 31.2(2023), 427–468, https://doi.org/10.54648/erpl2023018

Lievens, E., and V. Verdoodt, 'Looking for Needles in a Haystack: Key Issues Affecting Children's Rights in the General Data Protection Regulation', *Computer Law and Security Review* 34.2 (2018), 269–278, https://doi.org/10.1016/j.clsr.2017.09.007

Malgieri, G., *Vulnerability and Data Protection Law* (Oxford: Oxford University Press, 2023)

Mantelero, A., 'Children Online and the Future of EU Data Protection Framework: Empirical Evidences and Legal Analysis', *International Journal of Technology Policy and Law* 2 (2016), 169–181, https://doi.org/10.1504/IJTPL.2016.077189

OECD, *Recommendation of the Council of 23 September 1980: OECD Guidelines Governing the Protection of Privacy and Transborder Flows of Personal Data* (Paris: OECD Publishing, 1980), https://legalinstruments.oecd.org/en/instruments/OECD-LEGAL-0188

Poncibò, C., 'Remedies for Artificial Intelligence', in C. Poncibò, M. Ebers, and M. Zou (eds), *Contracting and Contract Law in the Age of Artificial Intelligence* (London: Bloomsbury, 2022), pp. 201–220

Prosser, W. L., 'Privacy', *California Law Review* 48.3 (1960), 383–423

Ranchordas, S., and M. Beck 'Vulnerability', in M. Kaufmann and H. Lomell (eds) *Handbook of Digital Criminology* (Berlin: De Gruyter, 2024), pp. 509–518

Solove, D. J., *The Digital Person* (New York: New York University Press, 2004)

Solove, D. J., 'Privacy and Power: Computer Databases and Metaphors for Information Privacy', *Stanford Law Review* 53 (2001), 1393–1462

Solove, D., *Understanding Privacy* (Cambridge, MA: Harvard University Press, 2008)

Stigler, G. J., 'An Introduction to Privacy in Economics and Politics', *Journal of Legal Studies* 9.4 (1980), 623–644

Sunstein, C., *Behavioural Law & Economics* (Cambridge, UK: Cambridge University Press, 2000)

Ursic, H., 'The Failure of Control Rights in the Big Data Era: Does a Holistic Approach Offer a Solution?', in M. Bakhoum et al. (eds), *Personal Data in Competition, Consumer Protection and Intellectual Property Law* (Berlin: Springer, 2018), pp. 55–83

Walker, R., *From Big Data to Big Profits: Success with Data and Analytics* (Oxford: Oxford University Press, 2015)

Warren, S. D., and L. D. Brandeis, 'The Right to Privacy', *Harvard Law Review* 4.5 (1890), 193–220

Westin, A., *Privacy and Freedom* (New York: Atheneum, 1967)

14. EU Sustainable Finance Regulation: An Analysis in the Context of Contemporary Debates in European Private Law

Jennifer de Lange-Collins[1]

Abstract

The adoption in 2015 of both the United Nation's Sustainable Development Goals and the Paris Agreement on Climate Change served to focus attention on a fundamental rethinking of many aspects of society. The financial system certainly did not escape scrutiny. Indeed, the European Commission launched its Sustainable Finance Action Plan in 2018 and a number of legislative enactments have subsequently been adopted. This chapter analyses these developments in the context of a number of contemporary debates as to the nature, purpose, and scope of European private law. Specifically, this contribution considers the following questions: does the EU approach to sustainable finance reveal a further instrumentalisation of private law and, if so, to what ends? Does the approach signal a movement towards or away from the Europeanisation of private law? What does the approach to sustainable finance reveal in terms of the EU's view on financialisation? To what extent does the approach indicate that financial regulation must have an economic rationale? And does the approach indicate a view as to the role of the consumer in the (sustainable) financial system?

1 Many of the themes discussed in this chapter are further explored in the author's PhD thesis, J. S. de Lange-Collins, *Great Expectations of Sustainable Finance: A Critical Analysis of EU Sustainable Finance Strategy and Sustainable Finance Regulation* (doctoral thesis, University of Amsterdam, 2024).

 https://doi.org/10.11647/OBP.0448.14

1. Introduction: Sustainable Finance, in the Context of Issues in EPL

The adoption in 2015 of both the United Nation's Sustainable Development Goals (SDGs)[2] and the Paris Agreement on Climate Change[3] turned attention to a fundamental rethinking of many aspects of society. The financial system certainly has not escaped scrutiny. Indeed, business leaders and politicians alike have championed the necessity of such a change. Mark Carney, for example, underlined that the financial system has an important part to play in managing climate change, which he famously referred to as the 'tragedy on the horizon'.[4] Meanwhile, the French minister for the economy went on to declare in 2017, that 'Finance must be green, or it cannot be at all'.[5]

The EU responded to this challenge with its 2018 Sustainable Finance Action Plan (the 'Action Plan'), setting out its view that a 'comprehensive shift' was necessary in how the financial system works. Consequently, measures including the Taxonomy Regulation and the Sustainable Finance Disclosure Regulation (SFDR) were adopted and many existing financial regulations amended in order to integrate sustainability into finance. The combined result of these legislative changes has largely been to increase the availability of sustainability information and to mandate the consideration of sustainability risks and sustainability preferences in the process of providing financial services and selling financial products.

These developments illustrate the role that European private law (EPL) can play in responding to current challenges. However, these developments can also be analysed to provide insights into the EU's position on a number of contemporary debates. In particular, this chapter will explore what the EU's approach to sustainable finance reveals with respect to its views on: (a) the instrumentalisation of private law, (b) the Europeanisation of private law, (c) the phenomenon of financialisation, (d) the proper use and purpose of financial regulation, and (e) role of the consumer in the (sustainable) financial system.[6]

This chapter is structured as follows. Section 2 sets out the main content of the Action Plan and the sustainable finance regulations introduced under that plan (the 'legal context'). Section 3 then critically analyses how the EU's approach to sustainable finance contributes to contemporary debates in EPL (the 'societal context'). Finally, the conclusions are presented in Section 4, with a number of points for further reflection suggested in Section 5.

---

2 United Nations, 'United Nations Resolution 70/1. Transforming Our World: The 2030 Agenda for Sustainable Development' (2015), https://sustainabledevelopment.un.org/content/documents/21252030%20Agenda%20for%20Sustainable%20Development%20web.pdf

3 United Nations, 'United Nations Framework Convention on Climate Change, 21st Conference of the Parties, Paris' (2015), https://unfccc.int/process-and-meetings/the-paris-agreement

4 M. Carney, 'Breaking the Tragedy of the Horizon—Climate Change and Financial Stability', Speech by Governor of the Bank of England and Chairman of the Financial Stability Board, at Lloyd's of London, Bank of England, 29 September 2015.

5 Bruno Le Maire, statement made at Climate Finance Day 2017.

6 With respect to the concept of European private law and the trends of Europeanisation and instrumentalisation of European private law, see Chapter 1 in this volume.

2. Legal Context: The EU Approach to Sustainable Finance

The European Commission initially set out its vision as to how a comprehensive shift in the financial system would be realised in the Action Plan. Specifically, the plan identified three objectives as key to realising such a shift. First, the amount of private funds allocated to sustainable investments would need to increase. Second, sustainability would need to be taken into account by risk managers as constituting a risk to the financial value of assets. Third, transparency and long-termism would need to be fostered. In order to achieve these objectives and integrate sustainability into finance, the Commission set out a plan to introduce a number of new financial regulations and to amend a series of existing legislative acts.

It is worth noting, for completeness, that the Action Plan has twice been updated by the Commission. Initially, pursuant to its 'Strategy for Financing the Transition to a Sustainable Economy' (the '2021 Strategy'),[7] and later in the form a communication entitled 'A sustainable finance framework that works on the ground' (the '2023 Package').[8] In reality, however, neither development signalled a major change of course. The 2021 Strategy in fact described its purpose as being to finalise and consolidate the foundations of the 'ambitious framework' laid by the 2018 Action Plan.[9] Similarly, the main contribution of the 2023 Package was to introduce further delegated acts under the already adopted Taxonomy Regulation and to propose a regulation concerning sustainability ratings, which had been noted as potentially necessary in the Action Plan. Therefore, the headline objectives of the EU's sustainable finance policy have remained consistent since 2018.

The following sections will outline those financial regulations that have been adopted pursuant to the Action Plan (as renewed from time to time).

a. Benchmarks Amendments

One of the first measures adopted under the Action Plan was an amendment to the existing Benchmarks Regulation. To understand the changes introduced it is useful to first understand the important role that benchmarks play in the financial markets.

Well-known benchmarks include interest rates such as the sterling overnight index average (SONIA) and the euro interbank offered rate (EURIBOR) and equity indexes such as the Dow Jones Industrial Average and the S&P 500. Such benchmarks are widely used to determine payment obligations,[10] as a reference for the creation of

7 Commission Communication, 'Strategy for Financing the Transition to a Sustainable Economy', COM (2021) 390 final, https://eur-lex.europa.eu/legal-content/EN/TXT/?uri=celex:52021DC0390

8 Commission Communication, 'A Sustainable Finance Framework that Works on the Ground', COM (2023) 317 final, https://eur-lex.europa.eu/legal-content/EN/TXT/?uri=CELEX:52023SC0209

9 See Commission Communication, 'Strategy for Financing', p. 20.

10 Interest rate benchmarks, for example, are used to set the rate to be paid by one party to another in loan contracts, including mortgages. Payments under derivative contracts may also be triggered dependent on the performance of a particular benchmark (which may relate to interest rates, equities or commodities for example).

portfolios and products,[11] and as a means of monitoring the performance of existing portfolios and products.[12] Since 2016, the Benchmarks Regulation has imposed certain obligations and standards on parties creating such benchmarks (so-called 'benchmark administrators'), broadly with the aim of safeguarding the reliability and transparency of benchmarks.[13]

The changes to the Benchmarks Regulation, adopted in November 2019, not only introduced standard criteria for the construction of two new benchmarks referred to as Climate Transition Benchmarks (CTB) and Paris-aligned Benchmarks (PAB),[14] but also required administrators of significant benchmarks to use their 'endeavours' to publish a CTB.[15] Furthermore, the amendments obliged administrators to explain how their benchmarks reflect or pursue environmental, social, and governance (ESG) objectives (or not).

b. The Sustainable Finance Disclosure Regulation (SFDR)

The Sustainable Finance Disclosure Regulation (SFDR) was adopted in late 2019.[16] Notably, the measure does not prohibit or mandate any particular activities, behaviours or products in order to meet the objectives of the Action Plan. Rather, as its name suggests, the SFDR requires certain parties operating in the financial markets to make sustainability-related disclosures. The regulation describes these disclosure obligations using a range of new (and sometimes rather complex) definitions. For ease of reference therefore, simplified descriptions of the terms referred to below are provided at the end of this section.

First, the SFDR requires 'financial market participants' and 'financial advisors' to make disclosures concerning the way in which they manage and consider sustainability. For example, such parties must disclose the way in which they manage 'sustainability risks' and how their remuneration policies are consistent with the integration of such risks.[17] Furthermore, they must explain how they consider the 'principal adverse impacts' of their investment decisions (or their investment advice) on 'sustainability

11 A fund manager may for example track the composition of a benchmark, investing in the assets of which the benchmark is composed.

12 For example, a fund manager may invest in a range of equities and then compare the performance of the invested portfolio against a certain benchmark, ideally in order to show that the fund has exceeded the performance of such benchmark.

13 Regulation (EU) 2016/1011 of the European Parliament and of the Council of 8 June 2016 on indices used as benchmarks in financial instruments and financial contracts or to measure the performance of investment funds and amending Directives 2008/48/EC and 2014/17/EU and Regulation (EU) No 596/2014, OJ L171, p. 1–65.

14 Regulation (EU) 2019/2089 of the European Parliament and of the Council of 27 November 2019 amending Regulation (EU) 2016/1011 as regards EU Climate Transition Benchmarks, EU Paris-aligned Benchmarks and sustainability-related disclosures for benchmarks, OJ L317, p. 17, published in the official journal on 9 December 2019.

15 Article 19(d) Benchmarks Regulation, as amended.

16 Regulation (EU) 2019/2088 of the European Parliament and of the Council of 27 November 2019 on sustainability-related disclosures in the financial services sector.

17 Article 3 and Article 5 SFDR.

factors'.[18]

Second, the SFDR requires the disclosure of certain information with respect to 'financial products'. Specifically, where a financial product promotes 'environmental or social characteristics', information must be provided to explain how the product actually pursues those characteristics. Similarly, where a financial product has 'sustainable investment' as its objective, the SFDR requires disclosure as to how such investments are made.[19] In practice, financial products promoting environmental or social characteristics are typically referred to as light green products and those pursuing sustainable investment are referred to as dark green products.

Key terms in the SFDR include the following:

- 'Financial market participants' include a range of players such as collective investment vehicles (commonly referred to as funds) and also, to the extent that they are offering specific services, banks.
- 'Financial advisors' is a wide term that includes financial market intermediaries, banks, and funds to the extent that such parties provide advice on investments or insurance.
- 'Sustainability risk' means an environmental, social or governance event or condition that, if it occurs, could cause an actual or a potential material negative impact on the value of an investment.
- 'Principal adverse impacts' are not defined in the SFDR but detailed guidelines are provided around this term in a separate delegated act.
- 'Financial products' include participations (shares) in funds, as well as pension products/schemes and managed portfolios.
- 'Sustainability factors' are described as including environmental, social, and employee matters, respect for human rights, anti-corruption, and anti-bribery matters.
- 'Environmental characteristics' and 'social characteristics' are not defined in the SFDR, although templates have since been developed to assist parties in making the required disclosures.
- 'Sustainable investment' means an investment in an economic activity that contributes to an environmental objective or social objective and does not significantly harm any such objectives, provided that the investee companies follows good governance practices. For such purposes, the SFDR provides guidance on (but does not define) the terms 'environmental objective' and 'social objective' and specifies that 'good governance' may include sound management structures, employee relations, remuneration of staff and tax.

---

18 Article 4 SFDR.
19 See Articles 8 and 9 SFDR.

c. The Taxonomy Regulation

The SFDR was swiftly followed, in June 2020, by the adoption of the Taxonomy Regulation,[20] which the Commission has alternatively referred to as creating a 'classification system', a 'common language', and a 'green list'.

Pursuant to the Taxonomy Regulation, economic activity may be considered environmentally sustainable to the extent that the activity is included in the Taxonomy and complies with four conditions.[21] First, the activity must contribute substantially to one of the following environmental objectives: (i) climate change mitigation; (ii) climate change adaptation; (iii) the sustainable use and protection of water and marine resources; (iv) the transition to a circular economy; (v) pollution prevention and control; or (vi) the protection and restoration of biodiversity and ecosystems. Second, the activity must not significantly harm any of those six environmental objectives. Third, the activity must be carried out in compliance with a range of internationally recognised standards including the OECD Guidelines for Multinational Enterprises and the UN Guiding Principles on Business and Human Rights. These standards are referred to as 'minimum safeguards' pursuant to the Taxonomy. Finally, the activity must comply with detailed requirements which are referred to as technical screening criteria (TSC) and are set out in hundreds of pages of delegated regulation.[22]

The Taxonomy Regulation is, however, more than just an elaborate definitional booklet. It also imposes obligations on certain parties. Specifically, a wide range of companies must publish an annual statement detailing the extent to which their economic activities are environmentally sustainable as per the Taxonomy definition of that term.[23] Furthermore, the Taxonomy requires those parties making light or dark green products available[24] to explain the extent to which those products are aligned with the Taxonomy.[25]

Finally, it should be noted that the Taxonomy does not provide any classification system or harmonised way of identifying environmentally unsustainable activities.

20 Regulation (EU) 2020/852 of the European Parliament and of the Council of 18 June 2020 on the establishment of a framework to facilitate sustainable investment, and amending Regulation (EU) 2019/2088, OJ L198.

21 See Article 3 Taxonomy Regulation. Note that the Taxonomy Regulation lists specific types of activity that may be considered to be environmentally sustainable. As a result, economic activities that fall outside of this list cannot be described as taxonomy-aligned.

22 See for example Commission Delegated Regulation (EU) 2021/2139 of 4 June 2021 establishing the technical screening criteria for determining the conditions under which an economic activity qualifies as contributing substantially to climate change mitigation or climate change adaptation and for determining whether that economic activity causes no significant harm to any of the other environmental objectives, published in the official journal on 9 December 2021.

23 See Article 8 of the Taxonomy Regulation. The types of undertakings subject to this obligation are defined as those also required to make certain periodic reports under the Accounting Directive. At the time of writing, however, the Commission is consulting on proposals to reduce the number of parties captured by this obligation.

24 As to which, see Section 2.b of this chapter.

25 See Articles 5 and 6 of the Taxonomy Regulation. Article 7 also requires a negative disclosure statement to be made where a financial product does not contribute to an environmental objective.

It also does not help to identify socially sustainable economic activities, although a number of reports have been produced with respect to the possibility of extending the Taxonomy in this way.[26] There is, in other words, no 'dirty' or 'social' Taxonomy at the present time but only a 'green' Taxonomy.

d. Miscellaneous Amendments to Existing Regulations

Pursuant to the Action Plan, amendments have also been made to a range of existing financial regulations. In particular, the Markets in Financial Instruments Directive (MiFID), the Units in Collective Investments Funds Directive (UCITSD), the Alternative Investment Funds Directive (AIFMD), the Solvency Directive, and the Insurance Distribution Directive (IDD) were amended in 2022 in order to embed sustainability into the financial regulatory framework.[27] Pursuant to these changes, parties including banks, investment funds, and pension providers are obliged to disclose how they consider sustainability risks and to ensure that prospective investors are asked to provide their 'sustainability preferences' as part of existing client due diligence procedures.

These developments were followed in November 2022 by a Corporate Sustainability Reporting Directive (CSRD), which made amendments to the existing Accounting Directive, Audit Directive, Audit Regulation, and Transparency Directive.[28] In summary, these amendments oblige a wider range of entities to report on so-called 'sustainability matters' and mandate independent audits of such disclosures. Pursuant to the CSRD, such matters are no longer referred to as 'non-financial' reporting but rather are considered 'sustainability' reporting.[29]

e. EU Green Bond Standard Regulation (EU GBS)

In October 2023, an EU Green Bond Standard Regulation (EU GBS) was also added to the suite of EU sustainable finance regulations, setting out requirements for issuers who wish to designate their bond an 'EUGB'.[30] Rather than introduce mandatory

26 See for example, Platform on Sustainable Finance, 'Draft Report by Subgroup 4: Social Taxonomy' (2021), https://finance.ec.europa.eu/system/files/2021-07/sf-draft-report-social-taxonomy-july2021_en.pdf and also Platform on Sustainable Finance, 'Final Report on Social Taxonomy' (2022), https://finance.ec.europa.eu/system/files/2022-08/220228-sustainable-finance-platform-finance-report-social-taxonomy_en.pdf

27 Specifically, the amendments made changes to existing delegated regulations adopted pursuant to each of these 'level 1' frameworks. See further Delegated Directive (EU) 2021/1270; Delegated Regulation (EU) 2021/1255; Delegated Regulation (EU) 2021/1253; Delegated Directive (EU) 2021/1269; Delegated Regulation (EU) 2021/1257 and Commission Delegated Regulation (EU) 2021/1256.

28 Directive (EU) 2022/2464 of the European Parliament and of the Council of 14 December 2022 amending Regulation (EU) No 537/2014, Directive 2004/109/EC, Directive 2006/43/EC, and Directive 2013/34/EU, as regards corporate sustainability reporting, OJ L322, pp. 15–80.

29 This is a subtle shift but one that reflects a trend towards recognising 'sustainability matters' as having a potentially material financial impact.

30 Regulation (EU) 2023/2631 of the European Parliament and of the Council of 22 November 2023 on

sustainability disclosures for all bonds, the regulation sets out requirements for issuers wishing to label their bonds as compliant with the EU GBS. In essence, additional disclosures are required and an external reviewer must assess compliance with certain standards.

f. Corporate Sustainability Due Diligence Directive (CSDDD)

Finally, a Corporate Sustainability Due Diligence Directive (CSDDD)[31] was, adopted in June 2024, following protracted negotiations. This Directive requires certain (large) companies to undertake due diligence with respect not only to their own activities, but also with respect to their suppliers and other 'business partners' and to take action to prevent, end or mitigate any actual or potential adverse impacts on human rights and on the environment. Entities within the scope of the Directive are also required to publish a so-called 'transition plan'.

Controversial points in the negotiations included whether financial institutions should fall under the scope of the CSDDD, the extent of directors' duties with respect to the issues covered in the Directive, and the question of civil liability for breach. Ultimately, financial institutions will remain out of scope in the near future, no direct amendments to directors' duties have been introduced under the measure and, although civil liability will be introduced for a failure to adhere to the requirements of the CSDDD, the thresholds for such liability have been significantly watered down.[32]

In summary, a fairly impressive number of sustainable finance regulations have been adopted, or existing financial regulations amended, over the course of the past five years or so.[33] The following section will critically analyse these regulatory developments in light of ongoing debates in the sphere of EPL.

3. Societal Context: Analysis of the EU approach to Sustainable Finance

There are many ways to analyse legal developments. One could, for example, undertake an economic analysis of EU sustainable finance regulation, examining the extent to which these rules have improved informational (or any other form of) efficiency. Alternatively, one could compare the EU approach on sustainable finance to the strategy pursued in third countries such as the UK or China, each of which has or

European Green Bonds and optional disclosures for bonds marketed as environmentally sustainable and for sustainability-linked bonds, OJ L2023/2631, 30 November 2023.

31 Directive (EU) 2024/1760 of the European Parliament and of the Council of 13 June 2024 on corporate sustainability due diligence and amending Directive (EU) 2019/1937 and Regulation (EU) 2023/2859.

32 At the time of writing, the Commission is consulting on proposals to reduce the scope of the CSDDD, including the provisions on civil liability.

33 Note also that this short overview does not purport to address all legislative actions taken under the umbrella of sustainable finance in the EU since 2018. Rather, it focuses on the legislative actions envisaged in the Action Plan. Amendments to the prudential framework are, for example, not discussed in this chapter.

is working on its own form of classification system for the identification of sustainable activities.

This chapter, however, uses a critical legal studies (CLS) approach, to analyse how the EU approach to sustainable finance provides insights into the position of the EU on contemporary debates in EPL. CLS should, however, not be confused with critique per se. Rather, its intention is to uncover underlying thought patterns, processes, and biases so that legal rules can be revised and recalibrated to better achieve their goals. This idea was explained by James Lucarello, who suggested that 'CLS is not about discovering the correct application of the law, but rather an ever-evolving conversation on what the law ought to be'.[34]

With this objective in mind, this section will explore what the EU's approach to regulating sustainable finance indicates with regards to its stance on the instrumentalisation of private law, the Europeanisation of private law, financialisation, the rationale of financial regulation and the role of the consumer in the EU legal order.

a. The Instrumentalisation of Private Law

Article 114 of the Treaty on the Functioning of the European Union (TFEU) allows the EU to adopt measures 'for the approximation of the provisions laid down by law, regulation or administrative action in Member States which have as their object the establishment and functioning of the internal market'. It is well-documented that a wide interpretation has been given to this legislative competence, with a variety of EU measures having been adopted on the basis that they allegedly contribute to the creation of a market in which goods, persons, services and capital are able to move freely across national borders within the EU. Consequently, commentators have been critical that the liberal use of Article 114 to justify legislative interventions reflects a practice of instrumentalising private law in the pursuit of a specific purpose: that of realising an internal market.[35] Indeed, this may be objectionable to the extent that one believes that the purpose of law is (or ought to be) wider.

In the face of such criticism, it is perhaps striking that the Commission has chosen to introduce many of its proposed sustainable finance regulations, including the SFDR and the Taxonomy, on the basis of Article 114. In this respect, one could certainly argue that the cause of sustainability has been seized on as yet another basis on which to pursue the singular objective of creating an internal market. However, a brief review of the alternative bases on which the EU could have acted reveals that its options were somewhat limited as a result of existing legislative competencies.

Certainly, use could have been made of the shared competence set out at Article 191

34 J. F. Lucarello, 'The Praise of Silly: Critical Legal Studies and The Roberts Court', *Touro Law Review* 26 (2010), 619–647 (p. 621).

35 See further Chapter 1 in this volume. The tendency of the EU institutions to over-stretch their competencies has been referred to as 'competence creep' by a variety of scholars. See, for example, on this issue more generally S. Garben, 'Competence Creep Revisited', *Journal of Common Market Studies* 57.2 (2019), 205–222.

TFEU. This basis for EU action provides that: 'Union policy on the environment shall aim at a high level of protection taking into account the diversity of situations in the various regions of the Union. It shall be based on the precautionary principle and on the principles that preventive action should be taken, that environmental damage should as a priority be rectified at source and that the polluter should pay'. This legislative basis as a ground for sustainable finance regulation raises a number of interesting possibilities. Use of this legislative competence would, for example, have shifted the emphasis from the importance of establishing an internal market to the importance of protecting the environment. Indeed, Article 191 TFEU would seem perfectly placed to tackle the various negative effects caused, but not compensated, by certain financial practices (so-called 'externalities'). This, however, is not the narrative of sustainable finance that the Commission advanced. Indeed, rather than illuminating and tackling the negative impact that the financial system can have on the planet when externalities go unaddressed, the Action Plan focused on the positive role that the financial system could play by re-directing financial resources to sustainable projects and managing sustainability risk. The financial system was essentially cast as environmental saviour rather than villain.

With respect to the social aspects of sustainability, regard could possibly have been had to Article 151 TFEU, which provides for shared competence between the EU and Member States with respect to '...the promotion of employment, improved living and working conditions, so as to make possible their harmonisation while the improvement is being maintained, proper social protection, dialogue between management and labour, the development of human resources with a view to lasting high employment and the combating of exclusion'.[36] However, this competence offered limited options for the Commission to drive its sustainable finance policies forward because he European Union is assigned a supportive and coordinating role in this area and, moreover, the Commission is not authorised to propose legislative interventions under the article.

Indeed, given the limited alternative competences and the tendency of the European Court of Justice to interpret the internal market competence rather generously,[37], one could argue that the EU made rather creative use of Article 114 in order to deliver legislation intended to contribute to a more sustainable financial system.

Understood in this light, the EU's use of the internal market competence as a legal basis for much of its sustainable finance legislation does not signal an undesirable instrumentalisation of private law. Rather, it signals a perhaps more fundamental problem with the suitability of the current competence sharing arrangements of the treaties in addressing contemporary issues. The Commission is essentially incentivised to frame new issues such as sustainable finance in internal market terms. The practice

---

36 Article 151(1) TFEU, see also Article 151(2) providing for both ordinary and special legislative procedures.

37 See S. Weatherill, *The Internal Market as a Legal Concept*, 1st edn (Oxford: Oxford University Press, 2017), in particular chapter 5, at section A (*The Breadth of the Market as a Legal Concept*).

of framing private law (in this case, financial regulation) within the internal market competence is therefore likely to continue unless the EU is granted wider powers to adopt legislation aimed at the sustainability transition. In the event that this is perceived as an undesirable instrumentalisation of EPL in pursuit of the internal market objective, the most appropriate solution, political obstacles aside, may in fact be to amend the TFEU.

b. The Europeanisation of Private Law

Since the landmark case of *Costa v ENEL* established the priority of EU law over national law,[38] the precise scope of such priority has been contested. Indeed, the increasing influence exercised by the EU on national private laws, or the 'Europeanisation' of private law, has continued to be a hotly debated issue.

Financial law, in particular, has undergone a process of Europeanisation in the years since the Global Financial Crisis (GFC) of 2007–2008 threatened to bring the global financial system to its knees. The EU has not only taken a leading role in shaping the way in which European financial markets are regulated but has shown an increasing preference for the use of regulations over directives.[39] Often, the use of regulations is presented as both proportionate and in line with the principle of subsidiarity given the importance of harmonised EU rules.[40]

The EU approach to sustainable finance signifies a continuation of this trend towards Europeanisation, with a clear reference for the enactment of regulations over directives where possible.[41] Indeed, both the SFDR and the Taxonomy were adopted as regulations, with the relevant impact statement accompanying those legislative proposals explaining that harmonised Union action was necessary to avoid market fragmentation through the proliferation of different standards and definitions. Notwithstanding the Commission's reasoning however, one can certainly question whether a full harmonisation approach to sustainability is the most logical option given the urgency of the transition and the great difficulty in achieving consensus as to what is to be defined as 'sustainable' at EU level. Indeed, progress has been slow with respect to the whether nuclear energy, clean coal, natural gas and bio-fuels ought to be

38 Case C-6/64 *Costa v ENEL* [1964] ECLI:EU:C:1964:66.

39 Note that as a matter of European law, Regulations have direct applicability, meaning that they do not need to be (and indeed may not be) transposed into national law whereas Directives are binding as to effect but allow discretion as to the way in which the relevant rules are transposed into national law.

40 See Article 5(3) TEU (Treaty on the European Union) and Article 5(4) TEU. See also Protocol (No 2) on the application of the principles of subsidiarity and proportionality, annexed to the Treaty on European Union and the Treaty on the Functioning of the European Union by the Treaty of Lisbon of 13 December 2007.

41 Indeed, it appears that directives have only been used where the Commission had no discretion to adopt the relevant measure in the form of a regulation. The legal basis for the CSDDD, as well as for the majority of the amendments introduced under the CSRD, was Article 50 of the Treaty on the Functioning of the European Union (TFEU), for example, which expressly requires the European Parliament and the Council to act in this area by means of directives.

recognised as 'environmentally sustainable economic activities',[42] while discussions on the social Taxonomy have all but ground to a halt. One can therefore wonder if such decisions are not better left with national governments, some of which may choose to act more decisively and swiftly in determining which activities may be recognised as sustainable.[43]

The ever-expanding reach and importance of EU law in the national legal orders of Member States is also reflected in a clause of the Taxonomy Regulation which obliges Member States (as well as institutions of the Union) to use the EU definition of environmental sustainability when introducing any new legal measures that set out requirements in respect of financial products or corporate bonds that are made available as environmentally sustainable.[44] The recitals to the Taxonomy Regulation explain that the rationale for such an approach is to avoid market fragmentation and to protect the interests of consumers and investors.[45] In effect, a choice has been made to secure the priority of the Taxonomy above potentially divergent national laws and classification systems.

It can be concluded that the measures enacted under the 2018 Action Plan reflect a tendency towards the Europeanisation of financial law. The Commission has repeatedly made its case when presenting its proposals that intervention at the EU level is not only necessary but adds value over a purely national approach. It is also clear that the use of Regulations has been favoured over Directives where possible, with the effect that less scope has been afforded to national legislatures to enact divergent rules. Nevertheless, it is also notable that, in this instance, the Europeanisation of financial law has not generally led to a displacement or abolition of national laws since many Member States had no (or limited) national laws providing for classification systems, sustainability disclosure or sustainability due diligence. In this sense, the case of sustainable finance perhaps demonstrates the value of Europeanisation and an EU legal order that can tackle emerging contemporary challenges more efficiently than separate national parliaments.

c. Financialisation

Financialisation broadly refers to the rise in importance of finance (and the financial system) in relation to the productive or 'real' economy. More specifically, Gerald Epstein has suggested that the term refers to '...the increasing importance of financial markets, financial motives, financial institutions, and financial elites in the operation of the economy and its governing institutions, both at the national and international

42 This problem of achieving concensus on thorny issues should not however be over stated, since it is at least in part addressed by the modular nature of the Taxonomy, which means that progress can be made on those sectors with respect to which there is consensus whilst further sectors may be added over time in order to reflect scientific and other developments.

43 Of course, the consequent fragmentation of the term may certainly be undesirable.

44 Article 1(2)(a) and Article 4 Taxonomy Regulation.

45 Recital 14 Taxonomy Regulation.

level'.[46] Although financialised economies may offer benefits, for example in terms of overall economic growth, they are also commonly associated with less desirable consequences such as high levels of speculation and debt, low levels of morality, increased inequality, decreased useful production, excess, and financial crises. As a consequence, the appropriate level of financialisation permitted, or encouraged, within (or by) EPL has been an issue of some debate.

The mass securitisation of housing loans offers one example of financialisation, as well as its consequences. In short, securitisation is a process by which loans (such as mortgages) are sold by the original lender to a newly incorporated special purpose entity (SPE). The SPE funds its purchase of the loans by issuing notes (securities), which are purchased by a range of investors. In turn, the SPE pays interest amounts to the investors and, all being well, returns the amount invested (the 'principal') to the investors after a fixed period of time. The SPE is able to fund these interest and principal payments to investors from the interest and repayments that it receives from the loan debtors (i.e. the individuals who originally took out the housing loans).

Such securitisation structures have clear benefits. First, they allow lenders (banks) to sell loans so that they may use the proceeds to make new loans to new borrowers. Second, the investors in such securitisation notes are able to take a limited amount of exposure to the housing loan market, which helps to expand the range of investment opportunities open to investors. Finally, the fact that the risk of non-payment of the loans no longer sits with one lender but is distributed throughout the market (to the investors) may be viewed as desirable risk-spreading.

However, the financialisation of housing loans also has drawbacks, as became apparent during the course of the GFC. First, it transpired that lenders who make loans with the intention of on-selling those loans to an SPE lacked the necessary incentives to adopt good lending practices. The so-called 'moral hazard' arose as a result of the fact the original lenders were not exposed to subsequent borrower defaults. Second, the use of housing loans as collateral to structure complex transactions was shown to have unintended, and unforeseen, consequences for the wider market. Specifically, as the appetite for these apparently profitable securitisation products soared in the pre-GFC period and financial market players became ever more creative, securitisation notes were re-packaged into new securitisations, resulting in products that became so complex that even those with significant financial market experience were unable, or unwilling, to properly analyse the risks involved in holding such investments. Furthermore, the ratings assigned to such re-packaged products by specialised credit rating agencies were generally not internally verified by financial institutions. Moreover, there was relatively little supervision of the expanding securitisation market by centralised regulators.

Ultimately, these issues of moral hazard, greed, over-reliance, and limited supervision led to a securitisation market that was, ultimately, unsustainable. As

46 G. Epstein, 'Financialization, Rentier Interests, and Central Bank Policy' (2002), https://peri.umass.edu/wp-content/uploads/joomla/images/publication/fin_Epstein.pdf

homeowners (largely those in the US) started to struggle with spiralling mortgage costs the market quickly descended into panic, with availability of credit drying up as a consequence. Lenders were simply unto provide new loans as they struggled to establish their own positions and financial health, a situation which particularly impacted consumers and small and medium sized enterprises (SMEs).

These problems came to symbolise 'financialisation' in the post-GFC period and the Commission ostensibly set out to tackle this issue with a number of proposals in the years that followed.[47]Securitisation, in particular, was a tarnished asset type and the EU enacted a new Securitisation Regulation intended to ensure that certain standards were applicable to all such deals in the future.[48]

Given the acknowledged dangers of financialisation, its tendency to dominate over the 'real' economy and its association with undesirable conduct, one may expect a sustainable financial system to be one which discourages over-financialisation and ensures that the financial system is used to serve the real economy rather than become an industry in and of itself which produces ever more complex products. Such a system could, for example, be based on a set of principles to safe-guard equitable financial practices, with rules intended to discourage windfall profits, ensure that all creditors receive a fair proportion in bankruptcy and prohibit economic activity that fails to conform to certain accepted standards. This is, however, not the version of sustainable finance that the European Commission has actively championed to date. Rather, the EU's approach could be described as a financialisation of sustainability.

In particular, in the EU's current version of sustainable finance, the role of the legislator is not to control or direct the market towards more sustainable forms of activity and behaviour but largely to facilitate. The narrative has been that if only sustainable investments could be identified more easily, 'the market' would select those options. As a result, financial regulation is crafted to assist the flow of standardised information. Indeed, sustainable finance regulations have introduced very few mandates beyond those to produce information.[49] Furthermore, those information obligations are incredibly detailed such that the available information is essentially targeted towards those sophisticated financial parties able to translate the avalanche of disclosures into their risk models when making and evaluating investments. The likelihood is that, in the absence of easily understandable labels, the information will be of little direct value to the consumer.

47 For example, pursuant to its Capital Markets Union project.

48 Regulation (EU) 2017/2402 of the European Parliament and of the Council of 12 December 2017 laying down a general framework for securitisation and creating a specific framework for simple, transparent and standardised securitisation, and amending Directives 2009/65/EC, 2009/138/EC and 2011/61/EU and Regulations (EC) No 1060/2009 and (EU) No 648/2012. Under this measure, limits apply with respect to the sale of securitisation notes to consumers, for example, and larger, sophisticated investors are subject to due diligence requirements before they may purchase a position in a securitisation. Furthermore, those parties originating securitisations are now obliged to ensure that they hold a 5% stake throughout the term of the transaction and a labelling system has been introduced to help investors identify those securitisations that can be regarded as simple, transparent, and standard (so-called 'STS Securitisations') [2017] OJ L347, pp. 35–80.

49 The soon to be adopted CSDDD is the main exception to this general trend.

Furthermore, the sustainable finance regulation that has been enacted is very much of a type that is enabling rather than prohibitive. Parties are not barred in any way from pursuing business or investments that are environmentally unsustainable, for example. Neither are there targets or obligations on any party to make even reasonable efforts to invest a proportion of their available investment capital in sustainable investments or to ensure that their economic activities are at least partially 'environmentally sustainable'. Similarly, no party that regularly creates financial products is obliged to ensure that it offers some percentage of dark or light green financial products. Certainly, benchmark administrators publishing one or more 'significant' benchmarks are required to use their 'endeavours' to publish a Climate Transition Benchmark (CTB)[50] and companies in-scope of the CSDDD will be required to actively address human rights and environmental abuses. Such 'hard' requirements remain, however, the exception rather than the rule.[51]

Essentially, the approach to sustainable finance taken by the EU is very much one which puts its faith in the market. The idea is that by providing standardised terms and mandating the disclosure of sustainability information, financial market players will be encouraged to create sustainable financial products which can be valued and traded. The approach reflects a conviction that sustainability should be understood as a risk to be 'priced' and that sustainable investments will be selected by investors if they are easily identifiable. In essence, the regulatory approach reflects the idea that sustainability can, and should, be commoditised—or, in other words, financialised.

d. The Rationale of Financial Regulation

Private laws of different types generally have recognised underlying policy goals. Often these goals must be balanced against one another, and one goal may be more dominant at a given time, as a result of prevailing political views. Contract law, for example, is frequently associated with a commitment to party autonomy and certainty, goals which must be balanced against fairness. Financial law, on the other hand, is most often connected with the pursuit of efficiency and it is widely accepted that financial regulation must have an economic rationale. In short, this means that financial regulation is generally only perceived as justifiable to the extent that a 'market failure' has occurred and no alternative solution is available to resolve such issue. There are, however, occasionally calls for the rationale of financial regulation to be reassessed. It has been suggested, for example, that financial law ought to pursue the goal of 'equity'.[52] Furthermore, the high-level expert group on sustainable finance advised in

50 Article 19(d) Benchmarks Regulation, as amended. Although even this obligation is currently under discussion, with proposals having been submitted by the Commission to remove Article 19(d).

51 In this respect, it is also notable that the CSDDD is under review at the time of writing, with proposals to reduce the scope and obligations introduced under such legislation.

52 J. Stiglitz and the Members of a UN Commission of Financial Experts, *Stiglitz Report: Reforming the International Monetary and Financial Systems in the Wake of the Global Crisis* (New York: New Press, 2009).

2017 that financial regulation would need to be 'repositioned' towards sustainability.[53] An analysis of the EU's approach to sustainable finance regulation however reveals a continued commitment to the idea that financial regulation must have an economic, rather than a legal, social, environmental, or other such rationale.

The most commonly recognised grounds for regulatory intervention are to: (i) increase efficiency, (ii) enhance investor protection, and/or (iii) safeguard financial stability. The economic rationale would identify the related market 'failures' as inefficiency, lack of investor trust, and instability respectively. An analysis of the EU's sustainable finance strategy and the regulations adopted thereunder show that the Commission has largely justified its regulatory output by reference to such language.

First, the Commission has argued that regulation is necessary to correct informational inefficiencies since the market has failed to produce sustainability information, thereby hindering investors who would otherwise invest sustainably. Second, the Commission has suggested that increased information and a common language around 'sustainability' is necessary to protect investors against the mis-selling of products as environmentally sustainable when they are not (so-called greenwashing). Third, there have been repeated references to the fact that mandating the production of sustainability information will allow sustainability risks to be managed, therefore safeguarding financial stability. For such purposes, 'sustainability risks' are understood as those sustainability issues that pose a threat to the value of financial assets.

Further, since the economic rationale teaches that regulation should not go further than is necessary to allow the market to correct itself, the EU's sustainable finance strategy remains relatively non-interventionist.[54] Additional disclosures have generally been the order of the day, seemingly on the basis that an informed market will self-correct to ensure that non-sustainable practices are afforded a cost and sustainable investments are selected in greater volumes. Notably absent in the Commission's narrative has been any argument that financial regulation is necessary, or justified, in order to pursue the goal of equity, or that sustainability is a policy goal of financial regulation in its own right.

In conclusion, the EU continues to adhere to the view that regulatory intervention in the market is legitimate only to the extent that a market failure, of a traditionally recognised type, has occurred. As such, the Commission has presented the lack of sustainable investment and the failure of the market to price sustainability risk into asset values largely as a matter of informational inefficiency. Moreover, regulatory interventions have been used conservatively and continue to be framed as a last resort solution to correct the free market rather than as a tool with which to steer the market more decisively towards sustainable financial outcomes.

---

53 EU High-level Expert Group on Sustainable Finance, 'Financing a European Economy', HLEG Interim Report (2017), https://finance.ec.europa.eu/system/files/2017–07/170713-sustainable-finance-report_en.pdf, p. 3.

54 As explained in Section 3.c of this chapter.

e. The Role and Nature of the Consumer

Finally, we turn to the characterisation of and role afforded to the consumer in EPL, which has also long been an area of debate. The EU has frequently cast the financial consumer as a rather rational actor, capable and motivated to sort through complex information in order to select the investments most suitable for him or her. Moreover, these consumers, acting on their own free will are understood as forming the 'invisible hand' of the market which serves to direct capital to its optimal use. Behavioural economists, however, have queried this depiction of the consumer and their role in the market. They argue that consumers often suffer 'bounded rationality', meaning that they neither will, nor indeed can, process complex information in a rational manner.[55] An analysis of the EU's sustainable finance strategy and regulations nevertheless suggests that the Commission remains faithful to a traditional characterisation of the consumer.

The tendency to assume an engaged, informed, and rational consumer is most evident in the amendments introduced in regulations such as MiFID, UCITS, and the AIFMD which aim to ensure that sustainability preferences are taken into account where consumers are provided with advice. Specifically, the consumer must be asked to indicate whether and to what to extent they would like a financial instrument presented to them: (i) to be 'Taxonomy aligned', (ii) to invest in 'sustainable investments' (as defined in the SFDR); or (iii) to take account of the 'principal adverse impacts' on certain 'sustainability factors' (and if so, how).[56] Not only is the consumer expected to understand all of this jargon, the Commission has confirmed that it is the intention that the client must determine his or her 'specific ambition' with regards to sustainable investing,[57] with advisors instructed to '...adopt a neutral and unbiased approach as to not influence clients' answers'.[58]

One obvious alternative to this agnostic state of affairs would have been to design a choice architecture favouring sustainable investments unless the consumer of financial products actively expressed a preference not to invest sustainably. Another would have been to assign financial advisors and intermediaries the task of actively soliciting sustainability preferences by providing guidance as to the potential benefits and drawbacks of selecting sustainable investments.

55 See further with respect to the the consumer (or the 'retail investor') the following: W. F. M. de Bondt and R. H. Thaler, 'Financial Decision-Making in Markets and Firms: A Behavioral Perspective', *Handbooks in Operations Research and Management Science* 9 (1995), 385–410, https://doi.org/10.1016/S0927-0507(05)80057-X; J. Baron, *Thinking and deciding*, 4th edn (Cambridge, UK: Cambridge University Press, 2007); and R. H. Thaler, 'Behavioral Economics: Past, Present, and Future', *The American Economic Review* 106.7 (2016), 1577–1600.

56 As per the definition of sustainability preferences as introduced into relevant legislation.

57 See European Commission, 'Questions and Answers: Taxonomy Climate Delegated Act and Amendments to Delegated Acts on Fiduciary Duties, Investment and Insurance Advice' (2021), https://ec.europa.eu/commission/presscorner/api/files/document/print/en/qanda_21_1805/QANDA_21_1805_EN.pdf, p. 4: 'The client should ultimately determine this specific ambition.'

58 ESMA, 'Final Report: Guidelines on Certain Aspects of the MiFID II Suitability Requirements' (2022), https://www.esma.europa.eu/sites/default/files/library/esma35-43-3172_final_report_on_mifid_ii_guidelines_on_suitability.pdf, para. 26, pp. 45–46.

Moreover, it remains unclear why the Commission assumes that consumers will, in sufficient numbers, choose to invest sustainably if asked about their preferences. One possibility is that investors are expected to have, or develop, a preference for sustainable investments because those investments are (or will eventually be) more profitable than non-sustainable investments. In fact, however, evidence supporting the view that sustainable investments achieve (or will in the future achieve) enhanced profit remain rather inconclusive. Indeed, consumers may have relatively short investment horizons meaning that investing for the long term, or for future generations, may not always be a realistic expectation.[59] An alternative explanation for the apparent assumption that merely enquiring about sustainability preferences will lead to greater sustainable investment is that the individual is expected to express a preference for sustainable investments for altruistic reasons. This explanation, however, would seem to indicate a willingness to sacrifice the well-meaning individual, who may in fact sustain personal investment losses, to the greater good. Whether this is, in itself, a sustainable approach to sustainability is questionable.[60]

In conclusion, the EU's approach to sustainable finance continues to assign a starring role in driving the transition to the rational, well-informed individual who is expected to exercise their free choice by sifting through the mountain of sustainability information to be made available under regulations such as the SFDR, Taxonomy, CSRD, and CSDDD, thereby spontaneously resulting in the allocation of a greater amount of private capital to sustainable investments. The same approach has failed to offer any convincing explanation as to why an individual would in fact choose to invest sustainably, particularly in the event that sustainable investments may carry greater risk and/or lower return. Moreover, the Commission has chosen to adhere to an out-dated understanding of the consumer despite evidence from behavioural economists that would indicate that the average consumer is rather ill-equipped to navigate the complex jargon introduced and unlikely to be motivated to process the volume of sustainability on offer.

4. Conclusions

Today, one can hardly imagine a world without EPL since it impacts matters across the EU from human rights to consumer rights and from housing to the financial system.[61] Debates continue also as to nature, purpose and scope of EPL, including of EU financial regulation, which constitutes a particular form of EPL. As discussions continue around these contemporary issues in EPL, of course, new societal challenges arise, demanding a response from EPL. This chapter has shown that by critically analysing

59 With respect to the 'questionable beliefs' on which the current approach to sustainability is based, see A. Bris, 'We Need a Realistic, Fact-Based Approach to Sustainability', *IMD* (25 April 2023), https://www.imd.org/ibyimd/magazine/we-need-a-realistic-fact-based-approach-to-sustainability/

60 With what we, as citizens, can logically and sensibly expect of one another when faced with societally important choices, see G. Hardin, 'The Tragedy of the Commons', *Science* 162.3859 (1968), 1243–1248.

61 See, for example, the contributions in this volume related to such issues including those of Chantal Mak, Guido Comparato, and Irina Dorumath (Chapter 5, Chapter 11, and Chapter 12 respectively).

those responses, we can better understand the position held by policy makers with respect to contested issues in EPL.

In particular, this chapter has shown that the EU's strategic and regulatory response to sustainable finance indicates a continued commitment to the instrumentalisation of private law in pursuit of the internal market objective, although it has also been noted that such an approach may largely be the product of the limited competences provided in the TFEU. The chapter has also noted that the approach reflects the further Europeanisation of private law, with the EU demonstrating a preference for regulations over directives and harmonisation of sustainability definitions and obligations. Furthermore, a continued commitment to financialisation has been observed with the concept of sustainability approached from the point of view that sustainability is a risk to be priced and a commodity to be traded. Reflections as to whether certain types of finance or financial practices ought to be limited or prohibited are notably absent in the EU's approach to sustainable finance. It has also been argued that the EU's approach to financial regulation has remained rather traditional. In particular, the view persists that regulatory interventions must have an economic rationale, such that the goal of safeguarding people and/or the planet is apparently regarded as an insufficient ground for financial law-making. Instead, sustainability rules have been adopted which mandate disclosure (to enhance informational efficiency) and encourage sustainability risk management (in support of financial stability). Finally, it has been argued that the EU's approach to sustainable finance regulation reflects an enduring depiction of the consumer as a rational and financially-engaged individual whose free choice will spontaneously drive capital in the direction of sustainable investments, with limited explanation as to why a consumer would choose sustainable investments over less sustainable alternatives—particularly in the case that the latter may render higher returns in the short term.

5. Points for Reflection

Q1: This chapter has taken a critical legal studies approach to the EU's approach to sustainable finance. Which alternative methodologies could be employed to study the EU's approach, and do you think such methodologies would be more or less appropriate?

Q2: Do you consider European, rather than national, legislative action to be the most effective manner of adopting sustainable finance rules and regulations? Why (not)?

Q3: Should financial regulation always have an economic rationale or does the challenge of transitioning to a sustainable financial system justify the use of financial regulation to meet alternative policy goals, in your opinion?

Q4: Do you agree that the EU's approach to sustainable finance constitutes a financialisation of sustainability?

Q5: What do you think can be expected of the retail investor in the sustainability transition? To what extent do you think the pursuit by individuals of their own preferences is likely to contribute to a more sustainable financial system?

Q6: Do you think that a comprehensive shift in the way the financial system works has occurred or appears to be underway as a result of the adopted regulatory approach?

Q7: If not, can you think of alternative, or additional, measures that could contribute to a comprehensive shift in and/or a deep re-engineering of the financial system?

Bibliography

Baron, J., *Thinking and deciding*, 4th edn (Cambridge, UK: Cambridge University Press, 2007)

Bondt, W. F. M. de, and R. H. Thaler, 'Financial Decision-Making in Markets and Firms: A Behavioral Perspective', *Handbooks in Operations Research and Management Science* 9 (1995), 385–410, https://doi.org/10.1016/S0927-0507(05)80057-X

Bris, A., 'We Need a Realistic, Fact-Based Approach to Sustainability', *IMD* (25 April 2023), https://www.imd.org/ibyimd/magazine/we-need-a-realistic-fact-based-approach-to-sustainability/

Commission Communication, 'Strategy for Financing the Transition to a Sustainable Economy', COM (2021) 390 final, https://eur-lex.europa.eu/legal-content/EN/TXT/?uri=celex:52021DC0390

Commission Communication, 'A Sustainable Finance Framework that Works on the Ground', COM (2023) 317 final, https://eur-lex.europa.eu/legal-content/EN/TXT/?uri=CELEX:52023SC0209

Epstein, G., 'Financialization, Rentier Interests, and Central Bank Policy' (2002), https://peri.umass.edu/wp-content/uploads/joomla/images/publication/fin_Epstein.pdf

ESMA, 'Final Report: Guidelines on Certain Aspects of the MiFID II Suitability Requirements' (2022), https://www.esma.europa.eu/sites/default/files/library/esma35-43-3172_final_report_on_mifid_ii_guidelines_on_suitability.pdf

EU High-level Expert Group on Sustainable Finance, 'Financing a European Economy', HLEG Interim Report (2017), https://finance.ec.europa.eu/system/files/2017-07/170713-sustainable-finance-report_en.pdf

European Commission, 'Questions and Answers on the Banking Package 2021' (2021), https://ec.europa.eu/commission/presscorner/detail/en/qanda_21_5386

Garben, S., 'Competence Creep Revisited', *Journal of Common Market Studies* 57.2 (2019), 205–222, https://doi.org/10.1111/jcms.12643

Hardin, G., 'The Tragedy of the Commons', *Science* 162.3859 (1968), 1243–1248

Lange-Collins, J. S. de, *Great Expectations of Sustainable Finance: A Critical Analysis of EU Sustainable Finance Strategy and Sustainable Finance Regulation* (doctoral thesis, University of Amsterdam, 2024)

Lucarello, J. F., 'The Praise of Silly: Critical Legal Studies and The Roberts Court', *Touro Law Review* 26 (2010), 619–647

Platform on Sustainable Finance, 'Draft Report by Subgroup 4: Social Taxonomy' (2021), https://finance.ec.europa.eu/system/files/2021-07/sf-draft-report-social-taxonomy-july2021_en.pdf

Platform on Sustainable Finance, 'Final Report on Social Taxonomy' (2022), https://finance.ec.europa.eu/system/files/2022-08/220228-sustainable-finance-platform-finance-report-social-taxonomy_en.pdf

Stiglitz, J., and the Members of a UN Commission of Financial Experts, *Stiglitz Report: Reforming the International Monetary and Financial Systems in the Wake of the Global Crisis* (New York: New Press, 2009)

Thaler, R. H., 'Behavioral Economics: Past, Present, and Future', *The American Economic Review* 106.7 (2016), 1577–1600, https://doi.org/10.1257/aer.106.7.1577

United Nations, 'United Nations Framework Convention on Climate Change, 21st Conference of the Parties, Paris' (2015), https://unfccc.int/process-and-meetings/the-paris-agreement

United Nations, 'United Nations Resolution 70/1. Transforming Our World: The 2030 Agenda for Sustainable Development' (2015), https://sustainabledevelopment.un.org/content/documents/21252030%20Agenda%20for%20Sustainable%20Development%20web.pdf

Weatherill, S., *The Internal Market as a Legal Concept*, 1st edn (Oxford: Oxford University Press, 2017), https://doi.org/10.1093/acprof:oso/9780198794806.001.0001

V. METHODS

15. Private Law and Political Economy

Marija Bartl

Abstract

This chapter discusses the 'political economic' approach to private law. The political economic approach is instrumental for the study of private law's role in making, and eventually remaking, different social institutions and processes, such as markets, global value chains, corporations, globalisation etc. In this chapter then, after situating the intellectual locus of 'private law and political economy', I first outline how law and political economy scholars view the social institution of markets, which is often the locus of their scholarly interest (Legal Context 1). Second, to exemplify the kind of inquiry that one may encounter in this line of scholarship, I ask what role private law plays in fostering either more emancipatory ('freedom') or more coercive ('exploitation') side of markets as social institutions. To do so, I start by discussing how private law enables the more coercive side of markets, by way of narrowing down what unfair exploitation and unjust enrichment stand for (Legal Context 2).[1] I then turn to outline how private law may foster more emancipatory side of markets, by means of expanding what 'private' stands for (Societal Implications).

1. Introduction: On 'Law and Political Economy' as an Approach to Studying Law

In recent years, one of the most prominent new trends in legal scholarship has been titled 'law and political economy'.[2] Political economy stands for the study of 'co-constitutive' relationship between politics, law, and economic practices and processes, in how societies materially and socially reproduce themselves. The lens of law then serves as an entry point for 'law and political economy' scholarship. However, law

1 R. L. Hale, 'Force and the State: A Comparison of Political and Economic Compulsion', *Columbia Law Review* 35 (1935), 149–201.

2 The tradition of the study of 'political economy'—that is, of the political constitution of economy—is historically the longest one, including famous economists and social theorists, such as Adam Smith, David Ricardo, Karl Marx, and Max Weber.

 https://doi.org/10.11647/OBP.0448.15

remains just that—an entry point—to a more complex reality that cannot be untangled without understanding the operation of economics or politics, as well the insights of scientific disciplines that study them.

Importantly, law and political economy is not an external perspective on law imported from a different discipline, such as is the case with law and economics (neoclassical economics/microeconomics), law and literature (literature/literary criticism), law and behaviour (behavioural psychology) and so forth.[3] Instead, it is an interdisciplinary perspective on society, which sees law, alongside politics and the economy, as elements that together co-constitute (a large chunk of) our social reality.

This integrative perspective is usually achieved by placing a particular social institution—such as the market, value chains, the corporation etc.—at the centre of the analysis. Law is then used as the entry point for studying how this institution is made to operate in society, including its emancipatory as well as coercive dimension.[4] A law and political economy approach thus (definitionally) cuts across the boundaries of scientific disciplines, using insights from law, economics, politics, geography, and religion, to understand how various social institutions are made and can be remade.[5]

In terms of the questions that scholars of law and political economy ask, one can find more traditional critical questions, such as a) what are the distributive impacts of existing legal categories, rules and principles in the market economy, that is, who stands to gain or lose (debtors, creditors, workers, employers, rich, poor, tenants, homeowners etc.)?;[6] usually followed up by more transformative questions, such as b) how does one change the distributive patterns of law if those, in confrontation with empirical realities, asymmetrically privilege certain groups above others?[7] More recently, the question occupying much scholarly attention has been c) what is the role of law in co-producing various economic and societal problems we face today, such as climate change,[8] growing inequality,[9] or exploitation along the value chain?, often followed by the inquiry d) how could law contribute to solving some of the societal problems it co-constitutes, including the socio-political routes for advancing such proposals for change?[10]

In this chapter I aim to do three things. First, I outline how law and political economy scholars view the social institution of markets, which is often the locus of their scholarly interest (Section 2). Second, to exemplify the kind of inquiry that one

3 M. Bartl and J. C. Lawrence, *The Politics of European Legal Research: Behind the Method* (Cheltenham: Edward Elgar Publishing, 2022).

4 S. Deakin et al., 'Legal Institutionalism: Capitalism and the Constitutive Role of Law', *Journal of Comparative Economics* 45 (2017), 188–200.

5 M. Weber and S. Kalberg, *The Protestant Ethic and the Spirit of Capitalism* (London: Routledge, 2013).

6 The question of law's distributive role was central to one of the predecessors of LPE, namely critical legal studies. The most important figures in that group are Duncan Kennedy, Roberto Unger, David Kennedy, all from Harvard.

7 Ibid.

8 See Chapter 1 in this volume.

9 See Chapter 11 in this volume.

10 For instance, at the University of Amsterdam, these questions are dealt with in a major research project titled Sustainable Global Economic Law.

may encounter in this line of scholarship, I ask what role private law plays in fostering either more an emancipatory ('freedom') or more coercive ('exploitation') side of markets as social institutions. To do so, I first discuss how private law enables the more coercive side of markets, by way of narrowing down what unfair exploitation and unjust enrichment denote (Section 3).[11] I then turn to outline how private law may foster more emancipatory sides of markets, by means of expanding what 'private' stands for (Section 4).

2. Legal Context

a. Markets are Legally Constituted

Law and political economy scholarship starts from an obvious, but in recent decades somewhat neglected, fact. Namely, markets are social institutions, that is, collective agreements about norms and behaviours in pursuance of a social objective.[12] If markets are social institutions, rather than some natural self-regulating systems, how shall we think about the objectives pursued by markets, and the ways by which they are pursued? To approach this question, we need to look back in history.

Market economies have emerged first at the level of states, as national markets (only in the 19th century for most of Europe),[13] and later expanded to what we often describe today as the 'transnational' or 'global market'.[14] Markets' existence and modes of operation depend on many things, such as the availability of transport, (information) technologies, and suitable geographies, to name a few. But most importantly, markets fundamentally depend on political will, rules, and enforcement that make it possible in the first place.

There can be no markets, as we conventionally understand them today, without private law, be that contract or property law, and the coercive state apparatus to back it up. These are the basic preconditions of market economies, as also stressed by the World Bank, which considers the rules of property and contract as central elements to the 'rule of law'.[15] Most market economies, however, that are typified by such a thin set of private legal rules, as the World Bank considers fundamental, would be very similar to the markets seen in 19th-century Europe: characterised by rampant exploitation of

---

11 Hale, 'Force and the State '.

12 J. Turner, *The Institutional Order: Economy, Kinship, Religion, Polity, Law, and Education in Evolutionary and Comparative Perspective*, 1st edn (New York: Longman, 1997).

13 P. S. Atiyah, *The Rise and Fall of Freedom of Contract* (Oxford: Oxford University Press, 1979).

14 C. Joerges, *Karl Polanyi, Globalisation and the Potential of Law in Transnational Markets* (Oxford: Hart Publishing, 2011).

15 'These are: "reforming laws" (i.e. drafting substantive laws, for simplicity often categorised under five main headings: property; contract; company; bankruptcy; and competition); and "reforming institutions" ("including courts, legislative bodies, property registries, ombudsmen, law schools and judicial training centers, bar associations, and enforcement agencies")', in G. Barron, 'The World Bank & The Rule of Law', *Development Studies Institute* 5.70 (2005), https://www.files.ethz.ch/isn/137920/WP70.pdf, p. 19.

the poor, including children, women, and racialised groups.[16]

Yet rampant exploitation has not been, and need not be, the only face of markets. In fact, whether this is the case will ultimately depend on rules and institutions (including private law) underpinning the market. In several European states, Canada, Japan, and to a lesser degree in Australia and the US, over the course of the 20th century, a number of laws were put in place to ensure that it is not those who control most capital[17] that dictate the acceptable levels of pollution in society, degree of safety at work or the minimum rates of pay. Equally, a strong representation of workers' collective interests via trade unions has also played a central role in ensuring that workers have benefited from increased social product in the post-World War II decades.[18] In contrast, in both the 'Global South' and many post-communist countries, the struggle for even rudimentary market regulation is still ongoing—often hampered (to say the least) by multinationals from the 'Global North' populating these 'emerging' economies, precisely to capitalise from this regulatory vacuum.[19]

Another important development we have witnessed over the past years and decades is the creation of 'regional markets', comprising more national markets, in many parts of the world (Latin America, Southeast Asia, Africa, Europe). The successful establishment of such markets requires an abundance of laws and public interventions. In the European Union (EU), for instance, the 'integration through law' [20] has been primarily directed at putting in place a *common* and later *internal* market—by liberalising the movement of goods, services, capital, and labour across the EU. This so called 'negative integration[21] has been complemented by 'positive integration',[22] which has tried to reinstate some of the protections previously liberalised away.[23] All these regulatory efforts by the EU have given shape to the internal market—enabling and constraining, emancipatory and coercive.[24]

The further liberalising push came from what we can call '(second) economic globalisation'. This has predominantly taken off over the past forty years, having been facilitated by the rulemaking and standard setting of several international institutions (including the World Trade Organisation, Organisation for Economic Co-operation and Development, International Labour Organisation etc.) across a number of key fields (including trade law, investment law, international labour standards, tax

16 E. P. Thompson, *Whigs and Hunters: The Origins of the Black Art*, 1st edn (London: Penguin, 1977).

17 By 'capital' you can understand: large companies, their management, rich individuals, large shareholders etc.

18 F. W. Scharpf, 'The Asymmetry of European Integration, or Why the EU Cannot be a 'Social Market Economy', *Socio-Economic Review* 8 (2009), 211–250.

19 J. P. Robé, *Property, Power and Politics: Why We Need to Rethink the World Power System* (Bristol: Bristol University Press, 2020).

20 J. H. H. Weiler, 'The Transformation of Europe', *Yale Law Journal* 100 (1991), 2403–2483.

21 See Chapter 3 in this volume.

22 See Chapter 4 in this volume.

23 T. Piketty, *Capital and Ideology* (Cambridge, MA: Harvard University Press, 2020).

24 In an interesting contribution, Kukovec discusses some of the distributive consequences of the internal market for the more recently acceded member states. See D. Kukovec, 'Law and the Periphery', *European Law Journal* 21 (2014), 406–428.

standards etc.) Equally the rules of 'private governance' (technical standardisation, private regulatory regimes, International Organisation for Standardisation (ISO) standards, financial standardisation etc.), gave further shape to this global market, stepping in where the public regulation was missing.[25] These rules work to furnish market actors with, for instance, a plethora of technical specifications or standard derivatives contracts that enable global trade and exchange. Overall, global markets, legally enabled but thinly shaped, make private autonomy and freedom of contract paradoxically at their strongest.

In a recent famous book in the law and political economy tradition, *The Code of Capital*, Katharina Pistor argues that globalisation is in fact private. [26] What she means by this is that globalisation is furthered by private law and private actors. In Pistor's account, globalisation is driven by transnational corporate legal practice, which shapes the contours of global markets in the interests of their clients, by skilfully employing the rules ('modules') of property, contract, bankruptcy, corporate law, and financial law from two main jurisdictions (New York and England) to create various private law instruments, such as derivatives, trusts, financial products etc. Relying thus mostly on freedom of contract, they use the modules of private law to 'code' assets (material or immaterial), adding value to them by attributing priority, guaranteeing durability, ensuring convertibility, and warranting universality of claims. Since such advanced legal services are available only to those who already possess high levels of capital, private globalisation drives inequality, insofar as it enables the rich to get richer, while leaving everyone else worse off.

Three important take-aways can be derived from the previous discussion. First, from the perspective of law and political economy, there are no 'free' markets. At least not as institutions somehow operating of their own accord without law and political intervention (the myth of 'self-regulation' and 'invisible hand'). Rather, many rules are in fact necessary to make markets/market economies exist and function.[27] Second, the objective of markets—to whose advantage/disadvantage they operate and with what consequences—will depend to a great degree on the rules (including laws) which they are made off. Third, the mediation between public and private power in the constitution of market operation is dependent on fundamental private law categories—such as protection of property, the enforcement of contracts, as well as rules on setting up and dissolution of legal persons—which will gain a greater importance in the global markets, where public regulation is less available.

25 The conventional knowledge is that since there are no 'public institutions' at a global level, such as those present at the national level, private governance needs to step in, to enable market functioning.

26 K. Pistor, *The Code of Capital: How the Law Creates Wealth and Inequality* (Princeton, NJ: Princeton University Press, 2019).

27 Joerges, *Karl Polanyi, Globalisation and the Potential of Law.*

3. Markets and Private Law

The emergence of market economies in the 19th century (for most European countries) was at least in part an emancipatory project, based on the idea of 'freedom' of contract. In that new era, people of a certain gender, age, and sex, were able to conclude contracts as free and equal individuals with equal standards of care and responsibility expected from them. This new institutional framework promised a break from the bonds of feudalism where status previously ruled. The contract was now to assume its place.[28]

The relationship between freedom and its opposite—coercion and exploitation (usually attributed to feudalism)—was anything but straightforward, however, even in market economies. While capacity to contract on equal terms remains fundamental, not only to day-to-day transactions, but to transformative projects as well,[29] the coercive dimensions of markets have been and are pervasive.

In the following two subsections, I will outline the uneasy relationship between freedom and exploitation in private law. I will argue that those markets based on a thin private law infrastructure are invariably the ones to show their most coercive and exploitative face, insofar as such markets are uninterested in the pervasive condition of economic duress and disregard 'social responsibility'. The awareness of this fundamental weakness of private law also serves as an invitation to both rethink private law as an institution in its own right, as well as produce other market-shaping rules that would remedy this myopic private law vision.

a. Freedom to Exploit: The Property Trap

When starting our law degrees, we are presented with private law as a body of rules enabling individual freedom, choice, and commerce. Exploitation is straightforwardly banished from it. In fact, in most private rulebooks in Europe (and elsewhere) you will find provisions such as this:

> DRAFT COMMON FRAME OF REFERENCE, II.-7:207: Unfair exploitation
>
> A party may avoid a contract if, at the time of the conclusion of the contract: (a) the party was **dependent** on or had a relationship of **trust** with the other party, was in **economic distress** or had **urgent needs**, was **improvident**, **ignorant**, **inexperienced** or lacking in. **bargaining skill** and (b) the other party **knew or could reasonably be expected** to have known this and, given the circumstances and purpose of the contract, **exploited the first party's situation** by taking an excessive benefit or grossly unfair advantage.[30]

---

28 M. Weber, *Economy and Society*, I (Oakland, CA: University of California Press, 1978); O. E. Williamson, 'The Economics of Organizations: The Transaction Cost Approach' (1981) 87 American Journal of Sociology 548.

29 P. Williams, 'The Obliging Shell: An Informal Essay on Formal Equal Opportunity', *Michigan Law Review* 87 (1989), 548–577.

30 Study Group on a European Civil Code and the Research Group on EC Private Law (Aquis Group),

If any one party uses dependency and trust on the one hand, or economic distress, urgent needs or ignorance on the other, to gain excessive benefit or unfair advantage out of the contract, that constitutes unfair exploitation. In such a case, the exploited party can ask a judge for a cancellation or a modification of such disadvantageous contract.

Yet, the elephant in the room is; what is not considered exploitation under this legal framework? In the economy we all well know, very few people (but the holders of large capital) are in a situation of no economic distress to take a job, for instance. Our economic system depends on there actually being a sufficient degree of economic distress, by a sufficient number of people, so that some people have to take up all kinds of contracts, including physically demanding, demeaning, and badly paid jobs. The US legal realist Robert Hale famously argued at the beginning of the 20th century that the system of exclusionary property rights ensures that those who have property, or productive capital, do not have to share it with others—unless those others without property or productive capital enter into some relationship of subordination (a wage contract) in order to provide themselves and their families with the most basic needs, such as food and shelter.[31] What remains of 'freedom' of contract in the case of such widespread economic necessity?

But even within the remit of this foundational paradox, what has historically been considered 'unfair exploitation' as opposed to 'freedom of contract' has changed considerably. In the past, children aged nine could work in mines, fourteen hours a day, six days a week—something entirely within the bounds of their (parents') 'freedom' of contract.[32] Today, such employment would be subject to criminal sanctions across the world—despite the fact it unfortunately still happens all too often.[33]

In many countries, minimum thresholds for age, pay and safety-at-work have been implemented through regulation—providing a different pre-configuration for the 'freedom' of contract. Regulating what is considered as belonging within the ambit of 'freedom of contract' is a reaction to the foundational duress on which market economy is based. Interestingly, however, many such pre-configurations of 'freedom of contract' have been taken out of what we consider 'general contract law'. In continental Europe, they are usually not found in civil codes, but have been confined to their own 'special' fields, such as labour law, tenancy law, consumer law, in order not to disturb the founding fiction that people are equal and free from duress of all kinds.[34]

Given this legislative handiwork, what today remains encompassed within the ambit

---

'Principles, Definitions and Model Rules of European Private Law: Draft Common Frame of Reference (DCFR) Outline Edition' (2009), https://sakig.pl/wp-content/uploads/2019/01/dfcr.pdf, p. 212.

31 R. L. Hale, 'Coercion and Distribution in a Supposedly Non-Coercive State', *Political Science Quarterly* 38.3 (1923), 470–494.

32 Atiyah, *The Rise and Fall of Freedom of Contract.*

33 See International Labour Organisation, 'Child Labour', *International Labour Organisation*, https://www.ilo.org/global/topics/child-labour/lang--en/index.htm

34 H. W. Micklitz, 'The Expulsion of the Concept of Protection from the Consumer Law and the Return of Social Elements in the Civil Law: A Bittersweet Polemic', *Journal of Consumer Policy* 35 (2012), 283–296.

of the 'unfair exploitation' as mentioned above? The provision is mainly applicable to the misuse of trust in personal relations, remaining oblivious to more structural types of inequalities.[35] It could be applicable, for instance, in cases of sham 'self-employment' across all kinds of delivery services. Yet, this has only ever exceptionally been the case. For instance, a Canadian court recently declared 'unconsciousable'[36] an arbitral provision determining the Netherlands as the applicable jurisdiction in a dispute between Uber and one of their drivers.[37] It is telling that this case caused great surprise, and critique, in common law systems:[38] these rules were intended for specific (individual and occasional) weaknesses and vulnerabilities of contractual parties rather than more structural inequalities. This also makes any other non-general-private-law route (for instance via labour law) a far more attractive forum to pursue such claims in places where they exist, such as the EU.[39]

b. Freedom to Enrich Yourself: The Privity Trap

Another way to look at how private law shapes markets, via the tension between freedom and exploitation, is to consider how it goes about distributing the benefits of social cooperation. This is particularly salient in the context of global markets and global value chains, where only a very thin layer of market-shaping laws exists. To demonstrate this, we will examine a famous US legal case.

In 2009, the California Court of Appeal rendered its judgement in *Doe v Wal-Mart*.[40] The case was brought as a class-action[41] by the workers of suppliers to Wal-Mart, a major discount supermarket chain in the US, for sweatshop conditions of their work. Due to the previous scandals, Wal-Mart had introduced a 'code of conduct' for its suppliers, requiring foreign suppliers adhere to local laws and standards regarding pay, hours, forced labour, child labour, and discrimination. The code of conduct further included a paragraph titled the 'Right to Inspection':

---

35 The examples in the Draft Common Frame of Reference Comments are of this kind. See Study Group on a European Civil Code and the Research Group on EC Private Law (Aquis Group), 'Principles, Definitions and Model Rules of European Private Law: Draft Common Frame of Reference (DCFR). Articles and Comments [Interim Edition]' Outline Edition', https://www.ccbe.eu/fileadmin/speciality_distribution/public/documents/EUROPEAN_PRIVATE_LAW/EN_EPL_20100107_Principles__definitions_and_model_rules_of_European_private_law_-_Draft_Common_Frame_of_Reference__DCFR_.pdf, pp. 215–218.

36 The common law doctrine of 'unconsciousnessability' may be seen as a parallel to unfairness in continental European legal systems, or 'unfair terms' in EU consumer contracts. Cf. H. Beale, *Contracts Law: Ius Commune Casebooks for the Common Law of Europe* (London: Bloomsbury Publishing, 2010).

37 *Uber Technologies Inc. v Heller*, 2020 SCC 16, [2020] 2 S.C.R. 118.

38 See D. Brodie, 'Fair Bargains and the Gig Economy', *University of Strathclyde* (15 July 2021), https://www.strath.ac.uk/humanities/lawschool/blog/fairbargainsandthegigeconomy/

39 See J. Toh, 'Another Win for Workers: Uber Drivers are Employees', *Social Europe* (22 September 2021), https://socialeurope.eu/another-win-for-workers-uber-drivers-are-employees

40 The decision, *Jane Doe, et al. v Wal-Mart, Inc.*, No. 08–55706 (9th Cir. 2009).

41 Class actions, as the procedural law institution, enable collective action claims in the US that should enable people to tackle also some more structural problems in the economy. Of course, the problems with this type of legal action remain considerable. See T. L. Russell, 'Exporting Class Actions to the European Union', *Boston University International Law Journal* 28 (2010), 141–180.

> To further assure proper implementation of and compliance with the standards set forth herein, Wal-Mart or a third party designated by Wal-Mart **will undertake affirmative measures, such as on-site inspection of production facilities**, to implement and monitor said standards. Any supplier which fails or refuses to comply with these standards or does not allow inspection of production facilities is subject to immediate cancellation of any and all outstanding orders, refuse [sic] or return [sic] any shipment, and otherwise cease doing business [sic] with Wal-Mart.

The claimants, suppliers' workers, contended that while Wal-Mart presented itself to the public as being socially responsible, it knowingly overlooked and ultimately benefited from the despicable conditions of their work. More specifically, Wal-Mart purposefully failed to monitor their suppliers based on their code of conduct—with only 8% of the audits being unannounced and most of the workers having been coached on how to respond to the auditors.

On this basis, the four courses of action were presented against Wal-Mart. First, that the claimants were third-party beneficiaries of the Code of Conduct. Second, that Wal-Mart was their employer. Third, that Wal-Mart was negligent in its duty to monitor. Fourth, that Wal-Mart was unjustly enriching itself at the expense of the claimants. The Court of Appeal found the claim unjustified on all four counts.

First, given that the Code of Conduct did not postulate that Wal-Mart had the obligation to monitor (i.e. Wal-Mart has no obligation but only a right to take affirmative measures), the workers could not have been the intended beneficiaries of the statement. By the parties to the agreement between Wal-Mart and its suppliers, the claimants could not be seen as third-party beneficiaries. Second, despite the claimants' contention that Wal-Mart exercised control over their day-to-day employment, the supply contract terms did not constitute (in the Court's view) such a level of control to merit a claim that an employment relationship had been established. Third, Wal-Mart was also not acting negligently vis-à-vis the conditions of work of the claimants—since it never undertook the obligation to monitor their work conditions to start with.

Finally, and most relevantly for our purposes, the claimants raised the question whether Wal-Mart had unjustifiably enriched itself at their expense. While they worked in deplorable conditions for little-to-no pay, Wal-Mart made huge economic profits. The Court responds to this somewhat bluntly, asserting that:

> The lack of any prior relationship between Plaintiffs and Wal-Mart precludes the application of an unjust enrichment theory here. [...] no other [than employment contract] plausible basis upon which the employee of a manufacturer, without more, may obtain restitution from one who purchases goods from that manufacturer.

What matters for the Courts is the lack of any prior direct bilateral, inter-pares relationship—the privity of contact. And yet, it is exactly this condition that makes private law the enabler of the exploitation in global value chains. In many sectors of economy, transnational or global value chains can be properly described as 'captive'[42]

42 F. Cafaggi and P. Iamiceli, 'Unfair Trading Practices in Food Supply Chains. Regulatory Responses

where the lead firms—such as Wal-Mart—exercise exorbitant power over the suppliers in all aspects of business production. They can usually change terms at will, dictate prices and production deadlines, and move to another producer as and when they please. In this context, having such a narrow definition of 'unjustified enrichment' makes it possible for companies such as Wal-Mart to set the contractual conditions unilaterally and grossly in their favour. This allows them to cream off the lion's share of benefits from social cooperation—whilst leaving workers in Bangladesh (for instance) extremely poor, dispossessed, unhealthy, and often dead.[43]

4. Societal Implications: Transforming Markets via Private Law

Today, private law enables deeply unfair distributive patterns (especially across the global trade sphere) where only a fraction of the global population enjoys some sort of protection. Unless one qualifies, for instance, as a protected worker or a consumer in a particular jurisdiction, very little can be expected from general private law. This situation is further exacerbated by the increasing prevalence of private international law rules, which enable the spread of general private law norms—but without its protections.[44] This private law myopia renders this body of rules a 'regressively distributive' institution: a set of rules that turn markets into systems of exploitation rather than emancipation, shifting both benefits of cooperation and power from the 'have nots' to the 'haves'.[45]

And yet, as this chapter made clear previously, this need not be the case. Historically, we have seen that markets, in all their forms (whether more coercive or more emancipatory, more cooperative or more competitive, more extractive or more generative), all inherently depend on a set of rules and institutions to shape their purpose and operation. One of the core insights of the law and political economy literature is, however, that if we truly want to make better use of markets as social institutions we need to go beyond just tinkering at the edges, adjusting the 'protective' rules only. These remain geographically bound and permanently the exception—forever trailing and failing to address the extractive activity taking place under general private law. As Pistor and Martijn Hesselink[46] both argue, we must go after general private law norms in their own right—contract and property law for sure, but also company, financial, insolvency law etc. Only if we change the ground rules can we think of more inclusive and fair forms of market economies.[47]

---

and Institutional Alternatives in the Light of the New EU Directive', *European Review of Private Law* 27 (2019), 1075–1113.

43 See Accord, 'Safe Workplace', *Accord on Fire and Building Safety in Bangladesh*, https://bangladeshaccord.org/

44 Pistor, *The Code of Capital*.

45 B. Milanovic, *The Haves and the Have-Nots: A Brief and Idiosyncratic History of Global Inequality* (New York: Basic Books, 2010).

46 See Chapter 2 in this volume.

47 Pistor, *The Code of Capital*.

How to do that? Most generally, what is required is the redefinition of what 'private' means. For instance, in company law scholarship, one has to open the backbox of corporate purpose and the role of profit as we increasingly see in the discussion on the importance of social enterprises,[48] steward ownership,[49] social purpose of companies[50] or social/solidary economy.[51] In property circles the questions of common, shared and public ownership—as opposed to exclusionary individual ownership—are gaining more attention.[52] At the same time, older questions of workers participation in the governance of firms, as well as economic democracy, are beginning to gain traction,[53] while reining in the excesses of global value chains via hard law (in both the UN and the EU) even stands a fighting chance of legislative success.[54] All these accounts and proposals aim to unsettle the conception of the 'private', opening private law to more social and socially responsible alternatives. They move the discussion away from transactionalism (to a more relational understanding), away from profit-making (to prioritising social purpose); and away from exclusionary property rights (to sharing and holding in common).

There are however also other transformative dynamics at play that will have a fundamental role in rethinking private law. Perhaps the most notable private law transformation of late stems from so called 'climate litigation'. Claimants in several EU member states have succeeded in relying on novel interpretations of rules on negligence, duty of care and causality, in order to mandate not only their governments,[55] but also the private parties to cut their CO2 emissions.[56] Another notable development is the 'rights of nature' movement, which has seen the rights pertaining to rivers, mountains or other ecosystems being introduced into national constitutions from Latin America

48 See European Commission, 'Social Enterprises', *European Commission*, https://single-market-economy.ec.europa.eu/sectors/proximity-and-social-economy/social-economy-eu/social-enterprises_en

49 See Purpose, 'Steward-Ownership. For an Economy Fit for the 21st Century', *Purpose Economy*, https://purpose-economy.org/en/

50 F. Laloux, *Reinventing Organizations: A Guide to Creating Organizations Inspired by the next Stage in Human Consciousness* (Millis, MA: Nelson Parker, 2014).

51 See Social Economy, 'The Social Economy', *Social Economy EU*, https://www.socialeconomy.eu.org/the-social-economy/

52 A. Di Robilant, 'The Virtues of Common Ownership', *Boston University Law Review* 91 (2011), 1359–1374.

53 D. Ellerman, *The Democratic Worker-Owned Firm: A New Model for the East and West* (Abingdon: Routledge, 2021).

54 For the UN, see Business & Human Rights Resource Centre, 'Binding Treaty', *Business & Human Rights Resource Centre*, https://www.business-humanrights.org/en/big-issues/binding-treaty/; For the EU, see European Commission, 'Corporate Sustainability Due Diligence', *European Commission*, https://ec.europa.eu/info/business-economy-euro/doing-business-eu/corporate-sustainability-due-diligence_en

55 See Urgenda, 'Landmark Decision by Dutch Supreme Court', *Urgenda*, https://www.urgenda.nl/en/themas/climate-case/; Other climate case summaries available at *Climate Case Chart*: http://climatecasechart.com/non-us-case/neubauer-et-al-v-germany/; http://climatecasechart.com/non-us-case/a-sud-et-al-v-italy/; http://climatecasechart.com/non-us-case/klimaticka-zaloba-cr-v-czech-republic/

56 See Clearly Gottlieb, 'Dutch Court Orders Shell to Reduce Emissions in First Climate Change Ruling Against Company', *Clearly Gottlieb* (30 June 2021), https://www.clearygottlieb.com/news-and-insights/publication-listing/dutch-court-orders-shell-to-reduce-emissions-in-first-climate-change-ruling-against-company

to New Zealand, giving such entities better institutional representation and a louder voice.[57] Finally, advocacy for the rights of future generations (those which will inherit a very different, slightly less inhabitable planet) has also gathered attention, both in case law and via new institutions, such as the Ombudsman for future generations.[58] These approaches expand the 'private' in another sense, adding a new set of issues and actors to whom we as societies owe respect and responsibility.

All these developments are not only worthy of study for theoretical interest (via bachelor or master theses, for instance) but are also laying the new ground rules for the behaviour of private and public actors, as well as re-shaping the markets and worlds that private law students are entering as we speak. Hence, it is worth paying attention to this transformative 'bread and butter' of future private law.

5. Points for Reflection

Q1: What is the political economy?

Q2: What is the role of law, and private law, in the making of the political economy?

Q3: What does it mean that private law 'constitutes' markets?

Q4: What do we mean by the 'distributive impacts' of private law?

Q5: What are the boundaries of freedom in private law—in national, regional and global contexts?

Q6: How does economic globalisation change the regulatory settlement achieved at the national level in many European countries?

Q7: What is the role and importance of private law for socio-ecological transformation?

Q8: Which private law field do you consider the most promising tool for transformation?

Bibliography

Accord, 'Safe Workplace', *Accord on Fire and Building Safety in Bangladesh*, https://bangladeshaccord.org/

Atiyah, P. S., *The Rise and Fall of Freedom of Contract* (Oxford: Oxford University Press, 1979)

Barron, G., 'The World Bank & The Rule of Law', *Development Studies Institute* 5.70 (2005), https://www.files.ethz.ch/isn/137920/WP70.pdf

57 L. Burgers, 'Private Rights of Nature', *Transnational Environmental Law* 11 (2022), 463–474.

58 See A. Vincent, 'Ombudsperson for Future Generations: Brin Intergenerational Justice into the Heart of Policymaking', *United Nations Chronicle* (11 June 2012), https://www.un.org/en/chronicle/article/ombudspersons-future-generations-bringing-intergenerational-justice-heart-policymaking

Bartl, M., and J. C. Lawrence, *The Politics of European Legal Research: Behind the Method* (Cheltenham: Edward Elgar Publishing, 2022), https://doi.org/10.4337/9781802201192

Beale, H., *Contracts Law: Ius Commune Casebooks for the Common Law of Europe* (London: Bloomsbury Publishing, 2010)

Brodie, D., 'Fair Bargains and the Gig Economy', *University of Strathclyde* (15 July 2021), https://www.strath.ac.uk/humanities/lawschool/blog/fairbargainsandthegigeconomy/

Burgers, L., 'Private Rights of Nature', *Transnational Environmental Law* 11 (2022), 463–474, https://doi.org/10.1017/S2047102522000401

Business & Human Rights Resource Centre, 'Binding Treaty', *Business & Human Rights Resource Centre*, https://www.business-humanrights.org/en/big-issues/binding-treaty/

Cafaggi, F., and P. Iamiceli, 'Unfair Trading Practices in Food Supply Chains. Regulatory Responses and Institutional Alternatives in the Light of the New EU Directive', *European Review of Private Law* 27 (2019), 1075–1113, https://doi.org/10.54648/erpl2019058

Clearly Gottlieb, 'Dutch Court Orders Shell to Reduce Emissions in First Climate Change Ruling Against Company', *Clearly Gottlieb* (30 June 2021), https://www.clearygottlieb.com/news-and-insights/publication-listing/dutch-court-orders-shell-to-reduce-emissions-in-first-climate-change-ruling-against-company

Deakin, S., et al., 'Legal Institutionalism: Capitalism and the Constitutive Role of Law', *Journal of Comparative Economics* 45 (2017), 188–200, https://doi.org/10.1016/j.jce.2016.04.005

Ellerman, D., *The Democratic Worker-Owned Firm: A New Model for the East and West* (Abingdon: Routledge, 2021), https://doi.org/10.4324/9781315709062

European Commission, 'Corporate Sustainability Due Diligence', *European Commission*, https://ec.europa.eu/info/business-economy-euro/doing-business-eu/corporate-sustainability-due-diligence_en

European Commission, 'Social Enterprises', *European Commission*, https://single-market-economy.ec.europa.eu/sectors/proximity-and-social-economy/social-economy-eu/social-enterprises_en

Hale, R. L., 'Coercion and Distribution in a Supposedly Non-Coercive State', *Political Science Quarterly* 38.3 (1923), 470–494

Hale, R. L., 'Force and the State: A Comparison of Political and Economic Compulsion', *Columbia Law Review* 35 (1935), 149–201

International Labour Organisation, 'Child Labour', *International Labour Organisation*, https://www.ilo.org/global/topics/child-labour/lang--en/index.htm

Joerges, C., *Karl Polanyi, Globalisation and the Potential of Law in Transnational Markets* (Oxford: Hart Publishing, 2011)

Kukovec, D., 'Law and the Periphery', *European Law Journal* 21 (2014), 406–428, https://doi.org/10.1111/eulj.12113

Laloux, F., *Reinventing Organizations: A Guide to Creating Organizations Inspired by the next Stage in Human Consciousness* (Millis, MA: Nelson Parker, 2014)

Micklitz, H. W., 'The Expulsion of the Concept of Protection from the Consumer Law and the Return of Social Elements in the Civil Law: A Bittersweet Polemic', *Journal of Consumer Policy* 35 (2012), 283–296, https://doi.org/10.1007/s10603-012-9199-4

Milanovic, B., *The Haves and the Have-Nots: A Brief and Idiosyncratic History of Global Inequality* (New York: Basic Books, 2010)

Piketty, T., *Capital and Ideology* (Cambridge, MA: Harvard University Press, 2020)

Pistor, K., *The Code of Capital: How the Law Creates Wealth and Inequality* (Princeton, NJ: Princeton University Press, 2019), https://doi.org/10.2307/j.ctvc777c1

Purpose, 'Steward-Ownership. For an Economy Fit for the 21st Century', *Purpose Economy*, https://purpose-economy.org/en/

Robé, J. P., *Property, Power and Politics: Why We Need to Rethink the World Power System* (Bristol: Bristol University Press, 2020), https://doi.org/10.46692/9781529213195

Robilant, A. Di, 'The Virtues of Common Ownership', *Boston University Law Review* 91 (2011), 1359–1374, https://scholarship.law.bu.edu/faculty_scholarship/2897

Russell, T. L., 'Exporting Class Actions to the European Union', *Boston University International Law Journal* 28 (2010), 141–180, https://www.bu.edu/law/journals-archive/international/documents/141–180.pdf

Scharpf, F. W., 'The Asymmetry of European Integration, or Why the EU Cannot be a 'Social Market Economy', *Socio-Economic Review* 8 (2009), 211–250, https://doi.org/10.1093/ser/mwp031

Social Economy, 'The Social Economy', *Social Economy EU*, https://www.socialeconomy.eu.org/the-social-economy/

Study Group on a European Civil Code and the Research Group on EC Private Law (Aquis Group), 'Principles, Definitions and Model Rules of European Private Law: Draft Common Frame of Reference (DCFR) Outline Edition' (2009), https://sakig.pl/wp-content/uploads/2019/01/dfcr.pdf

Study Group on a European Civil Code and the Research Group on EC Private Law (Aquis Group), 'Principles, Definitions and Model Rules of European Private Law: Draft Common Frame of Reference (DCFR). Articles and Comments [Interim Edition]' Outline Edition', https://www.ccbe.eu/fileadmin/speciality_distribution/public/documents/EUROPEAN_PRIVATE_LAW/EN_EPL_20100107_Principles__definitions_and_model_rules_of_European_private_law_-_Draft_Common_Frame_of_Reference__DCFR_.pdf

Thompson, E. P., *Whigs and Hunters: The Origins of the Black Art*, 1st edn (London: Penguin, 1977)

Toh, J., 'Another Win for Workers: Uber Drivers are Employees', *Social Europe* (22 September 2021), https://socialeurope.eu/another-win-for-workers-uber-drivers-are-employees.

Turner, J., *The Institutional Order: Economy, Kinship, Religion, Polity, Law, and Education in Evolutionary and Comparative Perspective*, 1st edn (New York: Longman, 1997)

Urgenda, 'Landmark Decision by Dutch Supreme Court', *Urgenda*, https://www.urgenda.nl/en/themas/climate-case/

Vincent, A., 'Ombudsperson for Future Generations: Brin Intergenerational Justice into the Heart of Policymaking', *United Nations Chronicle* (11 June 2012), https://www.un.org/en/chronicle/article/ombudspersons-future-generations-bringing-intergenerational-justice-heart-policymaking

Weber, M., *Economy and Society*, I (Oakland, CA: University of California Press, 1978)

Weber, M., and S. Kalberg, *The Protestant Ethic and the Spirit of Capitalism* (London: Routledge, 2013)

Weiler, J. H. H., 'The Transformation of Europe', *Yale Law Journal* 100 (1991), 2403–2483

Williams, P., 'The Obliging Shell: An Informal Essay on Formal Equal Opportunity', *Michigan Law Review* 87 (1989), 548–577, https://doi.org/10.2307/1289302

16. Methods of Comparative Legal Research: How to Set Up and Carry Out a Comparative Legal Research Project[1]

Marieke Oderkerk

Abstract

Since the 1990s comparative legal research has been one of the important pillars of the development of European private law. This chapter aims to discuss methods of comparative legal research that apply in the field of European private law and beyond. It is written for both beginner and advanced researchers interested in engaging in comparative legal research, providing guidelines on how to set up and carry out such a project in a methodologically sound way. It is based on the assumption that a methodology (in this case the methodology of comparative law) provides a researcher a clear set of guidelines (steps that need to be taken in a certain order) to reach a determined goal. This chapter sets out the various goals and types of comparative legal research and discusses step by step the methodological issues that have to be dealt with in the subsequent stages within a comparative research project. With regard to each methodological question context-related guidelines are provided on how to come to a scientifically sound and well-justified answer.

1. Introduction

Since the 1990s comparative legal research has been one of the important pillars of the development of European private law. Both projects by groups of academics such as the Commission on European Contract Law,[2] the Commission on European Family

1 This chapter is an adaption and updated version of my article 'The Need for a Methodological Framework for Comparative Legal Research: Sense and Nonsense of 'Methodological Pluralism' in Comparative Law', *RabelsZ* 79.3 (2015), 589–623.

2 The Commission on European Contract Law (the Lando Commission) has drafted the Principles of European Contract Law (PECL) which were presented in 1999. See Section 3 and Section 4.a.2 below.

 https://doi.org/10.11647/OBP.0448.16

Law,[3] and the 'Trento Group',[4] as well as many individual research projects in this field were and are based largely on comparative legal research.[5] This chapter aims to discuss methods of comparative legal research that apply in the field of European private law and beyond. It is written for both beginner and advanced researchers interested in engaging in comparative legal research, providing guidelines on how to set up and conduct such a project in a methodologically sound way. It is based on the assumption that a methodology (in this case the methodology of comparative law) provides a researcher a clear set of guidelines (steps that need to be taken in a certain order) to reach a determined goal. This assumption also reflects the literal meaning of 'method': a word that derives from the Greek word *μεθοδος*, comprising *μεθ* ('along which') and *οδος* ('way, road'), meaning 'the way along which'—in other words, the way towards (a certain goal).[6] The methodological guidelines are discussed within a framework that is based on the rationale that each comparative legal research project goes through the same series of stages within which—depending on the specific context of the research—various methodological guidelines apply to answer issues that need to be dealt with within the indicated stages.[7]

After a description of this methodological framework (Section 2), this chapter sets out the various goals and types of comparative legal research (Section 3) and discusses in the subsequent section (Section 4) step by step the methodological issues that have to be dealt with in the subsequent stages of a comparative research project. With regard to each methodological question context-related guidelines are provided on how to come to a scientifically sound and well justified answer. The chapter ends with a brief conclusion (Section 5).

---

3 The Commission on European Family Law (CEFL) was established by an international group of scholars in 2001. See Section 3 (and footnote 20) below. Recently also another academic network of European family lawyers has been founded that uses as its main methodology comparative legal research: FL-EUR, see https://fl-eur.eu/

4 This group is working on the 'Common Core Project'. See Section 3 and Section 4.a.2 (footnote 44), below.

5 See e.g. J. M. L. van Duin, 'Justice for Both Effective Judicial Protection Under Article 47 of the EU Charter of Fundamental Rights and the Unfair Contract Terms' (doctoral thesis, University of Amsterdam, 2020); O. Bueno Diaz, *Franchising in European Contract Law: A Comparison between the Main Obligations of the Contracting Parties in the Principles of European Law on Commercial Agency, Franchise and Distribution Contracts (PEL CAFDC), French and Spanish Law* (Munich: Sellier European Law Publishers, 2008).

6 J. Husa, *Introduction to Comparative Law*, 2nd edn (London: Hart 2023), p. 102.

7 In my view 'methodological pluralism' that is often considered as problematic in the literature on comparative legal research should be understood in this way: all comparative legal research projects go to the same stages but depending on the context of the research (which is mainly determined by the aim and topic of the project) within these stages different methods and techniques might apply. See M. Oderkerk, 'The Need for a Methodological Framework'.

2. A Methodological Framework for Comparative Legal Research

Although anybody with research experience—whether on a large or small scale in any field of (legal) science—knows that it is far from a linear process,[8] they will at the same time have felt the necessity of understanding which actions and decisions must be taken, and in what order, to achieve a specific scientific goal. Comparative legal researchers form no exceptions to this rule. It is mainly for this reason that in this chapter, first one overarching 'method' or 'framework' will be described in the sense of a series of steps or stages. Just as in other comparative fields of study, such as comparative linguistics, comparative literature, or comparative politics, this series of steps or stages follows logically from the fact that the researcher intends to make a comparison. In order to be able to compare one needs to *describe* the objects of comparison. To know which objects are to be described one needs first to establish the aim of the project and the selection method chosen for the objects of comparison. After an indication of the similarities and differences between the objects (i.e. the comparison), one has—since we assume the research project has a scientific character—to explain these differences and similarities. If the aim of the project is law reform one should consider a subsequent stage in which to evaluate the various solutions the objects produce, according to certain specific evaluation criteria. The stages that can thus be indicated are: the preliminary or preparatory stage, the stage of description, the stage of comparison, and the stage of explanation (and if necessary and depending on the goal of the research project, a stage of evaluation).

Consensus on this overarching method or framework of comparative legal research is apparent as several authors have indicated these stages, with only minor differences over the years.[9] Furthermore, the existence of this series of subsequent stages has

---

8 Husa, Introduction to Comparative Law, p. 100.

9 L.-J. Constantinesco, *Rechtsvergleichung: Die rechtsvergleichende Methode*, II (Cologne: Heymanns, 1972), p. 137: 'Der Prozeβ der Vergleichung durchläuft mehrere Phasen, die sich voneinander unterscheiden. [...] Die rechtsvergleichende Methode besteht darin, eine Vergleichende Untersuchung durch drei aufeinanderfolgende Stadien hindurch zu führen, nämlich: feststellen, verstehen, vergleichen.'; W. J. Kamba, 'Comparative Law: A Theoretical Framework', *International and Comparative Law Quarterly* 23 (1974), 485–519 (pp. 511–512): 'There are, [...], three main operations or stages involved in comparative law. The first may be called the *descriptive phase*. [...]. The second stage may, for convenience, be described as the *identification phase* and is concerned with the identification or discernment of differences and similarities between the systems under comparative consideration. The third stage is the *explanatory phase* under which the divergences and resemblances are accounted for'; K. Zweigert and H. Kötz, *An Introduction to Comparative Law*, trans. by T. Weir, 3rd edn (Oxford: Oxford University Press, 1998), p. 42; D. Kokkini-Iatridou et al., *Een inleiding tot het rechtsvergelijkende onderzoek* (Alphen aan den Rijn: Kluwer, 1988), p. 145. See also D. Kokkini-Iatridou, 'Some Methodological Aspects of Comparative Law: The Third Part of a (Pre-)paradigm', *Netherlands International Law Review* 33 (1986), 143–194 (pp. 179–181); E. Örücü, 'Methodology of Comparative Law', in J. M. Smits (ed.), *Elgar Encyclopedia of Comparative Law* (Cheltenham: Edward Elgar Publishing, 2006), p. 447: 'As a blueprint, it can be suggested that the following steps be followed in most comparative law research. Having decided on the scope of the comparison, the first step is the choosing of the concepts and identifying them. [...] Logically, conceptualization precedes description and comparison, identification, explanation, measurement and confirmation (theorizing or theory testing), which are the other steps in a simple process of comparison'; P. de Cruz, *Comparative Law in a Changing World*, 3rd edn (Abingdon: Routledge-Cavendish, 2007), pp. 240–248; M. M. Siems, *Comparative Law*, 3rd edn (Cambridge, UK: Cambridge University Press, 2022), pp. 15–28.

not been contested. The importance of the recognition of this series of stages as the overarching framework for comparative legal research cannot be overestimated. The framework is valid for comparative legal research in every field of law and for many different purposes. In other words, this framework does not vary according to the context of the research and thus has a monistic character.[10]

The methodological framework can be laid down in a simple timeline as follows:

> *Preparation—description—comparison—explanation—[evaluation: if the research has a normative aim]*

It must be stressed that in most cases this framework coincides with the framework for a research plan for the whole research project. In some cases, however, only a section or sections of the research project will consist of comparative research; e.g. in research projects in which an evaluation criterion is needed to test various normative arrangements, one may need first to establish the criterion by comparing several legal systems. In these cases the only comparative part is the section in which the criterion is established. In these and similar cases, the framework obviously only applies to the comparative part(s) of the project. Similarly, the goal of the project coincides only with the goal of the comparison if the project is entirely comparative. In other cases the goal of the comparison has to be determined for each comparative part of the research.

It is also important to realise that the sequence of the stages is indicative; in practice the findings in the descriptive stage will usually lead to adjustments to the decisions in the preparatory stage and, for example, the findings in the explanatory phase can lead to the fine-tuning of, or even adjustments to, the aim of the project.[11] This does not engender methodological problems as long as the researcher assiduously ensures that the choices made in all other parts of the project remain consistent.

The following sections will be dedicated to a discussion of the methodological choices that should be taken at various stages of the research.

Before entering into this discussion, a short paragraph will be dedicated to the determination of the goal of the comparative legal research project. The determination of the goal of the comparative project is not part of the framework. Nevertheless, and perhaps more importantly, the goal of a project (together with and as implemented by the research question) forms the basis of and gives direction to any project: all methodological choices—as will be shown in the following sections—are partly or completely determined by the goal of the comparison.[12]

---

10 See also Kokkini-Iatridou, 'Some Methodological Aspects of Comparative Law', pp. 143, 156.

11 See also Kamba, 'Comparative Law: A Theoretical Framework', p. 511: 'These phases are not always distinctly separated from each other, nor are they always dealt with in a particular order. They may all be intermingled in the same discussion'. Differently: Constantinesco, *Rechtsvergleichung: Die rechtsvergleichende Methode*, p. 138: 'Diese drei Phasen müssen in der angegebenen Reihenfolge durchlaufen werden. Jede stellt die notwendige Vorbereitung und die Vorstufe für die nächste Phase dar'.

12 This fact has been stressed before by many other authors: see e.g. Husa, *Introduction to Comparative Law*, p. 101: 'The choices made depend on the aims of comparison as well as on the comparatist's own knowledge interests, i.e. there is no one-size-fits-all method.'; V. V. Palmer, 'From Lerotholi to Lando:

3. Goals of Comparative Legal Research

No single universally accepted, unequivocal, homogeneous set of goals of comparative legal research has been identified by the literature on comparative law.[13] In my opinion, this fact[14] forms one of the explanatory factors for the lack of a sophisticated and/or elaborated comparative legal research methodology.[15] As stated above: the goal of a project forms the basis of and gives direction to any project.

In my view, it should be stressed that, as in legal research generally, two main types of goals can be distinguished in comparative legal research: normative and non-normative.[16] Within both categories, two subtypes can be distinguished.[17] Normative research refers to research projects with an evaluative and/or regulatory aim. All projects that aim, for example, to reform the law have both an evaluative or regulatory aim, or both. All projects that aim, for example, to reform the law have both an evaluative and regulatory aim. Researchers aim to find a better set of solutions to a certain legal or social problem in the selected legal systems. Along with indicating which solution is considered best, the researcher will indicate the form in which the solution should be adopted by the system that needs legal reform. Projects that aim to unify or harmonise the law do not always aim to identify the best rule.[18] However, although one could think of projects aiming at formulating a unified set of rules based only on the common core of the systems involved, in practice unification projects often

---

Some Examples of Comparative Law Methodology', *American Journal of Comparative Law* 53.1 (2005), 261–290; and M. Adams and J. Griffiths, 'Against 'Comparative Method': Explaining Similarities and Differences', in M. Adams and J. Bomhoff (eds), *Practice and Theory in Comparative Law* (Cambridge, UK: Cambridge University Press, 2012), pp. 279–301 (p. 279). See also K. Zweigert and H.-J. Puttfarken, 'Zur Vergleichbarkeit analoger Rechtsinstitute in verschiedenen Gesellschaftsordnungen', in K. Zweigert and H.-J. Puttfarken (eds), *Rechtsvergleichung* (Darmstadt: Wissenschaftliche Buchgesellschaft, 1978), pp. 395–429.

13 See also M. Reimann, 'The Progress and Failure of Comparative Law in the Second Half of the Twentieth Century', *American Journal of Comparative Law* 50 (2002), 671–700 (pp. 697–698): 'Once a basic canon is established, comparatists should seek to clarify, and agree about, their discipline's overall goals. [...] Currently, comparatists have come to no meaningful agreement about their ultimate intellectual goals. It is true that there are standard lists of the discipline's practical uses and educational benefits and I do not mean to belittle their importance, but they are not enough'.

14 In 2004 C. Valcke, 'Comparative Law as Comparative Jurisprudence: The Comparability of Legal Systems', *American Journal of Comparative Law* 52 (2004), 713–740, indicates as examples of scholars who have proposed an elaborate typology of various uses of comparative law: Frankenberg (1985), Bogdan (1994), Stone (1951), Bermann (1999), Kötz (1999), and Gerber (1998). However, none of these authors has come up with a set of goals that has been generally accepted and/or has been combined with a specific methodology.

15 This thesis is discussed and defended in my article 'The Need for a Methodological Framework'.

16 See also Zweigert and Puttfarken, 'Zur Vergleichbarkeit analoger Rechtsinstitute', p. 395 .

17 In practice, two or more aims may be combined in research projects. One can imagine a project that aims both to explain and to evaluate. In these cases the researcher needs to confirm that all methodological choices are sound in relation to both aims.

18 The European Commission does frequently stress that the aim of a certain harmonisation or unification project is to find 'best solutions'. See e.g. Commission Communication, 'A More Coherent European Contract Law', COM (2003) 63/16 final, https://eur-lex.europa.eu/LexUriServ/LexUriServ.do?uri=COM:2003:0068:FIN:EN:PDF, section 68. However in practice what is considered 'best' is often determined by the criterion of political acceptability.

aim to find the best rule which will be acceptable to all systems included. See, for example, the comparative research project of the Commission on European Contract Law (the Lando Commission) which drafted the Principles of European Contract Law (PECL) presented in 1999,[19] or the project of the Commission on European Family Law (CEFL), established by an international group of scholars in 2001.[20] If we consider multilateral treaties on global or regional issues as unification projects as well, a similar mechanism can be noted. For example, two major climate Treaties—the 1992 Framework on Climate Change and the 1997 Kyoto Protocol—were based on comparative legal research between national and international systems of law and resulted in borrowing two fundamental regulatory precepts from national law: integration and incentives.[21]

The two non-normative aims to be distinguished are: to describe and to explore.[22] The 'Common Core Project', also known as the 'Trento Project', has explicitly adopted a non-normative aim, much like the project that, in various ways, inspired it: the 'Cornell Project' by Rudolph Schlesinger, carried out in the 1960s.[23] Since its inception in 1999, the Common Core group has deliberately refrained from making normative comments by taking a neutral approach that focuses on the 'is' rather than on the 'ought', while, at the same time, devoting itself to the production of reliable information.[24] Explanatory projects seem to be rarer,[25] although an augmentation of

19 See M. W. Hesselink, 'The Principles of European Contract Law: Some Choices Made by the Lando Commission', in M. W. Hesselink and G. J. P. de Vries (eds), *Principles of European Contract Law; Preadviezen uitgebracht voor de Vereniging voor Burgerlijk Recht* (Deventer: Kluwer, 2001), pp. 5–95.

20 See K. Boele-Woelki, 'The Principles of European Family Law: Its Aims and Prospects', *Utrecht Law Review* 1.2 (2005), 160–168.

21 J. B. Wiener, 'Something Borrowed for Something Blue: Legal Transplants and the Evolution of Global Environmental Law', *Ecology Law Quarterly* 27.4 (2001), 1295–1372.

22 Zweigert and Kötz seem to identify only normative aims for comparative legal research. According to Podgorecki, they 'not only see the role of law too narrowly, but also are unable to reject the "normative glasses" which are typically worn by those who only apply the law. They state, "While sociology of law goes in for field studies and empirical observation of how things actually are, comparative law, though it has many different aims, is basically concerned with the question of how the law ought to be"' (Zweigert and Kötz, *Introduction to Comparative Law*, pp. 9–10); A. Podgorecki, 'Social Systems and Legal Systems—Criteria for classification', in A. Podgorecki et al. (eds), *Legal Systems and Social Systems* (London: Chroom Helm, 1985), pp. 1–24.

23 R. Schlesinger et al., *Formation of Contract—A Study of the Common Core of Legal Systems*, II (Washington, DC: Oceana Publications, 1968). See for a discussion of the methodology of the project also: R. Schlesinger, 'The Common Core of Legal Systems, An Emerging Subject of Comparative Study', in K. H. Nadelmann, A. T. von Mehren, and J. NN Hazard (eds), *XXth Century Comparative and Conflicts Law* (Leyden: Sythoff, 1961), pp. 65–79. See on this and other 'Common Core Projects': M. E. Storme, 'Common Core Projects', in J. M. Smits et al. (eds), *Elgar Encyclopedia of Comparative Law*, 3rd edn (Cheltenham: Edward Elgar Publishing, 2023), pp. 306–317.

24 M. Bussani and U. Mattei, 'Preface: The Context', in M. Bussani and U. Mattei (eds), *The Common Core of European Private Law: Essays on the Project* (Alphen aan den Rijn: Kluwer Law International, 2002), pp. 1–8 (pp. 1, 4).

25 John Henry Merryman was a relatively early proponent of explanatory projects. In his view, the most important goal of comparative legal research is 'explanation'. His understanding of the term explanation infers the making or testing of one or more general hypotheses that include an explanation, by empirical data (see J. H. Merryman, 'Comparative Law and Scientific Explanation', in J. N. Hazard and W. J. Wagner (eds), *Law in the United States of America in Social and Technological Revolution* (Brussels: Bruylant, 1974), pp. 81–104).

these types of projects is likely to take place in the coming years as projects carried out by an interdisciplinary research group often provide the most interesting scientific results.[26] Frequently these groups (often consisting of sociologists, legal scholars, and specialists in the (societal) topic at hand) are interested in answering 'why-questions' and are qualified to do so. Interesting examples are provided by a project by John Griffiths, Heleen Weyers, and Maurice Adams on *Euthanasia and Law in Europe*[27] and Richard Hyland's impressive book, *Gifts*.[28]

4. Methods and Techniques of Comparative Legal Research

In this section the methodological issues that have to be dealt with in the subsequent stages within a comparative research project will be discussed step by step following the basic stages of this type of research. As indicated above, the following sub-sections aim to provide with regard to each methodological question context-related guidelines on how to come to a scientifically sound and well justified answer.

a. Methods and Techniques in the Preparatory Stage

In the preparatory stage of a comparative research project, after it has been established that the comparative method is the correct tool—or at least one of the correct tools—for the research project, its goal and relevance will be made explicit and the topic, the research question (and its limitations), the systems to be included, and the way to identify the objects to be compared will have to be determined. In other words when the topic and research question have been formulated and if it has been determined that it will be fruitful or even necessary to apply the comparative method to the whole project or parts of the project, the first questions that need to be answered are: which legal systems will be included in the project (Section 4.a.1) and how will the objects for comparison be selected in such a way that a comparison of apples and oranges is prevented (Section 4.a.2)? Having found the provisional answers to the questions above, the researcher needs to determine the sources to include in the research (Section 4.a.3).

If the goal of the comparative research requires a stage of evaluation (i.e. if the aim of the research is normative) it will also be useful to determine the evaluation criteria in the preparatory stage (see Section 4.c).

---

26 In 1999 H. Kötz, 'Comparative Law in Germany Today', *Revue internationale de droit comparé* 51.4 (1999), 753–758 (p. 757) wrote: 'If one wants to remain realistic it must be said that while interdisciplinarity has come to be accepted increasingly by comparative lawyers as an indispensable tool of meaningful comparative legal research, performance has been lagging'.

27 J. Griffiths, H. Weyers, and M. Adams, *Euthanasia and Law in Europe* (London: Hart Publishing, 2008).

28 R. Hyland, *Gifts, A Study in Comparative Law* (Oxford: Oxford University Press, 2009).

1) The Selection of Legal Systems[29]

Both the question of the selection of the systems for inclusion in the comparison and the question of how to select the objects to be compared are the most frequently discussed methodological issues within the field of comparative legal research. The issue of the selection of legal systems is also one of the issues that is most addressed and recognised as problematic in practice.

Before discussing the guidelines which apply here, it is necessary first to address two different issues, both of which are related to the selection of legal systems and influence (in a subtle, yet undoubtedly important, way) the methodological thinking concerning the selection of legal systems: the notion of the 'legal system' itself and the issue of 'the comparability of legal systems'.

First, in the context of comparative law, the notion of a 'legal system' has traditionally been used—and is often still used—only in the sense of a legal system of a nation state.[30] It is, however, my contention that there are no methodological or logical obstacles to the inclusion, in a conception of a 'legal system', of transnational, supranational, and international legal systems. Comparative legal research projects are and have been conducted which include national, transnational, supranational or international legal systems (or a combination of these). Nevertheless, public international law scholars in particular seem to consider these sorts of projects as methodologically flawed or consider them not to belong to the field of 'comparative law'.[31] However, there are signs nowadays that this view has changed, even among public international law scholars.[32]

Related to this issue is the question: what is a 'legal' system? Since this topic is also intimately linked to the further issue of which sources should be included within the scope of the research, they will be considered together in the discussion relating to the latter issue.

Secondly, the issue of 'the comparability of legal systems' suggests that only a

---

29 This paragraph is partially based on my 2001 article on the selection of legal systems: M. Oderkerk, 'The Importance of Context: Selecting Legal Systems in Comparative Legal Research', *Netherlands International Law Review* 48 (2001), 293–318.

30 Zweigert and Kötz, *An Introduction to Comparative Law*, p. 2: 'Thus 'comparative law' is the comparison of the different legal systems of the world'; and at p. 4: 'Comparative lawyers compare the legal systems of different nations'.

31 Wiener was probably one of the first authors who noted that in practice comparative legal research is being done in the field of public international law but not recognised as such (Wiener, 'Something Borrowed for Something Blue', pp. 1301–1302). See for a concise overview of Comparative International Law: W. E. Butler, 'Comparative International Law', in J. M. Smits et al. (eds), *Elgar Encyclopedia of Comparative Law*, 3rd edn (Cheltenham: Edward Elgar Publishing, 2023), pp. 326–327. See also, and for further references: A. Momirov and A. Naudé Fourie, 'Vertical Comparative Law Methods: Tools for Conceptualising the International Rule of Law', *Erasmus Law Review* 2 (2009), 291–309.

32 Momirov and Naudé Fourie hold the view that comparative methodology as developed mainly by private law lawyers can be applied to comparative research in the field of public international law, and attempt to prove it by elaborating on the methodology they use in their own comparative legal research projects on the international rule of law: Momirov and Naudé Fourie 'Vertical Comparative Law Methods'. See for a recent broad view on legal systems, Husa in his *Introduction to Comparative Law*, p. 115. Indicative for his broad view is his use of the expression: 'large-scale organized normativity' as a synonym for legal system within the context of comparative legal research.

number of pre-selected legal systems should be eligible for inclusion in a particular comparative legal research project. Although this idea was rejected long ago[33] and most authors who write about the selection of legal systems explicitly state that all systems are eligible for selection, from time to time we still find echoes of the idea that only 'comparable' legal systems should be included in a comparative legal research project. Although one might think that both approaches (i.e. all systems are eligible for selection *or* only certain systems are eligible for selection) ultimately produce the same results in practice, it is important from a methodological point of view to avoid the comparability issue in this context. The main reason is that in order to have a sound justification for the selected legal systems one must clarify that in principle all systems are available for selection, but that the aim and topic of the research project (often combined in the research question), together with any practical reasons related to the context of the research, make a selection necessary.

It is important to stress that some authors refer to 'comparability of legal systems' in a different context. When Catherine Valcke focused on the issue of the comparability of legal systems in 2004, she discussed the necessity for comparative lawyers to determine what should be considered as law, and indicated that it is important to reject concepts of the law that would virtually block the possibility of conducting comparative legal research.[34]

The question of selecting legal systems is compared to other methodological questions, such as how to determine which objects should be compared in the selected legal systems, undoubtedly the least controversial. The guidelines offered in the literature are essentially similar and do not contradict each other.[35] We see that most guidelines refer to the topic or objective of the research project (or both), and to the personal abilities of the researcher or to the division of legal systems into legal families (or both).

On the other hand, only a few authors provide a systematic method and, even so, none of these methods has been indicated as the correct method to follow. At this juncture, I present some guidelines as an example of how guidelines for specific methodological choices can be developed within a methodological framework. These guidelines will take into account the majority of different types of comparative legal research projects and are the result of a confrontation between guidelines as presented in theory and as applied in practice. I do not suggest, however, that this will provide an exhaustive list of correct guidelines. My goal is to illustrate that it is possible to create a set of more detailed guidelines that refers to and is related to the characteristics of

33 See e.g. Kötz 'Comparative Law in Germany Today', p. 758.

34 Valcke convincingly defended the view that comparative legal research is only possible when one accepts a concept of law as jurisprudence (Valcke, 'Comparative Law as Comparative Jurisprudence', p. 731. See on this topic from a critical perspective: G. Samuel, 'The Epistemological Challenge: Does Law Exist?', in S. Glanert, A. Mercescu, and G. Samuel (eds), *Rethinking Comparative Law* (Cheltenham: Edward Elgar Publishing, 2021), pp. 1–30.

35 See however the interesting article by R. Hirschl, 'The Question of Case Selection in Comparative Constitutional Law', *American Journal of Comparative Law* 53 (2005), 125–155, which applies the social science case selection method to constitutional law.

different research projects. To be able to do so, one should first determine which factors vary between comparative legal research projects, the combination of which ensures that every research project is unique. The factors that can be distinguished are (1) the topic of the research project; (2) the experience and knowledge of the researcher(s); (3) whether the researcher works alone, in a group, or is part of an (official) body or commission; (4) the time available; and (5) the aim(s) of the research project. I will refer to this combination of variable factors as the 'context of a comparative legal research project'. A well-founded selection of legal systems should, in my opinion, refer to this context and be consistent. However, it is important to emphasise that not every factor has the same weight: a certain hierarchy should be acknowledged.

When selecting legal systems, the most important contextual factors are the topic and aim(s) of the comparative legal study. Arguments that refer to these factors produce the most objective and, therefore, most well-founded justification(s) for the selection. For a cogent selection of legal systems for a research project conducted by a French Ph.D. student in legal history on the freedom of speech, for example, the goal of the project must first be determined. The purpose can be characterised as descriptive if the main goal is to assess the influence of ideology on the development of the function and functioning of the freedom of speech rule. The combination of purpose and topic will determine the selection. Since a descriptive goal does not place any restriction on the choice of legal systems, the selection must be useful from the point of view of the topic.

Thus, if a comparative legal research project has a descriptive or explanatory objective (a non-normative objective), one should include systems in which one expects to find objects that relate to the topic of the study (*guideline 1*). For example, in a comparative research project on refugee law carried out for purely descriptive or explanatory reasons, one could include any system on the condition that the chosen systems deal with refugees in a relevant legal context.

If the ultimate objective of a comparative legal research project is evaluative or regulatory (or both), one should include in the selection the system which will be evaluated (and, if necessary that for which the new regulation is meant), together with at least one system that can function as a source of other, possible solutions (*guideline 2*). A system can function as a source for other solutions if two conditions are met. First, the topic under analysis must (in all likelihood) have reached a higher level of development in the system.[36] Secondly, in the selected systems the topic under analysis should not be integrated into a completely different legal, social, political or economic

36 This can be the case, on the one hand, if a certain legal institution has existed for a long time and has been kept up to date by—if necessary—frequent law reforms by the legislature or the judiciary, as is the case in the USA in the field of constitutional review. On the other hand, for certain particularly 'modern' topics such as cybercrime (for which there is no legal system with a long tradition), one could include all systems having pertinent legislation. In that case, probably all of these type of systems can inform on some level, but if there are too many one could think of selecting those that already have some experience with and/or a substantial literature on the topic, or those that have an extremely different regulation.

structure.[37] When a comparative research project focuses on the grievance procedures in large companies and the objective of the research is to improve the grievance procedures in Dutch company law, the selection of American law is unhelpful, as the American and Dutch grievance procedures are embedded in different social and legal structures, and fulfill different functions. American grievance procedures fulfill functions that cannot be 'transplanted' into the Dutch procedures because they are already fulfilled by other Dutch legal institutions. In this context, the Dutch and American grievance procedures lack an essential common feature.[38]

If the objective of a comparative legal research project is to harmonise or unify the legislation of several states or nations, and the comparatist is looking for the common core of the regulation of the topic under analysis (a compromise), the selection of legal systems is relatively easy: one should include all systems whose regulations one is seeking to harmonise or unify (*guideline* 3). However, should these criteria change if the systems to be harmonised are those of the European Union or of the United States, and the research has to be carried out by one or two researchers within two years? If one applied the above-mentioned guideline, one would have to study all twenty-seven Member States of the European Union or the fifty States of the United States of America (fifty-one legal systems if you include the federal legal system). Such statistics are bound to have a negative effect on the feasibility of research carried out by individual comparatists. Unfortunately, if the objective of the research is to identify the common core of the systems, these difficulties are unavoidable. Perhaps in a very small number of cases—depending on the topic of the research—one could select representatives of legal families (in the case of the European Union research) or representatives of *Lösungstypen*. This could only be completed after a preliminary enquiry that has led to the conclusion that the affiliated legal systems do not significantly differ from their mother legal system. Clearly, in most cases only a group of researchers would be able to execute this type of research.

If, on the other hand, the objective of a comparative legal research project is similar to the above-mentioned objective of harmonising or unifying the legislation of several states or nations (that is, one is not looking for the common core, but instead for the best possible regulation) one should include the systems for which the new legislation is intended and—if necessary—include systems that can teach us something (*guideline* 4). The first requirement (i.e. to include the system(s) for which the new legislation is meant) is less of a burden if one is looking for the best possible solution rather than searching for the common core of the systems to be unified or

37 The reason for excluding systems in which this is the case is that it is not reasonable to expect that 'a transplant' of an attractive regulation from this system to the system seeking reform will function well. This exclusion of this system could furthermore be justified by referring to the non-comparability of the topics in the two systems: the lack of a *tertium comparationis*. On *tertium comparationis* see Section 4.b.2 below.

38 This does not mean that this kind of research is completely useless: the study of the American grievance procedures could inspire the Dutch comparatist to suggest certain improvements of the Dutch regulations.

harmonised, because in this context one is not looking for a compromise, nor does one necessarily need to distinguish between the similarities and differences of each of the systems to be harmonised or unified. The second requirement (i.e. to include systems that can teach us something) was previously mentioned under *guideline 2*. This seems obvious, yet it is often overlooked. Take the example of a comparative legal research project dedicated to the regulation of a certain aspect of the legal systems of the European Union: if one aims to uncover the best possible regulation, one often selects only Member States. Furthermore, if these Member States have legal systems that have developed more favorable regulations regarding the topic under analysis, one can of course limit the selection to these systems. However, if there are non-EU systems that can meaningfully contribute to the discussion, they should be included as well.

The following guideline on comparative legal research in the context of public international law speaks for itself: if the objective of a comparative legal research project is to draft a treaty, one should include existing treaties on similar subjects. If the objective is to draft a treaty establishing an international organisation, one should study the founding treaties, the legal systems, and the legal practice of international organisations with similar purposes (*guideline 5*).[39]

The following guideline can be formulated for comparative legal research in the context of supranational law: if the objective of a comparative legal research project is to improve an existing supranational regulation, one should include this regulation and systems that provide relevant information (*guideline 6*). This means guideline 2 would apply also in this context. What justifies the reiteration of this rule for research aimed at improving existing legislation on a supranational level? The justification lies in the need to be aware that the systems to be included in the comparison should be relevant from the perspective of the supranational system under analysis. This seems clear, yet it can hardly be denied that comparatists are inclined to choose systems that are relevant from the point of view of their own national legal system in this context and not, as they should be, from the perspective of the supranational system that needs to be improved. For example, if the topic of a comparative legal research project is of a cross-border nature, such as a study on the rules on reporting environmental consequences, and the objective of the project is to improve an EU directive in this field, a French scholar should not only select German, Belgian, Italian, Spanish, and Portuguese law 'because these systems are of importance in France in the context of concrete reports on environmental consequences'. In this particular case, one should select systems that are geared to the topic, not simply the laws found in neighboring countries.

39 See G. A. Bermann, 'Comparative Law and International Organizations', in M. Bussani and U. Mattei (eds), *Comparative Law* (Cambridge, UK: Cambridge University Press, 2012), pp. 241–254 (pp. 242–243, 247). See also P. van Dijk, 'De rechtsvergelijking en het recht der internationale organisaties; enige methodologische notities', in R. Barents (ed.), *Orde: Liber Amicorum Pieter VerLoren van Themaat* (Alphen aan den Rijn: Kluwer 1982), pp. 77–98 (p. 82).

If compliance with the above-mentioned guidelines results in an excessive number of legal systems, one can make use of the notion of *Lösungstypen* or, in some cases, that of 'representative legal systems'. Personal reasons can only be advanced for the final selection (*guideline 7*). Compliance with guidelines 1–6 will often result in an exceedingly large number of legal systems. Whether the number of legal systems that can objectively be included in the research is too large depends on several factors, such as the scholar's legal or linguistic knowledge and experience. More importantly, the circumstances under which the research is to be carried out (such as the available time, the number of researchers and facilities for gathering materials) are relevant. In most cases, though, it will be necessary to restrict the selection of eligible systems.

One way to reduce the number of systems is the use of the notion of *Lösungstypen,* introduced by Ulrich Drobnig in 1969.[40] Drobnig takes the view that for each legal problem a few clearly different solutions are conceivable. Before a selection can be made, one has to determine which system represents which *Lösungstyp*. The research can then be confined to the analysis and comparison of these representative systems. This approach is attractive as the subject can be represented in a well-organised and insightful manner, and is applicable to every field of the law. The only, albeit significant, drawback to this method is that extensive preliminary research is necessary to establish which systems represent the possible *Lösungstypen*. This is an unavoidable problem arising in respect of all guidelines for whose application knowledge with regard to the way in which a system has solved a legal problem is necessary. Experienced legal comparative scholars' opinions and reference books such as the *International Encyclopedia of Comparative Law* can be of assistance in such instances.

A second way to reduce the number of systems included in a research study is the use of the notion of 'parent legal systems' or 'representative legal systems' in combination with the division of legal systems into legal families. This approach has its limits: one can use this notion only in comparative legal research projects with objectives that are non-normative. The disadvantage of this method is that representative or parent systems may have been overshadowed in the course of time by one or more 'affiliated systems' in the field of the topic of research. Research projects aimed at law reform (projects with normative aims) cannot afford to ignore these further-developed affiliated systems.

Personal reasons, such as the researcher's knowledge of languages, should, because of their subjective character, only be a factor in the final selection.

Because of the many factors that bring about the great variety among comparative legal research projects, it is not possible to advance a blueprint or detailed method for selecting legal systems to be included in each individual project. As has been shown above, however, it is possible to lay down guidelines that refer (in a more detailed way than those that can be found in the literature) to the different possible contexts which determine the character

40 U. Drobnig, 'Methodenfragen der Rechtsvergleichung im Lichte der "International Encyclopedia of Comparative Law"', in E. Von Caemmerer, S. Mentschikoff, and K. Zweigert (eds), *Ius privatum gentium* (Tubingen: Mohr, 1969), pp. 221–223.

of a particular comparative legal research project. It is hoped that these guidelines will not only help comparatists to make a sound selection, but also provide some indication on how to justify their selection. Naturally, 'sound judgment, common sense or even intuition',[41] are all highly useful, but these are not the only tools available. Guidelines based on the experience and sound judgment of others can shield scholars from inefficiency and error.

2) The Method for Determining the Objects to be compared[42]

Research reports rarely explicitly and thoroughly discuss the selection of the method to determine the objects to be compared,[43] although an exception must be made with respect to some large academic projects such as the 'Common Core Project' also known as the 'Trento Project'[44] and the project on European family law.[45] In comparative legal research methodology on the other hand, the issue of method selection is frequently discussed and is predominantly known as the method concerning the issue of comparability or commensurability. In effect, this issue is often discussed as being the *only* issue of comparative legal methodology. In these cases, when referring to the method of comparative legal research, one is actually referring to the method to determine the objects to be compared.[46]

In this section, I describe the issue of comparability and the methods for finding objects that can be usefully compared. My point of view takes into account the literature on this topic from the last century[47] onwards and (part of) the actual practice of comparative legal research. It is not my intention to present a thorough analysis of the various views concerning this issue.[48] In the context of this chapter, I only describe the content of several existing methods, how the right method should be selected and how it should be operationalized. In doing so, I will indicate any flaws that need further elaboration in comparative legal

41 Zweigert and Kötz, *An Introduction to Comparative Law*, p. 33

42 Parts of this section are based on section IV in M. Oderkerk, 'The CFR and the Method(s) of Comparative Legal Research', *European Review of Contract Law* 3 (2007), 326–331.

43 In the (few) cases in which a reference to the method used for the selection of the objects is made explicitly, the author usually restricts him- or herself to the remark that use of the 'functional method' has been made.

44 See the books in the series *The Common Core of European Private Law*: e.g. J. Cartwright and M. W. Hesselink (eds), *Precontractual Liability in European Private Law* (Cambridge, UK: Cambridge University Press, 2008).

45 See the books by the Commission of European Family Law (CEFL) in de series European Family Law. See also on the methodology used by the CEFL: Boele-Woelki, 'The Principles of European Family Law: Its Aims and Prospects', p. 160.

46 See also J. Husa, 'Farewell to Functionalism or Methodological Tolerance?', *RabelsZ* 67 (2003), 419–447; J. Husa, 'Functional Method in Comparative Law—Much Ado About Nothing?', *European Property Law Journal* 2.1 (2013), 4–21.

47 It is commonly agreed upon that Ernst Rabel was the first scholar to discuss the issue of comparability seriously (introducing the functional method).

48 On the functional method this has already been done by R. Michaels, 'The Functional Method of Comparative Law', in M. Reimann and R. Zimmermann (eds) *The Oxford Handbook of Comparative Law* (Oxford: Oxford University Press, 2019), pp. 339–382 (p. 345). See also among others Husa, *Introduction to Comparative Law*, pp. 122–132; D. J. Gerber, 'Sculpting the Agenda of Comparative Law: Ernst Rabel and the Façade of Language', in A. Riles (ed.), *Rethinking the Masters of Comparative Law* (Portland, OR: Hart, 2001), pp. 190–208.

methodology. I will also indicate how the answer to this methodological question is directly related to the goal and topic of the research and the selected legal systems.

Before describing the methods used to find the objects to be compared (that are recognized in both the literature and in practice), it is important to stress that it is impossible to discuss this issue of comparability from an abstract point of view. By its very nature 'comparability' is a concept that can only meaningfully be discussed in relation to the aim of the comparison. Two things are 'comparable' if it makes sense to compare them in light of the aim of the comparison. If the aim of the research project is to regulate a certain factual situation or societal phenomenon of a certain legal system, it is only useful to compare objects that fulfill an equivalent function (in this example the function being 'to regulate the societal phenomenon under consideration'). In other words, the objects to be compared in these contexts need to have at least a common function. The common element that the objects of comparison must share in order to make useful comparisons is referred to as *tertium comparationis*.[49] The *tertium comparationis* within these kinds of research projects is the 'function'. Methods that have been developed to find objects that share the same or similar function are called 'functional methods'. I will describe below three variants of the functional method that may be distinguished from one another. At this juncture, it is useful to point out that—although less discussed and recognized in legal literature—a valuable *tertium comparationis* in law is also considered to be 'form' or 'structure'. The method that aims at finding objects that have a similar 'form' or 'structure' has been called the 'dogmatic',[50] 'nominalistic',[51] or 'institutional method'[52] and is also used in practice, although it is not always explicitly labeled as such; these terms are undoubtedly used less frequently than the term 'functional method'.[53] There are also some authors who have pointed out that alongside the form and function, the 'effect' could also be considered a valid *tertium comparationis*.[54]

---

49 In this context the term *tertium comparationis* is often used. It is understood to mean: the common denominator, or the common propriety of the objects to be compared (*comparatum* and *comparandum*). See among others: V. Knapp, 'Quelques problèmes méthodologiques dans la science du droit comparé', in K. Zweigert and H.-J. Puttfarken (eds), *Rechtsvergleichung* (Darmstadt: Wissenschaftliche Buchgesellschaf, 1978), pp. 334–349; Husa, *Introduction to Comparative Law*, pp. 154–160; U. Kischel, 'Tertium comparationis', in J. M. Smits (ed.), *Elgar Encyclopedia of Comparative Law* (Cheltenham: Edward Elgar Publishing, 2006), pp. 484–491.

50 U. Drobnig, 'Möglichkeiten und Grenzen intersystemarer Rechtsvergleichung auf dem Gebiete des Zivilrechts', in G. Gutman and S. Mampel (eds), *Probleme systemvergleichender Betrachtung* (Berlin: Duncker Humblot, 1986), pp. 195–205 (p. 203): 'dogmatische Rechtsvergleichung'; M. Rheinstein, *Einführung in die Rechtsvergleichung*, ed. by R. von Borries, 2nd edn (Munich: Beck, 1987), pp. 32–33: 'dogmatische Betrachtung'.

51 M. Bogdan, *Concise Introduction to Comparative Law* (Zutphen: Europa Law Publishing, 2013), p. 47: 'nominalistic comparison'.

52 Constantinesco, *Rechtsvergleichung: Die rechtsvergleichende Methode*, p. 75 ('institutionelle Vergleichung').

53 D. J. Gerber, 'System Dynamics: Toward a Language of Comparative Law?', *American Journal of Comparative Law*, 46.4 (1998), 719–737 (p. 722): 'The function/context methodology initially developed by Ernst Rabel represents what can be considered the standard methodology, at least in Europe and the United States, [...]'.

54 Constantinesco, *Rechtsvergleichung: Die rechtsvergleichende Methode*, pp. 97–100; Kokkini-Iatridou,

It is paramount to stress that the choice for the *tertium comparationis* has not had, and should not have, anything to do with a 'traditional view' on methods or any personal preference of the researcher; the choice for the *tertium comparationis* should fit—or in more methodological terms—be consistent with the aim, topic and selected systems of the project. It does not make sense to label the group of researchers who have used the functional method in their comparative research as 'functionalists'. This term creates a wrong impression, that is that the choice of the functional method is based on a standing preference (personal or scientific, or both) and that the researcher will always, irrespective of the context of the research, use the functional method. Of course, the label 'functional' has been used to mark several kinds of research and methods, as Michaels' thorough research has proved,[55] but it should not be forgotten that in the context of the methods to be used to select the objects of comparison, there is, logically, no such group.

A first general guideline on how to select the right method to find the objects to be compared is to determine the aim and topic of the research project.

As was valid for the selection of legal systems, if the aim is descriptive there are no restrictions that follow: both form and function are valid *tertia comparationis*. If the aim of the comparison is to discover the influence ideology exerts on a certain legal rule, such as the right of freedom of expression, the selection of the *tertium comparationis* is only influenced by the topic: the object of comparison is this specific rule, and the researcher's aim is to determine the influence of ideology on the way it is interpreted. One must compare rules that have the same *form* to be able to perform this analysis and describe the results. The *tertium comparationis* is 'form', meaning that 'form' is the only element that necessarily must be similar. Other elements will be studied and will be part of the result of the comparison. Accordingly, if the *tertium comparationis* is 'form', this does not mean that the function will *not* be studied. On the contrary, it will be the more interesting aspect because it might differ. However, this has to do with the outcome of the comparison and is not related to the methodologically correct selection of the objects to be compared.

If the aim of the comparison is descriptive but the topic of the research is the regulation of a certain societal phenomenon, the *tertium comparationis* will not be form but *function* because the researcher will describe the (different or similar) regulation of a similar societal phenomenon in several legal systems. The researcher will thus describe those rules that deal with this situation. In this way, the *tertium comparationis* is not determined by the aim of the research: the researcher selects objects that have an identical function not because the aim of the project requires this but because the topic logically calls for objects that fulfill a similar function.

'Comparative Legal Research', p. 18; Kokkini-Iatridou, 'Some Methodological Aspects of Comparative Law', p. 159.

55 R. Michaels, 'The Functional Method of Comparative Law', p. 345. See also J. de Coninck, 'The Functional Method of Comparative Law: Quo Vadis?', *RabelsZ* 74 (2010), 318–350 and R. Michaels's response to this article: 'Explanation and Interpretation—A Response to Julie de Coninck', *RabelsZ* 74 (2010), 351–359.

If, on the other hand, the project has a normative (evaluative or regulatory) aim a functional method will have to be used. To be able to find a best solution or indicate a certain rule as the best, the researcher must have compared sets of rules that purport to fulfill an equivalent function.

In the legal literature and in practice one can identify three variants of the functional method. Their aim is the same, that is, to select objects that have a similar function. One can distinguish between the functional-institutional method,[56] the problem-solving approach, and the factual approach.[57] The difference between the problem-solving and factual approach, on the one hand, and the functional-institutional, on the other, is based on a difference in perspective or starting point. The former methods start from a specific problem or set of facts (case) and search for the solutions in the selected legal systems; the latter method starts from a legal institution or other part of the legal system (for example, a rule or principle) and searches for objects in the selected legal systems that fulfill an equivalent function.[58]

If one's topic is, for example, 'punitive damages' and one wishes to compare this legal institution with a functionally equivalent object in the French legal system, the functional-institutional method will be the most natural one. One starts by determining the function of 'punitive damages' (the punishment for and/or prevention of infringements of the law), and then one asks if the French legal system fulfills this function, if it does, how it does so (i.e. whether the private law of the French legal system contains elements, in whatever form, which aim to punish or to prevent future infringements of the law). If the answer is positive, it is then necessary to ask: how are these elements regulated?

One could, however, also come up with a set of facts (a hypothetical case). For example: a man purchases a hot water bottle for his baby, and the baby's nurse fills the bottle with hot water and places it next to the newborn. The hot water bottle leaks and the baby is burned severely and permanently disfigured. The parents initiate court proceedings against the seller and/or manufacturer seeking damages. How would this case be decided according to the law of the selected legal systems? This method is known as the factual approach[59] and has been used on a large scale by the Trento Group.

---

56 This term was introduced by Esin Örücü in 1988: A. E. Örücü, 'Theories and Presumptions of Comparability', in M. Aitkenhead (ed.), *Law and Lawyers in European Integration. A Comparative Analysis of the Education, Attitudes and Specialisation of Scottish and Dutch Lawyer* (Rotterdam: Erasmus Universiteit, 1988), pp. 20–39 (p. 25). In the same chapter she shows that the problem-solving approach and the functional-institutional method are only two exponents of the functional method: they are nothing more than 'two sides of the same coin', since the function of a legal institution (a rule or principle) is to solve a specific problem; see also E. Örücü, 'Methodology of Comparative Law', p. 43.

57 This method is well-known by Schlesinger's 'Cornell Project'. See Schlesinger, 'The Common Core of Legal Systems', and Schlesinger, *Formation of Contract.*

58 Gerber, 'System Dynamics: Toward a Language of Comparative Law?', p. 722: 'Originally designed to aid in the process of legal unification, this methodology basically asks how best to compare specific normative arrangements in one system with those in another. It directs the analyst to identify the social function of norms in order to provide a basis for making comparisons of specific normative arrangements'.

59 This method is well-known by Schlesinger's 'Cornell Project'. See Schlesinger, 'The Common Core of

What solutions are provided by the legal system to ensure (as far as possible) that consumers are protected from product flaws that may cause severe harm? If the research question is formulated in this way, one has translated the function of the legal institution into a societal problem, and the method used is called a problem-solving approach. It is also possible that the topic of the research project is a societal problem. One can think of the problem of the shortage of organ donors. In that case the problem-solving approach or factual approach are the obvious methods. The solutions that will be found will form the objects to compare (namely, the 'comparable objects') of the research project at hand. These will always be objects that are comparable at a functional level, because the function of the solutions is to solve the problem.

Importantly, the fact that these methods identify objects with a similar function does not mean that the objects are similar; they have a similar function and therefore can be compared in a constructive manner. However, it may well be possible that, ultimately, one reaches the conclusion that these two solutions with similar functions are actually quite different. It is, therefore, unfortunate that Konrad Zweigert and Hein Kötz introduced the concept of the *praesumptio similitudinis* within the context of the functional method.[60]

If one has used the functional method, one finds rules that may fulfill an equivalent function, although they will generally have a different form or structure. In other words, the way in which the function is fulfilled differs. What Zweigert probably meant—although it is necessary to read the texts he wrote on the *praesumptio similitudinis* for a certain perspective—is that this approach can be helpful as a tool as part of the functional method: Zweigert refers to it as a heuristic tool. If one starts a comparative legal research project with a certain topic in mind and this topic seems not to exist in one of the legal systems included in the comparative legal research project, one needs to check and rephrase the research question in functional terms because it is improbable that there is no institution, a set of legal rules or social rules, that fulfills a similar function in the selected legal systems. This may be helpful and indicative, but no more than that.

In the broad critical discussion of the functional method authors have further criticised the idea that the functional method is closely related to, or even the same as, the evaluation of the solutions found in the various legal systems.[61] At the present time,

---

Legal Systems', and Schlesinger, *Formation of Contract.*

60 The *praesumptio similitudinis*—the idea that with regard to classical private law issues one may expect to find similar solutions in all legal systems—was already introduced by Zweigert in 1960 in his 'Zur Methode der Rechtsvergleichung' (K. Zweigert, 'Zur Methode der Rechtsvergleichung', *Studium Generale* 13 (1960), 193–200 (p. 198), and was repeated in all editions of Zweigert and Kötz's *An Introduction to Comparative Law,* p. 40. This idea has been much criticised and has been linked to the best solutions issue. I agree with this criticism in relation to what this idea suggests (in the way it is described) since it is simply not true that even in 'classical private law' (meaning private law that is not heavily influenced by (moral) values)—apart from the question whether this kind of private law actually exists, one finds 'similar' solutions.

61 For an overview of the critique on the functional method see A. Peters and H. Schwenke, 'Comparative Law Beyond Post-Modernism', *International and Comparative Law Quarterly* 49.4 (2000), 800–834 (p. 801); and Husa, 'Farewell to Functionalism', p. 419.

most authors recognise that there is a clear distinction between the stage of evaluation of a comparative research project on the one hand (which is overtly and necessarily normative, see Section 4.c below), and the descriptive and comparative stage, on the other hand, both of which can be described as normatively neutral. Some authors, however, do point out that the selection and/or description of the *tertium comparationis* (social problem, factual situation or function) is also a non-neutral process (steered by the consciously or unconsciously known evaluation criteria).[62] How this process works in practice and why it should be considered to be unproblematic, as is stated in the literature,[63] (with the exception that the conduct of research always requires selection, and selection is always subjective) has not been clarified.

3) The Method for Determining the Sources to Include in the Research Project

Rodolfo Sacco, and later Stefan Vogenauer, have dealt most thoroughly with the methodological issue of what are, or should be, the sources of law to be included in the comparative legal research project.[64] Others have implicitly considered this issue by pointing out that the law is inextricably linked to its social context, which leads to the need to include all societal elements in which the legal rules included in the study are embedded. Some scholars have referred to this fact as one of the 'pitfalls'[65] or 'weaknesses of comparative law'[66] implying that legal comparatists are generally not adequately equipped to properly deal with this issue. Pierre Legrand seems to have drawn the conclusion that comparative legal research is basically impossible, primarily on the basis that it is fundamentally not possible to understand the law of other legal systems.[67]

Only a select number of authors ask where the line should be drawn between law and non-law, and what should be considered as law, and the sources of law in the field of comparative law.[68] According to some authors 'extra-legal rules' do belong to the objects of study of comparative legal research.[69] It is even stated that if one does

62 N. Jansen, 'Comparative Law and Comparative Knowledge', in M. Reimann and R. Zimmermann (eds), *The Oxford Handbook of Comparative Law* (Oxford: Oxford University Press, 2019), pp. 290–319 (p. 291).

63 Ibid.

64 R. Sacco, 'Legal Formants: A Dynamic Approach to Comparative Law (Installment I of II)', *American Journal of Comparative Law* 39.1 (1991), 1–34 (p. 1); S. Vogenauer, 'Sources of Law and Legal Method in Comparative Law', in R. Zimmermann and M. Reimann (eds), *The Oxford Handbook*, 2nd edn (Oxford: Oxford University Press, 2019), pp. 876–901. See also A. Gambaro and M. Graziadei, 'Legal Formants', in J. M. Smits et al. (eds), *Elgar Encyclopedia of Comparative Law*, 3rd edn (Cheltenham: Edward Elgar Publishing, 2023), pp. 452–458.

65 A. Watson, *Legal Transplants: An Approach to Comparative Law* (Edinburgh: T&T Clark, 1974).

66 B. Grossfeld, *The Strength and Weakness of Comparative Law* (Oxford: Clarendon Press, 1990).

67 E.g. P. Legrand, 'How to Compare Now', *Legal Studies* 16.2 (1996), 232–242 (p. 232). See also: M. Adams and M. Van Hoecke, 'Conclusion: Challenges of Comparison', in M. Adams and M. Van Hoecke (eds), *Comparative Methods in Law, Humanities and Social Sciences* (Cheltenham: Edward Elgar Publishing, 2021), pp. 252–254.

68 To this select group belong Kahn-Freund, Grossfeld and, specifically, Sacco and Vogenauer.

69 See E. Rabel, *Aufgabe und Notwendigkeit der Rechtsvergleichung* (Munich: Verlag der

not take these rules into account, one will acquire a distorted view of the studied legal system.[70] On the question of what should be considered as law, Sacco has developed a rather sophisticated method. Sacco's starting point is that the object of comparative legal research is the legal norm. The question he asks is: how does one determine which norm applies in a legal system? The norm cannot be distilled from only one legal source (such as legislation or legal doctrine), but always from a combination. The norm consists of several building blocks (*formanti*). In identifying these *formanti*, Sacco strongly advises the comparative lawyer to use the factual approach.[71]

Only relatively recently has the question of the sources of law in comparative law been discussed in a thorough way. The main conclusion was that the comparatist should consult the sources of law of the system under consideration as understood by the lawyers of that specific legal system.[72] This—disappointingly for the practitioner—is a very hard task (and might sometimes even be impossible, since lawyers of a certain system do not always agree on which sources are to be considered to be the sources of law).

To be able to phrase correct methodological guidelines at this stage one would need to determine what the aim of the project is and which objects have been selected. Based on these two elements combined, one can decide whether one needs to only include the sources of law as recognised by the system itself, or, in addition, various kinds of societal data that provide context to the objects under comparison. To repeat some basic guidelines: if the aim is regulation, information about how the rules function and why they function in a certain way is important, and must be included. The same is true if the aim is to provide an explanation. If the aim is to find the law—to describe how a certain topic is regulated—the study of the law in the books (meaning all sources that are considered as sources of law in the selected legal system) may suffice. More in-depth research is possible, but is perhaps not required methodologically.

Hochschulbuchhandlung Max Hueber 1925), p. 3: 'Der Stoff des Nachdenkes über die Probleme des Rechts muß das Recht der gesammten Erde sein, vergangenes und heutiges, der Zusammenhang des Rechts mit Boden, Klima und Rasse, mit geschichtlichen Schicksalem der Völker [...], mit religiösen und ethischen Vorstellungen; [...]'.

70 Grossfeld, *The Strength and Weakness of Comparative Law*, pp. 8–9: 'What is the object of our specialty? What have we in mind when we speak of German of Chinese 'law'? Are we to include extra-legal rules? Indeed we must, or our picture of the foreign legal system will be sadly distorted'; see also Kahn-Freund who pleaded in strong terms for the inclusion of 'non-law' in his inaugural lecture and also spoke about the avoidance of a distorted view of the legal system under consideration. O. Kahn-Freund, 'Comparative Law as an Academic Subject', *Law Quarterly Review* 82.1 (1966), 55–56.

71 See above, Section 4.a.2.

72 Vogenauer, 'Sources of Law and Legal Method in Comparative Law'. See also J. C. Reitz, 'How to Do Comparative Law', *American Journal of Comparative Law* 46.4 (1998), 628–631: 'In establishing what the law is in each jurisdiction under study, comparative law (and, for that matter, studies of foreign law, as well) should (a) be concerned to describe the normal conceptual world of the lawyers, (b) take into consideration all the sources upon which a lawyer in that legal system might base her opinion as to what the law is, and (c) take into consideration the gap between the law on the books and law in action, as well as (d) important gaps in available knowledge about either the law on the books and the law in action [...]'.

b. Methods and Techniques in the Stage of Description

The first stage of the actual comparative legal research consists of the selection and description of the objects of comparison in the selected legal systems. Assuming that the selection-method of the objects to be compared has been determined and the sources have been indicated, the methods and techniques relevant to the descriptive stage are related to the issues of representation and presentation.

1) Description of the Objects to Be Compared (Language)

All comparatists, even those who write in the same language as that of the legal language of all the included systems (for example, an author describing and comparing in the English language the English, Irish, and Australian legal systems), will have to deal with the issue of the natural language often failing to coincide with the legal language. How should one translate legal terms that have no equivalent in the target language? What, for example, should one do with Dutch legal terms such as *dwangsom*? Practical suggestions provided by the literature are: (1) arrive at one's own (literal) translation ('coercive sum'), (2) provide a description ('a penalty connected to a court order that has to be paid to the demanding party by the opposing party in case of non-compliance with a court order to do something or to refrain from doing something other than the payment of money'), or (3) invent a neologism ('incentive-fine').[73] Nonetheless, even in cases in which equivalents can be found (legal terms such as 'contract' or 'marriage'), one could ask whether the choice of this equivalent is methodologically correct. It could give the reader the misleading impression that both the name of the legal institution and the content are similar, which is not necessarily the case. Finally, it is remarkable that although a vast amount of literature exists on the issue of law and how it relates to language and legal translation,[74] it does not yet seem to have become an integral component of comparative legal research methodology.

2) Presentation of the Analysis of the Objects to Be Compared (Structure)

The question of how to present the analysis of the selected objects is a rather practical issue, with very few theoretical foundations. Two possible means of presentation are

---

73 Cf. Sacco, 'Legal Formants: A Dynamic Approach to Comparative Law (Instalment I of II)', pp. 10–20.

74 See H. E. S. Mattila, *Comparative Legal Linguistics: Language of Law, Latin and Modern lingua francas*, 2nd edn (Farnham: Routledge, 2013); B. Pozzo, 'Comparative Law and Language', in M. Bussani and U. Mattei (eds), *Comparative Law* (Cambridge, UK: Cambridge University Press, 2012), pp. 88–113 and further references. See also specifically others: Sacco, 'Legal Formants', pp. 10–20; G.-R. de Groot and C. J. P. van Laer, 'Legal Translation', in J. M. Smits et al. (eds), *Elgar Encyclopedia of Comparative Law*, 3rd edn (Cheltenham: Edward Elgar Publishing, 2023), pp. 524–529; G.-R. de Groot, 'The Influence of Problems of Legal Translation on Comparative Law Research', in J. Baaij (ed.), *The Role of Legal Translation in Legal Harmonization* (Alphen aan den Rijn: Kluwer, 2012), pp. 139–160; P. Legrand, 'Issues in the Translatability of Law', in Sandra Bermann and Michael Wood (eds), *Nation, Language, and the Ethics of Translation* (Princeton, NJ: Princeton University Press, 2005), pp. 30–50.

distinguished: successive and simultaneous.[75] Successive presentation involves a textual structure in which the findings of the study of the objects within the various selected legal systems are described one after another, for example in separate chapters. Each chapter is thus dedicated to one of the selected systems. Simultaneous presentation of the text is structured according to a range of aspects or features of the selected object. Each chapter is dedicated to one aspect or feature and contains the analysis of the feature of each of the selected objects of all the selected legal systems. In other words, the equivalents of the selected objects of all selected systems are discussed with regard to a certain specific aspect, in one chapter. As for the more suitable method in any given situation, much depends on the character of the selected topics and the extent to which they are embedded in the selected system. If the various aspects chosen for discussion are closely and yet complexly related, one could imagine that successive presentation would be the best choice; in this way the object is presented in its whole, with the interrelatedness of its various aspects clearly shown. Where it is possible to present the various aspects separately from one another without difficulty, readers are placed at an advantage because they can see immediately the differences and similarities between selected objects. Personal and/or aesthetic preferences may also play a role in the selection of the manner of presentation. There are no methodological restrictions related to this choice.

c. Methods and Techniques in the Stages of Comparison, Explanation, and Evaluation

As stated above, one of the functions of a methodological framework is to assist in ordering the existing knowledge on comparative legal methodology. This will help to uncover lacunae in, or less-elaborated parts of, comparative legal methodology. The stages of comparison, explanation, and evaluation provide good examples of parts that need the full attention of comparative legal methodologists because they are apparently underdeveloped. This section will consider how the stages have been discussed in the literature and will indicate viable options for further research. Before entering into the discussion, it is necessary however to point out that both the explanatory and evaluative stages need the help of other sciences in the elaboration of their methodology. Both the explanation of the differences and similarities between legal systems and the evaluation of the normative arrangements found in the selected legal systems will find their sources in fields of knowledge that lie outside the law. The sciences to be consulted will depend on the precise topic and the aim of the project (combined with its research question). In the context of this chapter these issues can—given their breadth—only be explored in a cursory fashion.

As the stage of comparison is the crucial and central stage of the comparative legal research, one would expect a large toolbox with specific methods and techniques

75 Kokkini-Iatridou, 'Comparative Legal Research', pp. 187–188.

for this stage. However, one often only finds the requirements for general scientific research; it is important to be as objective, precise, and clear as possible. Of course, one has to realise that a considerable set of tools has already been used in the earlier stages that directly or indirectly prepare for this crucial, 'proper' stage of comparison. If a sound selection of legal systems and objects to compare has been made and these objects have been adequately described after consultation of the right sources, various pitfalls have already been avoided. However, the question as to how to identify and analyse differences and similarities between the objects that have been selected and described has not been answered, or at least not thoroughly. Before discussing in brief the issues that would need to be elaborated, it seems necessary, especially in light of the relatively recent discussions in the literature,[76] to point out that being objective, precise, and clear should lead to the identification of *both* similarities *and* differences, even if (or perhaps even more so) the objective of the comparative legal research project is harmonisation or unification.[77]

Comparative legal methodology should concentrate first on developing firm rules on how to analyse a topic or question and identify its relevant parts in view of the comparison. Subsequently, it is necessary to develop techniques on how to build a grid ('a system') that enables the researcher to measure and describe differences and similarities. If, for example, a researcher compares the level of protection of a third party in the context of matrimonial property law of the selected countries, he or she would need a detailed schedule indicating both the situations in which the third party would need protection and the various possible levels of protection (such as, unconditional protection, conditional protection, or no protection). Here we could draw inspiration from discussions in other comparative sciences.[78] In particular, qualitative sociological research has done much to elaborate refined schemes of comparison.[79]

In the explanatory stage the researcher provides an explanation of the similarities and differences indicated in the previous stage. If the comparison has an explanatory aim, the presentation of the findings will form the conclusion of the comparative legal research project.[80] In projects with other aims, the stage will usually form the penultimate stage. The academic discipline of comparative law cannot and need not provide a method or technique here. Comparative methodology confines itself here to giving indications on what kind of factors might explain differences and

76 For a description of the discussion see: G. Dannemann, 'Comparative Law: Study of Similarities or Differences?', in M. Reimann and R. Zimmermann (eds), *The Oxford Handbook of Comparative Law* (Oxford: Oxford University Press, 2019), pp. 390–422.

77 Ibid., pp. 418–419.

78 Jansen, 'Comparative Law and Comparative Knowledge'.

79 See e.g. B. Rihoux, 'Qualitative Comparative Analysis (QCA) and Related Systematic Comparative Methods, International Sociology', *International Sociology* 21.5 (2006), 679–706. See on the relatively recent introduction of quantitative methods in comparative law and its various uses in this field: R. Whalen, 'Quantitative Methods in Comparative Law', in J. M. Smits et al. (eds), *Elgar Encyclopedia of Comparative Law*, 3rd edn (Cheltenham: Edward Elgar Publishing, 2023), pp. 277–283. See also Siems, *Comparative Law,* pp. 174–284.

80 See e.g. Griffiths, Weyers, and Adams, *Euthanasia and Law in Europe.* For a thorough description of their methodology see: Adams and Griffiths, 'Against "Comparative Method"', p. 279.

similarities between legal systems. Common factors are, for example, 'the economic system', 'the political system and ideology', 'religion', 'history and geography', 'demographic factors', 'co-influence of other means of control', and 'accidental and unknown factors'.[81] Clearly a researcher should make use of methods and techniques taken from other disciplines such as politics, legal history, legal sociology, legal anthropology, statistics, and economics. It might be the task of comparative legal research methodology to indicate the main methods and techniques of the various fields involved and refer to their main sources. It must be said that—though in the literature on comparative law the importance of the explanatory stage is generally stressed[82]—in individual comparative legal research projects an explicit or distinct section that explains differences and similarities is for the most part absent.[83] However, the leading authors in this field are in agreement that the stage of explanation is important for its theoretical and practical relevance.[84] Nevertheless, one often hears in practice that lawyers generally are denied the specific knowledge and the skills to be able to perform this task in a reliable way. Ideally, experts from various fields should cooperate with each other.[85]

In comparative legal research methodology more attention is being paid to the stage of evaluation than to the stage of explanation. In the stage of evaluation the objects (for example, legal solutions to societal problems or sets of rules that regulate societal phenomena or situations) are assessed. In the literature one finds three schools of thought on the question of whether an evaluation should necessarily be part of any comparative legal research project.[86] One position is that an evaluation does not belong to the comparatist's task.[87] According to proponents of this school of thought,

81 Bogdan, *Concise Introduction to Comparative Law*, pp.57–62. See also Constantinesco, *Rechtsvergleichung: Die rechtsvergleichende Methode*, pp. 292–322; Kokkini-Iatridou, 'Comparative Legal Research', pp. 155–175; Kokkini-Iatridou, 'Some Methodological Aspects of Comparative Law', pp. 185–189.

82 See e.g. Bogdan, *Concise Introduction to Comparative Law*, p. 55: 'One of the most interesting and most important tasks of comparative law is to attempt to explain such similarities and differences'.

83 In larger projects on the other hand, in which different researchers cooperate, these kind of explanatory parts are generally quite well elaborated.

84 Among others: Bogdan, *Concise Introduction to Comparative Law*, p. 55; Örücü, 'Theories and Presumptions of Comparability', p. 47; Kokkini-Iatridou, 'Comparative Legal Research', p. 155.

85 In a less ideal—but acceptable—situation the researcher should undertake an introductory course in the—for the research project at hand—most important field and/or use may be made—if possible—of literature, documents etc. provided in that field. In any case, the researcher should make clear which of the options described above has been chosen and how this may influence the results of the research.

86 Kokkini-Iatridou, 'Comparative Legal Research', pp. 176–179; Kokkini-Iatridou, 'Some Methodological Aspects of Comparative Law', pp. 189–193. See on value judgments in comparative legal research projects specifically: G.-R. de Groot and H. Schneider, 'Das Werturteil in der Rechtsvergleichung', in K. Boele-Woelki et al. (eds), *Comparability and Evaluation: Essays on Comparative Law, Private International Law, and International Commercial Arbitration: In Honour of Dimitra Kokkini-Iatridou* (Dordrecht: Kluwer, 1994), pp. 53–68.

87 One of the few comparatists who hold this view is the Italian comparative scholar Rodolfo Sacco (*Introduzione al diritto comparato*, 2nd edn (Turin: Giappichelli, 1980)). However, it should be noted that this view is not explicitly stated in later editions of his book (4th edn, 1990; 5th edn, 1992; 6th edn, 2015; 7th edn, 2019). From a theoretical point of view, Ernst Rabel is of the opinion that evaluation should be considered as a separate action, and not a part of the (scientific) comparative research project (E. Rabel, 'Die Fachgebiete des Kaiser Wilhelm-Instituts fur ausländisches und internationales

a comparison should be impartial and indifferent. However, it can be said against that position that whereas one can and should be as objective as possible in the first three stages of the comparative research, it is certainly possible to add subjective elements in the form of an evaluation in the final stage.

A second opinion found in the literature is that although evaluation should not be completely ruled out, it is rather difficult and furthermore not necessary.[88] It is difficult, because no abstract, absolute criteria governing the basis of an evaluation exist and, furthermore, because the decision as to whether one particular solution is better than another will depend on the purpose of the comparative research. It is quite possible that in the case of a harmonisation project, a particular solution will be considered to be preferable as it provides a compromise, whereas in the case of law reform another solution would be preferred.

The third and final opinion is the most common. According to this view, a comparative legal research project should always have a regulatory aim, and in those cases an evaluation necessarily forms part of the comparative legal research project. The fact that the evaluation is subjective is not regarded as being problematic, provided the researcher clarifies the criteria which will be relied upon, and reports on the other stages of research as objectively as possible. In this case, others will be able to draw their own conclusions and agree or disagree.[89]

In my view, in the case of comparative legal research with a regulatory aim, evaluation forms a necessary part of the comparative research. However, if the objective of a project is descriptive and/or explanatory (for example, to study the influence of ideology on a particular legal institution) the research project will need to end with a conclusion, rather than a critical evaluation of the solutions found in the selected legal systems.

For this stage—much like the explanatory stage—the academic discipline of comparative law provides neither methods nor techniques.[90] As observed in the discussion on the functional method in relation to the problem-solving approach, the selected criteria in this context will refer to the way the 'problem' is solved by the

---

Privatrecht', in M. Planck (ed.), *25 Jahre Kaiser Wilhelm-Gesellschaft zur Förderung des Wissenschaften III* (Berlin: Springer, 1937), p. 77). However, from a practical point of view he does not want comparatists to refrain from evaluating: 'Wir Juristen, seit jeher an Kritik gewöhnt und vom Wunsch nach Rechtsbesserung besessen, vermögen gar nicht, den Ausblick auf die sachlich richtigere Regelung uns zu versagen'.

88 Constantinesco, *Rechtsvergleichung: Die rechtsvergleichende Methode*, pp. 323–325.

89 Zweigert and Kötz, *An Introduction to Comparative Law*, pp. 31–47. See also Kurt H. Ebert, *Rechtsvergleichung, Einführung in die Grundlagen* (Bern: Stampfli, 1978); Kamba, 'Comparative Law: A Theoretical Framework', pp. 510–512; Kokkini-Iatridou, 'Comparative Legal Research', pp. 178–179; Kokkini-Iatridou, 'Some Methodological Aspects of Comparative Law', pp. 191–193.

90 In the same vein: Reitz, 'How to Do Comparative Law', pp. 624–625: 'It is important to bear in mind that comparison by itself is at best a "weakly normative" […]. [C]omparative studies may uncover interesting ideas for domestic law reform, but in the end the case for adoption of a foreign model cannot rest on the fact that many other countries have the rule of legal institution. The argument for domestic law reform has to be made in terms of normative claims acceptable within the domestic legal system, and probably the foreign transplant will have to be modified in significant ways precisely because each legal system reflects an at least partially unique legal system'.

rules. In other words: which option provides the best solution? This representation of the selection of the criteria seems to be too simplistic. Clearly, the problem is best solved when it is solved completely or when the societal situation is adequately managed. However, it is as important to identify *how* the problem is solved, if there are any (negative) side-effects, or if a specific legal and/or social context is required. This example shows that while the problem-solving approach does provide contours of the evaluation criteria, it does not pre-select a set of particular criteria. It is a general requirement of good research that the criteria according to which the assessment/evaluation is undertaken are made explicit. As long as the researcher is explicit in relation to the criteria, it cannot be said that the project lacks objectivity. It is undeniable that these choices will be subjective, but if they are described in a clear way readers can make their own decisions with regard to their importance. The criteria themselves are not provided by comparative legal methodology,[91] but can and should be found in theories of justice or good law-making, or both.

5. Conclusion

This chapter has presented a framework for comparative legal research indicating the methodological issues that have to be considered in the subsequent stages of a research project. The main goal of this contribution was to provide the (beginner) researcher with guidelines on how to set up and carry out a comparative legal research project in a methodologically sound way. In this contribution, I discussed how, in particular, the purpose and topic of the research direct the answers to the methodological questions. It became clear that in particular the purpose (normative/non-normative) of the comparison is guiding, but that especially in contexts in which the purpose does not give direction, the topic of the project and/or aspects related to the research or researcher (such as language skills, size and composition of the research group, duration or budget) determine(s) the choice of a method and/or the operationalisation of a specific method.

6. Points for Reflection

Q1: What is the difference between comparative legal research and Auslandsrechtskunde (the study of foreign law)?

Q2: To what extent do you agree or disagree with the following thesis? 'It is of paramount importance to first determine the aim of a comparative legal research project before selecting the legal systems to be included in the project'.

91 See also Jansen, 'Comparative Law and Comparative Knowledge', p. 337: 'Evaluation of the objects compared is not a part of the comparative process. Comparative knowledge may be used to justify normative statements, but comparison itself neither proves the truth of a belief nor reveals one legal rule or doctrine to be superior to others'.

Q3: Can you explain why, in a comparative legal research project with a normative aim, choosing a functional method to find the objects of comparison in the selected legal systems would be most advisable?

Q4: To what extent do you agree or disagree with the following thesis? 'The functional-institutional method, the problem-solving approach and the factual approach are essentially the same methods'.

Q5: According to Zweigert and Kötz 'the basic methodological principle of all comparative law is that of functionality'. Why do you think they hold this opinion?

Q6: Can you think of a reason why it could be disadvantageous to label methods as 'modern' or old-fashioned?

Bibliography

Adams, M., and J. Griffiths, 'Against "Comparative Method": Explaining Similarities and Differences', in M. Adams and J. Bomhoff (eds), *Practice and Theory in Comparative Law* (Cambridge, UK: Cambridge University Press, 2012), pp. 279–301, https://doi.org/10.1017/cbo9780511863301.013

Adams, M., and M. Van Hoecke, 'Conclusion: Challenges of Comparison', in M. Adams and M. Van Hoecke (eds), *Comparative Methods in Law, Humanities and Social Sciences* (Cheltenham: Edward Elgar Publishing, 2021), pp. 252–254, https://doi.org/10.4337/9781802201468.00018

Bermann, G. A., 'Comparative Law and International Organizations', in M. Bussani and U. Mattei (eds), *Comparative Law* (Cambridge, UK: Cambridge University Press, 2012), pp. 241–254, https://doi.org/10.1017/cbo9781139017206.014

Bogdan, M., *Concise Introduction to Comparative Law* (Zutphen: Europa Law Publishing, 2013)

Boele-Woelki, K., 'The Principles of European Family Law: Its Aims and Prospects', *Utrecht Law Review* 1.2 (2005), 160–168

Bueno Diaz, O., *Franchising in European Contract Law: A Comparison between the Main Obligations of the Contracting Parties in the Principles of European Law on Commercial Agency, Franchise and Distribution Contracts (PEL CAFDC), French and Spanish Law* (Munich: Sellier European Law Publishers, 2008)

Bussani, M., and U. Mattei, 'Preface: The Context', in M. Bussani and U. Mattei (eds), *The Common Core of European Private Law: Essays on the Project* (Alphen aan den Rijn: Kluwer Law International, 2002), pp. 1–8

Butler, W. E., 'Comparative International Law', in J. M. Smits et al. (eds), *Elgar Encyclopedia of Comparative Law*, 3rd edn (Cheltenham: Edward Elgar Publishing, 2023), pp. 326–327, https://doi.org/10.4337/9781839105609.comparative.international.law

Cartwright, J., and M. W. Hesselink (eds), *Precontractual Liability in European Private Law* (Cambridge, UK: Cambridge University Press, 2008)

Commission Communication, 'A More Coherent European Contract Law', COM (2003) 63/16 final, https://eur-lex.europa.eu/LexUriServ/LexUriServ.do?uri=COM:2003:0068:FIN:EN:PDF

Coninck, J. de, 'The Functional Method of Comparative Law: Quo Vadis?', *RabelsZ* 74 (2010), 318–350, https://doi.org/10.1628/003372510791090238

Constantinesco, L.-J., *Rechtsvergleichung: Die rechtsvergleichende Methode*, II (Cologne: Heymanns, 1972)

Cruz, P. de, *Comparative Law in a Changing World*, 3rd edn (Abingdon: Routledge-Cavendish, 2007)

Dannemann, G., 'Comparative Law: Study of Similarities or Differences?', in M. Reimann and R. Zimmermann (eds), *The Oxford Handbook of Comparative Law* (Oxford: Oxford University Press, 2019), pp. 390–422, https://doi.org/10.1093/oxfordhb/9780198810230.013.12

Drobnig, U., 'Methodenfragen der Rechtsvergleichung im Lichte der "International Encyclopedia of Comparative Law"', in E. Von Caemmerer, S. Mentschikoff, and K. Zweigert (eds), *Ius privatum gentium* (Tubingen: Mohr, 1969), pp. 221–223

Drobnig, U., 'Möglichkeiten und Grenzen intersystemarer Rechtsvergleichung auf dem Gebiete des Zivilrechts', in G. Gutman and S. Mampel (eds), *Probleme systemvergleichender Betrachtung* (Berlin: Duncker Humblot, 1986), pp. 195–205

Duin, J. M. L. van, 'Justice for Both Effective Judicial Protection Under Article 47 of the EU Charter of Fundamental Rights and the Unfair Contract Terms' (doctoral thesis, University of Amsterdam, 2020)

Ebert, K. H., *Rechtsvergleichung, Einführung in die Grundlagen* (Bern: Stampfli, 1978)

Gambaro, A., and M. Graziadei, 'Legal Formants', in J. M. Smits et al. (eds), *Elgar Encyclopedia of Comparative Law*, 3rd edn (Cheltenham: Edward Elgar Publishing, 2023), pp. 452–458, https://doi.org/10.4337/9781839105609.formants

Gerber, D. J., 'Sculpting the Agenda of Comparative Law: Ernst Rabel and the Façade of Language', in A. Riles (ed.), *Rethinking the Masters of Comparative Law* (Portland, OR: Hart, 2001), pp. 190–208, https://doi.org/10.5040/9781472559135.ch-007

Gerber, D. J., 'System Dynamics: Toward a Language of Comparative Law?', *American Journal of Comparative Law*, 46.4 (1998), 719–737

Griffiths, J., H. Weyers, and M. Adams, *Euthanasia and Law in Europe* (London: Hart Publishing, 2008)

Groot, G.-R. de, 'The Influence of Problems of Legal Translation on Comparative Law Research', in J. Baaij (ed.), *The Role of Legal Translation in Legal Harmonization* (Alphen aan den Rijn: Kluwer, 2012), pp. 139–160

Groot, G.-R. de, and H. Schneider, 'Das Werturteil in der Rechtsvergleichung', in K. Boele-Woelki et al. (eds), *Comparability and Evaluation: Essays on Comparative Law, Private International Law, and International Commercial Arbitration: In Honour of Dimitra Kokkini-Iatridou* (Dordrecht: Kluwer, 1994), pp. 53–68

Groot, G.-R. de, and C. J. P. van Laer, 'Legal Translation', in J. M. Smits et al. (eds), *Elgar Encyclopedia of Comparative Law*, 3rd edn (Cheltenham: Edward Elgar Publishing, 2023), pp. 524–529

Grossfeld, B., *The Strength and Weakness of Comparative Law* (Oxford: Clarendon Press, 1990)

Hesselink, M. W., 'The Principles of European Contract Law: Some Choices Made by the Lando Commission', in M. W. Hesselink and G. J. P. de Vries (eds), *Principles of European Contract Law; Preadviezen uitgebracht voor de Vereniging voor Burgerlijk Recht* (Deventer: Kluwer, 2001), pp. 5–95

Hirschl, R., 'The Question of Case Selection in Comparative Constitutional Law', *American Journal of Comparative Law* 53 (2005), 125–155

Husa, J., 'Farewell to Functionalism or Methodological Tolerance?', *RabelsZ* 67 (2003), 419–447

Husa, J., 'Functional Method in Comparative Law—Much Ado About Nothing?', *European Property Law Journal* 2.1 (2013), 4–21, https://doi.org/10.1515/eplj-2013-0002

Husa, J., *Introduction to Comparative Law*, 2nd edn (London: Hart 2023)

Hyland, R., *Gifts, A Study in Comparative Law* (Oxford: Oxford University Press, 2009)

Jansen, N., 'Comparative Law and Comparative Knowledge', in M. Reimann and R. Zimmermann (eds), *The Oxford Handbook of Comparative Law* (Oxford: Oxford University Press, 2019), pp. 290–319

Kahn-Freund, O., 'Comparative Law as an Academic Subject', *Law Quarterly Review* 82.1 (1966), 55–56

Kamba, W. J., 'Comparative Law: A Theoretical Framework', *International and Comparative Law Quarterly* 23 (1974), 485–519

Kischel, U., 'Tertium comparationis', in J. M. Smits (ed.), *Elgar Encyclopedia of Comparative Law* (Cheltenham: Edward Elgar Publishing, 2006), pp. 484–491

Kokkini-Iatridou, D., 'Some Methodological Aspects of Comparative Law: The Third Part of a (Pre-)paradigm', *Netherlands International Law Review* 33 (1986), 143–194

Kokkini-Iatridou, D., et al., *Een inleiding tot het rechtsvergelijkende onderzoek* (Alphen aan den Rijn: Kluwer, 1988)

Kötz, H., 'Comparative Law in Germany Today', *Revue internationale de droit comparé* 51.4 (1999), 753–758

Knapp, V., 'Quelques problèmes méthodologiques dans la science du droit comparé', in K. Zweigert and H.-J. Puttfarken (eds), *Rechtsvergleichung* (Darmstadt: Wissenschaftliche Buchgesellschaf, 1978), pp. 334–349

Legrand, P., 'How to Compare Now', *Legal Studies* 16.2 (1996), 232–242

Legrand, P., 'Issues in the Translatability of Law', in Sandra Bermann and Michael Wood (eds), *Nation, Language, and the Ethics of Translation* (Princeton, NJ: Princeton University Press, 2005), pp. 30–50, https://doi.org/10.1515/9781400826681.30

Mattila, H. E. S., *Comparative Legal Linguistics: Language of Law, Latin and Modern lingua francas*, 2nd edn (Farnham: Routledge, 2013)

Merryman, J. H., 'Comparative Law and Scientific Explanation', in J. N. Hazard and W. J. Wagner (eds), *Law in the United States of America in Social and Technological Revolution* (Brussels: Bruylant, 1974), pp. 81–104

Michaels, R., 'Explanation and Interpretation—A Response to Julie de Coninck', *RabelsZ* 74 (2010), 351–359, https://doi.org/10.1628/003372510791090256

Michaels, R., 'The Functional Method of Comparative Law', in M. Reimann and R. Zimmermann (eds) *The Oxford Handbook of Comparative Law* (Oxford: Oxford University Press, 2019), pp. 339–382, https://doi.org/10.1093/oxfordhb/9780198810230.013.11

Momirov, A., and A. Naudé Fourie, 'Vertical Comparative Law Methods: Tools for Conceptualising the International Rule of Law', *Erasmus Law Review* 2 (2009), 291–309

Oderkerk, M., 'The CFR and the Method(s) of Comparative Legal Research', *European Review of Contract Law* 3 (2007), 326–331

Oderkerk, M., 'The Importance of Context: Selecting Legal Systems in Comparative Legal Research', *Netherlands International Law Review* 48 (2001), 293–318

Oderkerk, M., 'The Need for a Methodological Framework for Comparative Legal Research: Sense and Nonsense of 'Methodological Pluralism' in Comparative Law', *RabelsZ* 79.3 (2015), 589–623, https://doi.org/10.1628/003372515x14339403063927

Örücü, E., 'Methodology of Comparative Law', in J. M. Smits (ed.), *Elgar Encyclopedia of Comparative Law* (Cheltenham: Edward Elgar Publishing, 2006), p. 447

Örücü, A. E., 'Theories and Presumptions of Comparability', in M. Aitkenhead (ed.), *Law and Lawyers in European Integration. A Comparative Analysis of the Education, Attitudes and Specialisation of Scottish and Dutch Lawyer* (Rotterdam: Erasmus Universiteit, 1988), pp. 20–39

Palmer, V. V., 'From Lerotholi to Lando: Some Examples of Comparative Law Methodology', *American Journal of Comparative Law* 53.1 (2005), 261–290

Peters, A., and H. Schwenke, 'Comparative Law Beyond Post-Modernism', *International and Comparative Law Quarterly* 49.4 (2000), 800–834

Podgorecki, A., 'Social Systems and Legal Systems—Criteria for classification', in A. Podgorecki et al. (eds), *Legal Systems and Social Systems* (London: Chroom Helm, 1985), pp. 1–24

Pozzo, B., 'Comparative Law and Language', in M. Bussani and U. Mattei (eds), *Comparative Law* (Cambridge, UK: Cambridge University Press, 2012), pp. 88–113, https://doi.org/10.1017/cbo9781139017206.007

Rabel, E., *Aufgabe und Notwendigkeit der Rechtsvergleichung* (Munich: Verlag der Hochschulbuchhandlung Max Hueber 1925)

Rabel, E., 'Die Fachgebiete des Kaiser Wilhelm-Instituts fur ausländisches und internationales Privatrecht', in M. Planck (ed.), *25 Jahre Kaiser Wilhelm-Gesellschaft zur Förderung des Wissenschaften III* (Berlin: Springer, 1937), p. 77

Reimann, M., 'The Progress and Failure of Comparative Law in the Second Half of the Twentieth Century', *American Journal of Comparative Law* 50 (2002), 671–700

Reitz, J. C., 'How to Do Comparative Law', *American Journal of Comparative Law* 46.4 (1998), 628–631

Rheinstein, M., *Einführung in die Rechtsvergleichung*, ed. by R. von Borries, 2nd edn (Munich: Beck, 1987)

Rihoux, B., 'Qualitative Comparative Analysis (QCA) and Related Systematic Comparative Methods, International Sociology', *International Sociology* 21.5 (2006), 679–706, https://doi.org/10.1177/0268580906067836

Sacco, R., *Introduzione al diritto comparato*, 2nd edn (Turin: Giappichelli, 1980)

Sacco, R., 'Legal Formants: A Dynamic Approach to Comparative Law (Installment I of II)', *American Journal of Comparative Law* 39.1 (1991), 1–34

Samuel, G., 'The Epistemological Challenge: Does Law Exist?', in S. Glanert, A. Mercescu, and G. Samuel (eds), *Rethinking Comparative Law* (Cheltenham: Edward Elgar Publishing, 2021), pp. 1–30, https://doi.org/10.4337/9781786439475.00005

Schlesinger, R., 'The Common Core of Legal Systems, An Emerging Subject of Comparative Study', in K. H. Nadelmann, A. T. von Mehren, and J. NN Hazard (eds), *XXth Century Comparative and Conflicts Law* (Leyden: Sythoff, 1961), pp. 65–79

Schlesinger, R., et al., *Formation of Contract—A Study of the Common Core of Legal Systems*, II (Washington, DC: Oceana Publications, 1968)

Siems, M. M., *Comparative Law*, 3rd edn (Cambridge, UK: Cambridge University Press, 2022)

Storme, M. E., 'Common Core Projects', in J. M. Smits et al. (eds), *Elgar Encyclopedia of Comparative Law*, 3rd edn (Cheltenham: Edward Elgar Publishing, 2023), pp. 306–317

Valcke, C., 'Comparative Law as Comparative Jurisprudence: The Comparability of Legal Systems', *American Journal of Comparative Law* 52 (2004), 713–740

van Dijk, P., 'De rechtsvergelijking en het recht der internationale organisaties; enige methodologische notities', in R. Barents (ed.), *Orde: Liber Amicorum Pieter VerLoren van Themaat* (Alphen aan den Rijn: Kluwer 1982), pp. 77–98

Vogenauer, S., 'Sources of Law and Legal Method in Comparative Law', in R. Zimmermann and M. Reimann (eds), *The Oxford Handbook*, 2nd edn (Oxford: Oxford University Press, 2019), pp. 876–901, https://doi.org/10.1093/oxfordhb/9780198810230.013.28

Watson, A., *Legal Transplants: An Approach to Comparative Law* (Edinburgh: T&T Clark, 1974)

Whalen, R., 'Quantitative Methods in Comparative Law', in J. M. Smits et al. (eds), *Elgar Encyclopedia of Comparative Law*, 3rd edn (Cheltenham: Edward Elgar Publishing, 2023), pp. 277–283, https://doi.org/10.4337/9781839105609.quantitative.methods.comparative.law

Wiener, J. B., 'Something Borrowed for Something Blue: Legal Transplants and the Evolution of Global Environmental Law', *Ecology Law Quarterly* 27.4 (2001), 1295–1372

Zweigert, K., 'Zur Methode der Rechtsvergleichung', *Studium Generale* 13 (1960), 193–200

Zweigert, K., and H. Kötz, *An Introduction to Comparative Law*, trans. by T. Weir, 3rd edn (Oxford: Oxford University Press, 1998)

Zweigert, K., and H.-J. Puttfarken, 'Zur Vergleichbarkeit analoger Rechtsinstitute in verschiedenen Gesellschaftsordnungen', in K. Zweigert and H.-J. Puttfarken (eds), *Rechtsvergleichung* (Darmstadt: Wissenschaftliche Buchgesellschaft, 1978), pp. 395–429

Index

About the Team

Alessandra Tosi was the managing editor for this book.

Adèle Kreager and Hannah Bergin proof-read this manuscript. Adèle compiled the index.

Jeevanjot Kaur Nagpal designed the cover. The cover was produced in InDesign using the Fontin font.

Jeremy Bowman typeset the book in InDesign and produced the paperback and hardback editions and created the EPUB. The main text font is Tex Gyre Pagella and the heading font is Californian FB. Jeremy also produced the PDF edition.

The conversion to the HTML edition was performed with epublius, an open-source software which is freely available on our GitHub page at https://github.com/OpenBookPublishers

Laura Rodríguez was in charge of marketing.

This book was peer-reviewed by two anonymous referees. Experts in their field, these readers give their time freely to help ensure the academic rigour of our books. We are grateful for their generous and invaluable contributions.

This book need not end here...

Share

All our books — including the one you have just read — are free to access online so that students, researchers and members of the public who can't afford a printed edition will have access to the same ideas. This title will be accessed online by hundreds of readers each month across the globe: why not share the link so that someone you know is one of them?

This book and additional content is available at
https://doi.org/10.11647/OBP.0448

Donate

Open Book Publishers is an award-winning, scholar-led, not-for-profit press making knowledge freely available one book at a time. We don't charge authors to publish with us: instead, our work is supported by our library members and by donations from people who believe that research shouldn't be locked behind paywalls.

Join the effort to free knowledge by supporting us at
https://www.openbookpublishers.com/support-us

We invite you to connect with us on our socials!

BLUESKY
@openbookpublish
.bsky.social

MASTODON
@OpenBookPublish
@hcommons.social

LINKEDIN
open-book-publishers

Read more at the Open Book Publishers Blog

https://blogs.openbookpublishers.com

You may also be interested in:

The Digital Public Domain

Foundations for an Open Culture

Melanie Dulong de Rosnay and Juan Carlos De Martin (eds),
Foreword by Charles R. Nesson

https://doi.org/10.11647/OBP.0019

Intellectual Property and Public Health in the Developing World

Monirul Azam

https://doi.org/10.11647/OBP.0093

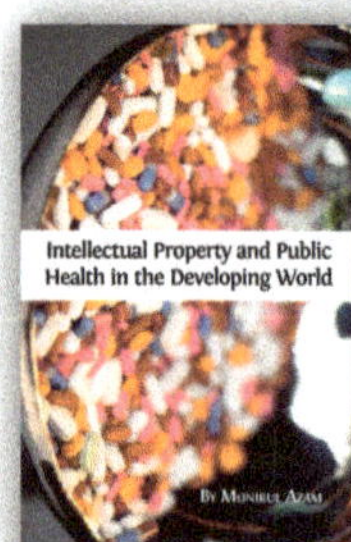

Circulation and Control

Artistic Culture and Intellectual Property in the Nineteenth Century

Marie-Stéphanie Delamaire and Will Slauter (eds)

https://doi.org/10.11647/OBP.0247

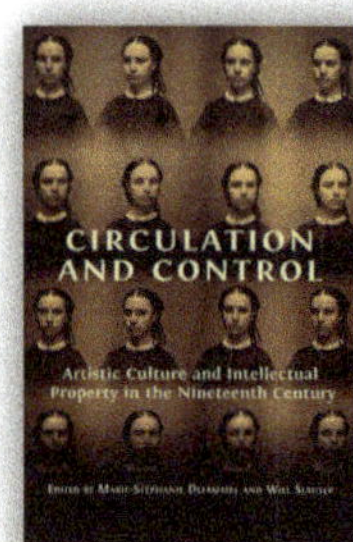

Privilege and Property

Essays on the History of Copyright

Ronan Deazley, Martin Kretschmer and Lionel Bently (eds)

https://doi.org/10.11647/OBP.0007

www.ingramcontent.com/pod-product-compliance
Ingram Content Group UK Ltd.
Pitfield, Milton Keynes, MK11 3LW, UK
UKHW062010041026
15591UKWH00017B/1257

9 781805 115052